W9-CNM-146

THE NEW
BOOK OF KNOWLEDGE

L
volume
11

THE NEW
BOOK OF
KNOWLEDGE

Grolier
INCORPORATED
NEW YORK

ISBN 0-7172-0505-3
Library of Congress Catalog Card Number: 73-8984

COPYRIGHT © 1974 BY  Grolier
INCORPORATED

COPYRIGHT © 1974, 1973, 1972, 1971, 1970, 1969, 1968, 1967, 1966
BY GROLIER INCORPORATED
Copyright © in CANADA 1974, 1973, 1972, 1971, 1970, 1969, 1968 by Grolier Limited;
1967, 1966 by Grolier of Canada Limited
COPYRIGHT PHILIPPINES 1974, 1973, 1972 BY GROLIER INTERNATIONAL, INC.

*All rights reserved. No part of this book may be reproduced
without special permission in writing from the publishers.*

PRINTED IN THE UNITED STATES OF AMERICA

The publishers wish to thank the following for permission to use copyrighted material:
The John Day Company, Inc., for "The Legend of the Blue Plate" from *Folk Tales from China*
by Lim Sian-tek, copyright © 1944 by the John Day Company.
E. P. Dutton & Co., Inc., and Routledge & Kegan, Ltd., for "The Mallard That Asked for Too
Much" from *Eastern Stories and Legends* by Marie L. Shedlock, copyright 1920 by E. P. Dutton &
Co., Inc., renewed 1948 by Arthur C. Jennings.
University of California Press for "Legend of the White Deer" from *Indian Legends of the
Pacific Northwest* by Ella E. Clark.
Henry Z. Walck, Inc., and Oxford University Press for "Roland and Oliver" from *French
Legends, Tales and Fairy Stories* by Barbara Leonie Picard.

Trademark
THE BOOK OF KNOWLEDGE
registered in U.S. Patent Office

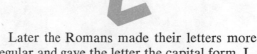

L, the 12th letter in the English alphabet, was also the 12th letter in the ancient Hebrew and Phoenician alphabets, and it was the 11th letter in the classical Greek alphabet. The Hebrews and Phoenicians called it *lamed*. The Greeks called it *lambda*.

Many language scholars believe that the Phoenician word *lamed* meant "goad," or "crooked staff," and that the letter was a picture of a goad. Others believe that it meant "the rod of a teacher." The letter *lamed* looked like this:

The Greeks based their alphabet on that of the Phoenicians. But they changed the forms of many of the letters and gave them new names. Unlike the Phoenician letters, which represented objects, the Greek letter names were just names for sounds. The classical Greek *lambda* looked like this:

It was used in eastern Greece. Different versions of the letter existed in other parts of the country. The form first used by the Romans when they adapted the Greek alphabet was the western Greek form of the letter. The Etruscans, who played an important role in the shaping of the Roman alphabet, also used this form of the letter. It looked like this:

Later the Romans made their letters more regular and gave the letter the capital form, L, that is used today.

In English the consonant sound of the letter is made by placing the point of the tongue against the ridge of the upper front teeth. The sound from the vocal cords passes over the sides of the tongue. The two main sounds of the letter in English are called the "clear" and the "dark" L. When the back of the tongue curves downward, as in the words *lumber, lake,* and *laugh,* the sound of the clear L is produced. The back of the tongue is raised toward the soft palate to produce the dark sound of the letter. Examples of words with the dark sound of the letter are *field, full,* and *cattle.* There are also some English words, such as *should* or *calf,* in which the L is silent.

The letter L is found in many abbreviations. In Roman numerals L stands for 50, and an L with a line above it (Ḹ) denotes 50,000. In English money an L with a cross bar (£) stands for pound (from the Latin *libra,* or "pound"). Lev. is the abbreviation for the Book of Leviticus, and LL.B. (for the Latin *Legum Baccalaureus,* meaning "Bachelor of Laws") is the degree held by lawyers. In dictionaries L is usually the abbreviation for Latin.

Reviewed by MARIO PEI
Columbia University

See also ALPHABET.

Labor Day parade on New York City's Fifth Avenue.

LABOR

Labor is the human activity that puts a roof over our heads, food in our mouths, and clothes on our backs. It generally refers to the work performed by people for other people. Workers receive payment in the form of wages and salaries. Farmers, doctors, lawyers, and owners of businesses are usually self-employed. Only about 10 percent of the working people in the United States are self-employed.

The word "labor" also has another meaning. When it is used to express the idea of workers acting as a group, it means the "labor movement" or "labor unions." If we speak of "labor's goals" or "labor's aims" or "labor's strength," we are speaking of this idea of group action as part of a labor movement.

Labor—both the workers and the labor movement—is tremendously important in the world's economy. In a true democracy labor is free. No worker can be forced to take a job or work for an employer against his will. He can quit his job if he feels he is not paid enough. In a totalitarian society labor is not free. The political system makes the individual less important than the state. The state dictates the terms and conditions of employment and of union organization as well.

▶ **HOW THE LABOR MOVEMENT BEGAN**

In ancient Greece and Rome slaves performed much of the labor. Food and shelter were provided by their masters in return. During the Middle Ages, too, serfs were required to work for the lord of the manor in return for protection. Life was rural. Laborers were tillers of the soil, not wage earners.

As trade increased, the town replaced the feudal manor as the principal place of employment. Merchants and artisans organized into associations, or guilds, for each craft.

Artisans and craftsmen performed their tasks at home or in small shops. They worked by hand. There were few factories and no large industries with many workers laboring together. The workers knew and understood the employer's problems.

The Industrial Revolution

Toward the end of the 18th century all this changed with the invention of several crude machines. These machines, used chiefly for spinning and weaving, revolutionized England's textile industry.

Machinery began to appear in other industries. Much of it was based upon the steam engine developed by Scottish instrument maker James Watt (1736–1819). Machinery could produce more goods faster than the individual worker. New methods of transporting and distributing goods were developed, all requiring the use of machines.

This economic and industrial upheaval is known as the Industrial Revolution. It began in England, then spread to Western Europe. By the beginning of the 19th century the Industrial Revolution had spread to the United States. It completely changed ways of living in the Western world. Handwork and small shops all but disappeared. Factories were built to house the machines, and both were expensive. Only a man with sufficient capital—wealth in money or goods—could afford to own the means of production. Work became more specialized; a worker needed only to learn the operation of one machine. He was no longer self-employed, but had to seek work from an employer. He was paid in wages for his services. Under these conditions the craft-guild system lost its usefulness.

Two classes of industrial producers developed from the Industrial Revolution. These were the owners and the wage earners. Factory workers were dependent upon their machines and their owners. They lost the satisfaction of individual creation and production. No longer did they have easy personal contact with the employer or boss. When workers had problems, they had no one who would listen to them.

Conditions in the early English cotton mills were particularly bad. Factory workers no longer had craft guilds to aid them. So they began to organize into unions. They felt that if they stood together their grievances and complaints would have a better chance of a fair hearing.

These trade unions were founded in the towns as small clubs of skilled craftsmen. Parliament passed a number of laws making all trade combinations, both workers' and employers', illegal. By the 1860's, however, the worker's status had improved. In 1868 the Trades Union Congress (T.U.C.) was formed in Manchester, England.

▶ LABOR IN THE UNITED STATES

There was a great need for unions in the early days of the republic. Men who had worked by hand or in the small shops found themselves out of work. Sometimes workers who had been replaced by machines angrily tried to smash them. They hoped in this way to get back their old jobs. A group of eight Philadelphia cordwainers, or shoemakers, formed the first union in 1792. It did not last a year.

One of the greatest difficulties that the early American unions had to overcome was the public attitude. Most people at that time were unfriendly to any organization of workers. Workers generally were thought of as servants who should do what the employers ordered. They should work long hours, from sunup to sundown—and for whatever pay the master was pleased to offer. Factory conditions were not as bad in America as in England. But they grew worse as industry increased. Many union workers were arrested and tried for the "crime" of attempting to help themselves. This

they hoped to do by forming unions and making demands on their employers. In 1806 the Philadelphia shoemakers were arrested, tried, and found guilty of "conspiracy to raise their own wages."

Today certain practices of some unions are criticized, but few people question the workers' right to form and run their unions. Public law recognizes and protects this right.

During the early years of the 19th century, unions began to form city-wide trade associations. The first was the Mechanics' Union of Trade Associations. It was founded in Philadelphia in 1828. These groups took an interest in politics and created a number of local labor parties.

Rise of National Unions. The fortunes of the labor movement rose in times of prosperity and fell in times of depression. The 1850's saw the formation of unions by the printers, stonecutters, machinists, and others.

After the Civil War, business boomed. Labor was in demand, and unions were active. There were 79 local unions in 20 states in 1863. In 1864 there were 170. The first important national labor federation was formed in 1866. It was headed by William H. Sylvis (1828–69). The union favored the 8-hour workday and putting an end to child labor, among other reforms. It became involved in political activities and went out of existence in 1872.

The 1870's were depression years. Unemployment was widespread. This resulted in strikes and violence. Disturbances in the anthracite coalfields of Pennsylvania were attributed to a secret organization known as the Molly Maguires. In 1877 there was a bitter strike on the eastern railroads against unfair rates and other practices. These events strengthened the general public's unfavorable attitude toward labor.

Knights of Labor

In 1869 several Philadelphia garment cutters under the leadership of Uriah S. Stephens (1821–82) founded the Noble Order of the Knights of Labor. Employers at that time were very unfriendly toward unions. So the knights began by being a secret organization. In 1878 it became a national federation. The Knights favored farmers' and producers' co-operatives, public ownership of

Samuel Gompers (*center, with cane*) leads a 1919 parade of AFL convention delegates.

utilities, and other reform measures. Their greatest contribution to unionism was the opening of their "assemblies," or local units, to all workers. Many were attracted by the appeal of labor's solidarity. Membership grew from about 10,000 in 1879 to over 700,000 in 1886.

The Knights then became involved in quarrels, strikes, and other difficulties with the national craft unions. On May 4, 1886, strikers from the McCormick Harvester Works in Chicago held a meeting at Haymarket Square. A bomb exploded, killing a number of people, including several policemen. Again there was a sharp public reaction against labor, even though the unions played no part in the riot. Terence V. Powderly (1849–1924), Grand Master Workman of the Knights, was a reformer rather than an organizer. He was not able to hold the Knights together. It finally went out of existence.

American Federation of Labor

A rival to the Knights, the Federation of Organized Trades and Labor Unions (F.O.O.T.A.L.U.), was launched in Pittsburgh in 1881. Its purpose was to promote the interests of the craft unions. One of its founders was a leader of the Cigar Makers' Union, Samuel Gompers (1850–1924). Five years later it merged with the newly formed American Federation of Labor (AFL). Gompers was elected president, and was re-elected every year except one until his death. William Green (1873–1952) and then George Meany (1894–   ) followed him into the presidency.

The federation was weakened by two vio-

Eugene V. Debs ran for U.S. president five times as the Socialist Party candidate.

SOME IMPORTANT DATES IN THE HISTORY OF UNITED STATES LABOR

1786 First recorded strike in U.S. history, by Philadelphia printers protesting a wage cut.

1792 First local union formed by Philadelphia shoemakers for collective bargaining.

1799 Philadelphia shoemakers win first union contract after 10-week strike.

1825 First women's union (tailoresses) organized in New York City.

1827 Philadelphia carpenters strike for 10-hour day.

1828 First city-wide trade association, the Mechanics' Union of Trade Associations, organized in Philadelphia; first statewide labor party, the Workingmen's Party, organized in Philadelphia.

1834 First national labor federation, the National Trades' Union, founded by union groups in New York City.

1842 *Commonwealth* v. *Hunt* decision in Massachusetts declares that strike of workers to improve their condition is lawful and not a criminal conspiracy.

1852 First national union, the International Typographical Union, founded.

1866 First important national labor federation, the National Labor Union, formed.

1869 Noble Order of the Knights of Labor founded in Philadelphia; carpenters in San Francisco use first union label.

1877 Strikes on eastern railroads.

1884 Bureau of Labor established.

1886 AFL formed in Pittsburgh; Haymarket "riot," Chicago.

1892 Strike at Carnegie Company plant, Homestead, Pa.

1893 American Railway Union organized by Eugene V. Debs.

1894 Strike against Pullman Company, Chicago; Federal troops called in; Labor Day made a legal holiday.

1898 Erdman Act passed providing for arbitration and mediation.

1902 Strike in the Pennsylvania anthracite coalfields.

1905 I.W.W. formed.

1913 Selzer Act established Department of Labor and set up U.S. Conciliation Service.

1914 Clayton Anti-Trust Act passed providing for regulation of monopolies.

1916 Adamson Act passed establishing 8-hour day for workers engaged in interstate traffic on railroads.

1919 Boston police strike—first strike of government employees; Pittsburgh steelworkers strike.

1922 Strike of anthracite and soft-coal miners.

1926 Railway Labor Act passed providing for establishment of the National Mediation Board.

1932 Anti-injunction Act (Norris-La Guardia Act) passed outlawing certain kinds of injunctions against unions.

1935 National Labor Relations Act (Wagner Act) passed safeguarding labor's right to organize and bargain collectively and creating the National Labor Relations Board; Social Security Act passed; CIO formed in Washington, D.C.

1937 Industrial arbitration tribunal of American Arbitration Association established.

1938 Fair Labor Standards Act (Wages and Hours Act) passed establishing minimum wages, overtime, and child-labor standards for employers engaged in interstate commerce.

1947 Labor-Management Relations Act (Taft-Hartley Act) passed amending 1935 National Labor Relations Act and restricting certain union practices, such as the closed shop.

1955 AFL-CIO merger.

1959 Labor-Management Reporting and Disclosure Act (Landrum-Griffin Act) passed.

1962 International Brotherhood of Electrical Workers, Local 3, won 30-hour week.

1966 Congress set new federal minimum wage (up to $1.60 an hour) and extended coverage of workers.

1973 House of Representatives approves increase of minimum wage law to $2.20 an hour by July, 1974, for millions of workers. President Nixon vetoes the measure as inflationary.

---

lent strikes. In 1892 steelworkers went on strike at the Carnegie Company plant at Homestead, Pennsylvania. Several hundred private police from the Pinkerton Detective Agency battled them. Plant Manager Henry C. Frick (1849–1919) was determined to crush the union—"If it takes all summer. . . . Yes, even my life itself." The strike collapsed. In 1894 federal troops put down a strike called against the Pullman Company in Illinois by workers and Eugene V. Debs (1855–1926) of the American Railway Union. But President John Mitchell (1870–1919) of the United Mine Workers led the long strike of Pennsylvania coal miners to a successful conclusion in 1902.

The AFL was also challenged by other labor groups, some of them political in nature. They accused it of being too conservative. Actually, the function of the AFL was to charter national unions. This gave the unions autonomy—the right to organize the men on a specific job. The AFL leadership did not believe that the federation should become involved in politics. On the contrary, the AFL and its associated unions devoted their energies to developing collective bargaining practices. These were strengthened in 1935 by the passage of the National Labor Relations Act (Wagner Act).

Industrial Workers of the World

Among those dissatisfied with AFL policies were Debs, William D. (Big Bill)

Philip Murray (*second from left*) and John L. Lewis (*far right*) were two of the labor leaders who met in 1947 to discuss the possible merger of the AFL and the CIO.

Haywood (1869–1928), and Daniel De Leon (1852–1914). In 1905 they founded the Industrial Workers of the World (I.W.W.). Its members were nicknamed Wobblies. The aim of the Wobblies was the overthrow of capitalism. They advocated direct action —strikes and sabotage—instead of collective bargaining. To their ranks they drew mainly unskilled labor from the West and radicals from eastern textile mills. After 1920 they lost members to the Communist Party and other left-wing groups. Organized labor also opposed the Wobblies, and they gradually lost their importance.

Congress of Industrial Organizations

Mass-production industries developed on a wide scale in the 1930's. The need for new methods of union organization became clear. Some AFL leaders argued that these new industries should be organized on a craft basis. This often meant 20 or more unions in a single factory. Each union would represent a particular craft. Other leaders thought that workers in these industries should be organized in mass-industrial unions. Each union would represent all workers in an entire industry. John L. Lewis (1880–1969) of the United Mine Workers headed this faction—the Committee for Industrial Organization. It was forced out of the AFL in 1937.

The same year, a successful drive to organize the steel industry was launched under the leadership of Philip Murray (1886–1952). An attempt to organize the Ford Motor Company followed. Strikers used an old tactic, the "sit-down" technique— instead of leaving the factory, they remained in it, next to their machines.

In 1938 the industrial union group changed its name to Congress of Industrial Organizations (CIO). Many workers flocked to join the AFL and the CIO during the 1940's. The end of World War II was marked by the end of wage and price controls—and by strikes. One result was passage of the Labor-Management Relations Act of 1947 (Taft-Hartley Act). This law restricted the calling of strikes that endangered the nation's safety, health, or welfare. John L. Lewis retired from the CIO presidency in 1940. Philip Murray succeeded him. Walter P. Reuther (1907–70) of the United Automobile Workers (UAW) became CIO president in 1952. The CIO followed many AFL policies. But unlike the AFL, the CIO believed in taking direct political action.

AFL-CIO

For several years many people had believed that the two giant labor organizations should merge. This they did in 1955. George Meany

George Meany (*left*), AFL-CIO president, and Walter Reuther (*right*), then vice-president, join hands at the AFL-CIO merger convention in New York City in 1955.

was named the first president of the combined American Federation of Labor-Congress of Industrial Organizations.

There are about 18,000,000 union members in the United States. Some 13,500,000 of them belong to the AFL-CIO in national and international unions. Not all unions are associated with the AFL-CIO. Certain unions belong to two minor organizations—the Confederated Unions of America and the National Independent Union Council. Others are independent. The most important independent union is the United Mine Workers (U.M.W.). The formerly independent International Brotherhood of Teamsters, joined with the United Automobile Workers to form the Alliance for Labor Action (A.L.A.) in 1968.

The AFL-CIO is the recognized spokesman of organized labor in the United States. It acts with the advice and consent of the national and international unions. "International" indicates that a national union also has locals in Canada and other countries. Some unions call themselves brotherhoods, associations, or guilds.

Some people were afraid that the merger of the AFL-CIO would give labor too much power. They did not realize that labor and management today are equally concerned with the nation's economic well-being. The unions operate educational, recreational, and medical facilities for their members. They also support programs in housing, civil rights, and full employment that benefit the entire community.

Labor Parties in the United States

Unions usually have worked for reforms through the established political parties. From time to time they have tried to develop a party of their own. However, the American labor movement is primarily a labor union movement. The unions are its most important element. It is not associated with any political party. This makes it different from the labor movements in most other countries.

The first labor party, the Workingmen's Party, appeared in 1828. The 10-hour day and free public schools were major issues in its political campaigns. Several other workingmen's parties appeared in various eastern cities, but none lasted long.

After the Civil War, labor continued to feel that the government was unfriendly to its aims. The destructive Railway Strike of 1877 convinced workers that political action was necessary. Workers and farmers joined to form the Greenback-Labor Party in 1878. They supported wider use of paper currency, the 8-hour day, and votes for women.

Many leaders of the various socialist groups were prominent European refugees who had left their native lands after the revolutions of 1848. In general they supported the economic aims of the unions. But they hoped eventually to transform America's capitalist society into a socialist worker's society. In such a social order the means of production would be owned by workers instead of by a private individual or corporation.

These views were held by the Socialist Labor Party, which was formed in the late 1870's. Disagreement within the party ranks led in 1898 to the appearance of the Social Democratic Party, which later became the Socialist Party. One of its leaders was Eugene V. Debs, organizer of the Pullman strike. He was the party's candidate for president of the United States five times. The Socialists cooperated with the unions. Many of their ideas were accepted by the union movement and the community. After World War I, however, a considerable number of the party's left-wing members joined Communist groups.

Several small labor parties sprang up in the 1930's. Most important of these was the American Labor Party. It supported progressive candidates of the major parties and in some cases nominated its own. Today labor works chiefly through the major political parties to achieve its aims. The voting power of union members is strongest in heavily industrial areas. Winning this "labor vote" is especially important in United States presidential elections.

American labor has played an active role throughout the most stirring periods in the nation's history—from post-Civil War days to the technological revolution of today. In protecting the vital interests of union members, it has advanced the well-being of all working people and of the country as a whole.

Union Organization in the United States

A labor, or trade, union is an association of wage earners in a trade or closely related trades. Its purpose is to protect and advance its members' interests with regard to wages and hours and conditions of employment. This may mean providing legal advice, taking political action, or influencing government representatives. A union's major work, however, involves **collective bargaining** with management. Today there are over 150,000 collective-bargaining contracts between employers and unions affiliated with the AFL-CIO.

Some industries employ large numbers of "blue-collar" workers. Among these are the construction, manufacturing, and transportation industries. Their unions are especially strong and active. Many "white-collar" workers are now organized. Groups of retail clerks, teachers, newspaper employees, actors, and office employees belong to unions.

Kinds of Unions. Craft unions represent all the jobs in a particular craft—carpenters, electricians, and so on. They may work in many different industries. National craft unions exercise so-called **horizontal** authority or command over their members. Industrial unions represent all the workers in one or more industries—the aircraft and automobile industries, for example. They work at many different jobs. National industrial unions ex-

Women took an active role in the labor movement in the early 1900's.

SOME IMPORTANT DATES IN THE HISTORY OF INTERNATIONAL LABOR

1791 **France:** Le Chapelier Law passed. This outlawed the organization of all private trade unions. Trade unions continued to exist illegally, and their leaders were often involved in law suits.

1799– **Great Britain:** Combination Acts passed. This
1800 made all trade groupings illegal.

1824 **Great Britain:** Combination Acts repealed. Government thought if unions were made legal, their appeal would be reduced.

1834 **Great Britain:** Grand National Consolidated Trades Union established. Tried to unite the workers, but failed.

1845 **Great Britain:** National Association of United Trades for the Protection of Labour founded. This also failed.

1864 **Great Britain:** International Workingmen's Association (First International) founded by Karl Marx in London. This tried to set forth Marx's ideas of socialism.

1868 **Great Britain:** Trades Union Congress (T.U.C.) formed at a conference of trades union organizations at Manchester. Another attempt to unite the workers. The American Federation of Labor (AFL) borrowed many ideas from the T.U.C.

1886 **Canada:** Trades and Labour Congress of Canada (T.L.C.) founded. Its goals were much the same as those of the AFL, which was founded in the same year.

1889 **Great Britain:** Dockers strike in London. Ends in an unexpected victory for strikers. Encourages the growth of unions.

1894 **New Zealand:** Compulsory system to settle disputes set up. This system favored unions.

1895 **France:** First trade federation, Confédération Générale du Travail (C.G.T.)—General Confederation of Labor—founded. In 1902 became the official national voice of labor in France.

1901 First conference of international labor organizations in Copenhagen. (Adopts title of International Federation of Trade Unions, I.F.T.U., in 1913. Headquarters in Amsterdam established in 1919.)

1907 **Canada:** Industrial Disputes Investigation Act passed. Set up compulsory investigation system in disputes involving railroads, public utilities, and coal mines. During World War II extended to all industries.

1919 International Labour Organisation (ILO) created.

1921 **Canada:** French Canadian Confederation of National Trade Unions (C.N.T.U.) formed in Montreal. This was composed of Roman Catholic and French Canadian labor groups.
Great Britain: Strike of miners defeated.

1927 **Canada:** All-Canadian Congress of Labour—later the Canadian Congress of Labour (C.C.L.)—formed.
Australia: Australian Council of Trade Unions (A.C.T.U.) founded at Melbourne.

1945 World Federation of Trade Unions (W.F.T.U.) founded in Paris. Controlled by the Communists.
Great Britain: Labour Party comes into power.

1949 Confederation of Free Trade Unions (I.C.F.T.U.) set up in London. Splits with W.F.T.U.

1956 **Canada:** Trades and Labour Congress (T.L.C.) and Canadian Congress of Labour (C.C.L.) merge. Form the Canadian Labour Congress (C.L.C.).

1957 **Italy:** Italian National Confederation of Labor Unions formed.

1961 AFL-CIO establishes foundation for development of union leadership in Latin America.

1965 African-American Labor Center established by AFL-CIO to expand assistance to African free trade unions.

1969 ILO receives the Nobel Peace Prize for its fight against poverty and unemployment.

---

ercise **vertical** authority and are called vertical organizations.

How Unions Operate. Local unions, or "locals," represent workers in the same area, such as a city or county. They hold meetings at a headquarters or hall, and there are regular elections of officers. If they can afford to, locals hire a full-time, paid representative, or "business agent."

Certain locals may join together to form a national union. National unions are governed by a convention that is held every year or so. Most of the 185 national and international unions in the United States are associated with a federation, the AFL-CIO. It has headquarters in Washington, D.C., and is governed by a convention that is held every 2 years. An executive council and committee and a general board govern the federation between conventions. Each of the associated unions conducts its own affairs and is free to withdraw from the federation at any time.

Union members pay monthly dues to the local union. Part is kept by the local; the rest is shared by the national union and the federation. Sometimes unions have a **checkoff** arrangement with employers. With the worker's approval, the employer deducts dues from his pay and turns them over to the union. Dues pay union operating expenses. They also provide funds to aid members during illness, old age, strikes, and periods of unemployment.

▶ ORGANIZED LABOR AROUND THE WORLD

In many parts of the world there are more agricultural workers than industrial workers in the labor force. Union organization in these areas is weak. It is strongest where the oldest and best-organized labor movements are found: in the industrial nations of North America and Western Europe and in Australia and New Zealand.

Many Countries Have Labor Unions

The distinctive feature of the Canadian labor movement is its close association with labor in the United States. Most union mem-

A protest meeting of Japanese miners in Tokyo.

bers belong to the Canadian Labour Congress (C.L.C.), which was formed in 1956. The headquarters of its international unions are located in Washington, D.C. In the province of Quebec there are also Roman Catholic, French Canadian labor syndicates that are similar to unions. The Confederation of National Trade Unions (C.N.T.U.), to which these labor syndicates belong, was founded in 1921.

In most countries outside North America the labor movement is associated with a political party. The Trades Union Congress in Great Britain, for example, is politically allied with the Labour Party. Sometimes a country may have several trade-union movements, generally split along religious or political lines. Japan and Mexico have a number of national federations and unions representing many shades of opinion. In France and Italy, as other examples, unions represent Roman Catholic, Socialist, and Communist viewpoints. The labor unions in the Soviet Union and in the Communist-dominated countries of Eastern Europe and Asia are not unions as that term is understood in a democracy. This is because their right to strike or bargain is limited. In the Soviet Union, for instance, strikes are not forbidden by law, but they are considered to be harmful to the best interests of the country.

In general, labor movements in Africa, Asia, and Latin America have come into existence only since 1900. These areas still are largely agricultural. Industry has made rapid gains in such countries as Japan, India, and Mexico, however, especially since World War II.

International Organizations

The first international labor organization was the International Federation of Trade Unions (I.F.T.U.). It was founded in 1901. After World War I the Russians established a rival group. In 1945 the British Trades Union Congress (T.U.C.), the American CIO, and the Soviet federation attempted to set up a combined organization. Four years later this split into two groups. One was the Communist-controlled World Federation of Trade Unions (W.F.T.U.); the other, the International Confederation of Free Trade Unions (I.C.F.T.U.). Rivalry between these two groups has encouraged the growth of unions in less developed countries. In these countries the I.C.F.T.U. has set up educational and training projects for workers.

Among the national organizations belonging to the I.C.F.T.U. are the British T.U.C., the Canadian C.L.C., and the American AFL-CIO. They are also members of the International Labour Organisation. The ILO was founded in 1919. It was associated with, but independent of, the League of Nations. Many nations that were not League members belonged to the ILO. When the UN was formed in 1945, the ILO became one of its specialized agencies. Its aim is to improve working and living conditions around the world. The ILO represents governments, employers, and workers. Its headquarters are in Geneva, Switzerland.

Prepared with the co-operation of
LOUIS HOLLANDER
Vice-President
Amalgamated Clothing Workers of America

See also ECONOMICS; GOMPERS, SAMUEL; GUILDS; INDUSTRIAL REVOLUTION; INDUSTRY; LABOR AND MANAGEMENT; SLAVERY; SOCIALISM.

LABOR AND MANAGEMENT

The **labor force** includes individuals who make their living by working for someone else and who are paid for their services in the form of wages or salaries. Not included are the self-employed—those who make their living from the fees they receive from their clients or patients.

In the early days of industry most business and industrial organizations were run and managed by the people who owned them. As organizations grew larger, corporations were formed. A **corporation** is an organization in which a group of persons is permitted by law to act as one person. A corporation is also permitted to sell shares of stock—representing ownership—in a business. In this way, many people outside an organization may actually "own" it.

As the corporations grew, it became necessary to hire people to manage them. These people work for salary, but their responsibilities are very much like those of the owner-manager. Their job is to represent the owner in running the business. They are said to belong to management.

Management, then, is the group of individuals within an organization that is responsible for directing the achievement of the goals of the organization—the production of goods and services. This group includes managers who are also owners of the company, as well as managers who are only employed by the company. The owner or president and the top officials clearly belong to management. To the workers within an organization, managers represent the owner or those who run the organization.

▶ THEY AGREE AND DISAGREE

Labor and management agree in some areas and disagree in others. Both have a common interest in keeping the general economy healthy. Both wish to see the economy grow, so that more goods and services are bought. This in turn means that more jobs are provided, bringing increased wages and salaries to the workers and increased profits to the owners. In an industry or business firm, labor and management have a common interest in producing goods or services that will sell. This means that they must be able to compete in quality, quantity, and price.

Some countries—the United States is an example—have a competitive economic system. In this kind of system a product must be able to compete successfully and efficiently against the products of other companies. A company will be successful if enough of the product is sold to pay the necessary expenses and to provide a profit as well. If a business or industry is not able to compete—its product may be poor in quality or its production may be particularly inefficient—it will fail. When a business or industry fails, its owners lose their money (investment), and its employees lose their jobs.

Goods and services are produced by owners and the people they employ working together. How much of the money (income) made by a business or industry should go to the owner and how much to the employee? Probably owner and employer have not been able to agree on this question since the first time one man worked for another. Today it is harder than ever to find an answer. Business organizations are much larger than they used to be. Instead of turning out a product all by himself, a workman specializes—he does only part of the work. It is on this question of how to divide up the income of a company that management and labor disagree.

▶ GROWTH AFFECTS LABOR-MANAGEMENT RELATIONS

Suppose that a man who owns tools, a building, and materials hires another man to make chairs. Both men are interested in producing chairs that people will want to buy. Both hope the business can sell enough chairs to make the money needed for it to stay in business.

The owner-manager and the employee will share the income. The owner-manager must get back the cost of the tools, the building, and materials. He must also put aside money to replace tools, repair buildings, and buy new material. He may also hope to save money or to be able to borrow money (which he can pay back with interest from the income of the business) so that he can expand the business. In return for the use of his money and his own services as manager he wants income in the form of profit—money left over after necessary expenses have been paid. Another part of the income must be paid as wages to the man who works for him.

Although owner-manager and employees share a common interest in the business and are dependent upon each other, each will hope to get as much money as he can for his services. They will reach an agreement as to how much the worker is to receive. This agreement is reached when the worker consents to work for the owner-manager at a certain wage.

The agreement will depend upon many things—the availability of workers (**labor supply**) and how many other jobs are open to the worker (**labor demand**). The wages being paid to other workers (**wage level**) must be taken into account, as well as the demand for the product (**product market**). Other considerations are the amount of profit coming to the owner and the amount he could earn by using his money and time in some other way. Changes in any of these factors may cause the owner-manager or the employee to try to change the original wage agreement.

The basic elements of labor-management relations are contained in this example of a single owner-manager and single employee. But when a business is successful and grows, its organization becomes more complicated.

The original owner may hire others to help manage the business for him. These members of management will share his goals and interests. More workers may be hired to make chairs. They, like the original employee, will want to get as much money as they can for their services.

The job of making the chairs may become specialized—each man doing only part of the job. One may make chair legs, one may make seats, one may make chair backs, one may put the parts together. The company may even start to make other products, such as tables and beds, which require workmen with different skills. These changes would make it necessary for management to decide upon several wage rates, not just one. The rates would depend upon the skills that are needed, for example.

Labor-management relations in a large business are more complicated than in a small business, but their basic elements do not change. In the one-owner, one-employee

---

SOME LABOR TERMS

Arbitration—An arrangement under which labor and management agree to refer disputes to an outside third party and to obey its decisions. The government orders **compulsory arbitration** for disputes that affect the public interest.

Checkoff—That part of a worker's wages that is deducted by the employer and paid directly to the union as dues.

Closed shop—A requirement that a company hire only workers who are union members.

Featherbedding—Union practice of requiring management to continue to employ workers who are no longer necessary. (A management term).

Fringe benefits—Vacations, pension plans, health insurance, and other extras provided for employees and paid for by the company.

Grievance—A complaint about wages, or similar matters, directed by labor against management.

Lockout—An employer's refusal to let his employees enter their place of work unless they accept his terms.

Open shop—A company's freedom to hire workers who have not joined a union and are not required to.

Pickets—People posted at a place of work or business by a labor union to dissuade nonunion workers from entering and to discourage the public from trading.

Seniority—Worker's rank according to length of service. The longer a worker is employed, the greater are his rights to job security, promotion, and favored treatment.

Strike or walkout—Workers' refusal to work in order to obtain certain benefits or concessions from their employer.

Strikebreaker—Person hired by an employer to do the work of an employee who is on strike.

Union shop—A requirement that a company hire workers who, if not union members already, must join a union within a certain time.

---

business, labor and management can talk directly with each other and solve all their problems. In the larger business there is apt to be less contact between labor and management, and it is harder to solve problems between them.

Labor's Position. Sometimes labor may have a strong position in bargaining with management. This may happen when the supply of labor is short, as in wartime, or when a particular skill is scarce. But the individual worker has little bargaining power, because he can only give or refuse to give his services. Only when he has other job opportunities does he have much influence in bargaining with management.

Management's Position. Management is in a stronger position in bargaining over wages and terms of employment because usually there are more people looking for work than there are jobs. It is management too that decides when to expand or hire more labor

Picket lines are public evidence that there is a dispute between union and management.

Walter Reuther, president of the United Automobile Workers (1946–70) speaking before a conference between his union and the management of General Motors.

and when to cut production and lay off or fire certain workers. Management may also decide to introduce tools or machines that take the place of human labor or that allows the same amount of labor to produce more.

▶ THE GOVERNMENT STEPS IN

The basic conflict between labor and management and the natural weakness in labor's bargaining position appeared early in the development of industrial society. Labor was plentiful, so wages were low and work hours were long. Women and children could be more easily exploited (underpaid or unjustly used) than men, and so suffered most. Of course, not all owners and managers were unkind. But if they did not do what everyone else did, their labor costs became too high. They could not compete with others and were forced out of business. These conditions led to many problems—exploitation of women and children, low wages, long hours, unsafe working conditions, unemployment.

Management says that it must be free to decide how best to use labor in the business organization. Labor, which depends upon continued employment in order to make a living, tries to limit the decisions management can make. Many managements, of course, look out for the well-being of their employees. Others think of labor as something to be used as cheaply as possible. In order to protect labor and to make the balance of bargaining power more equal, governments have passed certain laws.

The Worker's Rights and Safety

All industrial nations have laws to prevent labor from being exploited. The earliest laws of this kind had to do with the employment of women and children. These laws regulated working hours, wages, age at which children could start work, and such matters. Laws of central and local governments also set up health and safety standards.

Social Insurance

For most people any interruption of income because of injury, sickness, unemployment, or old age may cause economic disaster. Not all employers can afford programs that offer protection to their workers. So again governments have had to provide protection to some

degree. The earliest social insurance laws in the United States had to do with workmen's compensation. This provides medical care and limited income payments to workers who become sick or are injured or die as a result of conditions or an accident on the job. Such federal laws as the Railroad Unemployment Insurance Act (1938) and the Social Security Act (1935) provide payments during periods of temporary unemployment or permanent disability, or upon reaching retirement age. Private insurance sometimes provided by or through the employer gives compensation in cases of injury, accident, or death that are not connected with employment. These forms of social insurance have helped to soften the impact when a worker is temporarily or permanently out of a job.

Labor-Management Relations

The third type of government legislation aims to provide more balance to the labor-management bargaining relationship. When all the workers of an employer, community, or entire industry act together, they have a stronger bargaining position than does the individual worker. That is why labor unions developed.

The Wagner Act. The first permanent federal law governing labor-management relations in the United States (outside the railroad industry) was the National Labor Relations Act, or Wagner Act, of 1935.

The basic aims of the Wagner Act were to:

(1) prevent certain actions by management to make the development of unions difficult;

(2) guarantee the right of any group of employees to form a union and bargain collectively (together) with management;

(3) set up a federal agency, the National Labor Relations Board (NLRB).

The purpose of the NLRB was to provide employees with the means of deciding whether they wanted a union to represent them and to enforce other conditions of the act. These included preventing employers' using "unfair labor practices"—doing things the law forbids. An example of an unfair labor practice is the interfering with union organization by firing or refusing to hire a person because of union membership or activity. Several states adopted similar laws.

The Wagner Act and the NLRB speeded the growth of union activity and made the collective bargaining process more important. They made the balance between labor and management more equal. Some people believed that they gave the unions too much power. They thought certain changes were needed to protect the rights of management and of individual union members. So two new laws were passed.

The Taft-Hartley Act. The Labor-Management Act (or Taft-Hartley Act) of 1947 was passed following a wave of strikes in 1946 and 1947. It was an amendment to the Wagner Act.

The purposes of the Taft-Hartley Act were to:

(1) prevent major strikes that would cause public emergencies and look for ways of settling them;

(2) forbid some union practices that had been found to be unfair and check the use of some union tactics;

(3) permit labor and management to sue each other in federal courts for damages suffered as a result of breaking a collective-bargaining contract;

(4) require unions to file certain financial and organizational data with the United States Department of Labor if unions wished to use the administrative safeguards available in the act.

The Labor-Management Reporting and Disclosure Act. In 1959 the Labor-Management Reporting and Disclosure (or Landrum-Griffin) Act was passed. The purposes of this act were to:

(1) report more complete financial and organizational data;

(2) deal more effectively with corrupt practices of employers or unions and with undemocratic union procedures;

(3) change some of the curbs on unfair labor practices contained in the Taft-Hartley Act;

(4) make clear what authority the state and federal governments have over matters involved in labor-management relations.

These laws did not change the basic right of the worker to engage in union activities and to bargain collectively with management.

Collective Bargaining

In **collective bargaining** management meets with union officers representing labor to discuss hours, wages, conditions of employment, and other matters. When an agreement on these demands is reached between labor and management officials, it is put into a written **labor contract** and signed by both parties. It then becomes a legal agreement, which can be enforced in a court of law.

When the issues are wages, hours, and so on, bargaining takes place about the terms of the contract. But sometimes unions try to find new ways of dealing with new problems. Management also finds that new problems or new experiences with old problems often make it desirable to change the terms of contracts.

Management generally tries to keep or to broaden its area of decision making. Unions try to prevent management from doing this and in turn seek to broaden those decisions having to do with labor that are covered through collective-bargaining agreements. Besides bargaining with each other, labor and management often try to achieve their aims through government action or court decisions.

▶ ISSUES IN LABOR-MANAGEMENT RELATIONS

(1) Union security is always an important issue with unions. It includes the sections in collective bargaining agreements that are intended to protect the union as an institution. Management has always fought for an **open shop**. An open shop exists when management may hire a person who is not a union member, and the employee need not join a union. Unions have always felt that their greatest security rested in the **closed shop**—that is, an agreement that management will hire and keep only union members. The Taft-Hartley Act declared that the closed shop was not legal.

Most collective bargaining contracts provide for either a **union shop** or for **maintenance of membership**. Under a union-shop agreement management may hire anyone. However, all workers who are hired must join the union within a certain period of time, usually 30 days. They must also remain in the union as long as they are employed. Maintenance of membership is a somewhat weaker union-security agreement. Under it a worker is not required to join the union. But a worker who does join must keep up his membership

WORKERS COVERED

UNION STATUS

HOURS OF WORK

WAGE RATES FOR EACH
JOB CLASSIFICATION

SENIORITY RIGHTS

JOB
SECURITY

GRIEVANCE
PROCEDURE

FRINGE BENEFITS
(PAID HOLIDAYS
AND VACATIONS, ETC.)

SOME FEATURES OF A LABOR CONTRACT

in the union during the period of the union contract.

Unions generally look for the contract to provide for **checkoff** of union dues. This means that the employer deducts union dues from the employee's wages and pays them directly to the union. Under the Taft-Hartley Act the checkoff can be made only with the written consent of each employee.

(2) Employees also have a security issue — **job security**. The union generally tries to make sure that the contract limits management's right to fire or lay off an employee. A worker can be fired or laid off temporarily only under special circumstances. The firing or layoff, furthermore, is subject to review under the **grievance procedure**.

The grievance procedure is an important part of a union-management agreement. It outlines the course of action that the union and management representatives will take in trying to solve problems that arise under the contract. It is designed to permit settlement of

disputed issues during the contract without interrupting work. Sometimes the representatives cannot arrive at an agreement themselves. Many labor contracts state that when this happens, the issue will be referred to an outside third party who will not favor one side over the other. This third-party settlement is called **arbitration.** Both union and management must obey its decisions.

(3) Related to a worker's job security is **seniority**. This refers to the length of time a worker has been employed compared with that of the other workers. Seniority governs the order in which workers are laid off—those who have been employed the shortest time are laid off first. When the firm begins to recall (bring back) workers, those with the longest term of employment are recalled first. Seniority also counts in such matters as length of vacation, wages, and preference in promotion to better jobs. It is based on the idea that the longer a worker is employed by an organization, the greater right he has to continued em-

ployment and favorable treatment in other matters.

(4) **Fringe benefits** make up another important part of wage settlements. The term "fringe benefits" is used to describe such matters as holidays and vacations with pay, retirement pensions, medical care insurance, life insurance, and other related benefits.

(5) Workers and their unions are always fearful of unemployment. It may occur as a normal condition of employment—in construction, for example, bad weather stops work during the winter months. This is called **seasonal unemployment**. On the other hand, it may result from a drop in the general economy or the lack of demand for a certain product. This type of unemployment generally is considered to be temporary. Unions have tried to provide seniority guarantees in labor contracts to protect workers with long service. They have also tried to get labor contracts to guarantee a certain minimum period of employment or a minimum amount of income.

New methods and machines may cause unemployment by increasing the amount a worker can produce and thus lessening the need for so many workers. Such unemployment is called **technological unemployment** and usually is considered to be permanent. Here again, seniority is used to protect workers with long service. Unions have tried to develop contract provisions that oblige management to make some final payment to workers who have been permanently discharged. The idea behind this is to make it more costly for management to replace workers with new machines and methods. It would also give the workers funds to help support themselves while they are trying to find other jobs.

Many workers lost their jobs in the late 1950's and early 1960's because of **automation** (the automatic operation of machines by other machines), the newest and most complete type of technological change. This caused some unions and managements to develop special agreements to help soften the effects of job losses on workers. These agreements included such things as funds to pay for training for new jobs and special programs for placing jobless workers in new jobs.

Labor's fear of unemployment sometimes has led unions to resist new technological

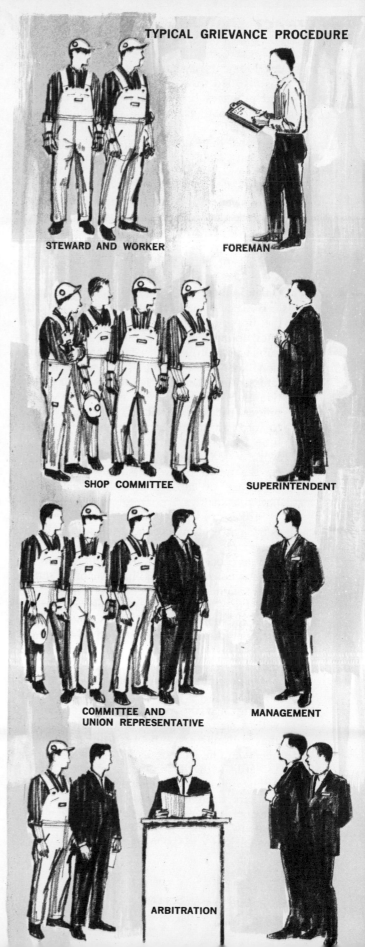

TYPICAL GRIEVANCE PROCEDURE

STEWARD AND WORKER   FOREMAN

SHOP COMMITTEE   SUPERINTENDENT

COMMITTEE AND
UNION REPRESENTATIVE   MANAGEMENT

ARBITRATION

developments. According to management, it has also led to contract terms on work rules and practices that force the hiring of more workers than are needed. Sometimes these practices have resulted in creating and keeping jobs that management thinks are unnecessary and in requiring the employment of substitute employees. Management calls such practices **featherbedding**. Unions generally explain that these employees are necessary to make sure of the quality of the work or to improve safety conditions, or that the hiring of these men is the usual practice of an industry or firm.

Union Tactics

Both unions and management today realize the importance of settling disputes without interrupting work. They are also sensitive to public opinion, which works through legislation and other channels to prevent such interruption. Seldom used now while a collective bargaining contract is in force is the unions' use of the **strike** (stoppage of work) to force an agreement by management. Also little used is the **lockout** (shutting down of work by management) to force an agreement by the union or workers. Such actions are forbidden by most contracts as well as by law.

Strikes or lockouts may occur when a union is trying to get management to accept it as the bargaining agent for a firm's workers. They may also occur when a new contract is being negotiated and disputes that cannot be settled by bargaining arise over its provisions. But even here, laws effecting labor make it difficult to take such action. The government also provides the services of skilled labor mediators to help both parties arrive at a settlement.

Unions put pressure on management in another way—by **picketing**. This means patrolling near the plant or place of business with a sign advising workers and the public that a dispute exists between union and management. One purpose is to force management to settle with the union through the use of public opinion. Another purpose is to prevent workers from continuing to work—a union member is not supposed to cross a picket line. Usually the use of picketing is regulated by law.

▶UNIONS AND LABOR-MANAGEMENT RELATIONS

In collective bargaining, management deals with its workers as a group rather than as individuals. It negotiates terms of wages and hours and conditions of employment with unions representing the workers, not with the workers themselves. Conditions of employment and of settling disputes that may arise are determined for the workers through the union and the collective bargaining process.

Unions also exercise an indirect influence on labor-management relations. Union leaders represent almost one third of labor. They are organized and have financial resources. Thus they often speak on issues or work for laws as economic, social, or political importance. As a representatives of all labor on matters of economic, social, or political importance. As a result of these activities unions have an influence over labor-management relations in such areas of governmental legislation as determination of the minimum wage required by law.

Unions also affect labor-management relations indirectly through their influence on workers who are not covered by union contracts. The terms of settlement of issues that are included in union contracts have an effect upon the wages and conditions of employment of other workers. If the production workers in a company get an increase under the union contract, management often gives a similar increase to office workers who may not be union members. One reason for this is the need to treat all workers alike, without discrimination. Another reason is that if such changes were not extended to nonunion workers, they might decide to join a union. Firms without unions may also try to keep up with or get ahead of union agreement terms in an effort to stop their workers forming a union.

In all countries where organized labor exists it has an influence upon labor-management relations that goes far beyond the direct effect it achieves through collective bargaining. It is clear that unions make up an important segment of a modern industrial economy.

ROBERT F. RISLEY
New York State School of Industrial and
Labor Relations, Cornell University

See also LABOR.

LABRADOR. See NEWFOUNDLAND; CANADA.

Belgian bobbin lace: Valenciennes.

French needlepoint lace: Point d'Alençon.

French bobbin lace: Chantilly.

LACE

Lace is an airy and delicate fabric made of fine threads stitched into lovely patterns. Lace is used to add beauty to many things we wear and use. It may be made by hand or by machine.

Handmade lace is usually made by one of two methods: the needlepoint method or the bobbin method. **Needlepoint lace** is made by drawing the design on a thick piece of paper backed by linen. The outline of the pattern is stitched onto the paper. The stitching is used as a framework. On it the lacemaker works with a needle and single thread, building up the pattern with looped stitches. When the work is completed, the framework stitches are clipped and the lace is lifted off the pattern.

Two of the most common needlepoint laces are Venetian and Alençon. **Venetian lace** usually has a delicate design of roses. Sometimes the design is raised. **Alençon** has flower patterns outlined by a heavy thread.

Bobbin lace is made with a large number of threads, each fastened to a bobbin (spool). The pattern is drawn on paper, and the paper is fastened onto a cushion. The end of each bobbin thread is attached to the cushion. Then pins are stuck into the cushion to keep the threads in position while the lace is being made. The lace is made with a pair of bobbins in each hand. These are moved from side to side to twist or interlace the threads.

As the work progresses the pins are moved farther along.

Probably the most beautiful of the bobbin laces is **Duchesse lace**, which has an exquisite allover design. **Chantilly lace** is a bobbin lace that has vine or spray patterns on a mesh ground. It is favored for evening dresses and bridal veils. **Cluny lace** is a fairly coarse bobbin lace. It is often used to trim children's dresses and household linens.

Machine-made lace usually copies the designs of handmade lace. A machine often used today is the Leavers machine, first patented in Britain in 1813. It is a very large machine, weighing about 17 tons and covering about 10 by 150 feet of floor space.

The first true handmade lace was probably made in Italy in the middle of the 1500's. Very soon afterward fine laces were being made in France. During the 1770's France and Belgium (especially Brussels) were the most important lace-making areas. Today handmade lace is made chiefly in Italy and Belgium. Machine-made lace is produced in England, France, and the United States.

LACQUERS. See VARNISHES AND LACQUERS.

LACROSSE

Lacrosse is a game that was developed by the North American Indians. It is the oldest organized sport in America.

When the French settlers of Canada saw it played, they called it lacrosse. The stick and net used in the game looked to them like a *crosse,* or crosier—the curved staff carried by a bishop. The modern stick has a handle and a triangular webbed net. Two sides of the net are attached to wooden side walls.

▶ PLAYING THE GAME

Lacrosse is played by two teams of ten players each—three attack, three midfield, three defense, and one goalkeeper. The length of the collegiate game is 60 minutes, divided into 4 periods, each 15 minutes long. The high-school game is 40 minutes long.

Each team tries to control the ball, which is about 8 inches in circumference, and to score by putting the ball into the opponents' goal. The ball is kept in play by being carried in a player's stick and eventually passed to a teammate who will shoot it at the goal. When the ball falls to the ground, a player can pick it up with a scooping motion of his stick. Any player may kick the ball, but only the defending goalie can bat the ball with his hand.

When throwing, a player does not usually face his target; his body is turned to the side. Passes are made in several ways. The long pass requires different motions from the short pass. The easily-blocked shovel pass is used for very short distances.

In catching, the head of the stick is turned so the entire net, or pocket, is prepared to receive the ball. While the player is running, the stick is turned upward and the ball is cradled in the pocket. Scooping—that is, picking the ball off the ground with the stick—is very important, since the ball is often loose on the field.

▶ TEAM OFFENSE AND DEFENSE

The three attackmen and three midfielders make up the attacking team. Their job is to carry out a play that will score a goal.

To get a man free for a shot, the three midfielders can use a weaving pattern. The opposing defensemen change position to cover them. To increase pressure on the defense, two attackmen behind the goal can also begin weaving. The other attackman remains near the crease, the 9-foot-radius circle around the goal (the goal is 6 feet wide).

The pass and cut is an effective play. An offensive player passes the ball to a teammate and fakes in one direction. Then he breaks for the goal and receives a return pass.

A screen, or pick, occurs when an offensive player blocks out the defenseman guarding another offensive player of the first man's team. This allows the latter to get free to take a close shot at the goal or to receive a pass in shooting territory.

The two attackmen who play behind the goal must control the ball when it is in their area. And they must look for chances to pass the ball to an open man. This is called feeding. They may feed the crease attackman, who might try for a goal. Or they may cut, or feed, a midfielder who is in a position for a shot.

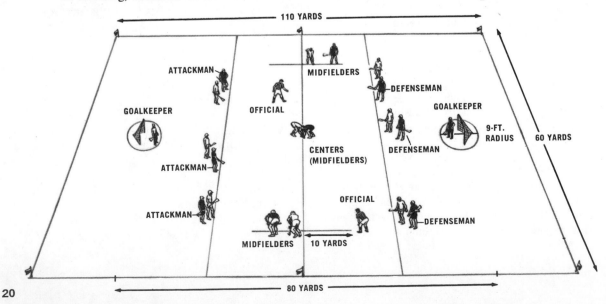

The attackmen must be able to dodge by their defensemen and come around to the front of the goal for a shot. They must also "back up" the goal. This means they must cover stray shots, missed passes, or any other balls that go past the goal.

The crease attackman usually plays several yards outside the crease. He tries to screen the goalie's vision on shots taken more than 10 yards from the goal. He must be ready to play rebounds off the goalie or loose balls in the crease area. Whatever feeds he receives should give him point-blank shots, because he plays so close to the other team's goal.

When the attack loses the ball, it begins riding the other team's defense—covering very closely to keep the defense from passing the ball or from clearing, or getting the ball out of their defensive territory to their attack.

The goalkeeper, three defensemen, and three midfielders make up the defensive unit of a team. (The three attackmen must remain on their side of the center line.) A team's defense must be unified and well co-ordinated to keep its opponent's attack from scoring.

Most teams use a man-to-man defense, in which each defensive player—with the exception of the goalie—guards one attacking player. In the zone defense, each man has an area to cover. He guards any offensive player who comes into this zone.

A defenseman should have quick reactions and good balance and must be fast and aggressive. He should play between his man and the goal and be in a position to see both his man and the ball. He should never rush or step into his opponent, thus allowing the man to dodge and break away from him.

When his opponent has the ball, the defenseman tries to dislodge it by "checking," or striking, the attackman's stick with his own, or he can use his stick to block the passes or shots his attackman may try.

Basic Rules

Length of Game. The game lasts for 4 periods—each 10 or 15 minutes—with a 2-minute rest between quarters and 10 minutes between halves. At each intermission the teams change goals. If the score is tied at the end of a regulation game, there is a 5-minute intermission, then play is continued. There are 2 overtime periods of 5 minutes each. If the score is tied at the end of the overtime, the game ends and is declared a tie.

Time-outs. Each team is allowed 1 time-out—2 minutes long—per period. The clock is also stopped under the following conditions:

(a) When the ball goes out of bounds.
(b) After a team scores.
(c) When a player is injured.
(d) When a penalty is being enforced.
(e) At the end of each period.

Scoring. A goal counts 1 point.

Face-offs. At the beginning of each period or after a goal has been scored, play is started by a face-off. The two center midfielders line up at the center of the field, each facing the goal his team will be attacking. They go into a crouch with their sticks on the ground. The heads of the sticks should be placed back to back. The players rest their gloved hands on the ground. The referee then puts the ball between the sticks. When he blows the whistle, the centers battle for possession of the ball, each trying to control it with his stick.

Ball Out of Bounds. A ball that goes out of bounds past a sideline or end line is not given to the team whose player touched it last, but to the opposite team. The only exception is a ball that goes out of bounds after a shot at the goal. It is given to the player who—when play is suspended—is nearest to the point where the ball goes out of bounds. This player's team is then in possession of the ball.

Offside. Each team must have at least three men on the attack half of the field and four men on the defensive half. If a team does not have enough men in either half of the field, an offside penalty is called. It is considered a technical foul.

Personal and Technical Fouls. A player who commits a personal foul is suspended from the game for 1 to 3 minutes, and the ball is given to the team that was fouled. Body checking from the rear, slashing an opponent with the stick, tripping, pushing, holding, unnecessary roughness, and unsportsmanlike conduct—all are personal fouls. Technical fouls include interference, touching the ball with the hand, and going offside. The player who commits a technical foul is suspended for 30 seconds or his team loses the ball.

ROBERT H. SCOTT
Lacrosse Coach, Johns Hopkins University

LAFAYETTE, MARQUIS DE (1757–1834)

The Marquis de Lafayette, who fought for the freedom of the American colonies, was also a brilliant leader in the French Revolution. He devoted himself to the cause of political freedom and human liberty perhaps more unselfishly than any other man of his time.

Marie Joseph Paul Yves Roch Gilbert du Motier, Marquis de Lafayette, was born on September 6, 1757, in the family château of Chavaniac in the Auvergne region of France. When Lafayette was 2, his father was killed fighting the British. At the age of 11 he was sent to military school in Paris. Two years later, on the death of his mother and grandfather, he inherited a fortune that gave him an income, in the currency of today, of more than $2,000,000 a year. At 16 the young Marquis was married to 14-year-old Adrienne Françoise de Noailles, whose family ranked second only to the ruling Bourbons of France.

▶ HE GOES TO AMERICA

In 1776 the tall, red-haired, freckle-faced Lafayette, now a captain of dragoons, decided to go to America to fight for the freedom of the colonies. He was impelled by curiosity, a hunger for glory, and sympathy for the American cause. Benjamin Franklin and other Americans in France encouraged this sympathy. Eluding agents of his father-in-law and of the king, Louis XVI, Lafayette and a few companions set sail from a Spanish port. They reached Georgetown, South Carolina, on June 13, 1777. From Georgetown, Lafayette and his party traveled 900 miles overland by coach and on horseback to Philadelphia. There the Continental Congress gave him a commission as major general.

Thus the 19-year-old Lafayette—whom George Washington came to love as a son—began the military career that made him an American national hero.

He first saw action at the battle of Brandywine, where he was wounded in the leg. After enduring the winter hardships of Valley Forge, he undertook an impossible assault on Canada. He then distinguished himself at the battle of Monmouth. In 1778 the French signed a treaty of alliance with the United States, and Great Britain declared war on France. Lafayette then returned home to use his influence for the American cause. The once disapproving Louis XVI welcomed him. Lafayette was able to arrange for 6,000 French troops to be sent to America under General Rochambeau, and returned to America to bring General Washington the news. Entrusted by Washington with the defense of Virginia, Lafayette successfully laid seige to the British army under Lord Cornwallis. The British general had contemptuously promised to capture "the boy." Instead, Lafayette was present at Yorktown on October 19, 1781, for Cornwallis' surrender. With American independence assured, Lafayette, then barely 24, returned to France.

But the clouds of a far bloodier revolution (that of the oppressed French people) hung over his homeland. Lafayette made one triumphant return to the United States before the French Revolution began in 1789. Throughout that terrible struggle he tried to achieve a constitutional government. This alone, he thought, could bring real liberty.

▶ THE FRENCH REVOLUTION

Lafayette was elected to the Estates General, the French assembly, as a representative of the nobility. Three days before the Bastille prison fell on July 14, 1789, he issued a declaration of the rights of man, patterned after Thomas Jefferson's. He added the royal white to the colors of the Paris revolutionary cockade, or badge, giving France its tricolor flag of blue, white, and red.

Lafayette allied himself with the Revolution and was elected commander of the National Guard, the people's militia. Yet he and his guardsmen repeatedly protected the royal family from the people during the stormy months that followed. Lafayette wanted a constitution, not assassination. When the King and Queen tried to escape, Lafayette brought them back under arrest. The nobility despised him because he had arrested his King. The people distrusted him because they believed that he had helped in the escape.

In September, 1791, Louis XVI signed the constitution limiting his powers. Lafayette then went home happily to Chavaniac.

But Louis had not learned that his absolute power existed no longer. When he started a highly unpopular war with Austria, the radical

Jacobin party, backed by the Paris masses, made him a virtual prisoner. The heads of those who defended the Bourbons began to fall beneath the guillotine. Soon the same fate would befall Queen Marie Antoinette and the King himself.

Lafayette was away commanding one of the three French armies against the Austrians. He wanted to lead his troops to Paris to restore the King to the power the constitution guaranteed him. But his men refused to follow. Learning that the Jacobins planned his arrest, Lafayette and some friends fled to Belgium. There they were captured by Austria's allies.

Lafayette spent the next 5 years in prison. Adrienne's pleas brought permission for her and two of their children to join him during the last 2 years. When Napoleon Bonaparte defeated the Austrians in 1797, Lafayette was released.

Back in France he soon found himself at odds with Napoleon, whom he considered a tyrant. He retired with Adrienne to farm her estate of La Grange, practically all that was left to them. From there he corresponded with friends in Europe and America until Napoleon's downfall in 1814 and the restoration of the Bourbons under Louis XVIII. In 1819 Lafayette was elected to the Chamber of Deputies. But his liberal stand made him hated by the Royalists, who defeated him for re-election in 1824.

That year Lafayette, with his son, whom he had named for George Washington, returned for a visit to the United States. He was greeted everywhere with an emotional and loving welcome the like of which was never to be seen in the United States again.

▶ LAST YEARS

Lafayette returned to France in 1825 and re-entered politics. Repressions by Louis XVIII led to the Revolution of 1830. Louis's successor, Charles X, was overthrown and Louis Philippe, whom Lafayette had supported, came to the throne. But when the new king went back on his democratic promises, Lafayette spoke out against him for usurping the people's rights.

Lafayette died in Paris on May 20, 1834. Royalist France would permit no demonstrations in his honor. But in the United States, flags flew at half mast and the Army went into mourning for 6 months, as it had after George Washington's death.

HODDING CARTER
Author, *Marquis de Lafayette,
Bright Sword for Freedom*

LAFFITE, JEAN (1780?–1826?)

Legend and mystery surround the life of the pirate Jean Laffite. Laffite was probably born in Bayonne, France, about the year 1780. As a young man he emigrated to Louisiana with his brother Pierre and opened a blacksmith shop in New Orleans.

Jean Laffite did not remain in New Orleans long. Soon he set up headquarters on an island in Barataria Bay in the Gulf of Mexico. He became the leader of a daring band of pirates who attacked British, Spanish, and American ships. The booty they seized was smuggled into New Orleans. There, Pierre, operating out of the blacksmith shop, sold the stolen goods for large sums of money.

During the War of 1812 the British tried to buy Laffite's help against the Americans. But instead Laffite offered his assistance to General Andrew Jackson in return for a full pardon for himself and his men. Much of the success of the battle of New Orleans in 1815 was due to Laffite's efforts, and the once-dreaded pirate was now hailed as a patriot. The United States Government kept its word, and Laffite's men were pardoned.

Within 2 years, however, Laffite turned again to piracy. In 1817 he set up new headquarters on the island that is now the site of Galveston, Texas. Soon he had attracted a band of about 1,000 men.

Determined now to rid the waters of Laffite's pirate ships, the United States Government sent an expedition to wipe out his headquarters. Laffite learned of the impending attack and, according to legend, escaped on his favorite vessel, the *Pride*. Some say that he settled in Yucatan, Mexico, but no further facts about his life are known.

LA FOLLETTE, ROBERT (1855–1925) AND ROBERT, JR. (1895–1953)

Robert M. La Follette, American political reformer and statesman, was born on June 14, 1855, in Primrose, Wisconsin. La Follette worked his way through the University of Wisconsin and opened a law office in Madison. From 1885 to 1891 he served in the House of Representatives. In 1900 he was elected governor of Wisconsin, a post he held until he became a senator in 1906.

Throughout his career he fought against dishonesty in government. Although a member of the Republican Party, he followed an independent policy. He pioneered in labor legislation and helped to draft laws to benefit workers and check the power of big business. He fought for changes in the tax laws. Under his leadership Wisconsin adopted an early income-tax system. His reforms were called the Wisconsin Idea.

In foreign policy La Follette believed America should stay out of the affairs of other countries. He voted against American entry into World War I. Later he opposed United States membership in the League of Nations and in the World Court. In 1924 La Follette received close to 5,000,000 votes as presidential candidate of the Progressive Party, a group he had helped to form. He died the following year while still serving as senator.

Robert M. La Follette, Jr., was born on February 6, 1895. After attending the University of Wisconsin, he served as his father's secretary. In 1925 he was elected to fill out the senior La Follette's Senate term.

Many of La Follette's views recalled those of his father. Strongly pro-labor, he helped to sponsor the Social Security bill and changes in the tax laws. Although he, too, believed that America should avoid foreign conflicts, he supported the war effort after the Japanese attack on Pearl Harbor.

In 1946 La Follette lost the senatorial nomination to Joseph R. McCarthy (1909–57). He died in Washington, D.C., on February 24, 1953.

LA FONTAINE, JEAN DE. See FABLES.

LA GUARDIA, FIORELLO (1882–1947)

Fiorello Henry La Guardia, congressman and three times mayor of New York City, was born in New York on December 11, 1882. His father, Achilles, who had come from Italy, was a bandmaster in the Army. La Guardia's boyhood was spent in Prescott, Arizona, where his father was stationed with the Army.

In 1898 Achilles La Guardia died, and Fiorello went to Europe with his mother. He worked for the American consulates in Budapest and Trieste and as consular agent in Fiume. In 1906 he returned to the United States. With a knowledge of seven languages, he became an interpreter for the Immigration and Naturalization Service while studying law at night. In 1914 the young lawyer ran for Congress as a Republican in a Democratic-controlled district in New York. As everyone expected, he was defeated. Stubbornly, he ran again in 1916. This time he was elected.

In 1917 La Guardia left to serve as an aviator during World War I. He returned to complete his term and in 1919 was elected president of the Board of Aldermen of New York. In 1922 he won election to Congress a second time. In Congress his liberal views antagonized the Republicans, and he was often attacked by the Democrats as well. Nevertheless, he was popular with the voters, who re-elected him four times.

In 1933 the Fusion Party, a reform party, nominated La Guardia for the office of mayor of New York City. He was elected, and with his boundless energy set to work to reform the city. He balanced the budget, fought graft, and cleared slums. New parks, low-cost housing projects, roads, and an airport were built. His methods annoyed some politicians, who called him a Napoleon. But he won the respect and admiration of the people of New York. His voice became well-known to city children when, during a newspaper strike, he went on the radio to read the comics to them.

La Guardia retired as mayor in 1945. The next year he was appointed director general of the United Nations Relief and Rehabilitation Administration (UNRRA). He died in New York on September 20, 1947.

LAKES

Lakes are inland bodies of water that occupy depressions in the surface of the land. These depressions are called basins.

Lakes result from the flow of water into low areas. Lake water comes largely from rainfall and melting snow. The water enters a lake basin through brooks, streams, rivers, underground springs, and groundwater.

Where the climate is humid, more water flows into a lake basin than is lost through evaporation. In this way lake basins tend to fill up. As the water rises it overflows and runs out at the lowest point or outlet. Finally the overflow reaches an ocean or a sea, except where the outlet discharges into a desert area.

Where the climate is dry, lakes lose water rapidly by evaporation. In desert regions many lakes are saline (salty). When the amount of water that flows into a lake is matched by evaporation, salty minerals are left behind in the lake. Such lakes become saltier with time.

Great Salt Lake in the United States contains over 20 percent mineral matter. Most of this is common salt. The Dead Sea in the Middle East contains more than 24 percent mineral matter. One third of this is common salt.

Some lakes are seasonal. They exist for a short time after heavy rains. During dry weather they shrink or disappear completely.

How Lake Basins Are Formed

Lake basins are formed in several ways: by changes in the earth's crust; by volcanic action; by glaciers; by waves and currents; by rivers; by groundwater; and by man-made dams.

Changes in the Earth's Crust. Many lakes are the result of faulting or warping of the earth's crust. Lake Superior in North America, Lake Titicaca in South America, and Lake Tanganyika in the rift valley of eastern Africa are examples of such lakes.

Volcanic Action. Sometimes lakes are created by volcanoes. A lava flow may block the outlet of a valley and form a lake basin. Sometimes the crater of an extinct volcano fills with water. Crater Lake in southern Oregon is a well-known example.

Glaciers. Many lakes occupy basins formed by glacial erosion. Examples include Great Bear Lake and Lake Winnipeg in Canada, all the Great Lakes in North America except Lake Superior, Lake Ladoga in the Soviet Union, and Lake Garda in northern Italy.

Thousands of small lakes are found where ice once deposited glacial drift and dammed up valleys. There are numerous examples of such glacial lakes to be found both in the northern part of North America and in northern Europe.

Waves and Currents. Along coastal areas waves and shore currents sometimes close inlets and temporarily create lakes out of bays and estuaries.

Rivers. The main stream of a river may build up its flood plain by depositing silt (mud and soil) when the river overflows. As a result, tributary valleys are flooded and lakes are formed.

Groundwater. In places where limestone underlies the land, groundwater may dissolve and remove enough limestone to produce great sinkholes that form lake basins. Florida in the southern United States contains many lakes of this type.

Dams. Lakes may also be artificial (man-made). A dam built across a river valley will block the flow of water and form a lake.

Artificial lakes are used as reservoirs to furnish water for cities miles away. They supply water to irrigate dry farmland. Generators built at damsites produce electricity. Huge Lake Mead in the western United States was formed by building Hoover Dam on the Colorado River, between Arizona and Nevada. When the Aswan High Dam in upper Egypt is completed, its reservoir will provide electric power and water to irrigate millions of acres of land.

How Lakes Disappear

Natural lakes are temporary features of the landscape. Outlets cut downward and drain the lakes. Inflowing streams tend to build up the bottom with silt. In time a lake may become so shallow that marsh vegetation takes over. The lake then turns into a marsh, or swamp, and finally disappears. However, very large and deep lakes, like the Great Lakes, are in no danger of being drained or filled.

Effect of Lakes

Freshwater lakes, whether natural or man-made, supply water to cities and industries. Large lakes, such as the Great Lakes, modify and temper the local climate. Lakes are a source of fish, waterfowl, and fur-bearing animals, which are taken for pleasure or profit. Lakeside locations offer recreational opportunities for people who enjoy fishing, boating, swimming, and ice-skating.

Some lakes receive sewage and wastes from cities and factories. We now know that such wastes present a serious threat to the ecology. Many governments are taking steps to clean up their lakes.

GUY-HAROLD SMITH
Ohio State University

▶ LAKES OF THE WORLD

Lake Albert is a long, narrow lake located in east central Africa on the border between the Congo (Kinshasa) and Uganda. It is one of the sources of the Nile River. The lake contains many food fish and is an important inland transportation route. Lake Albert was discovered by Sir Samuel Baker in 1864. He named it in honor of Prince Albert, husband of Queen Victoria of England.

The Aral Sea is a large lake of low salt content located in the desert region of central Soviet Asia. The lake is fed by two rivers: the Syr Darya and the Amu Darya. It has no outlet. The Aral Sea is an important source of sturgeon and other food fish. Aralsk in the Kazakh Soviet Socialist Republic is one of its chief ports. Formerly named the Khwarazm Sea, this lake is believed to have flowed into the Caspian Sea during glacial times.

Lake Athabasca forms a crescent across northwestern Saskatchewan and northeastern Alberta in Canada. It is fed from the southwest by the Athabasca River and is drained to the north by the Slave River. The lake is the fourth largest Canadian lake and is a popular nesting ground for wild geese.

Lake Baikal is in the Soviet Union, north of the Mongolian border. It is the deepest lake in the world and the largest freshwater lake in Eurasia. The long, narrow lake is fed by more than 330 streams, but the Angara River is its only outlet. The largest of its 27 islands is Olkhon Island, which is noted for its fish-processing industry. The lake contains seals, as well as salmon and other varieties of fish. A steamer service links its main ports during the ice-free months of the year.

Lake Balaton in western Hungary is the largest lake in central Europe. Its main tributary is the Zala River. It is drained by the Sio River, which flows into the Danube River. Vineyards cover its shores. The lake is navigable, contains many fish, and is a resort center.

Lake Balkhash is located in a desert region in the Kazakh Republic of the Soviet Union. It is 100 miles west of the Chinese border. The water is fresh where the Ili River enters the lake. Because the lake has no outlet, its water becomes salty towards the east. Salt and fish are the lake's chief resources. The lake is frozen 5 months of the year.

Lake Baikal in the Soviet Union.

Neftyanyye Kamni, an oil town built on pilings in the Caspian Sea.

The Caspian Sea, located in southwestern Soviet Asia and northern Iran, is the largest saltwater lake in the world. The present Caspian lies in a basin that was once part of a vast ancient sea. The lake has many tributaries but no outlet. The Caspian receives the Ural and Volga rivers from the north; the Terek, Sulak, Samur, and Kura rivers from the west, and the Sefid-Rud and Atrek rivers from the south. Nevertheless, because evaporation exceeds inflow, the lake level has decreased more than 7 feet in 35 years. The northern part of the lake is an important source of fish, and the entire lake is a major transportation route. Water from the Amu Darya reaches the Caspian by way of the low area known as the Uzboy and helps to maintain the surface at approximately 90 feet. Important Russian and Iranian ports are situated on the Caspian, and lumber, petroleum, grain, and dried fruits are the most common freight.

Lake Chad is a large, shallow, freshwater lake in north central Africa. It lies at the point where Nigeria, Cameroon, Chad, and Niger meet. It is fed by the Chari-Logone and the Komadugu river systems but has no visible outlet. The waters of Lake Chad sink underground to supply wells along the Bahr el Ghazal, a broad, depressed area. The size of the lake fluctuates according to season. Fish and natron (mineral) deposits are the only resources. Nets, basket traps, and spears are used for shallow-water fishing in the numerous swampy portions of Lake Chad.

Lake Champlain lies in a broad valley between the Adirondack Mountains and the Green Mountains. It forms part of the border between New York and Vermont, with an extension 7 miles into southern Quebec. During the glacial period the lake occupied the entire Champlain lowland. It is drained to the north by the Richelieu River and is connected with the Hudson River by the Champlain Canal. The surrounding region is fertile and is used for farmland or orchards. The lake attracts many summer tourists and is a link in the Hudson–St. Lawrence waterway. It was named for Samuel de Champlain, who discovered it in 1609. The lake was an important battle site in the French and Indian War, in the American Revolution, and in the War of 1812.

Lake Como, one of many lakes bordering the Alps, owes its origin to a mountain glacier. The glacier eroded a deep basin and blocked the outlet with debris. The lake is an Italian resort center famous for its beautiful scenery. It lies in north central Italy, surrounded by lofty Alpine peaks. The Adda and Mera rivers feed the lake, the Adda also being its outlet.

Crater Lake is a deep-blue, volcanic lake located in Crater Lake National Park in southwestern Oregon. It is the deepest lake in North America. The lake lies in a large pit, or crater, formed by the destruction of the summit of Mount Mazama—an ancient volcano. The lake is without outlet or inlet, and is kept filled by rain and snow. The shores are lined with multicolored cliffs that rise 2,000 feet above the surface of the water. These cliffs are encircled by towering mountains, some almost 9,000 feet high. Near the western shore Small Wizard Island, a small, inactive volcano with a 90-foot-deep crater at its summit, rises 776 feet above the water. These natural wonders, in addition to a scenic drive around the rim of the lake, make Crater Lake a popular tourist attraction.

The Dead Sea lies on the border between Israel and Jordan. It is 1,292 feet below sea level and is situated in part of a great depression that stretches north from the Dead Sea to the Sea of Galilee. The lake is fed by the Jordan River but has no outlet. Little rainfall and high evaporation rates cause the sea to be very salty. There is much mineral salt available and little, if any, wildlife. High hills rise from the eastern and western shores. To the south there is a chemical plant. The Bible refers to the Dead Sea as the Salt Sea, the Sea of the Plain, or the East Sea. In ancient times it was a navigation waterway.

The Finger Lakes are 11 long; narrow, glacial lakes that lie in west central New York State: Conesus, Hemlock, Canadice, Honeoye, Canandaigua, Keuka, Seneca, Cayuga, Owasco, Skaneateles, and Otisco. The lakes vary in size. Lake Seneca, with an area of 67 square miles, is the largest, and Lake Cayuga, 38 miles long, is the longest. The many waterfalls and other scenic beauties of the lakes make them a popular tourist attraction. The surrounding region is famous for its fruits and vegetables.

The Sea of Galilee, also called Lake Kinneret or Lake Tiberias, is a freshwater lake in northern Israel. The lake is 696 feet below sea level and is surrounded by mountains. Towns flourished along the lakeside during the time of Jesus, and the lake is frequently mentioned in the Bible. The village of Degania on its southern shore, founded in 1909, was the first collective settlement in Palestine. Ein Gev on the eastern shore is the site of Israel's annual music festival.

Lake Garda in north central Italy is the largest lake in Italy. It is fed by the Sarca River. Grapes and olives are grown in the surrounding region. The lake, a popular resort center, is surrounded by the high Alps.

Lake Geneva is bordered by Switzerland to the north and France to the south. It is the largest of the Alpine lakes. Surrounded by the Alps and the Jura Mountains, the crescent-shaped lake is a popular resort center. Many famous writers, such as Byron and Voltaire, have been inspired by its beautiful deep-blue waters.

The 425-foot-high Jet d'Eau—"jet of water"—rises from Lake Geneva in Switzerland.

Loch Lomond in the Scottish Highlands.

Native boats (dhows) on Lake Malawi (formerly Nyasa).

Crater Lake in Oregon's Cascade Range.

Native reed boats on Lake Titicaca in the Andes mountains.

Above: Lake Louise in Banff National Park, resort area in the Canadian Rockies. Right: Boating amid the floating gardens on Mexico's Lake Xochimilco.

Great Lakes. The five Great Lakes—Erie, Huron, Michigan, Ontario, and Superior—are described in the article GREAT LAKES in Volume G.

Great Bear Lake lies on the Arctic Circle in central Mackenzie District, Northwest Territories, Canada. Melting snows feed the lake, which is drained by the Great Bear River. Port Radium on the eastern shore is a uranium-mining center. Because of the severe climate the lake is navigable only 4 months out of the year.

Great Salt Lake, more than 4,000 feet above sea level, is located in northwestern Utah, east of the Great Salt Lake Desert. It is the largest salt lake in North America. Great Salt Lake is all that remains of a much larger glacial lake, Lake Bonneville. The lake is fed by the Weber, Bear, and Jordan rivers but has no outlet. This fact, in addition to high evaporation rates, makes its waters very salty. Because of the high salt content only shrimp live in the lake. The salt is used commercially. The great amount of salt in the water keeps swimmers from sinking. The lake attracts many tourists, and its southwestern shore is a resort center.

Great Slave Lake is located in southern Mackenzie District, Northwest Territories, Canada. It is fed by the Yellowknife, Slave, and Hay rivers, and drained by the Mackenzie River. With the exception of the forested western shore, the surrounding region and its many islands have only mosslike vegetation. The lake contains many fish, and supplies a growing fishing industry. The town of Yellowknife is a gold-mining center and the largest town in the Northwest Territories.

Ijsselmeer is a shallow freshwater lake in the north central Netherlands. A former branch of the North Sea, it was formed in 1932 from the old Zuider Zee by the building of the Ijsselmeer Dam between North Holland province and Friesland province. The lake is fed by the Vecht, the Ijssel, and the Zwartewater rivers. Some sections of the lake have been drained to give the Netherlands more farmland.

The Lakes of Killarney are a chain of three lakes in County Kerry, Ireland. The northernmost lake, Loch Leane, is famous for its island Innisfallen, described by the poet Thomas Moore. The ruins of Muckross Abbey lie near Loch Leane. The mountains of Kerry rise

Loch Leane, one of Ireland's Lakes of Killarney.

from the water's edge, and the lakes are famed for their scenic beauty.

Lake Ladoga, the largest lake in Europe (130 miles long), lies in the northwestern part of the Soviet Union. It receives the Svir and Vuoski rivers, and drains west into the Gulf of Finland via the Neva River. Storms and ice make navigation difficult in the winter, but important ports, such as Priozersk and Petrokrepost, have developed. Valaam Island in the north offers seclusion to a Russian Orthodox monastery. The lake is part of the White Sea-Baltic canal system.

Loch Lomond is the largest lake in Scotland (23 miles long). It lies in the highlands about 20 miles northwest of Glasgow. It is a popular resort center. At its southern end the lake has many wooded isles. Often shrouded in mist, the lake is famed for its beauty and has been the subject of many poems and songs.

Lake Louise is located in Banff National Park, Alberta, Canada. It lies on the eastern slope of the Rocky Mountains, 5,680 feet above sea level. Its quiet waters reflect the snowcapped peaks of the surrounding mountains. It is a popular resort center.

The Lake of Lucerne is an irregularly shaped lake in central Switzerland. The lake consists of three branches. The Reuss River flows into the lake from the southeast and out at the city of Lucerne. The four cantons (Uri, Schwyz, Unterwalden, and Lucerne) that touch the lake are called the Four Forest Cantons. Surrounded by mountains, the lake is a popular resort center.

The Lake of Lugano lies across the Italian-Swiss border. Fed by mountain streams, the lake drains to the west through the short Tresa River into Lake Maggiore. Steep mountains surround the northeast arm of the lake, and the beautiful scenery makes it a popular resort center.

Lake Maggiore, the second largest lake in Italy (40 miles long), lies in the north of that country and extends slightly into Switzerland. It receives water from Lake Orta, Lake Lugano, and Lake Varese. Sometimes called Lake Verbano, it is surrounded by the high mountains of the Alps. Its waters are filled with many kinds of fish. The beautiful towns located along its borders are popular vacation spots.

Lake Malawi is on the border shared by Malawi, Mozambique, and Tanzania. All three countries have important ports on the lake, which is entirely navigable. It is the third largest (360 miles long) of the lakes in the Great Rift Valley of eastern Africa. Lake Malawi is fed by small streams from the west. The Shire River, a tributary of the Zambezi River, is its only outlet. The lake level seems to undergo periodic changes.

Lake Manitoba, situated in southwestern Manitoba, Canada, is a remnant of an ancient glacial lake, Lake Agassiz. It is the third largest lake in the province (130 miles long). The lake has many important freshwater fisheries.

Lake Maracaibo in Venezuela is one of the largest lakes in South America (130 miles long). Famous for its petroleum deposits, the lake is one of the largest oil-producing areas in the world. This body of water, with the Catatumbo River, forms a major transportation route for products from the surounding area. A channel connects the lake with the Gulf of Venezuela. Because the natives lived in huts raised above the water on stilts, Spanish explorers called the area Venezuela, or Little Venice, as it reminded them of Venice, Italy.

Lake Mead is a long, narrow, freshwater lake that lies on the state line between southeastern Nevada and northwestern Arizona. It is one of the world's largest artificial lakes (115 miles long). The lake was formed by the building of the Hoover Dam on the Colorado River, at the western end of the Grand Canyon. The lake is used for flood control, irrigation, and power generation. It is a popular resort and recreation center of the National Park Service.

Loch Ness is a long, narrow lake (24 miles long) in central Scotland. It forms part of the Caledonian Canal system. Fed by the Oich, Enrick, and Foyers rivers, the lake drains into Moray Firth through the Ness River. The lake is surrounded by mountains. Some people believe that a huge monster lives in its waters.

Lake Nicaragua is located in southwestern Nicaragua. It is the largest lake in Central America (over 100 miles long). It receives the Tipitapa River and empties into the Atlantic Ocean through the San Juan River. The lake may become part of a proposed canal route across Nicaragua.

Lake Okeechobee in south central Florida is the second largest freshwater lake in the United States (35 miles long). Its Indian name means "big water." The Kissimmee River flows into the lake. Dikes have been built along the southern shore to prevent the fertile banks from eroding. The lake is popular for fishing. A series of canals leads to the Atlantic Ocean.

Lake Onega lies between Lake Ladoga and the White Sea in the northwestern part of the Soviet Union. Its southern shores are low and sandy, while the northern shores are rocky and indented with long, narrow bays. The lake is fed by the Vytegra, Shuya, Suna, and Vodla rivers and drains into Lake Ladoga via the Suir River. The lake has several ports, but ice makes navigation difficult during the winter.

Lake Pontchartrain lies in southeastern Louisiana, north of New Orleans. The Gulf Intracoastal Waterway crosses the lake and joins it to the Mississippi River at New Orleans by means of a canal. The lake receives part of the Mississippi floodwaters through the Bonnet Carre Floodway. The long Lake Pontchartrain causeway, which extends 24 miles over the lake, is the longest overwater highway in the world. The shores of the lake are dotted with popular resorts.

Lake Rudolf in northwestern Kenya occupies a relatively shallow part of the Great Rift Valley of Africa. It is fed by the Omo, Kibish, and Turkwell rivers, but has no outlet. Lake Rudolf is shrinking and becoming more salty because of a high rate of evaporation. Fish, crocodiles, and hippopotamuses live in its waters. The lake was discovered in 1888 by Count Teleki, who named it after the crown prince of Austria.

The Salton Sea is a shallow, salty lake lying 240 feet below sea level, located in southern California about 80 miles northeast of San Diego. It was once a vast, salt-covered depression, part of the ancient floor of the Gulf of California. In 1905 the Colorado River broke through a levee, and over the following 2 years the drainage created the Salton Sea. High evaporation rates reduced the size of the lake. Today drainage canals keep its level constant.

Lake Tahoe is located between the Sierra Nevada mountains of eastern California and the Carson Range of western Nevada. It is one of the most beautiful lakes in North America. Every year thousands of tourists vacation along the shores of Lake Tahoe and take advantage of the fine fishing and boating its waters provide. The lake, oval in shape and surrounded by picturesque mountain scenery, is a popular subject for artists. The Truckee River carries lake water into Nevada's Newlands irrigation project. Tahoe City on the western shore is one of several resorts on the lake.

Lake Tanganyika is the deepest lake in Africa (4,700 feet in depth) and the second deepest freshwater body in the world. It lies in east central Africa, forming the boundary between the Congo (Kinshasa) and Tanzania, and bordering Burundi to the north and Zambia to the south. All of the lake is navigable, and it is therefore circled by ports. Lake Tanganyika receives the Ruzizi and Malagarasi rivers. The Lukuga River, its only outlet, is often silted up, causing the lake's level to rise. Many edible fish are found in its waters. John Speke and Sir Richard Burton discovered the lake in 1858. In the 1870's Stanley and Livingstone explored the area.

Lake Titicaca in the Andes mountains is located between southeastern Peru and western Bolivia. It is the largest lake in South America (110 miles long) and the highest large lake in the world (12,500 feet altitude). The lake consists of two sections: Lake Chucuito and Lake Uinamarco. They are connected by the Strait of Tiquina, and together they form a major transportation system between Peru and Bolivia. The lake is fed in the east by the Suches River and in the west by the Coata and Ramis rivers. The Desaguadero River is its only outlet. Important towns, such as Puno and Guaqui, border its shores.

Tungting Lake, located in the northern part of Hunan province in China, is one of China's largest lakes. During the summer, or wet season, the floodwaters of the Yangtze River greatly increase the size of the lake. In the winter it dries to little more than a muddy plain. Its shores, low and marshy, are ideal for growing rice. The few lakeside towns are protected by embankments. The lake is very shallow and is gradually being filled with sediment from its tributary rivers.

Lake Victoria is the largest lake in Africa (250 miles long) and the second largest freshwater lake in the world. Most of the lake lies between Tanzania and Uganda. Only its northeastern corner extends into Kenya. The lake is a valuable source of fish for all three countries. Steamer service runs between its main ports: Kisumu (in Kenya), Entebbe and Jinja (in Uganda), and Mwanza, Musoma, and Bukoba (in Tanzania). Lake Victoria is the chief source of the Nile River. A dam at Owen Falls, completed in 1954, raised the lake's level over 3 feet and supplies electric power. John Hanning Speke, an English explorer, discovered the lake in 1858 and named it in honor of Queen Victoria of England.

Lake Washington is a freshwater lake in west central Washington. Seattle, the largest city in the state, occupies its western shore. The Lake Washington Ship Canal connects the lake to Lake Union and Puget Sound. Two bridges now span its waters. Along its shores are docking and ship-repair facilities.

Lake Winnipeg, a remnant of ancient Lake Agassiz, is in south central Manitoba, Canada. Fed by the Winnipeg, Berens, Red, Saskatchewan, and Dauphin rivers, it is drained by the Nelson River into Hudson Bay. Valuable timber grows along its shores, and fishing and shipping are important industries. Several vacation resorts are located along the shores of Lake Winnipeg.

Lake Xochimilco lies just southeast of Mexico City, Mexico. It consists of a series of canals separated from one another by small islands called floating gardens. These islands were once rafts (*chinampas*) on which Indians raised vegetables. The rafts are now rooted to the lake bottom. Today boating on the canals to the tune of *mariachi* bands is a popular tourist pastime.

Reviewed by GUY-HAROLD SMITH
Ohio State University

LAMB, CHARLES (1775–1834) AND MARY (1764–1847)

Charles Lamb, critic and essayist, was born on February 10, 1775, in London. His father was the clerk and servant of a judge. Charles attended day school until he was 7, then he went to a private boarding school called Christ's Hospital. There Charles formed his lifelong friendship with the poet Samuel Taylor Coleridge.

When Charles left school in 1789, he worked in South Sea House, a financial concern, where his brother, John, was a clerk. In 1792 he was made a clerk in the accountant's office of India House. Four years later a terrible event affected the rest of his life. His sister, Mary, in a fit of insanity, stabbed their mother to death. She was judged temporarily insane and would have been put in an asylum, but Charles became her guardian instead. His devotion to her meant they often had to move when people found out about her, and it meant that Charles could never think of marrying. Her attacks of insanity became more frequent as the years went by.

In 1796 four sonnets that Lamb had written were included in a volume of Coleridge's poems. More of Lamb's poems appeared in a second volume in 1797, and in 1798 *Blank Verse by Charles Lamb and Charles Lloyd* was published. Lamb's first real success came in 1807 with *Tales from Shakespeare*. Charles and Mary wrote the book together, Charles retelling the tragedies and Mary the comedies. Lamb also wrote a child's version of the adventures of Ulysses. His next book was *Specimens of English Dramatic Poets contemporary with Shakespeare* (1808). This proved Lamb to be an outstanding critic and writer.

When the *London Magazine* was founded in 1820, Lamb began writing essays for it, signing himself as Elia. These were later collected into book form. In 1823 the Lambs adopted an orphan girl, Emma Isola, who brought great happiness to them.

Lamb retired from India House in 1825. He died on December 27, 1834. His letters to his many friends were published after his death. They reveal his deepest thoughts. Mary lived until May 20, 1847.

LAMPS. See LIGHTING.

LANDSCAPE GARDENING. See GARDENS AND GARDENING.

LANGMUIR, IRVING (1881–1957)

Irving Langmuir was an American scientist and engineer. When asked why he worked so hard in science, Langmuir replied: "Whatever work I've done, I've done for the fun of it." He must have had a great deal of fun. His discoveries and inventions have added a great deal to our knowledge of the natural world and have affected all of us.

Irving was born in Brooklyn, New York, on January 31, 1881. His father was a businessman. His older brother, Arthur, was interested in chemistry, which attracted Irving's interest too. When he was 12, the family went to Europe for 3 years. Irving attended school in Paris. Irving—not yet a teen-ager—began to climb mountains in the Alps. This became a lifelong hobby, which he later combined with a scientific interest in meteorology, the science of weather.

Irving went to college at Pratt Institute in Brooklyn and the Columbia School of Mines in Manhattan. He studied metallurgy, the science and technology of metals. After obtaining his degree in 1903, Irving went to Germany and continued his studies at Göttingen University. His major professor was Walther Hermann Nernst (1864–1941), an outstanding chemist of the early 20th century.

In 1906, when Langmuir returned to the United States, about the only type of work open to a scientist was teaching. A few large industrial companies, however, were beginning to establish research laboratories. After 3 years of teaching, Langmuir took a position in the General Electric Company Research Laboratory at Schenectady, New York. He spent most of the rest of his life there.

At the time that Langmuir began his research for the General Electric Laboratory, the incandescent (glowing) light bulb had come into widespread use as the principal artificial light. The filaments of these light bulbs were tungsten wires, which were heated electrically until they became white-hot. These filaments did not last very long. In 1912 Langmuir discovered that their lifetime could be greatly increased by filling the light bulb with an inert gas, such as argon. (An inert gas does not usually react with other chemical elements.) This discovery decreased the cost

of lighting America by hundreds of millions of dollars a year.

From this spectacular discovery, made only 3 years after he began his research, Langmuir went on to make many others. He invented the atomic hydrogen welding torch. He developed a new kind of vacuum pump that made possible a whole new set of industries and greatly aided the development of radio and television. He and his fellow workers did much of the early work in rainmaking.

Throughout Langmuir's life he combined scientific studies with engineering applications. He believed strongly that if industry would support scientific research, it would profit greatly from the results.

In 1932 Langmuir received the Nobel prize in chemistry "for his discoveries and investigations in surface chemistry." The research that had led to this award had come out of his earliest studies on what happens to the surface of a tungsten light-bulb filament when it is heated. Langmuir died August 16, 1957.

DUANE H. D. ROLLER
The University of Oklahoma

LANGUAGE ARTS

In the United States the term "language arts" describes generally the English program at the elementary-school level. Most secondary schools simply use the more familiar term "English."

The language arts consist of all the forms of communication in which words are used. There are four language arts: listening, speaking, reading, and writing. Speaking involves the skills of speech. Both silent and oral reading are language arts. Writing includes handwriting and spelling.

Most of our communication today is oral. We talk and listen to one another much more frequently than we write. It is important, therefore, that children develop habits and skills of effective oral communication.

Listening. Listening involves attentive, accurate hearing and interpretation of what is heard. A person gains both information and pleasure from listening. Like reading, listening requires the listener to identify main ideas and related details, to make inferences, and to draw conclusions. Practice in directed listening develops critical and appreciative listeners and, in turn, it also develops more effective speakers.

Speaking. Speaking involves the selection and organization of ideas, and the ability to communicate these ideas orally. Effective speaking requires clear enunciation, correct pronunciation, and an audible voice. Speaking usually takes the form of conversation or discussion. It is not easy to tell one from the other in social situations. Most conversations tend to develop into discussions of a particular topic of interest to the listeners. The ability to express oneself clearly, make suitable comments, identify fact and opinion, and differ from others in socially acceptable ways is characteristic of a good conversationalist or discussant.

Oral communication also includes oral reading of prose and poetry, giving directions, making reports, reciting poetry, telling stories, and dramatics in one form or another.

Reading. Reading takes its place with listening as a major source of information and pleasure. In the process of learning to read, one masters the symbols of written language —letters of the alphabet and the sounds they represent. One also learns word meanings and sentence patterns. Understanding main ideas, recognizing and relating details, making inferences, drawing conclusions, and predicting outcomes are reading skills that children learn and practice in a language-arts reading program. Such a program has two main aims. First, it teaches children to read critically and at the proper speed. Second, it produces children who like to read and who read on their own as a form of recreation.

A student's fondness for reading is developed mainly through a literature program. Getting to know stories, poems, and plays of literary worth is the reward for learning to read. Literary appreciation develops slowly over the years. As the reader grows older and experiences more of life he gains a background for appreciating the experiences of others. Character study and plot interpretation help children to understand themselves and others.

Writing. Written expression involves the art of composition and the skill of recording the composition for another's reading. Writing letters; expressing one's ideas, opinions, emotions, and reactions; and writing original poems or stories are the usual forms of creative composition, or expressional writing. Giving directions, explaining or documenting a position or opinion, and sharing information are referred to as factual or expository writing.

Ideas, words, and sentence patterns must be recorded legibly and correctly. Manuscript writing, a form of handwriting using unjoined printed letters, is generally taught in the primary grades, with a later switch to cursive, or script, writing. In both forms the emphasis is on easily legible writing. Clear writing is a courtesy to the reader and a requisite for easy communication. The proper use of capital letters and punctuation marks is another aid to effective communication.

The language arts are interwoven. For example, a child's understanding and skill in listening and speaking influence his ability in reading. In turn, listening, speaking, and reading skills are reflected in his written expression.

MILDRED A. DAWSON
Co-author, *Children Learn the Language Arts*
See also HANDWRITING; READING; SPELLING.

LANGUAGES

Language is something taken for granted. Yet without it governments could not operate, businesses would close, trade could not be carried on, and science and industry would be a hopeless tangle. In fact, without language most human activity would cease.

The word "language" comes from the Latin word *lingua,* which means "tongue." The tongue is used in more sound combinations than any other organ of speech. A broader interpretation of "language" is that it is any form of expression. This includes writing, sign language, dance, music, painting, and mathematics. But the basic form of language is speech. Speech makes man different from all other animals. No human group is without a form of speech, while no animal group has ever succeeded in combining sound and meaning into the complex code that humans use. An animal can show joy, fear, dislike, or alarm through its voice, but it cannot carry the message beyond the immediate situation. Man can refer to the present, past, or future. He can deal with what is out of sight and millions of miles away. Man's speech becomes a particular language when two or more human beings decide that a certain sound or set of sounds shall have the same meaning for them.

▶ ORIGIN OF LANGUAGE

Where, when, and how language began is still a mystery, though there are many theories on the subject. One favorite theory is that early man imitated the sounds he heard in nature, such as the barking of a dog or the gurgling of a brook. Those who favor this theory believe that it explains why there are so many languages in the world. A rooster's crow may have struck the ear of one tribal chief in one way, but it may have sounded slightly different to another chief. Both men were probably able to convince their followers that their own imitation of the sound was the only correct one. Thus the sound a rooster made came to be "cock-a-doodle-doo" in English, *cocorico* in French, *cucuricu* in Rumanian, and *chicchirichi* in Italian.

Today there are nearly 3,000 separate spoken tongues. Some, such as English and Chinese, are spoken by hundreds of millions of people. Others, such as some of the native tongues of the American Indians, are spoken by only a few thousand or a few hundred people.

All languages have certain things in common, though their differences are enormous. They all consist of sounds produced by the vocal organs (the throat, nose, tongue, palate, teeth, and lips) and received by the ear. The vocal organs are capable of producing hundreds or perhaps thousands of different sounds. Each language group selects and uses only a small number of these—usually between 10 and 60. Different languages use different sets of sounds. People grow accustomed to the sounds of their own language. When they need to learn a new set of sounds, they find that their old language habits get in their way.

The sounds used by any language are arranged so that they produce words that have certain meanings. When the sounds of D, O, and G are lined up, they produce the word "dog." English-speakers agree that the spoken word "dog" represents a particular animal. If one English-speaker says "dog," another English-speaker will automatically see the image of a dog. But the same word will be meaningless to a Russian, who uses the word *sobaka* for the dog image, or to an Italian, who uses the word *cane.*

Words also have to follow certain rules. These are by no means the same in all languages. In English if you want to speak about more than one dog, you add the letter *s* and get "dogs." In Italian you change the last letter of *cane* to *i* and get *cani.* In English "I see him" has a certain meaning, and it is normal for English-speakers to arrange the words in that order. In Italian, however, it is just as normal to arrange the words so that they equal "I him see."

Despite their many differences, then, all languages have three things in common: a set of individual sounds, a particular way of ordering sounds into words or word units, and rules for such things as word endings or the arrangement of words in a certain order. To learn a new language, you must first learn to produce a new set of sounds. Then you must learn to accept new words for given meanings. Finally, you must learn new regulations for your new words. This is not really as difficult as it sounds. In fact, you have done it all before. As a baby, you began to imitate the sounds produced by your parents and other people around you. You connected the sounds with certain objects, actions, or ideas. You learned to string your words along in a certain way and to make changes in them when necessary for their meaning.

▶WRITING

The invention of writing gave man a'way to keep a permanent record of his thoughts. The oldest writing that we have any record of is that of the ancient Sumerians. The records go back at least to 3500 B.C. Sumerian writing was in the form of pictures that told a story or gave a message. Something similar is still used today in comic strips and in certain traffic signs. Modern picture writing, however, is usually helped along by written words—such as the captions in the comic strips and the words "School—Slow" written on the traffic sign that pictures a schoolhouse.

The original word pictures had no captions or any explanation based on speech. Nevertheless, the art of picture writing became so highly developed that even very abstract ideas could be expressed by it. The present-day Chinese system of writing has word pictures of this kind. The Chinese word "bright," for example, is a combination of the symbol for sun and the symbol for moon.

SUN 明 MOON

The Alphabet

An important advance in the development of language was made by the Phoenicians. They decided to let some of their picture letters stand for the sounds they used in their speech. This led to the first alphabet, a series of symbols that stood for the language's speech sounds. The oldest example of Phoenician alphabetic writing seems to be the one found on the stone coffin of the Phoenician king Ahiram, who ruled in the 11th century B.C.

An alphabetic system of writing, once it is put into operation, tends to change very little. Spoken language, on the other hand, is always

changing. The result is that there is often a great difference between the way words are written and the way they are spoken. The English spelling of the word "knight," for example, reflects the pronunciation of a thousand years ago. In those days the K was pronounced, the I sound was similar to the I in "it," and the GH represented a sound that has disappeared from English. The word is still spelled the old way, however, because writing habits change much more slowly than speech habits.

Language specialists have tried to overcome this problem with the International Phonetic Alphabet (IPA), in which each symbol stands for just one speech sound. In the IPA both "knight" and "night" appear as [najt].

English is far from being one of the oldest languages, yet even in its comparatively short life it has changed drastically. The opening words of the Lord's Prayer in Anglo-Saxon, the English spoken in the 6th or 7th century, are as follows: "Fæder ūre, thū the eart on heofonum, sī thīn nama gehālgod. Tōbecume thīn rīce. Gewurthe thīn willa on eorthan swā swā on heofonum." The Norman conquest of England in 1066 changed the whole course of the English language. French became the language of the upper classes until the beginning of the 14th century. Even then English was not used in writing. Only in the 15th century did English take the place of French and Latin in official documents. By then English had undergone tremendous changes in its grammar and vocabulary. Today the same lines of the Lord's Prayer look like this: "Our Father which art in heaven, Hallowed be thy name. Thy kingdom come. Thy will be done in earth, as it is in heaven."

All languages change. French, Spanish, and Italian were the Latin of Caesar and Cicero 2,000 years ago. English, German, Dutch, and the Scandinavian tongues were once the same language.

▶THE INDO-EUROPEAN FAMILY

More than half the world's population speak languages that are definitely related. This vast family of languages is called Indo-European because it includes tongues spoken by people from northern India all the way across Europe. The major languages of the

PRESENT-DAY INDO-EUROPEAN LANGUAGES

Americas, Australia, and New Zealand are also Indo-European, since they all came from European countries. The Indo-European group includes such different languages as Russian, Hindi, Persian, Armenian, Albanian, Greek, and Welsh.

There is no written record of an Indo-European language, but scholars have pieced together a language that they think must be very much like it. The Indo-European people may have lived in northern Europe around the shores of the Baltic. They were probably nomadic—that is, they wandered about a great deal in search of food. Some of them wandered to the south, others to the east and west. Eventually some went north and crossed the English Channel to what is now Britain. Wherever they went, a new language, based on the original Indo-European tongue, developed in its own way.

A Danish language scholar, Rasmus Rask (1787–1832), was the first to prove that all these languages were related. All the Indo-European languages are similar in three ways: in grammatical structure; in vocabulary, especially in certain key words, such as "father," "mother," "sister," and "brother"; and in sound patterns. One of the most important ways of showing that two languages are related is to show that certain sounds in one language are matched with certain sounds in another. For example, the relationship between English and Latin is shown in words that begin with P in Latin and F in English—compare the Latin *pater, pes, piscis* with the English *father, foot, fish*.

▶ OTHER LANGUAGE FAMILIES

The rest of the world's people speak languages that seem to be unconnected with Indo-European tongues. These fall into separate families. Chief among them are the **Semitic** and **Cushitic** families of North Africa and the Near East. The two most widely spoken Semitic languages are Hebrew and Arabic. Hebrew is the official tongue of Israel and the prayer tongue of Jews throughout the world. Various forms of Arabic are spoken in Morocco, Algeria, Tunisia, Libya, Egypt, Syria, Lebanon, Saudi Arabia, Yemen, Jordan, and Iraq. It is the sacred tongue of Islam.

The Cushitic family appears in parts of northeastern Africa. Cushitic languages are spoken by various groups in southern Egypt and the Sudan. However, the languages of Ethiopia belong to the Semitic family. Today there are probably about 150,000,000 people who speak Semitic and Cushitic languages.

A **Hamitic** group of languages was represented in ancient times by the Egyptian of the

Pharaohs. Other Hamitic tongues were spoken by the ancient Numidians and Libyans and throughout North Africa. Present-day Berber dialects, ranging from Morocco to Egypt and the Sahara, are Hamitic.

The **Uralic** family includes Finnish, Estonian, Lapp, and Hungarian. Some language scholars connect these languages with the **Altaic** languages (which include Turkish) in a **Ural-Altaic** classification. Other scholars prefer to keep the two families separate.

The **Sino-Tibetan** group includes all variations of Chinese, with close to 700,000,000 speakers, and Thai, Burmese, and Tibetan. **Japanese** and **Korean** are separate languages. The **Dravidian** languages, such as Tamil, Telugu, and Malayalam, are spoken in southern India. The **Malayo-Polynesian** family includes Malay, Indonesian, Javanese, Balinese, languages of the Philippines, and most of the languages of the Pacific.

African and American Indian languages are divided into many groups. Other small, separate families are **Caucasian**, which includes languages spoken in the Caucasus; the mysterious **Basque**, spoken by the people of the Pyrenees Mountains; and the native languages of Australia, Tasmania, and New Guinea. Some experts think that Basque is the sole survivor of a once widespread family of pre-Indo-European tongues.

▶ HOW LANGUAGES CHANGE

Languages are shaped and changed in many ways. New words are brought to a country through trade, war, or settlers from a foreign land. When the Romans conquered the nations of western and southern Europe, the languages of the conquered lands were replaced by the Latin of the Romans. Spanish became the major language of South America because most of the original conquerors and settlers came from Spain. In Brazil, where the Portuguese settled, Portuguese is the national tongue. English colonists made the United States an English-speaking nation.

To fit changing times, it is sometimes necessary to invent new words. The words "astronaut" and "television" did not exist 50 years ago. Words are also dropped from a language. This happens because they are no longer needed or because their meaning has been forgotten. Many words that were well-known in Shakespeare's time, such as "to trow," which means "to believe," are today unfamiliar to many people. Words also drop old meanings and take on new ones. "Meat," for example, used to mean any kind of food. Today it generally means only animal flesh.

Languages often borrow words from other languages. Many food names used in English, such as "omelet" and "crepe suzette," were borrowed directly from the French.

Occasionally new words are made by joining two old words together. "Brunch" is made up of "breakfast" and "lunch"; "smog," of "smoke" and "fog." Lewis Carroll invented many words of this kind. He called them portmanteau words. A portmanteau is a suitcase with two uses. It travels as an ordinary suitcase and opens up to be a clothes wardrobe. Portmanteau words carry two meanings in a single word. One of Carroll's best-known portmanteau words is "slithy" for "slimy" and "lithe."

Slang changes a language, too. Sometimes slang words or expressions are popular for a while and then are forgotten or fall into disuse, like "twenty-three skiddoo" or "the cat's whiskers." Sometimes they become a permanent part of the language, such as "okay" or "corny." Some language scholars think that all slang is acceptable. They argue that proper language is the language people are actually speaking, not the language they should be speaking. Others believe it is important to limit the use of slang in order to keep high standards of good speech.

Certain languages, like Interlingua and Esperanto, have been made out of other languages. Interlingua is based on English and the Romance languages. Esperanto was made out of words common to the chief European languages. It was named after its inventor, the Russian scholar L. L. Zamenhof (1859–1917), who called himself Dr. Esperanto ("the hoping one"). Both languages were invented in the hope that they would become international languages, spoken by people in every land. Languages like them are constantly being invented. None has become very popular.

MARIO PEI
Columbia University

See also GRAMMAR; UNIVERSAL LANGUAGES; WRITING; articles on individual languages.

LAOS

The flag of Laos tells a great deal about its country. The flag is red and bears the emblem of a white, three-headed elephant. The three heads represent the division of the ancient kingdom of Lan Chang into three parts, which today are united. The white parasol above the elephant's heads is a symbol of monarchy. The five-step stairway that the elephant stands on marks the first five commandments of Buddhism: No killing; No stealing; No telling lies; No adultery; No drinking. Their similarity to the Ten Commandments of the Old Testament shows that people the world over share fundamental values.

LAOS

▶ THE PEOPLE AND HOW THEY LIVE

The people of Laos belong to three racial groups. The largest group is made up mainly of the Lao, who are related in language and origin to the people of Thailand. This group makes up about one half of the Laotian population. The second racial group includes the mountain people, and they make up about 10 percent of the Laotian population. The third racial group consists of mountain people of Indonesian origin. They were called Kha ("slaves") by the Lao, and since independence they have been officially called Lao Thoeng, meaning "Lao of the highlands."

The population of Laos is estimated to be about 3,000,000. The Laotian farmers live in thousands of villages that range in size from a few families to several hundred. There are only a few cities in Laos. Vientiane, with a population of over 163,000, is both the administrative capital and the major commercial center of Laos. Luang Prabang ("town of the gold Buddha"), with a population of about 25,000, is the royal capital, where the king and his family live. Both capitals have airports but are not connected directly by all-weather roads. On the irrigated plains of the Mekong the population density is about 180 people for each square mile. But the average density for the country is about 30 persons per square mile.

Language, Religion, and Education

Most of the people in Laos speak Lao, which is closely related to the Thai language. The Kha people, however, speak dialects of the Mon-Khmer language, which is closely related to the language of Cambodia. In the marketplaces in the larger cities, foreign languages such as French, Chinese, Vietnamese, and English are also spoken.

Buddhism is the official religion of Laos. Nearly all Laotians are Buddhists. The Buddhist priests, or bonzes, do not marry. They live in the compounds of the wats ("temples"). Spirit worship (known as animism) is also practiced by the hill people and by some of the Lao as well.

Only a small percentage of the Laotians can read and write. Prior to the arrival of the French, schools were conducted in the homes and in the wats, where the Buddhist bonzes emphasized religion and morals. The French established a public school system and taught classes in French. Public school education has been compulsory since 1951. However, there are still not enough school buildings, teachers, and teaching materials to fill the needs of all school-age children.

The farm people live in bamboo huts built on stilts or piling. Here in the tropics, where the sunshine is abundant and temperatures are high, preschool children wear little if any clothing. They spend hours each day in rivers and irrigation ditches playing, swimming, paddling, and catching fish.

At an early age village children help with small family tasks. Boys and girls help adults with heavier jobs. They catch, clean, and cook fish and help cut bamboo shoots for food. By the time they are 13, most Laotian boys and girls are helping transplant and harvest rice and other crops. Early marriage and big families coupled with modern medical improvements account for the increase of population in this country.

Girls and women wear blouses and loose-fitting skirts. Women use strips of cloth wrapped around the waist to make skirts. On ceremonial occasions men wear *pha muang,* a silk or cotton strip that wraps around the waist and legs to make pants. Some men wear pants and shirts or jackets.

There are many religious rites and festivals during the year. The Laotian New Year is celebrated in April. *Vixakha Bouxa,* or *Boun Bang-Fay,* the festival that honors "the birth, enlightenment, and death of Buddha," comes at the time of the full moon in May. In July, *Khao Vassa,* the beginning of fasting, is celebrated. *Ho Khao Slak,* which comes in the autumn, is to Laotian children what Christmas is to American children.

FACTS AND FIGURES

POPULATION: 3,000,000 (estimate).

LANGUAGE: Lao (official), French.

GOVERNMENT: Constitutional monarchy. **Head of state**—king. **Head of government**—prime minister. **International co-operation**—United Nations, Colombo Plan.

NATIONAL ANTHEM: *Pheng Xat Lao* ("Lao National Anthem").

ECONOMY: Agricultural products—rice, corn, potatoes, citrus fruits, coffee, tobacco, cardamom, cotton, livestock (oxen, elephants, water buffalo, pigs). **Industries and products**—forestry (teak, other wood and wood products), tobacco products, rubber shoes, rice processing, lamé cloth, handicrafts (weaving, wood carving, pottery). **Chief minerals**—tin and rock salt. **Chief exports**—tin, cardamom, coffee, hides. **Chief imports**—foodstuffs, motor vehicles, machinery, electrical equipment, chemicals, textiles, metals and metal products, manufactured goods. **Monetary unit**—kip.

The migrations of the Indians from the west, the Chinese from the north, and the Indonesians from the south have influenced Laotian art, music, literature, and religion. Examples of Laotian art are often found in wats and pagodas. Many of these religious buildings have wall frescoes and carved wood-work.

The Laotians love music, especially singing. The most popular musical instruments are the flute and a bamboo harmonica called a *khene.* The Laotians do not usually engage in social dancing. They do, however, enjoy watching professional dancing troupes perform. There is much storytelling, since books are scarce.

▶ **THE LAND**

Laos is located in continental Southeast Asia. Communist China lies to the north and Communist North Vietnam to the northeast and east. Also bordering Laos are South Vietnam to the southeast, Cambodia to the south, Thailand to the west, and Burma to the northwest.

Laos occupies an area of about 91,000 square miles. Most of Laos is hilly and mountainous. The northern third of the country is the most rugged. Stretching in a northwest-southeast direction, the Annamese Cordillera mountain range runs through central and southern Laos into South Vietnam. The crest of this mountain range forms a water divide along most of the eastern Laotian border. Central and southern Laos slope westward from the Annamese Cordillera to the Mekong River.

About two thirds of the country is covered with forests, which provide a home for many wild animals, such as elephants, leopards, panthers, and tigers.

The Mekong, the largest river in continental Southeast Asia, marks the boundary between Thailand and Laos. Along its left bank are narrow alluvial plains, where one finds numerous rice fields, gardens and orchards, villages, and most of the Laotian cities. By natural flooding, the Mekong River irrigates the fields. The fish from its waters provide the protein to balance the daily rice diet of the Laotians. Sampans, light barges, and pirogues (canoes) cover the Mekong River and its tributaries and carry most of the freight. There are no railroads in Laos.

There are two distinct seasons in Laos: the dry season and the wet. The first lasts from November to April; the second, from May to October. Between October and March it is dry and cool. Temperatures range from 40 degrees Fahrenheit to 70 degrees. It is the best time of the year. Heat begins in March, and temperatures rise to the 90's. The monsoon comes in June and ends in October.

INDUSTRY AND PRODUCTS

Most of the farmers raise food for their own use. There is only a small amount of trade. A few people are employed in transportation, forestry, mining, and fishing. The handicraft industry provides an income for some people. The country is known for its lamé cloth, a fabric woven from metal threads mixed with silk.

Rice is the chief crop grown in Laos. In the Mekong Valley's irrigated fields, wet rice cultivation methods are used. On the mountain slopes dry rice cultivation is employed.

Corn is the second most important crop in Laos. Hemp, coffee, tea, tobacco, cardamom, citrus fruits, and cotton are also raised. Water buffalo, pigs, poultry, and some domesticated elephants are the main livestock. There is some cattle raising in southern Laos.

Tin and rock salt are the only minerals mined. But there are known deposits of iron, coal, copper, lead, and gold. Waterwheels turned by falling water are still in use. Electricity is not always available during the day in some cities.

Tin is the main export of Laos. Other exports include teakwood, green coffee, and the spice cardamom. Imports consist mainly of manufactured goods, processed foods, machinery, vehicles, and chemicals.

GOVERNMENT

Laos is a constitutional monarchy headed by a king. Executive power is actually exercised by a prime minister, who is appointed by the king. The prime minister is assisted by a council of ministers, or cabinet. The legislature consists of the National Assembly and the King's Council. The National Assembly, made up of 59 members elected by the people, is the principal lawmaking body. The King's Council, made up of 12 members, acts as an advisory body. The judicial branch of the government consists of a supreme court, an appeals court, and provincial courts.

HISTORY

In early times the people living in Laos were Indonesians who had moved northward from the islands of Indonesia. Sometime between the 13th and 14th centuries A.D., the Lao people from the north (China) arrived in the area of present-day Laos. They conquered the local Indonesian tribesmen and settled at the sites of the present cities of Luang Prabang, Xieng Khouang, and Vientiane.

Later in the 14th century a large kingdom called Lan Chang (Lan Xang) was organized by Prince Fa Ngoun (Ngoum), who also introduced the Buddhist religion to Laos. Lan Chang means "land of a million elephants." Early in the 18th century, Lan Chang was broken up into three kingdoms: Champassak, Vientiane, and Luang Prabang.

In the beginning of the 19th century, Siam (now Thailand) succeeded in dominating Vientiane and Luang Prabang. In 1893, by the treaty ending the Franco-Siamese War, Laos became a part of French Indochina.

During World War II the Japanese overran Laos. The French returned in 1946. Three years later Laos became an independent sovereign state within the French Union. In 1953 the country was invaded by Communist troops from North Vietnam. They were helped by the Communist-controlled Pathet Lao rebel group led by Prince Souphanouvong. In 1954 an international conference was held at Geneva. An agreement was reached to end the war. Laos gained its independence, and the fighting temporarily stopped.

Since independence Laos has been torn by civil war between the Royal Laotian Army, supporting the government, and Pathet Lao guerrillas, who are aided by North Vietnamese troops. The Vietnam War led to the bombing of the Ho Chi Minh trail, which runs through Laos into South Vietnam. In 1971, South Vietnamese troops—supported by United States artillery and air forces—entered Laos to attack this Communist supply route.

THOMAS F. BARTON
Indiana University
Reviewed by Permanent Mission of Laos
to the United Nations

LAPLAND

Lapland is a region, not a country. It lies in the far north of Europe, and it has no definite boundaries. The name "Lapland" is given to northern Norway, Sweden, and Finland together with the adjacent part of the Soviet Union. This region extends from the Norwegian Sea in the west to the White Sea in the east and from the Barents Sea of the Arctic Ocean in the north to the Gulf of Bothnia in the south.

▶ THE PEOPLE

As the region's name suggests, it is the home of Lapps—about 35,000 in number. Swedes, Norwegians, Finns, and Russians also live in the region.

The Lapps once roamed through south and central Finland, and along the Scandinavian Peninsula as far south as central Norway. Then the Finns and Scandinavians pushed the Lapp settlements northward. The Lapps were forced to retreat north of the Arctic Circle. They have remained there to this day.

There are four major groups of Lapps. The coastal Lapps live chiefly by fishing along the Arctic coast of Norway. The fisher Lapps earn their living mainly by fishing in the lakes and rivers of Sweden and Finland. The forest Lapps live by reindeer herding but do not wander far from their permanent settlements in the woods. The mountain Lapps are nomads and move about with their herds of reindeer.

There are about 4,000 mountain Lapps. Most of them live in Sweden. They spend the winter in permanent homes, wear fur clothing, and travel in *pulk*—lightweight canoe-sleds that are pulled by reindeer. When spring comes, these Lapps move north toward the mountains, away from the mosquitoes and flies of the forest. Formerly entire families moved with the herds, but nowadays only the men follow the reindeer. The homes of the nomads during the spring and summer are tepee-shaped tents. Since they cannot use sleds in spring and summer, they must walk from place to place. Most of the other Lapps live in permanent houses, like their Scandinavian and Finnish neighbors.

The Lapps have adopted the customs and languages of the sections in which they live. Their own language is closely related to that spoken in Finland, but different tribes speak different dialects. Lapp children in Finland go to Finnish schools. If a Lapp-speaking teacher is available, they get two Lapp lessons a week. In Norway and Sweden children are taught mainly in Lapp. When they reach higher grades, they begin to learn in Swedish and Norwegian.

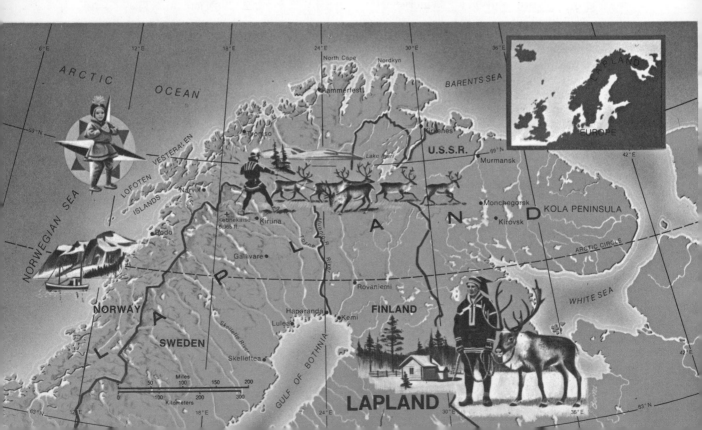

LAPLAND

In winter, many Lapps still dress in clothes made from reindeer skin and live a rather primitive life. But more and more Lapps are moving to settled areas to find better economic and educational opportunities. Even among the mountain Lapps fewer people take part in the reindeer drive each year, and the nomadic way of life is slowly passing.

▶ THE LAND

Lapland is a region of snowcapped mountains, rolling plains, rushing rivers, and sparkling lakes. The highest mountain is Kebnekaise (6,965 feet) in Sweden. Lapland's Arctic shores are steep and rugged for the most part. At Cape Nordkyn, for example, there are cliffs almost 1,000 feet high. In the mountains of Swedish Lapland there are many long and deep fingerlike lakes, which were formed by glaciers long ago.

In summer, temperatures average between 50 and 70 degrees Fahrenheit, while in winter they may drop to below zero. Precipitation varies from more than 60 inches on the western slope of the mountains to less than 20 inches over most of the region east of the mountains. Much of the moisture falls in the form of snow, which stays on the ground for as long as 6 to 7 months of the year.

Because much of Lapland lies north of the Arctic Circle, the midnight sun shines there during the summer. In the northernmost portions the sun circles the heavens for 2 months without setting. In midwinter the conditions are reversed. Although there are a few hours of twilight at midday, the sun does not rise at all. During this season the gloomy darkness is driven away by the light of the moon and stars, and by the brightness of the snow that blankets the ground.

▶ INDUSTRIES AND PRODUCTS

The reindeer is important in the economy of the Lapps. It once supplied the Lapps with everything they needed—milk, meat, clothing, and even knife handles from the antlers and thread from the sinews. Today the reindeer is raised mainly for meat or for sale.

Lapland's way of life has changed in recent years because the region has a variety of resources that are important to industry. For example, one of the largest deposits of high-grade iron ore in the world is located at

A Lapp boy learning to rope reindeer.

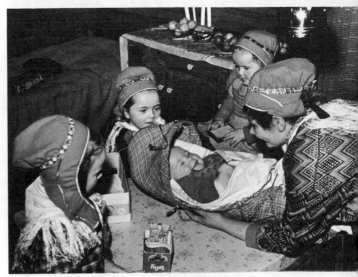
The family of a Lapp reindeer herder in Finland.

Kiruna in Swedish Lapland. Norway's largest iron mine is near Kirkenes, and many other metals are mined along the Skellefte River in Sweden. Timber is a major resource of Swedish and Finnish Lapland. Lapland's rushing rivers are the source of much hydroelectric power used in Sweden and Finland. In northern Norway fish is the most valuable export.

Lapland also has great resources in its spectacular scenery, midnight sun, and fascinating people. Today, thanks to modern communications, Lapland is becoming an increasingly popular tourist region.

VINCENT MALMSTROM
Middlebury College
Reviewed by EERO KORPIVAARA
Consul of Finland

See also FINLAND; NORWAY; SWEDEN; UNION OF SOVIET SOCIALIST REPUBLICS.

LARVA. See METAMORPHOSIS.

LA SALLE, ROBERT CAVELIER, SIEUR DE (1643–1687)

Robert Cavelier, Sieur de La Salle, was one of the most famous fur traders and explorers in the history of North America. He was the first white man to descend the Mississippi River to its mouth in the Gulf of Mexico.

La Salle was born in Rouen, France, in 1643. He was educated as a Jesuit missionary but left the religious life and went to Canada in 1666 or 1667. He received a grant of land near Montreal that was jokingly called La Chine (China) because he was so interested in finding a route across North America to the riches of Asia.

Like other fur traders of his day, La Salle combined exploration with fur trading. From 1669 to 1671 he traveled with French missionaries among the Iroquois Indians south of Lake Ontario. According to his own account, La Salle was the first white man to explore the Ohio River. He dreamed of building a great French fur empire in the Mississippi basin. In this he was encouraged by Count Frontenac, who arrived in 1672 to become governor of New France.

In 1673 Frontenac sent La Salle to invite the neighboring Iroquois tribes to a historic meeting at Cataraqui (now Kingston, Ontario). There peace was made between the Iroquois and the French. At Cataraqui, La Salle built Fort Frontenac. This post was important to the fur trade because it stood at the east end of Lake Ontario, where the St. Lawrence River begins. When the fort was completed, La Salle was put in command.

The next year, 1674, La Salle returned to France. He was made a noble, with the title Sieur de La Salle. Fort Frontenac and the surrounding lands were given him as his seigneury, or estate. There he built two ships to carry on the fur trade. La Salle and Frontenac were anxious to get control of the whole fur trade. They extended their enterprise into the upper Mississippi valley by building Fort Crèvecoeur on the Illinois River. This was the first establishment of the white man in the Mississippi valley. Earlier, on the Niagara River, just above the falls, La Salle had built the *Griffon,* the first ship to sail on the upper Great Lakes. But the *Griffon* was lost on Lake Huron on its maiden voyage.

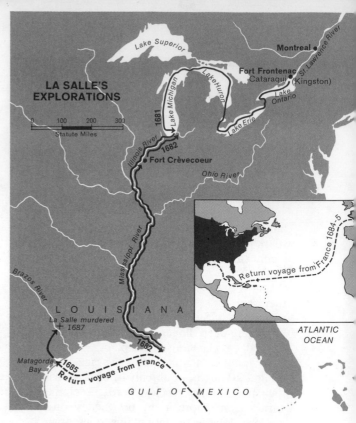

LA SALLE'S EXPLORATIONS

King Louis XIV had given La Salle permission to settle the Mississippi valley. But he did not begin his search for the mouth of the Mississippi River until 1682, after the French government complained that he was neglecting exploration. In that year he made his famous trip down the great river, which Jolliet and Marquette had explored in 1673. La Salle named the vast, newly discovered land Louisiana, after King Louis.

La Salle returned to France with news of his discovery. In 1684 he was sent out again with a party of settlers and four ships to start a colony on the Mississippi. The ships missed the mouth of the river and landed instead at Matagorda Bay on the coast of Texas—over 300 miles west of the Mississippi. Some of their supplies were lost in landing. Indian attacks and accidents killed many of the settlers. La Salle, with most of the surviving settlers, began a march across the country to reach the Mississippi. On the way, some of the men mutinied, and on March 19, 1687, La Salle was murdered.

JOHN MOIR
Carleton University (Ottawa)

See also MARQUETTE, JACQUES, AND LOUIS JOLLIET.

LASERS. See MASERS AND LASERS.

Rio de Janeiro, Brazil, is one of South America's most beautiful cities.

LATIN AMERICA

Government Palace in La Paz, Bolivia.

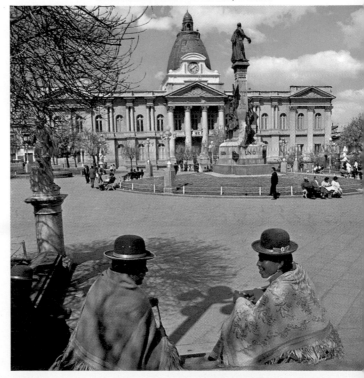

Government Palace in La Paz, Bolivia.

Latin America is a region of natural wonders, but it is also a region of problems. It is rich and it is poor. It has mountain ranges as bold as the Andes and rivers as broad as the Amazon. It has volcanoes as old as Popocatepetl in Mexico and as menacing as Irazú in Costa Rica. It has impenetrable jungles, like those in southern Guatemala, and deserts as long as the Atacama in northern Chile. Nearly three fifths of the world's bauxite, one fourth of its copper, and one fifth of its lead and oil come from Latin America. Much of the world's coffee, bananas, and sugarcane is produced in the area. But Latin America has little coal, and industrialization is a recent development. Latin America has the oldest universities in the Western Hemisphere; but half of its people cannot read or write. The average yearly income of the majority of the people is between $100 and $300. Yet nowhere else is population growing at a faster rate.

Latin America is a world where life seems

to stand still. But it is also a world of constant change and revolution.

Twenty-four independent countries (four of them members of the British Commonwealth) plus some island and mainland possessions of the United States, Great Britain, France, and the Netherlands make up the area called Latin America. The geography and the climate of Latin America vary greatly from place to place. The people and their languages differ, also. There is variety in religion, customs, institutions, and government. Latin America is many worlds. But like the United States, Latin America is a melting pot. Thus, it is one world as much as the United States is one world.

Origin of the Name "Latin America"

The term "Latin America" was first used in the early 19th century. It differentiated those American countries of southern European (Latin) origin from those of northern European or English origin. For this reason the possessions of the United States, Great Britain, France, and the Netherlands in Latin America itself are sometimes excluded from the term.

But there was another reason for the use of

Avenida Juárez is one of Mexico City's main thoroughfares.

Tegucigalpa, capital of Honduras, is the center of an agricultural and mining region dating back to Mayan times.

the term "Latin America." The first republic in the world was the ancient Roman republic of the Latins. This Latin republic—its laws, its organization, even its architecture for senate house and government palace—served as an inspiration to the Latin Americans in their struggle for independence. Latin America was "Latin" precisely because it looked back to the ancient ideal of freedom in the Latin republic. To this day the legal systems of the Latin-American republics are based on Roman law and the Code Napoléon. In contrast, legal practice in the English-speaking parts of the Caribbean is based on British law.

▶ LANGUAGES

Of the some 280,000,000 people living in Latin America, more than 170,000,000 speak Spanish and more than 90,000,000 speak Portuguese. Spain was the mother country of 18 of the independent Latin-American countries. Portugal was the mother country of Brazil. Language is therefore one of the elements many Latin Americans have in common. This also means there is a common culture. A Puerto Rican poet or an Argentinian novelist can be read by a Panamanian, a Honduran, or a Mexican.

But Latin Americans speak languages other than Spanish and Portuguese. English is the most important of these languages. About 7,000,000 people speak English. It is the official language of British Honduras and of Guyana, as well as of a number of the Caribbean islands, such as Trinidad and Jamaica. But it is also a second language for many millions more throughout Latin America. Some 7,500,000 people speak French, the official language of the Republic of Haiti, of French Guiana, and of the Islands of Martinique and Guadaloupe in the Caribbean. About 5,500,000 people of Chinese, Japanese, East Indian, Arabic, and Slavic origin speak their own languages in addition to the official language of the country where they are now citizens. Finally, millions of people of American Indian ancestry speak their own Indian language in addition to their country's official language.

Spanish and Portuguese. An Argentinian or a Peruvian can understand the Spanish of a Spaniard. A Brazilian can understand a native Portuguese. But Spanish and Portuguese as spoken in Latin America differ somewhat from the same languages spoken in Spain and Portugal. There are differences in speech pattern, rhythm, and accent. Anyone familiar with Spanish or Portuguese recognizes these differences. But he understands the language, just as a New Yorker understands a Bostonian, an Englishman, or an Australian.

Language and Environment. A language is like a mirror. Spanish and Portuguese reflect their New World environment in at least two ways.

First, there was the influence of the Indians, who were the earliest inhabitants of the Americas. Later there was the influence of Negroes, brought from Africa to work as slaves. Both groups, Indians and Negroes, are numerous in certain parts of Latin America. There are Indians in present-day Mexico, Central America, Ecuador, Peru, Bolivia, and Paraguay. There are Negroes in the Caribbean and in Brazil. Many words for foods, everyday things, and customs in Latin America come from the Indian or African languages. "Chocolate," for example, comes from the ancient Aztec word *chocolatl*. "Hammock" comes from an Indian Carib word, *hamaca*. The Cuban *ñáñigo* comes from an African word for priest.

Many of the Indians in Mexico, Guatemala, Bolivia, Peru, and Ecuador do not read or write Spanish. But most of them speak and understand it. One of the necessary changes taking place in Latin America is teaching the Indians to read and write Spanish. At the same time, every country with a large Indian population takes pride in remembering and maintaining its Indian heritage. Several million Latin Americans still speak Indian tongues. The most important example of this is in Paraguay, where almost the entire population is bilingual, speaking both Guaraní and Spanish. Other important Indian languages are Aztec, Tarascan, and Zapotec (Mexico); Aymara (Bolivia, Peru); Mayan (Mexico, Guatemala); and Quechua (Peru, Ecuador).

The French spoken in Haiti, known as Creole, differs from French as spoken in France. The Negro has added words and even elements of grammar of his own.

The Spanish, Portuguese, and French languages spoken in Latin America contain many new words that originated in America. Words that mean the same thing may differ from country to country. A Chilean says *huaso* for "cowboy." An Argentinian says *gaucho,* a Costa Rican *sabanero,* and a Colombian *llanero.* A Bolivian and a Peruvian say *oriente* ("east") when speaking of the frontier or last-settled part of a country. A Cuban speaks of *la manigua* ("the bush") when he means the frontier. A Venezuelan says *cambur* when speaking of a banana, but a Mexican says *plátano.* A public bus is called *guagua* in many parts of the Spanish Caribbean. But *camión* and *autobus* are common elsewhere in Latin America. A Brazilian says both *gaucho* and *vaquero* for "cowboy," and *matuto* for "backwoodsman." Creole French has *icit* for "here," *la pli* for "rain," and *moin* for "I."

▶ **THE PEOPLE**

The people of Latin America are as varied as their languages. In Latin America there are *criollos,* Indians, Negroes, mestizos, and mulattoes.

Criollos. Up to the 19th century persons of European descent born in Latin America called themselves *criollos.* It means "well-born" and differs from "creole," used in the French and British West Indies. The *criollo* felt closer to the mother country than to his place of birth. He thought of himself as Spanish or Portuguese. He sent his children to schools in Spain or Portugal. His home, dress, foods, and customs were modeled after the mother country's. But in the 19th century the Latin-American republics gained their independence (often under *criollo* leadership). Then most *criollos* began to feel closer to the country of their birth. In Mexico and Central America, in Cuba, Colombia, Venezuela, Bolivia, and Brazil, the word *criollo* is used today mainly for its historical importance. In each country independence and long internal struggle have finally molded the people into a nation. Elsewhere—in Argentina, Costa Rica, and Uruguay—large-scale immigration at the turn of the century (chiefly Italian and German) and after World War II (chiefly Chinese and Japanese) has made the person of foreign extraction as much a part of the country as anyone else. But Chile, Ecuador, and Peru still have a ruling class that clings to the tradition of a colonial aristocracy. In these countries the word *criollo* still has meaning.

Indians. Because Columbus imagined he had discovered a new route to India, he referred to the inhabitants of the New World as Indians. To this day they have kept the name.

The earliest Indians probably came from Asia many centuries before the time of Columbus. On the plateaus and high mountain valleys in Mexico, Guatemala, Colombia, Ecuador, Peru, and Bolivia, .great Indian

Boats woven of featherweight balsa reeds sail on Lake Titicaca, high on the Peru-Bolivia border.

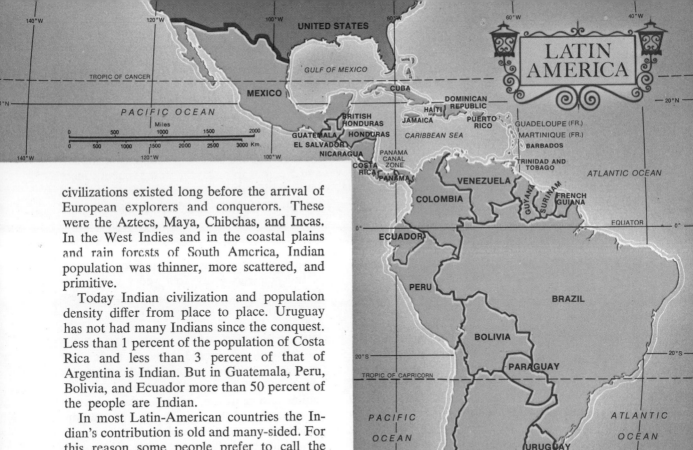

civilizations existed long before the arrival of European explorers and conquerors. These were the Aztecs, Maya, Chibchas, and Incas. In the West Indies and in the coastal plains and rain forests of South America, Indian population was thinner, more scattered, and primitive.

Today Indian civilization and population density differ from place to place. Uruguay has not had many Indians since the conquest. Less than 1 percent of the population of Costa Rica and less than 3 percent of that of Argentina is Indian. But in Guatemala, Peru, Bolivia, and Ecuador more than 50 percent of the people are Indian.

In most Latin-American countries the Indian's contribution is old and many-sided. For this reason some people prefer to call the region Indo-America. But this term is not entirely accurate. Costa Rica, Argentina, and Uruguay are largely European in origin. In Haiti, Cuba, Brazil, and the Guianas the Negro rather than the Indian has been the important influence on the life and culture.

Mestizos. Mestizos are Latin Americans of Indian and European ancestry. Mexico, the Central American republics of El Salvador, Honduras, Nicaragua, and Panama, and the South American republics of Colombia, Venezuela, Chile, Peru, Bolivia, and Paraguay are largely mestizo countries. The mestizo is the largest element in today's growing middle class. Many lawyers, political leaders, businessmen, teachers, doctors, scientists, priests, and artists in Latin America are mestizo.

Negroes. Negro slaves were brought from Africa to Latin America as early as the 16th century and as late as the middle of the 19th. They worked as slaves on plantations in the West Indies, in the coastal lowlands of Central America, in Brazil, and on the northeastern coast of South America. Some became legally free, although like the Indians they were subject to social discrimination and economic exploitation.

Haitians are mainly of Negro origin. Persons wholly or partly Negro are an important part of the populations of Cuba, Puerto Rico, the Dominican Republic, Panama, Jamaica, Trinidad, the Guianas, and Brazil.

Brazil is an example of an integrated Latin-American society. Many Brazilians are of Negro ancestry, but racial origin does not determine the social class to which a person belongs. Social position in Brazil, as in most of Latin America, is based on wealth.

Racial equality was achieved earlier in Latin America than elsewhere in the Western Hemisphere. But the ideals of democracy and self-government have not yet been wholly attained. The Latin-American republics continue to struggle for democracy. There are several reasons for this.

Colonial Government. The first reason has to do with Latin America's past. The colonial history of Latin America is very different from the colonial history of the United States or Canada. Three centuries of Spanish and Portuguese rule gave Latin Americans little experience in self-government.

In the Spanish and Portuguese colonies the king was supreme. The Spanish king ruled through the Council of the Indies and through the viceroys (governors appointed by the king). The Portuguese king governed through the Transmarine Council. The members of both councils were appointed by the king and lived in Spain and Portugal. The councils issued laws, supervised the church, and regulated trade and trade routes. The viceroy was the representative of the king and the council in the Spanish colonies.

This system of government meant that people born in the New World had little opportunity to govern themselves. A few *criollos* were appointed to the *cabildos,* or *senados da camara* (town councils), as *regidores* (town councillors). The mestizos had even fewer social and political rights. They were even less prepared for self-government. The Indians who worked for the landowners and mineowners were practically serfs; the Negroes, who worked on the plantations, were literally slaves. Thus, only the *criollos* gained some experience in government.

In the 19th century most Latin-American countries revolted and became independent republics. It was not surprising that the wars for independence were led by *criollos,* like Simón Bolívar, José de San Martín, and Francisco de Miranda, or by exceptional mestizos, like Miguel Hidalgo y Costilla (1753–1811) or José María Morelos (1765–1815). No war of independence was necessary in Brazil. The Portuguese court had moved to Brazil following Napoleon's invasion. Brazil is unique for this peaceful transition from colony to independent monarchy, and later from monarchy to republic.

The *criollo* class included the higher clergy, the wealthy landowners and mineowners, and the merchants. For the most part they were conservative. A few liberal *criollos* joined with the mestizos and sought the support of Indians and Negroes to make the new republics more democratic. Both groups, conservative and liberal, knew that the people were not ready for self-government. Lack of a common education and internal barriers like mountains, deserts, and jungles kept the people in each country from feeling truly unified.

Independence was followed by quarrels between liberals and conservatives. These were divided on the question of the relation between State and Church, on economic policy, and as to whether the states or the federal government should wield the greater power. The liberals opposed the Church's ownership of land and its control of education and marriage, whereas the conservatives supported the Church. The liberals opposed government control of the economy; conservatives, holding the reins of government, favored its control of investment and tariffs. Finally, liberals wanted less centralization of government; conservatives favored more centralization.

Coups d'état and dictatorships were common throughout 19th-century Latin America. Strong men, known as *caudillos,* ruled in Latin America. To this day many Latin Americans admire the strong individual who takes a political party into his hands and, with it, a nation.

Politics and Government Today. In most Latin American countries all adults, both male and female, are free to vote. In some countries voting is compulsory. In countries ruled by the military, elections are often suspended for an indefinite period.

The 20th century has seen the onset of many social revolutions on behalf of the peasant and worker and the rising middle class. The first occurred in Mexico in 1910. This was followed by revolutions in Argentina (1916), Chile (1920), Brazil (1930), Peru (1930), Guatemala (1944), Costa Rica (1948), Venezuela (1954), Colombia (1957), and Cuba (1959). Some of these revolutions were violent, some were peaceful; some were suc-

A Mexican fruit market.

A wool market in Peru.

A guitar stall in Bolivia.

Panama hats are made in Ecuador.

A *piñata* street party in El Salvador.

Religious procession in Guatemala.

Santiago, capital of Chile.

cessful, and some are still in the process of realization.

As a result of these revolutions or as a way of preventing new revolutions, governments in Latin America have begun to assume new functions. Education, land distribution, public housing, and foreign and domestic investment are undergoing changes that may benefit the majority of the people. Governments have also assumed new responsibilities—in social security, public health, and economic planning. With these changes the influence of the Latin-American republics in international affairs has increased. Only eight republics declared war against the Central Powers in World War I. But after the war all in time joined the League of Nations, and all declared war against the Axis powers in World War II. Today all the independent Latin-American countries are members of the United Nations. All except Guyana belong to the Organization of American States (OAS). (Cuba was suspended in 1962.) The Alliance for Progress, the Central American Common Market (CACM), and the Latin American Free Trade Association (LAFTA) are other examples of co-operation among the republics.

▶ TRADITION

The Latin American is both a very ancient and a very modern man. Sometimes he lives in a village shut in by great mountains or rivers. Here he is an Indian whose way of life is influenced by his ancestors. Those who live in towns and cities built under the Spaniards and Portuguese are most likely mestizos, combining an Indian and a European way of life. Those who live in cities made modern by new industries are either mestizos or the descendants of Spaniards, Portuguese, or more recent immigrants to the area.

Religion. Many of the world's religions are practiced in Latin America. Freedom of worship is guaranteed by the constitutions of the Latin-American states. Curaçao, a Netherlands possession, has the oldest synagogue in the New World, and Buenos Aires, Mexico City, and Rio de Janeiro have important Jewish communities. There are Hindus and Muslims in Trinidad and in Guyana; the religions of China and Japan are present in Argentina and Brazil. Protestant minorities exist in every country. But most Latin Ameri-

cans are Roman Catholic. The Spanish and Portuguese conquerors and settlers were intensely religious Catholics. Religion was also an important influence in all ancient Indian cultures. It was not difficult for Catholic priests and missionaries to convert the Indians to Catholicism.

In countries with large Indian populations —Mexico, Guatemala, Bolivia, and Peru— religion shows a mingling of Indian and Catholic practices. In Oaxaca, Mexico, for example, the Zapotecs use white lime to paint the outline of a cross around the body of the dead. The cross remains on the ground 9 days following the funeral. In rural Mexico a child's funeral requires that the body be dressed in the costume of the Virgin or of a saint. Toys and foods are buried in the grave. Folk dances and fireworks are customary. The family believes that when the child reaches heaven, he intercedes for those who love him. Births and marriages are celebrated with equal display of music and fireworks.

The Negro has also made religion a powerful influence in Latin America. He brought from Africa a great many gods whose worship he has combined with Christian beliefs and practices. Rural Cuba, the Dominican Republic, Haiti, and Brazil are places where the Negro and mulatto are an important part of the population. These countries practice Catholicism modified by Negro cults—voodooism, shango, macumba.

Family Life. Obedience in children and respect for authority in adults are part of the Latin American's upbringing. To help the father in the fields and the mother at home is the custom for children. There is a love of ceremony and tradition in family and social life.

One custom is followed after the birth of a Catholic child, whether he be rich or poor, urban or rural. He is baptized and named for the saint on whose day he was born. Frequently the names of other close members of the family are added, so that a child sometimes has five or six names.

In city and country the choice of a godfather and godmother is of the highest importance. Nothing brings two Catholic Latin Americans closer together than for one to be the godfather of his friend's child. The child's soul, welfare, education, and even his support are sometimes entrusted to the godparents. Baptism takes place in the church and is followed by a party. In the country this party includes a feast, dances, and songs. In the city it is customary to dance to popular music and eat sandwiches and cake.

Courtship and Marriage. Piety, gallantry, respect for parents, and courtesy are carefully cultivated in the Latin-American child.

Courtesy and gallantry are emphasized in courting a girl in Latin America. In many places the boy still needs the girl's permission to visit her at her window or the door of her house. If this is granted, he must also secure the permission of her parents. On her birthday he might court her with songs or surprise her with a midnight serenade. When asking for her hand in marriage, his parents or godparents must visit and ask her parents on his behalf. Several visits are required, the last often accompanied by gifts of food and wine.

Wedding ceremonies usually take place in church. But the preparations and the celebrations that follow a wedding vary from country to country, from religion to religion, and from region to region. A civil ceremony is considered as binding as a religious one. But most Catholic brides do not feel properly married unless there is a church ceremony.

In Latin America a girl does not lose her own family name when she marries. If Cecilia López marries Juan Díaz, she becomes Cecilia López de (of) Díaz. Her family name also lives on in her children. Her son Pablo, for example, would be known as Pablo Díaz López; her daughter Catalina, as Catalina Díaz López. All legal documents—baptismal records, school certificates, passports—bear this sequence: given name, father's family name, mother's family name. The status of women is improving throughout Latin America. Improvement varies from country to country and class to class. But more women are now engaged in careers in government, science, diplomacy, and business than ever before.

City and Country. A large part of Latin America is rural and agricultural. But great cities have always existed on the continent. Tenochtitlán in Mexico was built by the Aztecs. And the Incas built Cuzco in Peru.

The Spaniards destroyed many Indian cities. In their place they erected Spanish colonial cities.

New World cities are laid out in simple, straight lines radiating from a central square. The central square is called the plaza. On the sides are buildings that give form and authority to the city. On one side is the church. On another are the government buildings. On a third side are the homes of the wealthy. And on the fourth are the important business buildings. Streets are wide, suitable for parades or festivals. Most streets have covered arcades for the convenience of tradesmen. Santo Domingo (Dominican Republic), the oldest Spanish city in the Americas, is based on this pattern. So are Mexico City (Mexico), Lima (Peru), Bogotá (Colombia), and Caracas (Venezuela). Monasteries, convent schools, hospitals, bishoprics, and private homes are built on the streets leading away from the square. The simple dignity of white and pastel-colored houses and of the stonework or ironwork at doors and windows is typical of colonial Latin-American cities.

The early explorers' search for gold, silver, and diamonds in mountainous areas sometimes altered this city plan. Some of Latin America's mining towns, like Guanajuato and Taxco in Mexico, or Ouro Prêto in Brazil, cling to hillsides with exotic charm.

Population of Cities. Buenos Aires (Argentina), Mexico City (Mexico), and São Paulo and Rio de Janeiro (Brazil) have populations of over 3,000,000. Santiago (Chile), Caracas (Venezuela), Lima (Peru), Bogotá (Colombia), and Havana (Cuba) have populations of over 1,000,000 each.

Cities in Latin America, like cities anywhere else in the world, are a contrast of wealth and poverty. Beautiful plazas, modern public buildings, fine hotels, and handsome private homes are found in all the major cities. Low-income groups sometimes live in a sort of apartment house. This is the *vecindad* (tenement), a house often two stories high with a long patio. Families live around the patio. Sometimes four or five people occupy one room. Clotheslines and washing and bathing facilities, all found in the patio, are used in common by the *vecindad* residents. The middle-class home follows the design of the colonial house, though urban government projects have begun to use the plans of the modern apartment house familiar in the United States.

Slum areas are often found on the outskirts of the cities. People live in shanties. Streets are not paved. There are no sewers, and there is no running water. The slums are called *barriadas* in Spanish and *favelas* in Portuguese. These sections contrast with the beauty of the colonial houses and the opulence of the modern mansions and hotels. Most Latin-American countries have begun programs of slum clearance.

The large cities of Latin America are growing larger. New opportunities created by commercial and industrial development explain their growth in part. But the 20th-century social revolutions in Mexico, Costa Rica, Argentina, Bolivia, Cuba, Colombia, and Brazil have uprooted rural populations and sent them into the cities. As cities have grown larger the differences between a rural and an urban way of life have begun to disappear. Highways and roads connecting cities and the countryside are one consequence of larger cities. Another cause of less difference between a city and a rural way of life is the growth of newspapers and reviews throughout Latin America. Each city has at least one or two newspapers, and four or six are not exceptional in the capitals.

The Home

In the rural areas the materials and methods of building a home have changed little in centuries. The rural home is simple. It is made of logs, boards, or adobe. The roof is made of palm leaves, grass, stone, tree branches— materials readily available.

The typical city home is Spanish in origin. Thick stone walls keep out the heat. Several rooms open onto a central patio, a feature the Moors introduced into Spain. The patio is the center of the home. There the children play, mother and servants work at their household tasks, father and friends sit and converse. Flowers and other plants and birdcages decorate the patio. Kitchen, bedrooms, and living room open onto the central patio and receive the maximum of air and sunshine. The Latin-American home, no matter how modest, combines the outdoors and the indoors.

Homes of the wealthy are more elaborate. Huge doorways lead into an open hall. This hall, in turn, leads onto the patio. Columns and arches surround the patio. Sometimes there is a second patio, used as an orchard and for the servants' quarters. Ceilings in bedrooms are high. Walls are usually painted white, but doorways and floors are often decorated with colored tiles. Balconies and gates are made of wrought iron. The modern Latin-American home may use new materials —glass, marble, brick, concrete, steel. It may be provided with the newest conveniences of modern living. But its design still mirrors the pattern' of the colonial home.

Furnishings and Utensils. Many things used in Latin America's homes go back to pre-Columbian days. The **petate**, a straw mat common in Latin America, is the bed on which the Latin-American peasant is born, sleeps, and dies. The well-to-do Latin American uses a handwoven *petate* as a floor or wall decoration. Every home has a stone hearth, or a *brasero* or *fogón*. This is an iron stand or a raised stone platform on which charcoal or wood is burned for cooking. Rural homes in

The government of Paraguay, like those of all other Latin-American countries, is making an effort to educate all children.

Mexico and parts of Central America still have a three-legged stone mortar to grind corn for *tortillas,* or corn cakes. Smaller mortars are used for mashing vegetables and spices.

Latin Americans are fine craftsmen and still make many things by hand. Most cottons, woolens, glassware, silverware, ceramics, pottery, and toys are handmade rather than mass-produced. Latin-American designs are original and colors are bold, so the simplest dish has individual beauty. The pottery and ceramics of Latin America are unique and varied. Each region uses its own designs.

Foods and Drink. Corn (maize), avocados, potatoes, manioc (cassava), tomatoes, cocoa, and many varieties of nuts and fruits are some of the foods that are native to the Americas. Plantain, a bananalike fruit, is as widely used in the Caribbean as corn is in Mexico and Central America or as potatoes are in South America. Mangoes, breadfruit, papayas, and mameyes are only a few of the fruits eaten in Latin America. The tequila of Mexico (a strong drink distilled from a variety of the century plant), the *tiste* of Bolivia, and the wines of Chile are national drinks. Each country has developed its own national dishes. Argentina produces fine steaks. Chilean *empanadas* are flour dumplings filled with fish or meat, olives, and spices. Venezuelan *hallacas* are corn dumplings, also stuffed with meat and fish. *Mole,* or turkey in a pepper and spice sauce, is popular in Mexico. *Escabeche* is a fine Peruvian fish platter, and the *llapingachos* of Ecuador are potatoes stuffed with cream cheese and eggs. Soups and desserts are equally varied. Brazil's national dish is *feijoada,* black beans cooked with various meats and served with rice and a mixture of manioc, oranges, and other fruits.

Dress. In the rural areas men wear white cotton trousers and shirts and women wear long, full, dark skirts and white blouses. People in towns and cities dress like city people in Europe or the United States. But in a great many regions of Latin America garments of Indian style and design are still worn. Traditional folk dress is ornamented and brightly colored, and yet dignified and tasteful. The *quexquemel,* worn by the Indian women of Mexico and Guatemala, is made of two long pieces of cloth sewn together, with an opening for the head. This garment is worn over the shoulders like a cape. Short trousers and embroidered shirts tied at the waist are worn by the Indians in southern Mexico. Every country has its distinctive regional dress. The man's straw hat, varied in size and shape, is seen everywhere in tropical Latin America. Woolen caps for the men and derby hats for the women are common with the Indians in the cold, windswept Andes of Bolivia. Jewelry varies from modest strings of colored beads, shells, and coral to elaborate silver and gold earrings and bracelets.

Sports and Holidays

Each country has its own holidays to celebrate: independence day, the birth or death of a national hero, or the anniversary of an event in the nation's history. Children, workers, and government officials parade and listen to speeches. Band concerts in the evenings, excursions to the country, festive meals at home or in town—these are the pleasures of the holiday. Horseback riding, soccer (football), and jai alai are enjoyed by many people. Bullfights are popular in Mexico and Central America. Basketball, baseball, and boxing are increasingly popular sports.

Many of Latin America's holidays are religious. Every village, town, and city has its patron saint. Religious pilgrimages, folk dances, songs, and fireworks are familiar ways of celebration. New Year's Day, Carnival, Easter Sunday, All Soul's Day, and Christmas are some of the major holidays most Latin Americans observe.

On New Year's Eve the family dines at home and then goes to the plaza to watch the fireworks. At midnight the church bells announce the New Year and people attend mass. On New Year's Day merchants present gifts to their regular customers. Families give presents to those who have served them during the year—the postman, policemen, and servants. In the afternoon, visits are made to friends.

Carnival, or Mardi Gras, is a celebration introduced by the Spanish and Portuguese. People wearing masks and elaborate costumes parade through the streets. Gay parties are held in most homes. Carnival is a burst of joy and freedom before Lent, a 40-day period of self-denial. The carnivals of Trinidad, Haiti, Costa Rica, and Brazil are internationally famous.

On the outskirts of a large city in Honduras, women wash clothes in the river.

Ecuador's bananas (*left*) and Guatemala's coffee (*right*) are important Latin-American exports.

Argentina's Mar del Plata (*above left*), Puerto Rico's San Juan (*above right*), and Uruguay's Punta del Este (*below*) are among Latin America's sun-drenched and fashionable resort cities.

Easter Sunday is a high point in religious celebration. The day may begin with the burning of a papier-mâché Judas in the streets. It may close with an evening stroll in the plaza as the band plays. Young men break colored eggshells filled with confetti or perfume and shower the contents at the girls as they stroll in opposite directions around the square.

All Soul's Day is observed by visits to cemeteries. People bring flowers, foods, and pictures of the dead. In some places there are all-night vigils and prayers. Respect for the dead makes this one of Latin America's most solemn days.

In Brazil children receive gifts on Christmas Day. But in most Latin-American countries they receive their gifts on January 6, celebrating the visit of the three Magi. The children leave a bundle of hay or a pot of water for the Magi's camels. Santa Claus is a recent import to the countries of Latin America, and is known only to children living in the larger cities.

Christmas is a season of joy throughout Latin America, but nowhere does it last longer or have more magic than in Mexico. There the season begins on December 16. Each night the family and their guests act out Mary and Joseph's search for a lodging. There are prayers and songs. Candies, fruits, food, and punch are available for all guests.

The children enjoy breaking a *piñata* each evening. The *piñata* is a clay pot covered with papier-mâché and colored tissue paper and filled with candies, fruits, and coins. It may take one of many shapes—a head of lettuce, a donkey, a fish, a lyre, a ship, a stork. When it is broken, children scramble for the contents. It is the gay end to each evening from December 16 through Christmas Eve, when the family attends midnight Mass.

The Day

The Latin American is an early riser. Around 7 A.M. he has a breakfast of coffee and milk, hot chocolate with buns, or, in Central America and Mexico, *tortillas* and beans. If he can afford it, he has eggs and bacon. He works until 12 noon or 1 P.M., when he goes home to eat the big meal of the day. The food of the average Latin American is simple, robust, and pleasant. Often, but not always, it is highly spiced with hot peppers. The staple foods are rice, beans, eggs, beef, pork, lamb, fish, squash, tomatoes, and other vegetables. Fruit is abundant—some kinds are known only in tropical Latin America—and it accompanies the noon meal. The type of cooking depends on local resources and so, like everything else in Latin America, it has regional variations.

The Siesta. In most of Latin America people take a siesta during the middle of the day. Shops, businesses, and factories close down for 1 or 2 hours. Farm work stops. The Latin American eats his midday meal and then takes a nap or rests in the shade of a tree. Heat and altitude—not laziness—make this habit necessary. The workday begins early and ends later than it does in the United States. Brazil alone does not follow this pattern.

At 6 or 7 P.M. the Latin American eats a snack called a *merienda*. This may be coffee and bread, buns, cheese, or, in corn-producing countries, one of many local varieties of filled corn cakes. Dinner is eaten quite late in Latin America—9 or 10 P.M. or even later.

▶ A WORLD OF CHANGE

Latin America is a troubled region in the process of profound change. Its problems are many. It has one of the highest rates of population growth in the world. Its land is still not distributed fairly among the people. It lacks capital to invest in home industries. And it needs better education, health, and housing programs to combat illiteracy, ill-health, and poor housing. Countries that export only one main product, such as sugar, coffee, bananas, oil, or minerals, need to collaborate more with each other for better exchange of goods. Politically, many countries are struggling to find a form of government able to meet these problems. In a number of countries, military regimes have emerged and significant internal changes are taking place. Although many of these regimes are dedicated to social and political reforms, in some cases they have severely limited the freedom of the opposition.

Reviewed by FLORINDO VILLA-ALVAREZ
University of Rio de Janeiro

See also CARIBBEAN SEA AND ISLANDS; CENTRAL AMERICA; NORTH AMERICA; SOUTH AMERICA; articles on individual countries.

LATIN-AMERICAN ART AND ARCHITECTURE

The art of Latin America reflects the varied origins and rich traditions of the people who produced it. The Indians native to Latin America often were highly skilled stonecutters, potters, and weavers. After the Spanish and Portuguese conquests many artists came to the New World. They were trained in the finest European schools of architecture, painting, and sculpture.

Encouraged by vigorous church-building, Latin-American art developed quickly. The styles were set by the Europeans, but the brilliant colors and rich textures were often contributed by the Indians.

▶ ART AFTER THE CONQUEST

The conquest of the New World, which began in the early 16th century, was undertaken as much to spread Christianity as to find gold. Catholic missionaries arrived in the same ships with the soldiers. At first their monasteries were small and crude. Within a

Sculptured relief (17th century) on the Church of San Miguel, Pomata, Peru, is in early baroque style.

short time, however, the Spanish priests were using the building skills of the Mexican and Peruvian Indians to create monasteries, churches, and cathedrals of great size and beauty.

During the 16th century many thousands of churches and hundreds of monasteries were built in Latin America. Because whole Indian populations were converted at once, especially in Mexico, 16th-century churches were built with huge front courts for mass conversions.

The most striking feature of the early 16th-century church was its fortresslike appearance. The fortified walls showed the conquistadores' fear of Indian uprisings. These massive churches had ribbed and pointed arches—simplified versions of the European Gothic style. **Buttresses** (supports) lined the outside walls. The small, round windows were sometimes adorned with patterned designs.

Spanish art was greatly influenced by the Moors—North Africans who occupied Spain for 800 years. **Mudéjar**, the Spanish version of detailed geometric Moorish designs, was popular throughout the colonial period in Latin America. Especially handsome were the carved wooden doors and tile-covered church domes. These were done in *Mudéjar* style by highly skilled local craftsmen.

One of the best examples of early 16th-century art is the Augustinian monastery at Acolman in Mexico. The church looks like a high, narrow box. Inside, a series of magnificent **frescoes** (paintings done on plaster) decorates the **apse**—the part of the church that contains the altar. Nearby, monastic enclosed gardens, called **cloisters**, are surrounded by heavy, rounded arches.

▶ ART OF NEW SPAIN

When the conquest of Latin America was completed in the mid-16th century, the Spanish established colonies, or viceroyalties. New Spain (present-day Mexico and Central America), with its capital at Mexico City, was established in 1535. The Viceroyalty of Peru (now Peru, Bolivia, Ecuador, and Colombia), with its capital at Lima, was formed in 1544. Other colonies were formed later, but Mexico and Peru easily dominated all other colonial areas in art. As the church grew richer, monasteries became more luxurious, and more cathedrals were built.

Italian Renaissance forms influenced Spanish art and were widely used in the New World. Round arches, grooved columns, and a variety of lively decorative figures and flowers came into fashion. The Renaissance style added a graceful note to Latin-American buildings.

Another European style to come to Latin America with Spanish craftsmen and artists was **plateresque**—a combination of Gothic, Renaissance, and Moorish forms. The style is characterized by fine ornaments that look like the delicate work of silversmiths (*plateros*). Doorways and niches were decorated with rich designs and elaborate statues of saints, often painted bright colors.

In the late 16th and early 17th centuries there was a brief period during which churches became austere and ornaments were practically eliminated. But this style, known as **Herreran**, proved too severe for the Latin Americans. The people of the New World preferred exciting designs in their intricately woven colored blankets and monumental pyramids of the sun and the moon. It is not surprising, then, that **baroque** art—with its lavish decorations and dramatic effects—inspired the most outstanding and original buildings in colonial Latin America. Baroque was a bold, richly decorated, and dramatic style that was popular in 17th-century Europe.

All over Latin America baroque churches were built in a **cruciform** (cross shape), with a central dome and bell towers. The **facade** (front) was covered with carvings. The enormous baroque altarpieces were immensely complicated. Paintings or statues of saints were placed from floor to ceiling, connected by a series of twisted carvings. The cathedral interiors became great museums of sculpture, painting, metalwork, and costume.

Churrigueresque, a highly decorated Spanish version of baroque, came to the New World early in the 18th century. It became very popular because the exciting, swirling style suited the passionate religious feelings of Latin Americans. In the monastery of Tepozotlán, in Mexico, almost every square inch is carved, curled, or painted. The most

Detail of Antônio Francisco Lisboa's painted sculpture *Christ at the Last Supper* (1796–99), in a Brazilian church.

famous Churrigueresque art forms were the **retablos** (altar screens), which were lavishly carved from wood or stone. There were sometimes four or five glowingly colored and gilded *retablos* in a church.

By the 18th century the great town churches were no longer the only buildings of architectural importance in New Spain. As life became easier the people demanded beautiful private palaces and public buildings. The increasingly wealthy churches and private families wanted oil paintings. The demand was so great that artists were kept busy turning out paintings by the hundreds. In the rush to fill orders workmanship was standardized, and the same subjects were done over and over. This mass production brought about a serious decline in the quality of painting.

ART OF PERU

Like the Aztecs and Maya of New Spain the Inca Indians in the Andes mountains of South America had a highly developed art. Because the Inca traditions and religion were unlike those of the other Indians, the art of Peru had distinct qualities.

Spanish artists usually worked in what had been the large Indian capital cities. The Spanish destroyed the temple to the Inca god Wiraqocha in the ancient Inca capital of Cuzco. They built the cathedral of Cuzco over the ruins. The conquerors used the large, evenly cut stones from the Inca temple in the new cathedral. The squat towers and simple outlines of the cathedral also reflect the influence of the Incas.

The Indians of the Andes had a long tradition of carving stone in a flat, linear manner. Sometimes the monks allowed Indian craftsmen to use symbols from local custom and religion. It was hoped that the use of familiar designs on Christian works would help spread the faith. The Inca religious symbols of the sun and the moon may be seen on the facade of the church of San Lorenzo at Potosí, Bolivia. Instead of the usual angels, figures of sirens (unreal creatures with the head of a woman and the body of a bird) were placed over the doors. The sirens are playing native musical instruments.

Most baroque and later art in the Andes was less ornamented than other Spanish-American art of the same periods. An outstanding exception is the 17th-century monastery of San Francisco in Quito, Ecuador. Filling an area of four city blocks, it is one of the most elaborate monasteries in Latin America. San Francisco has four cloisters, each with altars and paintings. The facade of the church is long and low, with the massive quality of other Andean churches. Although the exterior is plain, the interior contains Mudéjar work on the ceiling and gilded woodwork throughout. The high altar is so immense that it flows over into neighboring parts of the church.

ART OF COLONIAL BRAZIL

War, lack of money, and the wildness of the countryside kept Portugal from developing her New World territory until the late 17th century. In Brazil there were few of the missionaries who had encouraged art so successfully in the Spanish colonies. Also, the Brazilian natives were not skilled craftsmen. For these reasons the art of Brazil did not begin to develop until early in the 18th century.

The church of the Third Order of St. Francis in Bahia, completed in 1703, is a fine example of early Portuguese art in the New World. The church has the typical Portuguese baroque balconies of **wrought iron** (iron that has been shaped and ornamented). Wavy scrolls decorate many corners.

Tall, narrow facades and whitewashed walls are characteristic of another distinctive Brazilian style, **coastal baroque**. Squared towers, large, ornamental doorways, and highly decorated French windows complete the exterior.

A third Brazilian style is associated with the 18th-century mining towns. Discoveries of gold and diamonds brought much wealth and activity to the region of Minas Gerais. Many elaborately decorated churches were constructed in the area. Their airy and graceful design was copied from the European style known as **rococo**. Local materials like quartz—a beautiful light-colored stone—and fine hardwood added special touches to the church decorations.

In the city of Ouro Prêto the famous architect-sculptor Antônio Francisco Lisboa (1730–1814) designed many magnificent churches. Lisboa was disfigured by an illness and was known by the name O Aleijadinho ("the Little Cripple"). The twin-towered church of São Francisco is typical of his style. It was built on a rectangular plan. The contrasting colors of the facade give the church a gay look. The main body of the building is light gray, while the towers, bases, and **cornices** (ornamental raised doorframes) are soft orange—all variations of a local stone. Imaginative decorative themes of garlands and scrolls and graceful window carvings and realistic sculpture are the trademarks of this outstanding artist.

19TH CENTURY

In the 19th century the Latin-American colonists gained their independence from Europe. It was a time of sudden and violent changes. Government buildings replaced the

A folk painting of Christ and the Madonna refreshing the martyrs, from 17th-century Peru. Collection of Claude Arthaud.

Madonna and Angels, a detail from a relief at the Church of Santo Domingo, Oaxaca, Mexico (late 16th through early 18th century).

Antônio Francisco Lisboa's Church of São Francisco (18th century), Ouro Prêto, Brazil.

Flower Festival, Feast of Santa Anita (1931), by Diego Rivera. Museum of Modern Art, New York.

Zapatistas (1931), by Orozco. Museum of Modern Art, New York. Below: A mosaic by Carlos Mérida decorates a modern government building in Guatemala.

church as the center of art and life, and Latin-American artists did more portraits and landscapes than religious paintings.

The most important 19th-century trend was **neoclassicism**, in which artists imitated the balance and calm of ancient Greek and Roman art. Neoclassicism was a reaction to the highly decorative baroque and rococo styles. Reformers of the new republics were interested in correcting evil in government, and the artists wanted to "correct" their old styles. They turned their backs on carved and gilded wood. Instead of using the old twin towers, churches were built with simple columned fronts, like Greek temples. Before, interiors of many brilliant colors had been streaked with masses of solid gold leaf. Now the church interiors were decorated in a more restrained combination of white and gold.

The Goya movement, named after the Spanish artist Francisco Goya (1746–1828), attracted many followers in Latin America. An artist who worked in this style was Antonio Salas (?–1860) of Ecuador. Artists were called upon to glorify revolutionary heroes and record successful battles. Salas painted the liberators of the Colombia area. Portraits and scenes from everyday life, called **genre** paintings, were also popular.

In sculpture Latin Americans were still turning to Greece and Rome for their models. But the landscape painters wanted to show the beauty of their own countries. The outstanding 19th-century painter was José María Velasco (1840–1912) of Mexico. His famous vistas (views) of the Valley of Mexico realistically represent the striking mountains and green valleys of his country.

▶ 20TH CENTURY

The Latin-American people had gained their independence from Europe. Yet a few families still controlled the land, and the farmworkers earned very low wages. A wave of social revolution and civil war swept Latin America as the poor tried to correct these injustices. Art played a great part in spreading the ideas of the revolutions. In Mexico, for example, the revolutionary government ordered murals for public buildings to explain the country's history. The leaders felt that even the poorest people should be allowed to enjoy art.

In 1922 the Syndicate of Technical Workers, Painters, and Sculptors was formed in Mexico. The syndicate tried to do away with European styles and replace them with truly Mexican art. The most famous artist of the group was Diego Rivera (1886–1957). He imitated the flat, linear Indian style and use of dramatic colors. In large historical murals that cover the courtyard walls of the President's palace in Mexico City, Rivera shows Spanish conquerors destroying Indian civilization. The murals glorify the Indian and the continuing revolution. José Clemente Orozco (1883–1949) applied broad sweeps of brilliant colors to frescoes and paintings. The violence and power that characterize much of his work are marks of modern Mexican painting. David Alfaro Siqueiros (1898–   ) participated most actively in workers' revolutionary movements. His anger at injustice is clearly expressed in his dramatic and sympathetic representations of laborers. In Brazil, Candido Portinari (1903–62) depicted everyday life in colorful scenes.

Since World War II there has been a wave of building in Latin America, notably in Mexico, Cuba, Santo Domingo, Venezuela, and Brazil. The use of **reinforced concrete**, an inexpensive manufactured product, has been widespread. Latin Americans, who have always loved rich textures, have quickly learned to use the most modern materials. In Brasilia, the new capital of Brazil, a team of architects including Lucio Costa (1902–) and Oscar Niemeyer (1907–) is creating exciting and daring reinforced concrete buildings right in the middle of the Amazon jungle.

The mixture of very modern structural forms and old materials like **azulejos** (colored and glazed tiles) is often seen in Latin America. Juan O'Gorman (1905–) is famous for his mosaic of over 1,000,000 colored pieces that covers the entire exterior of the library at University City, Mexico.

In Latin America, universities, schools, hospitals, and other community buildings are going up at a tremendous rate. These service buildings—like all Latin-American art and architecture—show a real concern for people and their needs and problems.

JOSEPH A. BAIRD
University of California

TANGO
(Argentina)

TEHUANTEPEC
WEDDING DANCE
(Mexico)

FREVO
(Brazil)

JOROPO
(Venezuela)

LATIN-AMERICAN DANCING

Dancing is one of the major forms of expression of those countries in the Western Hemisphere south of the United States. Different peoples and cultures have given Latin-American dance its variety and color. First, there were the native Indians; then the Spanish and Portuguese conquerors and settlers; then the African slaves. Finally, there were other and later European immigrants. The customs and beliefs of all these people are revealed in the dances we call Latin-American.

▶ **PRE-COLUMBIAN DANCE**

Most of America was inhabited by Indians at the time of the discovery of the New World. There were as many different dances as there were different peoples. Yet all dance had one characteristic: it was, above all, religious and ceremonial. Dancing and music were a vital part of the religions of the three most important pre-Columbian cultures. These were the Aztecs and Maya of Mexico and Guatemala, and the Incas of Peru, Bolivia, and Ecuador. Other Indians—those living on the Caribbean islands, for example, or in the Amazon basin—were more primitive and unsettled. But dance and music were important to all in nearly every happening of their daily lives.

Among the Aztecs, Incas, and Maya, dance

was an institution of the state. Young people were taught dancing, singing, and playing by priests, who were skilled teachers. Training was rigorous. A bad performance was considered an offense not only to the community but to the gods. The Aztec, Maya, and Inca states kept companies of dancers, and so did wealthy nobles. Thus, dancing was performed at state festivals and private celebrations. Among state festivals there were dances to the sun, for rain, and for a prince's marriage or a prince's death. There were dances for victory in war, for peace after a war, for a good harvest, and for immortality after death. There were also comic and satiric dances, which pantomimed a person, a custom, or an institution. Among private festivals there were dances for births, marriages, and deaths. In the absence of writing, pre-Columbian dance, like pre-Columbian painting and sculpture, was a way to give history and religion visible form.

▶ **DANCE AFTER THE CONQUEST**

At first the Spanish and Portuguese, whether soldiers, priests, or settlers, tried to suppress the Indian dances because they were not Christian. But today, just as in the days of Aztecs, Maya, and Incas, dancing and music are an important part of the lives of the Indians. In dance they express their Catholic beliefs and find recreation. Since the conquest, three kinds of dance have developed in Latin

America. First, there is a folk dance with Indian elements, particularly in Mexico, Guatemala, Ecuador, Bolivia, and Peru. Second, there is a mestizo dance, a mixture of Indian and European steps and styles. Finally, new native dances have developed in many areas. These dances are found in countries having few Indians—Argentina and Uruguay—and in those with large Negro populations, like Brazil and the Caribbean countries.

Indian Folk Dances

As they did before the conquest, Indians today often wear masks to represent animals, devils, or people. Dancing is not reserved for the professional. All people may take part in the acting out of ancient legends, battles, or events. "Los Voladores" (The Fliers), performed in various regions of Mexico, is only one of these old Indian dances. It is performed on the feast of Corpus Christi. The best-known version is performed at Papantla in the state of Veracruz. A special tall tree is chosen, cut, and brought to the village amid a religious feast. Ritual dances and music are performed. Five dancers climb the tree. One dances on a frame built on the treetop. The other four dancers, their feet tied to a rope, fly into space with arms outstretched as the rope unwinds from their bodies. The dance celebrates man's skill and courage. In Bolivia, dancing is still so important that no one can dance in the major festivals till he is 18 years old. To state that he is grown up, a Bolivian Indian only has to say, "I have already danced."

Mestizo Dances

The Spaniards and Portuguese who conquered Latin America brought many of their own dances with them from Europe. Soon Spanish and Portuguese dances and musical instruments were added to those of the Indians. The result was neither Spanish nor Indian, but mestizo—a mixture of both.

These dances based upon Spanish and Portuguese styles and traditions are found in all countries of Latin America. Some are so popular and so widely danced that they are considered national dances. In Mexico the famous "Jarabe Tapatío," or "Mexican Hat Dance," is an example of a national dance that uses the Spanish *zapateado*, or heel-beating steps. Many other national dances, such as the

cueca of Chile, the *marinera* of Peru, and the *sanjuanito* of Ecuador, are based on the *zapateado*. They tell a story of flirtation and courtship. The men wave handkerchiefs, snap their fingers, and beat their heels to attract the attention of their girl partners.

The *zapateado* is also a part of the *joropo* of Venezuela, the *seis zapateao* of Puerto Rico, the *gato* of Argentina, and many more. Other dances, such as the *pericón* of Uruguay, took their patterns and figures from European dances like the quadrille. They are favored by the gauchos, or cowboys, of South America.

Negro Latin-American Dances

With the introduction of slavery to Latin America the syncopated African rhythms were added to the Indian, Spanish, and Portuguese dances. In Africa religion was expressed through drumming and dancing dedicated to the worship of gods and ancestors. In Cuba, Haiti, Trinidad, and Brazil organized religious societies, or cults, known as voodooism, shango, ñáñigo, and macumba still perform dances in honor of African gods.

Gradually the rhythms of the drums began to affect the Spanish, Portuguese, and Creole dances and music. Thus a new type of dance, known as Afro-Cuban or Afro-Brazilian, developed. At first, dances such as the batuque in Brazil or the rumba in Cuba were intensely exciting and danced only by the lower classes. All of them were performed by groups of people, usually dancing individually without partners in a circle.

Early in the 20th century, however, the mixture of African rhythms and European melodies began to influence dance orchestras. The best-known dances of this type are Cuban and Puerto Rican: rumba, son, conga, mambo, and cha-cha-cha. Even the bolero, the popular "blues," or love song, of Latin America, added drums and percussion to its Spanish melody. The samba in Brazil includes several types of dances, from the strongly African batuque to the modern ballroom samba.

The only well-known Latin-American popular ballroom dance showing no African influence is the tango from Argentina. In Argentina, African slaves were not common. But the tango, like the Brazilian maxixe and samba and the Cuban rumba, began among the lower classes of the city. Now everyone in society dances it.

▶ **OLD AND NEW DANCE FORMS**

Once a year, carnival (Mardi Gras) brings thousands of costumed dancers into the streets to parade and dance the favorite and traditional rhythms of each country. Patron saints' days, local festivals, and holidays are all celebrated by typical dances and folk music. The music is played on instruments ranging from drums and percussion, guitars and *cuatros,* to the ancient pipes of Bolivia and the *rondadors* of Ecuador.

Many of the old dances are still seen, especially among the Indians of Bolivia, Peru, and Ecuador, and among the Negroes of the African cult societies. But the folklore of Latin America does not stand still. It is constantly changing as Latin America becomes more urban and modern.

Reviewed by AMALIA HERNÁNDEZ
Director, Ballet Folklórico de Mexico

LATIN-AMERICAN LITERATURE

Latin-American literature can be divided into two parts. There is Spanish-American literature, written in Spanish, and Brazilian literature, written in Portuguese.

▶ **SPANISH-AMERICAN LITERATURE**

16th Century. When Christopher Columbus discovered America in 1492, both Spain and Portugal entered an age of great cultural and literary splendor known as the Golden Age. The discovery and conquest of the great and untamed New World produced a literature about heroes and their actions. Conquerors set down their experiences in writing. Some of the men gave the straight facts of living history and wrote chronicles. Others, more poetic, sang of the great deeds they witnessed and wrote epics. The 16th-century chronicles and epics are the beginning of Spanish-American literature.

Naturally, the first man to write about America was Columbus himself. But the first important literary achievement was the *Letters of Report,* five letters Hernando Cortes wrote to the King of Spain describing the Spanish conquest of the Aztecs in Mexico.

Of the many chronicles some are important as literature and can compete even today in interest and suspense with any fiction. A vivid example is *Unknown Interior of America* by Álvar Núñez Cabeza de Vaca (1490?–1559?), in which he tells of his adventures in what is today the southern United States. Another chronicle that has come down to us is *Destruction of the Indies,* a book by the priest Bartolomé de las Casas (1474?–1566).

He pleads on behalf of the Indians, denouncing their mistreatment at the hands of the conquerors.

One of the most fascinating of all the chronicles of the period is *Summary of the Natural History of the Indies,* by the Spanish conquistador Gonzalo Fernández de Oviedo (1478–1557). Another interesting work is the book of one of Cortes' soldiers, Bernal Díaz del Castillo (1496–1584). Díaz's *True History of the Conquest of New Spain* tells the story of the conquest of Mexico in a colorful, candid way.

As for the epic, the most important was *The Araucana,* by the soldier-poet Alonso de Ercilla (1534–94), a Spanish nobleman. This poem celebrates the brave Araucanian Indians of Chile, against whom Ercilla fought.

Garcilaso de la Vega (1539–1616), called El Inca, was the son of a Spanish conqueror and an Inca princess. He gathered the history and traditions of the Incas into *The Royal Commentaries.*

17th and 18th Centuries. With the passing of the 16th century, life and literature in the new colonies began to take form. Both followed the pattern of the motherland. During the 17th century the fashion was for Gongorism, an ornate and complicated poetry, as written by the Spanish poet Luis de Góngora. Many writers imitated him, but one, a Mexican nun, Sister Juana Inés de La Cruz (1648–95), towered over all.

She had enjoyed the admiration of the glittering court of the Viceroy in Mexico City.

But when she was only 16 years old she entered a convent, where she spent the rest of her life. She wrote short religious plays, an autobiography, and beautiful, haunting poetry about her love of God.

Another important author of the colonial period was the hunchback Juan Ruiz de Alarcón (1580–1639). Born and educated in Mexico, he left for the mother country, never to return. In Spain he became a leading playwright of the Spanish Golden Age. One of his better works is *La verdad sospechosa* (*The Suspected Truth*), a play imitated by the French playwright Pierre Corneille in *Le Menteur* (*The Liar*).

19th-Century Romanticism. Between 1808 and 1825 Spanish America became free. Freedom brought with it not only revolutionary ideas but also new literary themes and styles that reflected them.

The first Latin American to express the new, radical thoughts was José Joaquín Fernández de Lizardi (1776–1827), author of a political journal, *The Mexican Thinker*. His most important work is *The Itching Parrot,* a novel about a boy's growing up.

Three men best represent the romantic poetry of the period. The first is the Ecuadorian José Joaquín Olmedo (1780–1847). The second is the Cuban José María de Heredia (1803–39). Heredia was the first romantic poet in the Spanish language to use the natural beauty of the Americas in his poems *In the Temple of Cholula and Niagara.* The third is Andrés Bello (1781–1865), a Venezuelan poet and scholar known for his poems that describe the tropics.

The outstanding name of the romantic period, however, is that of Domingo Faustino Sarmiento (1811–88), an educator and president of Argentina. His most important work is *Civilization and Barbarism: The Life of Juan Facundo Quiroga.* This biography deals with a dictator's henchman, the gaucho Facundo Quiroga. The gaucho is the Argentine counterpart of the North American cowboy, and his way of life is the basis of a school of writing known as gaucho literature. The poem *Martín Fierro,* by José Hernández (1834–86), is another narrative of gaucho life in the pampas.

The romantic struggle against tyranny is reflected by the life and work of the Ecuadorian Juan Montalvo (1832–89). His *Seven Treatises* contains the most important essays of this period. The best and still the most widely read novel of the time is *María,* by Jorge Isaacs (1837–95). In this popular work the author combines a melancholy atmosphere of love and death with the beauty of the Colombian landscape. In a class all to himself is the Peruvian Ricardo Palma (1833–1919). His *Knights of the Cape* is a sample of the excellent historical anecdotes he wrote in *Peruvian Traditions.*

Few dramatic works written during this period achieved prominence. Florencio Sánchez (1875–1910), born in Uruguay, was one of the few important playwrights.

The Turn of the Century: Modernism. The movement called modernism began in 1888 with the publication of *Azure,* by the Nicaraguan Rubén Darío (1867–1916). By joining old Spanish and new French poetry Darío forged a new, personal, and truly Spanish-American style that influenced all of Latin America. His masterworks are *Azure, Profane Prose,* and *Songs of Life and Hope.* Rubén Darío remains the giant of Spanish-American letters.

Before Rubén Darío four other important poets had begun to make a new literature: José Martí (1853–95), a Cuban national hero and an essayist and poet (*Simple Songs*); Julián del Casal (1863–93), also a Cuban; José Asunción Silva (1865–96), a Colombian; and the Mexican Manuel Gutiérrez Nájera (1859–95).

There are at least three other important names among the modernists. Two are poets —Amado Nervo (1870–1919), from Mexico, and the Peruvian José Santos Chocano (1875–1934). The third is the Uruguayan essayist José Enrique Rodó (1871–1917).

20th Century. Modernism came to an end with World War I. The new generation of poets had certain traits in common. They shunned rhyme, abstraction, and sentimentality. Their work in no way mirrored life, and they tried to achieve what they called pure poetry.

One who attained the greatest originality was the Peruvian César Vallejo (1892–1938), who wrote about his background, his life, and his knowledge of death. The most important of the modern poets are Neftalí Reyes (1904–   ), a Chilean, who writes under the pen name of Pablo Neruda, and Octavio Paz (1914–   ), a Mexican.

The 20th century is noted for women poets. The best-known is Gabriela Mistral (1889–1957), whose real name was Lucila Godoy. This Chilean poetess received the Nobel prize for literature in 1945, the first awarded to a Spanish-American writer.

The realistic novel became a strong form of literary expression in 20th-century Spanish America. Life close to primitive nature attracted writers' attention. Thus, we have the novels of the jungle, the best example of which is *The Vortex,* by José Eustasio Rivera (1888–1928), a Colombian. This novel gives a memorable view of the Amazonian jungle and the dangers of living in it.

Doña Bárbara, by the Venezuelan Rómulo Gallegos (1884–1969), is a novel of the prairies. This book describes the life of men in the tropical prairies of Venezuela. In this same category there is the Argentine novel *Shadows on the Pampas,* by Ricardo Güiraldes (1886–1927).

Uruguayan Horacio Quiroga (1878–1937) is known for his short stories. The background for his adventure tales is the jungle of northern Argentina.

The Mexican Revolution (1910) created a new kind of novel, one showing the struggle of the mestizo and the Indian for justice against the aristocratic overlord. An outstanding example is *The Underdogs,* by Mariano Azuela (1873–1952).

The social awareness born with revolution made the life and problems of the Indian very important to writers. Those countries with great Indian populations—Guatemala, Ecuador, Peru, and Bolivia, for example—produced a good many novels on the Indian's place in society.

In countries with less of an Indian problem the novelist cultivated the psychological and philosophical novel. This is especially true of Argentina, where Eduardo Mallea (1903–   ) and Jorge Luis Borges (1899–   ) have created a fiction dealing with the European character of Argentine society.

In the latter half of the 20th century, increasing numbers of Latin-American authors began to attain worldwide recognition through translations of their work. Among the writers who achieved prominence are the Cuban Alejo Carpentier (1904–   ), the Peruvian Mario Vargas Llosa (1930–   ), the Mexican Carlos Fuentes (1928–   ), and the Argentines Julio Cortázar (1916–   ) and Ernesto Sábato (1911–   ). Miguel Ángel Asturias (1899–   ) of Guatemala received the Nobel prize for literature in 1967.

▶ BRAZILIAN LITERATURE

Brazil was discovered in 1500 by the Portuguese. The Portuguese language, spoken in Brazil, is a Romance language. Like Spanish, it comes from Latin.

16th–18th Centuries. The conquest of Brazil was followed by a colonial period. During the 16th century the name of the Jesuit José de Anchieta (1534–97) is prominent among early writers. The most important author in the 17th century was another Jesuit father, Antônio Vieira (1608–97). With the 18th century came the Mineira school of poetry, so named after the province of Minas Gerais. This school extolled Brazilian nature, and José Basilío da Gama (1740–95), with the poem *O Uruguai,* is a good representative of the school.

19th Century. In 1822 Brazil became an independent country under its own emperor, Pedro I. This opened the country to the world. Romanticism began to appear, and with it a new consciousness of the Brazilian. Writers of the 19th century began to develop a new individuality of theme and style.

One of the two most important poets was Antônio Gonçalves Dias (1823–64), who idealized in his poems the image of the noble savage. The other outstanding poet was Castro Alves (1847–71). His love of liberty helped to free the Brazilian Negro slaves.

The romantic novelist José de Alencar (1829–77) saw Brazilian nature in epic terms in his novels *The Guarani* and *Iracema.* Later Euclides da Cunha (1866–1909) wrote a study of the Brazilian hinterland, *Rebellion in the Backlands.*

The towering literary figure of Brazil is Joaquim Maria Machado de Assís (1839–1908). Machado de Assís was a poor mulatto with little schooling. But his deep insight into human behavior makes his novels works of art. Many have been translated into other languages. Among his best-known works are *Epitaph of a Small Winner* and *Dom Casmurro.*

20th Century. Brazilian modernism appeared after World War I. In Brazil it meant a reaction against all previous literary models. Writing had been elegant, careful. Modernism made use of the manners and speech of the many different peoples of Brazil—Negroes, Indians, Europeans, East Indians. Mario de Andrade (1893–1945) and Oswald de Andrade (1890–1954) did a great deal to spread the movement. Graça Aranha (1868– 1931) and Jorge de Lima (1895–1953) were among the other followers of the modernist movement.

Among the novelists—all of them preoccupied with social problems—are José Lins do Rego (1901–57), Erico Veríssimo (1905–   ), José Américo de Almeida (1887–   ), and Jorge Amado (1912–   ).

Margarita Ucelay Da Cal
Chairman, Spanish Department, Barnard College

LATIN-AMERICAN MUSIC

The phrase "Latin-American music" is rich with familiar associations—the sounds of guitars, flutes, and drums.

Three worlds meet and mingle in Latin-American music. The first is quite old. It reaches back to the time before the discovery and conquest of America. This is the world of the native Indians. The second world came with the Spaniards and Portuguese, who brought the music of Europe to the New World. The third came with the African Negroes, who came as slaves to work in the mines and on the plantations of the West Indies and South America.

Thus, many races make and enjoy Latin-American music. It can be heard at marketplace or concert hall, at a family fiesta or a state ceremony. It is an art as well as a folk music. It is very old and very new; it is always colorful.

▶ **MUSIC BEFORE THE CONQUEST**

The Aztecs and Maya of Mexico and Central America and the Incas of Peru, Bolivia, and Ecuador were great painters, sculptors, and architects. They were also musicians. Stories of their gods and events of their history provided the subjects of music. It was heard at great religious and civic festivals. It was played to accompany dances or epic

REED PIPE

STEEL DRUM

MARIMBA

GUIRO

poems that told the stories of the people. Music also served to accompany the more personal and private lyric poems.

Not much is known about this music. But ancient chants can still be heard in remote parts of Latin America. These show that the scale was pentatonic—that is, only five (in Greek, *penta*) tones were used. Pottery, paintings, and archeological excavations show that the ancient Aztecs, Maya, and Incas had wood and skin drums of various sizes; wood and bronze bells; bone scrapers and shakers. The most sophisticated instrument was the marimba, an instrument similar to a xylophone. The marimba is made of wooden bars of different sizes, with hollowed gourds or pumpkinlike fruits hung from each bar to produce greater vibration. Wind instruments included reed pipes and panpipes—reeds of graduated lengths bound together that will reproduce the scale. There were also whistles, musical shells, and bird-shaped mouthpieces, now called ocarinas. There is no evidence of stringed instruments among the ancient Indians. The lute, the guitar, and the violin were brought by the Europeans.

▶ MUSIC SINCE THE CONQUEST

The Spaniards destroyed the Indian cities and suppressed the Indian arts. But they built cities, and they brought their own music and instruments. Soon the Indians adapted the new music and instruments to their own uses. After the 16th century the Negroes, brought in as slaves from Africa, added a new folk element to music. Two traditions of music began to grow side by side in the New World. The first was a folk music combining Indian or Negro elements with European elements. The second was an art music that remained largely European in style until the close of the 19th century. But with the opening of the 20th century, Latin-American composers turned to the native folk music for new inspiration and forms.

Folk Music

In Latin America nearly every song can be danced and every dance has words. Since gaining independence in the 19th century each country has evolved its own national music. This evolution reflects the mixture of races of the particular country. The *zamacueca,* or

cueca, of Chile, in 3/4 and 6/8 time, is very Spanish in feeling. So is the *pasillo,* a Spanish balladlike air sung in both Colombia and Venezuela. Mexico's *huapango,* a song and dance that uses the harp in addition to various guitars, and Mexico's *son* reflect the influence of Spain. The same is true of Argentina's dances, the *gato* and *cielito.*

But perhaps the best-known Latin-American folk music is the Mexican *corrido* and the Argentinian tango. The Mexican *corrido* is usually a narrative story set to a vigorous music. The words are about historical events and local, everyday happenings. The *corridos* are balladlike in form. The tango is very like Cuba's habanera; both are music in slow, syncopated 2/4 time. The tango, now a popular ballroom dance, grew up in the slums of Buenos Aires. In the best tangos not only the Spaniards but other Europeans—Italians, Frenchmen, and Jews, who immigrated to the country at the turn of the century—have found a means of self-expression.

The music of Brazil, Trinidad, Cuba, Haiti, the Dominican Republic, and Puerto Rico reflects the vitality and freshness of the Negro's contribution to Latin-American music. The infectious Brazilian samba, a favorite all over the world, is in a highly syncopated 2/4 time. The *macumba,* also Brazilian, is a dance rich with religious folk themes and so varied in meter that it is hard to classify. The *macumba* has begun to influence modern dance-band music.

The rumba and conga are Cuban and began as chants in African rituals. They, too, have been adopted by the modern city dance bands. The merengue of the Dominican Republic, a merry dance with regional variations, and the witty, bubbling, and dramatic calypso of Trinidad are other examples of rhythmic and instrumental color in Latin-American music. In Haiti drums are used at voodoo ceremonies in a music that is deeply religious—a music to invoke the aid and spirit of ancestors and gods.

The latest influence on Latin-American folk music is jazz. Mambo, cha-cha-cha, and bossa nova are among the best-known blends and mixtures of jazz with European melodies and Negro-Caribbean and Negro-Brazilian songs and dances.

Art Music

Colonial. The first art music heard in the New World was that of the parent countries, Spain and Portugal. Choir music, religious songs of praise to the saints (*alabanzas*), and Christmas songs were among the first forms. But as a society began to develop in the colony, the music of the royal courts and the town mansions also began to be heard.

The Portuguese influence in Brazil and the Spanish influence in the rest of Latin America dominated the development of colonial music. With independence in the 19th century, conservatories, opera houses, and concert halls were founded in Mexico City, Mexico; Bogotá, Colombia; Lima, Peru; and Rio de Janeiro, Brazil. Through music teachers and conductors the influence of Germany and Italy reached Latin America at the same time that it was reaching France, England, Spain, Portugal, and Russia.

The first important South American composer was the Brazilian Carlos Gomes (1836–96). He wrote *Il Guarany,* an opera about Indian life in Brazil. But its text was in Italian, and he imitated Italian music. In Mexico, Melesio Morales (1821–1908) and Aniceto Ortega (1838–75), among others, wrote on native subjects with the colorfulness of the Italians. However, the Spanish *zarzuela* (operetta) and *sainete* (comic opera) were also popular.

Modern. Encouraged by the social revolutions of the 20th century, Latin-American composers turned to their own folk music to create a new and modern national music.

Manuel M. Ponce (1886–1948) is greatly respected in his native Mexico as a pioneer of modern Mexican music. He composed the famous song *Estrellita,* as well as the symphonic trilogy *Chaupultepec* (1929) and the *Concerto of the South* (1941) for orchestra and guitar. But Mexico's world-renowned composer is Carlos Chávez (1899–   ). As a conductor and a teacher, he is a leader of the younger generation. In such works as *The Four Suns* (1926) and the *Indian* Symphony (1936) Chávez gave Mexico a music all its own. Other important Mexican composers are Silvestre Revueltas (1899–1940); Blas Galindo (1910–   ), who used folk themes; and Miguel Bernal Jiménez (1910–   ), composer of religious works.

Another world figure in Latin-American music is the Brazilian composer Heitor Villa-Lobos (1887–1959). He created a music rooted in national life but with an appeal for the whole world. A composer of many songs, symphonies, and suites, such as *Discovery of Brazil* (1937), he is most popularly known for *Bachianas Brasileiras* (1932–47), a series of Bachlike works on Brazil. Oscar Lorenzo Fernandez (1897–1948), Francisco Mignone (1897–   ), and particularly Camargo Guarnieri (1907–   ) have further enriched Brazilian musical culture.

A pioneer of music in Argentina was Alberto Williams (1862–1952), the grandson of an Englishman. He brought a fine European training to the composition of piano works based on Argentinian dances. Juan José Castro (1895–1968) and Juan Carlos Paz (1897–   ) brought the leading styles of modern Europe to Argentina. This influence ripened in the original and brilliant work of Alberto Ginastera (1916–   ), Argentina's most gifted composer.

In Uruguay nationalism in music began with Carlos Pedrell (1878–1941). But it was Eduardo Fabini (1883–1950) who achieved originality.

Elsewhere in South America noted composers are the Chileans Pedro Humberto Allende (1885–1959); Carlos Isamitt (1887–   ), who used Indian themes; and Carlos Lavin (1883–1964). In Peru the music of Raoul de Verneuil (1901–   ) is inspired by Indian life, and the work of Juan Vicente Lecuna (1898–1964) is strongly Venezuelan in spirit. Colombia has a composer of distinction in Guillermo Uribe Holguín (1880–   ).

The mixture of races and the drama and color of life in Central America and the West Indies have produced several noteworthy composers. Two of the best-known are the Cubans Alejandro García Caturla (1906–40) and Amadeo Roldán (1900–39).

To the outside world the music of Latin America appears as a many-colored world of brilliant sounds and flashing and exotic rhythms. Behind this display there is an art of composition that has brought into unity the art and folk music of Latin America.

Reviewed by LEO PERACCHI
Composer, *Musica di Cena para a Plaça*

LATIN LANGUAGE AND LITERATURE

Latin is the language that was used by the ancient Romans and carried by them to much of Europe, the Near East, northern Africa, and even Britain. Millions of people have spoken or studied Latin over the past 2,500 years. Although Latin is no longer used for everyday speech in the world today, it is the official language of the Roman Catholic Church, and it is read and studied in schools in many parts of the world.

Anyone who speaks English speaks some Latin without realizing it, for more than half the words in the English language and many legal and scientific terms come directly from Latin. Some Latin words in common use are: *animal, area, capital, fact, genius, labor, minus, orator, resolve, senator,* and *senior.* Many Latin words have come into English with a slight change of meaning: "arena" (which in Latin meant "sand"), "campus" ("field"), "sinister" ("left").

Alphabet and Structure

The alphabet we use every day came to us from the Romans. It was developed from a Semitic alphabet through a western Greek form of writing used by the Etruscans, who dominated early Rome. It had only 21 letters until Y and Z were added in order to be able to spell words borrowed from Greek. J and W were not used. I was both a vowel and a consonant (with the sound of our Y). There was no sound like our V. The vowel sound U, as in "put," and the consonant sound W, as in "wine," were written with the letter *u,* which in capitals was V. Thus the Latin word for light, *lux,* looked like LVX. Vowels (A, E, I, O, V) were pronounced as long or short, but consonants had only one sound each, and that was much the same as in English. C, G, and T were always "hard" in classical Latin, as in "call," "get," and "take." Later, in the Latin of the church, they were pronounced "soft," as in "cello," "gem," and "nation."

Words in the Latin language change their endings to indicate different meanings. This process is called inflection. Some English words inflect, too. For instance, the word "boy" adds *'s* to show the possessive, "boy's." Latin nouns inflect according to five patterns, called declensions. Each declension has endings that show the use of the word in each of six cases: nominative, for subject; genitive, for possession; dative, for indirect object; accusative, for direct object or with many prepositions; ablative, with other prepositions or for special uses; and vocative, to name a person or thing being spoken to. Latin verbs inflect according to four patterns, called conjugations. These endings on words make it possible to change the order of words around much more freely in Latin than in English.

Development

The Latin language was originally only one of many different languages spoken in Italy. It was the speech of the people who lived in the rich plain of Latium toward the mouth of the river Tiber in central Italy. These included the citizens of the city of Rome. The oldest complete books in Latin that have come down to us are the comedies of Plautus, written during the years around 200 B.C. They show that the early Latin language was not simple and crude, as we might expect. It was lively, energetic, and full of variety. It made up new words very easily. It did not stick closely to fixed rules of grammar or spelling. Since many of the cities in southern Italy were Greek colonies and the Greeks were more highly civilized than the Romans, Latin borrowed many Greek words, such as *architectus, philosophus,* and *scaena* ("scene" or "stage").

The authors of Rome admired Greek literature and did their best to imitate it. Most of them wanted to make the Latin language as graceful and expressive as Greek. Terence the dramatist, Lucretius the philosophical poet, Cicero the orator, and many others worked to improve Latin. They cut out ugly and awkward words. They set up clear and neat rules for correct spelling and grammar. They brought in Greek tricks of style that would allow them to express noble and beautiful thoughts. Thus, the Latin language did not just grow up like a tree in the woods. It was planned and cultivated like a garden. Each of the great Latin writers improved it in his own way.

Classical Latin is the Latin written and spoken by well-educated Romans from about 100 B.C. to about A.D. 150. (The word "classical" means "first-class.") During this time the best Latin books were written and the language was at its finest. It had fewer technical and scientific words but more poetic words than modern American English. Its sentences could be quite clear and straightforward, as in Caesar's *Notes* on his campaigns. They could also be very long, as in the most powerful passages of Cicero's speeches; and very complicated, as in some of Vergil's poetry. In ordinary conversation and in friendly letters the Romans used short and simple phrases. But for books and speeches they usually chose dignified and imaginative words. They made their style very elaborate and filled their words with double and triple meanings. They built their sentences into beautifully proportioned paragraphs, taking great care with sounds and rhythms.

Classical Latin has never died out as a literary language. All through the Middle Ages and the Renaissance right down to the present time, people have gone on reading and writing it. Many later poets (for instance, Milton and Baudelaire) have published poems in Latin, and in Europe prizes are awarded every year for the best poem and the best essay written in Latin.

However, from about A.D. 200 onward, Latin began to change in several ways. Civil wars and barbarian invasions damaged the Roman Empire in the west. Libraries were destroyed and schools were closed. The level of education dropped. Fewer people were able to speak and write correct Latin or read the classical books. The Latin language finally broke up into rough dialects spoken by the farmers, the poor, and the invading barbarians. (After many centuries these dialects grew into French, Italian, Portuguese, Rumanian, Spanish, and other modern tongues.)

Further changes were brought about by the Christians who spoke and wrote Latin. They invented many new words and stretched the meaning of old words to carry their new message. They also wanted to speak to the ordinary, simple people, so they used language that was very plain. Sometimes it was even wrong, according to the rules of classical Latin. The standard Latin translation of the Bible, the Vulgate (which means "popular"), is full of phrases and word forms that Cicero would have thought coarse or mistaken. But it was written for readers who were not necessarily Roman or even Italian and who were not so well educated as Cicero's friends and readers.

Thus the dialect spoken in central Italy grew into the language of nearly all Italy. Later it became the speech of all the western Roman Empire from Britain to North Africa. (Greek continued to be the language of most of the eastern provinces.) Finally it split up into classical Latin, a language read and written but not spoken; church Latin, the language of the western Christians; and the dialects that grew into the modern Romance languages.

Early Latin Literature

During the early period (before about 100 B.C.) Latin developed under the influence of Greek culture. Romans translated and adapted Greek works. They also wrote original patriotic histories and dramas in Latin. They invented poetic words and set up forms of drama, satire, and history.

Earliest Latin writings included the laws of the kings and the *Twelve Tables* (500 and 450 B.C.), but the first real literature in Latin was a group of translations. Livius Andronicus (284?–204? B.C.) was a freed slave from the south of Italy, where Greek was spoken. He translated the *Odyssey* into Latin for use as a schoolbook, and a Greek tragedy and comedy for a celebration in 240 B.C. The epic form was used by Gnaeus Naevius (270?–201? B.C.) for a patriotic poem on the First Punic War, and by Quintus Ennius (239–169? B.C.) for his poem on the history of Rome, *Annales*. Both men wrote or adapted dramas on Greek and Roman themes. Roman audiences loved the theater, but they preferred comedies. The greatest comic playwrights were Plautus (Titus Maccius Plautus, 254?–184 B.C.) and Terence (Publius Terentius Afer, 185–159 B.C.). Plautus, whose name means "Flatfoot," wrote many stories of mix-ups and tricks. People masqueraded in funny costumes, and slaves outwitted their masters. Terence's stories and characters were deeper and more serious. Much sterner was old Marcus Porcius Cato (234–149 B.C.), who wrote the first prose history, *Origines,* and a book on agriculture.

Literature of the Later Republic

Writers of the later republic (about 100–27 B.C.) showed continued Greek influence in

The players in the Roman theater wore masks.

Cicero delivering an oration in the Roman senate.

their forms and philosophical thinking, but they were strictly Roman in their energy and political and moral consciousness.

Lucretius (Titus Lucretius Carus, 96?–55 B.C.) wrote the first great philosophical poem in Latin. His six-volume *De Rerum Natura* ("On the Nature of Things") preached the Epicurean philosophy of a well-balanced, peaceful life and gave a scientific theory of the universe that was based on the proposition that all matter is composed of atoms in motion. It was all done in beautiful poetry with rich vocabulary and skillful use of rhythm.

A very different poet was Gaius Valerius Catullus (84?–54 B.C.). Catullus wrote many short and a few long poems, most of them very artistic and highly polished in the style of the Greeks. His love poems for his sweetheart Lesbia are filled with passion, adoration, and despair. The long art poems tell stories from mythology and are full of Greek words.

The greatest of all Latin prose writers, who set the style that is still considered the best classical Latin, was Marcus Tullius Cicero (106–43 B.C.). Cicero was most noted for his moving and powerful orations. These include his attacks on Verres and Catiline and his defense of his old teacher Archias. The speeches show precise sentence structure, long periods of carefully developed thought, very full vocabulary, and a stern dignity broken by occasional puns or jokes. As a professional orator Cicero wrote several books on the theory and practice of oratory. He also loved to read and discuss Greek philosophy. He wrote many books in Latin in which he reorganized and summarized the ideas of the Greeks. He made them into entertaining books of dialogues, pretending that he was recording conversations among friends. In his letters, published after his death, we catch Cicero completely off guard, writing to Brutus (whose assassination of Caesar he applauded), his brother Quintus, his friend Atticus, and other friends. The contents of the letters were occasionally formal but most often conversational, as on his grief over the death of his daughter or worry about a visit from Caesar.

Gaius Julius Caesar (102–44 B.C.) was most famous as a soldier and politician, but he deserves credit also as one of the best writers of Latin prose. His *Commentaries,* or *Notes,* on the Gallic and civil wars are written in clear, precise, straightforward, simple language and have been models for many later historians. Caesar was also an excellent orator, second only to Cicero.

Another historian of the period was Sallust (Gaius Sallustius Crispus, 86–34 B.C.), who wrote books on the conspiracy of Catiline and the war with Jugurtha. Sallust used a brief, tightly compressed style with many archaisms (imitations of very old words and spellings) and translations from the Greek. Publius Cornelius Nepos (100?–24? B.C.) wrote biographies of famous men, both Greek and Roman.

The Augustan Golden Age

The period of the reign of the first emperor, Augustus (27 B.C.–A.D. 14), brought peace and prosperity to the Romans after a century of civil war. Great advances were made in art and culture. Romans had a new patriotism and a new zest for living that were reflected in their writings. Roman writers completed their mastery of Greek forms to produce the greatest Latin poetry of all time. Augustus himself encouraged literature, and it was natural for the poets of his day to idealize his reign as a new golden age.

Vergil (Publius Vergilius Maro, 70–19 B.C.) became the greatest poet to grace the Latin tongue. His first works were poems on rustic life, *Bucolics,* and on farming, *Georgics.* Augustus himself asked the young poet to write a great national epic, and Vergil spent the last 11 years of his life composing the *Aeneid.* It is a long narrative poem in 12 books and tells the story of Aeneas, the legendary hero who came from Troy to found the Roman race in Italy. Vergil died before he finished revising the poem. He left orders that it was to be burned after his death (because he had not completed it as he wished), but the Emperor intervened. He had the poem edited by two of Vergil's friends and then published. Here and there it shows signs of being only partially finished. Even so, it is a masterpiece that has inspired hundreds of later poets and given delight to countless readers.

Another poet who received support and encouragement from the Emperor was Horace (Quintus Horatius Flaccus, 65–8 B.C.). Hor-

The *Aeneid* tells of the Trojans' battles in Italy.

ace wrote over 100 odes, or songs, in meters copied from the Greeks. Some are gay, some serious. They deal with many themes—love, religion, the search for true happiness, and, occasionally, the decline of Roman morality. Some of his shorter poems tell of his joy in simple country life and his delight in the Sabine farm given to him by the Emperor. Horace also wrote letters and satires (*Sermones*) in verse. He poked fun at many things, especially life in the city with its race for wealth and position. Horace's writings show much grace and skill blended with humor and worldly wisdom.

Albius Tibullus (54?–18? B.C.) and Sextus Propertius (50?–15? B.C.) wrote elegies—poems of love and sadness and strange visions—in a polished, sophisticated style imitating the Greeks. Tibullus wrote of simple country life and love, like Horace. Propertius wrote elegies in a violently emotional style with brilliant, eccentric turns of thought.

Ovid (Publius Ovidius Naso, 43 B.C.–A.D. 17?) wrote elegant little poems of love in elegiac meter, including his famous and rather scandalous *Ars Amatoria* ("Art of Love") and *Remedia Amoris* ("Remedy for Love"). Banished for some unstated offense against the emperor Augustus, Ovid wrote sad poems of his longing to be home. One of his more important books was the *Fasti,* an almanac in verse describing and explaining the religious celebrations of the Roman year. Ovid's most famous and enduring work is the 15-book *Metamorphoses*. It retells stories from mythology from the creation of the world to the deification of Julius Caesar. It is thanks to Ovid that we know as much of classical mythology as we do.

Livy (Titus Livius, 59 B.C.–A.D. 17) was a friend of Augustus' and the tutor of the later emperor Claudius. He wrote a history of Rome in 142 books, *Ab Urbe Condita,* covering over 700 years from the founding of the city to the death of Augustus' best general, Drusus, in 9 B.C. Only about one fourth of this work survives. Livy is a strong moralist and a devoted Roman patriot. His style is wonderfully varied and yet always sounds vivid and natural. He is at his best in describing big crowd scenes, such as battles and stormy senatorial debates.

The Silver Age

From about A.D. 14 to about A.D. 130 Latin writers continued to flourish but did not achieve the greatness of those of the Augustan Age. Lucius Annaeus Seneca (4? B.C.–A.D. 65), the emperor Nero's tutor, wrote nine tragedies filled with horror and violence, as in the drama of Thyestes, who unknowingly was served his own children to eat. Seneca also wrote several books on stoic moral philosophy and a satire about the emperor Claudius. Lucan (Marcus Annaeus Lucanus, 39–65), Seneca's nephew, composed a 10-book epic, *Pharsalia,* on the civil war between Caesar and Pompey. Petronius (Gaius Petronius Arbiter, ?–66?) wrote the *Satyrica,* a brilliant satirical novel about underworld life. All these writers were forced to commit suicide by Nero.

Aulus Persius Flaccus (34–62) wrote satires teaching stoic morals in private life. Martial (Marcus Valerius Martialis, 40?–104?), a clever Spanish poet who lived by his wits, produced 12 books of witty epigrams on the foibles and vices of Rome. The one surviving book of Quintilian (Marcus Fabius Quintilianus, 35?–95?) is a complete manual for the education of an orator. It is full of advice that is still valuable for speakers. Gaius Plinius Caecilius Secundus (62–113), Pliny the Younger, was also interested in oratory and wrote letters to be published, imitating Cicero. His uncle, Pliny the Elder (23–79), wrote an encyclopedic series of volumes on natural history.

Cornelius Tacitus (55?–117?), a friend of the younger Pliny and one of the great Latin historians, composed histories and annals covering most of the imperial period. Tacitus also wrote a biography of his father-in-law, Agricola, and a book on the Germans. Suetonius (Gaius Suetonius Tranquillus, 69?–140?) wrote biographies of famous men, especially the 12 Caesars who had been emperors up to his time. One of the greatest writers of this period was Juvenal (Decimus Junius Juvenalis, 60?–140?). His satires in verse ridiculed such things as the noise and filth of the city of Rome and the vanity of human wishes.

Later Latin Writing

After the Silver Age, Latin literature fell into a decline. Marcus Cornelius Fronto (100?–175?) practiced oratory and urged a return to archaic style. He influenced two other writers of the second century, Aulus Gellius, who produced a collection of essays called *Attic Nights,* and Apuleius, who wrote *The Golden Ass,* a fanciful story of a man turned into an animal.

Christian writers were trying more to persuade their readers than to produce lasting works of art. Tertullian (Quintus Septimus Florens Tertullianus, 160?–230?) wrote of Christian beliefs. Minucius Felix and Lactantius Firmianus in the 3rd century condemned pagan practices in their writings.

Perhaps the last of the literary Latin writers was Decimus Magnus Ausonius, a 4th-century professor who delighted in setting into Latin verse everything from the days of the week to a list of his ancestors. None of these writers can rank with the earlier ones for literary or artistic merit.

CAROL LAUER CHISDES
Wall Township (New Jersey) High School
Reviewed by GILBERT HIGHET
Columbia University

LATITUDE AND LONGITUDE

Imagine a motorist who needs help because his car has broken down in a city. He phones the local automobile club or service station and reports his location as "the intersection of Fourth Avenue and Main Street." The serviceman knows that Fourth Avenue runs north-south and Main Street runs east-west. Therefore he has no difficulty in finding our imaginary motorist.

Another man in trouble is the captain of a ship. A fire has broken out. He radios an S.O.S. But for him there are no street signs to mark his location. How is he to be found? He reports his location in terms of latitude and longitude. In this way he locates himself just as precisely on the ocean as the stranded motorist on land.

Just as streets and avenues are used to locate places in a town or city, so latitude and longitude lines are used to locate places on the surface of the earth.

The latitude and longitude location scheme for the earth's surface is a system of intersecting north-south and east-west lines. With such a system, an exact location can be given for any point on the earth.

▶ LATITUDE

Latitude is the distance north or south of the equator. The system begins by using the earth's North Pole and South Pole as its reference points. Halfway between the poles an imaginary circle is drawn completely around the earth. This circle runs east-west and is known as the **equator**. It divides the earth into a Northern Hemisphere and a Southern Hemisphere. The equator, then, is the main east-west line of the earth. Additional circles can now be drawn parallel to the equator. Because the circles are parallel to the equator, they are called parallel circles, or just **parallels**. Each parallel marks off a fixed distance north or south of the equator. This distance is called latitude. All points in the

Parallels (latitude) run east and west. Meridians (longitude) run north and south. These crisscross lines form a grid that helps us locate any place on earth.

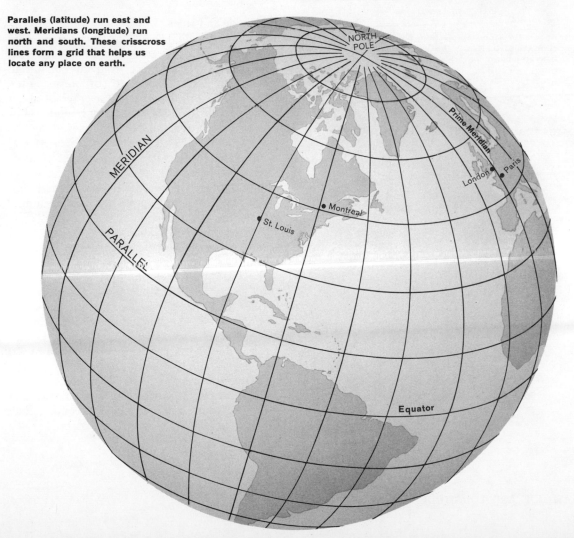

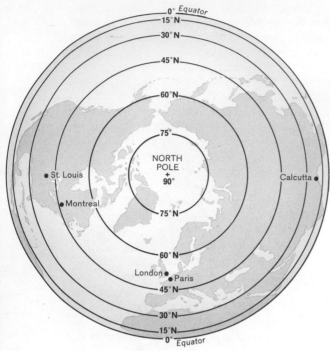

Polar Projection

Above: On a polar projection, parallels are shown encircling the earth. Below: On an equatorial projection, meridians are shown converging at the poles.

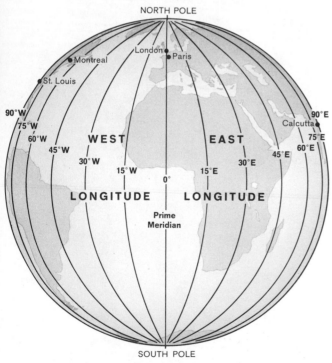

Equatorial Projection

Northern Hemisphere have north latitude. All points in the Southern Hemisphere have south latitude.

Latitude Units

Latitude is measured in circular degrees. A circle has 360 degrees. The distance from the equator to the North Pole or to the South Pole is one fourth of a circle around the earth and is therefore equal to 90 degrees (written 90°). The equator is the line from which latitude is measured. Its latitude is 0°. The North Pole has a latitude of 90° N, and the South Pole a latitude of 90° S. This is the highest latitude possible on the earth. A point midway between the equator and the poles has a latitude of 45° N or 45° S, depending on the hemisphere. A latitude of 30° means a location one third of the way from equator to pole, and so forth. On a globe or map the parallel circles usually mark off latitude every 10 or 15 degrees. However, the mapmaker may use any interval he feels is desirable.

Latitude and Miles

Even though latitude is always measured and expressed in degrees, it is easily converted into miles. The distance from the equator to either pole is 6,222 **statute** (ordinary) **miles**. Divided by 90, this gives an average of about 69.1 statute miles to a degree of latitude. (For simple approximations 70 miles may be used.) Because the earth is not perfectly spherical, the length of a degree of latitude changes slightly all the way from the equator to the poles. The earth is flattest at the poles. A degree of latitude is almost a mile longer there than at the equator.

If we know the latitude of a place on the map, we can estimate its distance north or south of the equator. Montreal is located about 45° N. If we multiply 45 by 70, we learn that Montreal is about 3,150 statute miles north of the equator. London is located about 51° N, and Paris about 49° N. London is therefore about 140 statute miles farther north than Paris (2 degrees multiplied by 70 miles).

Degrees are too large to measure precise distances on the earth. Therefore a degree is subdivided into minutes and seconds. Each degree of latitude has 60 minutes (60′). Each minute has 60 seconds (60″).

A minute (1′) is equal to about 1⅙ statute miles, or about 6,000 feet. A second is equal to about 100 feet. Latitude may be given more precisely in degrees, minutes, and sometimes seconds. The latitude of Montreal, for example, is 45° 31′ N.

▶ LONGITUDE

Latitude by itself tells only how far from the equator a location is. It places an object somewhere on an east-west parallel that is thousands of miles long and extends around the earth. To find the exact location, north-south lines are needed to run at right angles to the parallels and intersect them.

The north-south lines of our location system are called **meridians**. Each meridian is a half circle that runs north and south from the North Pole to the South Pole. The meridian meets each parallel at right angles. While parallels of latitude mark off distances in a north-south direction, meridians mark off distances in an east-west direction. But whereas the equator is a natural midway line from which to measure north and south distances, there is no natural midway line from which to measure east and west distances. However, all countries have agreed on a starting line. They use the meridian that runs through Greenwich Observatory, near London, England. This meridian is called the **prime meridian**, and its longitude is 0°. Every other meridian measures off a fixed distance east or west of the prime meridian. This distance is called longitude.

Longitude Units

Longitude, like latitude, is measured in degrees. The half of the earth that is east of the prime meridian has east longitude up to 180° (halfway around the earth). The half that is west of the prime meridian has west longitude up to 180°. The 180th meridian is the same for both east and west longitude. It is therefore not called east or west, but simply 180°. It lies directly opposite the prime meridian, forming a full circle around the earth with it. Halfway from the prime meridian to the 180th meridian is 90° W. This is about the longitude of St. Louis, Missouri. In the other direction, 90° E runs close to Calcutta, India. North America, South America, and Greenland are entirely in west longitude. Australia and most of Africa, Asia, and Europe are located in east longitude.

Longitude and Miles

At the equator 1° of longitude is 1/360 of the circumference of the earth and is therefore about the same length as 1° of latitude. Meridians, unlike parallels, do not stay the same distance apart, but come closer and closer together with increasing distance from the equator. They finally meet at the poles. This means that the number of miles in 1° of longitude is different for each latitude. The poles have no longitude because all the meridians meet there. Longitude degrees, like latitude degrees, are divided into minutes and seconds.

Location by Latitude and Longitude

When both the latitude and longitude of a place are given, an exact point on the globe is located. For example, the latitude of St. Louis, Missouri, is 39° N. Its longitude is 90° W. This locates St. Louis at the intersection of the parallel 39° north of the equator and the meridian 90° west of the prime meridian.

Longitude and Time

Because the earth rotates on its axis from west to east, the sun crosses each meridian at a different time. The rate at which the earth rotates is 360° in 24 hours, or 15° an hour. This means that two meridians 15° apart will have a difference in time of 1 hour. In fact, a navigator finds the longitude of his ship by determining the difference in time between his location and Greenwich, England. He reads his local time by the sun and Greenwich time from the chronometer, a very accurate clock always kept at Greenwich time. For example, if he sees that his local time is 3 hours earlier than the chronometer, he knows his longitude is 45° W. If his local time is 3 hours later than Greenwich time, he knows that his longitude is 45° east of the prime meridian.

SAMUEL N. NAMOWITZ
Author, *Earth Science*

See also EQUATOR; INTERNATIONAL DATE LINE; TIME.

LATTER DAY SAINTS, CHURCH OF JESUS CHRIST OF. See MORMONS.
LATTER DAY SAINTS, REORGANIZED CHURCH OF JESUS CHRIST OF. See MORMONS.
LATVIA. See UNION OF SOVIET SOCIALIST REPUBLICS.

LAUNDRY

Keeping clothes clean is always a problem. One way a housewife may solve this problem is to use the services of a commercial laundry. In some countries commercial laundries have operated for hundreds of years. Egypt had a laundry in 2000 B.C. Greece and Rome had launderers, called fullers, who washed and pressed clothing.

In some parts of the world laundries use the same primitive methods once used by the Egyptians. But many improvements have been developed in the commercial laundries of industrialized countries. One of the first improvements was a new type of ironer called a mangle, which appeared in England in the 1800's. From the late 1800's on, improvements in laundry machinery were added by British, French, and American inventors.

The first commercial laundry in the United States was set up in Troy, New York, around 1825 to wash collars made in the shirt-collar factories. The first United States power laundry was founded in California in 1851 to wash shirts for the gold-seeking forty-niners. One of the miners had little luck in his search for gold. With the engine from a wrecked steamer he rigged up a washer and agreed to wash shirts for gold dust as pay. Until the miner set up his laundry, dirty clothing was sent by ship to Hawaii to be washed, and it was 6 months before it returned.

REMOVING STAINS

BLOOD. Use cold water to sponge or soak the stain. Wash fabric in warm soapy water.

CHEWING GUM. Harden the gum with an ice cube, and rub it until it crumbles away, or use dry-cleaning solvent.

CHOCOLATE OR COCOA. Scrape off as much of the stain as possible with a dull knife. Then wash fabric in warm soapy water. Sponge stubborn stains on white fabric with hydrogen peroxide and rinse thoroughly.

FRUIT. Sponge the stains with cold water as soon as possible. Then wash the fabric. If the stain remains, use a bleach on it. Once a fruit stain has been ironed, it will probably not come out.

GRASS. Sponge the stain with alcohol and then wash it. Or wash the fabric in hot water and soap, rubbing the stain well. If this does not remove the stain, use a bleach.

GREASE. Rub the stain with detergent and then wash the fabric in hot water. If this does not work, sponge the stain with cleaning fluid.

ICE CREAM. Sponge the stain with cold water. Then wash the fabric in warm suds.

SOFT DRINKS. Sponge the stain with cool water. Dip white clothes into a chlorine bleach solution for 1 minute and then rinse well. Pour glycerin on colored fabrics. Let stand for ½ hour and rinse with water.

▶ TYPES OF LAUNDRY BUSINESSES

Hand Laundries. A hand laundry is the most common type of laundry. Hand laundries do fine finishing work. Some of them do their own washing, but most of them send it out to a large wholesale laundry.

Neighborhood Coin Laundries. Also a familiar sight in many neighborhoods is a laundry with a long row of automatic washers and dryers. Some of these laundries do the washing for their customers. In others the customers load the machines themselves. These laundries are called laundromats, launderettes, washaterias, or self-service laundries.

Commercial Wholesale Laundries. Large laundry plants do wholesale washing for neighborhood hand laundries and may do some dry cleaning for neighborhood dry cleaners. They also do work for hotels and restaurants. Almost all these laundries are in large cities.

Industrial Laundries. Some laundries own large quantities of work clothes, wiping towels, and similar items, which they rent to factories, garages, newspaper plants, and businesses. They wash only these supplies.

Linen-Supply Laundries. Linen-supply laundries own linens and uniforms that they rent out to doctors, dentists, hotels, and restaurants.

Diaper Laundries. In many areas laundries provide a continuous supply of clean diapers. Like the industrial and linen-supply laundries, these diaper laundries rent their supplies.

Family Laundries. The type of laundry most common in towns and small cities is the family laundry. The family laundry does almost any type of washing and ironing job the housewife needs done. All the ironing at family laundries is done by machine. Family laundries may also do some commercial work and linen-supply and industrial work.

▶ HOW THE LAUNDRY DOES ITS WORK

Sorting. First, the clothes are sorted. Colored clothing cannot be washed with white clothing. The colors might run and stain the white clothing. Silk and woolen clothing cannot be washed with cotton clothing. Cottons are washed at high temperatures that might damage other fabrics. Sometimes a load of wash is sorted into as many as 16 different piles.

Identification. In some laundries the wash is placed in a net bag and identified by a numbered pin. In other laundries each piece is marked. There are millions of different laundry marks. The police have been able to trace many criminals and identify many accident victims by tracing down laundry marks. Some police departments keep a file of local laundry marks.

Washing. Commercial laundries use many changes of water. Almost all washes receive at least two or three sudsings. Very dirty washes receive more sudsings. Large automatic machines are used. Soaps and detergents carefully selected for the type of water (hard or soft) and the fabrics being washed are fed automatically into the machines. After sudsing, the wash goes through three to five rinses to get all the cleaning agents out of the fabric.

Drying. Once the wash is clean, water is removed from it by spinning the washing-machine basket rapidly. Now the pieces are just damp enough to be ironed. Pieces that do not need to be ironed are tumble-dried in large drying machines. Some items, like woolen pieces, instead of being tumbled, are dried on special forms to keep them from shrinking.

Ironing. Sheets, pillowcases, and other flat pieces go through large flatwork ironers. Automatic folders may fold the flat pieces as they come out. Some of these ironers can iron 15 sheets in 1 minute.

Other ironing jobs are more difficult. There are many separate steps to pressing a man's shirt. One machine irons the collar. Another irons the sleeves and cuffs. Another does the backs, and another the fronts. Then the shirt is folded and wrapped. A set of shirt-ironing machines operated by three experienced workers can iron 150 shirts in an hour.

When the ironing is completed, all the pieces belonging to one customer are brought together and wrapped for delivery.

LEE JOHNSTON
American Institute of Laundering
See also DETERGENTS AND SOAP; DRY CLEANING.

LAURIER, SIR WILFRID (1841–1919)

Sir Wilfrid Laurier was Canada's first French-speaking prime minister. He was born on November 20, 1841, at St. Lin, Quebec, north of Montreal. He was elected to the Quebec legislature and in 1874 to the Canadian House of Commons. As the most promising young French Liberal, Laurier was made a cabinet member in the Liberal government of Alexander Mackenzie (1822–92) in 1877.

At that time Liberalism was unpopular in Quebec because some of the Roman Catholic clergy believed that all Liberals were against religion. In 1877 Laurier made an important speech showing that this was not true. His influence among Liberals grew until, in 1887, he was chosen leader of the party.

In the election of 1891 Laurier called for closer economic ties with the United States. This was an unpopular idea, and it helped defeat the Liberals. But in 1896 the Liberals won the election, and Wilfrid Laurier became prime minister. As prime minister, Laurier carried on many Conservative policies, such as favoring trade with Great Britain over trade with the United States. Canada was then growing very rapidly. Millions of people from Europe and the United States settled in the Canadian Prairie Provinces at the invitation of Laurier's government. Two new trans-Canadian railways were built.

In 1910 Laurier started a Canadian navy. The next year he proposed reciprocity—a form of free trade—with the United States. These two policies were very unpopular and caused his defeat by Sir Robert Borden (1854–1937) in the election of 1911.

As leader of the Opposition, Laurier supported Canada's war effort during World War I. But in 1917 the Liberal Party was split over the plan to conscript men as soldiers. When he refused to join a coalition (joint) government with the Conservatives, many English-speaking Liberals joined the Conservative Party. Laurier was left with few followers except those from Quebec. Laurier, who had always worked for Canadian unity, was bitterly disappointed at this. He died on February 17, 1919, an unhappy and defeated man.

JOHN S. MOIR
University of Toronto

LAVOISIER, ANTOINE LAURENT
(1743–1794)

During Antoine Laurent Lavoisier's 51 years he was a chemist, a politician, and a lawyer. He was also a farmer and a banker. But it is as a chemist that he is remembered and honored today.

Lavoisier was born in Paris, France, on August 26, 1743. He was the son of a wealthy lawyer. Antoine studied law as his father wished, but he also attended many lectures on scientific subjects. Soon after graduating from law school he decided to follow a career of scientific research.

To carry on research, Lavoisier set up one of the finest laboratories in Europe. He insisted on exact measurements in all his experiments. He would accept no idea unless it could be proved. In this way he helped introduce methods of exactness in chemistry.

In 1771 Lavoisier married Marie Paulze, a brilliant, gifted girl 14 years younger than he. She acted as his secretary and later made many of the drawings for his books. They had no children.

▶ LAVOISIER'S WORK IN CHEMISTRY

In the 18th century chemists did not understand clearly what happened when a fuel burned. They thought a burning fuel gave up a weightless substance called phlogiston. Lavoisier found this hard to believe.

In 1772, he noticed that certain chemicals gained weight when they burned. This meant that something must have been added to these chemicals, instead of being lost. But he could not find out what this was.

In 1774, Lavoisier learned that the English chemist Joseph Priestley had discovered a gas that seemed to help things burn. Lavoisier repeated Priestley's experiments and added his own. These experiments convinced Lavoisier that this gas—which he called oxygen—is necessary for burning. When a fuel burns, he said, it combines with oxygen. There is no such thing as phlogiston.

In 1783 Lavoisier learned that another great English chemist, Henry Cavendish, had obtained water when he burned a gas then called "inflammable air." But Cavendish's explanation of why this happened did not satisfy Lavoisier.

Lavoisier added some careful measurements of his own to Cavendish's experiments. Then he announced that water was a combination of two gases, oxygen and "inflammable air." (He soon renamed this gas hydrogen.)

Lavoisier also carried out important investigations into respiration, or breathing. He showed that the body uses breathed-in oxygen to burn food, which gives the body its heat.

Up to that time there was no one way of naming chemicals. Lavoisier worked with several other chemists to set up a system of naming chemicals. It is in use today.

Lavoisier had long been a member of an organization that was much hated by the French people. The organization was called the Farm-General. Among its duties was the collection of taxes for the king. In 1789 a revolution broke out in France against the king. At the height of the French Revolution the members of the Farm-General were arrested, tried, and sentenced to death. Lavoisier was among them. On May 8, 1794, he was beheaded.

Antoine Lavoisier did not make many discoveries of his own. But he gave correct explanations of the discoveries of others. His explanation of combustion, or burning, changed the whole science of chemistry. Our modern science of chemistry is based on his work.

DAVID C. KNIGHT
Author, science books for children
See also CHEMISTRY, HISTORY OF.

LAW AND LAW ENFORCEMENT

Laws are rules that define people's rights and responsibilities toward society. Laws are agreed on by society and made official by governments.

Some persons look on laws with fear, hatred, or annoyance. Laws seem to limit a person's freedom to do many things he would like to do. Though laws may prevent us from doing things we wish to do at the moment, laws also stop others from acting on wishes that might harm us. Laws make everyone's life safer and more pleasant. Without laws we could not hold on to our property. We could not go to bed at night expecting to wake up in the morning and find we had not been robbed. No stores in which we buy food, clothes, and other necessities could stay open and sell to us. Our banks would not be safe places for our money.

Social life would be impossible without laws to control the way people treat each other. It is not the laws that should be feared, but the trouble that comes to everyone when laws are broken. Once a citizen understands this, he will lose his fear or hatred of law. Understanding the need for good laws and the evil results of breaking laws is the first requirement of good citizenship and government.

▶ HOW LAW BEGAN

Philosophers once believed that in the earliest days of human life, mankind lived without laws in a "state of nature." Every man was free to do as he pleased, unless a stronger man stopped him by force. Life, described as a "war of all men against all men," became so unsafe that leaders created laws in order to protect life and property.

This is no longer believed to be true. Scholars now think that as soon as small groups of men began living together, they worked out rules for getting along with each other. In time, everyone accepted and supported the rules. Manners, customs, and beliefs controlled all living habits of the group. Such rules and habits of life are called folkways.

Folkways are probably the real beginnings of human laws, as well as of religion, morals, and education. Early men believed that folkways were revealed to them by their gods. This gave these rules a religious meaning, which made it very dangerous to break them. If a folkway was broken or violated, the violator had committed both a crime and a sin. The gods might punish him. Folkways gradually improved, and the groups that worked out the best folkways survived.

History of Lawmaking

As life became more complex, folkways became more complete guides to living. After thousands of years part of the important folkways were put into writing as the earliest laws. When people wrote down their laws, they began to realize that rules were made by men as well as revealed by gods. Written laws in Egypt date from about 3400 B.C. Written laws in Mesopotamia date from the period of the Sumerians (3500 to 2360 B.C.). The Babylonians produced the most famous of ancient written laws, the Code of Hammurabi, written about 1700 B.C. Among the Hittites written law goes back to around 1300 B.C. and among the Hebrews, 1200 B.C. In European history the most famous early written code was the Twelve Tables in Rome (about 450 B.C.). But the whole body of Roman law, stressing order and obedience to government, was not organized until about A.D. 530 at the order of the Emperor Justinian.

During the early Middle Ages most European countries were under feudal law. Some towns and small cities, which were usually controlled by guilds, made laws too. Special kinds of new laws grew up to deal with special needs. Mercantile law was a group of rules and regulations that governed the way merchants and traders conducted their businesses. These laws were designed to prevent cheating in trade. The Roman Catholic Church used parts of Roman law in their canon law (church law). Later, when wars became more frequent, men like Hugo Grotius (1583–1645) and Emerich von Vattel (1714–67) worked out systems of international law to try to prevent war.

Systems of national law began to appear in the later Middle Ages. The most famous was the English common law. As new nations arose in Europe a mixture of national laws and Roman law began replacing feudal law. At the end of the 17th century John Locke and others worked out a philosophical system

ARREST

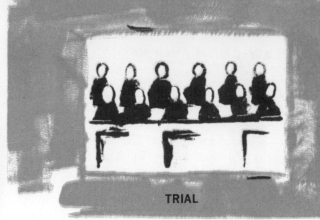

TRIAL

using the idea of natural law. It was based on the theory that life, liberty, and property must be protected. It influenced the writing of the American Declaration of Independence, as well as very important Supreme Court decisions since the Civil War.

English common law was the greatest influence on the growth of law in the American colonies, later the United States. Roman law was introduced by the French in Louisiana. It lasted there long after the United States bought Louisiana. Under Roman law a man accused of a crime was thought guilty until he proved himself innocent. English common law held that he was innocent until proved guilty.

As life grew more complicated with faster transportation and the rise of modern industry and big cities, more human acts and interests had to be ruled by law. This led to a great increase in the number of laws. Also, some old laws stayed on the books when there was no more need for them or group opinion no longer supported them. Many legal experts feel we now have far more laws than authorities can successfully enforce. They think that having too many laws makes it harder to enforce any laws.

▶ LAW ENFORCEMENT

Unless laws are enforced, they cannot protect us. Poorly enforced laws invite crime and violence. The breakdown of law enforcement could lead to a situation as fearful as the "state of nature" imagined by philosophers.

As law grows and changes, methods of law enforcement change, too. During the thousands of years before written law the leaders of primitive society enforced the folkways. Tribal leaders gave special groups the job of enforcement. Since folkways were believed to

be the law of the gods, priests took a major part in enforcing them.

Law enforcement has four steps: arrest of the suspect; decision about his guilt or innocence; sentencing, if he is found guilty; and execution of the sentence, or punishment. Primitive tribes seized a suspect when someone complained about him or when he was caught in a criminal act. They settled the question of guilt or innocence quickly. Sometimes they used torture, but not as often as people did later, in the Middle Ages. More common were trials by battle, or duels—fights between the accused and the injured or his representative. The winner was thought innocent, since people believed gods helped the innocent.

Primitive societies used many punishments. Serious religious offenses might bring the terrifying penalty of exile. This put the lawbreaker in a lonely place where his gods could no longer protect him. For personal injuries it was common to apply the *lex talionis* ("law of retaliation"), the ancient Biblical rule of "an eye for an eye and a tooth for a tooth." If a man knocked out someone's tooth, his own tooth would be knocked out in return. Today capital punishment for murder is based on this idea: If a person kills someone, he must pay with his own life.

If a member of one tribe wronged a member of another tribe, the offender's whole group was held responsible for the crime. This group guilt led to the blood feud. In a feud any member of the injured group could revenge the injury by attacking anyone in the offending group, as in war.

Late primitive societies also used fines. The German tribes worked out an elaborate system of fines known as wergild (blood money). The amount of the fine was set by the

SENTENCING

PUNISHMENT

seriousness of the crime and the rank of the injured man. It cost more to attack a noble than to attack a commoner.

With the rise of civil society in the Near East, Greece, and Rome, public authorities took over law enforcement. Usually there were judges and courts. Torture was widely used down to modern times. Judges relied on the direct testimony of witnesses. There was no jury trial as we know it, for this custom developed gradually during the later Middle Ages. Punishment was nearly always physical—whipping, mutilation, ducking in cold water, and so on. Capital punishment took many cruel forms.

Slowly law enforcement grew less arbitrary and punishment less cruel. In England law enforcement became the duty of constables, sheriffs, justices of the peace, and judges. With the rise of prison systems in the late 18th century, confinement could sometimes be substituted for brutal physical punishment. But in England as late as the first half of the 19th century, 200 crimes were still punishable by the death sentence. This injustice led to drastic reform of criminal law under Jeremy Bentham (1748–1832) and Sir Samuel Romilly (1757–1818) As cities increased in population city police systems grew bigger, too. The police began to do part of the work that had been done by rural officers, such as sheriffs.

▶ PROBLEMS OF LAW ENFORCEMENT TODAY

Changing needs bring changing police systems. Increase in the number of automobiles and better highways has resulted in traffic problems that have made it necessary to organize larger police forces. In the United States an efficient federal police system was gradually created to deal with crimes that crossed state lines. The federal system began to be greatly improved in the late 1920's by what is now called the Federal Bureau of Investigation. The FBI helps federal, state, and city police and serves as a model for the training of policemen and for research in scientific crime detection.

Today law enforcement has reached a crisis all over the world. In the older, more rural societies of the United States and of the countries of Western Europe, much behavior was controlled by custom and enforced by small personal groups—family, church, school, neighborhood. These groups no longer have so much control over the moral behavior of the individual, particularly the young person. Too few new community groups have grown up with sufficient power to replace the old authorities. At the same time, new conditions—dangers of city life, automobile traffic, drug abuse, lack of jobs and of recreational facilities—all increase crime, especially among the young.

As crime increases, citizens are faced more and more with the problem of planning law enforcement to protect both the individual and society. Most students of law agree that the best protection against crime is planned social change and law reform to reduce the causes of crime and encourage people to obey laws. Such a solution would join a sound system of law enforcement with forces working to prevent crime. To get such a solution, it is necessary for all citizens to understand the need for good laws and for their enforcement.

HARRY ELMER BARNES
Author, *The Story of Punishment*

See also COURTS; FEDERAL BUREAU OF INVESTIGATION; JURY; LAWYERS; POLICE; PRISONS.

1 Preparation of soil before seeding is important. Spade the surface to a depth of 3–4 inches.

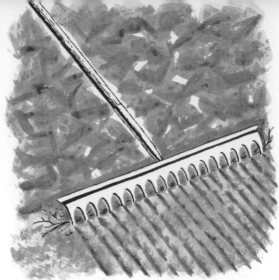

2 Rake the seeding surface to remove stones, large clods, and building debris.

4 Spread grass fertilizer liberally before or just after seeding. Follow directions given on the package.

5 Seeds must be spread uniformly and in proper amounts to ensure a smooth lawn.

7 Frequent watering is necessary to provide new seedlings with enough moisture for proper growth.

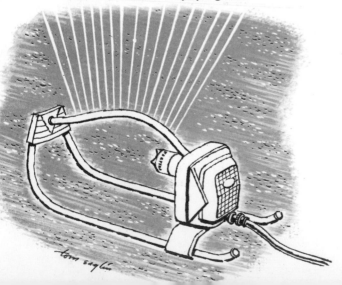

LAWNS

Until quite recently constant care was necessary to have a lovely lawn. Today, because of scientific developments, there are improved varieties of grass seed. There are chemicals that control weeds without hurting the grass. Insecticides keep hungry bugs from eating it. Fungicides prevent grass diseases.

Many people think that they must have topsoil to have a good lawn. Actually, anyone can grow a good lawn—even on 100 percent subsoil. The main function of soil is to anchor the roots, and almost any soil or

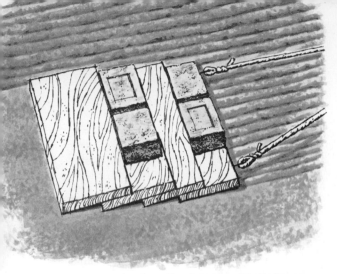

3 A weighted drag can be pulled across the seeding surface to make it level.

6 Lightly brush the surface with wire screening if you wish to cover the seeds.

LAWN PROBLEMS AND THEIR CAUSES

SYMPTOMS	CAUSE
Large areas dead in spring.	Smothered by tree leaves. Used for skating area in winter. Subjected to heavy foot traffic when frozen.
Leaves dusted with "flour."	Mildew. Slime mold.
Small, yellow spots on leaves.	Leaf-spot fungus.
Moldy or webby growth.	Snow-mold fungus (caused by combination of near-freezing temperatures and excessive moisture).
Mushrooms, toadstools, fairy rings.	Buried decaying organic matter (old roots or debris).
Turf thin.	Starvation. Poor drainage. Improper mowing (scalping). Cutworms or armyworms.
Narrow yellow streaks.	Missed areas when feeding. Excessive overlapping when feeding or using weed controls.
Moss and algae.	Low fertility. Poor drainage. Excessive shade.
Small, circular bumpy spots.	Earthworm casts. Ants.
Raised tunnels.	Moles. Mole crickets.
Bees.	Attracted by clover in lawn.
Patches of bent grass.	Volunteered. Introduced as impurity in seed mixture, soil, or sod.
Lawn weedy.	Turf in poor vigor (hungry). Turf mowed too close (scalped). Heavy weed infestation in area.
Mower cuts with difficulty.	Mower needs sharpening. Turf not cut frequently enough. Wild grasses have invaded. Turf kept too dry (fine-bladed fescue is particularly wiry when too dry).

subsoil can do this. As for nutrients, your grass depends upon you to supply what is needed. The kind of fertilizer you supply and when you apply it are far more important than the differences in the soils.

Weeds can be expected to appear whenever a thin or bare spot develops in the lawn. These weeds are volunteers (growing without human control) from seeds deposited long ago in the soil. Agricultural research has proved that weed seeds may remain inactive in soil for 25 to 50 years and then spring to life when proper conditions of warmth, light, and moisture are present.

Weeds can also appear in lush lawns if topsoil, manure, or compost (a mixture of decayed organic matter, such as leaves) is spread on the lawn. As a rule, the damage caused by the weeds offsets the good that the topsoil, manure, or compost may do.

Some weed seeds are carried by wind—sometimes for many miles. Buckhorn, plantain, and cocklebur seeds are sticky and adhere to clothing, shoes, and dogs. In this way they are moved from field to lawn, or lawn to lawn.

Fortunately, many kinds of annual weeds disappear with repeated mowing. Annual weeds complete their life cycle from seed to seed in a single year. The parent plant then dies. New plants start the next year from seeds already in the ground.

JOSEPH E. HOWLAND
Editor, *Lawn Care*

LAWYERS

The lawyer is a person with a very special knowledge of the law—both civil and criminal. Because of this knowledge the lawyer can help people plan their affairs in accordance with law. In other words, he helps people keep out of trouble as well as helping those who are already in trouble. He helps to ensure freedom of thought and action and to bring about peace between person and person, and person and government. He prepares agreements and contracts by which one person makes sure that another person will carry out his promises. He prepares wills and documents transferring property. He gives advice to people on domestic and family relationships and on business problems.

▶ A LAWYER'S WORK

Most of a lawyer's work is carried on outside the courtroom, although the cases the public usually hears or reads about are those that come to court. Court cases, like cases in a hospital, are the "sick cases." Most people do not get into the courts because they carry out their promises, are careful in their behavior, and obey the laws of society.

The lawyer presents or defends in court claimed violations of rights, or disputes arising out of differences as to what has happened or what is legal and just. In a civil action the court hears claims between private persons about private business, family matters (husband and wife, parent and child), and negligence or accident cases. Sometimes there are claims for or against government. In criminal cases lawyers either prosecute or defend public wrongs against the community, state, or nation, such as murder, robbery, criminal fraud, assault, and other crimes or offenses.

The lawyer is not only a champion and advocate of the rights of his client but also an officer of the court sworn to uphold the Constitution and the law.

▶ HOW LAWYERS ARE TRAINED

Most lawyers today are generally college-trained men who have completed a course in a law school. Each state has its own rules about training and admission. In some states, instead of going to law school, a person may substitute a long period of training in a law office, where he learns the various techniques and the basic knowledge that others get in a law school. This method was more prevalent many years ago when educational facilities were few and the body of law was small. President Abraham Lincoln is an outstanding example of a man who became a lawyer by learning in an office.

In law school, students learn how to analyze and present problems for decision. They are trained in disciplined, analytical thinking. They study prior rulings and precedents because the doctrine of *stare decisis* (reliance on precedent) is the basis of the English and American law. They study the Constitution, treaties, statutes, and court decisions. This reliance on precedents permits us to plan our affairs with certainty because we can be reasonably sure of the consequences of our acts, and so predict what the courts will enforce.

The law student takes basic courses dealing with such problems as torts, which means civil wrongs; contracts, which are the means by which a person makes sure that another person will carry out his promise; other specialized branches of contract law; and the law of estates and wills. There are also courses in public law, such as constitutional law, international law, law governing nations and business abroad, labor law, administrative law, and others. Almost every aspect of life's activities is discussed in a law-school course, because a lawyer during his practice is likely to become involved in many different fields, such as medicine, psychiatry, engineering, architecture, and accounting. He must learn how to study new subjects and absorb information and present it clearly, both in writing and in speech.

After a person has completed formal law-school training, he must take an examination to enable the state to check whether he has learned the fundamentals of the law. This examination, which is known as the bar examination, is difficult. A substantial number do not pass the first time.

Besides passing the bar examination, the applicant must show he is of good character. A committee appointed by the court checks on home training, college training, employment, and past behavior. The applicant is interviewed, and after his character is approved, he is then licensed to practice law. License to practice in one state does not automatically permit a lawyer to practice in another state.

▶ PRACTICING LAW

It is not uncommon that after a few years in general practice, a lawyer develops a special field of interest. Thus, a lawyer might specialize in tax law, trusts, estates, domestic relations, corporation law, family law, antitrust law, criminal law, or copyrights and patents. Some of the special fields require additional training in the law or other fields of scientific knowledge. If a man wants to practice patent law, he must know something about engineering, chemistry, physics, and similar subjects. Those who practice tax law usually have some experience or training in accountancy. Some serve first as an employee of a government tax department.

Lawyers who practice in the trial courts usually start either by entering the public service to work under a district attorney, county attorney, or corporation counsel, or by working in private practice under a trial lawyer, so that they become experienced in trial practices and procedures. This, too, is a specialized skill.

The training of a lawyer is so broad and so varied that many men use their legal education for entering other careers. Many lawyers enter public service and become civil service employees, devoting their lifetime to government service. Some enter the field of politics and run for public office or accept appointments in the executive branch of government. Of the 34 presidents of the United States, 24 were actually licensed to practice as lawyers. In the legislature of the United States, the number of lawyers is very large. To become a judge also requires law experience.

Some leave general law practice and become counsel to a corporation. Sometimes the lawyer becomes an executive and uses his training to make decisions, but no longer acts as a legal adviser.

In the United States a lawyer is sometimes called an attorney, attorney at law, counselor, counselor at law, solicitor, advocate, or barrister. These terms generally refer to the same person. In England and Canada there is a

> **What is meant by "Possession is nine points of the law"?**
>
> This is just an old, popular saying that means possession is a decided advantage. It does not refer to any actual principle of law or any set of legal points. The number nine does not mean anything in particular, either. Thomas Adams wrote in 1630, "The devil hath eleven points of the law against you, that is, possession."

difference between a solicitor and barrister. A solicitor engages primarily in advice, negotiations, drawing agreements, and office practice. The barrister is the trial lawyer, or courtroom counselor, who is usually employed by the solicitor and not by the client.

The lawyer, like the doctor, is governed by a code of ethics that requires him to maintain the highest standards of faithfulness, trust, honesty, and devotion to the cause of his client, and at the same time to be thoroughly fair with the court in which he acts and loyal to the Constitution and laws of the nation.

The lawyer is an agent of the person who employs him and is in a trusted position. The law recognizes the close, intimate relationship and protects the client so that what a client tells a lawyer is considered just as confidential and secret as what is told to a priest or doctor. A violation of the code of ethics is punished, even to the extent of disbarment, or taking away the lawyer's license.

The lawyer is an important man in the community and fills an important need. He enables the world's work to be carried on by protecting people from other people, and even from the state itself, if either tries to overreach, interfere with, or damage any of their rights guaranteed by the Constitution.

The law permits every man to be his own lawyer in a lawsuit, if he wishes. But this is not wise; it is as if a doctor were to operate on himself or a close relative. He could not be calm, collected, dispassionate, and unemotional, and therefore his judgment would not be of the best. This is why people say "A man who is his own lawyer has a fool for a client."

ARTHUR H. SCHWARTZ
Former Justice of Supreme Court
New York State

See also COURTS; LAW AND LAW ENFORCEMENT; WILLS.

IMPORTANT USES OF LEAD

LEAD-SHEATHED ELECTRICAL CABLE

BULLET

SOLDER

FISHING SINKERS

LEAD SOLDIER

PAINT

STORAGE BATTERY

LEAD PIPE

LEAD

Lead is a soft metal that serves many purposes in the home and in industry. It has several very useful characteristics: it can be easily melted and shaped, it will not rust, and it is heavy and dense.

The paint industry uses large quantities of lead compounds. Red lead paint is the standard protection against rust for all kinds of steel structures. White lead is one of the basic ingredients of house paints.

Lead melts at a lower temperature than most other metals. Solder, an easily melted mixture of lead and tin, is used to fasten metal parts together.

Lead is easy to shape and form and has good resistance to corrosion. These qualities make it useful for such things as drainpipes and coverings for power and telephone cables. The Romans used huge amounts of lead for water pipes. Many of these pipes have been dug up in Italy near Rome and Pompeii and in England, where the Romans once ruled. Some of this ancient pipe is in almost perfect condition. Our words "plumber" and "plumbing" come from the Latin name for lead, *plumbum*.

Bullets have been made of lead for many years. In fact, the word "lead" is a slang term for bullets. Lead is good for making ammunition because it is so dense and heavy. A lead bullet will fly straight and true through the air, while a bullet made of lighter metal might waver off course. Steel coverings, or jackets, are put on many lead bullets used in high-powered guns. Steel is harder than lead and helps the bullet penetrate deeper when it hits its target.

The heaviness of lead is also used in other ways. Lead weights are used to balance airplane propellers and automobile wheels and to help fishing tackle sink.

Lead is so dense that it can block dangerous rays from X-ray machines or from nuclear equipment. When standing behind a lead shield, a worker is safe from radiation. Lead-lined aprons are used to shield X-ray workers. Lead linings protect equipment that might be harmed by acids and other chemicals. The metal cannot be eaten away by these chemicals.

The most important use of lead is in electric storage batteries that provide and store up electricity needed to start automobiles, trucks, buses, and other vehicles. Much larger storage batteries are used for emergency power sources in hospitals, telephone exchanges, and industrial plants. Another important use of lead is in type for printing.

Combinations of lead and other materials play an important part in industry. A compound of lead and arsenic is a good insect killer. Lead oxide and silica are used in making fine glassware and the glaze on china. Tetra-ethyl lead, a compound of lead, carbon, and hydrogen, is well known as an anti-knock ingredient of gasoline.

Lead is a very versatile metal, but there is one thing it cannot be used for—containers for foods. This is because lead and its compounds are poisonous.

Sources of Lead

Lead is usually found in combination with other metals, especially with silver and zinc. The richest source of lead is a mineral ore called galena, a compound of lead and sulfur. Two other mineral ores, cerrusite and anglesite, are also important sources of lead.

Most of the world's lead is mined in the United States, the Soviet Union, Australia, Mexico, Canada, Yugoslavia, Germany, Peru, Sweden, Southwest Africa, Spain, and Italy. Lead ores are widely distributed around the world, however, and many other countries also produce some lead.

Because lead is practically indestructible, much of it can be used more than once. Old storage batteries, pipes, sheets, cable coverings, and solder are melted down, and the lead is re-used in new products.

Processing the Ore

Most ores are not rich enough in lead to be sent directly to the refinery. Usually waste

---

BASIC FACTS ABOUT LEAD
CHEMICAL SYMBOL: Pb (from Latin *plumbum*).
ATOMIC WEIGHT: 207.21.
SPECIFIC GRAVITY: 11.3 (slightly more than 11 times as heavy as water).
COLOR: Bluish-gray.
PROPERTIES: Soft and easily shaped; resists corrosion by seawater, air, and many chemicals; resists passage of radiation; fairly low melting point; chemical reaction of lead and its oxides with sulfuric acid allows storage of electricity.
OCCURRENCE: In combination with other metals, especially silver and zinc.
CHIEF ORE: Galena (compound of lead and sulfur).

rock and other materials must first be removed. Removing waste materials from lead ore is called concentrating the ore. The ore is crushed into small particles and mixed with water and oily chemicals. Blasts of air are blown through the mixture. The metal floats to the surface in a froth that is skimmed off. The waste materials sink to the bottom. With this process, ores that contain even small amounts of lead can be mined economically.

After waste materials are removed, the ore is roasted to remove most of the sulfur. Then it is smelted in blast furnaces and refined further to obtain the desired purity. Commercial grades of lead are from 99.85 to 99.99 percent lead. Lead of even higher purity—99.9999 percent—is also available for specialized electronic uses.

Lead in History

Lead has been used by men for many hundreds of years. The ancient Egyptians used it for solder and for making ornaments. Greeks, Romans, and Chinese used it in their coins. Women in ancient India used red lead as a cosmetic. The hanging gardens of Babylon were floored with sheets of lead to help hold moisture for the plants.

Long before bullets were invented, lead was being used in warfare. Pieces of lead were hurled from slings at the enemy, and molten lead was poured down from forts onto attacking troops.

ROBERT L. ZIEGFELD
Executive Vice-President
Lead Industries Association
See also ALLOYS; METALS AND METALLURGY.

What is the "lead" in a lead pencil?

The lead in a lead pencil is really not lead at all. It is graphite, a soft form of the element carbon. Graphite leaves a black streak on almost everything it touches. To keep the graphite from wearing away too fast, it is mixed with clay.

Why then is a lead pencil called a lead pencil? The answer is that long ago lead was used in pencils. Lead, being soft, makes a gray streak when it is rubbed on paper. Before graphite was discovered, lead was one of the best markers people had.

LEAGUE OF NATIONS

At the end of World War I most of the nations in the world saw the need for some kind of international organization to keep the peace. The idea of the League of Nations was sponsored by Woodrow Wilson, President of the United States during World War I. He was horrified at the untold destruction and suffering of World War I and wished to put an end to all wars. In order to accomplish this goal, he proposed that all nations of the world adopt an "all for one and one for all" rule called **collective security**. Under this rule, if one nation were to attack another, it would be the duty of all the others to come to the rescue of the victim and to stop the aggressor.

President Wilson went to Versailles, France, in 1918 to work toward establishing a League of Nations with America's allies in World War I—Great Britain, France, Italy, and Japan. The leaders of these nations agreed with Wilson that the world had to be made safe for peace and democracy and that a League of Nations should be established to keep the peace.

President Wilson then returned to the United States only to face a bitter disappointment. The United States Senate refused to go along with his idea, since many Americans wanted to stay aloof from world affairs and not have to worry about wars in other countries. President Wilson warned the Senate, however, that a future war would hurt the United States and involve Americans whether they liked it or not. Therefore the United States should be prepared to help prevent such a war from occurring. Nevertheless, the Senate rejected the President's plan. The League of Nations was born, but without the membership of the United States.

Organization

The League of Nations made the Palace of Nations in Geneva, Switzerland, its headquarters. The three main bodies of the League were the assembly, council, and secretariat. The League's organization also included the Permanent Court of International Justice, the Permanent Mandates Commission, the International Labour Organisation, and sections concerned with health, communications, and child welfare. The organization of the League was in many ways similar to that later adopted by the United Nations.

The League in Action

The most successful years for the League of Nations were from 1920 to 1930, when it dealt with disputes between Greece and Italy, Britain and Turkey, Greece and Bulgaria, and others. But the history of the League was an unhappy one.

In 1931 the Japanese attacked Chinese territory in Manchuria, and the League was unable to stop them. Mussolini, the Fascist dictator of Italy, invaded Ethiopia in Africa in 1935. The member states of the League made a half-hearted attempt to help Ethiopia by stopping the shipment of oil and other vital war materials to Italy. But the effort failed, and Italy withdrew from the League in 1937. When the Nazi leader Adolf Hitler invaded Austria in 1938 and annexed portions of Czechoslovakia a year later, the League was unable to stop him either. Germany had withdrawn from the League back in 1933. The Soviet Union attacked Finland in 1939. The League of Nations expelled the Soviet Union from membership, but by that time it was too late. World War II had started.

It is true that the League was not able to stop the aggressive actions of Japan, Italy, Germany, and the Soviet Union. But it must be remembered that the League was the first attempt by most of the nations of the world to join in an effort to preserve the peace. This first effort failed. But it served as an inspiration for a second try.

The League of Nations stayed in operation until 1946, when its job was taken over by the United Nations. After the end of World War II mankind tried once again. The United Nations, a much stronger and more vital organization than the old League, was established. The United States joined this new organization from the very beginning, and the United Nations has lasted and has steadily grown in strength and stature. The United Nations is the child of the League of Nations. This child is stronger than its parent, but without the parent there would have been no child.

JOHN G. STOESSINGER
Author, *The Might of Nations: World Politics In Our Time*

MEMBERS OF THE LEAGUE OF NATIONS
(* original member, January 10, 1920)

Afghanistan (admitted, 1934)

Albania (admitted, 1920; annexed by Italy, 1939)

* Argentina

* Australia

Austria (admitted, 1920; annexed by Germany, 1938)

* Belgium

* Bolivia

* Brazil (withdrew, 1926)

Bulgaria (admitted, 1920)

* Canada

* Chile (withdrew, 1938)

* China

* Colombia

Costa Rica (admitted, 1920; withdrew, 1925)

* Cuba

* Czechoslovakia

* Denmark

Dominican Republic (admitted, 1924)

Ecuador (admitted, 1934)

Egypt (admitted, 1937)

* El Salvador (withdrew, 1937)

Estonia (admitted, 1921)

Ethiopia (admitted, 1923)

Finland (admitted, 1920)

* France

Germany (admitted, 1926; withdrew, 1933)

* Greece

* Guatemala (withdrew, 1936)

* Haiti (withdrew, 1942)

* Honduras (withdrew, 1936)

Hungary (admitted, 1922; withdrew, 1939)

* India

Iraq (admitted, 1932)

Ireland (admitted, 1923)

* Italy (withdrew, 1937)

* Japan (withdrew, 1933)

Latvia (admitted, 1921)

* Liberia

Lithuania (admitted, 1921)

Luxembourg (admitted, 1920)

Mexico (admitted, 1931)

* Netherlands

* New Zealand

* Nicaragua (withdrew, 1936)

* Norway

* Panama

* Paraguay (withdrew, 1935)

* Persia

* Peru (withdrew, 1939)

* Poland

* Portugal

* Rumania (withdrew, 1940)

* Siam

* Spain (withdrew, 1939)

* Sweden

* Switzerland

Turkey (admitted, 1932)

* Union of South Africa

Union of Soviet Socialist Republics (admitted, 1934; expelled, 1939)

* United Kingdom

* Uruguay

* Venezuela (withdrew, 1938)

* Yugoslavia

The Palace of Nations on the shores of Lake Geneva. The buildings, former headquarters of the League of Nations, now are used by the United Nations.

LEARNING

A fourth-grader recites the multiplication facts. A scientist recognizes a star by its position in the sky. A diver springs from the end of a diving board into the water. You read the lines on this page.

All these acts are examples of skills and behavior that are shaped by learning. A skill is an ability you gain or develop. Behavior refers to all your activities.

Through the ages man's great ability to learn has helped him survive. He has been able to change his behavior as conditions around him have changed. When forced to move from one geographical region to another, he learned how to live under new conditions. As enemies threatened, he learned to protect himself.

Man's ability to learn has also set him apart from all other creatures. Through learning, man is able to build his basic abilities into new and more complicated skills. Man alone has invented tools and an alphabet. Man can learn quickly. He learns more and can master more difficult skills and knowledge than animals can.

Think of all the words you know. Think of the people you can recognize and name. Have you ever stopped to count the number of tools you can use and the number of games you can play? You can remember what your aunt gave you for your birthday. You know the national anthem, and you can recognize the smell of roses.

Human beings spend a large part of their lives learning, even when they are not aware of it. Only a small part of what you learn is learned in school.

▶ WHAT IS LEARNING?

It has been difficult for scientists to discover and explain the nature of learning. It is a very complicated process. Psychologists, who study the behavior of human beings and animals, are concerned with the problem of learning. Educators, too, are concerned with the subject. Naturalists, physiologists, and even engineers work on learning problems.

Although our understanding of learning is still not complete, a great deal is known. Learning has many different forms and takes place under many conditions. In general, it involves a change in behavior. When a change in behavior takes place as a result of learning, the change is usually a long-lasting one. Learning may mean that a number of small independent acts are arranged in a new order. This happens, for example, when you learn to play a new piece on the piano.

Learning may involve performing a familiar act in a new situation. If, for instance, you already know how to focus a microscope, it will be easier for you to learn to focus a telescope.

Learning may also mean not performing a familiar act in its usual setting. If a friend's telephone number is changed, you learn to stop using the old number.

There are some changes in behavior that result from normal growth and development. A newborn baby, for example, cannot follow a moving object with his eyes, but by the time he is 6 months old, he is able to turn his head and follow the object. A change of this kind is the result of growth and is not considered learning. Other changes in behavior may be caused by disease or by drugs. These are not thought of as learning, either.

▶ HOW DO WE LEARN?

Scientists and educators have developed theories to explain learning. Not all of these theories are alike. But in general, it is agreed that much learning can be described as forming habits. We say that a human being or an animal forms a habit when he learns to act in a certain way under certain conditions.

Scientists use special terms in explaining how learning takes place. Some of these terms are *stimulus, response, reinforcement, unconditioned reflex, classical conditioning, instrumental conditioning,* and *motivation.*

A **stimulus** is a signal that acts on the senses. A printed or spoken word may be a stimulus. The point of a needle against the skin might be called a stimulus.

The way a human being or animal reacts to a stimulus is called a **response**. A response is an act, usually a movement. The movement may be very slight, like the twitch of a muscle or the blink of an eyelid, or it may be more complicated, like the closing of a door. Learning is the building of new relationships between stimuli and responses.

There are stimuli that trigger responses without any learning. If you touch a hot object, for example, you will pull your hand away. A response that is produced by a stimulus without prior learning is called an **unconditioned reflex**. Unconditioned reflexes are of great importance in keeping human beings and animals alive and healthy.

Not all learning takes place under the same conditions, and not all learning involves the same kind of behavior. There are different kinds of learning. Two of the kinds that are best understood are classical conditioning and instrumental, or operant, conditioning.

Classical Conditioning

Classical conditioning was first demonstrated at the beginning of the 20th century by the great Russian physiologist Ivan Pavlov (1849–1936).

To understand classical conditioning, imagine that you are watching a laboratory experiment. A dog is standing on a table. The dog is loosely tied to an aluminum stand. Two painless instruments are attached to the dog's mouth. One instrument is used to record when the dog salivates—that is, when saliva flows in its mouth.

The other instrument is a very thin tube through which small amounts of a mixture of vinegar and water can enter the dog's mouth.

When the vinegar-and-water mixture is squirted into the dog's mouth, the dog begins to salivate. This is a natural reaction to the sour mixture. The saliva flows for a time; then it stops.

Then a door buzzer is sounded. The dog turns in the direction of the sound. No saliva flow is recorded. The buzzer is sounded again, and 1 second later some of the vinegar-water mixture is squirted into the dog's mouth. Still no saliva flows when the buzzer is sounded, but a great deal flows as soon as the vinegar and water enter the dog's mouth.

The same order of events is repeated several times. The buzzer is sounded, and 1 second later the liquid is squirted into the dog's mouth. Before long, the dog begins to salivate as soon as it hears the buzzer. The saliva flows now even if the buzzer is sounded alone and no vinegar-water mixture has entered the dog's mouth.

The sounding of the door buzzer has been closely linked in time with the squirting into the dog's mouth of a liquid that makes the dog salivate. Thus, the door buzzer alone can now cause the flow of saliva.

In this experiment the vinegar mixture is a stimulus and salivation is a response. Salivation is the dog's natural, or unlearned, response (unconditioned reflex) to the vinegar. The vinegar mixture is therefore called the unconditioned stimulus.

The door buzzer is a second signal, or stimulus. The dog is indifferent to it at first. But it is presented again and again before the unconditioned stimulus (the vinegar). In time, the door buzzer alone is able to produce the response of salivation. This response is learned. The learned response is called the **conditioned response**. The stimulus that produces it (in this case, the door buzzer) is the **conditioned stimulus**.

In the experiment the conditioned stimulus

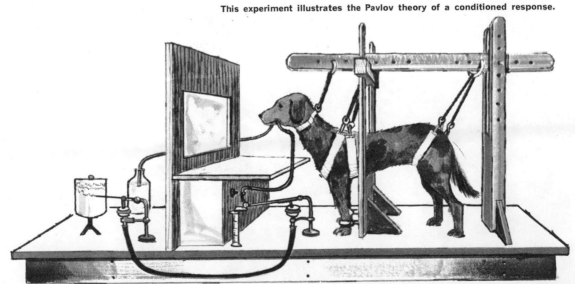

This experiment illustrates the Pavlov theory of a conditioned response.

is followed closely by the unconditioned stimulus. This procedure is known as **reinforcement**. The unconditioned stimulus (the vinegar) helps establish the relationship between the conditioned stimulus (the door buzzer) and the conditioned response (salivation at the sound of the buzzer).

But without reinforcement the conditioned stimulus may lose the ability to bring on the conditioned response. If vinegar is no longer squirted into the dog's mouth after the sounding of the door buzzer, the dog will soon stop salivating after the buzzer is sounded.

Failing to follow the conditioned stimulus with the unconditioned stimulus can cause the unlearning of a conditioned response. Scientists conducting an experiment may purposely cause this to happen. When they do, the process is called experimental extinction.

Many examples of classical conditioning can be seen in the behavior of human beings as well as animals. Strong emotional responses are often the result of classical conditioning. A number of responses, such as goose pimples, trembling, changes in heart rate, sweating, and flinching, are linked to the emotion of fear.

An inexperienced marksman, for example, may flinch as he begins to squeeze the trigger of his rifle. Loud noise is an unconditioned stimulus for flinching. The squeezing of the trigger becomes a conditioned stimulus for the same response.

In an experiment carried out by the American psychologist Dr. John Watson (1878–1958), a little boy was allowed to play with a tame white laboratory rat. In the beginning the boy enjoyed playing with the rat. Then, each time the boy began to play with the rat, a sudden, loud noise was made. In a short time the boy showed strong signs of fear whenever the rat was brought near him. He also cried and trembled whenever he saw a rabbit, a dog, or a fur coat. The fear response had spread to a number of furry things.

Later, the boy's conditioned fear response to the rat was removed. This was done by allowing the boy to become accustomed to the rat. The caged rat was brought into the room each day as the boy had his lunch. At first, the cage was left far from the boy. Gradually it was brought closer and closer. Finally the boy became used to the rat and was able to play with it once more.

Instrumental Conditioning

To understand instrumental conditioning, imagine that you are watching a second laboratory experiment. A hungry pigeon is placed in a box the size of a small television set. One side of the box is made of clear plastic so that the pigeon can be watched. Inside the box, in the center of one of the other sides, there is a round button about 1 inch across. The button has a small light bulb behind it. When this light bulb is turned on, the entire button is lighted up. Just below the

Dolphins have keen hearing and can "hear" differences in sizes of objects. A blindfolded dolphin is able to recognize the larger of two balls by means of its built-in sonar system. By pressing the lever nearest the larger ball, it gets reward of fish.

button there is a little opening through which grains of cereal can be fed to the pigeon.

At first, the button is dark, and the pigeon walks restlessly around the box. Then the button is lighted, and the pigeon quickly walks up to it and strikes the button with its beak. When this happens, the light behind the button is shut off and a few grains of cereal are fed to the pigeon.

The experiment is arranged so that grain is fed to the pigeon only after it has pecked the lighted button. If the pigeon pecks at the button while it is dark, the animal is not fed. This arrangement is the secret of the pigeon's prompt peck at the lighted button. Striking the lighted button helps the hungry pigeon get a few grains of cereal.

The principle behind instrumental conditioning is simple. In this experiment the pigeon has not been fed for several hours. It is hungry. Its hunger is called a **motivation**. A stimulus (the lighted button) is presented to the animal. When the animal performs the response its trainer wants (pecking the button), the animal is rewarded with food.

Providing food in a situation like this is called reinforcement because it seems to strengthen the relationship between the stimulus and the desired response. In many ways reinforcement is like a reward.

Instrumental conditioning describes learning that takes place because the learned response brings, again and again, a reinforcement, or reward.

Many of the skills and acts that human beings learn involve instrumental conditioning. The complicated acts we call manners are in this group. Children often learn the style of speaking or acting that will be pleasing to adults and bring rewards of praise or gifts. Adults may learn ways of behaving that will bring business and social success.

It has been shown by experiment that a principle like that of instrumental learning also affects our willingness to speak and what we say. Thus, if the person to whom we are speaking makes a pleasant, approving sound or smiles when we say certain words, we tend to say those words more often. In the classroom, when the teacher asks a question, a child who has often answered correctly is more apt to raise his hand than a child who seldom gives correct answers.

This chimpanzee was taught to work for poker chips, instead of food, as a reward. The chimp knows he can use the chip to get food from machine called Chimp-o-mat.

Verbal Learning

Verbal learning, or the ability to use words, is one of the most important parts of our lives. Only human beings have this ability.

Through verbal learning we are able to associate words with persons, places, things, and ideas. This kind of learning takes place when you learn to call someone by name or when you learn to call an object with a flat surface and four legs a table.

Through verbal learning we are also able to associate words with other words. The words "happy," "cheerful," and "gay" are associated with one another.

Much of our education involves verbal learning. Words provide a quick way to learn about the world around us. Once we have learned to call things by name, we can use the words as substitutes for the real objects in communication with others.

Verbal learning also makes it possible for us to form links in time. Through words we can learn about the experiences of people who lived long ago. Through words human beings who are not yet born will be able to find out what we learned about the world.

WHY DO WE LEARN?

In experiments in instrumental conditioning, hungry pigeons generally learn faster than those that have just eaten. Because hunger seems to drive the animals, it is often called motivation. People, too, have motivations. It has been found that people learn faster if they have a strong desire to learn. The need or desire that makes a person want to learn is a motivation.

A person's motivation to learn is not the same all his life. It changes as he develops. A young child, for example, may want to learn in order to win approval and acceptance from adults. He may want the reward of seeing his teacher smile or of hearing his mother praise him.

As children grow older their motivation usually changes. An older child no longer wants to learn simply to please others. He wants to learn in order to please himself. He wants to feel that he can master a subject. He wants to satisfy his curiosity about people and things around him. At the same time, he may be motivated by a desire for good marks or by the desire to go to a certain college.

Motivation comes from within a person. But teachers and parents can influence the child's motivation to learn. There are many ways to stimulate and keep alive the individual's motivation to learn. Encouraging a child, answering his questions, showing an interest in his interests, and helping him feel that he is a successful person are just a few of the ways.

Sometimes children who are bright and are capable of learning do poorly in school. They accomplish far less than they are capable of accomplishing. Studies have been made to try to find out why this is so. When a child underachieves—that is, achieves less than he is capable of—several problems are usually involved. The child lacks the desire to learn. But he may be troubled by other things. He may have a poor relationship with his parents and with boys and girls his own age. Or he may lack confidence in himself as a person and in his abilities.

In some homes or settings, learning is made difficult by unfavorable conditions, or it is not encouraged. In some cases failure may bring a child more attention than success. Good study habits have to be learned and encouraged.

The problem of the underachiever calls for understanding on the part of teachers and parents. If parents are unable to discover where the trouble lies, they may want to consult the school guidance counselor or an outside counselor.

Punishing a child is certainly not the best solution. At one time people believed punishment was the way to make a child learn. Through experiments it has been learned that rewarding good behavior is a much better way to help a child learn than punishing undesirable behavior. For example, a child who gives his mother all the change after a trip to the store and is praised for it is more likely to return all the change the next time. A child who keeps a dime for himself and is punished for it may repeat his behavior. In the terms of instrumental conditioning, rewards reinforce the behavior being rewarded. But

The rat in the "Y" maze (*right*) has more than one path to choose from. The correct choice will bring him to food placed at one arm of the "Y." The maze is connected electronically with computor in control room (*left*). Here the rat's behavior in the maze is recorded automatically and is studied by scientists. Rats are able to master the maze quickly.

Above: The hen has been taught to walk a tightrope to reach feeding box.
Right: The pigeon has learned to tap the sign corresponding to the color that was turned on.

punishment does not cause the child to unlearn the behavior for which he is being punished.

▶ HOW DO WE LEARN BEST?

Through experiments with animals and human beings, scientists have found out not only how we learn but also how we learn most easily. Knowing the conditions under which learning takes place most easily can help a student plan the way he will study.

In learning a skill such as typing or in memorizing a poem or a passage from a book, it is generally felt that people learn best if they practice for a certain length of time, then take a rest period, and then practice again. Less progress is made if the person practices in one long session without a break.

To learn a long poem or a part in a play, it is best to try to learn it one verse or part at a time, rather than as a whole.

It is much easier to learn if you understand the material you are learning and if it means something to you. Experiments have shown that people learn real words much faster than they do meaningless nonsense words.

Sometimes a particular method of study is especially suited to a particular subject. An important part of learning a skill, such as swimming, is practicing correct swimming form. We learn some skills by actually doing them. Some subjects like literature and history

are learned mainly through reading. But reading alone is not enough for a student who is learning a foreign language or studying the history of music. He must also learn through hearing the language or the music. To a student of art history, looking at paintings or slides of paintings is important.

At one time people thought that learning Greek, Latin, and mathematics exercised and strengthened the mind, just as working out with weights strengthens the muscles. This is now known to be untrue.

SENSE AND NONSENSE WORDS

I	II
perg	bird
quan	table
silm	child
mank	pear
ferd	baby
glif	road
joft	car
relk	farm
palt	apple

Look at list 1 for one minute. Close the book and write down what you remember of the list. Now open the book and look at list II for the same amount of time. Close the book and see how many words from this list you can write. From which list did you remember more?

Worms and mollusks are invertebrates and show some learning ability. Some worms can learn to change direction to avoid an electric shock. The octopus, a mollusk, is readily trained. It can learn to take crabs out of pots, run mazes, and differentiate between such forms as a circle, a square, and a triangle.

Insects, such as bees, wasps, and cockroaches, learn to find their way through mazes. Bees learn to go to a particular color which they associate with a food reward. They also learn the time of day when food can be obtained at a certain place.

Many fishes have color vision and can recognize each other by color patterns on the head. They can master maze and detour problems. Aquarium fishes learn the particular time for their feeding.

Amphibians (frogs, toads) and reptiles (lizards, snakes, turtles, tortoises) have been tamed. Frogs and toads learn to respond to those who look after them. Toads soon learn to recognize that some things, such as bees or hairy caterpillars, are inedible.

Birds have good learning ability and a great sense of direction. They can recognize common enemies. The jackdaw, raven, parrot, and others have a counting sense. Parrots, parakeets, and others can imitate sounds.

Among the rodents the rat has a superior ability to find its way through a complicated maze. The squirrel, like some birds, has a sense of numbers.

Among the hoofed animals (horse, pig, cow, giraffe, sheep, goat, and others) the horse and the pig show considerable capacity for learning.

Among the flesh-eating animals the dog shows superior talent for trainability. Cats can learn some skills by imitating other cats.

Among the ocean mammals the dolphin, or porpoise, is highly intelligent. It is playful and becomes friendly with humans. It has very keen hearing and seems capable of making imitative sounds.

Apes and monkeys have learning ability second only to that of man. One species of ape, the chimpanzee, can solve some problems that are difficult for monkeys and impossible for rats and lower mammals.

Man is the most intelligent of all animals. Only man can use language and an extensive set of symbols to communicate. Of all animals, man has the greatest capacity for profiting from experience and for thinking and planning ahead.

Reviewed by KENNETH COOPER
Department of Psychology, Brooklyn College

LEARNING ABILITY AMONG ANIMALS

An animal's intelligence is measured by how well it acts in a new situation and how it solves problems. Lower animals usually respond in the same way to the same stimulus. The scallop flaps its shells to get away from its enemy the starfish. The hungry octopus remains motionless until the unsuspecting crab, a favorite morsel, comes near. But these acts tell nothing about learning ability. Many animals, from a flea to an elephant, can be taught to perform tricks. But their learning capabilities vary widely.

A method much used by scientists to test learning ability in animals is the **maze**. A maze consists of a number of pathways. The animal must discover the path through which it will avoid discomfort or that will lead it to food or some other reward. The number of attempts the animal must make to find its way through the blind alleys of the maze, and how long he remembers what he has learned, tell something about the animal's learning and memory capacities.

Vertebrates, animals with backbones, are often superior to **invertebrates**, animals without backbones, in learning how to solve new problems. The chimpanzee is considered superior to all other vertebrates except humans in selective learning ability. Based on various testing procedures, next in order of learning ability come monkeys. There are wide differences in learning ability among individual animals of the same species. For example, some ants, bees, and cockroaches are brighter than other members of the same colony.

However, the ideas and habits you gain in one area of study can help you in another. This is called transfer of training.

Something you have already learned can help you learn something new. The principles of mathematics that you learn in elementary school will help you in solving problems in physics and chemistry later on. The way you learn to take notes and to outline may help you when you write long papers in college. Even the use of good methods of study can be carried over to your work the whole time you are in school.

▶ REMEMBERING AND FORGETTING

Remembering is closely linked to learning. People need more than the ability to learn swiftly and well. They must be able to remember what they learn.

Psychologists have tried to explain how people remember and why they forget many of the things they learn. No one has yet found all the answers, but there are several theories to explain remembering and forgetting.

It is believed that when a person learns something, a physical change of some kind takes place. A trace, or pattern, is left in the brain. According to one theory, memories or the traces memory may leave in the brain simply fade away in the course of time. Thus, things learned long ago are forgotten before things learned more recently. This is largely true, but there are enough exceptions to make scientists look for further explanations of forgetting. Old people, for example, often remember clearly events of their childhood, but they are unable to remember things they did only a few hours earlier.

According to another theory, memories of different things sometimes interfere with one another. When this happens, one displaces the other from memory. Something that you have just learned may cause you to forget something you already knew. Or something you have already learned may prevent you from learning and remembering something new.

The way you felt about a particular experience may also determine whether you remember it or forget it. In general, people are apt to forget things that are unpleasant or upsetting and remember things that are pleasant.

With some effort on your part, it may be possible to improve your ability to remember.

In trying to recall a simple thing like a name or a word, it often helps to stop trying to remember and to think of something else. The forgotten name or word may pop up in your memory. Or you may recall a name that is not the one you are trying to remember but resembles it in some way. It may start with the same sound as the correct word, or it may rhyme with it. Looking at different features of the incorrect word may help you recall the correct one.

In order to remember something you are studying, it helps to go over the material a number of times, even after you have mastered it. This is called overlearning. (You must be careful, though, to go over the material correctly each time. You do not want to repeat and learn a mistake.)

In studying to understand and remember, it is important for the learner to be active. This does not mean that he must move around the room. But he must be awake and alert, and he must pay close attention to the film or demonstration he is watching, the book he is reading, or the lecture to which he is listening.

Students have many methods for getting more out of study. They may outline a chapter in a textbook as they read it or underline key passages (if they own the book). When they listen to a lecture, they may take notes so that they learn and remember what they are hearing.

Sometimes students are even advised to go through special routines to help them retain what they study. One of these routines is called the **SQ3R method**. "S" stands for surveying, or skimming, the material to see what is covered and to look for important topics. "Q" stands for questions that the student is advised to make up for each heading or topic. "3R" stands for reading, reciting, and reviewing. This means reading through the material to find answers for the questions that have been made up. Reciting means stopping every so often and, without looking at the book, trying to recall the material that has been covered. The third "R," reviewing, means going over the material once it has been learned. Rereading and reciting may both be part of reviewing.

Students sometimes use another method to improve their memory of subjects they are studying. They invent categories into which they place the material they must learn. In studying the French Revolution, a student might invent such categories as "causes," "major events," "important figures," and "results."

People also help themselves remember facts by inventing special aids to memory, called **mnemonics** (from the Greek word for memory). If you wanted to memorize the names of the early presidents of the United States (Washington, Adams, Jefferson, Madison, Monroe, Adams, Jackson, and Van Buren), you might make up a saying like this: "When a just man makes a just vow." You would then remember the names, because the first letter of each word in the sentence stands for a president.

►ABILITY TO LEARN

People differ in their ability to learn. They differ in the amount of ability they have, as well as in the kind of ability they have. Some students can barely get passing marks in high school, while others earn all A's. Certain students are successful in mathematics and science but do poorly in literature and history. Other students do well in literature and history and poorly in science and mathematics.

It is hard to find out what causes these differences. Are they due to the person's background—to the kind of home or neighborhood in which he grew up and the kind of experiences he had? Or is a person's ability to learn passed on to him from his ancestors, along with such traits as the texture of his hair and the color of his eyes?

Most studies of these questions seem to point to the fact that both the conditions under which a person grows up (his environment) and the traits passed on to him from his ancestors (his inheritance) determine how well the person learns.

It is true that some families have an unusually large number of gifted members. But these families may live in homes in which there are books and other opportunities for learning. The parents may be concerned with their children's success in school. In other families there are generations of people with very modest abilities. In these families, interest in learning may not be encouraged.

Differences between boys and girls in ability to learn have also been reported. Generally, however, the differences have been small. Girls tend to have slightly better grades in elementary school, and they are slightly better in word skills than boys. Boys, on the average, get higher scores on mathematical learning tasks and in science and mechanics.

It is doubtful that the differences reported in learning reflect physical differences between boys and girls. It is more likely that the differences in learning reflect a general feeling among people in the Western world. Certain tasks are popularly felt to be best suited to girls and others best suited to boys.

It is thought by many people that children learn more easily than adults. But children are not necessarily the best learners. The ability to remember numbers, to memorize poetry, or to learn school subjects increases as people grow older. In many of these tasks a person can achieve nearly twice as much at the age of 20 as he can at the age of 10. After the age of 25 the ability to acquire new learning begins to drop somewhat. This drop continues for the rest of one's life. But it is not the same for all subjects. The ability to learn routine tasks falls off faster than the ability to learn meaningful material. It also seems to be true that people who are intelligent and well educated show less of a drop than others in ability to learn as they grow older.

We have seen that human beings learn in a number of ways. Classical conditioning, instrumental conditioning, and verbal learning are part of our daily lives.

The rapid growth of technical and other information in this century has made learning particularly important. But many questions wait for answers. Much research is going on in psychological laboratories. Psychologists want to know how memory works. In what way is an ability to learn affected by the skills we have learned before? Do human beings have certain inborn abilities that make it possible for them to learn some skills more easily than others?

The need for learning and remembering is especially important to students. Perhaps your task as a student will be made easier as more is discovered about learning.

ERNST Z. ROTHKOPF
Bell Telephone Laboratories, Inc.

See also ANIMALS: INTELLIGENCE AND BEHAVIOR; PSYCHOLOGY.

LEATHER

Leather is an animal hide or skin that has been tanned, or treated. The most important use of leather is for shoes. Many other articles are also made from leather: jackets, coats, dresses, skirts, handbags, and belts. Leather luggage is used for travel. Leather furniture is used in homes, offices, and automobiles. Wherever people play—in ball parks, stadiums, gymnasiums, golf courses—leather is a part of the playing equipment. Leather belting, tough but flexible, helps turn the wheels of industry.

▶ LEATHER FOR SHOES

Early men found that animal skins offered better foot protection than any other material. Animal skins were, in fact, about the only long-wearing material available. Today, though other materials are available, leather is still used for shoes and boots. About four fifths of the leather of the world goes into shoes.

This is because leather is both a comfortable and a healthful shoe material. Viewed under a microscope, leather is not seen as a dense mass. Instead, it is a fine network of millions of tiny fibers linked together. Leather can "breathe" because the tiny fibers permit a steady movement of air and water vapor. That is why all-leather shoes insulate feet—keeping them warm and dry in winter and cool and dry in summer. Foot perspiration evaporates through the leather's invisible pores.

▶ LEATHER ZOO

If all the different kinds of animals whose hides or skins are used for leather were brought together, they would make a good-size zoo. This leather zoo would have animals from every continent of the world and even from the oceans. The most important by far would be the cattle, sheep, and goats. Also in the leather zoo would be horses, hogs, kangaroos, alligators, snakes, lizards, and deer.

The word **hides** usually is used for the skins of large animals, as in cowhide or horsehide. The word **skins** is usually used for the smaller animals, as in goatskin, sheepskin, pigskin, and calfskin.

Cattle hides are the single most important

source of leather raw materials. The largest single source of cattle hides is the meat-packing houses of the United States. Other sources are Canada and Argentina.

Calfskin leather is finer grained and lighter in weight than cattle hide. It is extremely strong and handsome and is used for the most expensive shoes, handbags, and similar articles. The important sources of calfskin are the United States and Europe.

Kidskins are practically all exported from countries where goats are raised for milk and meat. India, South America, and Central Africa provide many kidskins. The skin of any goat, old or young, is known commercially as kidskin. Most suede leathers are kidskins buffed on the side that originally was next to the flesh.

The hide of the horse is used for shoes, jackets, and sports equipment. Most horsehides are from France and Belgium. Pigskin leather is produced from domestic hogs or from the peccary, a small wild hog of South America. The kangaroo, a native of Australia, provides the strongest of all leathers. It is used for track and baseball shoes. The skins of lizards and snakes, even of cobras and pythons, are also used. They provide leathers of unusual textures and colors for shoes, handbags, and luggage. Alligator leather was formerly very popular in high-quality leather goods. However, the alligator is now so near extinction that it has been placed on the U.S. government's list of endangered species.

Deerskin and buckskin both come from deer. Unusual leathers for many purposes are provided by water buffalo, ostriches, seals, and sharks.

▶ HOW IS LEATHER MADE?

Tanning turns animal hides and skins into soft, flexible leather. Tannin, the bark extract used in tanning, causes a chemical reaction in hides. Different types of leathers are produced by slight changes in the chemical processes.

By using the proper tanning agents, leather-makers can produce soft, supple, long-lasting leather for shoe uppers or the firm yet flexible leather needed for shoe soles. Dyes and finishes are put on during the leathermaking process. In this way a great variety of tones, textures, and surface effects can be produced in the leather.

STEPS IN PREPARING LEATHER
(SOME PROCESSES ARE NOT SHOWN)

HIDES ARE SALTED TO PRESERVE THEM FOR STORAGE AND SHIPPING

AT TANNERY, SALT IS WASHED OUT OF HIDES

HIDES ARE TREATED WITH LIME TO LOOSEN HAIR

VEGETABLE-TANNED HIDES ARE SOAKED IN VATS

CHROME-TANNED HIDES ARE TUMBLED IN CHEMICAL SOLUTION IN A DRUM

HIDES ARE SHAVED TO UNIFORM THICKNESS

Preserving the Leather

Before the hides are tanned, they must be preserved, or "cured." This is done in the packing house by salting the skins to prevent rotting.

Many hides and skins are still preserved by the old method of spreading the layers with salt. However, a new curing system is proving more effective. In packing houses where the new system is used, the hides and skins are soaked in a brine (salt) solution. In a few hours the brine penetrates the hides and skins and protects them from decay as well as they would be protected if covered with salt for 30 days.

Preparing the Hides

When the cured hides arrive at the leather plant, or tannery, they are washed and soaked in cold water. This is done for two purposes. First, it removes excess salt and any foreign materials. Second, it brings the fibers back to their natural shape (the curing dried them out of shape) and condition, so that they will absorb tanning agents readily.

To remove the hair the hide is soaked in a lime solution and scraped by a machine that has dull blades similar to those on a lawn mower. Any small pieces of flesh still sticking to the hide are removed by hand or by another machine. This machine has sharper blades than the one used for taking the hair off the hide. Various solutions and baths are used to remove the lime and salts still in the hide. Then the hides start through the tannery.

Tanning Methods

Most leather is made by two main tanning methods—vegetable tanning and chrome tanning. The type of work done in each method is different, the type of leather produced is different, and the two methods are used for different purposes. For these reasons tanneries usually specialize in either vegetable or chrome tanning.

Vegetable tanning uses extracts from the

HAIR IS REMOVED BY MACHINE

SCRAPS OF FLESH ARE SCRAPED AWAY

HIDES ARE DE-LIMED AND "BATED" IN ORDER TO BE SOFTENED

HIDES ARE PASTED ON GLASS PLATES, AND DRIED SMOOTH IN HEATED TUNNEL

"BOARDING" PRODUCES A GRAINED PATTERN

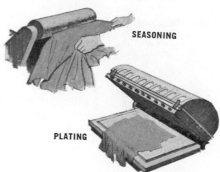

SEASONING ADDS COLORING AND POLISHING INGREDIENTS; PLATING GIVES EXTRA-SMOOTH SURFACE

bark and wood of trees. It is a long process that takes several months. It produces a firm leather that resists water. Most shoe soles, luggage, furniture, and belts to drive machines are made from vegetable-tanned cattle hides.

In vegetable tanning the hides are hung from racks or rocking frames that are set in vats until the hides soak up the tanning solutions. The skins are moved from vat to vat, with stronger solutions in each vat. After a time the hides are left to soak in layaway sections where the leather matures. After it is tanned, the leather is bleached and "stuffed." Leather is stuffed by adding several coats of compounds containing clay, mineral salts, corn sugar, mineral oils, and codfish oil. This adds weight to the leather and makes it last longer.

The **chrome-tanning** process is used to produce leather for shoe uppers, garments, and other soft leather articles. Chrome tanning is a rapid tanning method that requires hours and days instead of weeks and months.

During the process special qualities can be built into the leather. Chrome-tanned leather is very flexible, long-wearing, and does not scratch, scuff, or scar easily. Lightweight hides such as calf, sheep, lamb, goat, and pigskins are best for chrome tanning.

During the chrome-tanning process, hides and skins are tumbled in huge wooden drums partly filled with chromium salt solutions that turn the skins a light blue-green. Then the leather is cleaned, dried, and smoothed. After this it is ready for bleaching and dyeing.

A combination of tanning methods—vegetable and chrome tanning—is sometimes used to make especially soft leather.

Tanning Materials

The barks and chemicals used in tanning come from all over the world. The country that processes the most leather, the United States, imports over 60 percent of the tannin it uses. The bark of the quebracho tree, which grows in South America, makes up over three fourths of this tannin. Other imported barks come from mangrove trees in Southwest Asia and other tropical areas, wattle in Australia and South Africa, valonia in the Black Sea area, and gambier in Southeast Asia. In North America vegetable-tanning agents are obtained from oak, chestnut, and hemlock barks.

The tanning agents in the chrome process are chemicals prepared from chromite, the chief ore of chromium. Most chromite ore comes from many countries of Africa and from Greece, Brazil, New Caledonia, and other areas of the Pacific. There are a few chromite mines in the western United States.

Finishing Leather

Leather is highly valued for its beauty and suppleness as well as for the protective covering it offers. Most of the beauty of leather comes from its natural "grain," or pattern. This grain is different in different types of animals. Sometimes grains are pressed by hand or machine into smooth leathers.

To make leather shinier, waxes, resins, shellac, or other chemicals are applied. Dyes add color. The application of enamel paint called japan or of plastics gives patent leather its shiny surface. Suede leather is made when the flesh, or underside of the leather, is buffed or sandpapered to produce a nap. Suede leather is used for shoes, garments, and handbags.

▶ RESEARCH IN LEATHER

Research and engineering have improved the quality of leather, produced new varieties, finishes, and colors, and provided new products for everyday use. Some types of leather are treated to produce extremely high scuff resistance. Garment leathers are made soil resistant with new fluoride chemicals that cause leather to shed oil and grease stains. Washable leathers have been developed for shoes, gloves, and garments. Silicones make the upper leather of shoes waterproof without changing the leather's ability to "breathe." Leather for white shoes and for baseballs is made with zirconium.

▶ LEATHER THROUGH THE AGES

Skins were man's first clothing material. Early man also used leather for water con-tainers and for tents. Even before he raised wool-bearing animals or learned to plant flax for linen and spin the cloth, early man was able to tan leather.

Archeologists have found bits and pieces of leather—partly preserved leather jackets and cloaks and bottles—scattered as far and wide as ancient man wandered. Skillfully decorated leather sandals have been found in old Egyptian tombs. In bogs of Scotland men have found partly preserved leather garments worn by the ancestors of the present-day Highlanders. Water, grain, and other household items were stored in leather containers found in ancient Crete. The Bible and other writings of long ago mention leather tanning.

Twenty-five hundred years ago the Greeks had leather tanneries. Because of their bad odor the tanneries were placed outside the city walls. Greek, Roman, and Egyptian tanners all used limewater to help take the hair off hides, just as is done now. They scraped the hides to pull off the last of the hair. Oak and sumac bark extracts were used for tanning.

In the Middle Ages England became a center for leathermaking and for the export of leather. But England was not the only place where tanning was done. In Russia tanning was one of the most important industries. France, Spain, Italy, and Germany also had important leather industries.

During the Middle Ages England's leatherworkers organized trade guilds. The guilds tried to keep the making of leather a secret. By 1422 there were 11 different guilds of leatherworkers in London among all the 111 guilds listed. Entire sections of the city were cordwainers' or leatherworkers' neighborhoods. The word "cordwainer" means a worker in cordwain, or cordovan leather. Cordovan leather was the leather from Cordova, a city of Spain. Now the name cordovan is used for leather made of horsehide.

Some American Indians were expert tanners. They used leather for clothing, tents, boats, and many other purposes. All the leather made by these Indians was "buckskin tan." This leather was very soft and pliable and remarkable for its ability to keep out water.

The Indian women dressed the skins. Skins were collected, heaped in piles, and wetted. They were allowed to decompose until the

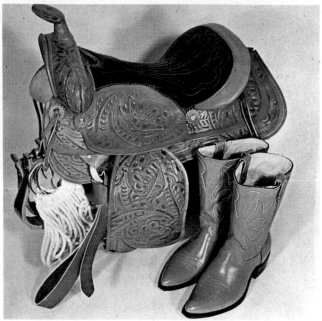

Leather is used for making strong, durable luggage.

hair was loosened. Then they were scraped with bone tools until both the hair and flesh sides were perfectly clean. After the skin was treated with a mixture of the brain and liver of the animal, it was softened by rubbing.

Although the Indians produced an excellent leather, they knew nothing of the bark tanning methods used in Europe. These were introduced by the French in Canada and the English in New England as early as 1623.

Until late in the 18th century, leathermaking was the same slow process known to early men. Then new discoveries made it different. In England the famous scientist Sir Humphry Davy (1778–1829) discovered that oak and sumac barks were not the only barks that could be used for tanning. He found that tannin was also in the bark of the hemlock and mimosa and in the wood of the chestnut and the quebracho trees. Sir Humphry's work was valuable for American tanners because American forests were full of hemlock and chestnut trees. For many years American tanners set up their plants in the midst of hemlock forests in Pennsylvania, New York, Michigan, and Wisconsin.

In the 19th century two Americans, Augustus Schultz and Robert Foerderer, following up discoveries in England, learned how to chrome-tan leather. Chrome tanning made it possible for tanners to produce lightweight leather of different colors. The chrome-tanned leather replaced the heavy bark-tanned leather used in shoe uppers up to that time.

Meanwhile, the invention and improvement of machinery made it possible to produce leather cheaper and faster than it had been produced before. A machine made in 1809 by Samuel Parker of Newburyport, Massachusetts, split leather to any thickness. Before that, hides were shaved down by hand to the desired thickness. With Parker's machine a worker's output increased from four hides per day to several hundred.

Now the United States makes more shoes than any other country. It makes 550,000,000 of the 3,000,000,000 (billion) shoes produced, about one sixth of the world's total. Other important shoe-manufacturing countries are Italy, Spain, the Soviet Union, Britain, Germany, and France. Other countries, where the making of shoes is not a major industry, have important tanneries, or they export such hides and skins as kangaroo, lizard, or kid.

WILLIAM RAPP
Director, Leather Industries of America
See also SHOES.

LEATHERCRAFT

Leathercraft is the art of making useful and beautiful articles from leather. It is one of the oldest crafts. Early man made foot coverings and clothing from leather. Through the centuries leather was used in many other ways. In the Middle Ages people drank from leather cups, wore leather armor, and rowed in leather boats.

As the uses for leather grew, people's skill in working with leather grew, too. Craftsmen began to decorate the articles they made so that they were pleasing to the eye as well as useful. American Indian women made practical garments from the hides of deer and bison. Porcupine quills were dyed and sewn in designs on the garments.

Today most of the leather shoes, belts, and jackets we wear are made in large factories. But skilled leather craftsmen continue to make fine articles of leather by hand. These include richly decorated saddles, harnesses, belts, and wallets. In addition, many children and adults enjoy leathercraft as a hobby.

▶ LEATHERCRAFT AS A HOBBY

Leathercraft is a hobby for everyone. Beginners can make such simple things as bookmarks, coin purses, or key cases. There are kits that contain the leather, tools, and directions needed to complete a project. The parts are cut and ready for assembly. All you have to do is lace them together.

More experienced craftsmen can make wallets, handbags, and a variety of other interesting things. They can also decorate the articles they make in a number of ways. Tooling, or pressing a design into moistened leather, is one of the most popular ways of

decorating leather. Calfskin, goatskin, cowhide, sheepskin, steerhide, and other kinds of leather can be used.

You can buy leather from a hobby shop or from crafts-supply firms that sell by mail. Send for a catalog so you will have information about leathers and tools.

▶ WORKING WITH LEATHER

For each article you plan to make, cut a template, or pattern, out of heavy paper or thin cardboard. Place the pattern on the piece of leather with which you are working, and trace around it with a sharp pencil.

Leather must be cut with a very sharp knife. You may use a knife made especially for leathercraft or any other knife with a sharp, pointed blade.

Cut the leather on a smooth-grained pine or maple board. Avoid any surface that has knots in it. These will turn the knife blade as you cut. Use a metal-edged ruler as a guide for cutting straight lines. Hold the knife firmly, and bear down so that you cut through the leather and into the wood. Curved lines must be cut freehand.

To make a simple bookmark, cut a strip of leather about 1 inch wide and 6 inches long. You may use it just as it is, or you may decorate it by cutting fringes in one or both ends.

Tooling

You can further decorate the bookmark by tooling it. This involves pressing a design into the grain, or finished, side of the leather with a special modeling tool. (The other side of the leather is the flesh side.) Leather must be moistened before it can be tooled. Place the leather on a piece of marble, tile, heavy plate glass, or stainless steel. Moisten the flesh side of the leather with a sponge until the piece is

thoroughly wet but not sopping. You should not be able to squeeze water out of it when you press your fingernail against a corner. Turn the leather over so that the grain side is uppermost.

Draw a design on a piece of thin tracing paper. This need not be complicated. It can be a simple initial. Place the paper over the leather so that the design is centered. Trace over the design with a pencil, but do not press too hard, or you may go through the paper.

Remove the paper. Then, using the pointed end of a modeling tool, go over the design to deepen the lines in the leather.

Flat Modeling

You may press down the area around the tooled initial or design so that it is raised and stands out. This process is called flat modeling. To do flat modeling, you will need a modeling tool with a spoon-shaped end. Working on the front, or grain, side of the leather, rub the area surrounding your design with small, circular motions.

Embossing

You can raise the initial or design still more by tooling it from the back, or flesh, side of the leather. This is called embossing. Turn the leather over and use the spoon end of the modeling tool to push the design out from the back. Hold the leather in your hand as you do this, working against the palm of your hand.

Texturing

You can also make the design stand out by texturing the background instead of pressing it down with a modeling tool. For texturing you will need a stippler. This looks like a cluster of nails set into a handle. To use the stippler, simply press the pointed ends of the tool into the moist leather. This will leave a group of dots. The more you stipple a particular area, the finer the texture will be. If you do not have a stippler, you can use the end of a blunt nail or a used-up ball-point pen.

You can also texture an area by stamping it with a background tool. One end of this tool has a fine texture imprinted on it. Place this against the moist leather, and strike the other end firmly with a wooden or rawhide mallet. (All stamping must be done on a wooden surface—never on glass.)

Burning

Another way to decorate leather is by burning. A special tool is used. It looks like a small electric soldering iron with a fine tip. Plug it into an electric outlet, and allow it to become hot. Then use the burning tool as though it were a pencil, drawing directly on the grain side of the leather. You may do this freehand, or you may trace your design on the leather beforehand. The leather should be clean and dry. The hot tool will scorch the leather, darkening it. The longer you leave the tool on the leather and the harder you press, the darker the impression. You must be very careful in using this hot tool.

HARRY ZARCHY
Author, *Creative Hobbies*

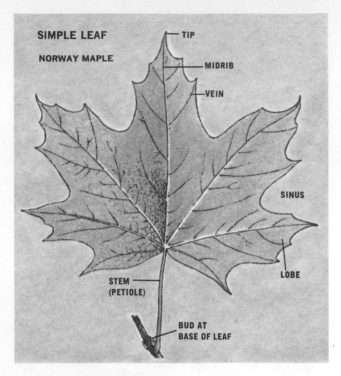

SIMPLE LEAF

NORWAY MAPLE

TIP
MIDRIB
VEIN
SINUS
LOBE
STEM (PETIOLE)
BUD AT BASE OF LEAF

LEAVES

A maple leaf, a pine needle, a fern frond, a spinach leaf, and a grass blade are all leaves. They resemble each other in important ways. Like most other leaves they need light for growth. They contain green cells that make food for the entire plant.

Yet each of these leaves looks very different from the others. Each kind of plant—from tiny moss to giant sequoia—has its own kind of leaf. This makes it possible to recognize plants by their leaves, somewhat as detectives identify people by fingerprints. Flowers and fruits also provide important clues for identification.

On these pages some common leaves are shown. These pictures will help you identify leaves that you find. You may also want to buy a guidebook to plants of the region in which you live. The leaves you find will never exactly resemble the drawings. However, if you note the appearance and arrangement of the leaves of an unfamiliar plant, you will have several good clues to its identity.

▶ LEAVES AS CLUES TO THE IDENTITY OF PLANTS

Pine trees and their relatives have leaves like needles or scales. Almost all other plants have either flat, very thin leaves or thick, very

fleshy ones. These are called **broad leaves** because they are broader than the needlelike leaves.

If you are making a leaf collection, you have probably started with broad leaves. As you may have noticed, there are two kinds of broad leaves: simple and compound.

Simple and Compound Leaves

Broad leaves have certain main parts. A maple leaf is a good example. The broad, flat part is called the **blade**. The blade is connected to the growing twig by a rounded stalk, the **petiole**. The petiole supports the blade and turns it to face the sun. A few plants, such as corn and grass, have no petioles. Their blades grow directly from the main stem.

The edges of a maple leaf are deeply notched, or indented. The parts of the blade between the notches are called **lobes**. Although the blade is lobed, it is all one piece. Scientists call any undivided leaf like this a **simple leaf**.

In some plants the blades are divided into a number of separate leaflets, or little leaves. Such a leaf is called a **compound leaf**. An ash leaf is a good example of a compound leaf. It

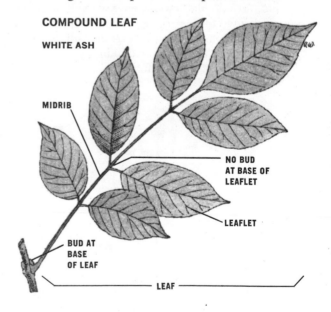

COMPOUND LEAF

WHITE ASH

MIDRIB
NO BUD AT BASE OF LEAFLET
LEAFLET
BUD AT BASE OF LEAF
LEAF

is made up of a number of leaflets arranged in two facing rows at each side of a **midrib**, or central stalk. One leaflet grows at the tip of the midrib. Some other kinds of compound leaves have no leaflet at the tip.

It is sometimes hard to tell a leaflet from a simple leaf. One way you can tell the two apart is by examining the base. Buds and branches develop at the base of a leaf. They never form along the midribs of compound leaves.

Warning: Poison

Before picking leaves for your collection, there are three plants with compound leaves that you must learn to recognize. If you touch their leaves (or any other part of the plant), you may get a blistering skin rash. The plants are poison ivy, poison oak, and poison sumac.

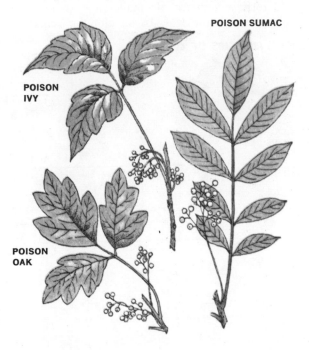

POISON SUMAC

POISON IVY

POISON OAK

Each poison-ivy and poison-oak leaf has three leaflets fanning out from the tip of the petiole. A poison sumac leaf has seven to thirteen leaflets.

Arrangement on the Growing Twig

On each kind of plant the leaves are usually arranged in a certain way. On apple trees, elms, and lindens, for example, the leaves are spaced out along the sides of the growing twigs. One leaf lies on one side of the twig, and the leaf above it on the other side. In other words, the leaves grow on alternate sides of the twig. They are called **alternate leaves**.

On other kinds of plants the leaves grow in

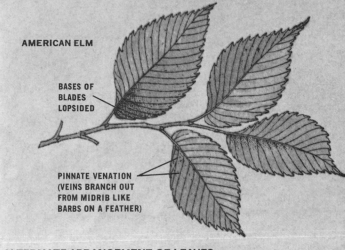

AMERICAN ELM

BASES OF BLADES LOPSIDED

PINNATE VENATION (VEINS BRANCH OUT FROM MIDRIB LIKE BARBS ON A FEATHER)

ALTERNATE ARRANGEMENT OF LEAVES

pairs—one leaf on one side, and the other leaf facing it on the opposite side of the twig. They are called **opposite leaves**. The opposite arrangement, like the alternate one, serves to keep any one leaf from completely shading another.

In still other plants three or more leaves grow in **whorls**, or circles, around the twig.

HORSE CHESTNUT

OPPOSITE ARRANGEMENT OF LEAVES

Shape and Size

Broad leaves come in many sizes, from leaves $\frac{1}{16}$ inch long to giant banana and palm leaves over 20 feet long. They come in many

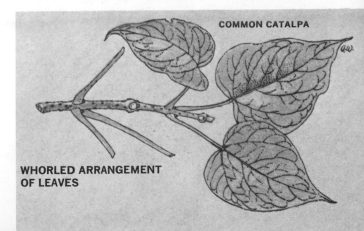

COMMON CATALPA

WHORLED ARRANGEMENT OF LEAVES

shapes, from almost perfectly round to long and narrow. The leaves of the common catalpa are heart-shaped. Those of the sweetgum are star-shaped. Other kinds of leaves may be shaped like eggs, baskets, or fans.

On certain plants, such as sassafras and mulberry, you may find leaves of several different shapes. For example, one sassafras may have both oval and mitten-shaped leaves. And some of the mittens may have a "little finger" lobe as well as a "thumb" lobe.

Edges

Holly and some other kinds of leaves have jagged teeth along their edges. The leaves of such plants as the iris and dogwood have smooth edges. Still other leaves have wavy or lobed edges. Some have rounded tips and some have pointed tips. Begonia and other leaves are lopsided—that is, they are wider on one side of the midrib than on the other. These differences are good clues when you are trying to identify a leaf.

Pattern of Veins

The arrangement of the veins is also helpful in identifying leaves. The veins usually stand out in ridges along the bottom side of the blade and sometimes along the top as well. In a maple leaf the veins fan out from the petiole and form a network of smaller and smaller veins through the leaf. In an elm the veins

SOME DIFFERENT SHAPES, EDGES, AND TIPS OF LEAVES

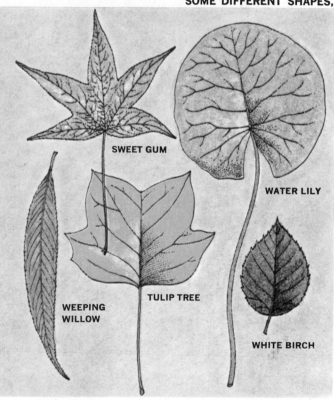

SWEET GUM

WATER LILY

WEEPING WILLOW

TULIP TREE

WHITE BIRCH

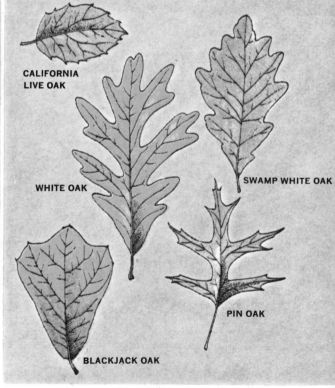

CALIFORNIA LIVE OAK

WHITE OAK

SWAMP WHITE OAK

PIN OAK

BLACKJACK OAK

THE DIFFERENT SHAPES OF SASSAFRAS LEAVES

PARALLEL VENATION OF PALM LEAVES

branch out from the midrib, like barbs on a feather. In palms, grasses, and other plants the veins run parallel to one another from petiole to blade tip. By examining each leaf to see whether the pattern of veins is parallel, featherlike, or fanlike, you have another clue to the kind of leaf.

▶ WHY DO LEAVES CHANGE COLOR?

In temperate regions in autumn, when days are warm and nights are cool, many plants lose their green color and take on brilliant hues of yellow, orange, red, and purple. During most of its life a green leaf produces food. Then, for reasons scientists do not completely understand, food production slowly stops. The substance responsible for the green color slowly breaks down. New coloring substances, which have been present but hidden by the green, appear. These substances produce the bright autumn colors.

▶ WHY DO TREES LOSE THEIR LEAVES IN THE FALL?

As the color turns, the cells across the base of each leaf gradually change. The petiole is weakened and finally separates from the twig. The leaf falls to the ground, where it slowly decays.

Just before or just after the leaf falls, a layer of cork forms and seals off the broken veins, thus protecting the twig. The cork forms a **leaf**

HOW TO MAKE AND KEEP A LEAF COLLECTION

Once you have identified a plant, carefully pick a perfect leaf for your collection. (Be sure to find out whether you need permission to pick the leaves.) Green leaves soon curl up and turn brown. If you want to keep them in a scrapbook, you must press them. For this you will need old newspapers and something heavy for pressing, such as books, bricks, or weights.

First, put several sheets of old newspapers in a layer on a table or shelf. Arrange the leaves on the paper so that they do not touch one another. Then cover the leaves with more newspapers. Put a board on top and weight it down with some heavy object.

Change the newspapers every day. Depending on the weather and the kind of plants, the leaves should be thoroughly dry in about a week.

Carefully mount the dried leaves on sheets of heavy paper. Arrange each leaf neatly on a separate sheet and fasten down the tip and the petiole with cellophane tape. Attach a label identifying the leaf and giving any other information you wish. These sheets may be bound in a loose-leaf scrapbook or placed in folders.

scar. In winter you can see a few corky dots where the veins broke off.

Many plants have a small supporting structure—the **stipule**—at the base of the petiole. When the stipule falls, it, too, leaves a scar. Its scar is long and thin rather than round.

Above the leaf scar you may see a new bud. Buds form during the growing season, just above the point where the petiole joins the main twig. In winter the bud remains closed up, protected by **scales**, which are a special kind of leaf. In spring, after a few weeks of warmth and light, the scales fall off and a new leafy twig develops.

This is true for most woody plants that shed their leaves. However, most plants with no

MAKING LEAF PRINTS

You can make prints of leaves in several ways.

One of the simplest ways is to make a rubbing of each leaf, as you would a coin.

Place the leaf, bottom side up, on a smooth, hard surface. Put a sheet of strong white paper over the leaf. Rub the paper with a soft dark-green or black crayon until you have a good print, showing the veins and margins of the leaf.

Label the sheet and put the rubbing in your scrapbook.

Here is another way to make a leaf print. Though it is somewhat more difficult, you will get very good prints with practice.

Fill a smooth, round bottle, such as a pickle jar, with cold water, and screw the lid on tightly. Smear the sides of the bottle with a thin coat of vaseline. Hold the bottle over a candle flame until it is thickly covered with soot.

Now place a leaf bottom side up on a piece of newspaper. Roll the sooty bottle slowly over the leaf. Be sure the leaf is evenly covered with soot.

Gently pick up the leaf and place it sooty side up on a clean newspaper. Cover the leaf with a sheet of paper. Take a rolling pin or clean round bottle, and roll it over the paper and leaf. You will have a print of the underside of the leaf.

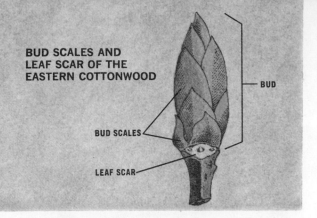

BUD SCALES AND
LEAF SCAR OF THE
EASTERN COTTONWOOD

— BUD

BUD SCALES

LEAF SCAR

trunks or branches die after each growing season. In some nonwoody plants, such as beans, the roots send up new shoots in the spring. In others new growth starts only from seeds.

Plants that shed all their leaves at one time are called **deciduous** plants. Those that do not shed all their leaves at one time are called **evergreen**. In evergreen plants—such as redwood, fir, or spruce—each leaf may grow for 4 or more years before it falls.

Most evergreen plants have narrow, needle-like leaves, although a few have broad leaves. Among the broad-leaved evergreens are rhododendron, holly, live oak, and sagebrush. The needles of some evergreens grow in **bundles**, or bunches. The number of needles in each bundle gives a clue to the kind of plant. In other evergreens each needle grows directly from a twig.

Whether attached separately or in bundles, the needles are arranged so as to keep one needle from shading another. The shape of the leaves also helps prevent this.

▶ **THE FOOD FACTORY**

All leaves, whether deciduous or evergreen, need light. They need light for energy to make food. Leaves are often called the food factories of plants. Sunlight keeps the food factories going.

In addition to light, leaves need certain raw materials. They get these materials in water from the soil and in the gas carbon dioxide from the air. Using energy from sunlight, the green substance in certain cells turns the raw materials into sugar.

In the process a certain amount of oxygen is left over. This oxygen goes into the air.

The process of food manufacture is called **photosynthesis**. The word is formed from two Greek words, *photos,* meaning "light," and *synthesis,* meaning "putting together." The green substance in the cells is called **chlorophyll**.

The sugar produced in the leaves is used by the plant in various ways. Some is used by the growing leaves. The rest is used by other parts of the plant.

A double pipeline of veins runs through the middle of the leaf. One pipeline carries water and dissolved minerals from the soil to the green cells. The other carries food materials to all parts of the plant.

Some food is stored in stems, roots, seeds, and fruits. Some is changed into materials for building or repairing cells. Some is "burned" to provide energy for these activities.

As the sugar is burned, water vapor and carbon dioxide are formed. These leftover gases are given off into the air. This is how it happens.

The food factory has walls—cell walls instead of bricks or concrete. A layer of cells

NEEDLELIKE LEAVES

BALSAM FIR
NEEDLES
ATTACHED
SINGLY

WHITE PINE
NEEDLES
IN BUNDLES
OF FIVE

PITCH PINE
NEEDLES
IN BUNDLES
OF THREE

SCOTCH PINE
NEEDLES
IN BUNDLES
OF TWO

REDWOOD
LOWER
BRANCHES

ALTERNATE
OR
OVERLAPPING
LEAVES

WHITE SPRUCE
NEEDLES
ATTACHED SINGLY

UPPER
BRANCHES

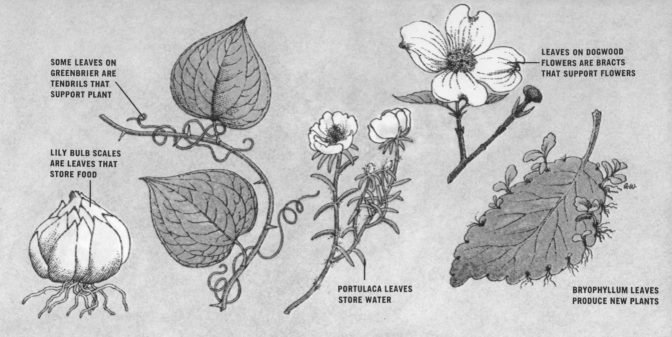

SPECIAL KINDS OF LEAVES

SOME LEAVES ON GREENBRIER ARE TENDRILS THAT SUPPORT PLANT

LILY BULB SCALES ARE LEAVES THAT STORE FOOD

LEAVES ON DOGWOOD FLOWERS ARE BRACTS THAT SUPPORT FLOWERS

PORTULACA LEAVES STORE WATER

BRYOPHYLLUM LEAVES PRODUCE NEW PLANTS

forms an **epidermis** (skin) around the outside of the leaf. Usually the epidermis is colorless. (If you are very careful, you may be able to peel a small portion off a living leaf.)

Gases move in and out of the food factory through small openings between certain epidermal cells. These openings are called **stomata**, a name meaning "mouths." The "lips" are a pair of **guard cells**. The guard cells are green, and their cell walls are thicker than those of other epidermal cells.

Using a small magnifying glass, you may be able to see some guard cells and stomata along the underside of a leaf. In general, leaves have far fewer stomata in the upper side than in the lower. Most tree leaves have no stomata at all in the upper epidermis.

The stomata open, close, and change shape, depending on various chemical changes in the guard cells. During the day the stomata are usually open. This allows the carbon dioxide needed for food production to enter, and leftover oxygen to pass out of, the leaf. The leftover gases from food burning also escape.

At night the stomata are closed, but small amounts of oxygen are drawn in and carbon dioxide and water vapor move out.

During the day, when the stomata are open, there is always a danger that a leaf will lose too much water. This is prevented to some extent by a waxy substance called **cutin**. The cutin covers the epidermis, protecting the inside of the leaf against drying out and against plant pests. In many plants fine silky or woolly hairs also cover the epidermis. The hairs collect rainwater and dew. In some plants they produce sticky or stinging substances that may protect the leaves against hungry animals.

▶ **SPECIAL KINDS OF LEAVES**

Certain leaves do not look very much like leaves. In some cases they do not carry on the work of food production. In the course of centuries of development most cactus leaves, for example, have become spines. These hard, round, thin structures no longer have green cells. They serve mainly to protect developing buds and keep off grazing animals.

Both leaves and tendrils of greenbriars and pea vines contain green cells. But the tendrils, which are a special kind of leaf, serve the plant mainly as supports. They coil around various things and so hold up the plant.

Other kinds of leaves support flowers, store food or water, and give rise to new plants. Still others, like those of pitcher plants and Venus's-flytraps, catch and digest insects and other small creatures.

Reviewed by WALTER SINGER
The New York Botanical Garden

See also FLOWERS AND SEEDS; PHOTOSYNTHESIS; TREES.

LEBANON

Lebanon is a small independent republic on the eastern shore of the Mediterranean Sea. Because the country is a crossroads between Asia, Europe, and Africa, its people have become good traders. Today Lebanon's capital, Beirut, is a strategic international air communications and transportation center. The natural beauty of the country has also made it "the playground of the Middle East."

▶ THE PEOPLE

The earliest known people in Lebanon were the Phoenicians. They arrived around 3000 B.C. and are referred to in the Bible as the Canaanites. Some Greeks settled on the coast and in the Bekaa plain after Alexander the Great conquered the region in 330 B.C. Then, in the 7th century A.D., Lebanon was conquered by the Arabs.

Today Lebanon is considered an Arab country, and its national language is Arabic. The country has a population of approximately 2,500,000. About half of the people are Christians, which makes Lebanon the only Arab country with such a large non-Muslim population. There are also several thousand Jews and about 90,000 Druzes, an Arabic-speaking group whose religion is a mixture of Islam and other faiths.

In addition to Arabic, most educated people speak either French or English and sometimes both. Syriac is used in some of the Christian churches. Over 75 percent of the Lebanese population can read and write. This literacy rate is much higher than that of most other countries in the Middle East.

Five years of primary schooling are required. Lebanese children attend either government or private schools. There are four excellent universities in the capital city of Beirut. The newest are the Lebanese University and the Arab University. The American University of Beirut was founded in 1866, and the University of St. Joseph, a French institution, was founded in 1875.

▶ THE LAND

Lebanon has an area of more than 4,000 square miles. From north to south the country

stretches 130 miles. Its greatest width from east to west is only 55 miles.

A narrow plain lies along its 140-mile coastline. In some places the plain is just wide enough for a road. The Lebanon mountains rise steeply from the coastal plain. The highest peak, Qurnat al-Sawda, is 10,131 feet high. The Anti-Lebanon mountains, on the Syrian border, are lower than the Lebanon mountains. Between these two mountain chains lies fertile Bekaa plain.

The Litani and the Orontes are the major rivers. The Litani River rises in north central Lebanon. It flows southwest across more than half the country and finally breaks through the Lebanon mountains and flows into the Mediterranean Sea. The Orontes River begins in the Bekaa plain near the town of Baalbek and runs north between the two mountain chains into western Syria.

Climate. Lebanon has a Mediterranean climate with cool, rainy winters and warm, dry summers. Temperatures on the coast average about 55 degrees Fahrenheit in January and

FACTS AND FIGURES

REPUBLIC OF LEBANON is the official name of the country.

CAPITAL: Beirut.

LOCATION: Southwest Asia. **Latitude**—33° 05′ N to 34° 45′ N. **Longitude**—34° 58′ E to 36° 55′ E.

AREA: 4,015 sq. mi.

POPULATION: 2,500,000 (estimate).

LANGUAGE: Arabic (official), French, English in commercial circles and government.

GOVERNMENT: Republic. Independent since November 22, 1943. **Head of state**—president. **Head of government**—prime minister. **International co-operation**—United Nations, Arab League.

NATIONAL ANTHEM: *Kullu na lil watan lil 'ula lil 'alam.* ("All of us for the country, glory, flag.")

ECONOMY: Agricultural products—citrus fruits, apples, olives, wheat, grapes, potatoes, tomatoes, barley, bananas, maize, figs, oilseeds, peas and beans, other fruits (plums, cherries, pears, peaches.) **Industries and products**—food processing, cement, oil refining, textiles, chemical and wood products, tourism. **Chief exports**—fruits, vegetables, paper and paper products, yarns and textiles. **Chief imports**—fuel, cereals, metals, textiles, machinery, vehicles, appliances, iron and steel products, chemicals. **Monetary unit**—Lebanese pound.

---

average about 85 degrees in August. It is cooler in the mountains, where the ground is covered by snow most of the winter. The mountains also receive more rainfall than other areas of Lebanon. Sometimes in late winter or early spring, a hot dry wind, called khamsin, blows in from the south. It raises the temperatures and brings unpleasant weather.

Natural Resources. Lebanon was once famous for its old and beautiful cedar trees. These trees became the symbol of the country and are shown on its national flag. Unfortunately, most of the trees were cut down in past centuries. Now they are seen only in groves where they are protected from further destruction. Today, Lebanon has to import nearly all its lumber.

There is little mining in Lebanon although deposits of iron ore have been found. Stone for building is an important natural resource.

▶ INDUSTRIES AND PRODUCTS

Trade is the largest source of Lebanon's income. Lebanon is the center for much of the buying and selling of the other Arab countries. This is one of the reasons Lebanese banks are world-famous. Another source of income is the tourist trade. The country's beautiful coastline and breathtaking mountains attract vacationers from all over the world. Today, Lebanon is famous for both winter and summer sports. Oil transportation also brings in a large share of the national income. Pipelines from Iraq and Saudi Arabia bring oil to Lebanese ports where it is loaded onto tankers for export. Small industries include textiles, cement, and food processing.

Citrus fruits and bananas are grown in the coastal plain. Apples, pears, peaches, grapes, cherries, olives, and vegetables grow on the lower slopes of the Lebanon mountains. Surplus fruit is exported to other Middle Eastern countries. Wheat and other grains are grown mainly in the Bekaa plain, but not enough is produced for local needs. As a result, much grain has to be imported.

Major Cities. Beirut is the capital, the largest port, and the commercial center of Lebanon. It has a population of about 700,000 people. The city grew around a good natural harbor, which was used in the past by Phoenicians, Greeks, Romans, and the Crusaders. At the end of the 19th century an artificial port was constructed, and the city began to grow rapidly. Today it covers several foothills of the Lebanon mountains. Its large international airport is located in an area of coastal sand dunes south of the city.

Tripoli, the second largest city and port, was originally a Phoenician colony. It has been an important trading center throughout the centuries. Today its oil refineries supply the country with gasoline and fuel oil.

▶ GOVERNMENT

The constitution of Lebanon provides for a president as the head of state, a Chamber of Deputies as the principal legislative body, and a prime minister as the chief executive officer. The president is elected by the Chamber of Deputies, and his term of office is 6 years. Members of the Chamber of Deputies are elected every 4 years by universal suffrage. Each Muslim and Christian sect is assured of representation in the Chamber. The executive powers are exercised by a prime minister appointed by the president. In practice, the

Downtown Beirut, capital and largest city of Lebanon.

president is always a Maronite Christian, the prime minister a Muslim of the Sunni sect, and the president of the Chamber of Deputies a Muslim of the Shia sect.

▶ HISTORY

In ancient times Lebanon was made up of several city-states, among which Byblos, Sidon, and Tyre were the most important. The Phoenicians, who founded a great empire, used these city-states as a base in the Mediterranean. At various times these states were conquered by Egyptians, Assyrians, Persians, and the Greeks under Alexander the Great. Later Lebanon became a part of the Roman Empire. It was during the Byzantine period that most of the people became Christians. In the 7th century A.D., Lebanon was conquered by the Arabs, and many Lebanese became Muslims.

Lebanon was occupied by French Crusaders from the 11th century to the 13th century. Then the Arabs drove out the Crusaders. Early in the 16th century the Arabs, in turn, were conquered by the Turks. In 1918 the British and French forces ended the Turkish rule of Lebanon.

After World War I Lebanon was placed under French rule as a mandate of the League

Above: The village of Becharre at the foot of snowcapped mountains. Below: The Hotel Saint Georges in Beirut, one of Lebanon's many modern hotels.

The Temple of Bacchus in Baalbek was built many centuries ago by the Romans.

Byblos, site of the ancient Phoenician city-state.

of Nations. In 1943 Lebanon achieved independence.

In 1958 the country faced internal revolt. Lebanon asked the United States for help, and 10,000 marines were sent. No shot was fired, and national peace was worked out later. Lebanon did not take part in the 1967 Arab-Israeli war. After the war Lebanon tried to maintain a moderate Arab position in the face of demands by Palestinian forces.

ALEXANDER MELAMID
New York University
Reviewed by THE PERMANENT MISSION OF
LEBANON TO THE UNITED NATIONS

LEE, ROBERT E. (1807–1870)

Robert Edward Lee was born at Stratford, the Lee family home in Westmoreland County, Virginia, on January 19, 1807. His father was the famous "Light-Horse Harry" Lee, one of George Washington's generals and one-time governor of Virginia. His mother, Anne Hill Carter, came from a family quite as famous as the Lees.

Robert attended school in nearby Alexandria and at the age of 18 went to the military academy at West Point. In 1829 he graduated second in his class and without a single demerit in 4 years. This was a record almost without equal in the history of the academy. In 1831 the newly commissioned lieutenant of engineers married Mary Randolph Custis, great-granddaughter of Martha Washington.

The 17 years that followed graduation from West Point were filled with routine engineering assignments. In the Mexican War (1846–48) Lee, now a captain, distinguished himself by his engineering skill and by his bravery on the battlefield. Then came several more years of routine service, the post of superintendent of the military academy, and command of the Department of Texas. In 1861 he was promoted to colonel.

▶ **A CONFLICT OF LOYALTY AND DUTY**

Then, when Lee was 54 years old and just about ready to retire, came the great crisis in his life. In 1861 the states of the Deep South seceded from the Union and set up their own nation, the Confederate States of America. When in April, 1861, Virginia seceded, Lee was faced with the most difficult decision of his life: should he stay with the Army of the United States or should he resign and go with his state? He did not believe in secession or in slavery. He was a soldier and the son of a soldier, and he had sworn allegiance to the United States. But he was a Virginian, too, his roots deep in the soil of his state.

Yet to Lee the question was a simple one. "With all my devotion to the Union," he wrote, "I have not been able to make up my mind to raise my hand against my relatives, my children, my home." To General Winfield Scott, commander of the United States Army, he said: "Save in defense of my native State, I never desire again to draw my sword."

It was in defense of his state that Lee was now called upon to draw his sword. He had refused field command of the United States Army. Now Virginia put him in command of all her forces, and Confederate President Jefferson Davis appointed him as his military adviser.

Lee was in Richmond, Virginia, the Confederate capital, when a Union army of 100,000 troops, under General George McClellan, advanced to the outskirts of the city. On May 31, 1862, the Confederate and Union armies locked in combat at the battle of Seven Pines. The Confederate commander, Joseph Johnston, was wounded, and President Davis appointed Lee to his place. Lee promptly gave the army the name it was to make immortal, the Army of Northern Virginia.

Beyond any general in American history, Lee combined qualities that make for military greatness. First, he had an almost unerring grasp both of grand strategy (the over-all military policy) and of tactics (the direction of troops on the battlefield). Second, he showed himself always willing to take the offensive and to take risks. Third, he displayed an astonishing understanding of what the enemy was up to; thus he was able to outguess and outwit the other side. Fourth, and perhaps most important, Lee inspired limitless confidence and devotion in his men. "He is the only man whom I would follow blindfold," said Stonewall Jackson. Lee had one other asset—a nobility of appearance and bearing. "He looked," said one Confederate general, "as though he ought to have been and was the monarch of the world."

Lee's immediate task was to save Richmond. His long-range task was to inflict such heavy losses on the Union forces that they would get fed up with the war and leave the

South alone. In a series of battles called Seven Days, Lee and Stonewall Jackson hammered McClellan's army and sent it reeling back. Lee's losses were heavy, but Richmond was saved. The whole Union strategy was thrown off balance, and there was a new spirit of confidence in the Confederacy.

Swiftly, Lee marched north. He caught a second Union army, under General John Pope, by surprise, and at Second Bull Run shattered the Union forces and sent them in full retreat to Washington, D.C. Now Lee decided to carry the war to the North. In September, 1862, the Confederates splashed across the Potomac River. General McClellan advanced to meet Lee with some 70,000 men. Lee had sent Jackson to capture Harpers Ferry, so his forces were smaller than McClellan's. The two armies met at Sharpsburg, Maryland, on a little stream called Antietam. All day long the Federals hurled themselves against the thin gray lines. As evening fell, Jackson's men came hurrying up from Harpers Ferry and saved the day for Lee. Yet it was not a clear Confederate victory, and Lee withdrew to Virginia.

Three months later a new Union commander, Ambrose Burnside, invaded Virginia. Lee moved swiftly to meet him near Fredericksburg and in a desperate battle gave him a terrible whipping. Next spring the Federals tried again under a new commander, "Fighting Joe" Hooker. In one of the most brilliant actions of the war, Lee met Hooker in the tangled woods called the Wilderness and rolled him back with heavy losses. It was Lee's greatest victory but a costly one, for he lost his ablest general, Stonewall Jackson.

▶ THE TURNING POINT OF THE WAR

Once again Lee prepared to invade the North. He crossed into Pennsylvania and ran into Union troops at the little town of Gettysburg. The battle of Gettysburg (July 1–3, 1863) was the worst fought of Lee's battles, partly because of mistakes by his generals. The result was a heavy defeat from which the Army of Northern Virginia never really recovered.

On May 4, 1864, the new Union commander, Ulysses S. Grant, headed for Richmond with an army of well over 100,000 men. With only 60,000 men Lee moved swiftly to stop him in the Wilderness. All month long the savage fighting went on, Lee outguessing Grant and stopping his advance. Altogether Grant lost almost 60,000 men, and Lee half that number. Yet The Wilderness was a Union victory. Grant could replace his losses, but Lee could not. Grant finally swung his great army across the James River to Petersburg and began to move on Richmond from the south. Lee hurried to meet him and halted him. There, in front of Petersburg, the two armies dug in for the autumn and winter.

By now the fortunes of the Confederacy were at low ebb. In February, 1865, Lee became commander-in-chief of all Confederate armies. But by then it was much too late for him to do anything effective. At the end of March, Lee decided that he must give up Richmond and retreat to the west. There he hoped to join up with remnants of other Confederate armies and make a last stand. As Lee hurried west along the Appomattox River, Grant pursued him. At the same time, Union General Philip Sheridan's cavalry raced ahead of Lee, blocking his retreat. Feeling that he could accomplish little more, Lee determined to avoid further bloodshed. On April 9, 1865, he met with General Grant at Appomattox Court House and surrendered what was left of his army. It was the end of the Confederacy.

▶ PEACE

"I believe it to be the duty of every one to unite in the restoration of the country and the re-establishment of peace and harmony," Lee wrote. He himself did his best for peace and harmony. In 1865 he accepted the presidency of Washington College (now Washington and Lee University) in Lexington, Virginia. He served as college president until his death on October 12, 1870.

Of all military leaders in American history, only George Washington can compare to Lee for qualities of spirit and of character. Honorable in all his actions, courageous and gallant in battle, patient in defeat, generous in victory, great in mind and in spirit, Lee belongs not only to the South but to the whole nation.

HENRY STEELE COMMAGER
Author, *The Blue and the Gray*

See also JACKSON, THOMAS JONATHAN ("STONEWALL").

LEEUWENHOEK, ANTON VAN (1632—1723)

One day in 1673 the Royal Society of London received a letter from Anton van Leeuwenhoek, the part-time caretaker of the Town Hall in Delft, the Netherlands. The learned members of the society were amused at receiving a letter from such a source. As they read on, their amusement changed to wonder. Leeuwenhoek was writing of a world no one had ever seen before. It was a world seen only through a microscope he had made.

The society encouraged him to write them more about his discoveries. This he did. For the next 50 years he continued to write. He told about the astonishing things he had seen with his microscopes.

Anton van Leeuwenhoek was born in Delft on October 24, 1632. By the time he was 22, Anton was married and owned his own dry-goods shop. A few years later he was appointed to his job at the Delft Town Hall. He ground lenses and made microscopes as a hobby. Later he gave up his dry-goods shop and devoted most of his time to grinding lenses.

Microscopes at that time were considered little more than scientific toys. The kind in use, the compound microscope, did not show things clearly. Leeuwenhoek made simple microscopes with only one lens. They were much better than the early compound ones. One of the amazing things about Leeuwenhoek's lenses was their size—about half the diameter of a pea.

Leeuwenhoek would spend hours peering through his tiny lenses. He looked at almost anything he could put under the lenses. He looked at the head of a fly, a piece of skin, a drop of rainwater, even the scrapings from his own teeth.

Leeuwenhoek discovered the one-celled animals we now call protozoa. He called them "animalcules" or "wretched beasties." He also discovered and made drawings of bacteria, but he could not explain what they were.

At that time people thought that certain forms of life came from air, mud, water, or decaying material. They thought life could even arise spontaneously—out of nothing.

But one day Leeuwenhoek examined some dirty rainwater under his microscope. In it he could see, as he wrote, "wretched beasties

. . . swimming and playing, a thousand times smaller than one can see with the eye alone." He was puzzled. Did they come from the sky?

To find out, he collected some rainwater that had just fallen. There were no "beasties" in it. But after several days some did appear. Leeuwenhoek correctly concluded that they did not arise spontaneously at all but were carried by dust in the air. After hundreds of such experiments he concluded that even the lowest forms of life must have a parent.

One time Leeuwenhoek looked at the tail of a tadpole through his microscope. He could see the flow of blood in the blood vessels. But he also noticed tiny, thin-walled vessels—capillaries—connecting the veins and the arteries. William Harvey, who had discovered the circulation of the blood about 1616, had not been able to see the capillaries because there were no good microscopes in his time.

In describing the capillaries, Leeuwenhoek confirmed the findings of the Italian scientist Marcello Malpighi, who had first seen those blood vessels through a microscope.

Leeuwenhoek lived to be 91 years old. He kept on working with lenses almost to his last day. He died in Delft on August 26, 1723.

DAVID C. KNIGHT
Author, science books for children

See also BIOLOGY.

LEGENDS

Myths, folktales, and legends are all closely connected and interwoven. Similar plots and characters occur in these three types of stories. However, myths are usually concerned with the gods and offer explanations of natural phenomena—for instance, how the wind or the oceans came to be. Folktales are mainly concerned with fictional characters that represent types—an old king, a wise man, a fool, and so on. Legends, on the other hand, tell of real people and places and often have a basis in history. Although folktales do not have to be set in a certain place, some are often connected with a definite locality. These tales form part of the folklore of that region.

With myths, legends, and folktales, it is sometimes difficult to tell where the stories of one type end and those of another begin. In tales about legendary heroes, gods and other divine beings often play important parts, either protecting or harming the hero. For example, in his wanderings Odysseus is aided by the goddess Athena and afflicted by the god Poseidon. Occasionally the hero himself is the incarnation, or human form, of a god. Rama is the incarnation of the Hindu god Vishnu. More often a hero is a god's child or foster child, and the hero takes on a trait of his father.

History

From the very earliest times men have told stories about great ones they admired. As the stories were told over and over, exaggeration crept in. The hunter who killed two wolves with his stone ax will later be held to have destroyed a pack. He who killed a serpent will become the slayer of a dragon. The warrior who defeated an enemy taller than himself will be remembered as a giant-killer. In time, as the real men concerned with these feats were forgotten, their deeds were transferred to someone else. Perhaps credit for the deeds went to some chief of the tribe. With so many feats to his credit, he became a superman. He was the hero of a whole group of tales. Even some of the myths would be retold with him in a leading role as a god.

Similar legends are found in places far distant from each other, and certain qualities of the legendary hero are met with time and time again. There are several reasons for this. First, people everywhere and in all ages have had a certain sameness of desires and interests. Second, as people have migrated they have taken their legends with them. Third, travelers moving from country to country have spread the tales.

As civilization progressed these stories became more elaborate. They pictured the ways of life of their tellers and hearers. They were handed down from generation to generation, each generation adding its share. On long winter evenings bards or scalds (tribes' poet-singers) entertained the chieftain and his warriors with tales. From these tales grew great epics and sagas—the *Odyssey,* the *Iliad, Beowulf,* the *Ramayana,* the *Volsunga Saga,* and others.

Why do legends change? With the spread of Christianity in Europe, the old pagan legends became Christianized. A clear example of this can be seen by comparing the *Volsunga Saga* and the *Nibelungenlied,* earlier and later versions of the same story. In the Middle Ages the code of chivalry also changed the tone of the legends. The pre-Christian Celtic tales about King Arthur were retold and romanticized during the Middle Ages.

At this time also, stories from the East greatly influenced European legends. Collections of Indian stories came to the West through Arabic and Persian translations. Returning Crusaders and warriors who had lived among the Moors spread the Eastern tales. The French romance *Aucassin and Nicolette* comes from a Moorish tale. Alongside old favorites, new tales continually sprang up around famous names and real people. This legend-making process continues even to this day.

The word "legend" comes from the Latin *legendus,* which means "to be read." Originally the term "legends" was applied to stories of saints and the miracles they performed. These stories were read in convents and monasteries at mealtimes. Some of these stories came from far older stories, dating from before the time of Christ. Some pre-Christian gods and goddesses have been absorbed into the persons of Christian saints. There is, for example, the Irish Saint Bridget. Her house burst into a flame that touched heaven, and when she took her vows as a nun a flame

Before the invention of printing, storytellers passed legends from one generation to the next.

shone above her. These stories come from myths about Brigit, the Celtic goddess of fire.

In time the term "legend" came to be used for any miracle story. Later still it described any traditional tale that was popularly believed to be based on history.

Subjects of Legends

Legends are supposed to be concerned with people who actually lived. However, legendary subjects range from the entirely imaginary hero to the real historical figure. Here are examples of several different types:

Manawyddan. Now a hero of Welsh legends, Manawyddan was originally a sea-god. He is an example of the gods who lose their deity when legends take over their stories and make heroes of them.

William Tell and Robin Hood. These two legendary heroes have no historical basis, in spite of efforts to prove that Robin Hood was the Earl of Huntingdon or one Robert Hood in the service of King Edward II.

Gilgamesh of Babylonia and King Arthur. These figures have a basis in history, but nothing is known of them other than the legends gathered about their names. The most famous of all legendary heroes, King Arthur was a British chieftain at the time of the Roman occupation. In the oldest legends concerning him Arthur is a semidivine warrior with poorly disguised gods as his companions. Gwalchmei (Gawaine) was a sun-god, Kei (Kay) was a fire-god whose nature was so hot that he remained dry in the rain and kept his friends warm by his presence.

Hruodland. Hruodland was a real figure about whom almost nothing authentic is known. All we know is that he was killed by the Basques in the Pyrenees, but he has lived on in legend as Roland, nephew of the Emperor Charlemagne.

Charlemagne, Theodoric, Attila, and El Cid. Charlemagne is one of the many historical figures whose deeds in legends are matched by his deeds in real life. Another in this class is

Theodoric the Goth, known as Dietrich of Berne in Teutonic legend. Attila the Hun is the Etzel of the *Nibelungenlied* and Atli in its Scandinavian version, the *Volsunga Saga*. In actual fact El Cid was a ruthless soldier of fortune who fought for both Moors and Spaniards. Legend presents him as a chivalrous champion of Spain against the Moors.

King Alfred and George Washington. Legends attach themselves to the names of some great men. There is the story of King Alfred's taking refuge in the hut of a peasant woman. Unaware of who her visitor was, the woman scolded and shouted at him when he failed to keep her cakes from burning. George Washington's hatchet, the chopped-down cherry tree, and "I cannot tell a lie" form the legend about America's first president.

Cycles of Legends

In the course of time many legends of different heroes have been grouped around one figure to form a cycle. Such has been the case with King Arthur, Charlemagne, Finn Mac Cool, Dietrich of Berne, and others. This sometimes results in tales in which the hero matters little. He is sometimes no more than a figurehead, as Arthur is in the adventures of many of his knights. This grouping together of legends can also bring about inconsistencies in story or character, when differing versions of a legend are combined into one narrative. For instance, in the *Volsunga Saga* Brynhild is a semidivine warrior maiden as well as the sister of King Atli. In the story of Lancelot, Elaine, originally one character, has become King Pelles' daughter and the maid of Astolat.

BARBARA LEONIE PICARD
Author, *French Legends, Tales, and Fairy Stories*

Four legends follow—one from France, one from China, one from America, and one from India. The French one tells of young Roland, nephew of the Emperor Charlemagne. The Chinese legend is one of many thousands storytellers have told in China for centuries. The American legend is told by the Umpqua Indians of the Pacific Northwest. The legend from India belongs to a series of legends about the rebirths of the Buddha. He was born in many different forms before becoming the Buddha, the founder of the religion called Buddhism.

▶ **ROLAND AND OLIVER**

In the days of the Emperor Charlemagne, Charles the Great of the Franks, who ruled France and Germany and fought so mightily against the enemies of Christendom, there lived a count named Girard. Count Girard held the city and the castle of Vienne and the land that lay about it, but he was no friend to his Emperor, and with his vassals and his knights he rebelled and made war on him. Charlemagne, much angered, called together his army and marched against Vienne, whilst Girard and his followers retreated into the city, defending the walls bravely. For many months the advantage fell to neither side, and time passed until the siege had lasted for two whole years, and many there were among the besiegers, as well as among the besieged, who longed for the war to be over. Yet the city could not be taken, so well was it defended, and Charlemagne, glad though he would have been to be at peace with all his subjects, could not bring himself to withdraw his army, lest it should seem as though he acknowledged himself defeated by a rebel.

With the Emperor's army were those who were considered the great champions of France: Duke Naimes, his most trusted counsellor, Ganelon, who later brought such sorrow on France, Ogier the Dane, Yve and Yvoire, Gerin, Engelier the Gascon, Turpin the Archbishop of Rheims, who could wield a sword in defence of his faith as well as any knight, Duke Samson and brave Count Anseïs: ten champions famed throughout France.

There, too, with Charlemagne was his young nephew Roland, son of the Emperor's sister Berthe. Roland had but lately been knighted and he was anxious to prove himself, yet so long as the siege lasted it seemed as though he would have little chance of showing his worth. The days went slowly for him, and with the other young knights and the squires he often left the camp and hunted in the woods near Vienne, or jousted with his companions; and among them there was no one more skilled at feats of arms than he.

Count Girard also had a nephew, Oliver, of an age with Roland; and one day, for an adventure, carrying plain arms, that he might be unknown, Oliver slipped unseen through the gates of Vienne and wandered into the Emperor's camp. Here in an open space he found Roland and his companions tilting together, and after watching for a while, he asked if he might join them. Though he was a stranger to them, they thought him one of the Emperor's men, and they lent him a horse and let him tilt with them. Soon it was apparent that Oliver surpassed them all. Not even Roland, who was accounted the best

among them, was more skilled with lance and sword.

The youths were loud in admiration of the stranger and asked his name, but he only smiled and would not answer. Then someone whispered that he might be an enemy, since in two years no one of them had seen him before. And the murmur went round amongst them, so that their friendly smiles were changed to suspicious frowns, and they crowded about him, demanding his name. Rough hands were laid upon him, but he broke free, and leaping on a horse, rode for his life towards the walls of Vienne.

'After him!' cried Roland. 'He must not escape. He is too good a prize to lose.' And the young knights rode after him swiftly with Roland at their head. Steadily Roland gained on Oliver, until he was upon him, and close beneath the city walls, Oliver turned to face his pursuers, and Roland, in triumph, raised his sword to strike. But at that moment there came a cry of terror from the walls above, and Roland looked up and saw a maiden, the fairest he had ever seen, standing on the ramparts, her hands clasped in supplication and her face pale with fear. It was lovely Aude, the sister of Oliver. 'Spare my brother Oliver,' she pleaded. And Roland, staring at her, slowly lowered his sword and

let Oliver ride on to the gates unharmed. 'I could not bring grief to so fair a maiden,' he said to himself.

During the days that followed, Roland thought much on Oliver and Aude, and wished that they had not been the Emperor's enemies. And for their part, they thought of Roland, and wished the war were at an end; and Oliver sought to persuade his uncle to peace.

After a time, his nephew's counsels prevailed, and Count Girard sent Oliver, well attended, to Charlemagne to ask that they might be accorded. 'If you will withdraw your army, sire, my uncle the Count will come forth from Vienne and swear allegiance, and he will serve you faithfully for all his life,' said Oliver.

But the Emperor, for all that he hated warring against his own vassals, could not find it in his heart to forgive Girard his rebellion so easily. 'Let Count Girard humble himself before me, and I will consider pardoning him,' he said.

'Sire,' replied Oliver, 'that would my uncle never do.'

'Then the war goes on,' said Charlemagne. But Duke Naimes spoke to him, counselling peace.

Oliver, standing before the Emperor, turned his head and looked at Roland and saw how he was watching him. He smiled and said impulsively, 'You and I are of an age and well matched. How say you, if our uncles are willing, shall we settle this war in single combat?'

'Gladly,' said Roland, and he begged the Emperor's permission. After thought, Charlemagne agreed. 'Go back and tell Count Girard,' he said to Oliver, 'that if you are victorious in this contest I will depart from his lands with all my army, and leave him in peace for ever. But if my nephew Roland is the victor, then must Count Girard lose Vienne and all his lands to me.'

'I shall tell him,' said Oliver; and he returned to the city.

And so it was decided that the outcome of the war should be determined by single combat between the two young knights, and a day was named upon which they should meet on a little isle in a river that ran between the camp and the city walls.

On the appointed day, Roland, armed and carrying his sword Durendal, which no blade could withstand, went to the islet to await Oliver. Soon Count Girard's nephew came out through the city gates, wearing the armour and bearing the sword which had been given to him by a good Jew of Vienne on the day he had been made a knight.

Eagerly all those from the Emperor's camp crowded about Charlemagne and the champions of France upon the bank of the river to watch the fight, whilst Count Girard and his family, and Aude with them, stood upon the walls of Vienne with the defenders of the city.

The two young men greeted each other courteously, and at once the battle began. They were indeed well matched, giving blow for blow; and at any one of their strokes a lesser knight would have fallen. Soon their shields were dented and their armour battered, links from their chain mail falling about them as they hacked with their good swords. But at last with a great stroke from Durendal, the strongest sword in all France, Oliver's blade was broken and he fell to his knees with the force of the blow. A cry of fear went up from the watchers on the walls of Vienne, but from the Emperor's knights a shout of triumph rose. Oliver thought, 'My last moment is come,' and he braced himself to meet the stroke which would end his life. But Roland flung Durendal aside. 'I cannot slay an unarmed man,' he said.

Oliver rose, and he and Roland tore up two saplings to serve them as clubs, and with these they continued their fight until the green wood was broken all to splinters. And then the young knights wrestled together, each striving unsuccessfully to throw the other, until, at midday, both locked in each other's grip, they fell to the ground at the same time, so that neither could be said to have thrown the other. They stood up, breathless and exhausted. 'The sun is high,' said Roland. 'It is too hot for fighting. Let us rest awhile.'

They took off their helmets and smiled at one another. 'I am happy,' said Oliver, 'that I am privileged to fight with so worthy an enemy.' And the two young men embraced and sat down upon the grass and talked together as though they had been old friends. Wine was brought to them from the city, and another sword for Oliver; and when an hour or two had passed and the sun was lower in the sky, they helped each other to arm again, and once more began their fight.

As before, neither proved the better, and for long the battle raged, until suddenly, stepping aside to avoid a blow from Oliver, Roland lowered his sword and said, 'Stay your hand awhile, for I feel a weakness come over me as though I had a fever, and I would rest.'

With courtesy Oliver set aside his sword. 'Rest for as long as you need, good Roland. I would not wish to be victor because you are unwell. Lie down and I will watch over you.'

Roland, who was merely feigning sickness in order to test Oliver, took off his helmet and lay down upon the grass. Oliver placed his shield beneath his head to serve him as a pillow and fetched water for him from the river in his own helmet.

Watching, Charlemagne thought, 'My nephew is vanquished and I have lost the day.' While from the walls of Vienne fair Aude watched with pity; for though her brother's cause was hers, from her first sight of him she had felt a great admiration for Roland, an admiration which she knew could very easily turn to love.

But Roland sprang to his feet and laughed. 'I did but try you, Oliver. And so courteously have you treated me that I wish we were brothers or friends, and not enemies.'

'Brothers we could be,' replied Oliver. 'If we both live through this battle, I will give you my sister for your wife, since there is no other to whom I would rather see her wed. And as for friends, are we not friends already in our hearts?'

They fell once more to fighting, and again the advantage lay with neither, and still they fought as the sun went down the sky and sank from sight. Through the twilight they fought, while the watchers strained their eyes to see them and could not tell one from the other; and on into the darkness, so that only the sound of metal clashing upon metal told that the battle still went on.

And then at last from the darkness there was silence, as with one accord they ceased their strife. 'Heaven does not mean that to either of us shall be the victory,' they said. And they threw down their weapons and embraced, swearing friendship for ever. 'Never again shall we take arms against each other,' they vowed.

Each of them persuaded his uncle to be at peace, and for love of them Charlemagne and Count Girard were accorded, uniting against their common enemies, the Saracens, who held all Spain and were attacking France. And on a happy May morning Roland and Aude were betrothed, to their great joy and Oliver's.

From the day of their battle Roland and Oliver were comrades in arms, riding together against the Saracens and fighting side by side, winning such fame that they were accounted amongst the champions of France, the foremost of the twelve. Roland was ever brave, brave to the point of rashness, and very proud, and he hated the Saracens with all his heart and never trusted them. But Oliver, though no less brave, was gentle and cautious and never set his own glory before the good of France. Many adventures did the two young knights have in the years they were together, and until the day they died they were never parted.

▶ THE LEGEND OF THE BLUE PLATE

China gave the world the first porcelain, and through the centuries her artist-potters have made porcelainware which for beauty of line and color has not been excelled or equaled by any other country.

Perhaps you have in your family one of those famous blue-and-white Chinese willow pattern plates which were so popular in your grandmother's time. And perhaps you have gazed at the sad, drooping willow trees, the quaint Chinese pavilions, and the beautiful arched bridge with the three running figures

on it, and wondered what all this means. There is a beautiful legend which explains it all.

Once upon a time, there was a noble Chinese mandarin who had a daughter named Koong-se, fair and beautiful as the moon. They lived in one of the pavilions shown on the blue plate. He wanted her to marry the son of a mandarin friend; but the maiden would not listen, for she had given her heart to her father's secretary, a handsome young man by the name of Chang.

Ah, love's course never runs smooth. . . . The angry father immediately had his daughter shut up in her chamber and dismissed the young man from his service.

The two lovers pined for and dreamed of one another. Out of her window the saddened maiden daily watched the drooping willows by the pond. One afternoon, over the water there came sailing a coconut husk, with a little sail attached to it, carrying a hidden letter. It was from the faithful Chang asking the weeping Koong-se to elope with him. The time was the next day.

In the morning Chang came as he had promised, and the two were soon running over the beautiful bridge for dear life. Yes, in the blue plate there are three figures on the bridge. . . . The third is the angry father chasing the eloping lovers!

Of course, they got away and married and were happy ever after!

▶ LEGEND OF THE WHITE DEER

In the early days of southwestern Oregon, the Colvig family, who had come west in a covered wagon, settled on land along the South Umpqua River. Near them was a small village of Umpqua Indians. One day, one of the white men killed and brought home a most unusual animal—a snow-white deer. When an old Indian neighbor saw it, he was distressed. "The man who killed that has a bad heart," he told the white family.

"Why?" they asked. (Both groups spoke in Chinook.)

"Because that deer is the angel of the Great White Spirit," said the old man, pointing toward the sky. Then he explained by telling this legend.

A long time ago, a dreadful sickness spread throughout the Umpqua tribe. Many of the people died. Few who had the illness lived. For many days and nights the sad death chant was heard in the tepees. Both young and old, hundreds of them, slept their last sleep.

At last the medicine men of the tribe decided what should be done. "We will leave our village," they told their people. "We will go up to the top of the Big Mountains. There we will be nearer the Great Spirit, and he will hear our prayers and our cries."

So the people took up their tepees and climbed to the top of the Big Mountains. The Big Water is just beyond the mountains. There in a mountain meadow they put up their tepees. But the death sickness followed them. It looked as if the whole tribe would be wiped out.

Then Teola, the chief's daughter, became ill with the death illness. Teola was loved by all her people. She was tall and straight as the arrowwood and as graceful as the willow tree. She was called the Little Mother of the Umpqua. All of her people grieved when the dreadful sickness touched her.

One dark night they thought that Teola would die. Around the fire in front of her tepee, the men of the tribe sat with their heads bowed and their hands clasped before them. Inside the tepee, the women chanted the death song as they marched round the bed of the dying girl.

Then a strange thing happened. A deer, white as snow, came out of the dark forest beyond the fire. Unafraid, it walked across the meadow to the people near Teola's tepee. Silent, wondering, the men watched the deer walk round the tepee three times. Each time it looked in at the dying girl.

The third time, the white deer entered the tepee, and the girl stretched out her hand toward it. The deer came close to her, kissed her lips, and then walked off into the darkness.

As soon as the white deer had gone, Teola rose from her bed and walked among her people. "I am well! I am well!" she called to them. "The angel of the Great White Spirit has kissed away my sickness!"

Since that time, my people, the Umpqua, have never killed a white deer. The white deer is sacred, to be protected and loved.

▶ THE MALLARD THAT ASKED FOR TOO MUCH

And it came to pass that the Buddha (to be) was born a Brahmin, and growing up was married to a bride of his own rank, who bore him three daughters.

After his death he was born again as a Golden Mallard, and he determined to give his golden feathers one at a time to enable his wife and daughters to live in comfort. So away he flew to where they dwelt, and alighted on the central beam of the roof.

Seeing the Bodisat, the wife and girls asked where he had come from, and he told them that he was their father who had died and been born a Golden Mallard, and that he had come to bring them help. "You shall have my golden feathers, one by one," he said. He gave them one and departed. From time to time he returned to give them another feather, and they became quite wealthy.

But one day the mother said: "There's no trusting animals, my children. Who's to say your father might not go away one of these days and never return? Let us use our time, and pluck him clean the next time he comes, so as to make sure of all his feathers." Thinking this would pain him, the daughters refused. The mother in her greed plucked the Mallard herself, and as she plucked them against his wish, they ceased to be golden and became like a crane's feathers. His wings grew again, but they were plain white; he flew away to his own abode and never came back.

LEGISLATURES

The word "legislature" comes from Latin and means "a body for proposing law." In other words, a legislature is a lawmaking body.

More than half the national legislatures in the world today are **bicameral**: that is, they are divided into two houses, or chambers—an

LEGISLATURES IN THE 20 MOST POPULATED COUNTRIES OF THE WORLD

COUNTRY	LEGISLATIVE BODY	HOUSES OF THE LEGISLATURE
Brazil	National Congress	Senate, Chamber of Deputies
China (People's Republic of)	National People's Congress	Unicameral
Egypt	National Assembly	Unicameral
France	Parliament	Senate, National Assembly
Germany (West)	Parliament	Bundesrat, Bundestag
India	Parliament	Council of States, House of the People
Indonesia	People's Consultative Assembly	Unicameral
Italy	Parliament	Senate, Chamber of Deputies
Japan	Diet	House of Councillors, House of Representatives
Mexico	Congress	Senate, Chamber of Deputies
Nigeria	No legislature at present	
Pakistan	National Assembly	Unicameral
Philippines	Congress	Senate, House of Representatives
Poland	Seym	Unicameral
Spain	Cortes	Unicameral
Thailand	Parliament	Senate, House of Representatives
Turkey	Grand National Assembly	Senate, National Assembly
Union of Soviet Socialist Republics	Supreme Soviet	Soviet of the Union, Soviet of Nationalities
United Kingdom	Parliament	House of Lords, House of Commons
United States	Congress	Senate, House of Representatives

upper house and a lower house. In most legislatures it is necessary for both houses to approve a bill before it becomes a law. This is not the case in the bicameral English Parliament, where only the House of Commons must approve a bill before it becomes a law. Some of the countries with **unicameral**, or one-house, legislatures are Austria, Finland, Spain, Portugal, and New Zealand.

In democratic countries the national legislature represents and expresses the will of the majority of the people. Members of legislatures are elected for different periods of time in different countries. The term of office averages between 2 and 5 years.

The world's oldest legislature, the Althing, was founded in Iceland in A.D. 930. The first modern legislature, according to many historians, was the meeting of the "Model Parliament" in England in 1295.

The name of the national legislature is not the same in every country. For example, in Japan the legislature is the Diet, in Canada the Parliament, and in Iran the Majles. The national legislature of most Latin-American countries is called Congress.

LEHMAN, HERBERT H. (1878–1963)

Herbert Henry Lehman was a man of three careers—business, philanthropy, and government. He was born in New York City on March 28, 1878, the son of a German immigrant who had prospered in the cotton business. Herbert attended private school and then Williams College in Massachusetts. Upon graduation in 1899 he went to work for a textile firm but devoted his free time to the Henry Street Settlement, a social welfare agency in New York City. In 1908 he entered the firm of Lehman Brothers, the family banking business. Two years later he married Edith Louise Altschul. They had three children.

With the outbreak of World War I in 1914 Lehman limited his business activities so that he could aid war refugees. In 1917 he received a captain's commission in the Army, and he was made a colonel in 1919. In the Army, Lehman helped supervise the purchase, storage, and distribution of supplies for the American Expeditionary Force (A.E.F.).

Lehman's political career was closely tied to that of Franklin D. Roosevelt. Lehman served as lieutenant governor of New York under Roosevelt from 1928 to 1932. When Roosevelt was elected president in 1932, Lehman was elected governor of New York. He was re-elected three times. As governor, Lehman supported labor reform, antidiscrimination laws, and social security.

In 1942, during World War II, Lehman became head of the newly formed Office of Foreign Relief and Rehabilitation Operations. His work led to the establishment of the United Nations Relief and Rehabilitation Administration (UNRRA). UNRRA provided aid to people uprooted by the war.

Lehman was elected senator from New York in 1949. He retired from the Senate in 1956 but remained active as a leader of the reform movement in the Democratic Party. Lehman died in New York on December 5, 1963. During his life he had contributed much of his fortune to charitable organizations.

LEMON AND LIME

Lemons and limes are citrus fruits with many uses. They flavor pies, puddings, frostings, candies, jams, and marmalades. They are served with fish and some kinds of meat. Lemon juice is used in salad dressings and in tea. Lemonade and limeade are popular hot-weather drinks.

Besides making many foods taste good, lemons and limes are good for health. For years sailors who went on long voyages faced the danger of scurvy. This was a dreaded disease that sometimes killed off more than half the men on board ship. No one knew the cause of scurvy. Then, in 1775, the famous

British explorer Captain James Cook (1728–79) took limes for his men to eat on a voyage to Cape Horn. He was one of the first to discover that limes prevent scurvy. Now we know that scurvy is caused by a lack of vitamin C, and that there is vitamin C in limes. From Cook's time on, English ships carried supplies of limes. Even today, "limey" is a slang term for an English sailor.

Lemons, limes, and citrons are citrus fruits, like oranges and grapefruit. Citrus fruits are native to southeastern Asia. Citrons (fruit with little pulp and a very thick peel) were brought to the Mediterranean area before Christian times. During the Middle Ages the Arabs brought lemons and limes into the area.

Columbus brought lemon seeds to the New World on his second voyage, in 1493. The seeds were planted on the island of Hispaniola, where they took root quickly and the trees grew vigorously. In the 16th century Spanish conquerers took the seeds to Mexico and Central America. The Spanish who settled in St. Augustine, Florida, in 1565 also planted lemon seeds. Portuguese settlers had planted lemons and limes in Brazil by 1540.

All citrus trees are evergreens with glossy green leaves. They have white or pink flowers. The skins of lemons, limes, and citrons are thick rinds that have many small glands filled with fragrant oil. The flesh of the fruit is pulpy.

The trees grow in hot, humid climates and also, when properly irrigated, in hot, dry climates. With a very good climate, lemon and lime trees bloom almost all the time. The fruit matures continuously through the year and is self-fertile.

Lemon and lime trees are expensive to care for. They must be carefully sprayed to protect them from insects and disease. They must be irrigated when the weather is dry. They must be protected against frost. Heaters and wind machines are kept ready for use at any time. Heaters are small oil burners that heat the air around the trees. Wind machines have fans that stir the air in the orchard so that the cold air does not settle and freeze the trees.

▶ LEMONS

The commercial growing of lemons was first developed in Italy. Many of the varieties known today have Italian names. Large quantities of lemons are also grown in Greece, Spain, and Turkey.

The first commercial lemon orchards in the United States were planted in Florida. The trees in these Florida orchards were destroyed in the severe freeze of 1894–95. The industry did not start again for 60 years. The early growers did not realize that lemons are more sensitive to cold than oranges are. Lemons must be planted in very warm, but not too humid, citrus-growing areas. The trees develop many diseases in humid weather. Since 1955 there have been new plantings of lemons in southern Florida.

In Florida lemons cannot be shipped as fresh fruit. This is because they ripen there in September, when lemons are no longer in heavy demand. The greatest use of lemons is during the hot months. Therefore, the juice of Florida lemons is made into frozen concentrate and stored until the following summer.

The lemon industry was set up in California in 1880, near the warmer coastal areas. Since that time the state has become the largest producing area of fresh lemons in the United States. In California lemons do not have to be picked all at the same time. The season extends over several months.

California lemons are carefully picked while they are still green by clipping the fruit from the trees. They are transported to cool, dry storage houses and cured for a long period of time. During storage the green fruits slowly turn to a beautiful waxy yellow.

In 1 year the United States produces an average of around 15,000,000 boxes of lemons (76 pounds to a box). Most of these are grown in the California-Arizona area. The Mediterranean area produces even more, averaging about 20,000,000 boxes a year. Lemons are also produced on a smaller scale in South America.

▶ LIMES

The lime industry has never been very large. Mexico is the leading producer and exporter of limes. In 1 year it produces over 3,000,000 boxes (80 pounds to a box). The West Indies and Egypt have lime orchards, but the fruits are chiefly used locally. There is a small lime industry in southern Florida.

The lime is more likely to be injured by cold

than is the lemon. Only the warmest and most humid areas can be used for lime growing.

There are two main varieties of acid limes. The most important is called the Mexican lime. It is a small, very sour fruit that grows on small, bushy trees. The other is called the Tahiti lime. It has larger fruit, from taller and lovelier trees.

Not all limes are sour. There are sweet limes, which are popular with people in Central and South America, India, and Egypt. Sweet limes have not been grown in Europe and the United States because there has been no demand for them.

▶ **CITRONS**

Citrons are used to make a candied peel. It is rarely used except in fruitcakes and some candies. Because they have a limited use, citrons are not commercially important. They grow wild in northern India, and a very few are cultivated in southwest Asia, southern Europe, and America.

A citron called ethrog is used as a religious symbol in the Jewish festival of Sukkoth, a harvest thanksgiving ceremony. The citron for this ceremony is raised on the Greek island of Corfu and in Israel.

Citrons need warmer weather than any other citrus fruit. The real citrus-type citron should not be confused with a watermelonlike plant of the same name that grows in the southern United States.

HARRY W. FORD
University of Florida Citrus Experiment Station
See also FRUITGROWING; ORANGE AND GRAPEFRUIT.

LENIN (1870–1924)

On November 7, 1917, a group of revolutionaries seized control of the Russian Government. Their success was due in large part to the efforts of one man—Lenin—who had long been working toward this goal.

Lenin was born Vladimir Ilich Ulyanov in Simbirsk (now Ulyanovsk) on April 22, 1870, one of six children of a middle-class family. His father was a school inspector with an honorary title as a hereditary nobleman.

In 1887, the year that Vladimir graduated from high school, his older brother was executed for taking part in a revolutionary plot. In the next few years Vladimir became interested in the theories of the German philosopher Karl Marx, who saw history as a class war between poor workers and rich employers. In 1891 Vladimir received a law degree from the University of St. Petersburg (now Leningrad). He never practiced seriously, however, for he was soon devoting most of his time to spreading Marx's ideas.

In 1895 Vladimir was arrested for his activities. He was sentenced to jail and then exiled to Siberia. There he completed one of his best-known works, *The Development of Capitalism in Russia*. When he was released from exile, Lenin went to Germany and Switzerland. He published a newspaper, *Iskra,* calling for the overthrow of the Czar. It was about this time that he began to use the pen name Lenin. During the following years he traveled throughout Europe, strengthening his position in the Communist movement. His supporters were called Bolsheviks, which means "majority group" in Russian.

When World War I began, Lenin called upon the working classes to turn the conflict into a struggle against the rich. In March, 1917, the Russian people revolted, forcing the Czar to abdicate. A provisional government took control. Lenin returned to Russia to unite the revolutionary forces. He issued his April Theses, calling for the transfer of political power to soviets, or councils of workers. Finally his followers seized control and established what they called a dictatorship of the working class. Actually, it was a dictatorship of a single party—that of the Communists. Civil war broke out between Communists and anti-Communists. In 1921 the conflict ended in victory for the Communists.

Until his death on January 21, 1924, Lenin ruled the Soviet state. His body lies in a mausoleum in Red Square, Moscow. Thousands of tourists visit the mausoleum every year.

Reviewed by BERTRAM D. WOLFE
Author, *Three Who Made a Revolution*

See also COMMUNISM; MARX, KARL; STALIN, JOSEPH.

LENINGRAD

Leningrad is a city that has known the storm and violence of history. At one time, when it was the capital of the Russian Empire, it was called St. Petersburg. Today it is named for V. I. Lenin, the man who changed the course of his country's history.

Leningrad lies at the mouth of the Neva River, which flows into the Gulf of Finland. It lies about 60 degrees north of the equator and is nearly as far north as Anchorage, Alaska. In winter the sun sometimes sets as early as 3 o'clock, and the days are very short, but in summer there is hardly any night at all. Then people like to sit in the parks until late in the evening or to stroll along the riverbanks.

From 1712 to 1918 Leningrad was the capital of the Russian Empire. Russian, French, and Italian architects designed its fine squares, broad streets, parks, and stately buildings. Czars and noblemen lived in palaces that contained hundreds of rooms. After the Russian Revolution in 1917 these buildings were taken over by the government.

The main avenue, the Nevski Prospekt, is lined with shops, apartment houses, and churches. The Nevski Prospekt opens into the great square in front of the Admiralty, a handsome building with a tall spire. The cathedral of St. Isaac with its high golden dome is nearby. Across the big square is the Hermitage, a world-famous museum. Next to the Hermitage is the enormous Winter Palace, where the czars lived until 1917. Behind the palace the Neva flows under some of the many bridges that connect different parts of the city. A bronze statue of Peter the Great on his horse looks across the river to the fortress of Saints Peter and Paul and the gilded spire of the cathedral inside the fortress.

Leningrad is a fine place for children. It has parks where children may play or watch a puppet show. The city also has an excellent children's theater, and there is nearly always a circus. One of the old palaces has been turned into the Palace of Pioneers for children. The building has workshops and studios, sports areas and dance rooms, and a theater where children produce their own plays.

▶ HISTORY

The city has had three names. It was called St. Petersburg until the beginning of World War I in 1914, when its German name was translated into the Russian, Petrograd. In 1924 it was renamed Leningrad in honor of V. I. Lenin (1870–1924), the leader of the Revolution.

St. Petersburg was founded in 1703 by Czar Peter the Great (1672–1725). When Peter

The Nevski Prospekt is Leningrad's main avenue.

Left: The Griboyedov Canal is one of the many canals that link different parts of Leningrad.
Right: A skating lesson in one of Leningrad's parks.

became the czar, Russia had no seaport except Archangel, a nearly useless port on the Arctic Ocean. Russia was far behind the rest of Europe in its development of art, science, and industry. Peter was determined to make his country equal to the other European nations. By making war on Sweden, he won some marshy land on the Gulf of Finland in 1703. In the same year he began to build his port city, which he wanted to be a "window looking on Europe." Although the land was often flooded and the climate unhealthy, he drafted peasants and prisoners to work for him and Russian families to settle there. So many workers died from disease that the city is said to be built on human bones. In 1712 Peter made the city his capital instead of Moscow.

Peter's successors developed St. Petersburg into an important seaport and industrial center. The court and the nobles lived in great luxury in their palaces, but the poor people and the workmen knew only poverty and misery. There were factories for shipbuilding, metalworking, and textile manufacturing. The workmen got very little pay, worked hard and long, and lived in miserable slums or in barracks near their work. This sharp contrast between splendor and misery was one of the causes of the Revolution of 1917.

In 1914, during World War I, Russia fought against Germany. Millions of men were killed, wounded, or captured in the war. And then in March, 1917, the people of Petrograd rebelled. They poured into the streets, asking for bread and peace. This was the beginning of the Russian Revolution. In March, 1918, Moscow became the capital of the country, and in 1924 Petrograd became Leningrad.

Leningrad's history has been dramatic and often tragic. In the summer of 1941 Nazi Germany invaded the Soviet Union, and in August its powerful armies besieged Leningrad. While the soldiers defended it, women and children and old people dug trenches and built fortifications. The city was besieged for 2½ years, but never captured. During the winter of 1941–42 it was blockaded for several months. There was no electricity, no heat, and no food except what was already in the city. Hundreds of thousands of people died of cold and hunger, but the living worked on in the factories—making arms, ammunition, and clothing for the soldiers. Children went to school and helped wherever they could. In January, 1944, the city was freed.

Leningrad is now busier than ever before in its history. The city's more than 3,950,000 people are proud of their bustling city and its flourishing industries: the manufacture of machinery, electrical goods, and chemicals, and shipbuilding. Leningrad's modern port, which is ice-free from April to November, is the most important in the Soviet Union.

ELIZABETH SEEGER
Author, *The Pageant of Russian History*
See also HERMITAGE MUSEUM; PETER THE GREAT.

LENSES

Thousands of years ago someone happened to look through a glass bead and noticed that it made things seem larger. The rounded bead was really a rough lens. Later, people found they could take bigger pieces of glass and give them a shape that would bring together the rays of the sun. Such "burning glasses" were used to start wood fires. Legends tell us that the ancient Greeks set fire to enemy ships by using large lenses in this way.

Still later, people learned that lenses could reveal unknown wonders. One of the first men to use lenses this way was Anton van Leeuwenhoek (1632–1723) of Holland.

Leeuwenhoek was a shopkeeper, but his hobby was the grinding and polishing of lenses. He used his lenses to build some of the first true microscopes. With these instruments he was able to make out details of plants and animals a thousand times smaller than anything the eye alone could see.

In a few drops of water from a puddle, he found a swarm of what he called little animals. (Actually, he was seeing what we call bacteria.) He looked at the tail of a tadpole through his lenses and observed the little threadlike blood vessels called capillaries. Leeuwenhoek's magnifying lenses opened up an unknown world.

Even before this, the great Italian scientist

Lenses are the most important part of a wide variety of instruments.

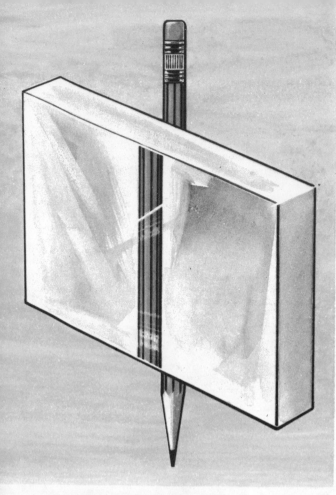

Figure 1. A pencil seems to be broken when seen through a thick plate of glass. This is because light rays are bent sharply when they pass from air to glass and from glass to air.

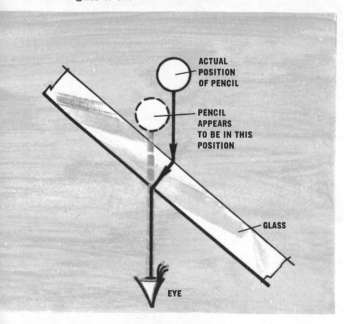

ACTUAL POSITION OF PENCIL

PENCIL APPEARS TO BE IN THIS POSITION

GLASS

EYE

Galileo (1564–1642) had put together lenses to build a telescope. He turned this instrument toward the sky and made several truly great discoveries about the sun, the moon, the planets, and the stars. Many of the things he found out about these objects in space were just as remarkable and unexpected as Leeuwenhoek's discoveries in the microscopic world. Galileo was the first to see the mountains and craters on the moon. He observed the dark spots on the face of the sun. He found several of the moons that circle the planet Jupiter. His discoveries had far-reaching effects on the beliefs of his time.

Lenses are usually the most important part of microscopes, telescopes, cameras, projectors, and a large variety of other **optical instruments**. The word "optical" means "making use of light." In order to understand how such instruments work, you must begin with a single lens. And even before that, you must recall certain things about light itself.

▶ REFRACTION OF LIGHT

Objects that give off light are called **light sources**. Light from a small source streams away in all directions, traveling outward as **light rays**. The light from a distant street lamp comes to you through the air. If all the air between you and the source is in about the same condition, the light rays will be straight lines. But if there are differences in temperature or in the amount of moisture in the air from place to place, the rays will curve slightly. In any case, as long as some rays get to your eye, you say that you see the source of light.

Besides being able to go through air, light can pass through many other transparent materials, such as water, plastics, or glass. Something special happens to light rays when they go from one transparent material into another. For instance, suppose you look at a pencil through a fairly thick piece of glass held at a slant. The part of the pencil behind the glass seems to be broken off and moved to one side.

The pencil, like anything else in the room, reflects light that it picks up from lamps or from daylight. When the reflected rays go into the glass, they bend sharply. And when they come out on the other side, they bend in the opposite direction (Fig. 1). This sudden change in direction of rays when they go from one transparent material into another is called **refraction**.

There is a simple way of describing how the refracted rays bend. Whenever a slanting ray goes from a thinner material (such as air) into a heavier one (such as glass), it bends sharply away from the surface. When a ray goes the other way—from a heavier material into a thinner one—it bends sharply toward the surface. If a ray does not come in at a slant but heads straight toward the surface that separates two different materials, it will go right through without bending. These facts about refraction are important in understanding how a lens works.

▶ LENS DEFINED

A **lens** is any piece of transparent material, such as glass, that has at least one smoothly curved surface. Cross sections of several kinds of lenses are shown in Figure 2. Some of the surfaces are curved outward and some are curved inward, and two of the lenses have a flat side. All these lenses can be divided into two groups. The first three shapes are thicker at the center than at the edges; they are **converging lenses**. The second three are thinner at the center than at the edges; they are **diverging lenses**. The word "converge" means "to bring together," and the word "diverge" means "to spread apart"—and that is just what these lenses do to light rays.

▶ CONVERGING LENSES

Figure 3 shows what happens to some parallel rays that are heading directly toward a converging lens. After passing through the lens, all the rays are moving in new directions except for the middle one, which keeps going straight ahead. All the other rays are refracted (bent aside) a little on going from the air into the glass and are refracted again in the same direction when they come out.

And here is the important thing that makes a converging lens very useful: it can send the rays toward a single point, called the **principal focus** of the lens. The distance of this point from the lens is called the **focal distance**. It depends on what the lens is made of and how the surfaces are curved. When you know the focal distance of a lens, you know a great deal about what it can do to light rays.

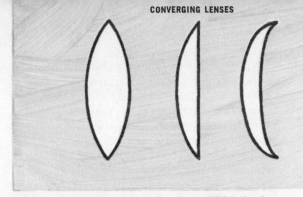

Figure 2. Converging lenses (*above*) are thicker in the center than at the outer edges. Diverging lenses (*below*) are thicker at the outer edges than in the center.

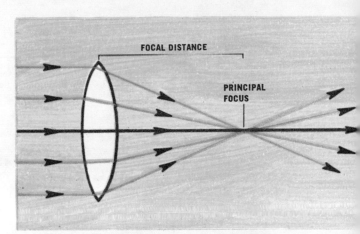

Figure 3. Converging lenses bring light rays together to a single point, or focus. When light rays travel in same direction as axis (center line of lens), focus is on the axis.

Figure 4. When light rays are not parallel to axis, focus is to one side of axis.

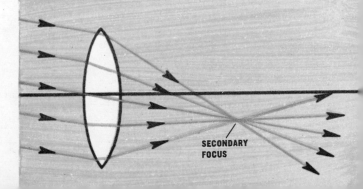

Rays coming from a very distant source are practically parallel, like the ones in Figure 3. A converging lens can bring them together to form a bright point of light. You can catch this point of light on a card held at the proper place behind the lens. If the card is not there, the rays simply go on and fan out again after crossing at this place.

The center line of the lens is called the axis. The parallel rays shown in Figure 3 are in the same direction as the lens axis. After going through the lens, they close down to the principal focus. What happens to parallel rays going in some other direction? They close down to another place that is a little off to one side (Fig. 4).

Any object, such as a tree or a person, is really a collection of many points, and each of these reflects light. A set of light rays coming from any one of these points can be gathered together again by the lens and sent to a certain place on a card held at the focal distance from the lens. The whole set of these bright points forms a light-picture of the object from which the rays came. Such a picture, which you see on the card, is called a **real image** of the object.

An ordinary magnifying glass is a converging lens. You can use it to form a real image of a lighted lamp on a card. Move the card slowly back and forth behind the lens until you see a sharp image. Notice that the image is upside down, as well as reversed from side to side. Figure 5 shows how this happens. Rays from the top of the object are brought to a focus below the axis. Rays from the bottom come to a focus above the axis. The same thing takes place in the sideways direction.

If the lamp is brought closer to the lens, the card must be moved farther away to get a sharp image. Instead of searching for the location of the image, scientists have worked out formulas that show in advance where the image will fall for any lens setup. They can also figure out how to shape a lens to give it a desired focal length.

▶ THE CAMERA

The setup using the magnifying glass and card is like a camera. In place of the lamp, there can be a person or a house or whatever you wish to photograph. The camera lens takes the place of the magnifier, and the film takes the place of the card.

In a good camera a combination of several lenses is used instead of a single lens to get a better image (Fig. 6). The whole set of lenses, firmly mounted in a metal tube, is called the **objective**. To focus a camera on a subject, the objective must be moved back and forth until

Figure 5. Image of bulb on card is upside down. Rays from top of bulb enter lens, are refracted, and focus below lens axis. Rays from bottom of bulb focus above lens axis. The same thing occurs in sideways direction. The focus is to one side of the axis, and so the image is reversed from side to side.

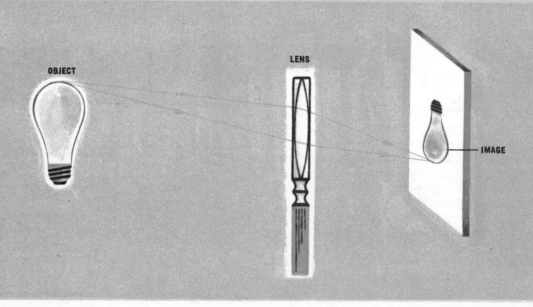

the image is perfectly sharp on the film. You cannot do this by looking at the image directly, because that would let light into the camera and expose the sensitive film. Instead, you use a distance scale marked on the objective, or a viewer or range finder mounted on the camera.

Some movie cameras and TV cameras are fitted with **varifocal objectives**. These make it possible to "zoom" in on a subject from far away, keeping it in focus all the while. This is done by moving some lenses of the combination back and forth, while the rest stay in place. The effect is the same as if the camera itself were moved toward or away from the subject.

In a camera objective, reflection of light from the various lens surfaces can be troublesome. Light reflected back and forth between the lenses may cause extra images and haze. To prevent such reflections, the lens surfaces can be covered with a very thin chemical coating. This sends most of the reflected light back into the lens, where it helps strengthen the image. If your camera objective seems to have a purplish color, it is a **coated objective**.

There is more to a camera than the objective and the film. A shutter lets light come through the objective just long enough for the image to register on the film. There is also an opening that can be changed in size to help control the brightness of the image.

▶ DIVERGING LENSES

If you try to do the lamp-lens-card experiment with a diverging lens, you find that there is no place where you can get a real image on the card. That is because a diverging lens spreads light rays apart instead of bringing them together.

Figure 7 shows what happens to parallel rays moving toward a diverging lens along its axis. After passing through, the rays fan out in a special way that makes all of them seem to be coming from a single point in front of the lens. This point is called the **principal focus** of the diverging lens. Its distance from the lens is the **focal distance**.

Other bundles of parallel rays, coming in at a slant with the axis, fan out in the same way after going through the lens. Each bundle seems to come from a different point off to one side or the other of the principal focus. A

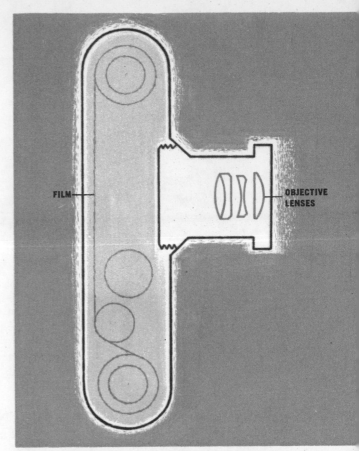

Figure 6. In many cameras a combination of lenses is used to give sharper images.

Figure 7. When light rays pass through a diverging lens, they fan out and seem to come from a focus in front of the lens.

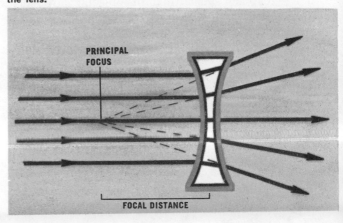

whole collection of such bundles, coming from various points of an object, forms a complete image. But this image is different in an important way from the real image formed by a converging lens—it cannot be caught on a card. For this reason it is called a **virtual**

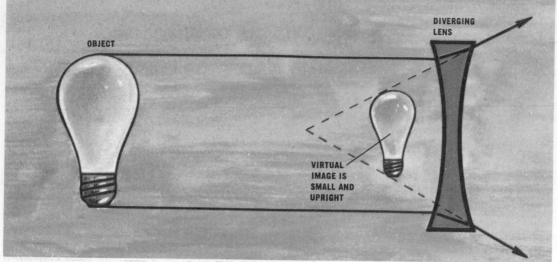

Figure 8. If you look directly through a diverging lens, you see a small upright image. Your eyes provide an extra set of lenses to bring light rays together.

image. This kind of image is only a collection of points from which the rays seem to come (Fig. 8).

Although a virtual image formed by a diverging lens does not show up on a card, it can be seen directly through the lens. That is because the eye furnishes an additional set of lenses to bring the rays together.

Look at any object through a diverging lens, such as one from a nearsighted person's eyeglasses. You will see a small, upright image. It seems to be located nearer to the lens than to the object itself. Diverging lenses always form virtual images that are right side up and smaller than the object. Figure 8 helps to show why this happens. Diverging lenses are almost always used in combination with other lenses.

▶ MAGNIFIERS AND MICROSCOPES

If you bring an object closer to a converging lens than the focal distance, you find that there is no longer any place where you can get a real image on the card. The reason is that rays from any point on the object have such a great spread that the lens cannot bring them together again on the other side. However, if you look directly into the lens, you see a much enlarged image of the object. This makes a converging lens useful as a simple magnifier.

Figure 9 shows what happens. Rays coming from any point on the object (here the wing of a fly) are refracted by the lens but still have a slight spread after going through. These rays seem to have come from a point that is located by extending the final rays backward. For example, in Figure 9 the rays coming from the

Figure 9. Converging lenses magnify objects placed between focus and lens. Light rays from object still have a slight spread after passing through lens, and they seem to come from a point behind actual object.

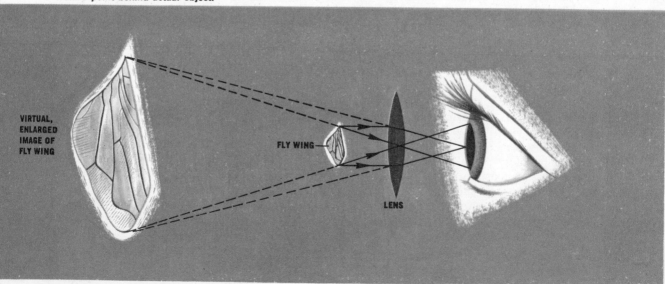

top of the wing can be traced back along the dotted lines to locate that part of the image. The same thing is true for the bottom of the wing and for all points in between. Your eye sees the complete image, which is virtual and enlarged. It is also right side up, which is convenient when the lens is used as a magnifier.

Leeuwenhoek's microscopes were simple one-lens magnifiers of this kind. In order to get better images and higher magnification, a combination of two converging lenses or sets of lenses must be used. A setup of this kind is called a **compound microscope**. That is the way all high-powered scientific microscopes are now made. Figure 10 shows how these instruments are constructed. A set of converging lenses of very short focal length is mounted at the bottom end of a tube. A second set of converging lenses, of moderate focal length, is mounted at the upper end. The tube can be moved slowly up or down by turning a knob. The first set of lenses forms the objective; the second set forms the **eyepiece**, or **ocular**.

To be examined, an object must be placed right under the objective. Then the tube is moved slowly up and down until the image is sharp. This image is virtual and very much enlarged. It is also upside down and reversed from side to side. It seems to be located some distance below the objective.

Modern compound microscopes used by biologists, geologists, and engineers can magnify things more than 2,000 times. This would make a single hair look as broad as the trunk of a tree. At high magnification only a small part of the object may be seen at one time.

▶ **THE TELESCOPE**

Telescopes are used to make distant objects appear nearer and larger. A **refracting telescope** has two sets of converging lenses, just as a microscope does. The important difference is that the objective system at the front end of the telescope has a very long focal distance, instead of a short one. As in the microscope, the final virtual image is upside down and reversed from side to side. This is troublesome for most uses of the telescope, and so a third lens is sometimes put in to make things appear in their normal position. A better way of getting this result is to reflect the rays back

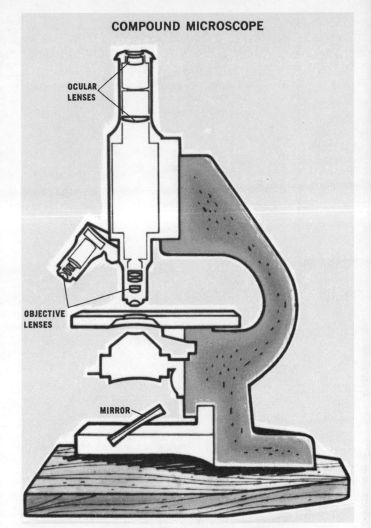

COMPOUND MICROSCOPE

OCULAR LENSES

OBJECTIVE LENSES

MIRROR

Figure 10. A modern compound microscope consists of two sets of converging lenses that can magnify an object more than 2,000 times.

and forth inside the instrument, using a pair of triangular pieces of glass, called **prisms**. At the same time this makes the instrument much shorter and more convenient to hold. A **prism binocular** is made up of a pair of such telescopes, one for each eye.

The biggest telescopes of all are the ones used in astronomy. These instruments must be able to take in enough light to make very faint or distant stars show up. This means that, in some cases, the objective must be several feet in diameter. It is very difficult to grind and polish lenses of this size because the surfaces must be accurate to within about one millionth of an inch. For this reason most of the very largest telescopes use a hollowed-out mirror in

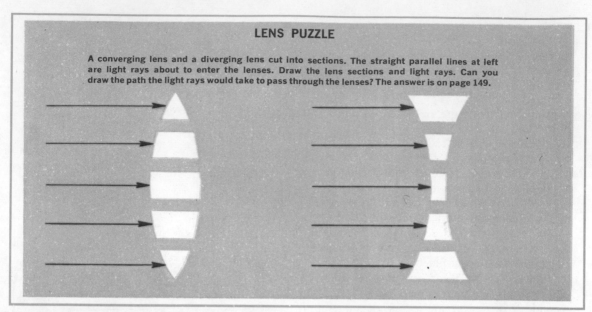

LENS PUZZLE

A converging lens and a diverging lens cut into sections. The straight parallel lines at left are light rays about to enter the lenses. Draw the lens sections and light rays. Can you draw the path the light rays would take to pass through the lenses? The answer is on page 149.

place of a set of objective lenses. Such an instrument is called a **reflecting telescope**.

▶ DEFECTS OF LENSES

No matter how carefully and exactly a single lens is made, it cannot give a perfect image. There are always shortcomings that prove troublesome under certain conditions. Such defects of lenses are called **aberrations**.

Rays going through the outer parts of a broad lens do not focus at exactly the same point as the rays nearer the axis. The result is that the image is not quite sharp, and this effect is known as **spherical aberration** (Fig. 11). The remedy is to block off the outer parts

of the lens by using a piece of metal that has a small, round hole in it. A better image is then formed because only the rays coming through the center of the lens are used.

That is what happens when you "stop down" the objective of your camera on a very bright day. Although this is done mainly to reduce the amount of light that comes in, it also cuts down spherical aberration. As a result, the image is sharper than it would be with the objective "wide open." However, if there is not much light, stopping down the objective would make the image too weak. Then the only practical remedy is to use lenses that have been ground to a special shape by

Figure 11. Light rays entering at the edges of the lens do not focus in the same place as the rays entering the center. This is a defect called spherical aberration.

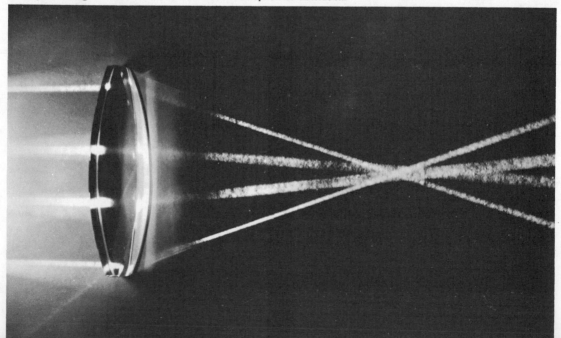

hand. Such lenses are expensive and are ordinarily used only in research instruments.

The images seen through a toy telescope or microscope often have annoying colored edges. This is another defect of lenses, called **chromatic aberration**. Ordinary daylight is really a mixture of all colors of the rainbow. When a ray of daylight enters a lens, the various colors in the light are refracted by slightly different amounts. Each color comes out again as a separate ray going in its own direction. Although the difference is quite small, it is enough to make the focal length of a lens noticeably different for each color. This means that there is no one place where all the colors come together to form a sharp image.

Chromatic aberration is often corrected by using a special combination of two lenses in place of one. One of the pair must be a converging lens made of a lightweight kind of glass. The other must be a weakly diverging lens made of heavier glass. Each lens cancels out most of the color-spreading of the other, so that the image is sharp and fairly free of color. Lens pairs of this kind are found in instruments of high quality. Sometimes sets of three and four lenses are used for even better color correction.

There are several other lens defects that an optical engineer must try to reduce or eliminate. In designing a new lens system, he may first make calculations to find which shapes and combinations will do what is needed. Then he traces some rays through the lenses on a large drawing of the setup. By such trials he finds a design that makes the lens errors as small as possible. The final test is to grind the lenses, mount them carefully, and try the system under the conditions of actual use.

▶THE EYE AND VISION

There is one optical instrument that nobody has ever been able to make. Yet it is by far the most important and useful of all. It is the eye. Your eye is like a color television camera because it can form images of things that are continually changing, and it can show them in their own colors.

Each eyeball is held in its socket by a set of muscles. The muscles can turn the eyeball, making the axis point in various directions. Figure 12 shows a cross section of the eye. Just behind the transparent front surface there

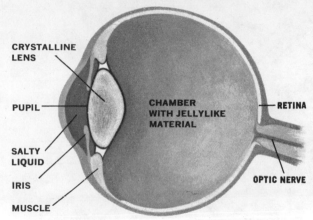

CROSS SECTION OF THE HUMAN EYE

Figure 12. The human eye is made up, in effect, of three converging lenses—the liquid behind front surface of eye, the crystalline lens, and the jellylike substance in main chamber of eye.

is a salty liquid. Next comes the **crystalline lens**, built up of layers of tissue. And behind this is the main chamber of the eye, filled with a thin, jellylike material. The liquid, the crystalline lens, and the jelly act like a set of three converging lenses. They form images on the inner back surface of the eye, which is

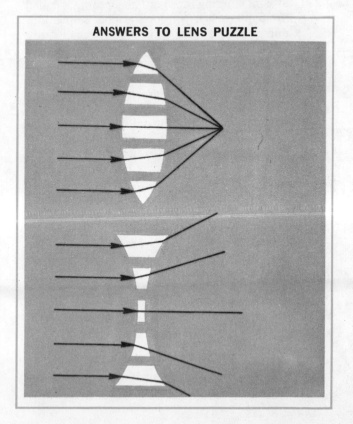

ANSWERS TO LENS PUZZLE

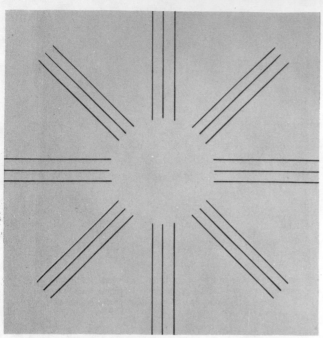

Figure 13. These lines will not appear equally clear to a person with astigmatism.

called the **retina**. From there, millions of nerves send sight messages to the brain.

Just in front of the crystalline lens is a small, round opening that controls the amount of light entering the eye. This opening is called the **pupil**. When you look at your pupils in a mirror, they appear to be black, because you are looking into the dark, inside part of the eyeball. The pupil is surrounded by two sets of muscles, which form the colored part of the eye. These muscles automatically change the size of the opening to regulate the amount of light entering. In bright sunlight the pupil may close down to ⅛ inch or less. In a darkened room it may open up to more than ¼ inch. In this way the pupil acts like the automatic "stop" on some cameras.

You focus a camera for various distances by moving the objective in or out. The eye changes focus in a different way. When you look at something nearby, muscles around the edge of the crystalline lens squeeze it up and shorten its focal length until the image is sharp. The muscles relax and let the lens flatten out again when you focus on a distant object.

There is a limit to how much the lens can be squeezed up. This **power of accommodation** allows a normal eye to focus on objects as near as about 10 inches without undue strain. With the help of a magnifying lens you can bring things much closer and yet see them clearly. The power of accommodation gets less as a person grows older, making it more difficult to focus sharply on nearby objects.

A **farsighted** eye is one that can give clear images of distant things but not of those that are fairly near. The reason may be poor power of accommodation. Or it may be an eyeball that is too short, front to back, for a sharp image to form on the retina. In either case the remedy is to use eyeglasses with converging lenses, to help bring the rays together properly.

Some eyes are **nearsighted** and cannot form sharp images of objects that are more than a few inches away. Usually this is because the eyeball is too long, front to back. This condition is helped by eyeglasses made of diverging lenses, which spread the rays slightly so that a clear image results.

Another quite common eye defect is called **astigmatism**. In this case the front surface of the eyeball is not evenly rounded in all directions. Look at the pattern of lines in Figure 13. If you have astigmatism, the various sets of lines will not appear equally sharp. One group will be clearer than all the others, while the group that crosses it squarely will seem fuzzier than the rest. Astigmatism can be corrected by using eyeglass lenses that are curved more in one direction than in another.

An eye may need correction for nearsightedness or farsightedness and for astigmatism at the same time. The two lens shapes that are needed can be ground into the same piece of glass. In recent years contact lenses have come into greater use. These are small, thin lenses that rest on the eyeball itself. They float on the layer of moisture (tears) that covers the eyeball, and are almost invisible to other people.

▶ WHAT YOU HAVE LEARNED ABOUT LENSES

There are two special ways that lenses can refract light rays coming from an object. A converging lens can bring the rays together to form a real image. A diverging lens bends the rays so that they all seem to come from a virtual image.

A real image formed by a converging lens can be caught on a card placed where the rays cross. It is always upside down and reversed from right to left. The image formed on the film by the objective of a camera is real.

Images formed by a diverging lens are always virtual. They are right side up and are not reversed from right to left.

The principal focus of a lens is the place where the image of a far-off object is formed. The distance of this point from the lens is called the focal distance.

Lenses can be combined to construct various optical instruments. The compound microscope uses a set of very short-focus lenses as an objective, and an ocular. The refracting telescope uses a very long-focus objective and an ocular. All these lens systems are converging. A prism binocular is really a pair of refracting telescopes. There are many other kinds of optical instruments.

Single lenses have certain defects, such as spherical aberration and chromatic aberration. These can be corrected by using only the center part of the lens, by using certain combinations of different types of lenses, or by grinding the lens surfaces to special shapes.

The eye acts like a set of converging lenses, forming real images on the retina. If an eye cannot focus sharply on nearby objects, it is farsighted, and a converging eyeglass helps. If an eye cannot focus sharply on objects more than a few inches away, it is nearsighted, and a diverging lens helps. Astigmatism results when the front surface of the eyeball is not evenly rounded in all directions. The remedy is to use an eyeglass lens that is curved in a way that makes up for these defects.

IRA M. FREEMAN
Rutgers—The State University
See also LIGHT; MICROSCOPES; TELESCOPES.

CONTACT LENSES

A contact lens is a small disk or cup of thin plastic that is curved to fit over the cornea of the eye. (The cornea is the transparent outer layer of the eyeball, covering the pupil and iris.) The shape and thickness of the contact lens are adjusted to an individual's eye in order to correct faults of vision.

For many years efforts had been made to develop corrective lenses that would be safe and comfortable when worn on the eyes. But a satisfactory design was not developed until 1948.

From the 1880's until the 1930's many different kinds of contact lenses were made. Some were of blown or ground glass, and later ones were of glass and plastic combined. Most were designed with an outer band that rested on the sclera, or white of the eye. But all of these early contact lenses were heavy and uncomfortable.

The first important improvement came in 1938, when contact lenses were made of lightweight molded plastic. In 1948 Kevin Tuohy, an optical technician in Los Angeles, California, made a further improvement. He introduced a contact lens that had no outer band. The lens was smaller in size than the cornea of the eye and was held in place over the cornea by the eye's own moisture.

Since 1948 smaller contact lenses have been developed. Modern contact lenses are about $\frac{1}{3}$ inch across and about $\frac{1}{125}$ inch thick.

Today millions of people wear contact lenses. Because these lenses can barely be seen, they have a special advantage for people who need glasses but do not like their appearance in them.

Contact lenses may be worn after cataract operations and to correct such conditions as nearsightedness and farsightedness, astigmatism (uneven curving of the cornea), and keratoconus (cone-shaped cornea). A single lens may be worn to cover a disfigured eye.

Many athletes wear contact lenses for sports, such as football and basketball, in which ordinary eyeglasses are unsafe.

To avoid their injuring the eyes, contact lenses should be fitted and checked by a qualified eye doctor. Fitting includes taking measurements of the curve of the cornea. Wearers of contact lenses should also be taught the proper way to insert, re-center, and remove the lenses. Because people's eyes—especially children's—change with time, contact lenses should be rechecked regularly.

Reviewed by MYER MEDINE, M.D.
Associate Attending Surgeon
New York Eye and Ear Infirmary

LEO XIII, POPE (1810–1903)

Pope Leo XIII was born Gioacchino Pecci on March 2, 1810, in Carpineto, Italy, to a family of the minor nobility. He received his education at Jesuit schools, where he proved himself a bright student with a gift for languages. He studied law and received his doctorate in theology before entering the service of the Papal Government.

In 1838, after serving a successful term as governor of Benevento, Monsignor Pecci was transferred to Perugia. In 1843 he became an archbishop and Papal Nuncio to Belgium. After a few years in this post he returned to Perugia as archbishop. In 1853 Pope Pius IX made him a cardinal.

On February 20, 1878, Cardinal Pecci became Pope Leo XIII. At once he took steps to improve the poor relations that existed between the Holy See and almost every government in Europe and Latin America. Especially difficult were relations with the Kingdom of Italy, which had seized the Papal States in 1870.

The new Pope soon proved himself a skillful statesman. His expert diplomacy met with much success. He helped to bring about the end of religious conflict in Germany and tried to get French Catholics to accept the new Third Republic as their lawful government. He arranged the settlement of a dispute between Germany and Spain over the Caroline Islands. Only in Italy, where he would not accept the loss of the Papal States to the new Italian kingdom, did his efforts fail.

Pope Leo XIII took a deep interest in the social problems of his day. Among the greatest of his contributions are his brilliant encyclicals, or papal letters. The most famous of these, *Rerum Novarum,* discussed social progress and the conflict between workers and employers. Leo upheld the rights of the working man. He revealed his approval of trade unions and laws designed to improve the lot of the laborer. Above all, Leo showed great understanding of the new ideas spreading throughout the Western world.

Pope Leo XIII was a generous patron of scriptural and philosophical studies. He opened the archives of the Vatican to historians from all countries. He took an especially friendly interest in the English-speaking countries and was the first pope to write sympathetically of democracy. He is generally regarded as one of the ablest of all the popes. His 25-year reign was one of the longest in Catholic history.

MSGR. FLORENCE D. COHALAN
Cathedral College

LEONARDO DA VINCI (1452–1519)

Perhaps no one in history achieved so much in so many different fields as did Leonardo da Vinci. An outstanding painter, sculptor, and architect, he also designed bridges, highways, weapons, costumes, and scientific instruments. He invented the diving bell and tank, and—though they could not be built with the materials of the time—flying machines. He made important discoveries about the structure of the human body.

From his notebooks we can tell that Leonardo approached science and art in the same methodical manner: after studying a problem, he made many sketches to help him find a solution. He saw no difference between planning a machine and a painting, and he became an expert in every field that interested him.

Leonardo da Vinci was born in the town of Vinci, Italy, in 1452. His father was a successful government official, and his mother was a peasant girl. Leonardo spent his early years on his family's farm. Free to explore in the fields and streams, he grew to love the outdoors. He had a keen interest in how things work. He bought caged birds in the marketplace and set them free. He did this because he could not stand to see birds in cages and also because he wanted to learn exactly how birds fly.

By 1469 Leonardo had moved with his father to Florence, where the young man was apprenticed to the painter and sculptor Andrea del Verrocchio (1435?–88). In the 7 or more years Leonardo spent in Verrocchio's studio he was especially inspired by his teach-

Self Portrait, drawn in red chalk by Leonardo da Vinci.

there. He painted court portraits, supervised pageants, designed costumes, built machines of war, and even installed central heating in the palace. He also supposedly played the lyre and sang to entertain the Duke and his friends.

While in Milan, Leonardo worked on his magnificent painting, the *Last Supper.* Because he worked slowly, Leonardo painted in oil on a damp wall instead of using the **fresco** technique (painting with watercolors on wet plaster). This experiment was not successful, and the painting began to peel soon after Leonardo's death. Although it is now badly damaged, it is still an extraordinary picture. By cutting out all unnecessary details Leonardo emphasized the drama of the event.

One of Leonardo's greatest interests was the study of the human body. At first, like other artists of the 15th century, he studied the outward appearance of the body. Then he became fascinated with its inner structure and dissected corpses to find out how the body was put together. His studies of the heart, in particular, were very advanced. Leonardo looked at plants as closely as he looked at men

er's imaginative sculpture. By 1472 Leonardo was listed as a master of the painters' guild. A few years later he painted such a beautiful angel that Verrocchio, his master, is said to have given up painting for good.

After this Leonardo's skill as a painter must have been known, for he painted an altarpiece, *The Adoration of the Kings,* for the monks of Saint Donato of Scopeto. The *Adoration* had a tremendous influence on younger painters. The Virgin Mary is shown in a large landscape. She and the three kings stand out among the many figures because of Leonardo's use of **chiaroscuro**—contrasts of light and dark. He made many drawings for this work. What we see today is only the first stage, for Leonardo left the painting unfinished in 1481. Leonardo often abandoned works, regardless of their state of completion. After he had solved a particular problem, he went on to other projects that interested him.

About 1482, Leonardo left Florence to enter the house of Lodovico Sforza, Duke of Milan. He performed a variety of services

Virgin and Child with St. Anne and the Infant St. John, by Leonardo da Vinci.

Model of a printing press, built from Leonardo's 15th-century design.

Leonardo's design (*right*) and a modern model (*above*) of a parachute.

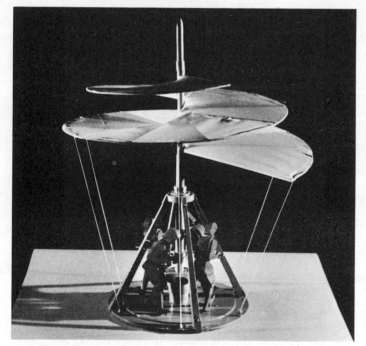

Leonardo's drawing (*right*) and a modern model (*left*) of a helicopter that he designed hundreds of years before a flying machine was actually built.

and animals, and he made many discoveries about plant growth.

Soon after he arrived in Milan, Leonardo began to write down things that interested him. His notebooks show the great variety and originality of his scientific observations. He illustrated his theories with very beautiful and exact drawings. By studying his drawings of machines, 20th-century engineers, with modern materials, have been able to build models that work perfectly. The notebooks are hard to read because he used mirror writing. He did not want his ideas to be stolen.

Leonardo's life in the court of Milan was

suddenly interrupted in 1499 by the invasion of the French Army. Leonardo's patron, Lodovico, was taken prisoner, and Leonardo fled to Venice. The next year he went back to Florence, still an active center of art. He was given a commission to paint an altarpiece for the church of the Annunziata. When his full-scale drawing of the Virgin and Child with St. Anne was placed on public view, people filed by for 2 days and admired it enthusiastically.

Leonardo briefly served Prince Cesare Borgia in Rome as a military engineer. In 1503 he returned to Florence, where he spent a few very productive years. The most outstanding and only completed painting of this period is his portrait of a Florentine lady, the *Mona Lisa*. This portrait is famous for the delicately painted features of the lovely face and for the rich **sfumato** ("smoky") effects of the mountainous landscape in the background. While in Florence, Leonardo was commissioned to paint a battle scene on a wall of the Great Hall of the Palazzo Vecchio. Again Leonardo experimented, this time with wax paint. The work began to melt even before he finished it.

It is said that Michelangelo wept and the city council was plunged into gloom. Leonardo was disappointed, but as a scientist he knew that to achieve success a man must expect some experiments to fail.

In 1513 Leonardo was invited to Rome by Giuliano de' Medici, a brother of Pope Leo X. There he continued his experiments. Sometime in 1516 Leonardo left Italy to become chief painter and engineer to the King of France. King Francis I gave Leonardo a château near Amboise, where he was free to carry on his experiments.

While in France, Leonardo became paralyzed. He had to stop painting, but his mind remained active. During his last years he received countless visitors, who listened with awe to the master's brilliant ideas about art and science.

Renaissance men set impossibly high goals for themselves. Leonardo da Vinci, the man who came closest to reaching all of those goals, died in his French château on May 2, 1519.

Reviewed by AARON H. JACOBSEN
Author, *The Renaissance Sketchbook*

LEOPARDS

Leopards are often considered the most dangerous of all the big cats. They weigh about 100–175 pounds and are some 7 feet long. But although smaller than lions and tigers, they are sly, savage fighters.

Leopards usually have yellowish brown coats covered with large and small black spots. Some leopards—the black panther of Southeast Asia, for example—are entirely black. (Leopards are known as panthers in some regions.) A litter (from one to four young) may have both black and spotted leopards.

Leopards spend much of their time in trees. From the branches on which they lie hidden, leopards leap on the animals that pass underneath. They may eat the animal on the spot, or they may store part of the meat in a tree and eat it later. Leopards eat a variety of animals—among them cattle, sheep, monkeys, antelope, dogs, and birds.

Leopards live to be some 20 years or so old. They are more common than lions or tigers and are found in a greater variety of places. They live in parts of Asia and in most of Africa. A few may still roam the Caucasus, east of the Black Sea in Europe.

Similar Animals. There are two other species of cats that are also called leopards. They are the snow leopard and the clouded leopard. They look like common leopards but differ in skull structure and in other details.

The snow leopard is about the same size as the common leopard. It is found in cold, mountainous areas of Central Asia. Its long, thick coat is grayish white, marked with broken black spots. These spots are larger and fewer than those of the common leopard.

The smaller clouded leopard lives in southeastern Asia. It is grayish yellow, with darker spots, stripes, and other markings. For its size, this leopard has very long fangs.

Reviewed by ROBERT M. MCCLUNG
Author, science books for children
See also CATS.

LESOTHO

Lesotho, controlled by the British since 1884 and called Basutoland, became an independent state on October 4, 1966.

▶ THE PEOPLE

Lesotho has a population of approximately 1,000,000. About half are Basotho, a people of Bantu stock. As Lesotho cannot yet support its large population, many Basotho must leave their country and work in the gold mines of the Republic of South Africa.

More than half the people of Lesotho are Christians. The rest practice local religions. A great majority of the children attend primary school. As a result 60 percent of the people can read and write. A university in Roma is shared with Botswana and Swaziland. The capital and chief city is Maseru.

▶ THE LAND

Lesotho has an area of 11,720 square miles and is about the same size as Belgium. The Republic of South Africa surrounds Lesotho. Its western region is a plateau that occupies about one third of the country and has an average elevation of 5,000 feet. The eastern two thirds of the country is mountainous and much higher. In the Drakensberg range, the highest peak is over 11,000 feet.

The climate is dry. On the plateau the average temperature is 60 degrees Fahrenheit. In the mountains it is somewhat lower. Annual rainfall averages about 30 inches. The heavy rains fall from October through April.

▶ PRODUCTS

About 1,000,000 acres are suitable for farming and grazing. The chief summer crops are maize, sorghum, and beans, while in the winter wheat and other grains are raised. Yields are low due to poor farming methods, so grain is imported from South Africa. Since soil erosion is a constant danger, dams have been constructed and hills terraced to stop erosion in many areas.

Sheep, goats, and cattle are grazed. A small horse similar to the Shetland pony is raised to transport goods and people. There are few industries. Wool from sheep and mohair from goats are important exports.

▶ HISTORY AND GOVERNMENT

The Basotho are descendants of several groups that moved into the mountainous area of Basutoland during the 19th century. These groups were united between 1815 and 1830 by Moshesh, a chief of great ability. By 1837 the Boers of South Africa reached Basutoland. After several wars with the Boers, Moshesh appealed to the British for help. Subsequently Basutoland was given British protec-

Basotho women wearing traditional "kobos," or blankets, in a post office in Maseru.

tion (1868). When the Union (now Republic) of South Africa became independent in 1910, Basutoland remained a British colony.

A general election to the National Assembly was held in April, 1965. Following this the colony became self-governing. In May, 1965, Prime Minister Leabu Jonathan and his cabinet took office. Britain retained control of foreign affairs, defense, and internal security until independence was granted in 1966.

After independence, some of Prime Minister Jonathan's policies were criticized. In the January, 1970, elections, the opposition party under the leadership of Ntsu Mokhelhe won over half of the votes, defeating Jonathan. Stating that he was fighting Communism, Jonathan declared a state of emergency, suspended the constitution, and jailed his opposition.

Lesotho's Parliament consists of two houses: a Senate and a National Assembly. All legislation is initiated in the National Assembly. The Senate can only amend bills and send them back to the National Assembly.

HUGH BROOKS
St. John's University (New York)

LESSEPS, FERDINAND DE (1805–1894)

Vicomte Ferdinand Marie de Lesseps was the man responsible for planning and administering the building of the Suez Canal. De Lesseps was also connected with the development of the Panama Canal. For many years of his life he was in the French diplomatic service.

Ferdinand de Lesseps was born at Versailles, France, on November 19, 1805. He was the son of a French diplomat who was very active in government affairs. His family was related to people in high government positions. His cousin Eugénie Marie de Montijo de Guzmán (1826–1920) became the wife of Emperor Napoleon III in 1853. De Lesseps was educated at the College of Henry IV in Paris. In 1825 he entered the French consular service. As a young man he served several years in Egypt.

In 1849 de Lesseps was sent as French ambassador to the new republican government of Italy. Then there was an election in France, and the government suddenly changed its policies. De Lesseps was recalled from Italy—in disgrace, because he had been connected with the old policies. He felt that he had been treated unfairly, and he resigned from diplomatic service.

In 1854, when de Lesseps was still without a position, he went to Egypt at the invitation of Said Pasha, an old friend of his who was the Egyptian viceroy. For many years de Lesseps had been thinking of the possibility of constructing a Suez canal. He had found the idea of a Suez canal in the memoirs of one of the engineers of Napoleon I, and it had struck his imagination. Said Pasha gave him the concession to build the canal. By 1858 de Lesseps had formed a French construction company and had raised much of the money he needed. The work began in 1859 and took 10 years to complete. The canal finally opened on November 17, 1869.

Later, de Lesseps was chosen by an international geographic congress to head a private company that would cut a canal across the Isthmus of Panama. Although de Lesseps was 74, he started the job energetically. But the problems of the project were greater than he had expected them to be. His bad temper and rigid thinking made the situation even worse. In 1889 the company dissolved, and de Lesseps was tried by the French Government for mismanaging and misusing funds. For political reasons he was given a prison sentence. But he was in such poor health that the sentence was suspended. De Lesseps went to his home, La Chênaie, in central France, where he died on December 7, 1894.

During his lifetime de Lesseps wrote three books about the Suez Canal. He was a member of the French Academy, of the Academy of Sciences, and of many scientific societies. For his efforts he was awarded the Grand Cross of the Legion of Honor by the French and presented with the Star of India by Queen Victoria. When he died he was well respected in spite of his difficulties with the construction of the Panama Canal.

See also PANAMA CANAL AND ZONE; SUEZ CANAL.

Philad.ª July 5. 1775

Mr Strahan,

You are a Member of Parliament, and one of that Majority which has doomed my Country to Destruction — You have begun to burn our Towns and murder our People. — Look upon your Hands! — They are stained with the Blood of your Relations! — You and I were long Friends — You are now my Enemy — and

I am, Yours, B Franklin

Reproduced on this page are three letters written by famous people. The top letter, sent by Benjamin Franklin to an old friend during the early months of the Revolutionary War, reveals Franklin's bitterness toward the British. The letter at the lower left is a comforting note of sympathy written by Abraham Lincoln to Mrs. Bixby, whose sons were killed during the Civil War. Franklin Roosevelt, when he was not quite 8 years old, wrote the letter at the lower right to his mother.

Executive Mansion
Washington, Nov 21. 1864

To Mrs Bixby, Boston, Mass,

Dear Madam,

I have been shown in the files of the War Department a statement of the Adjutant General of Massachusetts that you are the mother of five sons who have died gloriously on the field of battle I feel how weak and fruitless must be any word of mine which should attempt to beguile you from the grief of a loss so overwhelming But I cannot refrain from tendering you the consolation that may be found in the thanks of the republic they died to save I pray that our Heavenly Father may assuage the anguish of your bereavement, and leave you only the cherished memory of the loved and lost, and the solemn pride that must be yours to have laid so costly a sacrifice upon the altar of freedom

Yours very sincerely and respectfully,
A. Lincoln.

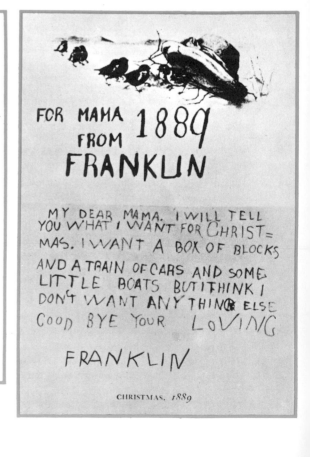

FOR MAMA 1889
FROM
FRANKLIN

MY DEAR MAMA. I WILL TELL YOU WHAT I WANT FOR CHRIST=MAS. I WANT A BOX OF BLOCKS AND A TRAIN OF CARS AND SOME LITTLE BOATS BUT I THINK I DON'T WANT ANY THING ELSE GOOD BYE YOUR LOVING

FRANKLIN

CHRISTMAS. 1889

LETTER WRITING

Letters help us to make friends and to get along well in the world. A letter can jet you across the miles for a visit with a friend or your family. It can say thank you or apply for a job or issue an invitation.

Letters are written for both personal and business reasons. It is important to know the proper form to use for each type of letter. Good letter writing can be learned. Some people write so well that they make an art of letter writing.

▶ FRIENDLY LETTERS

A friendly letter contains five parts: the heading; the salutation, or greeting; the body of the letter; the complimentary closing; and the signature of the writer. A friendly letter would look something like this:

> 9 Pinckney Street
> Boston, Massachusetts
> September 6, 1965
>
> Dear John,
> When I started this letter, I thought I had very little to tell you, but . . .
> You should have been here yesterday. Dad brought home . . .
>
> Your friend,

Heading

The heading has three parts: the writer's street address or the number of his post office box; his city, zone number, and state; and the date. Notice that very few punctuation marks are used—just a comma between the city and state and one between the day of the month and the year. If a zone number follows the name of the city, the comma comes between the zone number and the state. If a ZIP code number is used instead of a zone number, it should follow the name of the state.

Salutation

The salutation is the greeting. It tells to whom the letter is written. It begins at the left-hand margin and is followed by a comma. A letter to an adult might begin "Dear Grandmother" or "Dear Mr. Phillips." A close friend may be greeted with "Dear Ted" or "Dear Lucy." A letter to an entire family may begin "Dear Folks."

Body

The body of the letter gives the news. It has as many paragraphs as there are topics. The writer shows that he is changing topics by indenting the first line of each paragraph.

The body of the letter is of the utmost importance. It is you on paper. Reread your letter before you send it. Read it over first to be sure all your ideas are stated clearly and well. Then check for any errors in spelling or punctuation. Be sure, too, that your handwriting can be read easily.

Complimentary Closing

The complimentary closing is your way of saying good-bye. It must be right for the person to whom you are writing.

"Lovingly," "With love," "Your friend," "Your loving son (or daughter)"—these are correct closings for letters to people close to you. "Sincerely" or "Sincerely yours" is used for people you do not know well. "Cordially" is "Sincerely" with an extra dash of warmth.

Notice that the complimentary closing does not begin where a new paragraph begins. It begins just far enough away from the left-hand margin to give a balanced look to the page. A comma always follows the complimentary closing.

Signature

The signature is your name in your own writing. Even in a typewritten letter your signature must be handwritten.

Planning the Letter

Planning a letter helps you to remember what you want to include. Keep the plan simple—just a few topics, such as "The Family," "Fun at School," "Camping Out Last Weekend." Each topic will require at least one paragraph. Start with whichever topic would most interest the person to whom you are writing. Grandmother wants news about the family and about you. Your best friend wants to know what you have been doing and thinking. The news may be the same in each letter you write, but the arrangement and emphasis will differ.

Before you start, be sure to read over the last letter you received from the person to whom you are writing. It is always annoying when a writer fails to answer questions.

Writing the Letter

A friendly letter must sound like a lively conversation. A good letter writer tells about everyday happenings as if they were movies or plays. He puts in just enough description to make the reader feel he can see what the writer saw, hear what he heard, smell what he smelled, and feel the way he felt. The most exciting writing can be put into a letter. If you learn to write such a letter, your friends will look forward to hearing from you.

There are any number of ways to begin your letter. You can start right off with your first planned topic. Be sure to bring your reader into the first paragraph.

> Dear Bud,
>
>   I wished a dozen times last week that you were at camp with us. We had so much fun! But we'd have had even more fun if you had been there.

Or you can begin by setting a mood.

> Dear Janey,
>
>   I'm baby-sitting. It's twelve o'clock, and every sound sets my teeth on edge. If a branch creaks outside, I'm sure it's a burglar. If the wind knocks at the door, I stiffen with fright. That's why I'm writing to you. You never seem to be afraid of anything.

Never begin a letter with the weak excuse that you have not had time to write. Anyone could get a letter written if he really wanted to.

Try not to write a letter when you are in a bad mood. By the time the letter reaches its destination, your mood will have changed. And the letter certainly will not make the reader glad to receive it.

Make letter writing a regular habit. Long silences worry families and displease friends.

Addressing the Envelope

> Peter Martin
> 9 Pinckney Street
> Boston, Massachusetts
>
>   Mr. John Pond
>   R.D. 2
>   Jaffrey, New Hampshire

After you have written the address on the envelope, check it carefully. Is it legible? Is it complete? Write the return address, too.

Thank-You Notes

A fifth grader once remarked that the reason it was more blessed to give than to receive was that the receiver had to write the thank-you note.

Many people dread to write thank-you notes, but sometimes it is easier to say thank you in writing than in person. There are three simple steps to follow.

(1) Say thank you for the gift, mentioning something particularly pleasing about it.

(2) Explain, if you can, how you are going to use it.

(3) Chat a bit so that your ending will not be too abrupt.

>   416 Locust Drive
>   La Crosse, Wisconsin
>   October 4, 1964
> Dear Aunt Mary,
>   How clever of you to send me blue beads! I was planning to wear a blue sweater and a plaid skirt to the harvest festival next Saturday, and the beads will match perfectly.
>   Our harvest festival is going to be bigger than ever this year. We're having exhibits of farm products, arts and crafts, books, and flower arrangements. In the evening there will be folk dancing and games. You should be there!
>   Thank you again for your thoughtful gift.
>   Your loving niece,
>   Susie

Bread-and-Butter Notes. A bread-and-butter note is a must after you have stayed in someone's home. Begin by saying thank you and then mention the highlights of your visit. Probably you will also wish that your hosts may soon be your guests.

Mary Ann, her parents, and her brother, Mike, visited their cousins in the country. Afterward Mary Ann wrote to thank them.

>   134 Sandburg Drive
>   Chicago, Illinois
>   September 5, 1965
> Dear Cousins (all five of you),
>   We've talked about nothing since we got home except the wonderful time we had visiting your farm. I get so lonesome for the pony I dream about him. Mike is counting the weeks until next summer. He misses the cows the most.
>   Do come to visit us as soon as you can, though it isn't so much fun in Chicago.
>   Thank you for a lovely visit. You can tell I enjoyed it, because I gained two whole pounds!
>   Your cousin,
>   Mary Ann

Notes of Appreciation. Some people write notes of appreciation at Christmas or Thanksgiving or on a birthday. If you are a paper boy, you might write to your favorite customer. If you are a baby-sitter, maybe you have a favorite family. Perhaps a teacher has been especially kind to you. A doctor or nurse who took care of you or your camp counselor might appreciate a note, too. Even the president of the United States likes to get a note of appreciation.

This is a note a Boy Scout sent to his Scoutmaster.

> Box 19
> Stamps, Arkansas
> April 9, 1963
>
> Dear Mr. Burns,
>
> I want to thank you for giving me the courage to own up to breaking Mrs. Cox's window. I worked to pay off the damage, and now I have a regular job with her.
>
> You are a big help to all the Scouts in our troop. We may not show it, but we really appreciate all you do for us.
>
> Your friend,
> Charley

Invitations

Most invitations—to a birthday party or to a dinner at home or to spend the weekend—are informal. They can be written simply, telling the time, date, and place, and expressing the hope that the person being invited will be able to come. Some invitations—to a ball or a diplomatic reception or a church wedding—are formal. They follow a set pattern and must be answered in a certain way. For instance, a formal invitation to a wedding looks like this:

> Mr. and Mrs. Philip Clark Holmes
> request the honor of your presence
> at the marriage of their daughter
> Alice
> to
> Mr. Kent Amory Bond
> Friday, the ninth of June
> at four o'clock
> First Presbyterian Church
> New York

An invitation to a church wedding does not have to be answered, but if you are also invited to the reception, you must send a reply. Usually a small card is enclosed with the invitation.

> Reception
> immediately following the ceremony
> 525 Park Avenue
> R.S.V.P.

R.S.V.P. stands for the French words *Répondez s'il vous plaît,* meaning "Please reply." Your reply should be written by hand on the first page of a folded sheet of note paper. Space the words just the way they are in the invitation.

> Miss Melissa Hopkins
> accepts with pleasure
> Mr. and Mrs. Philip Clark Holmes's
> kind invitation for
> Friday, the ninth of June

If you cannot attend, the second line should say "regrets that she is unable to accept." In most cases it is courteous to mention your reason for not being able to attend.

Get-Well Notes

A get-well note to someone who is sick should be cheerful. Here is the way Richard began one to his friend Al:

> Hi, Pal!
>
> Hurry up and get those bones knitted or crocheted or whatever. School is dead without you. We haven't had a laugh in a week. The girls are all looking sad.

Sympathy Notes

Sooner or later a friend of yours may lose a grandparent or some other loved one, and you will want to say how sorry you are. Your note should express sympathy without making your friend feel any worse.

> Box 17
> Putney, Vermont
> May 10, 1966
>
> Dear Sue,
>
> Mother read in the paper last night about your Aunt Mary. I know you and your family will miss her very much. I remember how glad you always were when she came for a visit.
>
> Come to see us if you can and stay awhile. We should love to have you.
>
> Your friend,
> Verne

Pen-Pal Letters

Many people have discovered that it is fun to write to someone in another part of the world. They call themselves pen pals. Their letters help them to understand the way people in other countries live and think. Your school or your local newspaper can probably help you to find a pen pal.

In your first pen-pal letter you will want to introduce the members of your family to your new friend. Try to make a word portrait of each one.

As you get acquainted you can share experiences and future plans. A pen-pal letter is a sharing between friends.

5120 English Street
Madison, Wisconsin
October 6, 1964

Dear José,

I am so happy to write to a boy who lives in Argentina. My sister Ann studies Spanish in high school and she has promised to help me write to you in Spanish.

If we are going to be pen pals, you must meet my family. They are all here in the living room. The slightly bald man in the leather chair, reading his newspaper, is my father, Charles Clarke. He's the manager of a large department store in Madison. He looks quite severe right now, but he's really not.

Mom is pretty and full of life. She's always working at something. Tonight she's patching the trousers I tore at the ball game yesterday.

Ann is doing her homework at the desk. She has red hair and is quite vain about her looks.

The little boy asleep in front of the television set is Lonny, my 7-year-old brother. The only time he's quiet is when he's asleep.

I'm in the sixth grade at school. I like math and physical education best of all.

I hope you will answer my letter and tell me about your family and life in Argentina.

Your new friend,
Chester

▶ BUSINESS LETTERS

From time to time you will need to write a business letter. You may want to order something or apply for a job or request information.

A business letter has six parts. It has the same five parts as a friendly letter, plus an inside address. This is the same as the address put on the envelope. The salutation is followed by a colon instead of a comma, and the complimentary closing is more formal. Your name should be typed below your handwritten signature to be sure it can be read.

The letter should be typed or written carefully. Read it over to check the spelling, grammar, and punctuation. Keep the letter short, but give all the necessary information.

Here are some sample business letters.

130 West 57th Street
New York, New York
July 8, 1965

Jones and Company
2468 Church Avenue
St. Louis, Missouri

Dear Sirs:

Please send me the model kit #5905 advertised in your spring and summer catalogue. I am enclosing a check for $2.95 in payment.

Very truly yours,
Barbara Effron
Barbara Effron

362 Ash Avenue
Milford, Connecticut
June 3, 1964

Mr. Thomas Cook
Farm Machines, Inc.
28 Main Street
Milford, Connecticut

Dear Mr. Cook:

Your advertisement in this morning's *Courier* interests me very much. I am 15 years old and a sophomore at Winchester High School. Last summer I worked as a stock boy in the parts department of a large garage. The experience would help me in the stock job you have open.

If you wish to arrange an interview, I could come to your office any day after 3 o'clock. School closes on June 21.

Respectfully yours,
Jay Bennett
Jay Bennett

19 Cotswold Close
Singapore 10, Malaysia
April 19, 1965

United Nations Information Office
United Nations Secretariat Building
United Nations Plaza
New York, N.Y. 10017

Dear Sirs:

Our class in school is preparing a program on the activities of the United Nations. We plan to make a chart of the different member organizations and present dramatizations of the work they do. We should appreciate any information you can send us.

Thank you for your assistance.

Yours truly,
Nancy Ferguson
Nancy Ferguson

Your library has collections of letters written by famous people. They will help you see how important a letter can be.

MAUREE APPLEGATE
Wisconsin State College at La Crosse

LEWIS, JOHN L. (1880–1969)

John Llewellyn Lewis, one of the most powerful labor leaders in the United States, was the son of an immigrant Welsh coal miner. Born in Lucas, Iowa, on February 12, 1880, Lewis left school after the 7th grade to help support his family by working in the mines. At the age of 21 he traveled widely throughout the western states working at various jobs. Lewis married Myrta Edith Bell, a former schoolteacher. Mrs. Lewis has been credited with directing her husband's reading and helping him to rise to the top as a labor organizer. The couple had two children, John and Kathryn. Kathryn served for many years as her father's secretary.

In 1906 Lewis was chosen a delegate to the national convention of the United Mine Workers of America. During the years that followed, he held many posts in both the U.M.W. and the American Federation of Labor (AFL). In 1920 he became president of the mine union and served in that post until 1960, when he took the title of president emeritus. In 1935 Lewis played a leading part in the creation of a new kind of labor organization called the Committee for Industrial Organization, known today as the Congress of Industrial Organizations (CIO). This group differs from earlier federations in that it is set up along industry, rather than trade, lines.

Lewis was sometimes criticized by other labor leaders and the public for what seemed to be his ruthless methods. During World War II, for example, Lewis called four major strikes in the coalfields. Charged with disrupting American industry when strikes were prohibited, he defended himself by pointing to the gains he had made for the miners.

Lewis was a tireless fighter for the rights of the worker. Under his direction unions in the steel and automobile industries were organized. His persuasive powers as a bargainer won for the workers higher wages, better conditions, and many other benefits. One of his great assets was his gift of oratory. With his great, booming voice, eloquent phrases, and shaggy hair, Lewis was often called "the roaring lion of labor." He died on June 11, 1969, at the age of 89.

See also LABOR.

LEWIS, SINCLAIR (1885–1951)

The novels of Sinclair Lewis pictured life in the American Middle West for readers all over the world. One of his novels, *Babbitt,* brought him the Nobel prize for literature in 1930. Lewis was the first American to receive it.

He was born in Sauk Centre, Minnesota, on February 7, 1885. A lonely, awkward, pimply, red-haired boy, he spent most of his time reading. When he was in his teens, he began writing verses.

After two terms at Oberlin Academy he entered Yale in 1903. He wrote stories and poems for the college literary magazines and became an editor in his junior year. He also wrote for the New Haven *Journal and Courier* and spent two summers working on cattle boats going to England. In his senior year he left Yale and got a job in New York as assistant editor of a magazine called *Transatlantic Tales.* He then went to Panama to work on the canal but did not find a job. He returned to Yale and graduated in 1908.

He worked in various parts of the country before taking a job reading manuscripts for Frederick A. Stokes Company in New York. After his first novel, *Our Mr. Wrenn,* was published in 1914, he became an editor for George H. Doran Company. He left in 1916 when enough of his writing had been published to make him feel he could work independently. He was married to Grace Hegger in 1914 and divorced in 1928.

The publication of *Main Street* in 1920 caused a sensation. It was followed by *Babbitt* (1922), *Arrowsmith* (1925), *Elmer Gantry* (1927), and *Dodsworth* (1929). All of them portrayed in detail a particular side of American life and angered those who felt they were being attacked. Most of Lewis' other books were not of the same high quality.

In 1928 Lewis married the writer Dorothy Thompson. They were divorced in 1942. Lewis spent most of his later years in Europe. He died in Rome on January 10, 1951.

LEWIS AND CLARK EXPEDITION

When Thomas Jefferson (1743–1826) became president of the United States in 1801, he set about making an old dream come true. This was a dream of sending an expedition to explore the little-known territory west of the Mississippi River.

Between 1783 and 1792 Jefferson had encouraged plans for three such expeditions. Each had ended in failure. In January, 1803, he asked Congress for $2,500 to pay for an expedition that might journey as far as the Pacific Ocean. The request and its approval were kept secret because most of the region to be explored still belonged to France. This vast area, lying between the Mississippi River and the Rocky Mountains, was called Louisiana in honor of Louis XIV of France.

Jefferson hoped for many results from western exploration. He wished to open the territory to the American fur trade. Russian and British fur traders had already established a foothold in the region known as the Oregon Country. Jefferson hoped too that the members of the expedition would make friends with the Indian tribes they might meet. These contacts would be helpful to fur traders. These goals were broadened after the purchase of Louisiana in May, 1803. Now that this unexplored territory belonged to the United States, Jefferson ordered the expedition to collect information about the plants, animals, climate, and geographical features. The party also was instructed to follow the Missouri River to its source and seek an all-water route to the Pacific.

Jefferson appointed his private secretary, Meriwether Lewis (1774–1809), to head the expedition. As co-leader, Lewis chose William Clark (1770–1838), a younger brother of Revolutionary War hero George Rogers Clark (1752–1818). Both Lewis and Clark were officers in the United States Army and experienced frontiersmen. They selected about 40 adventurous young men, several of whom had military experience, to become members of the expedition.

The Expedition Gets Underway

The party set up winter quarters near St. Louis. They built three riverboats, held rifle practice, and became skilled in ways of meeting frontier hardships. Aboard the boats the men stored nearly 100 barrels of provisions, a supply of guns, ammunition, tools, drugs, and medical instruments, and 21 bales of goods for trade with the Indians. Then they started up the "Big Muddy"—the Missouri River.

Some 5 months later they built a blockhouse, Fort Mandan, near the present site of Bismarck, North Dakota, where they spent the winter. In the spring of 1805, 15 or 16 members of the party returned to St. Louis with specimens of plant and animal life collected along the way. The rest set out on the journey west. French trader Toussaint Charbonneau and his Shoshone Indian wife, Sacajawea (or Sacagawea), went with them as guides. Sacajawea (whose name means "bird woman") had been a captive of the Minnetaree tribe. She agreed to act as translator for the party when it reached Shoshone country and to lead the party through the Rockies.

During that summer the little band traveled through territory never before seen by white men. On June 13 the men gazed on the Great Falls of the Missouri, over 80 feet high. Then they pushed on to the headwaters of that river.

By this time the men were eager to reach the Shoshone villages. They needed supplies, guides across the Rockies, and horses. Soon they would be unable to proceed farther by boat. At last the expedition found the Shoshone on the banks of the Salmon River. The Indians seemed frightened at first but quickly became friendly when they recognized Sacajawea. They gave the white men horses, supplies, and guides.

The Pacific Reached

The expedition crossed the Rockies through the Lemhi and Lolo passes into the valley of the Clearwater River. Here they met the friendly Nez Percé Indians, who gave them food and shelter. The expedition members built dugout canoes, in which they followed the Clearwater to the Snake River and traveled down the Columbia River. On November 7, 1805, they reached the Pacific Ocean—or so they thought. Actually, what they heard were the roaring waters at the mouth of the Columbia River. A few days later they came to the ocean—"this great

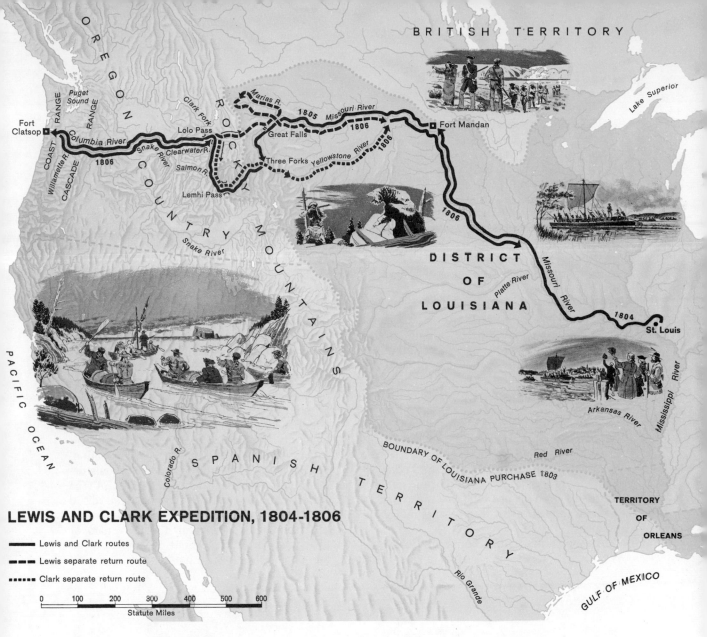

LEWIS AND CLARK EXPEDITION, 1804-1806

- —— Lewis and Clark routes
- --- Lewis separate return route
- ····· Clark separate return route

| 0 | 100 | 200 | 300 | 400 | 500 | 600 |

Statute Miles

Pacific Octean," as Clark wrote in his journal, "which we been so long anxious to see." Before winter set in, they built Fort Clatsop at the mouth of the Columbia River.

In March, 1806, after more than 4 months of rain, fog, and drizzle, the homeward journey began. In the valley of the Bitterroot River the party divided into two groups. Clark's went south to the three forks of the Missouri River, then to the Yellowstone River. Lewis' group went north of the Missouri and crossed the mountains through the Lewis and Clark Pass. On September 23, 1806, the entire expedition arrived at St.

Louis. After 28 months of travel the historic journey had come to an end.

The Lewis and Clark expedition gained valuable scientific information and added to the geographical knowledge of the Missouri and Columbia valleys. It established friendly relations with a number of Indian tribes and gave the American fur trade a new frontier of activity. Finally, it began a new age of exploration and trailbreaking, which made possible the settlement of the Far West.

OTIS K. RICE
West Virginia Institute of Technology

See also LOUISIANA PURCHASE.

LIBERIA

Liberia, independent since 1847, is Africa's oldest republic. Since 1821, when American Negroes first established communities there, Liberia has had close ties with the United States. Liberia was founded by an antislavery group as a home for freed American slaves. Its capital, Monrovia, was named in honor of James Monroe, who was then president of the United States. Today American technical assistance and capital continue to play an important role in the economy of Liberia.

▶ THE PEOPLE

Liberia has a population of approximately 1,150,000. It is made up of two major groups: the descendants of the Afro-American settlers and the indigenous (native) people. The Afro-Americans, descendants of the original settlers, are of Negro and Caucasian (white) ancestry. Intermarriage has led to the fast assimilation of the two groups. The majority of the people are descended from the original inhabitants. These indigenous tribes are governed by their tribal chiefs. Today the political and social leadership of the nation is shared by both groups (the descendants of the Afro-American settlers and the indigenous people).

Although a small minority of Europeans, Americans, and Lebanese play an important part in the economy, education, and religious affairs of the country, only people of Negro ancestry may become citizens. Women enjoy complete economic, social, and political equality. They have distinguished themselves in the national legislature and in government posts both at home and abroad.

Originally the immigrant Afro-Americans lived mostly in coastal cities, because of the lack of roads leading inland. With improved transportation and roads, their descendants now live in all parts of the country. Most people in the cities speak English, wear European clothing, and live in houses ranging from poor to luxurious, depending upon their earning abilities. Most of the Liberians are Protestant Christians. Many years ago children received a primary and sometimes secondary education at missionary or public schools. Today education is compulsory for all children through grade school. All schools, including the rural ones of the interior, are supervised by the Ministry of Education, which also gives annual grants to the assisting missionary schools. The textbooks of the entire school system have been standardized by the government. For higher education Liberian youths can attend the University of Liberia at Monrovia. About 15 percent of all the people living in Liberia can read and

A modern section of Monrovia, the capital of Liberia.

write. Some tribes continue to send their children, at a certain age, to traditional schools that provide practical education in agriculture, homemaking, and tribal tradition. These schools are called *poro* (for boys) and *sande* (for girls). They are staffed with teachers who are specialists in the cultural arts of their own tribes. Children attend these in addition to their regular schools.

The skills taught at the traditional schools were once limited to tribal members. But now the government attaches so much importance to the indigenous cultural arts that efforts are being made to preserve them. The folk music and dance are being taught to professional local dancers. On several occasions these dancers have appeared before audiences and visitors. A center for the display of native masks, handicrafts, dances, and arts has been established outside Monrovia.

Soccer, tennis, and basketball are nationwide sports. Monrovia has several large movie houses. The nightclubs are also popular places.

Most of the tribal people live in small villages in the interior. A village is usually a group of round mud huts with palm-thatched roofs. Family ties are very strong. Each member plays a part in the livelihood of the village. The men clear timber from the fields and plant the rice. The women help harvest the crops and cook the food. The old men make fish traps. The young boys carry water and drive the monkeys, baboons, and weaverbirds away from banana plants. The boys also tend goats. A tribesman who once produced only enough rice, cassava, yams, millet, and palm kernels to satisfy his family's needs is no longer limited to this. With modern equipment and new agricultural methods the tribesman may become a farmer with a surplus. His profits now enable him to buy a car and a radio and to build a modern home. Young men often work on rubber plantations or in the iron mines. Although tribal religions are still practiced, Christianity and Islam (the faith of the Muslims) are winning converts.

Tribal life is sometimes full of joy. All-night song and dance festivals are frequently held. Performances by "bush devils" dancing on stilts are a great favorite of the people. Colorful garments are seen everywhere. Ornate clay designs are used to decorate

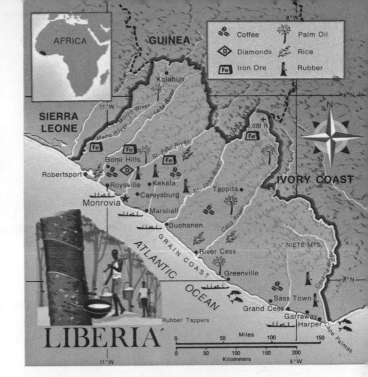

houses. Artistic talent is also seen in carved wooden tools and masks. Folktales and proverbs are passed on from generation to generation.

Tribal life is at times one of fear. Wild animals and diseases, such as malaria, yaws, and leprosy, are constant physical threats to the tribal people. Fears caused by belief in magic, witchcraft, and taboos are sometimes even greater.

▶ LAND AND RESOURCES

Liberia, with its area of 43,000 square miles, is about the size of Newfoundland. It lies about 300 miles north of the equator, on the western bulge of the African continent. It is bounded on the northwest by Sierra Leone, on the north by Guinea, on the east by Ivory Coast, and on the south by the Atlantic Ocean.

The country is divided into two land regions. One is a low-lying strip that stretches about 40 miles inland from the coast. Beyond this the land rises to a rough plateau about 800 feet above sea level. In many places the plateau is broken by small hills and mountain ranges. One of these mountains, Nimba, has an elevation of about 4,200 feet.

The coastal zone has a tropical climate. Almost 200 inches of rain fall from April through October. The average annual temperature of the country is 80 degrees Fahrenheit.

Deer, gazelles, elephants, monkeys, leopards, pythons, and many other wild animals are found in the forests. Liberia also has a rare species of pygmy hippopotamus. Other than goats and chickens, there are few domesticated animals.

Iron-ore deposits in Liberia are among the world's richest. The mines at Bomi Hills and Nimba have been supplying steel mills in Europe and the United States. Some diamonds and gold have been discovered in the post-World War II period.

Rubber remains one of Liberia's most important export crops. For many years it was almost the only source of revenue for the Liberian government. The major rubber producer in the country, the Firestone Plantations Company, was established in Liberia in 1926. Thousands of Liberians are employed by the company. Firestone also distributes rubber-plant seedlings to farmers. To diversify the agricultural economy, coffee, bananas, and other crops are being grown by Liberian and foreign planters.

The free port of Monrovia plays an important part in West African commerce. This man-made harbor was built during World War II with United States assistance. Up to that time Liberia was relatively isolated from the outside world. Also, very few of Liberia's rivers are navigable. Therefore, much of the country's interior had no contact with the coast. The deep ravines and broad rivers near the coast made road building difficult too. Two railroad lines now connect the coast with important sources of iron ore in the interior. Major airlines connect the country with all parts of the world. Internal air traffic also is growing rapidly. Highways have been built, despite difficulties, and trucks carry products between cities. Most goods that are moved within the villages, however, are still carried by hand.

Cities. Monrovia, the capital of Liberia, is situated near the mouth of the St. Paul River. The climate is hot and rainy from May to October and hot and dry from November to April. Monrovia is the cultural and educational center of Liberia. Because of its fine harbor, it is also the chief port and commercial center of the country. A large percentage of Liberian products are exported

An outdoor market in Monrovia.

from Monrovia. Roberts Field, Monrovia's airport, was built during World War II.

In addition to Monrovia, other important port cities are Robertsport, Grand Cess, Harper, River Cess, Buchanan, Marshall, Greenville, and Sass Town. Tappita, Roysville, Garraway, Careysburg, and Kakata are other large towns.

▶ GOVERNMENT

The structure of the government of Liberia is very much like that of the United States. There is a president, a legislature, and a supreme court. The legislature is made up of an 18-member senate and a 52-member house of representatives. The counties, districts, and municipalities are administrative districts of the national government. Most officials are appointed by the president.

▶ HISTORY

Modern Liberia's history began in 1821, when the first settlers landed near Monrovia. These pioneer settlers were sponsored by an antislavery group called the American Colonization Society. Thereafter, for 100 years, the United States provided Liberia with diplomatic and financial aid to meet the threat from European colonists and from the local tribal people. The United States, however, did not make Liberia a colony. In 1847 the

Many adults who speak tribal languages are also learning to read and write English.

settlers declared Liberia independent. A constitution was adopted, and Joseph Jenkins Roberts was elected first president. The recognition of Liberian independence by the European powers saved the country from further outside encroachment. The United States under President Lincoln first exchanged diplomats with Liberia during the American Civil War.

Liberia took part in both world wars. During World War II it was one of the major suppliers of natural rubber for the Allied powers. The airbase at Roberts Field was an important link in the Allied supply lines between America and the Middle East.

William V. S. Tubman became president of Liberia in 1944. He did much to expand the political rights of the people. Tubman, having served as president for more than 25 years, died while still in office, July, 1971. Liberia is a charter member of the United Nations and has become an important leader of the African countries in that organization.

J. GUS LIEBENOW
Indiana University

Reviewed by CHRISTIE W. DOE
Ambassador, Permanent Mission of Liberia
to the United Nations

FACTS AND FIGURES

REPUBLIC OF LIBERIA is the official name of the country.

CAPITAL: Monrovia.

LOCATION: Western Africa. **Latitude**—4° 30′ N to 8° 30′ N. **Longitude**—7° 50′ W to 11° 50′ W.

AREA: 43,000 sq. mi.

POPULATION: 1,150,000 (estimate).

LANGUAGE: English, tribal languages.

GOVERNMENT: Republic. **Head of government**—president. **International co-operation**—United Nations, Organization of African Unity (OAU).

NATIONAL ANTHEM: "All Hail, Liberia, Hail."

ECONOMY: Agricultural products—rice, cassava, coffee, bananas, millet, sugarcane, cacao, piassava fiber, palm kernel, rubber. **Industries and products**—cocoa, coffee, rubber, bricks and tiles, cement, soap, wood products, textiles. **Chief minerals**—iron ore, diamonds, gold. **Chief exports**—iron ore, rubber, diamonds, palm kernels, cocoa, piassava, coffee. **Chief imports**—manufactured goods, machinery and transport equipment, food, chemicals, mineral fuels, beverages, tobacco, oils and fats. **Monetary unit**—Liberian dollar.

LIBERTY, STATUE OF

On Liberty Island in New York Harbor stands the huge statue of Liberty Enlightening the World. It was presented by the people of France to the people of the United States on July 4, 1884. With its lofty concrete pedestal and base, it rises to a height of 305 feet. The statue wears a crown of spikes. The broken shackles at its feet represent Liberty's victory over tyranny. In the left hand is a tablet with

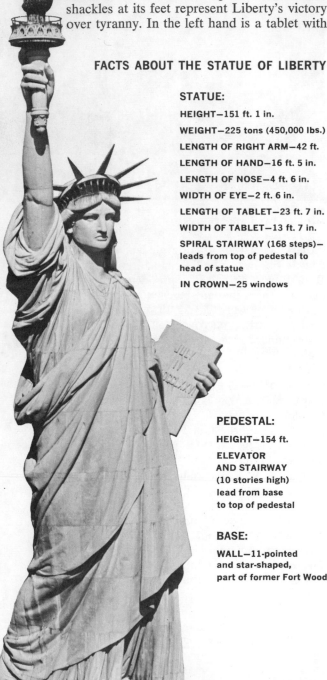

FACTS ABOUT THE STATUE OF LIBERTY

STATUE:

HEIGHT—151 ft. 1 in.

WEIGHT—225 tons (450,000 lbs.)

LENGTH OF RIGHT ARM—42 ft.

LENGTH OF HAND—16 ft. 5 in.

LENGTH OF NOSE—4 ft. 6 in.

WIDTH OF EYE—2 ft. 6 in.

LENGTH OF TABLET—23 ft. 7 in.

WIDTH OF TABLET—13 ft. 7 in.

SPIRAL STAIRWAY (168 steps)— leads from top of pedestal to head of statue

IN CROWN—25 windows

PEDESTAL:

HEIGHT—154 ft.

ELEVATOR AND STAIRWAY (10 stories high) lead from base to top of pedestal

BASE:

WALL—11-pointed and star-shaped, part of former Fort Wood

the date July 4, 1776, in Roman numerals. The right hand holds the torch of freedom.

In 1865 French historian Edouard de Laboulaye (1811–83) suggested the French gift as a memorial to American independence and as a symbol of friendship between the two countries. When sculptor Frédéric Auguste Bartholdi (1834–1904) sailed into New York Harbor, he realized that it was the perfect setting for a monument. This would be the figure of Liberty, standing at the gateway to the New World. To raise money for the statue, the Franco-American Union was formed in 1875. It was decided that the French would construct the statue and bring it to the United States; the Americans would build the pedestal. By 1882, Frenchmen had contributed 1,000,000 francs ($250,000) for the statue.

Bartholdi first made study models. One, reproduced in bronze, may be seen on the Pont de Grenelle, spanning the Seine River in Paris. Then the statue was built in sections. Thick copper sheets were hammered over wooden molds. By 1884 work was completed. A year later the statue was shipped in 214 cases to the United States.

An American fund-raising committee was formed and a site chosen—old Fort Wood on Bedloe's Island (renamed Liberty Island by Congress in 1956). Lack of funds brought work on the pedestal to a standstill late in 1884. But the required amount had been raised by the following August—2 months after the statue arrived in New York—bringing the total to $250,000. On October 28, 1886, the statue was dedicated by President Grover Cleveland.

The Statue of Liberty became a national monument in 1924. It is maintained by the National Park Service, U.S. Department of the Interior, and is open daily. At the statue's base is the American Museum of Immigration, honoring those who have come in search of liberty and opportunity. Liberty Island is reached by ferry from Battery Park at the lower tip of Manhattan.

Reviewed by THOMAS M. PITKIN
Statue of Liberty National Monument

PLAQUE—poem, "The New Colossus," by Emma Lazarus, ending:

"Give me your tired, your poor,
Your huddled masses yearning to breathe free,
The wretched refuse of your teeming shore.
Send these, the homeless, tempest-tost to me,
I lift my lamp beside the golden door!"

LIBERTY BELL

The Liberty Bell is one of the most prized symbols of the American past. Today it stands silently in a little room on the ground floor of the Independence Hall tower in Philadelphia. In 1776 it rang to proclaim the Declaration of Independence. The bell rang for the last time in 1846 on George Washington's birthday.

The Liberty Bell has had several names. First it was called the State House Bell. The Pennsylvania Assembly ordered it for the new State House (now Independence Hall). Thomas Lister of London cast the bell for a price of more than $300. It arrived in Philadelphia in 1752. The bell weighed over 2,080 pounds and was over 3 feet tall.

No one had ever rung the bell, so the new owners tested it. When the clapper struck the sides, the bell cracked. Two local workmen recast it. But they added too much copper and had to recast it again. Finally, in 1753, the bell was hung in the State House belfry.

The bell rang on July 8, 1776, when Philadelphians celebrated the Declaration of Independence. The thought of a bell ringing out for freedom fired men's imaginations. The bell became a symbol of the American Revolution. When the British took Philadelphia in 1777, patriots rescued the bell and rushed it out of town. According to a local tradition, it was hidden in the basement of a church in Allentown, Pennsylvania, until Americans regained Philadelphia.

The Liberty Bell rang in 1783 to announce that the United States had won independence. From then on, the bell rang on all important patriotic occasions. It rang on every Independence Day, July 4. It rang to mark the birthdays of great men. And it tolled the people's grief when great men died.

In 1835 the bell cracked while tolling the death of John Marshall, the fourth Chief Justice of the United States. After a period of neglect, men repaired the bell. Around this time the abolitionists (people who wanted to free the Negro slaves) were becoming active in Philadelphia. The sentiment in Pennsylvania was so strongly antislavery that the bell was given its present name—the Liberty Bell. The bell had stood for independence from England, but it now began to symbolize a larger fight for freedom.

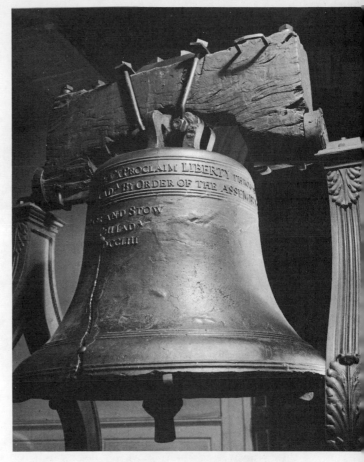

An attempt was made to fix the bell in 1845–46, but it cracked again as it rang for George Washington's birthday in 1846. This time no one was able to fix it. It was taken down from the belfry. After being placed in various parts of Independence Hall, the bell was finally set upon a framework on the ground floor of the tower in 1915. The wooden yoke that holds the bell was weak with dry rot. Steel bars were added to give the yoke strength. Wheels are hidden under the framework so that the bell can be moved in case of fire.

Now people come from all over the world to visit the Liberty Bell. They remember its proud past and examine the zigzag crack running almost from top to bottom. And they can see that the words from the Bible around the bell's top—"Proclaim Liberty throughout all the Land unto all the Inhabitants thereof" —mean as much for the future as for the past.

Reviewed by M. O. ANDERSON
Superintendent
Independence National Historical Park

LIBRARIES

Libraries have developed over the centuries in answer to man's never-ending search for knowledge. In a free society the books on a library's shelves have the power to inspire man to heights of imagination and invention. Books are man's link with the past, his roots in the present, and his guide to the future.

This article on libraries is divided into four main sections: (1) the modern library and its services; (2) how to use your library; (3) librarians and what they do; (4) a history of libraries.

▶ THE MODERN LIBRARY AND ITS SERVICES

In this section these kinds of libraries and their services are described: public libraries; state and regional libraries; school, college, and university libraries; and special and research libraries.

Public Libraries

Children's Services. The children's room is a friendly place. Books, carefully selected by the children's librarian, range from fairy tales and animal stories to *The Adventures of Tom Sawyer* and *Little Women*. There are books about the earth, the stars, outer space. There are stories about machines and occupations. There are tales about peoples of many lands and other times.

One of the most popular activities in the children's room is the weekly story hour. From the collection of stories old and new the librarian carefully chooses reading best suited for the group. A program of stories and games for preschoolers, aged 3 to 5, is one of the newer services for children.

Many boys and girls enjoy reading clubs. They are especially suitable for older boys and girls brought together by a common interest in dramatics, poetry, or a hobby, such as stamp collecting. The librarian helps a group organize its club and then guides the members' use of books that tie in with their interests. To encourage reading during summer months, many libraries have vacation reading clubs.

Knowing how to locate books and information in a library is a valuable skill. The librarian teaches children how to use the card catalog and find books on the shelves. Older boys and girls are introduced to reference tools, such as the *Readers' Guide to Periodical Literature,* encyclopedias, and other sources of information often needed for schoolwork.

In some communities over 90 percent of the elementary-school children are registered users of the public library. In the United States children borrow more than half the books circulated by public libraries.

Young Adult Services. At some fairly flexible point boys and girls leave the children's room to enter the world of adult books. Many make the switch at the completion of the eighth grade or entrance to junior high school. A number of libraries have a separate department for young adults. Other libraries set aside a section of the adult department. Whatever the arrangement, its object is to bring young people and good books together.

About 30 percent of the book collection for young adults is written especially for the teen-ager. About 70 percent consists of adult books on science, sports, humor, adventure, and other subjects of interest.

The public library provides reference service for young adults, sharing this responsibility with the school library. Many public libraries also offer a variety of special programs based on the varied out-of-school interests of teen-agers. Informal group-discussion programs are conducted on dating, etiquette, sportsmanship, and other topics. Often the young people, through a council of representatives, take part in planning the programs. Educational film showings and musical record programs are also favored by young people. Reading clubs further develop the young adults' special interests.

Librarians visit high schools and give talks in classrooms or the school library. A talk, skillfully telling just enough about a book to arouse interest in reading it, often brings students to the library.

Adult Services. The main purpose of the first public libraries in the United States was to lend books to adults for their enjoyment and self-improvement. The lending of books is still a major function, and libraries strive to satisfy adults' varied needs and interests. Librarians offer reading guidance to adults through personal consultation, book lists, and displays. Some librarians write book reviews for newspapers and give book talks on radio and television.

The modern public library provides reference service to help adults find the answers to questions. People from all walks of life look more and more to the library as a reliable source of information. Many libraries answer short questions of fact over the telephone, a great convenience for the busy adult.

The public library also serves various adult groups. For example, a librarian may set up a display of books on child care at a meeting of the local parent-teacher association. Libraries that have meeting rooms often sponsor their own programs for adult groups. Discussions of current events, film forums, concerts, and lectures are some of the activities offered. No admission fee is charged, and the programs are open to all adults. A number of organizations—neighborhood councils, old-age clubs, hobby groups—use the meeting rooms, making the library a lively center of community activity.

Special Services of Modern Libraries. Some

Libraries and librarians offer a variety of services to users of all ages.

The inside (*above*) and outside (*below*) of a bookmobile. These libraries on wheels reach people without access to other libraries.

libraries provide blind people with books in braille. They also offer "talking books"— books that enable a blind person to hear a book through the spoken word on a phonograph record. Forty-two libraries throughout the United States are regional distributing centers from which blind people borrow books and records. Some "talking books" are recorded on magnetic tape.

Educational services form a part of many library programs. Great Books and Junior Great Books programs are held in some librar-ies. Others offer rapid-reading courses and the newer devices of teaching machines and pro-gramed learning.

In urban centers libraries give special attention to the needs of educationally disadvantaged people. Informal storefront libraries to attract nonreaders, books in easy English, and tutoring programs to improve reading skill are typical of the services provided.

State and Regional Libraries in the United States

In addition to local public libraries, each state of the United States has its own library. Originally the state library was intended to serve state government officials with information relating to their work. This is still a major purpose, but today's state library does more. It offers expert advice and assistance to local communities in establishing a public library or improving one already in existence. Other state library functions include lending books to libraries that request them, encouraging co-operation among local libraries, and collecting and preserving official state papers.

Many sparsely populated areas of the United States cannot afford a local public library. In these areas regional and county libraries have been set up. The county library serves a single county or part of it. The regional library extends its services over two or more counties. Over 1,000 county and regional libraries serve about half the counties in the United States. Generally these libraries have a headquarters building in a county seat or in another central location. Headquarters arranges for numerous small book-deposit stations to be spread throughout the area.

Bookmobiles—buses or trucks that serve as libraries—are also widely used. A bookmobile carries a small book collection and calls, usually once a week, to give library service at schools, shopping centers, and other conveniently located points.

Interlibrary Co-operation. Every library, regardless of size, can benefit from co-operation with other libraries. One form of co-operation groups several libraries into a federation. The federation, or area, plan enables people of certain communities to use any library in the federation. Readers gain the advantage of the combined resources and services of several libraries. Economy and efficiency through centralized buying and processing of books are other benefits possible in a federation.

Many libraries co-operate by entering into a formal agreement known as a contract. A common form of contract involves a large library and a small library. Under the terms of the contract the large library gives services to the smaller one—book ordering, storytelling for children, and reference service, for example.

Libraries often borrow books from each other to meet the readers' special needs. This important form of co-operation, known as interlibrary loan, is widely practiced. For some types of valuable material—manuscripts or journal articles—a photostatic copy is sent instead of the original.

Federal Assistance. To help extend library service to farm and rural areas, the United States Congress in 1956 passed the Library Services Act. In time this law provided federal funds up to $7,500,000 per year to aid the states in setting up libraries in communities of less than 10,000 population. By 1963 an estimated 38,000,000 people had benefited from new or improved public library service as a result of the federal assistance. There were still, however, about 18,000,000 people without public library service, and about 110,000,000 had inadequate service.

In order to correct this situation more quickly, Congress, in January, 1964, passed the Library Services and Construction Act. The law provided more than $50,000,000 for the following fiscal year. The funds were to be used for building new public libraries as well as for improving service in existing libraries. All communities, large and small, urban and rural, were eligible for assistance under this act.

The Act was amended in 1966 to include financial aid for setting up regional, state, or interstate co-operative networks of libraries. It also provided funds to improve library service to physically handicapped persons and to establish libraries in institutions such as hospitals and prisons. Funds under this law are allotted to the states in proportion to their population.

Mechanical Devices and Equipment

Charging Machines. The modern library has various mechanical devices and special equipment to improve service and reduce costs of operation. Routine tasks performed regularly and often, such as the charging of books to borrowers, are most readily mechanized. Thus, charging machines are widely used. They enable libraries to check out books speedily and to keep an accurate record of the books in circulation.

A librarian and two young adults in a library's listening area.

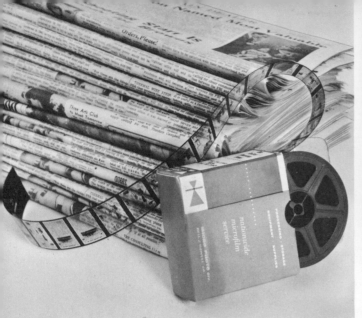

Microfilm copies of newspapers help solve storage problems.

The print is enlarged to readable size on microfilm readers.

Microtechniques. As the quantity of books and other printed matter grows each year, it becomes more difficult for libraries to store the material and locate it when needed. To help solve this problem, modern science is devising new methods of storing and finding information. One of these methods calls for the use of Microcards. It is possible to place the text of an entire book on eight cards. The cards, the same size as library catalog cards, measure 3 by 5 inches.

Books, magazines, or other printed materials are first photographed on film. After the film is developed, it is cut into strips, and the print is transferred through a contact process to the face of the Microcards. The size of the print is so greatly reduced that one card can hold 80 pages of a book. A Microcard reader that enlarges the print is used to read the cards. The Atomic Energy Commission as well as public, university, and industrial libraries are among the users of Microcards. A similar microform, also popular, is called microfiche.

Another of the materials commonly used by libraries is microfilm. Publications such as magazines and newspapers are photographed on rolls of microfilm. Greatly reduced in size, they take up only a fraction of the space needed for the regular printed publications. To read the microfilm, one places it in a microfilm reader.

Microfilm is also used in rapid searching for facts or other specific information. In most systems a code identifies the printed matter on the microfilm. The code is recorded on the film alongside the information to which it relates. Requests for information are also coded into a machine. The request is matched with the proper information through a searching unit that scans the film at high speed. When the code on the film matches that on the request, the film stops. The image may then be shown on the screen of a reader. In some systems a copying machine may then be used to print out the information.

The use of magnetic tape and electronic computers is one of the rapidly developing methods for storing and finding information. Economy of storage space and speed in locating information are outstanding features of these systems. Symbols representing about 12,000,000 letters of the alphabet can be recorded on a reel of magnetic tape measuring only 10½ inches in diameter. Tape-handling devices rush the tape at a speed of 200 to 300 inches per second past a reading and recording instrument. Thus a standard reel containing 2,400 feet of tape can be scanned in less than 3 minutes. Electronic computers sort and then print out information to match requests.

Photocopy Machines. Students, research workers, and others who come to the library for information often need to take notes from books and magazines. As a time-saver for these people many libraries have installed photocopy machines similar to those used in business offices. The machines are simple to operate and quickly reproduce a page of print. Usually there is a small fee for each page copied. Some of the photocopiers are of the coin-operated, self-service type.

Libraries in the Schools

Have you seen a modern school library lately? It may have a carpet on the floor, study carrels, listening booths, a conversation pit. There may not be many books on the shelves because most of them will be in use.

Modern teaching methods require students to read from a wide variety of sources rather than from a single textbook. To meet such requirements, the school library supplies study materials, such as reference books, pamphlets, magazines, newspapers, clippings, records, films, and filmstrips. It is a materials and service center to assist teachers in carrying out the school program. Beyond that, the library encourages good reading habits for leisure time. Supervised reference or research work in a school library makes it a workshop or laboratory, essential to all grades of student abilities and interests. School libraries are objective in providing materials. Collections contain reading matter that presents opposing viewpoints. Also on hand are materials representative of many religious, ethnic, and cultural groups. By offering such variety, school libraries help develop informed and responsible citizens.

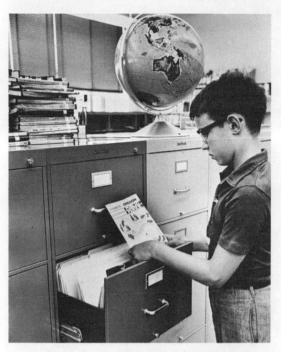

At the highest level of qualification the school librarian is both a teacher and a librarian. He has been trained to take part in school curriculum planning, to consult with teachers, and to provide important guidance for students in self-directed education.

Staffs of student assistants or library clubs are organized to offer students chances to take part in library activities. The clubs arrange for book displays and exhibits and talks by authors and illustrators. The librarian visits classrooms, tells stories, and gives book talks to stimulate interest in "free" reading. Best of all, the school librarian provides effective instruction and practice in how to use a library, helping the student develop lifetime library habits.

Elementary-School Libraries. Not many years ago only about one third of the elementary schools in the United States had libraries. In recent years, however, the number of elementary-school libraries has been steadily growing. The increase has been due largely to the financial aid from the federal government through the Elementary and Secondary Education Act of 1965. Since the act was passed over

10,000 elementary-school libraries have been established.

In some parts of the country, schools without libraries receive assistance from the public library. Classes are sent to the public library for instruction in use of the library. Sets of books, specially selected for the various grades, are lent to classrooms by the public library on a long-term basis.

It is now generally recognized, however, that the elementary-school library program is a fundamental part of the total educational program. Quality education calls for an abundance of reading material. Modern educators feel that the centralized elementary-school library with a professional librarian in charge would clear up many educational problems.

Secondary-School Libraries. There are libraries in about 97 percent of the high schools in the United States. Accreditation standards for schools are set by state education departments and educational associations. These standards have encouraged school officials to establish and improve high-school libraries. Some schools are trying to meet the 1969 national standards drawn up jointly by the American Library Association and the National Education Association. These standards recommend that there be at least 20 books per student, various quantities of audio-visual materials, and one professional staff member for every 250 students. Under the 1969 standards the school library is known as the media center and the professional staff are media specialists.

High-school libraries offer a variety of services to meet curriculum needs and to awaken interest in books. Some stay open all day and in the summer. Others start new methods of teaching and using the library. Certain high-school libraries circulate textbooks, paperbacks, and encyclopedias. They may provide teaching teams of librarians and teachers for regional materials centers. They may experiment with new audio-visual materials and vocational guidance assistance.

College and University Libraries. A college or university is often rated by the quality and size of its library. Special collections—such as those for law, engineering, and so on—are housed in separate departmental libraries. All together, they form one library system. A library system profits by co-operation among its separate smaller libraries. Over-all service is improved, and there is access to many more books.

Among the largest and most notable university libraries in the United States are those at Harvard (over 7,600,000 books), Yale (about 5,000,000), and Columbia (over 4,360,000).

Special Libraries

"Putting knowledge to work," the slogan of the Special Libraries Association, aptly describes the function of the special library. A large number of business, industrial, and professional organizations maintain libraries. The librarian is often selected for his knowledge of a subject field such as banking, chemistry, electronics, physics, or advertising.

Materials for a special library are obtained in a variety of forms. Up-to-date information is required. Thus, newspaper clippings, technical journals, technical reports, government documents, and other current materials are much used in addition to books. To help members of the organization keep abreast of new developments the librarian may prepare brief digests or abstracts of the latest articles and may index reports and other data.

Among the many well-known United States firms that have excellent libraries are General Motors, the Boeing Company, *Newsweek,* and Bell Telephone Laboratories.

Children from a local school receive instruction in the use of a public library.

Documentation

Libraries and a number of industrial firms and government agencies are trying to solve the problems of limited space, cost of personnel, and the need for rapid access to information. To do this they employ a wide range of techniques referred to as "documentation." These techniques are used in addition to the usual library methods of getting information from books—indexing, classifying and cataloging, abstracting, the making of lists or bibliographies, and what is called reference or "literature" searching.

These book techniques, though basic, are not readily adaptable to automatic or machine retrieval.

Documentation, on the other hand, is librarianship that supplies information by the use of mechanical devices, computers, and the like. Documentation is particularly suited to storing certain types of information—the names of chemical compounds, law cases, and similarly specialized facts.

The documentalist has to decide what information goes into the machines. He has to design a system of operations on a scale suitable for economical use of the machines. He has to alphabetize, classify, and code the data to be put into the machine. He has to provide for access to it.

Films or magnetic tapes are excellent for storing a large amount of information in a small space. But films and tapes, like the papyrus roll of long ago, present difficulties in locating material. A number of access methods require cutting the film into strips. Various selecting devices—the rapid selector or the electronic selector—locate specific frames upon the roll of film and reproduce them automatically.

Still another way to store information is to code it onto notched or punched cards. To bring out different parts of the data, these cards can be sorted by mechanical or electrical methods. Some types of cards can be used as input to electronic computers for sorting and arranging.

Photocopying machines are widely used to supply information for library patrons. They also perform the clerical routines of book ordering, charging and discharging books, and so on. These copying devices, coupled with new radio and television techniques, espe-

Vatican Library archives have 8 miles of bookcases.

cially those of the communications satellites, are being tested for the transmission of information. Someday it may be practical for a book in New York to be reproduced instantaneously in Chicago.

Research Libraries

The research library is an indispensable tool of scientists and scholars. It provides the basic information they need to conduct their studies and investigations. Research libraries have collections in many subject fields. They take in the whole range of available knowledge.

National libraries have important research collections. In the United States the Library of Congress, Washington, D.C., is, in effect, the national library. Its collections contain over 14,000,000 books and pamphlets and about 45,000,000 other items. Through the National Union Catalog, maintained by the Library of Congress, research workers can locate over 10,000,000 books in about 700 libraries in the United States and Canada.

The national library of England is the British Museum, which operates strictly as a reference and research library. It is allied with the National Central Library, through which books may be borrowed. Also renowned

Above: The Dag Hammarskjold Library building, UN Headquarters, New York City. Below: An open-stack section of the Bell Telephone Laboratories Library in Holmdel, New Jersey.

A U.S. Information Agency library in Katmandu, Nepal.

among European national libraries for their valuable research collections are the Lenin State Library of the U.S.S.R. and the Bibliothèque Nationale of France.

Large university libraries—such as Harvard, Yale, Columbia, and Michigan—have developed significant research collections. Among public libraries, the New York Public Library, the nation's largest, possesses rich collections in many fields and is of major importance as a research library.

University libraries co-operate with other research libraries in setting up depository, or storage, centers to which they send little-used books. Through such co-operation the participating libraries gain valuable space in their own buildings. They also increase their resources since they may use any of the books in the depository library. The Midwest Inter-Library Center is an outstanding example of this kind of co-operative venture.

Highly important to research workers are the union catalogs in regional bibliographical centers, such as those in Seattle, Philadelphia, and Denver. Through these catalogs books owned by any of the co-operating libraries can be located.

The papers of presidents of the United

The circular Main Reading Room of the British Museum, London.

States have great research value. Although the Library of Congress has many presidential papers, it has become customary to establish libraries especially for such collections. These presidential libraries, located in the native states of the presidents, offer rich sources of historical material on the various administrations.

United States Information Libraries

To promote friendly relations and improve international understanding, the United States Government has opened libraries in about 80 countries throughout the world. These libraries form a vital part of the United States Information Service program, and their services are free to all.

The collection of each library includes United States Government documents and pamphlets; magazines and newspapers; and dictionaries, encyclopedias, and other reference books. There are also books on history, government, sociology, science, and many other subjects. Books are specially selected to meet the needs and interests of the people in each country. In some cases the library serves as a counterpart of an American public library, in others as a research collection.

BERNARD SCHEIN
Deputy Director, Newark Public Library (N J)

The Library of Congress, Washington, contains over 12,000,000 books and periodicals.

Children filling out book slips.

A library card.

▶ HOW TO USE YOUR LIBRARY

No one can hope to know everything. But answers can be found to most of our questions. Libraries bring information on every subject within reach of those who know how to use them.

Libraries have been planned so that information can be found easily and quickly. Whether you are reading for pleasure, for special information, or for a school assignment, the proper book or other kind of source is available in the library. To make the best use of a library, you should know what it offers, how it is planned, and how the books are arranged.

You can become a public library borrower as soon as you can write or print your name on a card that the librarian or the desk assistant will give you. You are then issued your library card. Each time you want to borrow books, show the card to the clerk at the circulation desk. This desk, near the main door of the library, is where the books are charged in and out. A record is made of the books taken. The books are stamped, or slips are put in them, which tell when they must be returned. Some schools offer a discussion of the library and its rules before pupils make their first visit. These rules change a little from library to library, but basic rules help the greatest number of people get along well in a particular library. Some rules are about the care of books.

Care of Books

The books in a library are meant to be used by many people. Young people and adults alike should treat the books with care. A few rules must be remembered if books are to be handed on in good condition to the next reader. First, learn to take the book off the shelf by the middle of its spine. This is the narrow back strip that faces outward as the book

stands on the shelf. Second, open the book carefully so that the binding does not break. Third, turn the pages carefully by holding them at the upper right-hand corner.

Citizenship in the Library

A library is a public place. Certain rules help make it quiet and orderly, a place where a number of people can get work done. Some libraries request readers to leave books they have used on the table. A library helper, trained in this work, puts them back in place. Other libraries like readers to return books to the shelves and help keep them in order.

Parts of Books

Consider the books in terms of their parts. You will find a use for each one.

The pages before the text of a book are its **front matter**, usually arranged in this order—title page; copyright; dedication; preface or foreword; table of contents; lists of maps, charts, or illustrations; introduction; and half title (the title repeated).

The book's full title appears on the **title page**. A good nonfiction title tells you what the book is about. Usually the name of the author (or sometimes the editor), the name of the publisher, and the date of publication are on the title page. From this page the librarian gets the information that goes on the catalog card.

The **author** is the writer of the book. There may be more than one author to a book. In some cases an organization is considered the author of publications issued in its name.

If the book is a collection of the works of several writers, then the person responsible for making the collection is called its **editor** or **compiler**. In a publishing firm a person who prepares an author's manuscript for the printer is also an editor.

Often a book has an **illustrator** who has drawn the pictures. The title page of the book will have the name of the illustrator. Some authors illustrate their own works.

The name of the **publisher**, the **place**, and sometimes the **date of issue** are generally at the bottom of the title page. They are called the book's imprint.

The **copyright** date is given on the title page or on the back (verso) of the title page. The abbreviation © is often used. If up-to-date nonfiction material is needed, check this copyright date.

In a **dedication** the author compliments a friend, relative, or interested person by dedicating his book to him.

The **preface** or **foreword** is a short note in which the author can tell his reader the purpose of the book, its sources, and what it is to cover. It is customary to acknowledge here the services of those who helped in writing the book by contributing information, correcting proofs, and so on. Prefaces and forewords often honor librarians and educators. Their names add to the book's authority.

The **table of contents** lists the divisions of the book—its chapter headings or main subjects—with their page numbers. In a well-arranged book the table of contents serves as a kind of outline. It provides key words and topics. It helps in choosing a book suited to your purpose. Often it serves as a quick locating device for specific information.

Lists of **maps**, **charts**, or **illustrations** cannot be found in every book, but they are very useful, when given, for locating visual aids for your topic. Charts and figures put much information into a small space.

A book's **introduction** offers a preliminary presentation of the general subject matter. It is

PARTS OF A BOOK

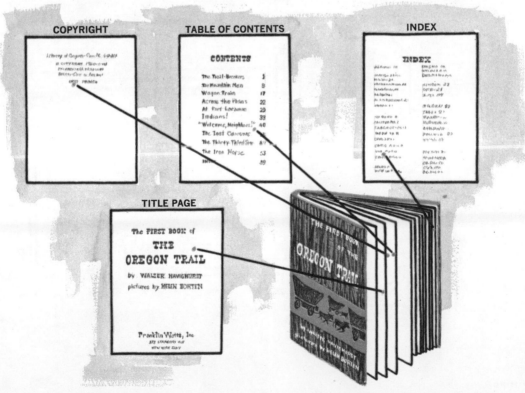

COPYRIGHT

TABLE OF CONTENTS

INDEX

TITLE PAGE

sometimes written by an authority other than the book's author.

A section added at the end of a book to explain or illustrate part of the reading matter is called the **appendix**. It can be charts of statistics, lists, diagrams, additional text, and so on.

A **bibliography** is a list of books or articles used by the author in writing the book. It can also be a list of recommended books related to a certain topic. The lists are usually at the end of the book or article or are noted in footnotes.

A **glossary** lists and defines the difficult words used in a subject field. Glossaries are found near the end of a book or article.

An **index** is a list of names and subjects in alphabetical order at the end of a book. Each entry is followed by one or more page numbers on which the item is treated. Use the index to find out if a book contains information you need or to find again information you remember having read.

How Books Are Arranged

You may go directly to the bookshelves to select a book. Labels on the shelves tell where certain kinds of books are: Biography, History, Science, Stories, Fairy Tales, Easy Books, and so on. But the librarian is always happy to help. Many librarians have already helped by arranging books according to a system. Do you want a book about animals or about the Oregon Trail? A storybook, perhaps? It is nice to find it yourself. Also, browsing among related books enlarges your knowledge. You might see something else you want.

Books are placed on the shelves according to their subjects and for the convenience of the readers most likely to use them. Some public library books may have J or Juv on the spine. These letters stand for juvenile. Books so marked belong in the children's (juvenile) department rather than in the adult department. Sometimes there are copies of the same book in both departments.

All the letters and numbers on the spine of a book have a special meaning. Books of fiction are together, arranged alphabetically from left to right by the first letter of the author's last name. For example, all of Charles Dickens' books are in one place. They in turn are arranged alphabetically by title. *David Copperfield* will come before *Great Expectations*. On their spines these books

A LIBRARY FLOOR PLAN

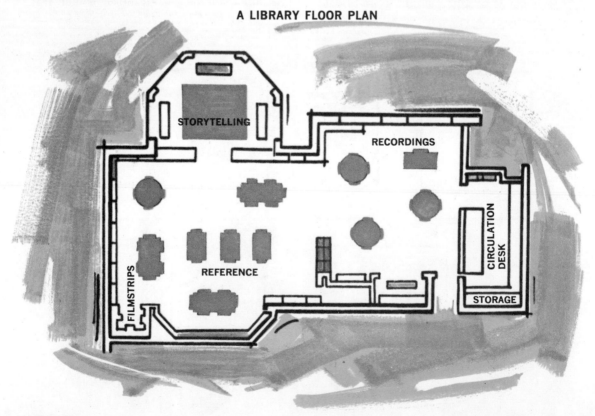

HOW THE DEWEY DECIMAL SYSTEM CLASSIFIES NONFICTION BOOKS

Melvil Dewey worked out a system of book classification that many libraries use. He chose certain numbers and subjects in order to group together nonfiction books on the same subject. Dewey chose the subjects by pretending to be a prehistoric man and then asking questions he thought such a man would ask.

100 Who am I?
PHILOSOPHY AND PSYCHOLOGY
(Man thinks about himself.)

200 Who made me?
RELIGION
(Man thinks about God.)

300 Who is the man in the next cave?
SOCIAL SCIENCES
(Man thinks about other people.)

400 How can I make that man understand me?
PHILOLOGY (Language)
(Man learns to communicate with others through words.)

500 How can I understand the world about me?
SCIENCE
(Man learns to understand the world about him.)

600 How can I use what I know about science?
APPLIED SCIENCE AND USEFUL ARTS
(Primitive man learned to make fire and weapons. Later, men learned about the wheel, medicine, crops, cooking foods, and making all the things we use.)

700 How can I enjoy my leisure time?
FINE ARTS AND RECREATION
(Primitive man had time to do things he enjoyed. He learned to make music, paint, dance, play games.)

800 How can I give my children a record of man's heroic deeds?
LITERATURE
(Man told stories and made up poems about his ancestors and the people he knew. Later, man put these into writing for all people to read.)

900 How can I leave a record for men of the future?
HISTORY GEOGRAPHY BIOGRAPHY
(Man began to write about events that had taken place in all countries and about the people who were part of those events.)

000 **GENERAL WORKS**
The numbers up to 100 are used for bibliographies, books about books, and for books that contain information on many subjects—encyclopedias and other reference books. All reference books have R before the number.

---

may have F or Fict for fiction and also the letter D for Dickens

Books of biography and autobiography—stories of people's lives—are together on their own shelves. They have the letter B for biography or the number 92 on their spines. Below this letter or number is the first letter of the last name of the person the book tells about—A for Adams, F for Frémont, W for Washington, in alphabetical order along the shelves.

Collected biographies, many lives in one book, are also in one group. They have 920 on their spines. Below that number is the first

letter of the last name of the person who made the collection. So these books are in alphabetical order by the author's initial.

A third group of books is called nonfiction. These books are about every subject imaginable, and some single books discuss several subjects. The librarian must decide under which subjects to classify the book so that it can be found most easily. Most libraries use a plan called the Dewey Decimal System, devised some years ago by Melvil Dewey.

Dewey Decimal System. The Dewey system is called a decimal system because of its use of 10's. The 10 main classes of the Dewey system are each divided into 10 divisions. New subjects can be added anywhere and each group can be subdivided almost indefinitely by 10's into smaller sections and subsections. This is made possible by using a decimal point after the first three numbers, as in this example.

900	History
970	History of North America
973	History of the United States
973.4	History of the United States, 1789–1809
978	History of the Western States
979	History of the Pacific States
979.5	History of Oregon

The 600 to 699 numbers are for books about applied science. This covers inventions, medicine, engineering, agriculture, industry, and others. Books that deal with aircraft are given the number 629.1, and books about automobiles 629.2. These numbers are called **class numbers**. All books on the same subject will have the same class number. This number is always marked on the spine of the book.

But since there may be many books on the same subject written by different authors, the library may add a letter under the number. This is the first letter of the author's last name. The books are arranged on the shelf according to their class numbers, and then in alphabetical order, according to the author's initial. For example, books of folk songs by Beatrice Landeck, Jean Ritchie, and Ruth Seeger would be shelved in this order:

784	784	784
L	R	S

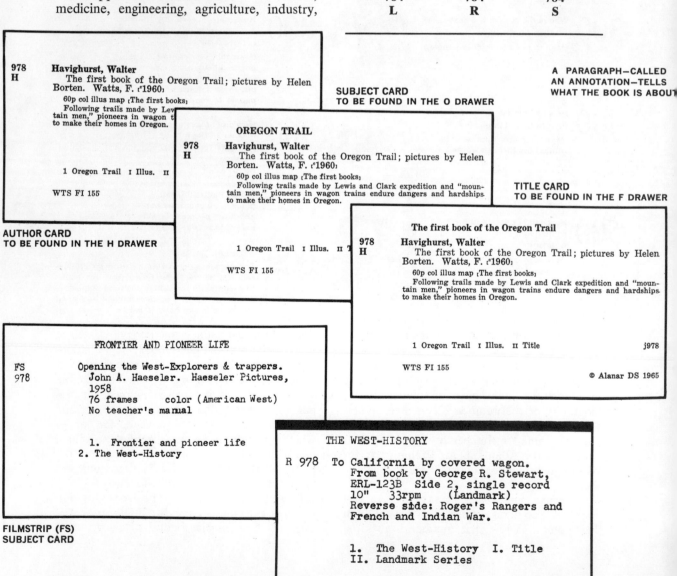

978
H
Havighurst, Walter
     The first book of the Oregon Trail; pictures by Helen Borten. Watts, F. ₍1960₎
     60p col illus map ₍The first books₎
     Following trails made by Lew[...]
tain men," pioneers in wagon t[...]
to make their homes in Oregon.

1 Oregon Trail ɪ Illus. ɪɪ

WTS FI 155

AUTHOR CARD
TO BE FOUND IN THE H DRAWER

OREGON TRAIL

978
H
Havighurst, Walter
     The first book of the Oregon Trail; pictures by Helen Borten. Watts, F. ₍1960₎
     60p col illus map ₍The first books₎
     Following trails made by Lewis and Clark expedition and "mountain men," pioneers in wagon trains endure dangers and hardships to make their homes in Oregon.

1 Oregon Trail ɪ Illus. ɪɪ T[...]

WTS FI 155

SUBJECT CARD
TO BE FOUND IN THE O DRAWER

A PARAGRAPH—CALLED
AN ANNOTATION—TELLS
WHAT THE BOOK IS ABOUT

TITLE CARD
TO BE FOUND IN THE F DRAWER

The first book of the Oregon Trail

978
H
Havighurst, Walter
     The first book of the Oregon Trail; pictures by Helen Borten. Watts, F. ₍1960₎
     60p col illus map ₍The first books₎
     Following trails made by Lewis and Clark expedition and "mountain men," pioneers in wagon trains endure dangers and hardships to make their homes in Oregon.

1 Oregon Trail ɪ Illus. ɪɪ Title   j978

WTS FI 155   © Alanar DS 1965

FRONTIER AND PIONEER LIFE

FS
978
Opening the West-Explorers & trappers.
John A. Haeseler. Haeseler Pictures,
1958
76 frames   color (American West)
No teacher's manual

1. Frontier and pioneer life
2. The West-History

FILMSTRIP (FS)
SUBJECT CARD

THE WEST-HISTORY

R 978 To California by covered wagon.
From book by George R. Stewart,
ERL-123B Side 2, single record
10"   33rpm   (Landmark)
Reverse side: Roger's Rangers and
French and Indian War.

1. The West-History I. Title
II. Landmark Series

RECORD (R)
SUBJECT CARD

The class number of the book plus the author letter is known as the **call number.** The call number tells exactly where the book is on the library shelves. Remember, however, that books of individual biography are arranged by the initial letter of the subject's last name.

Reference Books. If you were asked to make a short report in school on bees, dust, or helicopters, where would you get your information? Of course there are many books on these subjects that you could read. But the best place to find brief information, or an overview of a big subject, is reference books. They contain the most important facts about a great many subjects. There are different kinds of reference books in the library—atlases, almanacs, dictionaries, encyclopedias, and indexes. Such books are used by many people who want to look up facts quickly. For this reason these books are kept together in a section of shelves. Generally they are not allowed to be taken from the library. They are usually marked R or Ref for reference above the Dewey class number. *The World Almanac and Book of Facts,* for example, would have this marking on its spine:

Ref.
317
W

Some books are put "on reserve" so that they can be used by anyone while the library is open. Only under special rules, which the librarian will explain, can they be taken from the library.

The school library and the children's room of the public library will also have magazines, arranged by title on special racks. There will be file cabinets of pamphlets, pictures, and newspaper clippings which the librarian has collected and arranged by subject. These can often add much up-to-date information and visual aid to classroom reports.

Card Catalog

In addition to knowing how to select material directly from the shelves or special collections, it is necessary to know how to use the card catalog. This is really a special list of all the books the library owns. It is a guidebook for the library.

There are catalogs in book form. Instead of walking all about a store, one can look at a Montgomery Ward or Sears Roebuck catalog

Each drawer of a card catalog is labeled with guide letters that tell what cards are in it. For example, the top left drawer contains the A–Ark cards.

and select what he wants. A telephone directory is another kind of catalog for finding a person's street and phone number. Library catalogs are sometimes in book form also. Some—the *Children's Catalog,* for example —are made for use in many libraries. The librarian will show them to you upon request.

In certain libraries it is usually more convenient to have a card catalog in a file cabinet with several drawers. There are cards for each book in the library, a card for the author, a card for the title of most books, and cards for the subjects of fiction and nonfiction books. When the library gets a new book, its cards are filed in their proper alphabetical places, word by word, in the card catalog, and the catalog is up-to-date. All these cards usually have the call number of the book in the upper left-hand corner, indicating where the book will be found.

Guides. The guide letters on the outside of the trays of the card catalog tell which letters they contain. These trays are arranged in the cabinet in alphabetical order. Whether you are looking for the title, author, or subject card, it will be found in the appropriate drawer, filed alphabetically by the word method.

Generally the single trays may be taken out of the cabinet and put on a sliding shelf or nearby table. This makes it easier to look through the cards.

Card catalogs also have inside guide cards. These cards, which stand up higher than the others, have single letters of the alphabet, parts of words, or whole words on them.

Inside guide cards show exactly where you are in the alphabet. **Games** would be back of the G card, between **Gale** and **Gandhi**.

There are three possible ways of finding the cards for a book—by looking for its author, its title, or its subject card. Have pencil and slips of paper when you are ready to begin. Copy the call number, the author, and the title of the book. This will prevent return trips to the card catalog.

Where to Look. When the title of a book or a subject heading begins with the articles *a, an,* or *the,* look under the first letter of the next word. *The West—History* would be found under W. *A Candle in the Mist* would be found under C.

Numbers are arranged as they are spelled. Look for a book title beginning with the number 2 under the letter T for two, as in *Two Logs Crossing.*

If the title begins with an abbreviation like Dr., Mt., or St., look for it as if the abbreviation were spelled out: Dr. as Doctor, Mt. as Mount, St. as Saint. Names like McBride are filed as if they were spelled MacBride.

If the subject has many parts or subheads look for the subject cards first and then the cards for subheads.

The West
The West—Discovery and Exploration
The West—History

Subheadings may be aspects of a subject, as in the examples above. On the other hand, they may be a form of writing or period divisions, as in the examples below:

Indians of North America—Biography
(form division)
United States—History—1815–1861
(period division)
The West—Fiction (form division)

A student uses the card catalog on a research project.

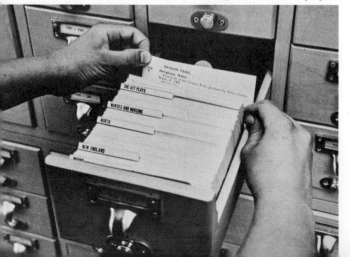

If the subject has more than one word—as in New York—look for the first word, New. All the New's—New England, New York, New Zealand—will come before Newark and Newfoundland, that is, word by word, short words before long ones.

The catalog also has cards that say "See" and "See also." These are cross-reference cards. They do not have call numbers because they refer to other *cards,* not to specific books. The "See" cards guide the reader from one heading that is not used in this catalog to another that is used to express the sense of the heading better.

Pioneer life
See
Frontier and pioneer life.

The "See also" cards guide you to additional related subjects.

Overland journeys to the Pacific
See also
Oregon Trail.

A Library Research Project

Research is investigation that results in your discovery of knowledge new to you, if not to the world. The project described below teaches a method used in research.

Suppose that your class is studying the westward expansion of the United States. For your report you want information about the Oregon Trail. Westward expansion is a big topic. It is wise to select an interesting corner of it. Your history textbook will give general study guides to the topic: what the Oregon Trail was, who used it and when, why and how it was followed. From these guides you will learn key words and special names that will lead to more materials, if you need them. Keep them in mind. The first step in research is to select the proper headings under which information on your topic will be located.

At the library go first to the card catalog's O drawer for the Oregon Trail, the specific heading. Here, between **Oregon** and **origin**—not under "the," remember—are cards for books with the class number 978. Go to those shelves in the history section and select these books.

In the section labeled 978 there will be additional books on the history of the western states. The *general* headings in the card catalog for these books are "The West—History" or "The West—Discovery and Exploration" if they deal only with discovery and exploration in the West. They may also contain chapters or sections on the Oregon Trail.

Some of the books—*Winning of the West* by McCracken, for example—offer background material on the part the Trail played in the West's history. Books about other overland journeys to the Pacific will be found in section 978—accounts of the Santa Fe Trail and the Chisholm Trail, for instance.

The card catalog may also have headings "The Oregon Trail—Stories" or "The Oregon Trail—Fiction." You might select a book here and then find it on the fiction shelves. Be sure to keep a record of all the books you use. These will become the bibliography at the end of your report.

The next step in your research is to look in the catalog for the key words and special names kept in mind from your first reading on the topic. Look for the Lewis and Clark Expedition under L for Lewis. Such a book will have the number 973.4 for that period of United States history. It would probably tell how the expedition blazed the way for the Oregon Trail.

Or you could look for the names Lewis, Meriwether, and Clark, William; or for Frémont, John C., whose report shaped the network of paths into a trail; for Whitman, Narcissa, the first white woman to make the journey; or for Sacajawea, the Indian woman who accompanied the expedition. These books will probably have B or 92 as class numbers and will be found in the biography section.

The annotations on the catalog cards (the short paragraph telling what the book is about) will help you decide if the book will add to your report. Annotations may also remind you of other key words and special names.

The word "pioneer" has probably appeared often in your research. Some catalogs have a "See" reference card guiding you to Frontier and pioneer life under F. A book like Franklin Folsom's *Famous Pioneers* will be listed here with the class number 920, collected biography.

Class number 979.5 indicates books on Oregon. A book on that state would tell something about the trail and might have pictures of places of interest related to it.

If you decide to write about how the people traveled along the trail, then you must think of other specific key words, such as covered wagon, pony express, carriages, and carts. These books would have the class number 383 for postal communication and 388.3 for transportation.

Should you want to buy a book on your topic or want to go to another library, ask the librarian to let you see the *Subject Guide to Books in Print*. Look under the same headings you looked under in the card catalog. Keep a record of the books that you would like to see—that is, the author, title, imprint (publisher and date), and cost for each book. Having such a record makes it easy to look up the books by title or by author in another library.

You now have a choice of books. But a research project means that you use all the resources of the library that apply to your topic. After the card catalog has been checked, using key subject words, check more of the library's guidebooks. Some of the books to be consulted are the *Readers' Guide to Periodical Literature,* the *Abridged Readers' Guide,* or the index to the *National Geographic* for a magazine article that you can use. *Granger's Index to Poetry* and the *Song Index* will give poems or songs on your subject. The librarian will help you with these and with the picture file and the vertical file, a file for pamphlets, clippings, and the like. There may also be films, filmstrips, records, or tapes that your class could use. These would be listed in the card catalog or in a special A V (Audio-Visual) book catalog in the reference section.

The reference section also has fact books, such as the atlases that give maps of the routes west. The biographical dictionaries, particularly the *Dictionary of American Biography,* will have more detailed information on persons. Use it especially for brief accounts of lives of those about whom no books have been written. *The Oxford Companion to American Literature* has brief accounts of persons, characters, and events that you may come across in your reading.

Bibliography. Your report will have a bibliography, a list of books about your topic.

Some of the books used in your research have bibliographies. They may suggest books to add to your search. Look for them by title, by author, or by subject. Expect to gain more leads as you begin to read and examine the material carefully and as you work on the outline for your report. Compare the different books and articles. Evaluate them and decide which are the most suitable. The bibliography for your library research project will look something like this.

Bibliography

1. Albert, M. "First Man Across." Boys' Life 52:18-19, June, 1963.
2. Dorian, Edith. *Trails West and Men Who Made Them*. New York, McGraw-Hill, 1955. Pp. 66-71.
3. Havighurst, Walter. *First Book of the Oregon Trail*. New York, Franklin Watts, 1960.
4. The Opening of the West (Filmstrip). Life, 1954. 61 fr. col.
5. "Smith, Jedediah Strong," in *Dictionary of American Biography*, Vol. 9. New York, Scribner, 1958 P.290
6. To California by Covered Wagon. From book by George R. Stewart, ERL-123B, Side 2, single record 10" 33 rpm. Landmark Records.

Little by little, with such topics as the Oregon Trail, and with other topics in different subject fields—science, art, or music—you will learn to use the same basic library tools—the reference books, the card catalog, the picture files, magazine files, and audio-visual materials. You will learn to select what you need by examining the books and materials themselves.

The library is set up for a kind of self-service to give you this great freedom of selection and to help you become independent in your study and research. But librarians sincerely hope that you will ask them for any help you need.

MARY VIRGINIA GAVER
Graduate School of Library Service
Rutgers—The State University

▶ LIBRARIANS AND WHAT THEY DO

Librarianship deals with both books and readers. Several pioneers in the field helped win for librarianship recognition as one of the learned professions.

Famous Pioneers in Librarianship

Melvil Dewey (1851–1931) was a man of wide interests, responsible for many library firsts in his long career. While serving as librarian of Amherst College, he devised the Dewey Decimal System of Classification. He was instrumental in founding the American Library Association. Later, as librarian of Columbia College in New York City, he established, as a part of Columbia University, the first school for the training of professional librarians.

William Frederick Poole (1821–94), a contemporary of Dewey's, also had a distinguished career. He, too, was one of the founders of the American Library Association and served as its president from 1885 to 1887. Besides organizing such famous libraries as the Newberry Library in Chicago, the Chicago Public Library, and the library of the United States Naval Academy, he carried on a lifelong controversy with Dewey. The two men disagreed about the techniques and philosophy of librarianship. Perhaps Poole's most lasting contribution to the profession was the compilation of the first general index to periodicals, *Poole's Index to Periodical Literature*.

John Cotton Dana (1856–1929) brought innovations to the operation of libraries and to the services they offered. In contrast to many librarians of his time, he believed that books should be used rather than gather dust on shelves. He served on the staff of the Denver Public Library and was later librarian of the Springfield, Massachusetts, and the Newark, New Jersey, public libraries. He helped found the Special Libraries Association and served as its first president. Dana also served as president of the American Library Association in 1895–96.

Although he was a surgeon, **John Shaw Billings** (1838–1913) made great contributions to society in the field of librarianship. After the Civil War he had charge of the Surgeon General's Library in Washington, D.C. Billings increased the collections from

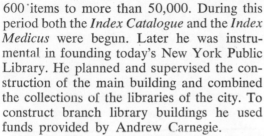

600 items to more than 50,000. During this period both the *Index Catalogue* and the *Index Medicus* were begun. Later he was instrumental in founding today's New York Public Library. He planned and supervised the construction of the main building and combined the collections of the libraries of the city. To construct branch library buildings he used funds provided by Andrew Carnegie.

Charles Ammi Cutter (1837–1903) served for many years as librarian of the Boston Athenaeum, one of America's foremost private libraries. Among his great contributions to the field of library science was the development of a system of classification. He also developed a letter and number system to represent authors' names. This number, called the "Cutter number," is used in many libraries. His book *Rules for a Printed Dictionary Catalogue,* written in 1875, is still one of the most important works in its field. Cutter was a co-founder of the American Library Association and helped establish the *Library Journal.*

Modern Librarianship

A librarian must have a broad knowledge of books, journals, documents, and other graphic materials related to his special field of work. He must know how to organize these materials so that they can be found quickly for readers. He must know how to go about finding information ranging from single facts to reports of highly specialized research studies. He must be familiar with the types of published materials and the scope and coverage of different publications. He knows the reading levels of materials as well as the reading interests of various age and job groups. The librarian decides where to look for information. Shall it be a dictionary, a yearbook, the card catalog? Or shall it be a specialized encyclopedia, a bibliography of books for children, or the catalogs and indexes to government documents?

The quantity of printed material, always large, has become a flood. To control the flood requires all the ingenuity that librarians and technologists can muster. In libraries as in business and industry, possibilities of automation are under study. Machines are already taking over some of the business aspects of libraries and may soon help with such library records as card catalogs, indexes, and bibliographies. These developments by no means imply that librarians will no longer be needed. Quite the contrary is likely to be true, as the machines can do only what they are told. Rather, librarians will need to acquire new skills just as libraries will need new types of equipment to meet new conditions.

Unlimited Future

Recent developments in the handling of scientific information have produced new terms, such as documentalist, information scientist, and science information specialist. These are names for people who perform a kind of librarianship. Some research libraries require a librarian with a degree in chemistry. Other libraries need people fluent in little-known languages. Only the linguist-librarian can process certain materials from the Middle East, Far East, and Africa. If librarianship keeps pace with the future, almost limitless kinds of specialization will be needed.

Changes in teaching methods in schools of all levels have vastly increased the student demand on libraries and librarians. This demand promises to increase. Growing populations and the automation of agriculture and industry will send more and more adults back to school to train for new vocations. With a changing society that requires new emphasis on education and research, librarianship has an assured future.

In years to come, librarianship will perhaps offer an even more stimulating and interesting way of life than it has in the past. The physical surroundings are usually pleasant, and the environment offers challenging intellectual association.

Who Should Be a Librarian?

Librarianship offers a wide variety of activities as well as many kinds of specializations. Therefore, librarianship has a place for people with a wide range of aptitudes and interests. Some librarians, because of highly specialized knowledge, spend most of their working day in a remote corner of the stacks of a large research library. They sort and identify valuable manuscripts and books, organizing these materials for scholarly use. These librarians may have little or no contact with regular library users. On the other hand, librarians working at reference and circulation desks are in constant contact with users. These positions require librarians who enjoy working with many kinds of people and who can remain calm and courteous under pressure.

In the early years of the development of librarianship, its leaders were men. Later, as with teaching, librarianship tended to be regarded as a profession primarily for women. More recently the proportion of men is increasing, with approximately 15 of each 100 positions filled by men. Some library schools report that 50 percent of those enrolled are men, indicating that the proportion of men in the profession will rise still further.

Many positions in libraries require clerical and technical skills rather than professional training. The maintenance of the card catalog, for instance, involves a great deal of typing and filing. The actual operation of the circulation system is usually handled by desk-assistants. Professionally trained librarians supervise these positions. In some instances professional librarians have to perform clerical duties. To avoid this, librarians are giving much attention to making the best possible use of staff. Perhaps the aid of machines and trained clerical assistants will keep librarians free to use their special skills fully.

Almost all library positions carry some administrative responsibility. Many small public libraries and the majority of school libraries employ only one professional librarian. This person must be able to plan and carry out all the activities of a library. These duties may include book selection, acquisition, cataloging, and classification. Then there are circulation and reference duties, as well as supervision of the clerical and desk assistants. Finally, the librarian must work with trustees or school officials for over-all planning. In large library systems, some with more than 100 professional positions, the librarian may specialize in a particular aspect of librarianship. This could be work with children, cataloging, or a particular subject—such as music or law. The director of a large system often spends his entire time administering the many services and work of the staff specialists. The librarian-administrator, although not actually performing any of the professional librarian's tasks, must know library operations and also possess the personal qualities of a good administrator.

How Do You Become a Librarian?

Most persons in Canada and the United States become librarians by attending library school after graduation from a 4-year college. Library schools accredited by the American Library Association require a minimum of 1 year of professional study.

Various combinations of college programs are acceptable if the emphasis is on academic rather than vocational subjects. For example, courses in history, economics, government, literature, foreign languages, and the sciences are preferred to courses in education, business administration, or home economics. Combinations of courses in education and a major in an academic subject field are especially useful for the prospective school librarian. Because many libraries contain materials in languages other than English, it is important, if not essential, that a librarian have a fair knowledge of at least one other language.

In addition to the accredited library schools, many colleges and universities offer courses in library education for the student certain that he wants a career in school librarianship. These courses, at both the graduate and undergraduate levels, are usually intended to qualify the student for work in a school library only.

Job Possibilities in the United States

A small profession, librarianship has about 80,000 fully qualified practitioners in the United States. It offers, however, an extremely wide range of types of positions. For example, one may prepare to work in a public, school, university, special, or government library. One may be the only librarian in a school or industrial library or one of several hundred in large systems. Libraries are located in small towns, large cities, and on college campuses in every state in the United States as well as in every branch of government. The armed services and the State Department offer opportunities for librarians to serve in foreign countries.

Although librarians form a relatively small occupational group, librarianship has been growing faster than almost any other profession. In fact, the demand for library-school graduates has been outstripping the supply for a number of years. As a result, qualified graduates receive numerous offers of positions, and advancement is rapid. Librarians with undergraduate majors in the sciences and school and children's librarians are especially in demand.

Professional Associations

Librarians have a number of professional associations. The largest of these, the American Library Association, has about 27,000 members. It was first organized in 1876.

One of the most important functions of a professional association is to set up specifications for the training of its members. The specifications are enforced by accrediting certain library schools. Besides controlling entry into the profession through this system, ALA also establishes standards of service for particular kinds of libraries. It further encourages the maintenance of these standards and the general improvement of the profession. Librarians in Canada and the United States working together in the American Library Association have established comparable standards for libraries and library education in the two countries. Other English-speaking countries tend to follow the British pattern. One becomes a member of The Library Association if he successfully completes his professional library training and then passes an examination.

Besides its headquarters office and permanent staff located in Chicago, the American Library Association maintains a branch office in Washington, D.C. The staff of this office works directly with members of Congress to secure legislation that will help libraries. The association also encourages research studies of various aspects of librarianship. It publishes these studies as well as other material of interest to librarians.

Anyone with an interest in libraries can join the American Library Association. The body is governed by officers and a council elected by the membership. The association has 13 divisions. There are divisions for types of libraries (school, public, college, or university) and types of library work (cataloging, reference, and the like). Each summer ALA holds its main meeting in a city of the United States or Canada. It also has a midwinter meeting each year.

There are a number of other important library associations with more specialized interests and activities. The Special Libraries Association, established in 1909, has more than 5,000 members. This group is connected primarily with libraries serving business, industry, and government. The Catholic Library Association specializes in library service to Catholics and Catholic institutions. Many states and some regions have separate organizations for furthering librarianship and libraries in their particular geographic area. The New England Library Association is such a group. Some large cities, such as New York and Washington, D.C., have local library clubs that combine social and professional activities.

These various organizations are interrelated in a very informal fashion but frequently cooperate through joint committees in matters of common interest. Although this may seem like a complex of organizations, an individual will belong to only a few of the groups. With such a variety from which to choose, any librarian is sure to find one or more opportunities to meet with other librarians to discuss mutual problems and interests.

A few publishing houses cater especially to the needs of librarians. Besides the important indexes—*Readers' Guide to Periodical Literature, Education Index, Biography Index,* and the *Book Review Digest*—the H. W. Wilson Company also publishes the *Wilson Library Bulletin.* This periodical has long been popular with librarians. The R. R. Bowker Company compiles current information about libraries in its *Annual.* Here one may find salary ranges, size of collections, budgets, and number of employees for all kinds of libraries. Bowker's *Books in Print* and other titles in this series are in constant use in libraries. Their *Library Journal* combines articles of interest along with reviews of new books.

Professional Publications

All members of the American Library Association receive *American Libraries,* the association's official bulletin. It contains information about the activities of the Association, programs of meetings, reprints of important speeches given at meetings, articles, and advertising of particular interest to the membership. Each division of the Association has a publication of special interest to its membership. Another kind of periodical published by the American Library Association is *The Booklist and Subscription Books Bulletin.* It specializes in reviewing books and serves as a selection guide for the librarian.

The Special Libraries Association publishes for its members a periodical called *Special Libraries.* It includes, along with the business and news of the Association, articles and advertising that will appeal to librarians serving business, industry, and government.

RICHARD H. LOGSDON
Director of Libraries and Professor
of Library Service, Columbia University

IRENE K. LOGSDON
Librarian and Director of the Instructional
Materials Center, Ridgewood
High School (N. J.)
Co-authors, *Library Careers*

▶ A HISTORY OF LIBRARIES

To some people the word "library" means a collection of books upon a shelf. But a library is more than a mere collection of books. To become a library the collection must be classified and arranged in a certain way so that the information in it will be easily available to the reader. And the library need not be a collection of books alone. Throughout its history the library has contained such varying materials as the clay tablet, the scroll of papyrus, and the parchment codex as well as the printed book.

Babylonia and Assyria

To Sir Austen Henry Layard (1817–94), the British archeologist and diplomat, we owe what we know of one of the earliest libraries in the history of civilization. During the 1840's he conducted excavations in Babylonia and Assyria. He discovered a public library containing about 10,000 clay tablets at the site of the ancient city of Nineveh. The library was largely the work of Ashurbanipal, the famous king of ancient Assyria, who ruled from about 669 to 626 B.C. His kingdom was known far and wide for its wealth, power, art treasures,

Papyrus scrolls were the "books" in this library of ancient Egypt.

and learning. His great-grandfather Sargon II founded the library there during the 8th century B.C., but Ashurbanipal organized and greatly enlarged it. In time the art of writing on clay tablets came to Egypt through the military conquests of kings, such as Ashurbanipal, and the peaceful visits of traveling businessmen.

The clay tablets were heavy to carry, but they were much less perishable than such fragile writing materials as papyrus. Because the tablets survived we know a great deal about the libraries of ancient Babylonia and Assyria. The libraries, housed in temples and palaces, were presided over by men called "men of the written tablets." One of the first was Amil-anu, a man of Babylonia. The collections reflected affairs of daily life, especially trade and religion. Many tablets developed out of a simple need for record keeping. Others told exciting and heroic stories.

When the temples and palaces of Nineveh, Ur, Telloh, Susa, and Erech fell during the ravages of war or moldered into ruin, their libraries were long forgotten. Then in the 19th century archeologists unearthed them, and the tablets were decoded by such men as Sir Henry C. Rawlinson (1810–95) and Georg F. Grotefend (1775–1853).

Ancient Egypt

We know much less about the libraries of ancient Egypt because its form of book was the perishable papyrus scroll. This type of scroll was used in other countries around the Mediterranean, including Greece. The Romans called it *volumen,* meaning "roll." *Volumen* is the Latin source for the English word "volume." In some countries papyrus remained popular until the early Middle Ages.

One of the most famous libraries in ancient Egypt was the one in the temple of Horus at Edfu (now Idfu), begun around 237 B.C. This "House of Papyrus," containing scrolls on astronomy, astrology, religion, and hunting, had its own catalog, cut into a stone wall. Archeologists working at the Karnak Temple at Thebes, in central Egypt, discovered an inscription for a "House of Books" there. Others unearthed the tombs of two librarians, father and son. The job of librarian was apparently hereditary. Like many administrators of temple libraries, these men were priests.

Libraries had existed in Egypt before the time of the temple libraries. The nobles of the feudal age may have gathered and maintained their own collections as early as 2000 B.C. For example, King Ramses II, who died in 1225 B.C., had a library of sacred literature. The library has vanished. There were other libraries at Tel el Amarna, Dendera, Giza, and at Heliopolis, near Cairo. Heliopolis was important for its libraries of literature and philosophy.

Ancient Greece

The first public library in the history of Western civilization was probably founded by Pisistratus, the tyrant of Athens. His government did much to stimulate the growth of art and literature in the 6th century B.C. By the end of the 5th century B.C. books could be obtained in Athens, and some Athenians had become book collectors. Such distinguished men as Euripides, Euclid of Athens, Nicocrates of Cyprus, and Polycrates collected books on a modest scale. But it was Aristotle (384–322 B.C.) who brought together the first great private library of ancient Greece. His collection grew from his need to gather source materials with which to carry on his research and teaching. As a result, his Peripatetic School in Athens had a sizable library that helped it become a center of research and study in every field of knowledge of the time.

After Aristotle died, the library underwent various travels and misfortunes. It was transported to Asia Minor, was returned to Athens, and was finally taken to Rome by Sulla, the Roman general and dictator (138–78 B.C.). In Rome it was used by Tyrannio, the teacher of Strabo, the Greek geographer.

The greatest library of the ancient world was that at Alexandria, Egypt. It was founded by Ptolemy I (367?–283 B.C.). During his reign the city of Alexandria became the capital of Egypt and a place where scholars from all over the known world gathered. Ptolemy I's son, Ptolemy II (309–246 B.C.), greatly enlarged the collection and improved the library and the museum. Galen, a Greek physician of the 2nd century A.D., tells us that the library was constantly enlarged by the requirement that every ship entering the harbor give up any manuscripts on board.

Two buildings housed the collection. Part was located in the royal residence, the rest in a building near the temple of Serapis. By the time of Callimachus, who died around 240 B.C., the collection numbered around 400,000 volumes in the larger building alone. Callimachus arranged and cataloged the library. While Julius Caesar was in Alexandria, in 47 B.C., fire destroyed about 40,000 volumes from the library that were stored near the arsenal. Perhaps it was an accident, for the books had probably been intended for shipment to Rome.

Rivaling the library of Alexandria was the library of Pergamum in Asia Minor, founded by King Eumenes II, who died about 160 B.C. Its 200,000 volumes were later added to the library of Alexandria when Mark Antony presented them to Cleopatra. So strong a rival in scholarship was Pergamum that it is said the Alexandrians embargoed supplies of papyrus to Pergamum. The resourceful citizens of Pergamum turned to the use of parchment. Parchment is made from animal skins from which the hair has been removed. The skin is then stretched and rubbed with pumice and chalk. The English word for parchment comes from a corrupted version of "Pergamum." Little by little, parchment took the place of papyrus in popularity because it lasted much longer. Its vogue lasted until the use of paper became widespread.

Ancient Rome

The discovery of parchment led to the invention of the codex. A codex is a bound manuscript book of sheets of parchment sewn together along one side. The parchment codex was easy to carry as well as to preserve. The Romans later carried the codex to every corner of their empire.

But that time was still far away. Before a civilization can have books and libraries, it must have a literature, and for hundreds of years the Romans had no literature. The first libraries in Rome were spoils of war, brought back by generals as part of their loot. Many of these books, written in Greek, spread the influence of Greek literature and thought among the Romans. So did the presence of Greek refugee scholars and exiles in Rome.

Julius Caesar (100?–44 B.C.) is usually credited with planning to found the first public

A medieval library.

library in Rome, with Varro (116–27 B.C.), the most learned Roman scholar of his day, in charge of it. But Caesar was assassinated before he could carry out his plan. Asinius Pollio (75 B.C.–A.D. 5) founded the first public library in Rome, during the reign of Emperor Augustus (63 B.C.–A.D. 14). The library was formed with the loot taken from the Parthini when Pollio defeated them in Illyria in 39 B.C. An ancient guidebook reveals that there were at least 28 public libraries in Rome by A.D. 400, many of them in temples. Some of the libraries had thousands of volumes, looked after by slaves and freedmen. As part of their work, these men sometimes copied manuscripts.

The most celebrated library founded by any Roman emperor was the Bibliotheca Ulpia. It was the project of the Emperor Trajan (A.D. 53?–117). Located in Rome, the library had its walls decorated with busts of authors. Magnificent porticoes formed a part of the structure. There were large separate collections of Latin and Greek manuscripts.

Often the Roman libraries were located near and connected with temples. Manuscript rolls were placed lengthwise on cupboard shelves or were stood up in boxes shaped like cylinders. The title of each roll could be seen on a tag fastened to it. Reading rooms often faced the east. This was partly for religious reasons. Also, the morning light made it easier for scholars to read, and the light helped ward off the dampness that is such an enemy of books.

The Middle Ages

Dampness and darkness were not the only enemies of libraries and books. Barbarians and theft took their toll of the Roman libraries. Theodosius the Great (346?–395), the Roman emperor, closed the pagan temples and with them the libraries. When the Goths and Vandals came down from the north and sacked Rome, the last of the libraries vanished. Many manuscripts survived because they were hidden away or copied by monks in their scriptoria, special rooms used for writing.

Some of the earliest Christian churches had libraries, including those at Jerusalem and at Nola in southern Italy. But the collections were very small, often no more than the Scriptures. The early Christians also maintained reading rooms, or *secreta,* in connection with their churches. Only fragments of classical literature survived, and after Christianity became the official religion of the Romans, the pagan authors were neglected. Much of the Western world's classical tradition disappeared, never to be recovered.

The Roman nobleman Cassiodorus (487?–

Vienna's Imperial Library during the 17th century.

583) held high office under Theodoric the Great. Cassiodorus was the first important force in establishing scriptoria and monastic libraries. He played a large part in passing on the classical heritage to the Middle Ages by setting up the first scriptorium for the copying of manuscripts. Cassiodorus also laid down rules for the care and preservation of books.

Modest in size, the monastery libraries seldom numbered more than several hundred volumes. They contained lives of the saints, medieval chronicles, rules of the monastic orders, church law, medieval encyclopedias, the Old and the New Testaments, and classical works, quoted as authorities in Christian writings. To prevent theft, precious volumes were often chained to the shelves, as telephone directories are sometimes chained today. A typical book was the parchment codex. It lasted a long time, it was easy to carry, and unlike the papyrus scroll, it had no unfavorable associations with pagan writings.

During the later Middle Ages the monastery libraries and scriptoria gradually lost their importance. One reason for this was the invention of printing from movable type by Johann Gutenberg (1400?–68?), probably around 1436 or 1437. Books became much cheaper and easier to come by. Slowly paper took the place of parchment as writing material.

Paper had reached Europe about the 12th century, although it had been invented by the Chinese as early as A.D. 105. A boom in trade and manufacturing gave rise to a middle class of business and professional men. Many of this group hungered for books that would instruct them and amuse them as well as prepare them for the next world. The rise of the university library in the 13th century also contributed to the decline of the monastic library.

Renaissance and Reformation

Only the wealthy could afford to collect large numbers of books during the Middle Ages and the Renaissance. For these few, scholars scoured the corners of the known world for Greek and Latin manuscripts. Often the scholars then edited them and translated them into the language of the people. These private collections provided a start for the great national and university libraries of Europe.

France. The first important national library was France's Bibliothèque Nationale. This developed from the libraries of such early French kings as Charles V, Charles VI,

Charles VIII, and Louis XI. Francis I (1494–1547) was the first to bring the royal libraries together at the palace of Fontainebleau and to name a librarian, Guillaume Budé (1468–1540). During the reign of Louis XIV (1638–1715) the library was doubled in size by Jean Baptiste Colbert (1619–83) and moved to its present site in Paris. Following the French Revolution, it became national property. The Bibliothèque Nationale was first opened to the public twice a week in 1692. Since 1859 it has been open to readers 7 days a week. Now divided into eight departments, the library owns over 6,000,000 books. By law one copy of every book published in France is deposited in the Bibliothèque Nationale.

England. The roots of the first great university library in England—the Bodleian Library of Oxford University—also go back to the late Middle Ages. It was then, in 1444, that Humphrey, Duke of Gloucester, gave his last collection of books to Oxford. The library itself did not open until 1488. During the stormy reign of Edward VI (1537–53) it was destroyed. Through the efforts of Sir Thomas Bodley (1545–1613) it reopened on November 8, 1602. Since 1946 the Bodleian has had a new building, containing about 2,000,000 books and 40,000 manuscripts. The new structure also houses models of buildings, coins, literary curiosities, and portraits of famous historical figures. Its Shakespearean and Biblical collections are famous.

Italy. In 1440, about the time that the Bodleian Library was founded, Cosimo de' Medici established Italy's first library open to the public. It was located in the cloisters of San Marco, in Florence. De' Medici also gathered the collection that, in the 16th century, grew into the famous state-supported Laurentian Library in Florence. This collection is housed in a spacious building designed by Michelangelo. It is a suitable setting for such treasures as the manuscripts of Vergil, Cicero, and Dante.

Another well-known Italian library, the Vatican Library, dates back to Pope Damasus I (304?–84) in the 4th century. Under Pope Nicholas V (1397?–1455), a patron of art and literature, the library began to prosper. Under another pope, Pius XI (1857–1939), the collections were for the first time properly reorganized and cataloged, with the help of the United States Carnegie Endowment for International Peace. Although in numbers of books and manuscripts the Vatican Library cannot compete with some of the national libraries in Europe and the United States, it more than equals them in the number of its rare books and manuscripts.

The British Museum

With the collection of Sir Hans Sloane, a physician, as its core, the library of London's British Museum was founded in 1753. Six years later it opened its doors to the public. Here one finds the Harleian collection of

Interior court, Bibliothèque Nationale, Paris.

Library (*foreground*) of Panama University, Panama City.

manuscripts and legal documents. Sir Robert Bruce Cotton's coins, books, manuscripts, and antiquities are among its treasures. These and other priceless objects and the 60,000 volumes given by King George IV have helped make the library one of the world's greatest.

The British Museum is in the Bloomsbury section of London. Completed in 1847, it is classic in style. Since it is one of four depository libraries in Great Britain, the library of the British Museum receives free of charge a copy of every copyrighted book published in the United Kingdom. Sir Anthony Panizzi (1797–1879), one of its best-known librarians, designed the famous circular reading room that opened in 1857. He also laid down the 91 rules that in 1839 became the basis of the library's enormous catalog.

The United States and the Western Hemisphere

The oldest library in the Western Hemisphere is the San Marcos University library in Lima, Peru, which the Spanish founded in 1551. The North American continent's first library was established in Quebec City, Quebec, in 1635. Not long afterward, in 1638, the Harvard University library began with about 400 volumes, which John Harvard had left to the new college in Cambridge, Massachusetts. By the end of the 17th century the college of William and Mary in Williamsburg, Virginia, also boasted a library. By the middle of the 18th century Yale University, New Haven, Connecticut, had a considerable collection.

Toward the close of the 17th century the Reverend Thomas Bray of England had sent parish libraries over to the colonies for the benefit of Anglican clergymen and their congregations. In this way about 34,000 volumes reached the colonies. They were widely distributed in those sections of the South where many Anglicans lived.

Throughout the American colonies many homes had small libraries by the early 18th century. Booksellers had shops in such centers as Boston and Philadelphia, and peddlers sold cheap editions from door to door throughout the country. A few Americans, such as Cotton Mather in Boston and William Byrd in Virginia, had large private libraries. Believing that books should instruct, the colonists collected mostly sober and useful books—such as sermons and political pamphlets. The first printing press had been set up in Cambridge, Massachusetts, in 1638. Philadelphia and New York had presses before the end of the 17th century. Before 1765 book production was flourishing in all the American colonies.

Public Libraries. The American public library movement got off to an early start in 1653. It was then that Robert Keayne, a Boston merchant, established a public library that served the Bostonians for several generations.

Benjamin Franklin founded the American colonies' first subscription library in 1731. He and other Philadelphia citizens contributed a book collection that would circulate freely among themselves. Thus the Library Company of Philadelphia began. Other important subscription libraries followed, the Redwood Library in Newport, Rhode Island, in 1747 and the Charleston Library Society in South Carolina in 1748. All of them exist today. To the west, in Amesville, Ohio, a "coonskin" library flourished in 1804, when settlers along the Ohio River traded coonskins for books from Boston merchants. In many American cities laborers and mechanics or skilled craftsmen pooled their small funds to form their own lending libraries.

The free public library supported by public taxation arrived on the United States scene long after the subscription library. Not until the middle of the 19th century did free public libraries really gain a foothold. New Hampshire, Massachusetts, and Maine had the earliest ones. Peterborough, New Hampshire, set up the first tax-supported library in 1833, and within a few years a number of state and city governments had followed. By 1875 there were 2,000 free libraries owning more than 1,000 books each. By 1900 the free libraries numbered 5,400.

The giant among New England public libraries is the Boston Public Library, which opened in 1854. Its organization into both reference and circulating departments set the pattern for later public libraries. The New York Public Library, now the largest in the United States, was founded May 23, 1895. The Astor and Lenox libraries formed the basis of its collection, and it was further aided by the Tilden Trust.

The free public library of Peterborough, New Hampshire, dates back to 1833.

Left: The V. I. Lenin Library, Moscow. Right: Suburban children at a bookmobile, Budapest.

The children's section of a library, Dacca, Bangladesh.

A college library in Yaba, Nigeria.

A modern public library in Skokie, Illinois.

Much of the growth of public libraries in the United States was due to Andrew Carnegie, the Scottish-born industrialist and steel magnate. He contributed over $5,000,000 to the building of libraries on the condition that towns would set up and properly finance such libraries by taxes. Another factor was the passage of state laws authorizing townships to create libraries. New Hampshire passed the first such law in 1893.

Library of Congress. The 6,457 volumes of Thomas Jefferson's library formed the heart of the collection of the Library of Congress at Washington, D.C. This library is considered the national library of the United States. The purchase of Jefferson's books in 1815 re-established the library, founded by act of Congress in 1800 and burned by British soldiers in 1814. The third largest library in the world, the Library of Congress as a depository library receives two copies of every book published in the United States.

School Libraries. The school library movement began in 1835 when a number of states passed laws providing for a small collection of reference books for school districts. These libraries were gradually replaced by public libraries. Then at the beginning of the 20th century a new educational trend encouraged the development of school libraries. Public librarians promoted the movement, working with the National Education Association, the National Council of Teachers of English, and the American Library Association.

A School Library Section of the American Library Association was established in 1914 and the first school library standards were formulated in 1920. The number of high-school libraries increased in the 1930's. A few elementary-school libraries were set up in suburban areas in the late 1920's and the 1930's. Changes in school curricula led the American Library Association to a formulation of national standards in 1945.

In 1951 the American Library Association set up the American Association of School Librarians. In 1960 it became a department in the National Education Association, while keeping its affiliation with the American Library Association. At that time committees formulated a new statement, *Standards for School Library Programs*. This statement was revised in 1969 and entitled *Standards for School Media Programs*. The new statement recommends that schools have a learning-materials center with books as well as non-book media such as films, recordings, maps, and lantern slides. The school library would be called the media center and the librarian the media specialist.

CHARLES MORITZ
Editor, *Current Biography*

LIBYA

Libya is an independent country situated in northern Africa. This country with a rich historical heritage has come into new importance because of large oil deposits found beneath the sands of its desert region.

The People and How They Live

The people of Libya are mainly Arabs and Berbers. Their family ties are very strong. Each tribe or large family group is headed by a sheikh, who is respected and obeyed by all members of the family.

Many Libyan men and women do not meet before they are married, but enter into marriages arranged by members of their families. In the past the women were never seen by anyone except members of their own families. They never went out in public unless they were completely covered by a long, loose robe called a *lahaf* (*barracano*). Only their eyes were allowed to show. Today the life of women is slowly changing. In the larger cities and towns women now appear in public wearing modern-style dresses.

One of the most important reasons for this change is education. During the Italian colonization only a very small percentage of Libya's people knew how to read. Very few children went to school, and few girls received any education. Today this is changing, and all boys and girls are able to attend school. In 1956 the University of Libya was established in Benghazi. Students, both male and female, come here to study science, business, literature, law, engineering, and art. There also is a religious university attended by many students from other African countries.

Islam is the official religion of Libya. The people believe in one God, Allah, and in the Koran, which is the Holy Book. Religion is very important to the Muslim people, who pray five times a day. Their house of worship is called a mosque. However, it is not necessary for them to go to a mosque to pray. When the time for prayer comes, they merely stop what they are doing and kneel down, facing the holy city of Mecca, which is in Saudi Arabia. Every Muslim dreams of being able to go to Mecca one day. A Muslim who has been there adds a special word, *Haj,* to his name. Muslims also celebrate a special holy month called Ramadan. During this month they must fast during the daytime, and eat and drink only at night.

One of the most colorful festivals in Libya is the *Mez* (*fantasi*), a custom that goes

Most Libyan women in small towns and villages still wear the traditional *lahaf*.

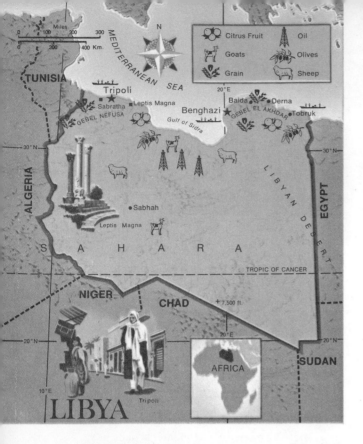

Map legend
- Citrus Fruit
- Goats
- Grain
- Oil
- Olives
- Sheep

back to the 7th century, when proud Arab warriors charged across North Africa. At this festival the men dress in the fine clothes worn in ancient times, place beautiful silver rugs on the saddles of their horses, and do trick riding.

Tea-drinking plays an important part in the life of the people. Traditionally at least three cups of tea were served. Each cup had a different taste and smell. However, this custom is changing, and black coffee or a soft drink may now be served in place of tea. The traditional Libyan dish, couscous, is made of wheat and a sauce of meat, red pumpkin or squash, boiled eggs, and *filfil,* or red pepper. Other favorite dishes are whole roast lamb stuffed with rice, almonds, pine nuts, and spices; and *bazin,* made of steamed wheat or barley and a sauce of stewed vegetables and meat. The dining room in rural areas is often a palm grove. Indoors, cushions are used as chairs, and tables and trays are placed on oriental rugs.

Nearly 80 percent of the people of Libya

Oil is the most important source of income in Libya, where 90 percent of the land is desert.

earn their living by farming or by raising animals. The chief crops are barley, wheat, olives, dates, potatoes, peanuts, and citrus fruits. Tomatoes, carrots, peppers, and other vegetables are also grown.

Raising animals is the most important occupation of farmers in the region of Cyrenaica. Animals are also raised in parts of Tripolitania. The farmers keep sheep and goats as well as camels, cattle, donkeys, and horses.

▶ **THE LAND**

Geographically, Libya is divided into the regions of Tripolitania in the northwest, Fezzan in the southwest, and Cyrenaica in the east. There are no rivers or lakes in Libya. Only a few oases water this dry country.

The Mediterranean Sea and the Sahara desert have a great influence on the Libyan climate. The coast has a Mediterranean type of climate. It is warm with rain during the winter. Most of the interior has a hot, dry climate. A hot desert wind, called the *ghibli* blows from the south and raises the temperature. Temperatures as high as 136 degrees Fahrenheit have been recorded near Tripoli. The climate of the highlands is much cooler. Sometimes it even snows in the mountains in the northwestern part of the country.

Dates, olives, oranges, lemons, and several kinds of vegetables are grown along the coast. South of the coastal area there are gray and green shrubs and bushes. Yellow flowers called *laila* also grow here. A long grassy plant called esparto grows on the hillsides of the northwestern mountains. This grass is used in making cord, baskets, and paper.

In the highlands there are animals common to North Africa, such as the hyena, the jackal, and the fennec, a small, light-colored fox with large ears. Porcupines and desert rabbits are also found here. Farther inland there are gazelles and antelopes.

Very little of Libya's land can be used for growing crops. Over 90 percent of the country is desert. Only a very small part of Libya has enough water for farming. In other sections there is barely enough to support grazing animals. Nevertheless, farm products are important exports. Libya exports peanuts, olive oil, livestock, hides and skins, esparto grass, almonds, seeds, and citrus

FACTS AND FIGURES

LIBYAN ARAB REPUBLIC is the official name of the country.

CAPITAL: Tripoli and Benghazi are dual capitals.

LOCATION: North Africa. **Latitude**—19° 30′ N to 34° N. **Longitude**—9° 30′ E to 25° E.

AREA: 679,360 sq. mi.

POPULATION: 1,870,000 (estimate).

LANGUAGE: Arabic (official), English, Italian, Berber.

GOVERNMENT: Republic, under military rule. **Head of state**—Revolutionary Command Council. **Head of government**—prime minister. **International co-operation**—United Nations, Arab League, Organization of African Unity (OAU).

NATIONAL ANTHEM: Al-Nashid al-Watani ("The National Anthem").

ECONOMY: Agricultural products—cereals (barley and wheat), tomatoes, dates, potatoes, citrus fruits, peanuts, olives, vegetables. **Industries and products**—fishing (sponges, tuna, sardines), food processing, olive oil, fish canneries, flour mills, tanneries, soap, livestock, handicrafts (carpets, jewelry), tobacco. **Chief mineral**—oil. **Chief exports**—oil, peanuts, citrus fruits, almonds, esparto grass, olive oil, hides and skins. **Chief imports**—machinery, transport equipment, textiles, chemicals. **Monetary unit**—Dinar.

fruits. Some years the crops are ruined because it does not rain at all in large sections of the country. In many parts of Libya farming is possible only because water is stored under the ground.

Fishing along Libya's Mediterranean coast is also important. Tuna, sardines, and sponges are taken from the sea.

Libya's industries make its farming and fishing products into goods to be sold. Olive oil, canned fish, tobacco, and flour are produced, and hides and skins are cured.

In the late 1950's vast oil reserves were discovered in Libya. This valuable mineral is now produced and exported in increasing quantities. Today, Libya ranks as one of the world's most important producers of oil.

Tripoli, Libya's largest city and chief port, is also the center of industry. Arabic-style buildings with round domes and towers called minarets stand next to modern office buildings. Flowering trees and brightly colored bushes add to the beauty of this city.

Benghazi is the second largest city. Like Tripoli it has modern houses, bright streets

Tripoli, on the Mediterranean Sea, is one of the dual capitals of Libya.

An ancient Roman theater at Leptis Magna.

and shops, and new movie theaters, restaurants, and gas stations.

Tripoli and Benghazi serve as dual capitals of the country. Beida, a town in the northern part of Cyrenaica, has been greatly enlarged by the Libyan Government.

Ancient Roman ruins are found in several of Libya's cities. Roman temples and theaters can be seen at Sabratha and Leptis Magna near Tripoli. Greek ruins are found in Cyrenaica.

▶ HISTORY

In ancient times the Greeks ruled the part of Libya that is now the region of Cyrenaica. The Phoenicians ruled Tripolitania. Later the Romans conquered both and added them to the Roman Empire. In A.D. 643 Arabs conquered Libya and ruled the country until it was conquered by the Turks. From 1551 to 1912 Libya was ruled by the Turks as part of the Ottoman Empire. The Turks united Fezzan, Tripolitania, and Cyrenaica under one pasha, or governor. In 1911 Italy declared war on Turkey and invaded its African possessions. Turkey lost the war, and in 1912 Libya was ceded to Italy. For the next 20 years the people of Libya carried on armed resistance against their Italian rulers.

During World War II the Allies fought against Italy and Germany in Libya. A Libyan army took part in the struggle beside the Allied troops. After the Allies defeated the Germans and Italians, the British governed Cyrenaica and Tripolitania. The French governed Fezzan.

In 1949 the United Nations decided to join the regions of Libya into a single independent nation and voted for Libya's independence. In December, 1951, Libya became an independent country. Four years later it became a member of the United Nations. Until 1969, Libya was a constitutional monarchy, ruled by King Idris I. In September of that year, a military coup overthrew the government and deposed the King. The revolutionary junta declared the country a republic, and named it the Libyan Arab Republic.

▶ GOVERNMENT

The Libyan Arab Republic is administered by the Revolutionary Command Council. It consists of 12 members whose chairman is also the prime minister and the minister of defense.

JOHN WESLEY COULTER
Professor Emeritus, University of Cincinnati
Reviewed by WAHBI EL BOURI
Ambassador of Libya to the United Nations

LICHENS. See FERNS, MOSSES, AND LICHENS.

LIE, TRYGVE (1896–1968)

Trygve Lie, Norwegian lawyer and statesman, gained worldwide prominence as the first secretary-general of the United Nations. He was born in Oslo on July 16, 1896, the son of a carpenter who died when Trygve was a boy. Young Trygve went to school in Oslo. Always interested in politics and people, he was chosen president of a branch of the Labor Party when he was a 16-year-old high-school student.

In 1914 Lie entered the University of Oslo as a law student. He became a labor lawyer, and after he received his degree he spent many years gaining valuable experience in settling disputes between workers and employers. In 1935 he entered government service as minister of justice. Later he served in the posts of minister of trade and minister of supply. During World War II he was one of the last government officials to leave Norway when the Germans invaded his country. As foreign minister of the Norwegian government-in-exile in London, he arranged several treaties between Norway and the Allies.

Lie's reputation as an international diplomat began when he led his country's delegation to the San Francisco Conference, which adopted the United Nations charter in 1945.

The following year, at the first session of the United Nations General Assembly in London, he was elected secretary-general. His term was marked by his keen understanding of international problems and his forceful efforts on behalf of world peace. In spite of repeated attempts, however, he was unable to maintain the support of the delegation from the Soviet Union, and in 1953 he resigned.

Back in Norway, Lie returned to public service within his own government. In 1955 he was appointed governor of Oslo and Akershus. He was Norway's minister of industry (1963), and minister of commerce from 1964 to 1965.

Lie's wife, a former social worker named Hjördis Jorgensen, died in 1960. The couple had three daughters.

In his many different positions both at home and abroad Lie earned a reputation as a forceful administrator and a skillful arbitrator. A strong believer in peace through international understanding, Lie was most of all a dedicated public servant. In his inauguration speech as secretary-general of the United Nations, he aptly described his own philosophy with these words: "I am the servant of you all."

LIECHTENSTEIN

The tiny country of Liechtenstein has often been called a miniature Switzerland because of its charming Alpine landscape. Its snowy peaks and rushing mountain streams contrast with the carefully tended fields in the Rhine Valley and the vineyards and orchards on the mountain slopes.

THE PEOPLE

The inhabitants of this tiny country tucked in the Alps between Switzerland and Austria are friendly and hospitable. Even strangers are greeted on the street with a smiling *"Grüss Gott"*—"God Bless you" in German, the language of Liechtenstein. Like their Swiss neighbors, the Liechtensteiners are reliable and hardworking. The family is the center of everyday life.

The people of Liechtenstein are fond of music. Almost every village has its own group of men and women who meet once a week to sing folk songs. Nearly every village has a small orchestra or a brass band. On Sundays little Liechtenstein has a festive air. Farmers, townspeople, and mountain folk put on their Sunday clothes. Many women wear their traditional embroidered costume with its big ribboned bonnet. The bells of all the churches and chapels throughout the country call the people—almost all of them devout Roman Catholics—to Mass.

On their way to church, women and children leave flowers at the many open-air shrines and crucifixes along the roads. Flowers of all kinds and colors—geraniums, begonias, carnations, and petunias—add color to the large wooden porches of the Swiss-style chalets, the windowsills of the bright stucco houses, the entrances of restaurants, and the public parks.

THE LAND

Liechtenstein is situated on the right bank of the Rhine River, which separates it from Switzerland. A range of the Alps forms the eastern and northern border with Austria. The whole country covers about 61 square miles. Liechtenstein may be small, but it rises high. Some of its mountain peaks stretch over 8,000 feet above sea level.

Except for a few small resorts in the mountains, all the major settlements are in the Rhine Valley and on the adjoining hills. Vaduz, with a population of almost 4,000, is the capital of the country. It is also the home of the ruling prince and the seat of government. The art gallery in Vaduz contains some of the prince's art collection. It is one of the greatest private art collections in the world. Other important towns are Schaan, Balzers, Triesen, and Eschen.

INDUSTRIES AND PRODUCTS

Until about 40 years ago Liechtenstein was mainly an agricultural country. Today the income of about half the population comes from the industries in the Rhine Valley. Sleepy little villages have been transformed by the building of factories. The chief products include precision instruments, such as calculating machines, and machines for various industries. Other products of Liechtenstein's factories are textiles, chemicals, drugs, dentures, dairy products, canned food, sausage casings, furniture, and ceramics.

Tourism is also important to Liechtenstein's economy. There are comfortable hotels, inns, motels, and well-equipped camping sites. The roads are in excellent condition. The country is crossed by the international railroad linking Zurich, Switzerland, with Vienna, Austria.

In short, Liechtenstein is a well-to-do little

The main street of Vaduz, the capital of Liechtenstein.

country with a standard of living that is among the highest in Europe. In spite of the country's rapid industrial growth, many people still raise cattle, tend their fields, or grow excellent wine grapes.

GOVERNMENT

Liechtenstein is a principality because it is ruled by a prince. The present ruler, Prince Francis Joseph II von und zu Liechtenstein (1906–   ), came to the throne in 1938. A 15-member parliament, the Landtag, is elected by direct vote for a 4-year period. The cabinet, which is responsible to the prince and the Landtag, has four members: the chief and deputy chief of the government, appointed by the prince and approved by the Landtag, and two councillors, who are elected by the Landtag.

HISTORY

In prosperous little Liechtenstein, history is not something that happened long ago and has been forgotten. The medieval castles that dot the land and the popular tales woven around them are faithful reminders of the past. The oldest parts of the prince's palace in Vaduz, for example, date from the 13th century.

The county of Vaduz and the barony of Schellenberg were ruled by several different families until 1699. In that year the Austrian Prince John Adam of Liechtenstein took possession of the barony of Schellenberg. In 1712 he added the county of Vaduz to his

LIECHTENSTEIN

realm. In 1719 the Holy Roman Emperor Charles VI (1685–1740) allowed Prince John Adam's successor, Prince Anton Florian, to unite these two regions in the Principality of Liechtenstein. Liechtenstein was a part of the Holy Roman Empire until 1806, when the ancient empire was dissolved. Liechtenstein was a member of the German Confederation (1815–1866) and then was allied with Austria.

At the end of World War I, Liechtenstein ended its treaties with Austria. In 1921 the Swiss franc replaced Austrian money as the currency of Liechtenstein. Because Liechtenstein is too small a country to keep diplomatic representatives in foreign capitals, it is represented abroad by Switzerland. Swiss customs officials have collected duties on Liechtenstein's Austrian frontier since 1924. The administration of the postal, telegraph, and telephone systems is in Swiss hands, also. Only the postage stamps, which are much sought after by collectors all over the world, are issued directly by Liechtenstein.

DOROTHEA SPADA
Journalist, *Die Stuttgarter Zeitung*
Reviewed by WALTER KRANZ
Chief, Press and Information Office
of the Liechtenstein Government

FACTS AND FIGURES

PRINCIPALITY OF LIECHTENSTEIN is the official name of the country.

CAPITAL: Vaduz.

LOCATION: Central Europe. **Latitude**—47° 03′ N to 47° 10′ N. **Longitude**—9° 28′ E to 9° 38′ E.

AREA: 61 sq. mi.

POPULATION: 20,000 (estimate).

LANGUAGE: German.

GOVERNMENT: Constitutional hereditary monarchy. **Head of state**—prince. **Head of government**—prime minister.

NATIONAL ANTHEM: *Liechtensteinische Volkshymne* ("Liechtenstein People's Hymn").

ECONOMY: Agricultural products—corn, potatoes, wheat, vegetables, wine. **Industries and products**—textiles, wood, precision instruments, chemicals, drugs, dairy products. **Monetary unit**—Swiss franc.

You can easily tell which of these are living and which are nonliving. But do you know what makes them different? Do you know in what ways they are different?

LIFE

What is life? This is a simple question to ask. It is not so simple to answer. In fact, it is so difficult that no scientist can yet answer it in a satisfactory way.

We can, however, explore the question.

Perhaps the best way to start is by asking a different question. For example, what is a human being? Suppose that you try to describe a person you know. You may begin by saying he has a certain height, weighs so many pounds, is thin or fat. He has hair that is blond or dark, curly or straight. His eyes are blue, brown, or gray. He wears this or that sort of clothes. He is intelligent or stupid, talks a lot or is quiet, and so on.

When you have finished, you will have told enough so that someone else can recognize this person. But you probably will have taken certain more important things for granted. For instance, this same human being has a head, neck, and trunk. He has a pair of arms and a pair of legs. He has two eyes and two ears, but only one nose and one mouth. Yet even if you

add these things, you have still said nothing about what makes this person alive.

The surface things are easy to see and describe. The things that make someone alive are difficult to understand and more difficult to explain. Yet living beings have certain features in common. By studying these features scientists hope one day to understand what life is. They also hope to learn how life began.

▶ LIVING BEINGS ARE CHEMICALLY ACTIVE

Scientists speak of all living beings as organisms. A human being is an organism. So is a mouse, a fish, an insect, or a worm. So is a tree, a daisy, or a fungus. So are bacteria and other tiny creatures invisible to the unaided eye.

All these living beings share some important features. That is one reason why scientists use the word "organism," thus giving each living being a name in common with every other living being.

Besides, the very word "organism" suggests that each living thing is organized. That is, its parts are arranged in certain ways and do certain work within the organism as a whole. No matter how simple an organism appears to be, it is very highly organized.

However, organization does not in itself make a substance alive. The parts of a watch are organized and each part has a function. But a watch is not alive. To be alive a substance must be active.

The activity of an organism is chemical. And it takes place inside the organism. You cannot see it. Yet this chemical activity is a continuous process. Without it the organism would not be alive.

Activity Takes Energy

A watch also has internal activity. Yet the watch is not alive. Its activity is mechanical: springs drive a system of cogwheels; the cogwheels turn the hands. The hands of an ordinary watch move only if the spring is wound up. Otherwise the watch runs down and stops. Energy (winding) must be put into the watch so that energy (movement of the hands) can be produced.

So it is with a living organism. Energy must continually enter the organism so that the invisible living machinery keeps going. If the supply of energy fails, the machinery stops. This means that the organism dies. Without

energy there can be no activity. Energy of some sort must continually flow into a living organism. Energy, then, is needed for life.

Activity Requires Material

Matter, too, is continually flowing through an organism. In this sense a living being can be compared with a river. A river consists of water contained by a riverbed. It has shape (the riverbed) and material (the water). The water flows through the riverbed. The river may look the same. Yet its material is always changing. The water at any one spot is never the same water. New water continually enters the upper end of the river, flows through the riverbed, and enters the sea at the other end. Water evaporates from the sea, falls again as rain or snow, and runs downhill with the pull of gravity.

So it is with life. A living organism has shape and substance (material). New material is continually flowing into living substance. The new material takes the place of older material, which is continually being pushed out or used up. Living material changes continually. Life is something that is happening. It is a process.

The same sort of process can also be observed in a candle flame. Matter (hydrogen and carbon from the paraffin and oxygen from

A watch, a river, and a candle are nonliving. Yet all share certain characteristics with living things. Can you name these characteristics?

Growth occurs when new living matter is building up faster than old breaks down, as shown in these photos of mushrooms taken over a span of 5 days.

the air) burns, forming the flame. The flame has shape and color. It gives off heat and carbon dioxide. It exists only as long as new material enters. If the supply of oxygen is cut off or if the paraffin becomes used up, the flame goes out.

Continual replacement of old material with new is as much a characteristic of life as is the flow of energy. The flow of energy and matter through an organism is called **metabolism**.

Material Needs Replacement

An organism grows if the new material flows in faster than the old material moves out. This is somewhat like heavy rains pouring water into a river faster than the water flows into the sea. The water level rises and overflows the riverbank. In other words, the river grows. As long as an organism is increasing in size or weight, it is growing. New living matter is building up faster than the old is breaking down. This is the kind of growth that you can see.

Once an organism has become full size, new material builds up at about the same rate as the old material breaks down. The organism stays the same size. It no longer grows. The flow of energy and matter continues, but it gradually slows down.

Finally, old material breaks down faster

than new material builds up. The organism ages and finally dies.

Something is needed to replace aging and dying organisms. Living material is able to make copies of itself. This process, called **reproduction**, has something in common with growth. But in reproduction only part—usually a small part—of a living organism is involved. In plants and animals these parts are commonly seeds and eggs. They give rise to new organisms of the same kind as the parents. In all living beings the process of reproduction makes new, similar organisms, which replace older organisms. Otherwise life would disappear.

Reproduction is one of the most important features of life. Living beings are characterized by certain processes. These are metabolism, growth, and reproduction. To be fully alive a thing must be chemically active, it must increase in size, and it must be able to duplicate itself. In other words, an organism is alive if it can metabolize, grow, and reproduce.

Many things remind us of living beings in one way or another, although these are not truly alive. Matter and energy flow into a candle flame, for example. The flame is chemically active, but it cannot reproduce itself. Crystals grow—but that is all they do. Viruses can reproduce—but only under certain conditions.

A virus is a small particle, very much smaller than any living organism, smaller even than the smallest kinds of bacteria. Most of the time it is not active. However, when it comes in contact with the right sort of living material, the virus may enter the material and reproduce. Then it gives rise to many more virus particles. Thus, a virus has one of the most important characteristics of life. But it is active only when it is inside truly living material. It lacks the other important features of life.

▶ **WHAT IS LIVING MATTER MADE OF?**

Living material usually exists in the form of cells. Most cells are microscopic in size but are very complex. In general, though, we can say that a cell has a central nucleus, surrounded by a mass of cytoplasm. Most of the life processes of the cell are carried on in the cytoplasm. The cytoplasm, in turn, is surrounded by an outer cell membrane. Large animals and plants consist of many billions of such cells. Many small organisms consist only of single cells. Still other organisms are composed not of cells but of fine threads of living matter. This is true of mushrooms and some other fungi, for example. Yet even in such organisms the living matter usually consists of many nuclei embedded in cytoplasm.

The basic living material that makes up the cells of bacteria, butterflies, roses, humans, and all other organisms is the same. A rose differs from a butterfly mainly in the way its material is put together.

Materials like brick, stone, cement, wood, nails, and glass can be put together to make a chicken house or a great cathedral. The same materials can be used to make very different buildings. And so it is with living matter. The elements in all organisms are the same. Only the proportions are different.

On earth there are about 90 elements that occur naturally, ranging from hydrogen, which is the lightest, to uranium, the heaviest.

Living matter is mostly made up of the lightest and most common elements. The chief ones are hydrogen, carbon, nitrogen, and oxygen. These form the main building materials. A few somewhat heavier, rarer ele-

Living material can reproduce itself. Sunflower (*left*) produces seeds, from which more plants grow. Frogs produce eggs (*right*), from which tadpoles hatch.

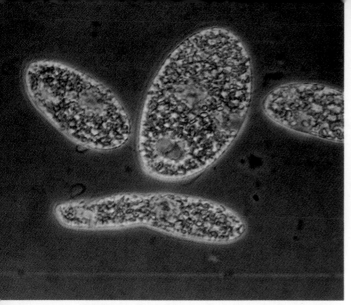

Some flagellates take in food, as animals do. Others, like these, make their own food, as plants do.

Green plants get the necessary outside materials in the form of water, carbon dioxide, and dissolved compounds of nitrogen and other elements. They use the energy of light. This process is called **photosynthesis**. It is carried on in the plant cells by means of chlorophyll (which gives plants their green color).

During photosynthesis the energy of light is used to split molecules of water into oxygen and an active form of hydrogen. The hydrogen combines with carbon dioxide, forming carbohydrate. This starts the production of more and more complex compounds, including the amino acids. These are the building blocks for making the all-important proteins.

Most of the oxygen split off from the water molecules is not needed. It is released into the surroundings. Scientists think that most of the oxygen in the atmosphere is a waste product of photosynthesis.

Animal life depends on plant life. Animals cannot manufacture their own proteins, carbohydrates, and other compounds directly from water, carbon dioxide, and nitrates. They must start with more complex building units. They must get their raw material from other organisms. These other organisms may be either living or dead.

Some animals feed directly on plants. Some are meat-eaters that feed on plant-eaters. Still others feed on both plants and meat. That is why we say that animal life depends on plant life. The plant proteins and carbohydrates must be split up into their building units, which are the amino acids and simple sugars. In other words, proteins and carbohydrates must be digested. Then, from these building units the animal organism produces its own proteins and carbohydrates.

It needs a source of energy to do this. Animals have no chlorophyll and make no use of the energy of light. Their energy comes from the food material. An animal gets chemical energy when sugar and some other compounds are broken down into carbon dioxide and water. It uses up oxygen in this process. Consequently, all animal life takes in oxygen and gives off carbon dioxide. Plant life takes in carbon dioxide and gives off oxygen. This is the great difference between plants and animals.

They are different also in that, as a rule,

ments are also important. These are sulfur, chlorine, phosphorus, iron, magnesium, sodium, potassium, and calcium. They are used in smaller quantities. You might think of them as the mortar, electric wiring, and plumbing materials in a building.

Three main kinds of chemical compounds make up most living material. These are carbohydrates, fats, and proteins. Carbohydrates and fats are made up of three of the four most common elements: carbon, hydrogen, and oxygen. Proteins require nitrogen as well, usually with a little sulfur to hold them together in special ways.

To these compounds we should add a fourth—water itself. Living matter consists mostly of water. Even with the bones included, your body is more than 67 percent water. A jellyfish is more than 95 percent water. This water is bound up in the framework of the living material itself.

▶ **DIFFERENCES BETWEEN PLANT AND ANIMAL LIFE**

The main problem of all living organisms is to get the basic elements needed for metabolism, growth, and reproduction. Every organism takes in matter from the outside. It must then use the elements to make the kinds of proteins, carbohydrates, and fats that it needs.

For this chemical work each organism must take in matter containing the needed elements. It must also have a supply of energy.

animals move from place to place and plants do not. Most animals must move about to find plant material or other animals that feed on plants. This also means that they respond to their surroundings to a much greater extent than do plants. However, plants are sensitive to such things as touch, chemicals, light, and gravity.

Not all animals move about. Some become attached to the floor of the sea or of fresh-water lakes and ponds. These creatures get their food from the water as it flows by. Sponges, which seem more like plants than animals, are a good example.

Some organisms are like plants in some ways and like animals in others. One example is the group of single-celled organisms called the flagellates. Their name comes from the flagellum, a tiny whiplike thread by means of which they move. Some flagellates are like plants. They have chlorophyll and manufacture new material from water and carbon dioxide. Other flagellates lack chlorophyll.

Like animals, they take in ready-made organic material, usually bacteria.

Another borderline case is the large group of well-known organisms called fungi. This group includes the mushrooms, toadstools, and molds. Their cells and methods of reproduction are more like those of plants than of animals. They live and grow more like plants. Yet they have no chlorophyll and do not photosynthesize their own material. Fungi absorb material from other organisms either living or dead. In this way they are more like animals.

▶ HOW DID LIFE BEGIN?

For a long time people have wondered how life first began on earth. Today's scientists think that life came into existence very slowly, over millions and millions of years, when the earth itself was very young. Their present theory is that simple gases may have combined chemically and that life slowly evolved from these chemical compounds.

How did life begin? Scientists think that ultraviolet light and lightning acted on gases in the atmosphere of the young earth, forming building blocks of life.

HEAT

ULTRAVIOLET
LIGHT

ATMOSPHERIC
GASES

LIGHTNING

WATER

Copying probable conditions of early earth, Stanley Miller produced amino acids in a laboratory in 1953.

and carbon dioxide. Experiments have been designed to copy conditions that may have been present in the young earth. These conditions included the gases, heat, rain, and lightning. Scientists exposed mixtures of the gases to ultraviolet light and electric sparks. They found that after a time the gases combined to form sugars, amino acids, and other organic compounds. These compounds are, of course, important building blocks for all life.

This finding shows a link between nonliving and living matter. From this beginning scientists are now building in the laboratory more of the compounds found in living matter. The more evidence they can produce, the more they can be sure they are on the right track. Perhaps someday they may even be able to answer the question: What is life?

N. J. BERRILL
McGill University

See also AGING; BODY CHEMISTRY; CELL; KINGDOMS OF LIVING THINGS; PHOTOSYNTHESIS.

In the earliest period of the earth's existence, scientists say, the atmosphere was very different from what it is now. It had no oxygen but consisted of other gases—perhaps methane, ammonia, and water or perhaps nitrogen

LIFE, ADAPTATIONS IN THE WORLD OF

Animals and plants, as a general rule, are suited to their surroundings. Rabbits live on land and breathe air; in water they drown. Fish thrive in water but quickly suffocate out of it. Ferns live well in damp, shady places but not in deserts. Cacti do well in dry, semidesert regions but not in forests.

The range of places in which life can exist is enormous. The conditions for life vary from place to place and from time to time—even in the same place. Plants and animals in any particular place must be suited to the local conditions. And to survive and reproduce their own kind, they must be able to deal with changes that occur. In other words, they need to be **adapted** to their surroundings. Otherwise their species (kind) would become **extinct** (die out).

▶ ADAPTATION TO SURROUNDINGS

Animals are fitted to their surroundings in various ways. Reptiles offer a good example. They were the first four-legged vertebrates (animals with backbones) to roam freely over the land millions of years ago. There used to be many more kinds than there are at present.

Today there are still a good many different kinds, each adapted to living in a particular way. If these species were not well adapted, they would not have survived.

Most lizards run freely on their four legs. They breathe air through lungs. They lay relatively large eggs protected by shells. When little lizards hatch, they are able to run around like their parents. Lizards are well adapted in a general way to living on land.

Some lizards are adapted to living under more special conditions. The horned lizard, for example, is fitted for life in the dry Southwest of the United States. All organisms need water, and there is little water in the desert where this animal lives. However, its heavy "horned" skin prevents loss of water. The lizard gets small amounts of water in the animals it eats. Its waste materials are dry, so little water is lost. During the heat of the day the lizard protects its body against drying out by burrowing into the sand. Its behavior and its body structure are specially adapted to life in the desert.

Still other reptiles have become adapted to very different conditions. For instance, some

Ferns (*above*) grow well in damp, shady places but not in deserts. Cacti (*right*) grow well in dry, desertlike areas. Each type of plant is adapted to its surroundings—it is suited to particular conditions, as are animals.

turtles live in the sea. A sea turtle has a heavy protective shell, like its land relatives. But both its front and hind legs have become flippers for swimming. Yet a sea turtle still must breathe air and lay its eggs on land.

Millions of years ago the front feet and legs of certain reptiles changed in another way. They became wings. These creatures, the pterosaurs (winged reptiles), were adapted for flight. They are now extinct.

However, in another group of reptiles the front legs and hands also became wings, somewhat different in design. Gradually backbones and other structures changed. Slowly these creatures developed into the kinds of birds we see around us today.

DIFFERENT ADAPTATIONS TO SIMILAR CONDITIONS

Birds have become well adapted for flight. So have bats. The forelegs of these two animals have become wings. But their wings developed in different ways.

Insects, too, have become adapted for flight. Unlike birds and bats, insects have no backbones. Their bodies are supported by a tough outer covering. In general, they have two pairs of wings, grown from the upper side of the middle part of the body.

Each species of organism is adapted in its own way to its surroundings. For example, tarpon and sea anemones are animals that live in the sea. The tarpon, which is a fish, propels

Tarpon, a fish, is adapted to life in water. It swims about to find its food.

Sea anemone has a different adaptation for food finding. It waits for food to come near its tentacles.

itself through the water in search of food. To do this, it uses powerful muscles along each side of its tapering body and at the base of the tail. It uses its fins to keep on an even keel. (The very shape of a fish is an outstanding example of adaptation. It is the body shape that moves through water most rapidly.)

Unlike fishes, sea anemones do not move around in search of food. An anemone has the shape of a long sac. Its closed bottom end clings to a rock or other surface. The mouth opening is at the other end, surrounded by a ring of tentacles. These are sticky and bear stinging cells. The tentacles reach out in all directions, for food may arrive from anywhere.

Unlike fishes, an anemone has no head, brain, eyes, or jaws. An animal that doesn't go anywhere has no need of such things. An anemone remains attached and waits for food to come within reach of its tentacles. It spends almost no energy getting food. It is perfectly adapted for what it needs to do.

A tarpon and a sea anemone represent different but equally successful ways of living in the same watery surroundings. Each is well adapted for life in the sea. Moreover, as this example shows, there is often more than one way to adapt, even to very similar conditions.

Tarpon and shark are fishes; icthyosaur, an extinct reptile; dolphin and seal, mammals. Water dwellers all, they developed the same general body shape.

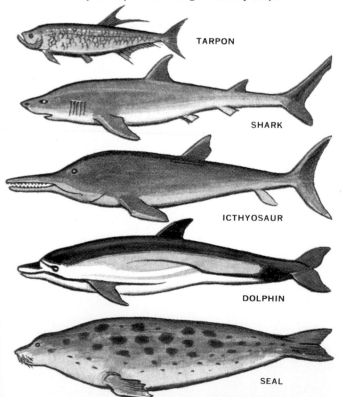

TARPON

SHARK

ICTHYOSAUR

DOLPHIN

SEAL

▶ADAPTATION TO CHANGE

In general, conditions of life in the sea change very little. On land they are constantly changing. New animals may arrive in a particular place and compete for existing food supplies or prey on other animals. Some animals may leave and others may die out for some reason. Over a long period of time the climate may change. Each species as a whole will survive only if it adapts to the new conditions. This is true also when animals and plants spread into places where conditions are different.

The term **adaptation** is often used to mean the process by which species of organisms become adapted to their surroundings. This process is very slow, and the results show only after many generations. If a species of organism fails to adapt quickly enough, it may become extinct.

Adaptation results partly from the fact that the offspring of any set of parents differ from one another in many small ways. (This may be seen in a family of dogs.) Some individuals in any family and in any population, or group, of the same species may be better suited to live in a certain place than others. In other words, in one environment (surroundings) some offspring get along better than others. Therefore they will be more successful in producing and raising healthy offspring of their own. If the environment does not change, the offspring most like the parents will probably do best.

On the other hand, if conditions are changing, the offspring that are most unlike the parents may be better suited in many small ways to the new environment. They in turn will be more successful in producing offspring. And some of their offspring will be more successful than others, and so on.

Very slowly, generation by generation, certain varieties of offspring will have been favored by the changing conditions. Eventually a change will result in the nature of the organism, a change that one can see and recognize as an adaptation to the new environment. Thus new species of organisms **evolve**, or develop, by a process of **natural selection**.

Natural Selection

The process of natural selection goes on in an entire population of a particular species,

Giraffe's long neck may be an adaptation to long legs, for feeding and drinking.

and not merely in a few individuals. The workings of this process may be seen in the case of the European cuckoo. This bird does not build a nest and hatch its own egg. Instead, it lays its single egg in the nest of another kind of bird. It is important that the cuckoo egg look as much like the eggs of the host bird as possible. Host birds tend to desert their nests if they notice a strange egg.

Cuckoo eggs vary somewhat in color. Some eggs happen to look a little more like the host birds' eggs than others. Those most like the hosts' eggs are less likely to be noticed, and so more likely to be hatched. Now, after untold generations of cuckoos, the eggs match the host eggs nearly perfectly.

As a result of natural selection, the European cuckoo lays blue eggs in Finland, where the host birds, redstarts and whinchats, lay blue eggs. In Hungary the host bird is the great reed warbler, whose eggs are greenish, blotched with brown and black. The cuckoo eggs are similar. In England cuckoos use the nests of many kinds of birds, such as pipits, warblers, and wagtails. These birds all produce rather plain-looking eggs, and so do the cuckoos.

▶ ADAPTATION TO ADAPTATIONS

One part of an animal's body may be a special adaptation to other parts of its body and so to the nature of the animal as a whole. For example, a giraffe's most notable features

are its long legs and long neck. The long legs enable the giraffe to travel very fast and so to escape its lurking enemies, lions and leopards.

At one time it was thought that the giraffe's long neck was an adaptation for feeding on the top parts of certain common African trees. Even though the giraffe's long neck does enable its mouth to reach these parts, the neck may actually have evolved in another way.

During thousands of giraffe generations, the legs gradually became longer. But giraffes still had to drink water and to feed on grass and other low plants. Their mouths had to be able to reach the ground no matter how long the legs or how high the body from the ground. The neck gradually grew longer. The long neck, some scientists say, is therefore a special adaptation to the longer legs. The long legs are an adaptation that aids the animal in escaping its enemies. Both adaptations aid in the continued survival of this species.

▶ ADAPTATION FOR SELF-PROTECTION

Success in staying alive long enough to breed and so help to produce the next generation is the most important thing for the survival of any population. To do this, an animal must succeed in getting food. It is equally important to avoid becoming the food of some other creature.

Generally speaking, there are three ways to avoid being eaten. One is to move fast enough

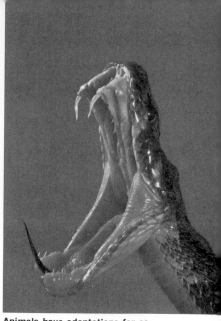

Animals have adaptations for escaping danger or attacking. Poison glands and fangs, like those of cottonmouth (*above*), make possible an attack on animal larger than the attacker. Rhino (*left*) is seldom attacked because of its very large size and very thick hide.

Camouflage protects the walkingstick. It also protects the caterpillar.

Brown coat of weasel (*left*) turns white (*right*) as snowy northern winter approaches.

to escape. Another is to be too big for most other kinds of animals to eat. And the third is not to be seen. In the animal kingdom there are many examples of each kind of adaptation.

Escape

Many large animals, such as giraffes and deer, rely on speed to escape from their enemies. The quick escape is also seen in many smaller animals. For example, in frogs, fleas, and grasshoppers the hind legs are very large. They enable the animal to jump high and fast when alarmed. Shrimps, crayfish, and lobsters flip their tails violently and so shoot rapidly backward. Many fishes flip their tails and shoot forward. All such special adaptations of the body enable the owner to escape danger and so go on living.

Large Size

Large size may be a protection against the danger of being eaten. It is very difficult for an animal to kill and eat another animal that is as large as—or larger than—itself. This is possible only for attackers equipped with special adaptations, such as poison glands, or with weapons, such as teeth or fangs.

Most fishes can feed only on smaller creatures that can be swallowed whole—shrimp, crabs, and other fishes. As a rule, a fish of a certain size can feed on any water-living creature smaller than itself. At the same time, it can be eaten only by an animal larger than itself.

The largest animals, such as whales and elephants, are rarely attacked except by man or by very ferocious creatures. Killer whales and tigers have powerful jaws and teeth. With these special adaptations killer whales can attack larger whales, and tigers can attack elephants.

Elephants, rhinoceroses, and hippopotamuses are protected by very thick skin, or hide, as well as by their very large size. They also have other special adaptations that suit them for life as a whole. For instance, their legs are like sturdy pillars holding up the great body weight. Slender legs like those of a giraffe would be no good at all. As in the case of the giraffe, one part of the body has become adapted to the character of the animal as a whole.

Camouflage

To be invisible is the least expensive way to protect oneself. Sudden speed uses up a lot of energy, and large size requires great quantities of food.

Protective coloring is very good camouflage, especially when combined with unusual body shapes. Many caterpillars, for instance, have the same color as the plant on which they feed. Some even have the same shape as the twigs they crawl on. Those creatures that look most like their surroundings are the most likely to be overlooked by insect-eating birds.

Camouflage serves the same purpose in adult insects, particularly moths. During the day these animals rest on the bark of trees. Generally they have the same sort of light and dark pattern seen in the bark. Their wings have an irregular outline. These things make it hard to detect a moth on a tree.

One of the most striking examples of camouflage can be seen in a flounder. This fish lies on the sea floor on its left side. Both eyes are on the upper or right side of the head. The underside of the body is pale, and the upper side dark. The fish's coloring blends with the sand, mud, or gravel of its surroundings.

Even more remarkable, it can change its color and appearance whenever it moves to different surroundings. Numerous small pigment (color) cells are scattered through the skin. Each star-shaped cell can expand (open up) or contract (close up). When all the cells are contracted, the spots of pigment are too small to be seen. Then the flounder's skin looks pale. When all the cells are expanded, the pigment spots cover the whole skin; the skin then has a dark brown color. According to what the flounder sees, the pigment cells are stimulated to imitate the appearance of the surroundings. This protects flounders from other fishes and from diving birds.

Few other animals can change color quickly in this way. Certain frogs and shrimps can do so, as can mollusks such as the octopus, squid, and cuttlefish. Nevertheless, most animals have the same need to remain as invisible as possible. This is true whether they are in danger from other animals or must creep up unsuspected on them. Tigers' stripes and leopards' spots make these animals less visible in the light and shade of the jungle.

A DEMONSTRATION OF CAMOUFLAGE

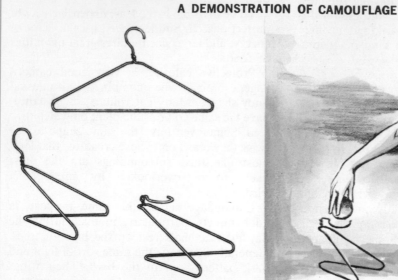

To see the way coloring protects animals from their enemies, try this simple demonstration. You will need three smooth potatoes of the same size, three wire coat hangers, and some white paint (or a paring knife if you have no paint).

To Make the Animals

Bend the coat hangers to form stands for the potatoes as shown in the drawings. Set up the stands on level ground out of direct sunlight. Adjust the wire so that the hanger will stand steadily, the hook forming a cradle for the potato body. Carefully balance the potatoes in their cradles.

Coloring the Animals

(1) Sprinkle handfuls of earth over the animals until they are the same color as their surroundings.

Walk away from the animals, pacing off about 25 feet. Turn around and look at the animals. Can you see them? Which part is the least visible?

(2) Now take two of the potatoes. Holding each one firmly, dip one half into white paint. Let the paint dry before continuing the experiment. (If you have no paint remove the dark peel from half of each potato. Repeat the experiment immediately before the white potato darkens.)

Place the potatoes white side down in their cradles. Sprinkle with earth, being careful not to get earth on the white part. Walk away from the animals. Which of the three is most visible?

(3) Now place one of the part-white potatoes white side up in its stand. Walk away from the animals. Which is most visible now?

In northern regions where the landscape is brown and green in summer and white in winter, color protection good for one season may be bad in another. Weasels, Arctic foxes, snow hares, and birds such as the ptarmigan shed their brown hair or feathers at the end of summer. They grow white coverings for the winter and then change back again when spring comes. In this way they become almost invisible against their surroundings.

▶ADAPTATION TO OTHER ORGANISMS

Through the process of natural selection, each species of plant and animal has slowly—over many generations—become adapted to its surroundings, both living and nonliving. A

honeybee, for instance, is adapted for life on land and in the air but not for life in the water. That is, it has legs for walking, wings for flying, and air tubes for breathing. In these ways it is like most other insects.

An adult honeybee, however, has other features that suit it for its own particular way of life and no other. It has special mouthparts for getting nectar from flowers. It has hairs and brushes that pick up pollen at the same time. It can live entirely on sugars. It can make and mold wax into shelters for food and young. And it lives as a member of a closely co-operating social colony (the hive). All these special adaptations make the honeybee different from most other insects. Through natural selection it has become adapted to living in a world of flowers.

Butterflies, moths, and some other insects are also adapted to this world of flowers. Such nectar-feeding insects differ in various ways. Some have long tongues; others have short tongues. Some are large in size; others are small. Their particular traits suit them for feeding on certain flowers and not on others.

The flowers, too, have become adapted to nectar-feeding insects. When a bee collects nectar, pollen is generally deposited on its body. The bee then carries the pollen to the next flower it visits. It is important that the pollen produced by one plant reach the flower of other plants of the same species. This results in greater variety among the seeds of that plant species, and so helps that species to survive. Without insects many plants could not produce seeds at all.

Through the process of natural selection flowers have become adapted to particular kinds of insects. Clover and other flowers have nectar in deep pockets that generally only bumblebees can reach. Other flowers, such as columbine, have nectar in deep tubes that only the very long tongues of butterflies can reach. Large, light-colored lilies with deep throats open at night. That is when long-tongued moths feed.

Birds, like insects, are well adapted for life

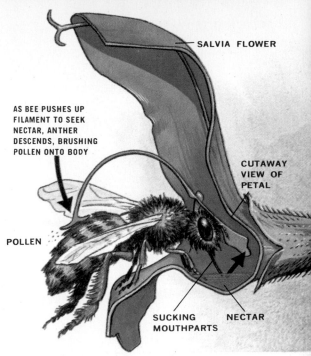

SALVIA FLOWER

AS BEE PUSHES UP FILAMENT TO SEEK NECTAR, ANTHER DESCENDS, BRUSHING POLLEN ONTO BODY

CUTAWAY VIEW OF PETAL

POLLEN

SUCKING MOUTHPARTS   NECTAR

Adult honeybee is like other insects in many ways, but has special adaptations for getting nectar.

on land and in the air. They are further adapted to these general surroundings in many small ways. For instance, bills have become adapted to many different kinds of food. Birds differ in their choice of nest site as well as choice of food. This means that in a small area of wooded land, for instance, many kinds of birds can live together without exhausting

Birds' bills are adapted to different kinds of food. (1) Woodpecker seeks insects in tree bark. (2) Warbler catches small insects. (3) Owl hunts mice. (4) Hummingbird sucks nectar. (5) Robin catches worm. (6) Sparrow eats seeds on ground.

Chipmunk (*above*) is chiefly a ground dweller and can live in same area with tree-dwelling squirrel (*below*).

trees for insects. At night, owls pounce on mice scurrying in litter and underbrush.

Robins build their nests in shrubs and in the forks of trees. Sparrows and juncos nest on or near the ground. Hummingbirds nest on branches near running water, and so on. Each kind of bird has its own manner of making a nest and of caring for its eggs and young.

Each kind of bird carries out its necessary activities in its own way. Each has its own **niche**, which means that each has its own particular circumstances and habits. An American robin, for example, feeds on worms and insects on the ground, and nests in low branches of trees; woodpeckers dig for insects in the bark of trees and nest in tree holes. The more kinds of trees and shrubs growing in a certain forest, the more different kinds of birds and other animals will be found living together side by side. And each plant and animal plays a part in the activities of that forest area as a whole.

▶ EACH ORGANISM HAS ITS OWN NICHE

Chipmunks and red squirrels live together in the woods. Both are able to climb trees and run on the ground. However, chipmunks spend most of their time on the ground and rarely climb. For safety they usually run to a nearby burrow or rock crevice. Squirrels spend most of their time in the trees and very little on the ground. They climb for safety.

Thus chipmunks and squirrels do not compete with one another. Each has specialized in its habits and to some extent in its choice of food. Each has its own niche.

Red squirrels and gray squirrels, on the other hand, both occupy the same niche. They compete with one another for food and for shelter in the treetops. Usually one species is more successful than the other. In England, for example, the gray squirrel (introduced from North America) has to a great extent taken the place of the native red squirrel.

Niches of the Seashore

The way organisms occupy different niches within the same environment is readily seen on rocky seashores between the level of high and low tide. This **intertidal** (between the tides) **area** is a particular kind of environment. It is under the sea for some time each day and exposed to the air for some time. In most

supplies of food and water and without destroying one another.

During the day robins, with their long, powerful beaks, pull earthworms out of the ground. Sparrows and juncos eat small seeds on the ground. Hummingbirds suck nectar from flowers. Warblers search trees for small insects. Woodpeckers, with their sharp beaks and long tongues, dig through the bark of regions of the earth the tide rises and falls twice each day.

Near the level of low tide the shore is exposed for a short while only. It is covered by the sea most of the time. Near the level of high tide the shore is exposed most of the time and is covered by the sea only for a little while each day. Midway between high and low water the shore is exposed to water and air for equal periods of about 6 hours each, twice a day.

The plants and animals that live in this intertidal area have had to adapt to these various degrees of exposure to air. At every level between high tide and low tide conditions are somewhat different, and the kinds of organisms are different.

Near the high-tide level there are usually no plants growing. However, seaweeds (algae) are cast up by the tide itself and provide food and shelter for countless sand hoppers, or beach fleas. (And the sand hoppers supply food for various shore birds.) On higher rocks, where there is little or no seaweed, barnacles and blue mussels are usually anchored firmly to the rock surface. Both kinds of animals close up when the tide falls. In this way they stay wet inside their shells until the sea again covers them.

At lower levels various kinds of algae occupy different niches, depending on how well they can do without water. The seaweed itself forms a curtain over the rocks. Beneath it many creatures find cool moisture, which enables them to survive until the tide rises. Winkles, whelks, small starfish, and certain kinds of sea anemones are found in such places.

Down near the low tide level, particularly in rock pools where some water remains, there live many of the creatures found beyond the intertidal area. In short, each level has its own populations of organisms, each adapted to particular living conditions and thus filling a particular niche.

▶ SUCCESSFUL ADAPTATIONS

When a plant or animal is perfectly adapted to its surroundings, it is important that its nature remain unchanged—at least so long as the surroundings do not change. Any change in a well-adapted organism would not improve its chances for survival. It would probably hurt them.

Certain kinds of organisms apparently have not changed at all for hundreds of millions of years. This is not surprising, for their surroundings have changed very little in all that

Intertidal area is underwater for some time each day and exposed to air for some time. Organisms living in this area have had to adapt to this situation.

Two survivors from the past—lungfish (*left*) and horseshoe crab (*right*). Neither has changed much in 200,000,000 to 300,000,000 years.

time. For instance, though coastlines have changed since the earth was young, flat sandy seashores have undoubtedly always existed somewhere. Two animals in particular became adapted to living in such sand flats millions of years ago. They have stayed almost the same for all this time.

Baboon, like other higher primates, has good use of hands and a well-developed brain.

One of these creatures is the stalked lamp shell, or *Lingula*. This animal has lived in such places for 500,000,000 or 600,000,000 years. It lived in them when fishes did not exist at all. It is living in them still.

The horseshoe crab, or *Limulus,* has remained almost unchanged for more than 200,000,000 years. It lived before the first dinosaurs crawled about on land, and long before the first birds and mammals.

In shallow, still waters in South America, central Africa, and Australia live the remains of a large population of fish that lived in similar surroundings all over the world about 300,000,000 years ago. These survivors are the lungfishes, which have lungs as well as gills for breathing.

From certain ancestors of these fish developed the four-legged vertebrates of the land. From other kinds developed the bony fishes of the freshwaters and seas. A few lungfishes lived on, with little change, in those parts of the world where certain conditions persisted.

Fossil remains of these species have been found in rocks formed in ancient times. Thus scientists can see that these organisms have changed very little for millions of years. And because they have changed so little, they are commonly called "living fossils." Of course, individuals of these species are still very much alive.

▶ FAILURES TO ADAPT

Many kinds of organisms have successfully adapted to changes in their environment. And some have survived unchanged because they can still find the right age-old conditions.

However, the history of past life on earth is

also a story of failures. Failure to adapt to new conditions leads to extinction. In fact, many more kinds of organisms have become extinct than have survived. The rocky sediments of the earth's crust are studded with the fossil remains of many kinds of extinct organisms, as well as with those of ancestors of living, or recently living, kinds.

Extinction can result from many causes. A change in climate, if it lasts long enough, may kill the plants on which certain animals depend for food and shelter. For instance, during the past 10,000 years the once grassy plains of the Sahara have become sandy deserts. Few organisms adapted to the new conditions, and this African region has become uninhabitable for most kinds of animals and plants. Today elephants, lions, zebras, giraffes, and many deerlike creatures can survive only south of the Sahara desert. Their former range has become greatly reduced.

During the last 1,000,000 years the great glaciers of the Ice Age advanced over much of North America and Europe. The glaciers changed conditions of life, and many organisms that once inhabited certain regions did not survive. Others survived the ice but perished when the ice melted, leaving floods of water.

Long before these events, many kinds of reptiles grew to giant size. You may have seen the fossil skeleton of a *Brontosaurus* or a *Brachiosaurus* in a museum. These dinosaurs were two of the largest animals ever to walk on the earth. They fed on plants. Other dinosaur species, like the ferocious *Tyrannosaurus*, which stood about 20 feet tall, preyed on the giant plant-eaters. Altogether, such giant reptiles were masters of the earth for 100,000,000 years. They had no enemies other than themselves. Yet finally they disappeared. Only small kinds of reptiles remained.

No one is yet sure why the dinosaurs became extinct, and we may never know. There may be several reasons. One is that these reptiles had enormous bodies but very small brains. The dinosaurs may have become too big for their own good. Another reason is that the plant-eaters needed a great deal of food, perhaps more than they could find. As a result, they became fewer and fewer as time went on. And so did the flesh-eaters that preyed on them. Another reason may be that small mammals destroyed and ate too many of their eggs.

Scientists do know that when the dinosaurs disappeared, the mammals took their place as the dominant creatures of the land.

Mammals are a large group of air-breathing animals with backbones. Unlike most animals, mammals are warm-blooded. Nearly every kind of mammal gives birth to living young. And all mammals produce milk, on which the young feed. Mammals are the only animals that produce milk. They are also the only animals that have hair. These and many other features are all adaptations. The adaptations have made it possible for mammals to be the most widely successful of the land animals.

▶ THE DEVELOPMENT OF THE PRIMATES

As the mammals spread out, many different kinds developed, including the primate group. All primates are now—or were once—adapted to living in trees. In this group are classed apes, monkeys, and some little-known tree-living creatures, such as the lemurs of Madagascar and the spectral tarsier of southeastern Asia. Scientists include man in this group also.

In the tropical and semitropical forests of long ago, some small mammals began to climb trees. Perhaps they wanted to get food, such as fruit, insects, or birds' eggs. Perhaps, too, they had to escape enemies on the ground.

Gradually their legs and feet became better suited for grasping branches and climbing. Little by little these creatures became adapted for living in the trees.

They no longer could rely on their sense of smell to warn them of danger or to track other animals through the underbrush. Instead, they relied on their senses of sight and hearing. Their noses became flatter, and their eyes became larger and set more toward the front of the face. Unlike their ground-living relatives, whose eyes were set at either side of a longish snout, the tree-dwellers could look directly ahead and focus both eyes on the same object. This meant that they gained a sense of space and distance. This three-dimensional vision was an advantage in judging distances, when a mistake in jumping from one branch to another could be fatal.

With stereoscopic (three-dimensional) vision these creatures could also focus on objects held close up in the hands. And hands good for climbing were good for holding things, such as food. The sense of touch became more developed. As these mammals examined and handled objects with eyes and hands, the brain developed. In particular, the parts of the brain concerned with vision became highly developed. Unlike a dog's brain, which is ruled mainly by a sense of smell, the sort of brain found in primates is ruled mainly by stereoscopic vision.

Mammals with this eye-hand brain became adapted for life in the trees in other ways too. Climbing, running, and jumping through trees required other changes in the body.

The hind legs, which had acquired handlike feet, were used more and more to support the body. Balancing on the hind legs was gradually done with more and more skill. The forearms were used more and more to reach out or up to grasp other branches. The forearms became longer and stronger. At the same time, hands and arms had to turn easily at the wrist and shoulder for swinging from branch to branch. (You can observe these movements in yourself next time you climb a tree or swing along a bar in a gymnasium.)

In some such ways, through a process of natural selection, some ground-living mammals became adapted to living in trees, and creatures something like present-day monkeys and apes came into existence.

Eventually some tree-living primates left the trees. They became adapted to life on the ground. Now their need was to run swiftly in order to capture small animals for food and to escape from large ones. Gradually these primates became sprinters, capable of sudden and rapid running. The legs became longer. Large muscles developed in the calf and thigh. The handlike feet became stronger for running instead of holding branches. Heels developed that made standing still and upright easier.

With all these adaptations to life on the ground, the brain grew larger. These mammals could better remember past experiences and plan future actions. Hands became more and more skillful. They began to shape stones for tools and weapons. In some such way, scientists say, man gradually came into existence.

The story of the long, slow development of the higher primates illustrates an important rule: adaptation usually means making something old over into something new. The first automobiles looked almost exactly like the horse-drawn carriages they replaced—except that a combustion engine in front took the place of the horse. Automobiles have been improved in various ways, but they have not really been changed. Like horse-drawn carriages, they carry people from place to place.

So it is with primate development. The early ground-living mammal became improved as it lived in the trees. But it still remained a mammal.

The tree-living primate became improved as it lived on the ground. But it kept the adaptations acquired among the trees and put them to use on the ground. The adaptations of the past are not really lost, but are slowly added to and changed.

▶ MAN CHANGES THE ENVIRONMENT

Man himself, like all other organisms that once lived or now live on earth, is the result of many adaptations to changing conditions. Man can look at the birds and the stars. He can make machines that will fly through the air and perhaps reach the planets. But, scientists say, without skillful hands that were once feet and without stereoscopic vision that was once useful in jumping through trees, this would not be possible.

The human species as a whole continues to become adapted to changes. However, today man himself causes most of the changes. To a large extent he can alter and shape his own living conditions to suit himself. Most other organisms must suit themselves to their environment.

Man changes the environment constantly in one way or another. He cuts down forests to get wood for his buildings. He levels hills to make his highways. He drains swamps to make land for his crops. He dams rivers, digs canals, and so on. In the process he destroys the niches of many other organisms.

Then, too, as his numbers increase, man with his domestic animals and crops takes up more and more space. Other organisms are crowded out. Still other organisms are destroyed by overhunting and by poisoning.

Among the first creatures to perish were the

Farming (*left*) and building (*right*) are two ways man changes the environment.

flightless birds of ocean islands. These included the dodo of Mauritius and two of the largest birds that ever lived, the elephant bird of Madagascar and the moa of New Zealand. Slowly but surely the larger wild animals of the world are approaching extinction. Every year since 1900 one species of mammal has disappeared somewhere in the world. Man himself has become the cause of extinction.

N. J. BERRILL
McGill University

See also EVOLUTION; FOSSILS; GENETICS.

LIFE, DISTRIBUTION OF PLANT AND ANIMAL

Most of the earth's surface is covered by water. The waters may be deep or shallow, dark or light, cold or warm, clear or muddy, calm or stormy. They may be salt or fresh—although they are mostly the salty waters of the earth's oceans.

Land covers less than a third of the earth's surface. It may be warm or cool, high or low, wet or dry. It may be open grassy plains, deep forests, deserts, or snow-covered mountains.

Life in some form is found almost everywhere. However, for life to exist, certain conditions must be present.

The right temperature is one of these conditions. All living things must remain within certain limits of temperature. Living material must not be "cooked" by heat or frozen.

Another condition is water. All living things require water. Few can live in the hottest, driest deserts. And few can live in places where water is locked up as snow and ice.

Light is essential for green plants. So are certain minerals. Green plants need light for photosynthesis—the process by which they build their own food. Where there is no light, no green plants are to be found.

Animals need a source of food. They cannot exist in places where they cannot get food. Animal life depends on plant life. Some animals feed directly on plants. Others feed on plants indirectly, as when they eat other animals that eat plants.

Thus, the right temperature, water, light, and food are necessary for life. Their presence in various degrees is responsible for the way plants and animals are distributed, or spread out, in the different regions of the earth.

▶ THE THREE MAIN ENVIRONMENTS

Animals and plants may live in salt water, in fresh water, or on land. The saltwater environment (surroundings) consists of all the seas and oceans of the world. Apart from a few

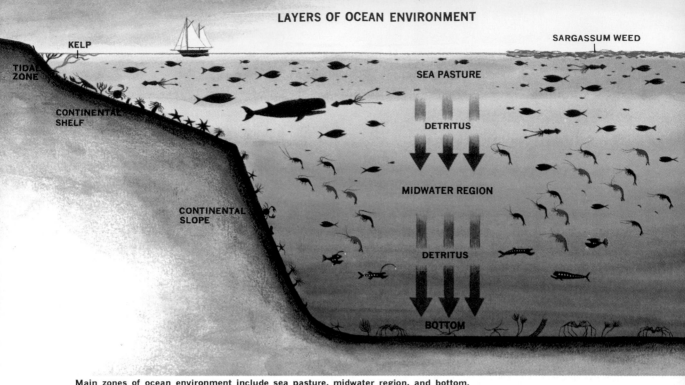

LAYERS OF OCEAN ENVIRONMENT

KELP

SARGASSUM WEED

TIDAL ZONE

SEA PASTURE

CONTINENTAL SHELF

DETRITUS

MIDWATER REGION

CONTINENTAL SLOPE

DETRITUS

BOTTOM

Main zones of ocean environment include sea pasture, midwater region, and bottom.

salty lakes, such as the Great Salt Lake in Utah and the Dead Sea in Israel, the seas and oceans are linked to one another. As a result they form one huge, continuous body of water.

The fresh waters consist of inland lakes and ponds, rivers and streams. They are generally above the level of the sea and flow downward to sea level. They are separated from one another either by land or by the saltwater oceans. Altogether, the fresh waters take up a very small part of the earth's surface.

The land consists of continents and islands. These are mostly surrounded by water and separated from one another. Few land plants and animals are able to cross these watery barriers unless carried by an outside agent, such as the wind, or able to fly.

As a general rule, most land animals cannot live in the sea or in fresh water. They need oxygen from the air. However, a few kinds of animals that once lived on land have adapted to life in the water. This is true of seals, walruses, whales, and sea turtles in the ocean; it is also true of turtles, alligators, and to some extent hippopotamuses in fresh water. These animals must surface frequently or keep their heads above water to breathe air.

Freshwater creatures are usually unable to live on land. They get their oxygen from the water, and most breathe through gills. They cannot breathe on land. Nor can they usually live in the oceans. They cannot tolerate (stand) the saltiness.

Finally, marine (saltwater) animals cannot live on land or in fresh water. They need the salt ocean, and they get oxygen from the water. They cannot tolerate the lack of salts in fresh water, and they cannot get oxygen on land.

There are some exceptions to this. Salmon spend the early part of their lives in fresh water and also breed there. But they spend most of their time feeding in the seas. Freshwater eels spend most of their adult life feeding in freshwater ponds and lakes, but go back to the sea to breed.

Animals and plants differ according to where they live—fresh water, salt water, or land. Even within one environment the distribution of plants and animals varies, depending on particular regional conditions.

▶ THE OCEAN ENVIRONMENT

The sea covers the greater part of the earth's surface. It also is the original home of life. At one time—more than 450,000,000 years ago—life existed only in the seas and fresh waters. Later, animals and plants spread onto the land. So it is not surprising that there are still many more living things in the sea than on the land. This is particularly true of animal life.

Marine Plants

In the ocean, plant life is limited by supplies of light. There is enough sunlight for plant growth at depths of 200 to 300 feet below the surface. (The exact depth depends on such things as waves and the clearness of the water.) Below these depths there is generally not enough light. However, in the upper layer of water is found the "pasture of the sea." Here many kinds of animals feed on the plants.

Throughout most of the ocean, the sea pasture consists mostly of single-celled organisms, such as diatoms and dinoflagellates. These cannot be seen without the aid of a microscope. But their tremendous numbers make up for their small size. Certain kinds of dinoflagellates give off a flash of light when disturbed. Many together cause the phosphorescent light of the sea at night.

Seaweeds are found mainly along the shores of the ocean, either above the low-tide level or in shallow depths below that level. Most seaweeds do not travel with the tides. Unlike the single-celled plants, most remain in one place. They are usually anchored to rock or to stones on the sea floor. They grow upward toward the light.

In some regions conditions for seaweed growth are excellent. This is true, for example, off the California coast and in the Strait of Magellan in South America. In these two regions giant seaweed, known as kelp, grows upward toward the surface from depths of 100 feet. The kelp forms an underwater forest in which many kinds of animals find food and shelter.

Some kinds of seaweed grow unattached to the sea floor. One is a species of sargassum weed found in the Sargasso Sea and in certain other oceanic regions. The Sargasso Sea lies in the southern part of the North Atlantic Ocean. It is bordered to the north by the Gulf Stream as that current winds eastward from the coast of North America to the seas of northwestern Europe. To the south the Sargasso Sea is bordered by the North Equatorial Current as it sweeps westward from the bulge of Africa toward the Caribbean. Between these two great currents the sea slowly turns round and round. Floating in this huge eddy are large

Below: Like this rockweed, most seaweeds are found along the shores, anchored to rocks or stones.

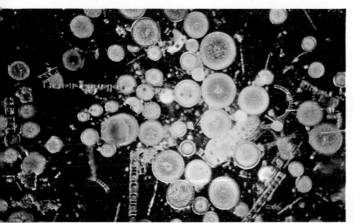

Above: Single-celled organisms, such as diatoms, make up major part of sea pasture. Below: Sargassum weed, unlike most kinds of seaweed, is not anchored in place but floats in large masses.

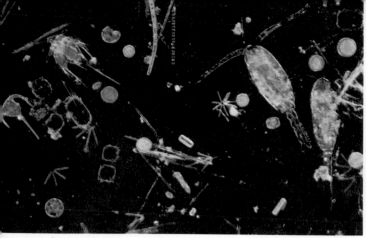

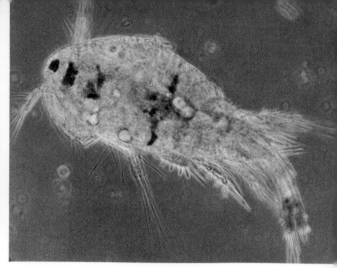

Plankton (*above*) consists of tiny organisms that drift in the sea. Copepod (*right*) is often found among plankton. They are shown here greatly enlarged—copepod is some 120 times its actual size.

Cuttlefish, of midwater region, often swims near bottom and feeds on crustaceans.

Most marine animals live in the upper layer of the sea. Small creatures feed on plankton and are in turn fed on by larger creatures. Marine animals of the midwater and bottom regions depend for food on the fine remains of plants and animals that sink from above.

Squid, a mollusk, swims backward and feeds on fishes in sea pasture.

Shrimp, a midwater dweller, may feed on the bottom.

Armored sea robin, a bottom-dweller, feeds on small crustaceans.

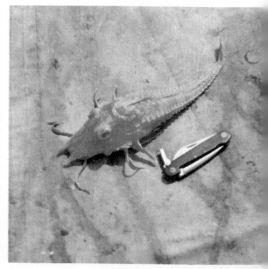

masses of sargassum weed. This seaweed is kept afloat by small air bladders scattered through the leaves. Altogether, it forms a sort of floating seaweed jungle that protects and feeds a large variety of animals. Most of these creatures have the golden-brown color of the sargassum weed itself and thus are concealed from hungry enemies.

Seaweeds, whether attached along the shores or floating in eddies, form only a small part of the total plant life of the ocean. By far the greater part is made up of the tiny organisms of the sea pasture. Most of the animal life of the sea is dependent, directly or indirectly, on this microscopic plant life.

Marine Animals

The marine animals inhabit three general regions, or layers. They may live in the sea pasture. They may inhabit the underwaters at depths of about 300 feet to 12,000 feet. They may live on the ocean floor itself, at depths that may approach 18,000 feet.

The Sea Pasture

The great bulk of marine animals live in the uppermost layer in seas and oceans. Countless copepods (small crustaceans, or shellfish) feed directly on the sea pasture. So do many other animals without backbones and very young stages of fish. These creatures provide food for all kinds of other animals—for example, arrow worms and sea butterflies. They serve as food for fishes of various kinds and sizes—from small herring to large tarpon, and from small mackerel to their giant relatives, tuna.

Fishes, in turn, are fed upon by larger fishes and by squid, both large and small. Squid, like octopuses, are related to other mollusks, such as clams, snails, and sea butterflies. Arrow-shaped, the squid swim backward by a sort of jet propulsion. Finally, feeding on the copepods, fish, and squid alike are the air-breathing whales and porpoises.

The Midwater Region

The very deep midwater region is dark and cold. Animal life depends for food, directly or indirectly, on **detritus**—the fine remains of dead animals and plants—that slowly sinks from the upper regions. The most numerous creatures are crustaceans, particularly prawns

and other shrimplike animals, and mollusks, such as sea butterflies and cuttlefish. Among the most abundant are the various kinds of small fishes. In general these animals are black or red—in this region red appears to be black. Some of these midwater animals are nearly blind. But many have quite large eyes, designed to catch any stray flashes of light. Many kinds have light-producing organs. Some use their small "flashlights" to attract prey, while others use the lights to keep in touch with their own kind, probably for mating purposes.

The Bottom

On the bottom there is no light, and the temperature is just above freezing. Conditions for life are very much the same everywhere on the bottom and are more or less unchanging. The bottom itself is usually very soft ooze. The food reaching this region is detritus from the surface layer.

Animal life consists mainly of glass sponges, sea pens, sea anemones, and other animals that can support themselves on stalks above the bottom ooze. Starfishes and long-legged crustaceans move about on the bottom. Various kinds of worms burrow in the mud itself. Most of these creatures feed on the detritus by swallowing the ooze, as do the worms, or by sifting it from the water, as do sponges.

The Continental Shelf

Seas are usually shallow near the continents. Such a coastal area is called a continental shelf. The shelf forms a sort of underwater platform, going out from the shore itself to a depth of no more than several hundred feet. It is on this platform and in the waters above it that much of the world's fishing is done.

On the bottom are carpets of shelled mollusks and crustaceans living together with starfishes and brittle stars and many other animals without backbones. The waters above teem with fishes and squid, the sea temperature determining whether cold- or warm-water kinds are to be found. The greatest numbers of animals live in the cold seas of the Arctic and the Antarctic. However, relatively few kinds are found there.

In the warm waters of the tropics there is

much less marine life but many more kinds. And it is in the tropics alone that coral reefs are found. These reefs are made up of the limy skeletons of corals, animals similar to sea anemones. Corals can grow enough to form reefs only in places close to the surface where the temperature is above 70 degrees Fahrenheit—or about as warm as the sea can be.

The Supply of Salts

In a general way, animal and plant life is distributed throughout the regions of the ocean. But some regions contain more life than others. The upper layer, where light penetrates, may be full of plant or animal life. But this depends on the supply of certain salts (phosphates and nitrates). In fact, the upper layer can be almost empty of life.

The salts necessary for plant life come mostly from two sources. Rivers wash soil down from the land into the sea and so continually add salts to the ocean water. Great currents of water well up from the ocean depths, carrying salts. Wherever great rivers enter the sea or currents well up, salts are plentiful and there is a rich growth of microscopic plant life. And so there is a variety of marine animals.

Numerous large rivers empty into the North Atlantic and Arctic oceans. These regions contain abundant marine life. The Pacific Ocean receives little material from rivers. Therefore it contains fewer plants and animals. This is true for the Pacific Ocean as a whole, although not for every part.

Along the west coasts of the Americas winds drive the water far offshore, and deep water wells up from below to replace it. The upwelling current of western South America is known as the Peru Current (also as the Humboldt Current, after its discoverer). The current carries water that is rich in salts. The result is an abundance of plant and animal life. The marine animal life is so rich that it supports tremendous colonies of seabirds. Great coastal fisheries are based on it, both off the coast of California and off the coast of Chile and Peru.

Near the equator the Peru Current swings from its northward course along the coast. It streams westward toward the Pacific islands, carrying its teeming life with it. When Thor Heyerdahl and members of his expedition set off westward from the coast of Peru, their raft, *Kon-Tiki,* was swept along in this current. The men were able to catch all the fish they needed

WORLD OCEAN CURRENTS AND RIVERS

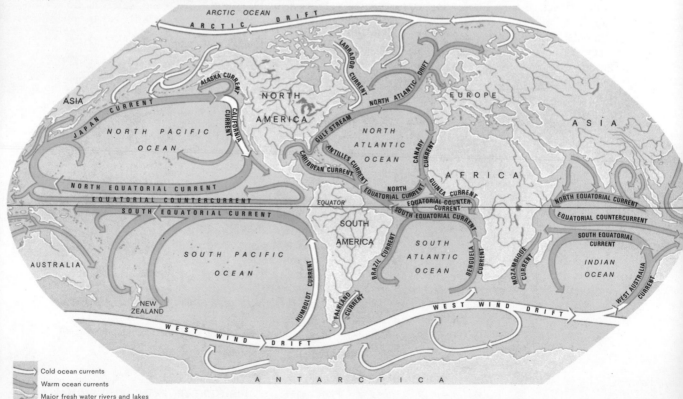

Cold ocean currents
Warm ocean currents
Major fresh water rivers and lakes

for food. If they had started out farther north or south, they would have found little marine life at all in their voyage westward. When Sir Francis Drake first sailed across the Pacific Ocean, he started from a point near present-day San Francisco. He and his crew did not see even one fish during their entire voyage to the Moluccas Islands. Large areas between the main currents that sweep across the ocean usually lack the salts needed for plant life—and so for animal life.

Most of the ocean is like that—with relatively little life. It is a mistake to suppose that there is no limit to the amount of life in the ocean or that life in the ocean is abundant everywhere. There is abundant life only in certain regions—and those are regions where man has already set up his fisheries.

▶ THE LAND ENVIRONMENT

On land there is some form of life almost everywhere, although life is limited—as it is in the oceans—by such things as temperature, light, and food. Life on land is also limited by supplies of water. The vast dry reaches of the Sahara and Arabian deserts are almost without life. The icefields of Greenland and Antarctica are equally inhospitable.

However, conditions for life are much more varied on land than they are in the ocean. And so there are many more kinds of plants and animals.

Plants and Animals Spread Across the Land

Almost any kind of organism (living thing) will in time spread across the land. Some kinds of organisms fail to survive in new areas. Others thrive. Still others develop new traits that enable them to adapt better. Gradually, new kinds of organisms may appear, each suited to living within certain limits.

Plants, of course, do not move about on their own. They spread as the result of outside agencies. Wind, water, and animals carry the seeds from place to place.

Birds and other small animals feed on berries. Many of the berry seeds pass undamaged through the animals' digestive systems. They are finally dropped somewhere, often far from where the parent plant grew.

The wind scatters the seeds of many more kinds of plants. These are plant seeds that can drift in the air. Two good examples of these

Plant seeds spread in many ways. Wind scatters the parachutelike seeds of dandelion.

Winged maple tree seeds form on the tree . . .

. . . and travel on the wind some distance from tree.

are the dandelion seed, which is parachute-like, and the maple seed, which is winged.

Wind and birds (and other animals) spread seeds over long distances, even across desert or water. Sometimes water itself carries seeds, as in the case of the coconut palm.

The seeds of this tree are of giant size—they are the coconuts themselves. Many coconuts drop at the base of the palm; they may root and grow up nearby. But others at the edge of the sea are washed away; they drift across oceans to some distant island or

Coconuts may be washed away and carried to a distant shore, where they take root.

continent. That is why most of the islands of the Pacific and Indian oceans have a fringe of coconut palms along their shores.

Some very small animals, such as insects, may be blown miles from their home area by the high winds of hurricanes and tornadoes. Or their eggs may be carried by water to new regions. However, animals generally move from place to place by flying, walking, running, crawling, burrowing, or swimming.

If it were possible to travel from the southern part of Africa to the southern part of South America, almost any kind of animal eventually would do so, as long as food and other necessary things were available along the way. Animals would do so even if it took 10,000 years and countless generations. And in fact this has often been possible, even though the barriers are too great at present.

The Main Regions of the Land

The regions of the land are mostly separated from one another by the seas or by other natural barriers. As a result, the kinds of plants and animals found on one continent or island differ, often very greatly, from those on another. For example, the animals in South America are almost entirely different from those in North America.

Scientists divide the world into five or six general regions, according to the distribution of life in each. For each region has its own kinds of animals and plants, although many small creatures are distributed in more than one region of the earth, and many are found everywhere.

The largest of the regions is usually called the **Holarctic** or whole northern area. It includes North America (with most of Mexico), Europe, North Africa, and Asia north of the Himalayas. The timber wolf, moose, elk, bear, rabbit, and other animals are common to all parts of this region. So also are many plants, such as birches and maples.

The other regions are much smaller than the Holarctic, as you can see on the map. The **Oriental region** consists of southeastern Asia (India, southern China, Malaysia, and parts of Indonesia). It is the haunt of the tiger, Indian elephant, gibbon, and orangutan, for example. The **Ethiopian region**, consisting of most of Africa and the Arabian Peninsula, contains giraffes, zebras, antelopes, gorillas, chimpanzees, lions, and African elephants. The **Neotropical region** consists of Central and South America. Its animals include sloths, armadillos, anteaters, guinea pigs, and monkeys that can grasp branches with their tails. The **Australian region** stands out even more.

LAND REGIONS OF ANIMAL LIFE

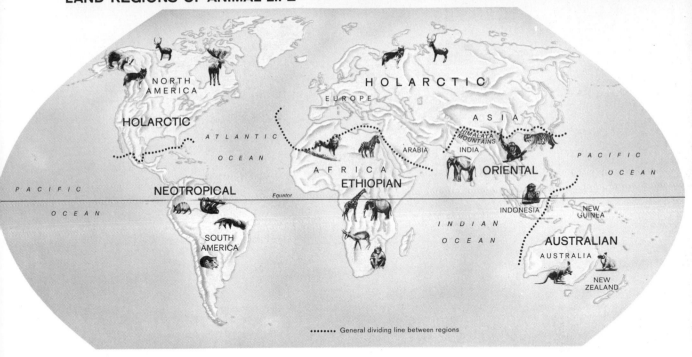

.... General dividing line between regions

It consists of Australia, New Guinea, and New Zealand. Many kinds of animals are found in this region and nowhere else, as, for example, kangaroos, koala bears, and many other pouched animals.

Barriers Preventing the Spread of Life

Within each region there are geographical and climatic barriers to the spread of plants and animals. For example, in tropical rain forests conditions generally are favorable to life. The temperature is warm, and rainfall is heavy during much of the year. Food supplies are ample. This is true in the great river basins of the Amazon in South America and the Congo in Africa.

Yet the forests and rivers themselves favor some organisms and not others. A forest may afford food and protection to leopards and monkeys. But it is not a good place for animals that feed by grazing on plains and that run fast to escape their enemies. The forest growth presents a barrier and source of danger to such animals.

In the same way, a river may serve as passageway and food source for alligators and hippopotamuses, but present a barrier to animals unable to swim. Thus, a land form that favors one kind of animal or plant may be a barrier to the spread of others.

Deserts are barriers for most animals and plants and may keep them from spreading into other suitable regions. (The camel is one exception to this. It has adapted for long periods of travel without food or water, and thus can get across a desert.)

Tropical rain forest is favorable to many kinds of life but a barrier to others, such as grazing animals.

MOUNTAINS AS CLIMATIC BARRIER TO SPREAD OF LIFE

WIND

RAIN

MOUNTAIN RANGE

DESERT

OCEAN

Rain falls as moisture-laden air rises up mountain; descending dry air causes desert to form. Beyond "tree line" low temperatures and strong winds prevent spread of life.

Mountain ranges, too, are barriers, especially if they are high and lack low passes. Mountains serve as climatic barriers. The higher the mountain is, the colder the temperature is and the stronger the winds are. For instance, forests, together with the animals they shelter, go up a mountainside just so far. Beyond this point low temperatures and strong winds make tree growth impossible. Above this "tree line" the mountains are nearly bare and may be covered with snow and ice.

Going up a mountainside is much the same, climatically speaking, as traveling toward the North Pole. The increasing cold first stunts, then stops plant growth.

The sea is an important barrier to movement from one region to another. Its waters are salty and undrinkable. They also stretch much farther than any river. Many birds are able to fly long distances and may even cross oceans, from one land mass to another and back again. But with this exception, land animals and plants are normally unable to cross the seas to settle in new regions.

Island-hopping

Some animals do occasionally cross water from one land area to another. This happens if there are islands in between. Island-hopping depends, as a rule, on the drifting of logs or of tangled masses of plant matter and soil across water—for instance, a chunk of riverbank may break off and drift seaward with the currents.

Rafts of this sort almost certainly carried a few South American lizards and tortoises to the Galápagos Islands. These islands lie in the Pacific Ocean, about 600 miles west of South America. From the original South American creatures eventually developed the kinds of giant lizards and tortoises that are found only on these remote islands. The monkeys of South America probably arrived from Africa in some such way.

A long time ago a few pouched mammals somewhat like the opossum seem to have drifted from one island to another, off southeastern Asia. Eventually they reached Australia. Once there, having no competition from other kinds of mammals, they developed in all kinds of ways. Some became runners; others, jumpers, climbers, burrowers, or flyers. Some creatures became meat-eaters and others became plant-eaters. So animals developed that are found only in the Australian region.

Land Bridges

Scientists have found no evidence that Australia was ever joined to the continent of Asia. However, at times in the history of the earth there have been low land bridges between certain other continents.

Today the narrow and shallow Bering Strait separates Siberia from Alaska. At times in the past there has been a land bridge between them, though only the chain of the Aleutian islands remains of it.

At the present time there is a land bridge at the Isthmus of Panama. At other times this land connection between the two Americas has been broken.

However, during many tens of millions of years in the past, one land bridge or the other or both have been in existence. This allowed animals to pass freely in both directions between the Old World and the New, and between North and South America. Whenever both bridges existed, animals could pass by land from the Cape of Good Hope at the southern tip of Africa all the way to Cape Horn at the southern tip of South America. (That is why the continents of Africa, Asia, Europe, and the Americas are sometimes called the World Continent.)

The passageways and breaks have been important in the rather strange-seeming distribution of many kinds of animals. So have the great climatic changes of the past.

The ancestors of camels came into existence in North America. From there they were able to travel into South America across one land bridge and into Asia across another. From Asia they spread into Arabia and North Africa. They spread from the place of their origin practically throughout the World Continent, except for central and southern Africa.

Then came the Ice Age, when great sheets of ice covered much of the earth. It eventually caused the camels to die out in the northern, colder lands. Today camels are found only in northern Africa, the Arabian Peninsula, central Asia, and the highlands of South America. The South American kinds of camels are the llamas and alpacas. No living kind of camel is native to North America or northeastern Asia. Only the fossil bones of early camels remain in these places to tell their story. If scientists did not know the past history of camels and of the earth itself, they would be unable to explain the present distribution of camels and llamas.

Another example is seen in the elephants. Their original home was east central Africa. From there elephants of one sort or another spread to other regions of the earth, crossing the land bridge from the Old World into the New and finally wandering far down into South America. Mammoths, one kind of large elephant, were once common in Siberia, North America, and along the Andes in South America.

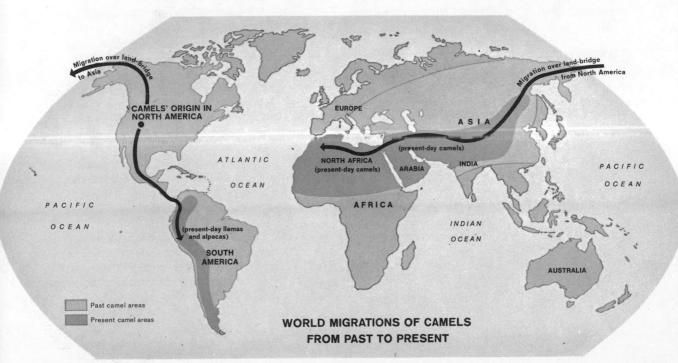

WORLD MIGRATIONS OF CAMELS FROM PAST TO PRESENT

Without natural enemies, rabbits overran Australia after man brought them in.

Once again the Ice Age changed conditions. However, in the case of the elephants it was not the cold itself that caused their disappearance in many areas. Rather, it was the great thaws that followed. In the huge swamps created by the thaws the heavy elephants sank and perished before they could reach higher ground. Today elephants survive only in Africa and in India.

Breaks in Distribution

The breaks that have occurred between parts of the World Continent have also affected the distribution of plants and animals. For example, many millions of years ago primitive mammals spread from North America into South America. Then the Central American land bridge broke up. The mammals in South America were cut off from their relatives to the north. They were isolated on their continent for a very long time. Gradually they developed in special ways suited to their particular surroundings. So it was that animals such as sloths and anteaters, found today only in South America, came into existence.

When the land bridge again appeared, new mammals from the north crossed the bridge and invaded the south. Among these were the camel, the mammoth, and the saber-toothed tiger. At the same time a few of the southern forms crept north. In this way North America gained the opossum and armadillo.

▶ MAN CHANGES THE DISTRIBUTION OF LIFE

In recent times the natural distribution of life on land has been changing. This is largely the result of man's activities, deliberate and accidental. Wherever man goes, he takes along his gun and his dog. He usually takes along some uninvited guests, such as rats and lice. Man changes the natural distribution in a region by thoughtless killing. Then too, some native animals cannot compete with man's animal companions.

New animals may be introduced to a new region with unforeseen results. For example, settlers introduced the rabbit to Australia. Having no natural enemies, the rabbits soon overran the countryside, destroying millions of acres of pasture. Another example is the introduction of the Japanese snail into the Pacific islands during World War II. Now the snail is seriously damaging plant life and is out of control. Normally animal numbers are controlled by disease organisms, certain kinds of organisms attacking each kind of animal. But when an animal is introduced to a place where its controlling organisms are lacking, it multiplies unchecked.

On the other hand, some diseases are carried from place to place as a result of human travel. Plant diseases newly brought to an island or continent may cause the death of many native plants. As a result, animals that depend on those plants also disappear.

It is almost impossible for man to make a change in natural environments, except for the worse. The situation is always too complicated to be understood in advance.

N. J. BERRILL
McGill University

LIFE, FOOD CHAINS IN

All living things need food. Food builds up the body and keeps it going. Without food an active organism (living thing) quickly wears out.

The life of an organism can be compared to a long and hard football game. In the game many players perform difficult and tiring tasks. Fresh players take the places of tired ones. The game goes on. But suppose there are no replacements. Then players will drop out of the game one by one. The game will eventually stop.

So it is with a living organism. Old material must be replaced. New material must be added. This process of replacement must continue, not just for growth of the organism, but also to keep life going.

▶ THE RAW MATERIALS

The basic materials needed by all living organisms are hydrogen, carbon, nitrogen, and oxygen. In addition to these elements, sulfur, phosphorus, salts, and iron and certain other metals are needed, but in much smaller amounts.

Green plants get these elements mainly in simple chemical compounds from the air, soil, and water. Special green cells take energy from light, usually sunlight. The plants use this energy and the raw materials of the chemical compounds to produce their living material. All green plants, whether growing in water or on land, produce food by this process of **photosynthesis**. Such plants are known as **producers**.

Animals cannot produce their own living material from the raw materials of the earth. They depend on plant life, directly or indirectly.

Animals are **consumers**, or eaters. Those that feed directly on plants are called **first-level consumers**. A grasshopper eats leaves; a mouse eats seeds. These animals are examples of first-level consumers. Animals such as frogs and cats prey on animals that feed on plants. They are **second-level consumers**. **Third-level consumers** are those that prey on the second-level consumers, and so on.

Food used by animals—whether it comes from plants or other animals—is very different from the nonliving raw materials used by the plants. It contains highly complex materials that make up a living organism. These organic materials include carbohydrates (sugars and starches), fats, proteins, and vitamins.

At first these materials are not exactly what the animal needs for replacing its own particular kind of material. So before the food materials can be used, they must be digested, or broken down into somewhat simpler chemical building blocks. Then these blocks

Left: Grasshopper, a first-level consumer, eats leaves. Center: Frog, a second-level consumer, eats grasshoppers and other plant-eating insects. Right: Snake, a third-level consumer, preys on frogs and other second-level consumers.

can be used for building new animal material. It is as if you carefully took down an old building and then used the bricks, stones, planks, tiles, and nails to make a new building of a different sort.

To split up food material and build it into living matter, animals need energy. They also need energy for other kinds of work, such as moving about. Animals get their energy from the food itself. So while some of the chemical building blocks are used for making new living material, other building blocks are used as fuel for producing energy.

▶ PYRAMIDS OF LIVING MATERIAL

In plants the raw materials are used mostly to form new plant material. In adult animals the food material is used mostly to run the living machinery. Only a small part actually goes to make new animal material.

For example, in a pig eating 10 pounds of corn most of the food material is used up for energy. No more than 1 pound of new pig material is produced.

The corn plant is a producer. The pig is a first-level consumer. A man eating the pig in the form of pork, ham, sausages, and bacon is a second-level consumer. Just as it might take 10 pounds of corn to make 1 pound of pig, so it takes 10 pounds of pig to make 1 pound of man. For 9 pounds of pig meat are used to keep the living machinery going during the time that 1 new pound of human material is being made.

If you put these two stages together—corn to pig and pig to man—you can see that it takes 100 pounds of corn to make 1 pound of man. This is assuming, of course, that the pig, and not the man, eats the corn.

Living material passing from corn to pig to man forms a sort of pyramid. The producer (corn) represents the broad supporting base of the pyramid. The first-level consumer (pig) forms the next layer, and the second-level consumer (man), the top. Each consumer level contains about $\frac{1}{10}$ the food material of the level below.

Scientists use pyramids like this simple one to show general relationships between producers and consumers. Such a pyramid tells little about how many different kinds of organisms are represented in each layer. But it shows the total amount of living material present in the various layers. It also shows that there is less food material at each layer as food moves up through the pyramid. This food material is divided up among an increasingly small number of large creatures rather than among an enormous number of smaller ones. For as a rule, the individual organisms of the second consumer layer are larger than the organisms in the first consumer layer. There are also fewer second-level consumers than first-level consumers. And there are fewer and larger organisms still in the higher consumer layers.

Let us take as an example the life in a forest. Grass, trees, and other plants form much of the living material present. Then come the first-level consumers, such as aphids and other tiny insects that feed on plants. These animals are very small and extremely numerous. They provide plenty of food material for the second-level consumers. The animals in this layer include spiders and beetles. Insect-eating birds are fewer and larger. The hawks and weasels that prey on the birds are relatively scarce. The ticks and lice that feed on a hawk or weasel are very small and numerous. Yet added together they weigh less and occupy less space than the animal on which they feed.

FOOD PYRAMID

1 POUND

↑

10 POUNDS

↑

100 POUNDS

Consumer levels among inhabitants of the forest.

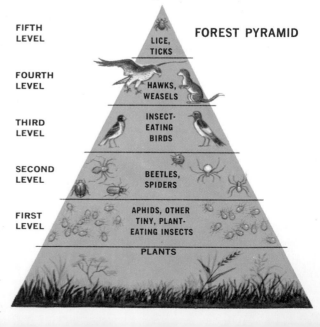

FOREST PYRAMID

FIFTH LEVEL — LICE, TICKS

FOURTH LEVEL — HAWKS, WEASELS

THIRD LEVEL — INSECT-EATING BIRDS

SECOND LEVEL — BEETLES, SPIDERS

FIRST LEVEL — APHIDS, OTHER TINY, PLANT-EATING INSECTS

PLANTS

►FOOD CHAINS

The path of the food material from the base to the top of a pyramid is known as a **food chain**. In the forest pyramid some of the food materials are linked in a simple chain like this:

plants—aphids—beetles—birds—hawks—lice

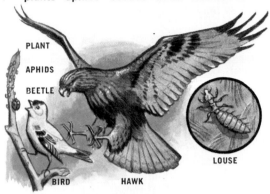

PLANT
APHIDS
BEETLE
LOUSE
BIRD   HAWK

FOOD CHAIN ON LAND

Few food chains are that simple.

In the cold Antarctic seas certain shrimp-like animals, known as krill, feed on diatoms (microscopic plants). The krill usually grow to a length of 1 or 2 inches and are very abundant. Great blue whales eat the krill, sifting the small animals out of the water through huge hairy sieves in their mouths. The food chain here, too, is very short. The links are simply:

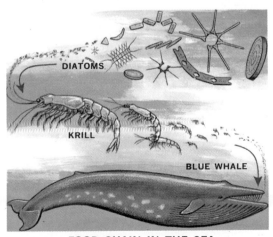

DIATOMS

KRILL

BLUE WHALE

FOOD CHAIN IN THE SEA

As a result, the whales are more numerous than they might be if they had to pursue the small fish that feed on the krill—or the larger

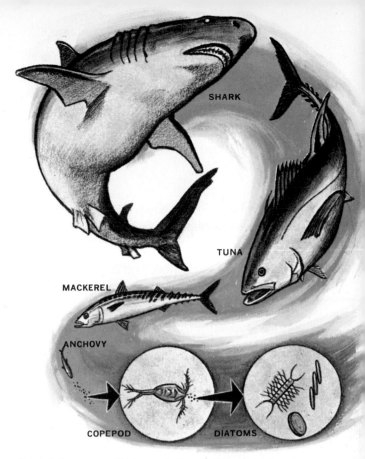

SHARK

TUNA

MACKEREL

ANCHOVY

COPEPOD   DIATOMS

Food chains are usually longer in the sea than on land.

fish that feed on the small fish or the squid that feed on the larger fish. However, the whales are less numerous than they might be if man did not overhunt them.

The shorter the food chain is, the more food material there is for the animals at the top of the pyramid. Less material has been used up in producing energy. If the food chain is long, less material remains, and there are fewer animals at its end.

In the sea, food chains are usually longer than they are on land. The billions of organisms that make up the "sea pasture" are extremely small. Instead of being bulky plants that a large animal can readily eat, these organisms are microscopic. Usually only very small animals are able to feed on them. A large animal would use up more energy just trying to eat enough plants than it would get from the food itself.

However, on land the food chain is short. The first-level consumers are often the largest animals. Deer, antelope, cattle, elephants, and giraffes graze directly on grass and other plants.

▶ BREAKING THE FOOD CHAIN

Like any chain, a food chain is only as strong as its weakest link. Insects feed mostly on vegetation. In turn, the insects are the main source of food for many birds and other creatures. Insects are a link in many food chains.

Man battles constantly against insects that destroy crops and carry disease. One way to control the insect population is by the use of DDT and other insecticides. But this breaking of the food chain has unwanted results. The number of birds and other insect-eaters is reduced because less food is available. Some of the insecticide may be washed into streams, where it kills the larvae (young) of water insects. Small fish, such as young salmon, need these larvae for food. The lack of larvae results in a lower number of salmon.

A food chain may be cut at either end. Killing the predators at the top, such as hawks, wolves, or mountain lions, results in a huge increase in the number of animals that are normally their prey. These creatures, such as rodents or deer, multiply more quickly and so create an imbalance in the community. The most serious changes, however, come about when the base of a chain is destroyed. When a forest is cut down, or a swamp is drained, a whole community of plants and animals may disappear.

▶ THE RAW MATERIALS OF LIFE

Even though plants use raw materials and animals consume plants year after year after year, supplies of raw materials do not run out. Although no individual organism lives forever, life goes on and on.

As each individual organism comes to the end of its existence, it is consumed by certain other organisms. Certain bacteria and fungi break down dead and waste materials into simpler substances. If these organisms did not decompose, or decay, once-living material, eventually all the raw materials needed for life would be used up. Life would cease.

Materials of life are used over and over. Only sunlight is newly supplied.

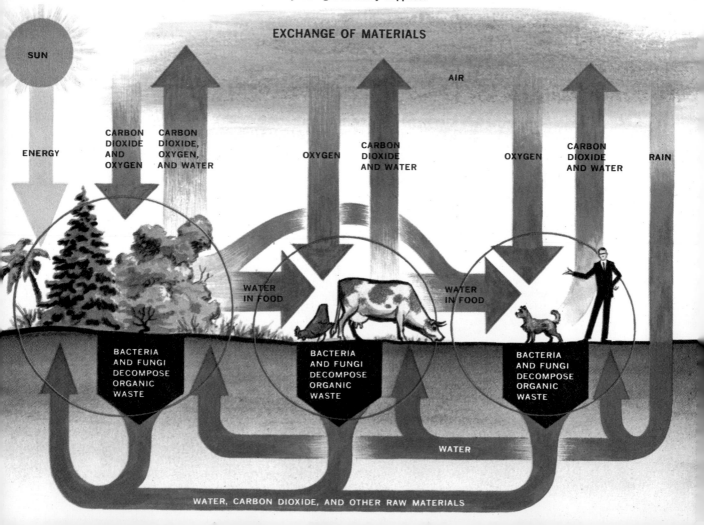

EXCHANGE OF MATERIALS

SUN

AIR

ENERGY

CARBON DIOXIDE AND OXYGEN

CARBON DIOXIDE, OXYGEN, AND WATER

OXYGEN

CARBON DIOXIDE AND WATER

OXYGEN

CARBON DIOXIDE AND WATER

RAIN

WATER IN FOOD

WATER IN FOOD

BACTERIA AND FUNGI DECOMPOSE ORGANIC WASTE

BACTERIA AND FUNGI DECOMPOSE ORGANIC WASTE

BACTERIA AND FUNGI DECOMPOSE ORGANIC WASTE

WATER

WATER, CARBON DIOXIDE, AND OTHER RAW MATERIALS

As it is, bacteria and fungi make the raw materials available again. Thus, the pathway of food is circular. Decay organisms complete food chains, however long or short.

One might say that living organisms keep spending the same money (raw materials) over and over again. Each time, the "money" may be spent on somewhat different things. But the things have to be turned into money again before being re-used.

At any particular time and place the total amount of living material may be limited by the amount of new materials and light available to plants. And on the earth as a whole, both on land and in the sea, the total amount of living material is limited.

Only the energy of sunlight is in continuous and unlimited supply. Energy from the sun forever pours into living plant cells and drives the living machinery to make its complex organic substances. The sun is the true power line that keeps plant life going—and so, in turn, the animal life that depends on the plants. Bacteria and other organisms return the raw materials to the soil and water, where they are available for further use. Solar energy and organic decay together make it possible for life to continue.

N. J. BERRILL
McGill University

See also BACTERIA; BODY CHEMISTRY; MICROBIOLOGY; PHOTOSYNTHESIS.

LIFE, RHYTHMS AND CLOCKS IN PLANT AND ANIMAL

The fiddler crab makes its burrow in beaches, salt marshes, and mud flats along the coasts of the United States. About as large as a silver dollar, this animal probably gets its name from the male's oversized claw. When defending himself or courting a female, the crab waves this claw around much like a fiddler playing his violin.

Twice each day, with much claw waving, fiddlers scurry up and down the beach feeding. This event happens when the ebbing tide uncovers their beach homes.

When the tide comes in again about 6 hours later, the fiddlers retreat to their burrows. There they hide quietly, safely out of reach of striped bass and other fish that find fiddler crabs particularly delicious.

The fiddlers' feeding and hiding behavior seems to be timed to the rise and fall of the tides. When something repeats itself over and over again, it is said to have a **rhythm**. For example, the feeding and hiding behavior of the fiddler crab has a rhythm. These events are an example of an animal rhythm. The regular rise and fall of the tides is a rhythm of the physical surroundings.

Fiddler crabs have a second rhythm. This one is timed to the sun. In the morning as it grows light, the fiddlers' shells become dark-colored. The crab's shell remains dark all day. About the time of sunset the color of the shell rapidly lightens, and it stays light all night.

This change of shell color has a rhythm. This rhythm is timed to the 24-hour day.

▶ RHYTHMS AND SURVIVAL

Both rhythms of the fiddler crab—the feeding and hiding, and the change of color—help the crab survive in its home area. The crabs are adapted (fitted) to the rhythms of their surroundings.

All living things, plant or animal, are adapted to life in a certain environment (surroundings). An important part of adaptation is the timing of various activities. For example, most seeds sprout in the spring. This gives them time to grow and to produce flowers and fruits before the cold weather begins. Scientists believe that all living things have similar rhythms, adapted to the rhythms of their environment.

▶ DAILY RHYTHMS

The earth rotates on its axis, in relation to the sun, once in 24 hours. As a result, there are repeated and regular changes in day and night, temperature and humidity. Some animals, such as human beings, dogs, and most songbirds and butterflies, are adapted for activity during the hours of daylight. Cats, bats, rats and mice, moths, and cockroaches are a few animals whose most active periods come at night.

Plants, too, have daily rhythms. Morning-glory blossoms close up when sunlight hits them at a certain angle. And just when the morning glories are closing, the bright blossoms of portulacas begin to open. Some flowers, such as the evening primrose, open in the evening and stay open until the sun's rays shine directly on them again. All these rhythms, which seem to be timed by the changes in light, temperature, and humidity in the course of a day, are called daily or **solar-day rhythms**.

▶ TIDAL RHYTHMS

The fiddler crab reacts to the tide in one way. Clams, mussels, barnacles, and snails react to the tide with a different rhythm. When they are covered by the rising tide, they open their shells. They feed by pumping water through their bodies and straining out the tiny particles they eat. When they are left exposed by the ebbing tide, these animals close up tight. This protects them from drying out during the hours of exposure and from the animals that would eat them.

On the tidal flats of the Atlantic coasts of France and Spain there is a flatworm that has single-celled green plants living in it. These tiny plants make food for both themselves and the worm. Green plants need sunlight to make food. So when the tide is out and the beaches are exposed, the worm crawls part way out of its hole and lies exposed to the sun.

▶ YEARLY RHYTHMS

As the earth orbits the sun its motion and the tilt of its axis result in still another series of rhythmical changes—the seasons. The farther

Yearly rhythm: in spring, salmon swim upstream to spawn.

one travels north or south of the equator, the easier it is to see seasonal changes in length of day, temperature, and humidity during the year. Some rhythms of living things are adapted to seasonal changes and are called **yearly**, or **annual**, **rhythms**.

Most annual rhythms have to do with producing and raising young and with finding food. For example, salmon run each spring to the rivers and streams of the Pacific Northwest for spawning. Great flocks of geese and ducks migrate southward each fall to new feeding grounds. Such biological activities are important to the survival of living things. They are timed to the season of the year most favorable for each species (kind) of living thing. Scientists believe that all living things have annual rhythms.

▶ MONTHLY RHYTHMS

Our calendar is marked off in months of 30 or 31 days. But there is another month, marked off by the moon. This is called the **synodic month** and is about 29½ days long. As the moon goes through its phases from one new moon to the next, there is a rhythmical change in the amount of light it reflects on earth. There is also a change in the height of the tides.

The gravitational attraction of the moon on the earth is the main cause of tides. Twice each month—once when the moon is full and again when it is new—there are a few days when high tides are higher than usual. These are called **spring tides**, although the name has nothing to do with seasons. Many animals that live in or near the sea have rhythms adapted to this 29½-day lunar month and to the changing heights of tides.

There are two animals whose biological rhythms are so precisely timed to synodic monthly and tidal rhythms that their stories sound almost like tall tales. One is the palolo worm that lives in the southwestern Pacific Ocean near the island of Samoa. The other is the grunion, a small fish about as long as a man's hand. The grunion lives in the ocean off the coasts of California and Oregon.

Palolo worms release their eggs and sperm each year in October and November during the last quarter of the moon. This spawning happens so regularly that the Samoans have names for the days when it occurs and declare

Solar-day rhythm: morning glories open in early morning sunlight (*above left*) and close (*above right*) when sunlight hits them at a certain angle.
Tidal rhythm: fiddler crabs feed on beach (*left*) when tide ebbs. When tide is rising, fiddler scurries to safety of burrow (*below*), away from hungry fishes.

a holiday to gather the worms, which they like to eat. There is a kind of palolo worm that lives in the Atlantic. It spawns in summer during the full moon.

The grunions' spawning, too, is timed to rhythms of moon and tide. Just after the spring tides from March through July the grunions appear in great schools. On moonlit nights when the tide has reached its highest point and has begun to go down, thousands and thousands of grunions swim to shore on the waves. They are washed up and left stranded for a few minutes until another wave comes rolling in. While on the beach the females deposit their eggs in the warm, moist sand. Then, with a mighty effort the grunions flop back into the next surf and are carried out to sea.

Tidal and monthly rhythm: palolo worm (*below*) lives in southwestern Pacific. These worms release their eggs and sperm each year in October and November during the last quarter of the moon. (Moon affects tides.)

Grunion spawning is timed to moon and tides.
Left: Grunions lay and fertilize eggs on beach.
Above: Eggs lie buried in warm, moist sand.

Since the tide has already begun to ebb, no other wave will reach the eggs that night. No other tide will come up that high until the next spring tide. The eggs remain safely buried in the warm moist sand for at least 2 weeks. During that time the tiny fish develop. When the waves of the next spring tide reach them, the eggs burst open and the tiny fish swim out to sea.

▶ LIVING THINGS MEASURE TIME

From studying such rhythms in living things, scientists have discovered that many, if not all, of life's most important activities are timed to take place with the rhythms of the physical surroundings. They have made a further and puzzling discovery. They have found that when a plant or animal is taken out of its natural surroundings and kept in a laboratory, its behavior follows its natural rhythm. This is true even when the creature is shielded from all changes of light, temperature, tides, or humidity.

Some experiments of this kind have been done with fiddler crabs. Scientists placed the fiddlers in large glass jars and kept them in

Fiddlers seem to have an internal clock. In experiment they continued to move and change color on schedule, although shielded from clues about tides and light.

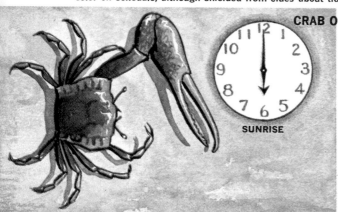

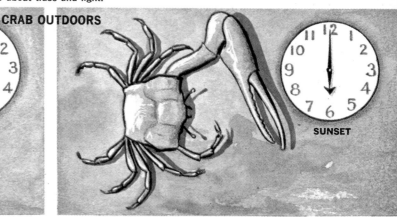

CRAB OUTDOORS

SUNRISE

SUNSET

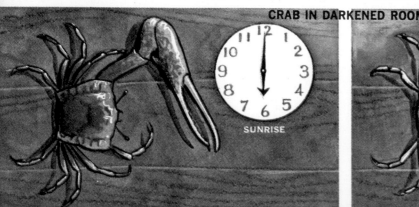

CRAB IN DARKENED ROOM

SUNRISE

SUNSET

photographic darkrooms. There, shielded from any clues about the tides or daylight and dark, their rhythms continued. When tides were high on their home beach, the crabs rested quietly at the bottom of the jars. When the tides were low, the crabs moved about restlessly. The color of their shells became darker and lighter in perfect rhythm with the sunrise and sunset the animals could not see. It seems as if the crabs can measure both the 6¼ hours between high tide and low tide and the 24-hour period of the day.

Crabs are not the only living things known to have such timing ability. It is also found in rats, mice, hamsters, and cockroaches. These animals are normally active at night. Their periods of activity are timed to the nighttime where they live. Placed in dim light that never changes, these creatures become active when the sun goes down outside.

Some plants, too, seem to measure the passage of time. Bean seedlings have what is known as a **sleep rhythm**. That is, they raise their leaves as daylight arrives and let them droop at night. When bean plants are screened off from all changes in light, temperature, and humidity, the sleep rhythm continues. The plants raise and lower their leaves with the changes of day and night outside.

▶ **BIOLOGICAL CLOCKS**

Many scientists think that all living things have the ability to behave on a regular schedule. However, it is not easy to account for the regularity of the rhythms and the fact that they

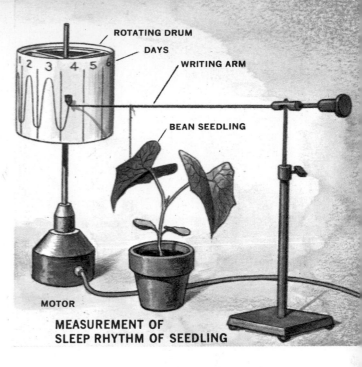

Apparatus for recording sleep rhythm of bean seedling. Raising and lowering of leaves is reflected in movement of writing arm and record on drum.

continue when all obvious outside clues are screened off. These scientists have suggested that living things must have built-in **biological clocks** or, in the case of monthly or annual events, **biological calendars**.

Resetting Biological Clocks

Biological clocks resist most efforts of scientists to experiment with them. This, of course, makes it very difficult to learn anything about them. However, they can be reset. For example, a human being's clock is reset

Biological clocks can be reset. Light in laboratory was turned on at night and off during day. Fiddler crab soon reversed its color changes to accord with light.

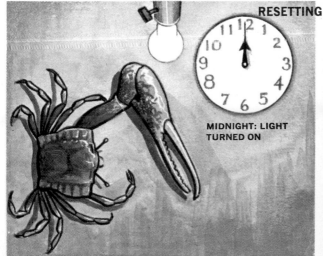

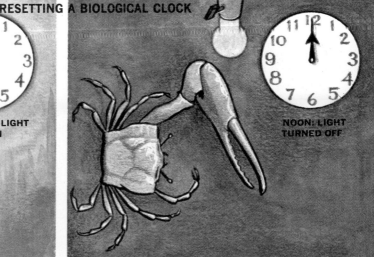

RESETTING A BIOLOGICAL CLOCK

MIDNIGHT: LIGHT TURNED ON

NOON: LIGHT TURNED OFF

Scientists are trying to understand how such migrants as these snow geese find their way over long distances to breeding and feeding grounds every year.

every time he flies from New York to London. In New York his normal 24-hour rhythm of sleep and waking and all his other important body activities are set to the daylight hours of the eastern coast of the United States. When he gets to London, the day begins 5 hours earlier. The New Yorker's rhythms are out of step with his surroundings by about the same amount of time. In other words, his clock is still working, but it is set for New York rather than London. However, within a few days his body rhythms will gradually shift into step with the sun time in England.

The same kind of resetting also takes place in the biological clocks of other animals and plants. This may be shown in a simple experiment. An animal or plant is placed in a laboratory, shut off from outside natural light influences. Light is turned on during the daylight hours of some other part of the world. It is turned off during the night hours. After a few such 24-hour days the creature's clock will be set to the laboratory-produced hours of light and dark.

A biological clock can be reset so that activities start and stop at any hour of the day. However, the time between starting on one day and starting on the next day always remains about the same. An experiment with mussels makes this clear.

Mussels are moved from one beach to another. At the second beach the tides rise and fall about 6 hours later than they do at the home beach. For a few days the mussels open at the wrong times—but always with the same amount of time between these openings. Finally the mussels become adjusted to their new location. Their clocks have become reset to the tidal rhythms of the new beach.

An experiment with bees also shows how the biological rhythms continue. Honeybees normally stay in their hives at night and feed during the day. They can be trained to come to a dish of sugar and water at any particular time during the daylight hours—or at any two times. Once they have been trained to come to the dish at certain times, they will continue to do so even if the sugar and water have been taken away. But this training will work only if the experimenter follows the bees' natural 24-hour rhythm. Bees cannot be taught to feed every 19 or 20 hours.

Waking Bean Seedlings

An experiment with bean seedlings shows another kind of resetting of living clocks. In this experiment scientists grew bean seedlings in an unchanging dim light. When this plant was in its nighttime position, with its leaves lowered, a scientist exposed it to very bright light for a few minutes. The bean plant began to raise its leaves. When the light was turned off, the leaves drooped to the sleep position once again. But 24 hours later, at just the same time of night, it raised its leaves for a few minutes. It did this for several days without any further exposure to the bright light. The bean biological clock had been set to time an additional 24-hour rhythm.

Resetting Biological Calendars

Scientists have experimented with annual rhythms, as well as with daily and tidal rhythms. Since most seasonal changes involve the length of daylight and the temperature, scientists can reset many annual rhythms by changing the amount of light or the temperature in a laboratory.

For example, the lengthening hours of daylight in spring set off the mating and nesting behavior in birds. If birds are exposed to lengthened periods of light in some other season, they get ready to nest. This happens even in midwinter.

Chrysanthemums bloom naturally in the fall, but it is possible to buy these flowers at any time of year. Flower-growers simply cover the plants with a dark screen to shorten their day. This brings them into bloom.

▶ CLOCKS AND COMPASSES

Some animals apparently use their clocks to find distant places and to move in a straight line toward them. Many birds and fish in particular migrate each year to breeding and feeding grounds hundreds or even thousands of miles distant. Their uncanny ability to do this has puzzled scientists for years.

Ships and airplanes out of sight of land may navigate (steer their course) by the sun in the daytime and by the stars at night. This is possible because the angle between the horizon and the sun or a star is different in different places and at different times. The navigator can tell where he is if he knows exactly what time it is. Knowing the time is important because the earth rotates about 15 degrees every hour. The position of the sun or stars keeps changing as they are observed.

Experiments with birds, fish, and insects show that some animals use the sun as a compass. A few are known to use the stars also, and even the moon, as a compass. But animals are in much the same fix as human navigators; the position of the sun, moon, or

star shifts for them, too. Experiments seem to show that animals use their various biological clocks to time a gradual change in the angle of the sun, moon, or star in relation to their course.

In one experiment a homing pigeon's clock was reset 6 hours by creating in a laboratory the night-and-day schedule that existed in a region a quarter of the way around the earth. When the bird was released, it flew off immediately. But it headed in a direction that was about at right angles to that of its home.

Explaining Biological Clocks

During the past 100 years there have been many experiments to find out if biological clocks and calendars exist, and if so, where they are located in the plants and animals and how they work.

Scientists believe that biological clocks are a kind of inherited ability, passed like any other trait from one generation to another. They point out that when generations of a certain species live in the same environment for millions of years, the species slowly becomes adapted to its surroundings. Its important life activities become adjusted to the rhythms of the physical environment. These rhythms become part of the inherited behavior of the species.

But how does a biological clock continue to measure time accurately when a creature is shielded from outside influences such as length of day or rise and fall of the tides? Two main explanations have been developed. Both fit the facts, but scientists have yet to find which is the correct theory.

Some scientists believe that the biological clocks are timed by chemical and physical changes inside the living creature. If this is so, these changes must be of a very special kind that is not yet understood.

For example, most of the activities of living things are influenced by temperature. This is particularly true of cold-blooded animals, such as the fiddler crab. A fiddler crab is much more active in warm water than in cold. But experiments have shown that its biological clock keeps good time over a wide range of temperatures, from very warm to almost freezing. The same holds true for the clocks in plants.

Experiments have been done with certain

chemicals that change the activities of animals in many ways. These chemicals have no effect on the clocks. They neither speed them up nor slow them down.

Many scientists argue that if the clocks were really an inherited ability and were part of the body chemistry, they would probably be changed in some way by temperature and chemicals. These scientists offer a different explanation.

They point out that animals and plants are always influenced by forces in the environment, no matter what steps are taken to shield them from it. Let's look at the fiddler crab again. Suppose it is responding not to the tidal rhythm, but in some manner to the daily change of relationship between earth, moon, and sun that causes the tides. If the crab responds to gravity rather than to the tidal ebb and flow, there is no possible way to shield it. Gravity cannot be shut out.

Then what about its color change? Surely if the crab is shut up in a dark room, it cannot get any clues about day and night. This is not so certain. Recently it has been discovered that there are changes from day to night in the earth's natural magnetic, electric, and radiation fields. It has also been discovered that living things are sensitive to these changes. Thus, the rhythms of the fiddler crab and other plants and animals may be not just inherited abilities, but very special ways of detecting and responding to the forces of the physical world.

All scientists agree that animals and plants can and do time their activities. Whether they time them by a special inherited chemical timing system or in response to outside forces is harder to prove. But whatever the final explanation, many, if not all, of the important activities of life seem to be timed to occur rhythmically. These biological rhythms are closely tuned to the natural rhythms of the physical environment.

FRANK A. BROWN, JR.
Northwestern University

See also BIRDS (Through the Year with Birds); HIBERNATION; HOMING AND MIGRATION.

LIFE, WEBS OF

Every living thing—from the largest whale and the heaviest elephant down to the smallest bacterium and diatom—has its own way of life. The way of life depends partly on its own form and activities and partly on its environment (surroundings). For no organism (living thing) lives entirely on its own. Every organism is affected by all that surrounds it—whether living or nonliving. And in turn each organism has some effect on its surroundings. Each organism is part of a complex **web of life**.

An organism's environment is made up in part of such things as water, temperature, and light. These things usually change with the seasons and together make up the climate. The climate of a particular place affects every kind of organism living there. The geography of the place, the kind of creatures that lived there in the past, the force of gravity, and other such things are also important.

At the same time, every organism lives as part of a **community**, or group, of other organisms. These organisms, too, make up part of the surroundings. Within the living community each organism competes with other organisms for food, water, and other needs. Each lives as best it can and, if possible, produces young.

Therefore, when we study an animal or plant in its natural surroundings, we are really studying much more. We are studying a web of life. A scientist who studies these webs of life is called an **ecologist**. His subject is **ecology**, which comes from two Greek words meaning "study of the home, or surroundings."

▶THE NONLIVING ENVIRONMENT

Among the most important nonliving things affecting all forms of life are water and temperature. All living material, no matter what kind, consists mostly of water. Whether an organism lives in water or on land, its cells contain water and must have water for their various activities. Therefore an organism must be able to get new supplies of water.

Temperature is also important. It sets limits

to life. For every organism there is a temperature range within which life activity is possible. If the organism is exposed to temperatures above or below that range, its life activities cease. Generally speaking, animals and plants can live actively only in the temperature range between the freezing and boiling points of water. And most kinds of life can live actively only within a much smaller range than that.

Freezing usually causes ice crystals to form in living cells, and so destroys them. (Sometimes living things can be frozen so quickly that ice crystals do not form in the cells. The living things may then become only apparently lifeless and recover when warmed up again. For example, Alaskan blackfish can be frozen for weeks and revive after a thaw.)

At temperatures even much lower than boiling, the living material usually cooks. (This happens, for example, when an egg is put in hot water. Its material sets hard.)

Within such limits, changes in temperature cause living activities to go faster or slower. They speed up when the temperature rises and slow down when it falls. For example, ants run faster in the summer than in the spring. Fish eggs develop faster in warm water than in cold. Yet if the temperature gets too high, the living activities begin to slow down, and death may follow.

Food and Energy

In addition to a supply of water and the proper temperature, all living organisms need raw materials and energy for the replacement

Every organism is part of a community and competes for food, water, and other needs. Drawing shows part of a food web. Note how complex even this part of the web is.

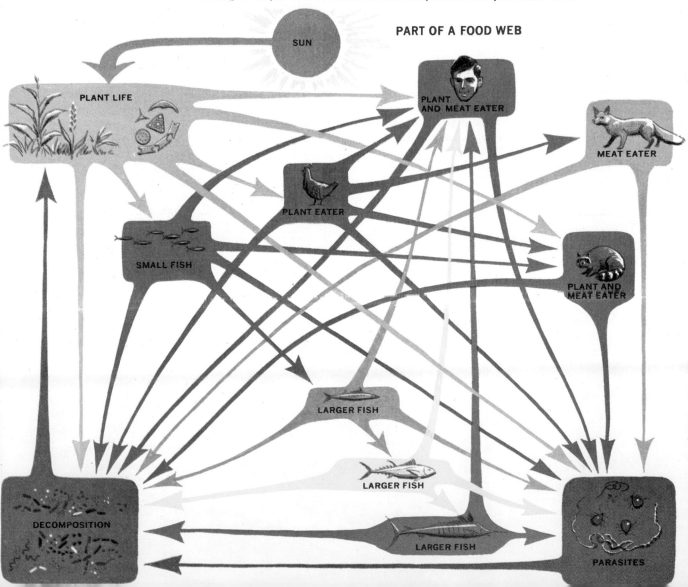

PART OF A FOOD WEB

SUMMER   AUTUMN

SPRING   WINTER

Foxes can use many kinds of food. Drawing shows how fox's diet varies with season and available food.

only special kinds. For example, beavers generally eat only the inner bark of willow, poplar, and other trees. The koala of Australia feeds on eucalyptus leaves. Female horseflies feed only on the blood of mammals (animals that nurse their young).

Then, too, many kinds of foods are seasonal. They may be abundant in spring and summer, but not in fall and winter. Animals depending on these foods must change their feeding habits accordingly or else die. In winter some animals become inactive or hibernate. Some change to other kinds of food. Still others travel to regions where they can find their own special kind of food.

Space

All living organisms need space in which to live. Animals and plants need space if they are to grow well and to produce young. An animal may also need space in which to escape from its enemies. But as a rule, a certain amount of space is necessary simply so that an animal will get enough food. This is clear, for instance, in the behavior of a small mammal such as the chipmunk.

A chipmunk lives in a burrow that shelters it from cold or wet weather and from enemies. The burrow serves as a place to store seeds collected for winter. It is the center of this mammal's world. The chipmunk gathers food within a certain distance all around its burrow. This area is its home territory. A chipmunk needs a home territory of a certain size all to itself if it is to get enough food.

and growth of their own substance. Green plants get raw materials from air, soil, and water. They take energy from sunlight. Thus plants compete for the same things: sunlight, minerals in soil or water, and water itself.

Animals get food and energy from plants or from animals that feed directly or indirectly on plants. However, animals differ greatly in their needs. Each kind of animal has its own particular needs, and each individual must have a certain amount of the right kind of food.

Some animals, such as houseflies, rats, and foxes, can use many kinds of food. Others use

Animals and plants need space in which to live. Chipmunk, like other animals, establishes a home territory and chases away other chipmunks that invade it.

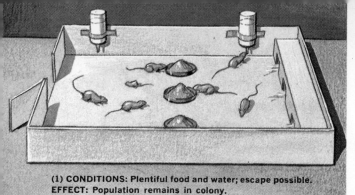

(1) CONDITIONS: Plentiful food and water; escape possible.
EFFECT: Population remains in colony.

(2) CONDITIONS: Shortage of food and water due to over-population; escape possible.
EFFECT: Migration from colony.

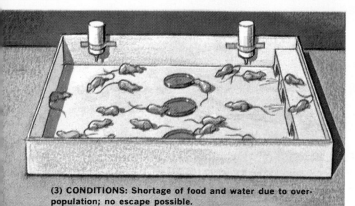

(3) CONDITIONS: Shortage of food and water due to over-population; no escape possible.
EFFECT: Decrease in birthrate.

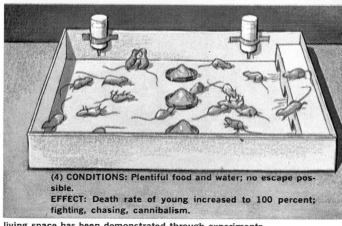

(4) CONDITIONS: Plentiful food and water; no escape possible.
EFFECT: Death rate of young increased to 100 percent; fighting, chasing, cannibalism.

The importance of having enough living space has been demonstrated through experiments with rats placed in pens. Overcrowding usually endangers plants and animals.

For this reason, a chipmunk chases away any other chipmunk that invades its home territory. Likewise it is chased away by other chipmunks if it invades their territories. If a chipmunk did not behave this way, too many of them would be collecting food in one area, and there would not be enough food for all. All would be half starved and probably unable to produce young. The chipmunk population would die out.

As it is, each chipmunk in control of its home territory is usually healthy. Only those chipmunks unable to find a territory of their own lack the food they need.

It is important to have enough living space. Overcrowding endangers animals and plants, even when there is enough food for all. Experiments have shown that rats placed in an overcrowded pen may fight, neglect their nests and young, and die. In similar experiments mice stopped producing young. However, there is some evidence that animals born in an enclosed space can multiply and endure overcrowding without becoming destructive toward one another.

The competition for living space can be seen among the trees of any forest. Trees need water and sunlight and air. A tree that stands by itself in a field has healthy branches growing from all sides and roots spreading widely in the soil. In a forest where it is crowded in by other trees the same kind of tree usually has a long, straight trunk. Its side branches are small and unhealthy, except at the very top. There the healthy branches and their leaves make a green crown. Young trees growing up within a forest often have too little space. They are spindly and may die without ever growing tall enough to get the light they need.

THE LIVING COMMUNITY

In any particular forest, desert, swamp, pond, rock pool, shallow sea floor, or other environment, living organisms will form a community of a particular kind. In each such community there will be some plants upon which various kinds of animals feed. There will be other creatures that feed upon the plant-eating animals. There will be still other

LAYERS OF ANIMAL COMMUNITY IN A TROPICAL RAIN FOREST

EMERGENT LAYER

BIRDS OF PREY
INSECTS

CANOPY

MONKEYS
SQUIRRELS
BIRDS
INSECTS

UNDERSTORY

APES
CATS
SNAKES
ANTELOPE
FROGS
LIZARDS
PIGS
INSECTS

FLOOR

INSECTS
WORMS

160 FT.

120 FT.

30 FT.

0 FT.

organisms that cause decay among the dead organisms. All these organisms are related to one another in a complex web of life. And each web overlaps with smaller and larger webs of life.

Many large communities of both land and water are made up of smaller communities. A forest, for example, is a large community. Various small communities exist within it. Certain insects live in the treetops, feeding on the leaves. Other insects are found in the lower branches; others are found in the bark; others feed in the leaf litter at the bottom; and still others, in the soil. At each layer larger animals feed on the insects. Woodpeckers get insects from the bark, thrushes get them from the ground, and so on. At each layer various small animals, such as squirrels and birds, may find shelter—a place to sleep and to breed. Each group of animals at each layer forms a small community.

As a rule, some one or two forms of life in the larger community influence the forms in the smaller communities. In a pine forest, the pine tree is dominant. It influences the community by shading other plants and the ground. To a degree it changes the climate and so the living activities of the community. It sheds pine needles, and these make the soil acid. Because of the conditions it produces, only a limited number and kind of other plants and animals can live in a pine forest. Ecologists would call this a pine forest community.

Plant Life in a Freshwater Pond Community

Quite another kind of community lives in a freshwater pond. Yet if the pond lies at the edge of a pine forest, life in one community closely affects life in the other.

A freshwater pond provides a particular environment for a small community of plant organisms. A pond is a hollow in the land,

Community of plant and animal life in a freshwater pond.

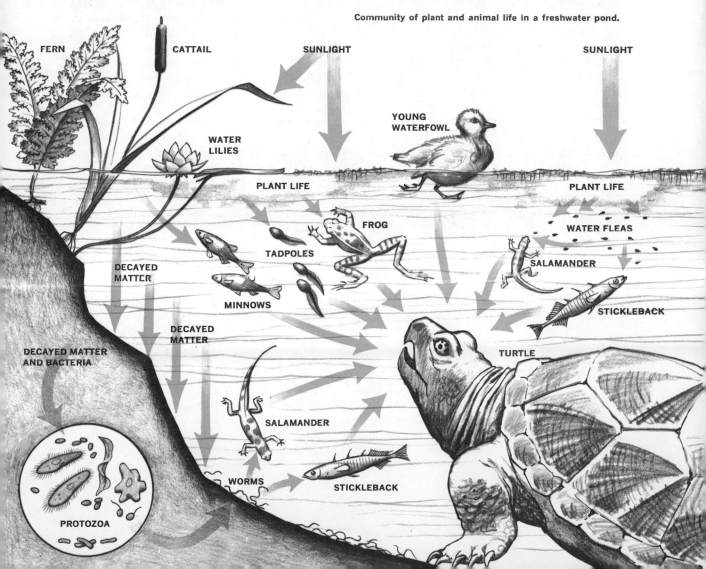

FERN
CATTAIL
SUNLIGHT
SUNLIGHT
YOUNG WATERFOWL
WATER LILIES
PLANT LIFE
PLANT LIFE
WATER FLEAS
FROG
DECAYED MATTER
TADPOLES
SALAMANDER
STICKLEBACK
MINNOWS
DECAYED MATTER
TURTLE
DECAYED MATTER AND BACTERIA
SALAMANDER
WORMS
STICKLEBACK
PROTOZOA

containing a small body of water. Several feet below the surface is a shallow margin, or rim. Ferns, cattails, water lilies, and similar plants grow along the margin, with roots in the mud and leaves at or near the surface. Small floating plants, such as duckweed, may cover much of the pond surface, with leaves at the surface and short roots dangling in the water. Tiny single-celled plants thrive in the upper layer of the water, often giving it a slightly greenish tinge.

The plants get raw materials from the water or from the mud and ooze at the pond bottom. The plants will keep growing as long as there are enough raw materials and sunlight and as long as the water temperature stays well above freezing. But as the end of summer approaches, the days become shorter. There is less light. The water becomes cooler. When the water temperature becomes too cold, plant growth will cease.

It will also cease if certain food materials become too scarce. The droppings of birds and other animals may add needed food materials from time to time, and plant life then becomes more productive. Plant life of a pond increases and decreases in a seasonal way. And it varies somewhat from year to year.

When plant life dies off for one reason or another, it decays. Decay is caused by the action of certain kinds of bacteria in the water and in the ooze at the pond bottom. As a rule, plants die at the end of summer and the decay process goes on during the winter. In the spring, when there is enough light and warmth for plant growth, the raw materials used up the year before are ready to be used again.

In northern regions, where the difference between summer and winter climates is great, the seasonal change in the plant life of a pond is striking. In tropical and subtropical regions, where the amount of light and warmth stays about the same all year long, the processes of growth, death, decay, and new growth go on all the time.

Other Life in the Pond

A pond also contains other kinds of life. Some kinds are microscopic and others may be large. What each feeds on depends mainly on its size.

Along the muddy bottom and the under-sides of larger plants are hundreds of thousands of single-celled protozoa. These tiny creatures feed on smaller protozoans or else on bacteria. And feeding on the protozoa are many-celled creatures, such as various kinds of freshwater worms. The decaying matter that forms much of the bottom ooze also provides food for these creatures. This matter is a rich source of food for small organisms.

Microscopic single-celled plants provide a rich supply of food for animals able to sift it from the water. Water fleas (small cousins of shrimps and crabs) usually swim about gathering such plant cells. At one time or another there are usually frog and toad tadpoles browsing on the plants in the shallower water. Certain fish, particularly some kinds of minnows, also eat plants.

Then there are animals that feed on the plant-feeders. Sticklebacks and other fish feed on the water fleas. So do young salamanders, relatives of frogs and toads. They also eat the worms at the bottom. In any pond there may also be a turtle or two feeding on the fish, on frogs, and on young water birds.

Altogether many kinds of animals exist, all dependent in some way on plant life and on one another. Plant life, in turn, is dependent on energy from the sun. Life in the whole pond changes continually as the seasons pass and as various populations increase and decrease. But as long as light and heat pour in from the sun, life never dies out. It is constantly renewing itself, using the old materials over and over again. Living and nonliving parts of the community all form part of its complex web of life.

A Prairie Community

A pond is one example of a living community. A tropical rain forest, a saltwater marsh, an oak and hickory forest, and a northern tundra are four others. A prairie community is yet another.

The basic life of a prairie consists of the grasses. Energy from the sun passes into the green cells of grass plants. There it is used to change minerals from the soil into new plant material. When the grasses die, bacteria break down the dead material and return its basic substances to the soil. As in the pond and in all other living communities, the processes of growth, death, and decay work continually

Frog.

Toad.

Turtle.

Tadpoles.

Mother mallard duck and young.

CREATURES THAT LIVE IN OR NEAR FRESHWATER PONDS

Underwater view of plant life and young sunfish.

Tiger salamander.

Paramecia

Diving beetle.

Garter snake.

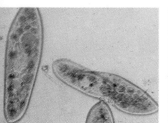

Yellow perch.

Crayfish.

together to make new life out of dead material.

And as in the pond, the plant life supports various kinds of animal life. Countless aphids (small insects) feed on the sap of the grasses. The aphids are eaten by young and adult forms of ladybird beetles. The ladybird beetles in turn are eaten by various ground beetles. Birds such as the horned lark and grasshopper sparrow feed on the beetles. And these birds may be eaten by marsh hawks. Fleas and lice and other organisms may feed on the marsh hawks. And when the hawks or the fleas or any other living thing dies, bacteria return the dead material to the soil.

The Grasslands of Africa

A somewhat similar community is found on the plains of Africa. These grasslands extend across central Africa. The grass and other plants support large populations of animals. Herds of many kinds of antelope, zebras, giraffes, and other creatures graze on the grass. Preying on them are lions and leopards (and man). Vultures, jackals, and hyenas feed on what the great cats leave of their kill. Sooner or later death overtakes all plants and animals, and their substance decays.

All the big game animals, together with many smaller kinds of creatures, depend directly or indirectly on plant growth. Plants in turn depend on raw materials in the soil, particularly on certain mineral salts. These salts are in short supply in the African soil, and water, too, is often scarce. Shortage of water may reduce the size of the herds. Then more water is available for plant use. And so eater and eaten tend to remain well balanced in the African grasslands.

▶ **THE BALANCE OF NATURE**

How much life exists in a community depends partly on its area. A water community, for instance, may be that of a small pond or of the enormous continuous oceans of the world. Each such community depends on the sun for energy and on various other nonliving factors. The total number of living organisms in any community depends on how much raw material is available for plant use.

In any community the various organisms are linked in a complicated web of relationships. These are usually in delicate balance with one another. If the natural web is disturbed, the results may be disastrous. As a rule, the various populations of organisms tend to adjust to seasonal and other changes, and the whole community stays in balance. Most disturbances come from man's activities. And man is interfering with nature all the time.

For example, man has interfered with the natural communities of the northern forests. He has cut down trees and killed animals, disturbing the natural balance.

Unless man interferes, a natural balance exists between deer and their enemies.

Spraying DDT controls harmful insects but also upsets natural balance of communities.

In an undisturbed forest, white-tailed deer feed on plants of various kinds. Wolves and mountain lions prey on the deer. When deer are very numerous, their enemies become numerous too, because there is so much to feed upon. The deer and their enemies stay in balance with one another.

Then man enters the scene. He looks on animals such as wolves and mountain lions as harmful. He kills as many as possible. When the animals that feed on deer are killed, the deer multiply without check. Soon the large deer population has eaten all, or nearly all, the plants available for food. Then the deer begin to starve. Now, instead of a good-sized, healthy population kept in check by natural enemies, there is a half-starved, unhealthy population.

Another example of man's interference with natural communities is the use of chemical insecticides. DDT, for instance, is sprayed to kill crop-destroying and disease-carrying insects. Grass in the sprayed areas may be eaten by cows. As a result, the milk of some cows has been found to contain too much DDT. The insecticides also collect in the tissues of birds that eat the sprayed insects. Some of the affected birds produce eggs that do not hatch. The number of birds decreases, cutting down the food supply of other animals. More and more, the use of these insecticides is being outlawed.

Whether intended or not, almost every change that man has made in natural webs of life has turned out to be a disaster for the communities involved. Man, of course, is part of the world's living community. Everything he does affects all the rest of it, just as any change in the community or climate around him affects his own well-being. Thus, by changing natural communities, man may harm himself. This makes it important to learn as much as possible about the natural webs of life on this planet, about the living and nonliving things in our surroundings.

N. J. BERRILL
McGill University

See also KINGDOMS OF LIVING THINGS.

LIGHT

Light is what enables you to see. It carries messages to your eyes that tell you what is going on in the world. Anything that gives off light of its own is called a **source of light**. The sun is the biggest and brightest natural source that you can see. It was the main one for the first men on earth, and today most other sources are only substitutes for the sun.

From earliest times people knew of lightning and of the light from the stars, but these were not useful sources, like the sun. The first man-made source was probably the flame from burning wood. Later, people used oil lamps, candles, gas flames, and then various kinds of electric lamps in order to carry on their activities after the sun went down.

Scientists and philosophers have always wondered what light really is. In ancient times they thought it was some sort of "feeler" sent out from the eyes. Later they realized that all visible objects give off something that the eyes are able to pick up.

▶ **LIGHT TRAVELS IN STRAIGHT LINES**

Light spreads directly outward from a source, moving in straight lines rather than in curved paths. A **shadow** is a result of the way light travels. If you stand between a lamp and a wall, a fairly sharp shadow of your body appears on the wall. The shadow is the dark space where your body blocks the light from the lamp. The edge of the shadow can be traced by imagining straight lines drawn out from the lamp and just touching the edge of your body all around (Fig. 1).

If the light source is big and quite near, there will be two parts to the shadow—a black inner part and a gray edge. (Fig. 2). Double shadows of this kind are especially noticeable when the source is a fluorescent lamp tube.

A double shadow also forms when there is an **eclipse** of the sun. This usually happens twice a year, when the moon comes directly between the sun and the earth. The black shadow of the moon is long and tapering, like the pointed end of a pencil. It makes a spot only 50 to 100 miles wide where it hits the earth. As the earth turns and the moon moves onward this spot sweeps over the ground on a long, curved path. Anyone who happens to be in this path will see the sky darken. The sun will be completely hidden while the shadow passes. All around the moving black spot there is a much larger, gray half-shadow. For people in the gray area, the sun is never entirely covered. They receive light from the part of the sun that is not hidden by the moon.

A shadow is cast when an object blocks the light from a light source.

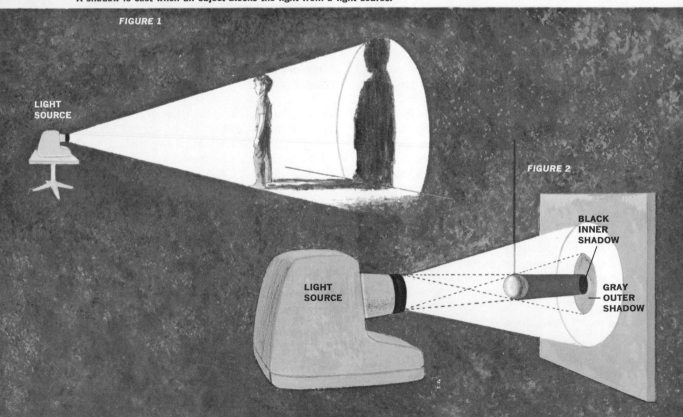

FIGURE 1

LIGHT SOURCE

FIGURE 2

LIGHT SOURCE

BLACK INNER SHADOW

GRAY OUTER SHADOW

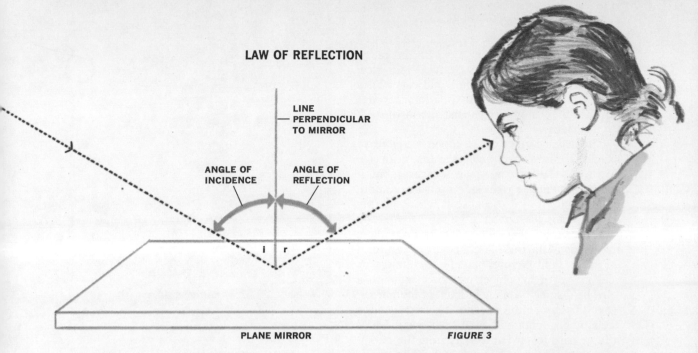

LAW OF REFLECTION

LINE PERPENDICULAR TO MIRROR

ANGLE OF INCIDENCE

ANGLE OF REFLECTION

i | r

PLANE MIRROR

FIGURE 3

The angle of incidence (i) is equal to the angle of reflection (r).

▶ **REFLECTION AND MIRRORS**

Straight lines can be drawn to show the direction in which light is moving. Light traveling along a straight line is called a **ray of light**. As long as the light travels in empty space or in any material that is the same all the way through, the rays stay perfectly straight and keep their original direction. One way to change the direction of the rays is to let light bounce off the surface of an object. This throwing back of light is called **reflection**.

You see the stars, planets, and the moon by light they send to your eyes. The stars are very hot and glow brightly; they send out light of their own. But the planets and the moon do not glow; they are seen only because they reflect sunlight. In the same way, you see most of the things around you because they reflect daylight or lamplight.

Plane Mirrors

Any smooth, shiny reflecting surface can be called a **mirror**. The surface may be either flat or curved.

If the surface is flat, it is called a **plane mirror**. A small plane mirror can be used to reflect a bright spot of sunlight onto a nearby wall. The spot of light moves around on the wall as the mirror is tilted in various directions. The rays change their direction sharply when the light is reflected from the mirror.

A ray that heads squarely toward a plane mirror is reflected straight back in the opposite direction. A ray that hits the mirror at a slant will bounce off, making the same slant with a line drawn perpendicular to the mirror (Fig. 3). According to the **law of reflection**, the angle of incidence is always equal to the angle of reflection and the two rays are directly opposite each other. This law explains why rays from an object reflected in a mirror seem to come from its **image**, which is a sort of copy of the object. The image in a plane mirror has the same size and shape as the object and appears to be just as far behind the mirror as the object is in front.

Hold some writing up to a mirror and you notice that it reads backward. The image is reversed—its right and left sides are exchanged. The image in a plane mirror is always reversed side to side but never up and down.

Plane mirrors are useful whenever it is necessary to change the direction of light rays. They are an important part of many instruments, such as the periscope, sextant, and range finder.

Curved Mirrors

Look at a shiny metal spoon. Both sides reflect light. Each surface is really a curved mirror. The back of the spoon is a **convex**

mirror and shows you a small image of yourself right side up. Convex rear-view mirrors are used on bicycles and cars. They are better than plane mirrors for this use because they show things that are farther off to the sides.

The inside surface of the spoon is a **concave mirror**. It shows you an image that is upside down. A shaving mirror is concave, but it shows your image right side up when you are not too far from it, because it is less sharply curved than the spoon.

There is another difference between these two kinds of mirrors: A concave one can form an actual light-picture, called a **real image**. A real image of an object can be caught on a card held some distance in front of the mirror. Test this by setting a shaving mirror on a table, facing a lamp about 10 feet away. Move a large card toward and away from the mirror until you get a sharp image of the lamp on it (Fig. 4). Notice that this image is upside down as well as reversed side to side.

A searchlight reflector is a concave mirror placed a short distance behind a small, very bright source of light. If the mirror has the right shape, all the reflected rays are sent out in a strong, parallel beam. Used for the opposite purpose, a concave mirror can gather incoming light or radio and television signals from a great distance. Huge mirrors of this kind are part of modern astronomical telescopes.

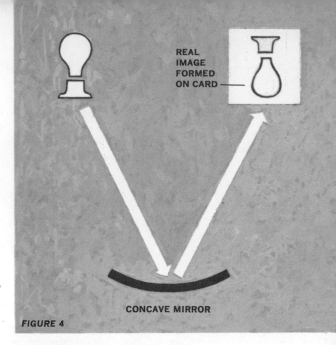

REAL IMAGE FORMED ON CARD

CONCAVE MIRROR

FIGURE 4

▶ REFRACTION

A shiny metal surface reflects almost all the light that hits it. But certain other materials let some of the light go right on through. Such materials are **transparent**. Air, water, glass, and certain plastics are familiar examples.

When light goes from one transparent material into another, the rays change their direction sharply. This change is called **refraction**. A ray striking a pane of glass at a slant will bend *toward* the perpendicular as it enters the glass. This happens when light goes from air into glass. It happens in all cases

Image of a candy mint in curved mirrors. Left: A convex mirror forms an image that is smaller than the object. Shape of the image shows it has been squeezed together from side to side. Right: A concave mirror forms an image that is larger than the object. Shape of the image shows it has been enlarged from side to side.

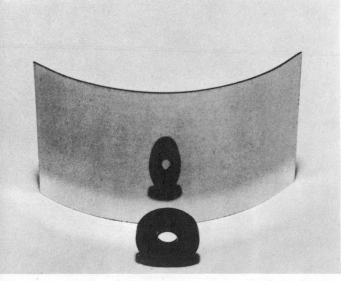

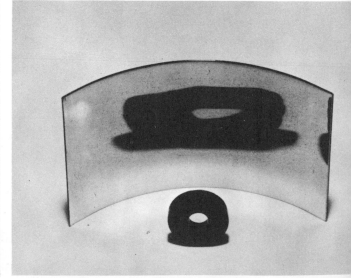

Light rays are refracted (bent) when they go from one transparent material (air) into another (glass). They are refracted again when they leave the glass.

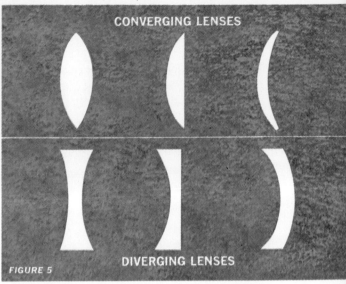
CONVERGING LENSES

FIGURE 5

DIVERGING LENSES

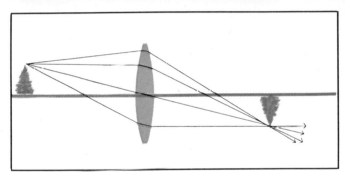
Light rays entering a converging lens are refracted and made to converge at a single point on the other side of the lens. This refraction produces a real image that is upside down and reversed from side to side. (Diagram shows path of rays coming from tip of tree only.)

where light enters a denser material. When the light comes out again on the far side, the rays bend in the opposite direction, swinging *away* from the perpendicular.

The amount of the bending depends on the materials and on the direction of the incoming rays. Different materials refract light by different amounts, which can be measured accurately. A scientist in a food laboratory can tell the difference between butter and margarine by measuring how much they bend light. A diamond refracts light more strongly than almost any other transparent material. Experts can measure the refraction of a jewel and tell if it is genuine or false.

Refraction of light by the air produces some interesting effects. Because of differences in temperature and pressure, the air is denser at some places than at others, and light going through is refracted. When you ride in a car on a hot summer day, you may notice what seems to be a pool of water on the road ahead. This is not water at all, but light from the sky refracted up to your eye by the heated air near the pavement. There is an opposite effect when the air near the ground is cooler than the rest. Then a distant cliff or tower will seem to loom up to a great height. Such effects are called **mirages**.

▶ **LENSES**

Long ago, people discovered that an object appeared to be larger if they looked at it through a glass bead. Such a bead is really a crude **lens**. A lens is any piece of transparent material that has at least one evenly curved surface. Figure 5 shows several lenses. Each is cut through the center to show its shape. The top three are examples of **converging lenses**. The bottom three are **diverging lenses**. "Converging" means "bringing together" and "diverging" means "spreading apart," and that is what these lenses do to rays of light.

Converging Lenses

When parallel rays head directly toward a converging lens, they are refracted in various amounts, depending on where each one hits the lens. But after going through, they all head for a single point on the other side. This point is called the **principal focus**. Its distance from the lens is called the **focal distance**.

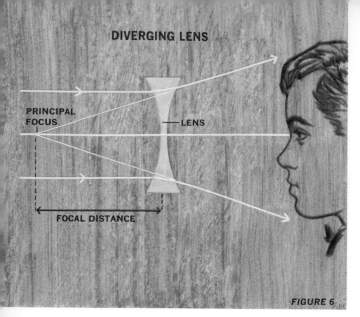

DIVERGING LENS

PRINCIPAL FOCUS

LENS

FOCAL DISTANCE

FIGURE 6

Rays that spread out from any point on an object can be bent by a converging lens so that they come together again at a single point on the other side. This happens for all parts of the object and gives a complete real image on a card held at the proper place. This image, like the one produced by the shaving mirror, is reversed up and down as well as side to side.

When an object is placed a certain distance from the lens, a sharp image will be formed a definite distance away. If either one of these positions is known, the other one can be found by the lens formula:

$$\frac{1}{p} + \frac{1}{q} = \frac{1}{f}$$

Here p is the distance of the object from the lens; q is the distance of the image formed; and f is the focal distance of the lens.

The arrangement of object, lens, and card really amounts to a **camera**. In a camera the card is replaced by a sensitive film that traps the image and gives a permanent picture when the film is developed. There is also a light-tight box to enclose the film and a shutter to control the amount of light that enters. A camera is usually focused by moving the lens back and forth until the image on the film is sharp.

Diverging Lenses

Suppose the lamp-lens-card experiment is tried with a diverging lens. There is no place where a real image forms on the card. That is because a diverging lens spreads the rays

instead of bringing them together. Parallel rays fan out in a special way after going through a diverging lens. All the rays seem to come from a single point located in front of the lens rather than behind it (Fig. 6).

In the same way, any object placed in front of a diverging lens will not give a real image. Instead, there will be a small image on the same side of the lens as the object. This is called a **virtual image**. Although it cannot be caught on a screen, a virtual image can be seen by looking through the lens from behind. A diverging lens has a principal focus and a focal distance, just as a converging lens has.

▶ **OPTICAL INSTRUMENTS**

About 300 years ago the Dutch amateur scientist Anton van Leeuwenhoek (1632–1723) used single lenses to make the first **microscopes**. With these instruments he was able to observe many interesting things, including tiny plants and animals that had never been seen before.

The great Italian scientist Galileo (1564–1642) used lenses to construct a **telescope**, with which he made many truly great discoveries in astronomy.

As scientists became more familiar with light rays, they found ways of putting together lenses and mirrors to form various **optical instruments**.

The prisms in binoculars correct the reversed image produced by the converging lens.

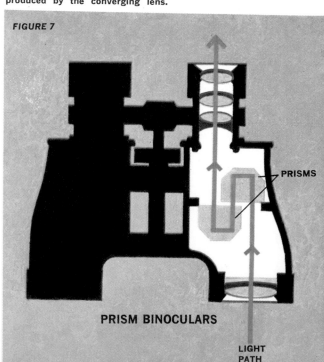

FIGURE 7

PRISMS

PRISM BINOCULARS

LIGHT PATH

The high-powered **compound microscopes** used in science today are quite different from the rough models made by Leeuwenhoek. There are two sets of lenses, each made up of several parts. The use of combinations of lenses allows the designer to correct certain defects and thus get better images. Modern microscopes used by biologists, geologists, and engineers can magnify objects as much as 2,500 times.

Telescopes usually have two sets of lenses, just as microscopes do. However, in a telescope the front lens combination has a very long focal distance. The image seen by the eye is upside down and reversed from side to side, as is the image in a microscope. A good way of turning the image around is to use two triangular pieces of glass called **prisms** to reflect the light back and forth. Two such telescopes, one in front of each eye, make up a **prism binocular** (Fig. 7).

The largest telescopes used in astronomy are somewhat different in design. These instruments must be able to gather enough light from very faint, distant objects to make them visible to the eye or to register in a photograph taken through the telescope. This requires a front lens system several feet across. Grinding and polishing accurate lenses of this size is very difficult and expensive. So most of the large instruments use a concave mirror in place of the first lens system. This kind of device is called a **reflecting telescope**.

One of the first reflecting telescopes was made by the famous English scientist Isaac Newton (1642–1727). Its mirror was only about 1 inch across and had a focal distance of about 6 inches. The mirror of the great reflecting telescope at Mount Palomar in California has a diameter of nearly 17 feet and a focal length, or distance, of 55 feet. It was completed in 1949 at a cost of $6,500,000.

▶ THE EYE

The human eye is the most important and useful of all optical instruments. The eye acts as a converging lens system to form an image on the **retina**, which is the sensitive inner surface of the eyeball. Millions of nerves send messages from the image to the brain. The **pupil** is the round opening at the front of the eyeball. A muscle changes the size of the pupil to control the amount of light that enters the

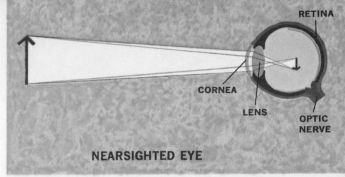

NEARSIGHTED EYE

In a nearsighted eye the image is focused in front of the retina. In a farsighted eye the object's image would be focused behind the retina.

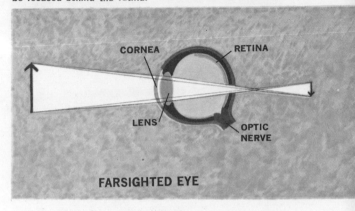

FARSIGHTED EYE

eye. In this way the pupil acts like the automatic "stop" on some cameras.

A camera is focused by moving the lens system back and forth. The eye changes focus by squeezing up or relaxing a muscle around the edge of the lens. This makes the lens thicker for looking at nearby objects and thinner for viewing distant ones.

The eye often has defects that can be helped by the use of suitable eyeglasses. A **farsighted eye** cannot see nearby objects clearly. Then a converging eyeglass lens can be used to bring the rays together properly on the retina. A **nearsighted eye** cannot form clear images of anything more than a few inches away. To correct this, a diverging eyeglass lens is used.

Often the front surface of the eye is curved somewhat unevenly. The result is a defect of vision called **astigmatism**, in which parts of the image are fuzzy. This condition is corrected by an eyeglass lens that is curved more in one direction than another.

▶ THE SPEED OF LIGHT

In times past some scientists believed that light could go from one place to another instantly. Others thought it had a definite speed, but one that might be too fast to

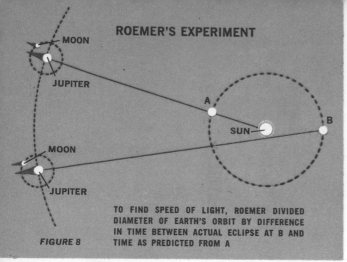

ROEMER'S EXPERIMENT

TO FIND SPEED OF LIGHT, ROEMER DIVIDED DIAMETER OF EARTH'S ORBIT BY DIFFERENCE IN TIME BETWEEN ACTUAL ECLIPSE AT B AND TIME AS PREDICTED FROM A

FIGURE 8

Roemer measured the speed of light by observing one of Jupiter's moons.

measure. About 350 years ago Galileo tried an experiment. He placed two men about a mile apart, facing each other. Each man had a lantern, closed by a shutter. Then, at a signal, one man opened the shutter and his light shone out. As soon as the second man saw the beam, he uncovered his own lantern. Standing next to the first man, Galileo tried to measure how long it took the light to go both ways. He could get no definite result because, as we now know, light travels much too fast to be measured in this way. It took thousands of times longer for the man to move his shutter after seeing the signal than it did for light to go the whole distance.

A few years later a Danish astronomer named Olaf Roemer (1644–1710) was able to prove that light really takes time to go from one place to another. By observing one of the moons of Jupiter as it came out regularly from behind the planet, he found that light travels almost 10,000,000 miles in a minute (Fig. 8).

The first accurate measurement of the speed of light was made only a little more than 100 years ago by the French experimenter H.

L. Fizeau (1819–96). He used the basic idea of Galileo's test, but he replaced the men and their lanterns with a fast mechanical shutter and a mirror that sent the light back from a nearby hilltop. This experiment was repeated by another French scientist, Léon Foucault (1819–68), who used a spinning mirror in place of the shutter. The result was a speed of about 186,000 miles a second—not far from the more exact results of today.

Some of the most accurate measurements of the speed of light were made nearly 50 years ago by the American physicist Albert Michelson (1852–1931). He improved the spinning-mirror method and sent a light beam back and forth between two mountains that were 22 miles apart. After the invention of radar, experimenters were able to show that radar signals travel exactly as fast as light. This means that the speed of light can be measured by electrical methods. The best figure at this time is 186,282 miles a second. Scientists think this cannot be off by more than about 2 miles a second.

▶ ELECTROMAGNETIC WAVES

In Newton's time scientists often had long discussions about the true character of light. Some of them believed that light sources sent out tiny particles that could bounce off reflecting surfaces or go through transparent materials. Others thought that light is some kind of wave. Nowadays scientists know that the wave idea can explain what light does, while Newton's particle idea cannot.

Light waves must be of a very different kind from waves on water or sound waves in the air. For one thing, we know that they are able to travel even in empty space. It turns out that light waves are made up of electrical and magnetic forces traveling along together. They are one kind of **electromagnetic wave**.

GALILEO'S EXPERIMENT TO MEASURE THE SPEED OF LIGHT

INTENSITY OF LIGHT

Light waves, streaming out from a source, can travel to distant places and make things happen there. In scientific terms, light waves carry **energy**. A flying missile has mechanical energy. A hot furnace has heat energy. Foods and fuels have chemical energy. The atoms of matter themselves have nuclear energy locked up inside them.

Some of the heat energy of the sun is continually changing into light energy. When the light waves strike the earth, part of their energy changes back to heat again. Lamps of various kinds also change a part of their heat energy into light. The strength of a lamp or other light source is measured in **candles**—a name that goes back to the old days of wax candles. A reading lamp may have a strength of about 50 candles.

The amount of light energy an object receives depends on how far away the source is. Suppose a single candle shines directly on a flat surface one foot away. Then it lights this surface with an intensity (brightness) of one **footcandle**. Because of the way light waves weaken as they spread out from a source, the intensity in this example becomes only 1/4 footcandle at a distance of 2 feet, 1/9 footcandle at 3 feet, and so on (Fig. 9).

If the surface is slanted, instead of being perpendicular to the incoming rays, the intensity at each place is less. This is the main reason for the difference between summer and winter temperatures on earth. The sun's rays come in at a greater slant in winter, because

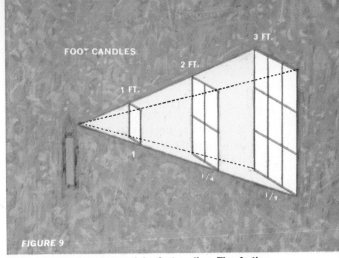

FIGURE 9

Light intensity is measured in footcandles. The farther away a surface is from the light source, the less the intensity of the light.

the surface of the ground is tilted away from the sun. As a result, the same amount of energy is spread over a larger surface, and there is less heating.

The illumination from a clear sky is about 1,000 footcandles, and from direct sunlight about 10,000 footcandles. The human eye is so sensitive that it can detect an illumination of only 1/10,000,000,000 footcandle.

DISPERSION AND COLOR

Light from the sun or from any very hot source is called **white light**. Some experiments by Newton first showed that white light is really a mixture of light of all colors. He darkened his room and let a narrow beam of sunlight come in through a small hole in a window shade. When he placed a glass prism

A beam of white light directed through a prism is dispersed into a color spectrum.

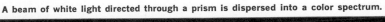

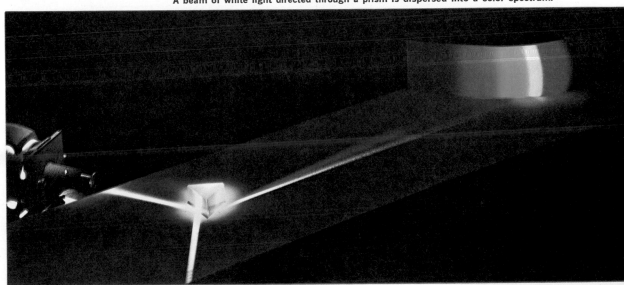

in the path of this beam, he noticed a bright patch of color on the opposite wall. This patch was made up of all the colors of the rainbow—red, orange, yellow, green, blue, and violet, in that order. Each shade blended gradually into the next without a break. Newton named this spread of color a **spectrum** (plural: spectra).

He correctly believed that these colors were all present in sunlight to begin with, but showed up only after being spread out by refraction in the prism. Each color is refracted a slightly different amount, red least and violet most. The resulting spreading-out is called **dispersion**. Without dispersion, the mixture gives the appearance of white (absence of color) to the eye.

It was only after Newton's time that the real explanation of color was found: Color is determined by the **wavelength** of the light (Fig. 10). The wavelength of light corresponds to the distance between one crest and the next in a wave traveling on water. While water waves may be many feet long, the light waves that the eye can detect are measured in millionths of an inch. The shortest visible waves are violet, with a wavelength of about 15 millionths of an inch. The longest are red, with a wavelength of about 28 millionths of an inch.

In between are all the colors of the spectrum, and each shade has its own wavelength.

Most of the colors we see in our surroundings are not of a single wavelength but are mixtures of many wavelengths. When white light falls on an object, some wavelengths are reflected and the rest are **absorbed** by the material. A piece of red cloth, for example, absorbs almost all wavelengths except a certain range of red ones. These are the only ones that are reflected to your eye.

Colored pieces of glass absorb part of the light passing through them. They are called **color filters** because they absorb certain wavelengths and let others pass through.

Many familiar colors are not found in the spectrum but are mixtures of groups of spectrum wavelengths. Purple is a mixture of red and violet; brown is a mixture of red, orange, and yellow. Different shades of any color can be made by adding some white light; for instance, a mixture of red and white is pink.

Mixing light of different colors is not the same as mixing paints (or pigments). A mixture of blue and yellow paints looks green because that is the only color that is not completely absorbed by the two kinds of paint.

THE COLOR OF VISIBLE LIGHT IS DETERMINED BY ITS WAVELENGTH

FIGURE 10

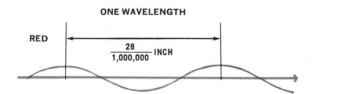

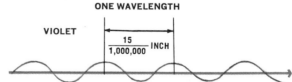

SPECTRUM OF VISIBLE LIGHT

COLORED LIGHTS CAN BE ADDED TOGETHER TO MAKE WHITE LIGHT

FILTERS OR PIGMENTS ABSORB, OR SUB-TRACT, LIGHT UNTIL NO LIGHT REMAINS

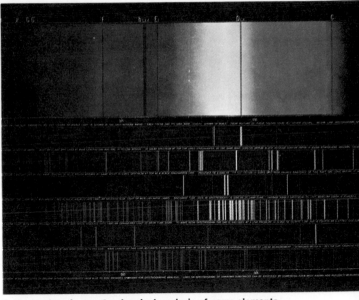

Patterns given by spectrochemical analysis of some elements.

Spectra

When white light from a glowing solid or liquid goes through a prism, it forms a **continuous spectrum**—one that has no breaks in it. But if the source is a thin material such as a gas or vapor, the spectrum is a set of bright lines separated by dark spaces. The light comes to the prism through a narrow slit, and each bright line is an image of that slit. There is one image for each wavelength that is present in the light. The separate lines in the spectrum of a gas show that only certain definite wavelengths are given out.

Each kind of material has its own pattern of spectrum lines. These patterns, once they are known, can be used to tell which materials are present in a sample. In this way, a chemist can make a **spectrochemical analysis** of a substance in much less time than he can make a regular chemical analysis. Besides, the spectrum can identify a substance from only a tiny speck. For such reasons, this method has become a valuable tool in steel mills, in chemical plants, and even in police work.

Some of the most remarkable uses of the spectrum are found in astronomy. A spectroscope is attached to a large telescope. The eye lens is replaced by a camera to photograph the spectrum lines. In this way the astronomer can find out the chemical makeup of distant planets, stars, gas clouds, and other objects in the sky.

There is still more information that an astronomer can get from the spectrum: he can tell how fast a star or other light source is moving. Light waves from a star that is moving toward the earth are crowded up and appear a little shorter, while waves from a source that is moving away are stretched out and appear to be a bit longer. This is called the **Doppler effect**, after Christian Doppler (1803–53), the scientist who worked it out over 100 years ago. These changes are small, and the light must be spread out into a spectrum in order to reveal them. The spectrum lines are shifted toward the red if the source is going away, and toward the violet if it is approaching. The amount of this shift can be used to figure out the actual speed of motion.

Infrared Radiation

About 150 years ago the English astronomer Sir William Herschel (1738–1822) held a thermometer at several places in the spectrum of sunlight and found that the temperature was highest near the red end. Then he held the thermometer just outside the red limit. To his surprise, he saw that the heating effect was even greater there than anywhere in the spectrum itself. This meant that sunlight must contain a strong, invisible radiation whose wavelength is even greater than that of red light.

Radiation of this kind belongs to a part of

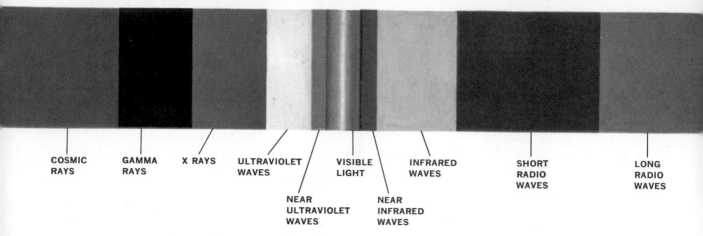

COSMIC RAYS | GAMMA RAYS | X RAYS | ULTRAVIOLET WAVES | NEAR ULTRAVIOLET WAVES | VISIBLE LIGHT | NEAR INFRARED WAVES | INFRARED WAVES | SHORT RADIO WAVES | LONG RADIO WAVES

the spectrum called the **infrared**. Infrared waves are given off strongly by glowing, hot objects such as the sun, electric lamps, and flames. Even things that are not hot enough to glow—such as electric irons and hot pavements—send out strong infrared radiation.

There are delicate instruments of various kinds that can detect and measure infrared radiation. Some can measure the temperature of a single star or detect a high-flying airplane by the radiation from its motors. Cameras with special photographic films can pick up the infrared and take clear pictures of distant scenes even through haze. The longer waves are able to get through the mist, which scatters aside all the ordinary light.

The Ultraviolet

A short time after the discovery of the infrared, other radiations were found just outside the violet end of the visible part of the spectrum. These waves, shorter than those of violet light, are called **ultraviolet**. When ultraviolet rays strike certain minerals, they are changed to longer waves that are visible. Many minerals, oils, plant juices, and other materials can do this. Such materials are **fluorescent**.

A fluorescent lamp tube has a coating of this kind on its inner surface. When an electric current passes through the gas in the tube, ultraviolet radiation is given off. When these waves hit the coating, they make it send out a strong, visible glow.

Sunburn is caused by ultraviolet rays in sunlight. In small amounts they have a good effect because they form vitamin D in the skin. Ultraviolet radiation can kill bacteria and is used for purifying foods and water and even the air in hospitals. Special "sun lamps" or "germicidal lamps" are used for producing the strong radiation that is needed. Police scientists use ultraviolet light for detecting bloodstains, forged documents, and faked oil paintings.

X Rays and Gamma Rays

In 1895 a German physicist, Wilhelm Roentgen (1845–1923), discovered a range of radiations whose wavelengths were very much shorter than even the ultraviolet's. Roentgen was not experimenting with sunlight and prisms but with a special high-vacuum tube. When current was sent through the tube, he noticed that a piece of mineral some distance away would glow. This happened even when he wrapped the tube in heavy cardboard to hold back any visible rays. Apparently some unknown radiation from the tube was causing the glow.

Roentgen named the new radiation **X rays**. He found that these rays could pass through many materials, such as wood and cloth. They could even go through the body and cast shadows of the bones on a screen coated with fluorescent material.

The discovery of X rays caused a sensation. Soon doctors were using the rays when setting broken bones. Today a well-equipped X-ray department is found in every large hospital.

Roentgen was interested mainly in learning what the rays really were. He was able to prove that they could be reflected like light. Later it was shown that they are electromagnetic waves with wavelengths hundreds of times shorter than those of visible light.

Not long after Roentgen's discovery it was found that certain minerals continually give off radiation that is even more penetrating than X rays. The work of the French scientists Pierre (1859–1906) and Marie (1867–1934) Curie finally led to the discovery of radium and several other chemical elements that send out these rays. This is called **natural radioactivity**. Most of the other elements are not naturally radioactive, but when they are placed in a nuclear reactor, they change to radioisotopes, which continue to give off strong radiations for some time.

Part of the radiation is in the form of electromagnetic waves, about 100 times shorter than X rays and much more penetrating. They are called **gamma rays**. This radiation can go through a steel plate several inches thick. X rays and gamma rays are useful for looking deep into materials and for locating and destroying harmful growths such as certain tumors and cancers. Engineers use X rays and gamma rays to locate defects inside metal machine parts.

▶ ELECTRIC WAVES

Electricity can be made to surge rapidly back and forth in an electric circuit. When these surges are fast enough, electromagnetic waves are sent out from the circuit in all directions in space. In some ways these **electric waves** prove to be like light. They travel in straight lines and can be reflected from surfaces.

In 1901 the Italian experimenter Guglielmo Marconi (1874–1937) sent a weak electric signal across the Atlantic Ocean—the first "wireless" message. That was the beginning of the great radio and television industry of today. The waves used in regular broadcasting are up to a quarter of a mile long. Television programs are carried by groups of electric waves that are from about 1 foot to 18 feet long. Waves less than about 1 foot long are called **microwaves**. Some of them are used in **radar**.

In recent years scientists found that electric waves were coming to the earth from various directions in space. Large concave mirrors called **radio telescopes** were built to gather the waves. With these instruments more than 2,000 radio sources were discovered. The waves are thought to be sent out when stars or groups of stars explode or collide far out in space. The sun and some of the planets are also found to be radio sources.

Beginning with the study of the visible spectrum, science has been able to extend the electromagnetic spectrum. It now goes down as far as wavelengths 1,000,000,000 (billion) times shorter than the ones the eye can see and up as far as some that are 100,000,000,000 (billion) times longer. All these waves are of the same basic electromagnetic nature, and all travel through space at the same speed.

▶ DIFFRACTION

A close look at the edge of a shadow can show that it is slightly fuzzy and that there are very fine, narrow stripes close to the edge. These observations were first made by the Italian scientist Francesco Grimaldi (1618?–63) about 300 years ago. They show that light actually does bend very slightly around corners. Grimaldi gave the name **diffraction** to this bending of light that takes place as the light passes the edge of an object.

An explanation of diffraction did not come until about 150 years later, when scientists realized that it could happen only if light was made up of waves. All kinds of waves—water waves, sound waves, and so on—bend to some extent when going past the edge of an obstacle or through an opening.

A mixture of wavelengths of light can be

A razor blade, highly magnified, shows diffraction of light by a sharp edge.

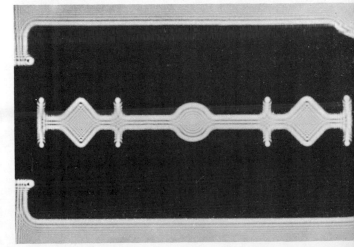

spread out by passing the light through a prism, as explained above. There is another way to sort out waves, and that is to use diffraction. It works for waves of any kind. If a mixture of waves is sent through a narrow slit, the long waves spread out more than the short ones. In order to separate the various wavelengths sharply, there must be a great many slits placed close together, side by side. Such a set of slits is called a **diffraction grating**. Modern gratings for light waves are made by a special machine that uses a diamond point to scratch thousands of very fine, parallel lines on a metal mirror. Diffraction gratings of this kind may have as many as 50,000 lines per inch.

Light from a source is sent through a narrow slit to the grating. The different wavelengths in the original light are diffracted off at various angles to form a line spectrum on a screen or on a photographic film. The positions of the spectrum lines are carefully measured. Then, knowing the spacing of the lines on the grating, scientists can compute the wavelength of each radiation.

When X rays were first produced, their wavelengths could not be measured very accurately. Ruled gratings suitable for light waves are much too coarse for X-ray work. Then it was found that natural crystals of certain minerals could be used to diffract X rays. The atoms of a crystal are regularly spaced, with just the right distance between them to give good diffraction of X rays. However, instead of giving a row of bright lines, as a ruled grating does, a crystal produces a regular pattern of spots. By measuring this pattern, scientists can find the X-ray wavelengths.

▶ INTERFERENCE OF LIGHT

The delicate coloring of a soap bubble, or of an oil spot on a wet pavement, is caused by the **interference** of light hitting a very thin layer of transparent material. Some of the light is reflected from the front surface of the layer and some from the back, as the illustration shows (Fig. 11). When these two sets of waves join up again, they may happen to be exactly in step with each other. In this case they reinforce each other, and the result is bright reflected light. But if the two sets of waves come back exactly out of step, they can-

cel each other out. No light is reflected at that place.

Whether there is reinforcing or canceling out at any particular spot depends on the thickness of the layer there. For each place only one color will have the right wavelength to cancel out, leaving a mixture of all the other colors. At another place the thickness of the layer of material may be different, and a different color will cancel out.

Some of the prisms and mirrors used in fine optical instruments must have surfaces that are flat to within a few millionths of an inch. The flatness can be tested by using interference. During the polishing process the surface is tested from time to time by putting it against another piece of glass that is known to be exactly flat. Interference of the light reflected from the two surfaces causes a series of light and dark bands to appear. When all the bands are straight and parallel, the piece that is being polished is truly flat.

Scientists have designed special instruments that use the interference of light for making very accurate measurements. These instruments are called **interferometers**. They form patterns of bright and dark bands, which can be measured to give the length of an object to the nearest millionth of an inch. An interferometer attached to a large telescope has been used to measure the diameters of stars. Some giant stars are found to be hundreds of times as big as the sun.

▶ POLARIZED LIGHT

In most of the familiar kinds of waves, something moves back and forth at a steady

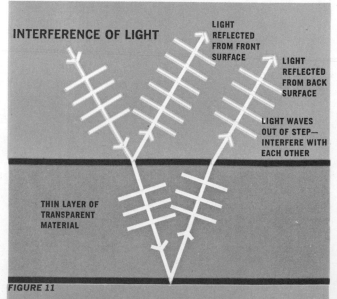

INTERFERENCE OF LIGHT

LIGHT REFLECTED FROM FRONT SURFACE

LIGHT REFLECTED FROM BACK SURFACE

LIGHT WAVES OUT OF STEP— INTERFERE WITH EACH OTHER

THIN LAYER OF TRANSPARENT MATERIAL

FIGURE 11

rate. For example, when water waves travel along the surface of a lake, there is an up-and-down motion at each place as the waves pass. When sound waves travel through the air, there is a very slight push-and-pull motion as the waves go by.

For a long time scientists wondered whether the movement in a light wave was *along* the direction in which the light traveled, similar to the push-pull motion in sound waves, or *across* this direction, like the rise and fall of water waves. Finally, certain experiments showed that whatever action takes place in light waves must be *crosswise* to the direction of travel.

Two flat slices were cut from a certain kind of crystal and held in a beam of light. While observers looked through both crystals, one of the crystals was slowly turned. When this was done, the beam changed regularly from bright to dark and back to bright again, time after time.

The diagrams show why this happens (Fig. 12). Each crystal has a sort of grain running in one direction. When light waves strike the

first crystal, only the forces that happen to be along its grain can get through. When these straightened-out waves hit the second crystal, they can come through if the grain of this crystal is lined up with the first, but they are held back if the grain of the second crystal is crosswise to the first. That explains why the brightness changes regularly as one crystal is turned.

Light from an ordinary source has its crosswise forces in all possible directions. Sending the light through a crystal combs out everything except the forces in one direction, and the result is called **polarized light**.

Besides showing that the forces in light waves are crosswise, polarization has many interesting uses. A manufactured sheet of material called Polaroid is used in place of the natural crystals used in early experiments. It is made of very tiny mineral crystals embedded in a plastic film. This material is used to make special sunglasses that cut out the glare from a lake or a pavement. When sunlight is reflected from a surface, it becomes partly polarized. The polarizing material in the sunglasses is set to cut out this light while letting through ordinary, unpolarized light from the surroundings so that everything else can be seen clearly.

Polarized light can help an engineer design a machine part or the framework of a bridge. He makes a model of the part out of a piece of clear plastic material. Then he places it between two polarizing sheets that have been set crosswise so that when a beam of light is sent in, none of it can get through.

Now the same kind of force is applied to the model that the real piece will get in actual use. The strains on the model change the light path so that some light can get through to form a pattern of light and dark bands (Fig. 13). The

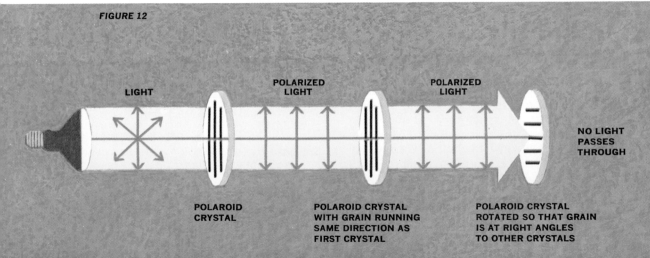

FIGURE 12

LIGHT

POLARIZED LIGHT

POLARIZED LIGHT

NO LIGHT PASSES THROUGH

POLAROID CRYSTAL

POLAROID CRYSTAL WITH GRAIN RUNNING SAME DIRECTION AS FIRST CRYSTAL

POLAROID CRYSTAL ROTATED SO THAT GRAIN IS AT RIGHT ANGLES TO OTHER CRYSTALS

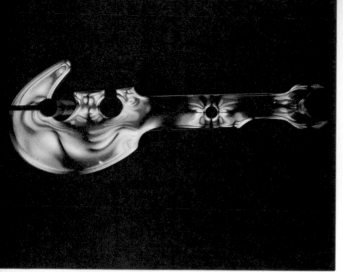

Figure 13. Pattern of light in plastic model of wrench.

Crystals magnified and viewed in polarized light. Above: Tartaric acid. Below: Vitamin B₁.

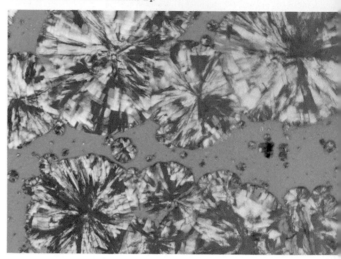

bands are narrow and close together where the strain is greatest. A study of this pattern shows how to shape the piece properly.

▶THE QUANTUM THEORY

The idea that light is some kind of wave motion explains reflection, refraction, dispersion, diffraction, interference, and polarization in every detail. There can be little doubt about the wave nature of light and all other electromagnetic radiations.

However, in 1900, a German physicist named Max Planck (1858–1947) found that waves do not tell the whole story. He was trying to explain how a hot object gives off radiation. In this, he found it necessary to assume that the radiation is sent out in little bundles, or packets, instead of in a steady stream. Each little flash of energy is called a **quantum** (plural: quanta), and the idea suggested by Planck has now become known as the quantum theory.

A single quantum of radiation energy is so small that the energy stream really seems to be steady. For example, even from such a weak source as starlight about 60,000,000 quanta enter your eyes each second, and the light looks perfectly steady.

The startling quantum idea was not accepted at first, but in time scientists found that it explained many other discoveries. It cleared up many questions about spectra that had had no answer before. Einstein was able to use the quantum theory to explain the kind of action that is now used in a **photocell**—a device for changing light energy into electrical energy.

Today physicists are forced to think of light as waves for some purposes and as quanta for other purposes. Neither idea by itself is able to explain everything that is observed. Waves explain fully what happens when radiation passes through space or through a material. But the quantum idea must be used to describe how radiation originates and what happens to it when it is absorbed in matter.

Light and other kinds of electromagnetic radiation involve some of the most complicated events in nature. So it is no wonder that neither waves nor quanta alone can describe everything that is observed. Nevertheless, scientists hold out the hope that some day they may find a way to combine these two ideas into a single theory that will cover everything in this field.

IRA M. FREEMAN
Rutgers—The State University
See also ECLIPSES; LENSES; MASERS AND LASERS; MICROSCOPES; MIRAGE; TELESCOPES; X RAYS.

Portland Head Lighthouse in Maine was built in 1787 by order of George Washington.

LIGHTHOUSES

Thousands of years ago the ancient Egyptians kindled fires on high hilltops to guide their ships at night. As water traffic increased on the Nile the Egyptians built stone towers to serve as lighthouses. Priests tended the flames that burned all night in the towers. The priests and the guiding fires were both considered holy by the ancient Egyptian mariners.

About 280 B.C. the Egyptians constructed the tallest lighthouse ever built in ancient—or modern—times. This was the Pharos of Alexandria, one of the seven wonders of the ancient world. The lighthouse, built on the island of Pharos near Alexandria, was over 400 feet high. At the top of the tower open fires were kept burning. They served as a beacon for Mediterranean mariners for about 1,500 years.

Today most nations operate some form of lighthouse, to help mariners at night determine the positions of their ships. Lighthouses are located in fixed positions on known locations. Each lighthouse has its own identi-fying flashing signal. Lighthouse engineers know the amount of pressure that winds and waves cause on any surface area. They erect buildings and beacons that can endure the pounding of seas and outlast the battering of storms.

▶ LIGHTHOUSE CONSTRUCTION

John Smeaton (1724–92), a British engineer, designed the first modern lighthouse in 1756. This was built on a submerged foundation—the famous Eddystone Rock outside Plymouth, England. The lighthouse was made of huge blocks of interlocking stones held together with bars of iron. Smeaton's basic design for building a lighthouse on an underwater foundation has been copied by every country throughout the world.

Lighthouses are built on mud, on soft sand, on lonely sections of rockbound land jutting out to sea, and on submerged rocks that seldom protrude above water. Lighthouses are

The giant lens in Makapuu Point Light, Hawaii, reflects light 28 miles out to sea.

built where there is a good view of the ocean, so that the light is visible over great areas. Lighthouses built on shoals, coral reefs, and sandbanks are usually made of masonry and concrete. Cylinder, or hollow-caisson, construction is used for underwater foundations that support the lighthouse towers. Huge steel cylinders are riveted or welded together on shore, towed out to sea on a barge, and then slipped into the water. One end stands on the sea bottom, and the other is above the surface of the water.

▶ LIGHTS

Lighthouse beacons have ranged from primitive signal fires to candles, oil lamps, and electric incandescent bulbs many times household size.

A Frenchman, Augustin Fresnel (1788–1827), in 1822 designed the first modern lighthouse lens, the Fresnel lens. This lens concentrates the light beam and makes it visible for many miles. This type of lens is still used today.

The lens is made of glass held together by bronze fittings, with from 1 to 24 inner circles called bull's-eyes. Triangular prisms of glass are placed around the bull's-eyes. The lens, driven by a suspended weight, a clockwork motor, or a small electric motor, rotates smoothly. As the lens rotates, each bull's-eye sends out a shaft of light. Unlimited combinations are obtained by using different numbers of bull's-eyes and different speeds of rotation.

Flashing navigation lights are white, red, green, or a combination of these colors. A ship's captain, after sighting and timing a light with a stopwatch, consults his light list. He identifies the light, takes an accurate bearing, and is able to figure out his exact position. The timed characteristics of lights are: fixed; fixed and flashing; flashing; group flashing; quick flashing; and interrupted quick flashing.

Electric incandescent lamps use bulbs of up to 1,500 watts each. The bulbs are placed inside the lens. Lighthouses using electric lamps were once also equipped with kerosene lamps, in case of electricity failures during storms. Today generators and storage batteries provide emergency electric power.

In isolated, wave-swept places and treacherous shoals where it is impossible for lighthouse keepers to live, automatic acetylene burners were formerly used. These brilliant lights were able to flash 100 times a minute. The burners had valves that automatically turned them on every evening and off every morning. Today batteries and electric eyes have replaced the acetylene burners. Lights go

Where is the Eddystone Light?

This famous light, forerunner of the modern lighthouse, still stands in the harbor outside Plymouth, England. It was built in 1757 by John Smeaton, a British engineer.

Two wooden structures preceded the present stone lighthouse. The first was destroyed by a storm. The second, begun by John Rudyerd in 1706 and completed in 1709, was later destroyed by fire.

While Rudyerd's men were building the lighthouse they were taken prisoner by a French warship. The captives were brought before King Louis XIV, who said, "Your work is for the benefit of all nations. I am at war with England, not with humanity." He returned the prisoners to England to complete their task.

In 1959 a 600,000-candlepower light was installed in Eddystone. The lamp sends out a flash every 10 seconds. The beam is visible for 17 miles.

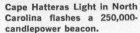
Cape Hatteras Light in North Carolina flashes a 250,000-candlepower beacon.

This new type of light tower, used in Buzzards Bay, Massachusetts, may replace lightships. The platform is supported on legs driven into solid bedrock.

on automatically at night and go off at daybreak.

▶ SOUND GUIDEPOSTS

When fog engulfs the sea, a light, no matter how bright, is of little help to the mariner. Sound must then be used to guide ships.

During the 18th century lighthouse keepers fired cannons once every hour to warn ships of danger during a fog. Some lighthouse keepers rang handbells. Today fog signals have been perfected so that warning sounds can be heard many miles out at sea.

Fog signals have different sounds and their own identifying numbers of blasts. Foghorns with deep steady tones and sirens that sound like fire engine signals give fog warnings. The diaphone, one of the most effective fog signals, has two tones—a high screech and a low grunt. The high note can be heard for 7 miles. The low note can be heard even farther. Lighthouse stations also use radio beams that transmit warning sounds through the densest fog.

▶ LIGHTSHIPS

Lightships lie at anchor, positioned where lighthouses are impossible to erect. Lightships carry the same warning equipment as light stations. Lights, radio beacons, and radar are

Calais Lighthouse, France, overlooks the Straits of Dover.

used for guidance. Buoys equipped with long-range automatic lights have replaced some lightships, which are expensive to maintain.

Lightships go nowhere. They are anchored in position with chains and heavy anchors except when they move to or from stations.

Where is the Boston Light?

Boston Light on Little Brewster Island at the entrance to Boston Harbor was the first lighthouse to be built in the colonies. The first lighthouse keeper was George Worthylake, who lived on Little Brewster with his wife and daughter. In 1718 all three were drowned in a storm that swept over the island. Benjamin Franklin, at the age of 13, described the tragic story in a ballad called "The Lighthouse Tragedy." Franklin sold copies of the ballad on the Boston streets. In June, 1776, during the American Revolution, British soldiers blew up the lighthouse. It was rebuilt in 1783, after the war.

During World War II Boston Light was extinguished, as a security measure. It was resumed again in 1945, with a 110,000-candlepower electric light flashing every 30 seconds and visible for 16 miles. Other equipment at Boston Light includes an air siren and a 2,000-candlepower auxiliary light, built in 1890.

Lightships are made of steel and painted bright red with white letters. They are among the strongest ships afloat. Lightship crews are kept busy maintaining the lights, electrical equipment, foghorns, and the ship's hull.

▶ LIGHTHOUSE AUTHORITY

In the United States, lighthouses and lightships are under the jurisdiction of the Coast Guard, which patrols the seacoast and the Great Lakes. The United States Coast Guard also operates electronic aids to navigation in some foreign countries, including Spain, Iceland, Turkey, Japan, and several African nations.

Lights that are manned by trained civilian personnel or Coast Guard members are officially called light stations. Lights that are unattended or have part-time help are usually referred to as lighthouses. A civilian employed part-time by the Coast Guard to attend a light station is called a lamplighter. A civilian employed full-time is called a keeper. Coastguardsmen assigned to light-station duty lead the disciplined military life of soldiers or sailors in uniform. They are on duty at least 6 to 12 hours a day. More and more of the light stations are now being converted to automatic operation.

Light-station keepers and coastguardsmen report weather conditions, check equipment, and look over machinery. Men on duty in the watch room of a light station have an unobstructed view of the surrounding sea. If visibility decreases enough to endanger the lives of mariners, the fog signal is started.

On calm, clear days the men are assigned duties outside the light station. Care is taken both inside and outside a light station to keep it immaculate. Machinery, floors, and lenses shine. The whitewashed look of a light station is kept up by frequent painting and scrubbing. Some light stations have quarters for wives and families of enlisted men, officers, and keepers.

Years ago some women tended light stations. Most of them were widows of lighthouse keepers. The last woman lighthouse keeper in the United States was from Maryland. She retired in 1948 after serving 23 years.

Reviewed by Aids to Navigation Division
United States Coast Guard

LIGHTING

When your room is dark, you can turn a switch and at once see easily. It was not always so easy to have light. And in many parts of the world it still is not easy. Once men struggled to break the blanket of night with a flickering torch or the small, fluttering flame of an oil lamp. Even so recently in history as the time of Abraham Lincoln, there was little lighting available. When Lincoln wanted to read at night, he had to use the fire in the fireplace for light. No wonder most people went to bed as soon as the sun went down.

Now people can read at night. They can also thread needles, paint pictures, and walk upstairs in safety. They can watch a basketball game in a gymnasium. They can go outside to a floodlighted stadium and watch football.

Emergency tasks can be done at night when good light is available. A surgeon can operate, if necessary, in the middle of the night as easily as in daytime. In fact, modern hospital operating rooms have no windows. Day and night lighting are the same. Good lighting permits all sorts of tasks to be done any time under easy seeing conditions.

▶ THE TORCH

The earliest lighting of all came from a wood fire. If a man needed to have light away from the fire, he picked up one of the burning sticks and had a torch. Men learned that torches dipped into animal fats lasted longer and threw a stronger light. Torches were used for many, many years. About the year A.D. 450, tarred torches were used to light the streets of Antioch. This Greek city in the Near East was the first in the world to have its streets lit. Torches like these were still being used in the Middle Ages.

Another natural torch material was the candlefish, which was used in Alaska. The candlefish was dried and held in a split stick. It was so oily that it held a good flame. The stormy petrel, a seabird found in the Shetland Islands, was used in the same way.

A Polynesian torch is made of candlenuts strung in single file on a bamboo strip. The candlenut is a very oily nut, just as the petrel is a very oily bird. The candlenuts burn slowly from top to bottom.

American Indians used pine knots for light. Early American settlers followed the practice. Pine-knot torches were made of thin slices of wood from pine trees. They were so full of pitch and turpentine that they burned with an especially bright, clear flame. Unfortunately, they also dripped pitch and gave off much black smoke.

▶ OIL LAMPS

The first oil lamps were open stone dishes with wicks of reeds or plant fibers. These lamps gave the light used by the cavemen when they painted pictures deep in caves.

Lamps have been found from as long ago as 3000 B.C. Some of these early lamps were made from shells or from the skulls of small animals. Conch shells were especially useful for lamps. They have a perfect shape for holding a good amount of oil and for supporting a wick. Hardened clay dishes were used next. When metalworking was developed, lampmakers made metal lamps.

The first oil used in these early lamps came from animals. In northern areas the fat of birds, whales, and fishes was important. In warm regions vegetable oils from olives, linseed, grape seeds, and coconuts were used. Butter made from water-buffalo milk is still used for oil lamps in India. Fish oils are still used in South America and other parts of the world.

One natural oil believed to have been used in lamps is rock oil. This is unrefined petroleum. Rock-oil lamps smoked, were dirty, and gave off bad odors.

In early America the oil lamps were filled with whale oil. The demand for whale oil caused the growth of the whaling industry. By the first half of the 19th century the whaling industry was very important in the United States. New England whalers made fortunes in one of the most exciting and dangerous jobs a man could have.

As the demand for whale oil grew, better lamps were invented for burning it. A lamp with two wicks, which gave a better light than the one-wick lamps, was made by Benjamin Franklin.

▶ RUSHLIGHTS

A waxed reed, something like a candle, was called a rushlight. It is difficult to know how

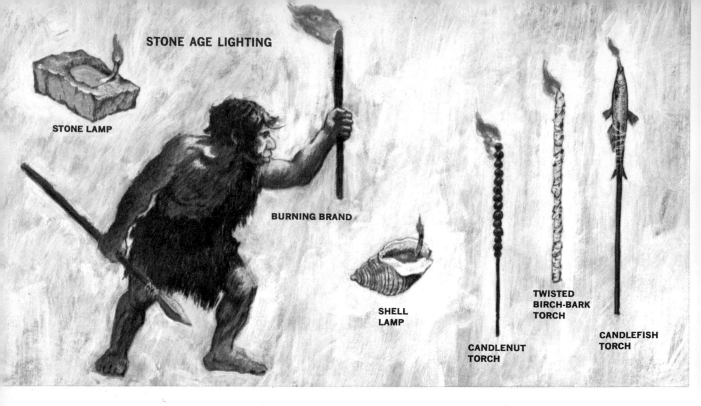

STONE AGE LIGHTING

STONE LAMP

BURNING BRAND

SHELL LAMP

CANDLENUT TORCH

TWISTED BIRCH-BARK TORCH

CANDLEFISH TORCH

old rushlights are. Their remains do not keep well in the soil or in caves. But enough traces of them have been found so that we know that they were used in Europe before the Middle Ages. Rushes grew in many parts of the world. As they were plentiful in the New England states, they were often used for lighting in the early colonial period.

To make a rushlight, part of the rush stem was peeled away, leaving a narrow section that held the pith or center stem together. This stem was perfectly round and about $\frac{1}{16}$ inch thick, and served as a wick. It was dipped in melted fat or tallow (fat from cattle or sheep) several times, until the coating was about $\frac{1}{8}$ inch thick.

The flame of the rushlight was about twice as large as the flame of a kitchen match. The rush wick ordinarily burned to ashes without being messy, but sometimes charred chunks would fall from it. Rushlights were very cheap and easy to make but were replaced by candles whenever possible.

▶ CANDLES

The candle was not used as early as torches, lamps, and rushlights. The first candles were apparently reeds or stalks filled with tallow or with beeswax from beehives. They were much like rushlights. The ancient Egyptians had wickless candles made of lumps of tallow wrapped with rags to keep them from melting apart as they burned. The Romans used candles made with wicks.

Candles were made in decorative styles and colors. Some, in glass containers, were used for religious purposes. These were 3 or 4 inches in diameter and burned for hours. Some candles were as tall as 10 feet and lasted for years.

Now most candles are used for decoration. Candles especially add to the gaiety and warmth of the decorations for holidays and other special occasions. Many religious groups use candles for ceremonies and pageants.

One trade secret among candlemakers was discovered about 1874. Several strands of a woven wick were treated with a chemical, nitrate of bismuth. This made the end of the burnt wick bend over and burn up completely. Before this, candles had to be trimmed every few minutes or they smoked badly. Trimming was done with a scissorlike tool with a box on one side. The box caught the bits of wick that the scissor blades snipped off.

The material used for candles in the early days of America was tallow, or if the family was wealthy, beeswax or spermaceti. Spermaceti was a wax from the sperm whale. Most candles today are made of wax combined with

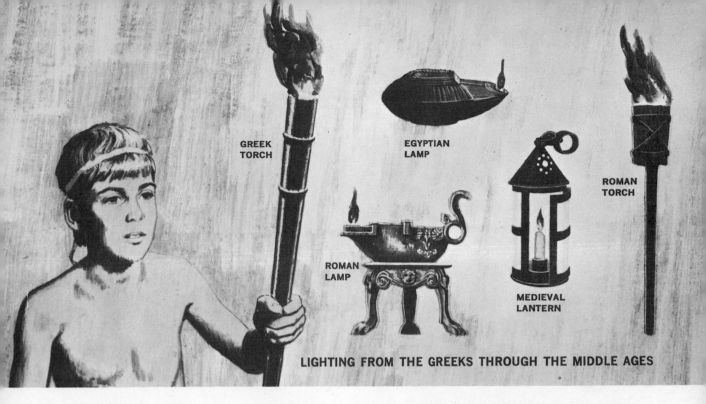

LIGHTING FROM THE GREEKS THROUGH THE MIDDLE AGES

GREEK
TORCH

EGYPTIAN
LAMP

ROMAN
TORCH

ROMAN
LAMP

MEDIEVAL
LANTERN

stearin, a product made from paraffin. Stearin increases the burning rate because it makes the wax melt faster. Bayberry candles, made from the wax given off by boiled bayberries, are still made in New England. They burn with a pleasant odor. (Any candle is useful for burning away tobacco smoke and clearing the air very quickly.)

▶ LANTERNS

Lanterns, protective cases for lights, were common from at least the 5th century B.C. They were lit with candles or oil lamps. Lanterns were designed in many different shapes. Cylindrical lanterns and square types with conical tops were popular. They were made of many materials—metal, wood, pottery, and even leather. Wealthy men had slaves go before them on their evening walks to carry a lantern. With their feeble flames and dark frames, lanterns could have given but little light. Sometimes the sides were fitted with thin plates of mica or horn. Later on, glass was used.

Candle lanterns held three, sometimes four, candles, but most often only one. Before glass-sided lanterns were perfected, tin lanterns were typically used. These had holes punched in their sides. The light shining from hundreds of tiny holes made a beautiful, lacy pattern on the ground, but the light was almost too feeble for a person to walk safely or ride horseback. Later lanterns had "bull's-eyes" of glass with thick centers. They gave a spotlight effect.

Ships' lanterns were made of heavy glass and metal. Sometimes the lantern was attached to the compass on a stand called a binnacle. Other lanterns aboard ship were (and still are) red- and green-sided. This tells sailors which way a ship is headed.

In wealthier homes in the 17th and 18th centuries, elaborate lanterns were used indoors in halls and entrance ways. Large dining rooms might have three lanterns hanging from the ceiling. Each time one had to be lit or put out, a servant would need to climb a stepladder, moving furniture out of the way if necessary.

Nowadays electric lanterns are very important in railroading. Railroad lanterns are carried by brakemen who ride in the caboose at the end of a long train of freight cars. The brakeman swings his lantern a certain number of times to signal the engineer in the locomotive cab to go ahead, to back up, or to stop.

▶ KEROSENE LAMPS

Before 1859 the best lamp oil that money could buy was whale oil. Unrefined petroleum

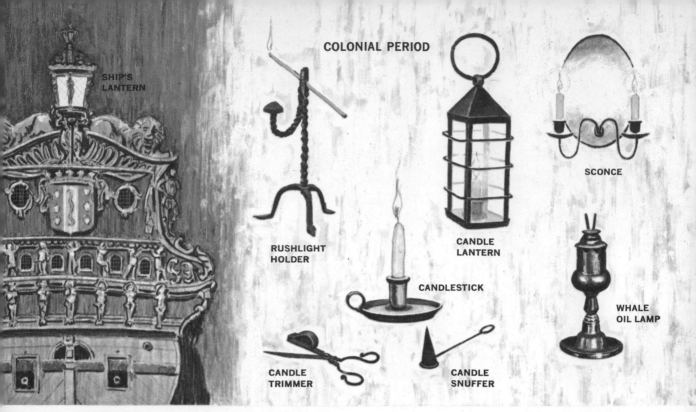

SHIP'S LANTERN

RUSHLIGHT HOLDER

CANDLE LANTERN

SCONCE

CANDLESTICK

WHALE OIL LAMP

CANDLE TRIMMER

CANDLE SNUFFER

had been used in lamps for many years, but it gave a feeble and dirty flame. In 1859 great quantities of petroleum oil were discovered in Pennsylvania. Shortly before this it had been learned that kerosene could be separated out of petroleum.

Kerosene gave a better light than had ever been known before. People could more easily read by it in the evening. Oil refining became an active business, supplying kerosene around the world. By 1890 there were 94 petroleum refineries in the United States, the first country to drill wells for oil.

At first kerosene was burned in open lamps. The open flame flickered and was dangerous to use. Then glass chimneys were made for kerosene lamps. The flame became steady and gave more light. With a glass chimney to protect it from the wind and a little roof to protect it from the rain, kerosene lamps could be used outdoors for street lights. A lamplighter had the job of lighting them every evening and turning them out in the morning.

Kerosene lamps had flat wicks. By the turn of a small knob the wick could be raised and lowered and the lamp's light could be adjusted. This was a great advantage over other lighting. A circular wick, which allowed air to circulate inside as well as outside of it, made a lamp that burned much brighter. This was the

Argand oil lamp, invented in Geneva by Aimé Argand (1755–1803) in 1784. It was used in lighthouses and in great oil chandeliers, as well as in homes and offices.

In homes of the early 1800's, candles and oil lamps were rival light sources. In the average home there was a large oil lamp on a table in the center of the living room. There father read his paper, mother sewed or knitted, and the children read or played games. But when the children went upstairs to bed, they carried a candlestick to light their way. Candles were safer than oil lamps to carry about. If an oil lamp was dropped, the burning oil might set the house on fire.

In areas of the world where there is no electricity, kerosene lamps are still used. And in many homes with electricity, especially homes in country areas, kerosene lamps are kept on hand. When electric wires do not operate in heavy storms, the kerosene lamps are used. Kerosene lanterns are sometimes used on highways to show detours or repairs in the roadway. Even now there are farmers who carry a lantern to the barn when they are milking the cows or doing other chores. A legend still persists that the terrible Chicago fire of 1871 was caused by Mrs. O'Leary's cow kicking over an oil lantern in the barn. No one really knows how the fire started, but

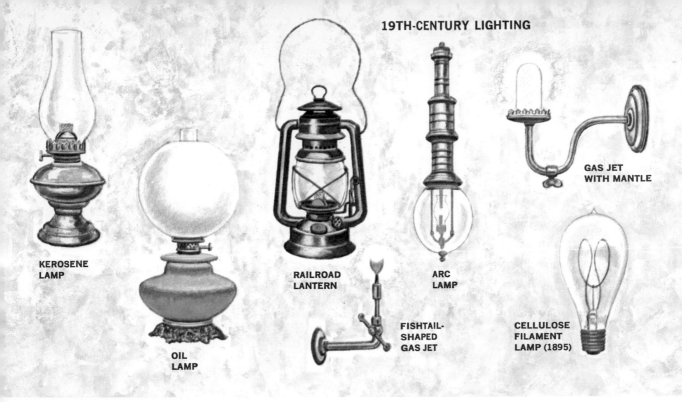

KEROSENE
LAMP

OIL
LAMP

RAILROAD
LANTERN

FISHTAIL-
SHAPED
GAS JET

ARC
LAMP

GAS JET
WITH MANTLE

CELLULOSE
FILAMENT
LAMP (1895)

kerosene burns quickly, and the fire could have started with such an accident.

▶ GAS LIGHTING

Many times in history when men drilled wells for water they accidentally discovered gas. To do so was always considered a misfortune, since it meant redrilling. Men knew that it was gas that caused "burning springs"—the flames that sometimes appeared in the air over boggy or rocky areas. Burning springs frightened and amazed people. It evidently did not occur to anyone that this burning gas might make a good light or fuel.

Late in the 1700's men learned how to make gas from coal. With this new discovery of gas, men began to think how they might use it. Many experiments were made. By 1813 the Westminster Bridge in London was lighted with gas. The bright, unusual lights astonished the people. But not many people used this new lighting in their homes until about 50 years later. The main problem was that the pipes in which gas traveled were leaky. Leaking gas was very dangerous and frightened people. Gas in large quantities makes people suffocate and also explodes very easily. However, gaslight was so much brighter than kerosene light that it was soon used for lighting streets.

Many natural-gas wells were found. Manufactured gas was made by distilling petroleum as well as by heating coal. Both natural gas and manufactured gas were growing competitors of oil in the United States up to 1910. Fishtail-shaped gas jets on the ends of pipe brackets that swung out from the wall were the pride of many householders. But the bare flames were dangerous, and they flickered. They made sooty spots on the ceiling. Later, white-glass and clear-glass globes that enclosed the flames made cleaner gas lamps.

If the flame from a gas lamp was blown out instead of being shut off, gas would fill the room. "Don't Blow Out the Gas!" was a familiar sign in hotel rooms, a warning to country people unused to city conveniences.

In 1885 Carl Auer von Welsbach (1858–1929) of Austria invented the gas mantle. It was a loosely woven cotton cover for gas jets. The threads were filled with chemicals. They glowed so brightly that the light was increased about five times. This mantle is the one used in gasoline lanterns today, and also in the post lanterns in some front yards.

Gas was seldom used outside cities. It was difficult and expensive to lay the gas piping for long distances. Even now, when gas is a common fuel for heating and cooling, it is not often used in rural communities except where bottled gas can be supplied. Electricity is used instead.

ELECTRIC LIGHTING

We think of electric lighting being used everywhere, but it is estimated that more than half the people of the world are still without it. Perhaps small atomic power plants can eventually be built to light those regions of the world still getting along with flame sources such as kerosene lamps, oil lamps, or candles. Another way to do this may be with sun generators. These are powered by sunlight energy, which charges large storage batteries. The batteries provide electricity for use at night.

The First Electric Lights

The electrical lighting industry began with Thomas Alva Edison's (1847–1931) first practical incandescent lamp in 1879. Many scientists knew how electricity worked. They had been trying to make electric lamps. But no one had been able to make one that worked well. Work done by a British physicist and chemist, Sir Joseph Wilson Swan (1828–1914), may have helped Edison in his invention.

Edison tried again and again before he found how to make a lamp filament last more than a few hours. He used hundreds of materials. One day he even tried a whisker from the beard of one of his assistants. Finally he tried sewing thread from Mrs. Edison's sewing basket. He carbonized the thread. It worked! That first lamp lasted for 40 hours. Edison and his assistants watched it all day and half the night.

The carbonizing was the secret of the successful lamp filament. Later lamp filaments were made of carbonized wood from selected Japanese bamboo. The carbonizing was done by rolling the thin strips of wood in fine carbon and then heating them for hours in an iron mold in a furnace. Later, carbon filaments were made of cellulose squirted through a die (a mold). Cellulose is made from cotton or wood fiber.

Filament Lamps

The type of electric lamp made by Edison is called a filament lamp. A filament lamp lights when a thread inside it heats up to incandes-

INCANDESCENT FILAMENT LAMP

cence—that is, when it heats so brightly that it glows with light. There have been big improvements in filament lamps since the time of Edison. Edison's lamp used a carbon filament. Carbon filaments could not operate at a high enough temperature to be very efficient. Tungsten filaments were more efficient, but they broke easily. In 1910 a way was found to draw tungsten wire through dies. This made a strong tungsten filament. As a result, tungsten replaced carbon as filament.

Edison's first lamps had vacuums in them. That is, the air was pumped out of the bulbs and then they were sealed. This was done to keep the filament from burning up by combining with the air's oxygen. But although the vacuum protected the filaments from burning up, they still evaporated. When the filament became hot, particles escaped from its surface and settled on the glass of the lamp. After a time the inside of the lamp became blackened by these particles. Finally the filament broke in two, so that no current could pass through. The lamp was "burned out."

Then in 1913 an American scientist named Irving Langmuir (1881–1957) filled a lamp with inert gas. (An inert gas is one that does not react easily with other substances.) The pressure of the inert gas tended to keep tungsten particles from escaping from the filament.

As a result, the lamp lasted much longer than a vacuum lamp.

Edison himself had experimented with lamps filled with the inert gas nitrogen. They had not been successful. To get a good light from a nitrogen-filled lamp, the filament had to be thick. Yet a thick filament used up too much current. Langmuir solved this problem too. He designed a filament that was thick and thin at the same time. Taking a thin tungsten wire, he coiled it into a spiral, like a coil spring. The spiral, which had as much surface area as a thick filament, glowed brightly. Yet the thin wire of which it was made drew little current.

Today all filament lamps are filled with inert gases, usually a mixture of nitrogen and argon. Lamps larger than 25 watts have coiled filaments.

Carbon Arc Lamps

The electric arc lamp was a strong rival of Edison's rather small bulb. A simple arc lamp was made of two carbon rods about ½ inch thick held vertically so that the ends touched each other when the current was off. When the switch was closed, the rods were mechanically drawn apart. This drew an arc of light between them. The arc light was a continuous spark as bright as a tiny sun. Because the carbon rods burned away rather rapidly, a feeding device was necessary to move the rods as they burned. To keep the arc stream steady, they had to be the same distance apart all the time. The first arc lights burned in the open air, but later ones had glass globes around them.

Except in some factories and other large workplaces, arc lighting was not practical to use indoors. It made smoke and fumes. But the lights were very much bigger than Edison's light. This made arc lighting a favorite for lighting streets in the 1890's and early 1900's. Nowadays, carbon arc lights are used in movie projectors and for large theater spotlights.

Automobile Lighting

The first automobiles used coach lamps with candles in them. There were no headlights. Kerosene lamps soon replaced the candles. Kerosene lamps gave a feeble light, but it was better than the candlelight had been. With such poor lighting, few cars were used after dark.

Car headlighting was made possible in the early 1900's with the invention of an acetylene gas generator. The gas generator had a double brass tank with water in the top half. The lower half held chunks of calcium carbide. Calcium carbide was a material that resulted when limestone was heated with coke in the then newly invented electric furnace. As water from the top of the tank dripped on the carbide, acetylene gas was created. The gas was piped to the burners in the headlights. Only when the generator had been in operation a few minutes could the headlights be turned on.

Before long, bottled acetylene gas, called Prest-o-lite, was used. The gas, contained in a tank strapped to the running board, was adjusted with a small wrench called a Prest-o-lite key. At dusk all motorists stopped their cars at the side of the road and lighted their

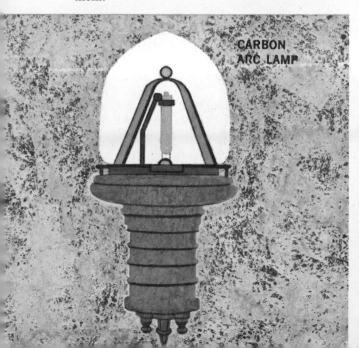

CARBON ARC LAMP

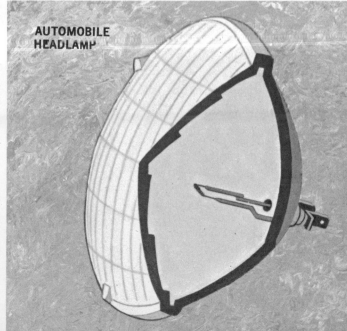

AUTOMOBILE HEADLAMP

lamps. It was a difficult thing to do on a rainy, windy night, especially for a person who was alone and had no one to adjust the pressure at the tank.

In 1911 Charles F. Kettering (1876–1958) developed the electric generator-starter-battery system now in universal use on automobiles. In the early cars five or six lamps were the most that could be used. Today between 20 and 30 lamps are used on each car, depending on the make and model.

For about 30 years automobile headlights were made as metal reflectors with small enclosed bulbs in them. The reflector directed the light rays straight ahead of the car. Glass covered the front of the headlight. In 1949 a new lamp was made—in one piece. This was a large, thick-glass lamp that combined all three parts—reflector, filament, and lens. The first models were made from pyrex-glass cooking dishes. The new, tough glass made it possible to mold very accurate reflectors and lenses. Now cars travel at night with powerful lights that shine far ahead of them.

Quartz-Iodine Lamps

The newest tungsten-filament bulbs, called quartz-iodine lamps, are tubular in shape, only 3/8 inch in diameter, and only a few inches

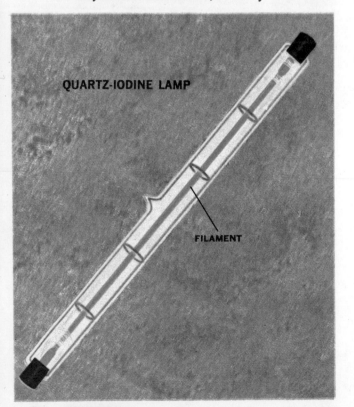

QUARTZ-IODINE LAMP

FILAMENT

long. Quartz-iodine lamps provide a brilliant light for their size and are often used for floodlighting. They are among the lights used to light New York City's Shea Stadium. The first quartz-iodine lamps were used on the wing tips of jet airplanes. A 500-watt lamp of this kind is about as large as a lead pencil.

The bulbs get so hot that glass cannot be used for them. Only quartz can take the high temperatures. The gas mixture in the tube includes iodine. The iodine, when hot, combines with the evaporated tungsten. Tungsten ordinarily evaporates from any filament as the lamp is burned. But quartz-iodine lamps are just as bright at the end of their lives as they are when new. The secret is that when hot iodine combines with the evaporated tungsten, tungsten iodide (a colorless gas) is formed. This gas is broken down by the heat inside the bulb. This puts the tungsten back on the filaments, and the whole cycle starts over again.

Fluorescent Lamps

Fluorescent lamps have tiny filaments at both ends of a long glass tube. The tube contains a drop of mercury that becomes mercury vapor when the lamp is lit. Special chemicals on the filaments rapidly release electricity into the lamp. The electricity jumps from one end of the lamp to the other. The jump of electricity is like a flash of lightning. In a fluorescent lamp there is a miniature lightning flash 120 times a second all the time the lamp is lighted. The flashes come so quickly that the light looks as if it were perfectly steady.

The flashes of light produce ultraviolet energy—rays that our eyes cannot see. The tube of the fluorescent lamp is coated inside with white phosphor powder. The powder coating changes these invisible rays to white light.

Because fluorescent light comes from a long tube, it is soft and melts shadows. Harsh shadows are made only by small, bright spots of light. Fluorescent light is now used in many homes, stores, schools, offices, and streets.

Much more lighting is used today than was used in the past. Not only is lighting cheaper than it used to be, but lighting experts have found that people work better under suitable lighting.

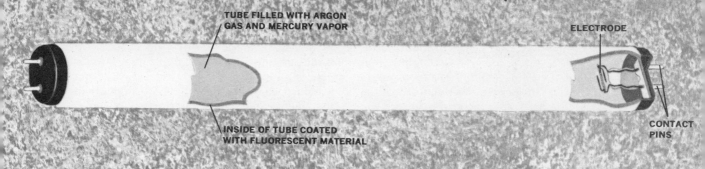

TUBE FILLED WITH ARGON
GAS AND MERCURY VAPOR

ELECTRODE

INSIDE OF TUBE COATED
WITH FLUORESCENT MATERIAL

CONTACT
PINS

A **footcandle** is a standard measure of the amount of light. It is the light on a surface 1 foot away from a candle made of special materials and burning at a certain rate. Where 50 footcandles might have been used a few years ago, today 100 to 200 footcandles of lighting are recommended.

All electric lighting systems produce heat. Lighting systems that use 100 footcandles or more of light produce enough heat to affect a building's heating and cooling systems. The latest designs of office and factory lighting fixtures combine lighting, heating, and air-conditioning systems. These combination systems are called space conditioning.

Electroluminescent Light

The strangest lamp of all is called electroluminescent. It is the first electrical device to change electricity into light without first heating a wire, as in an incandescent lamp, or creating an arc, as in a fluorescent tube. Electroluminescent lamps look like thick pieces of plastic or plastic-coated glass plates. They are made in three layers, like a sandwich. The middle layer is a coating of phosphor powder like the powder used in fluorescent lamps. When the current is on, the phosphor glows with a dim light. A lamp 2 inches square makes an excellent night-light.

Mercury Lamps

Mercury lamps are used for lighting in streets, tunnels, and factories. In the mercury lamp the electric current moves along the mercury vapor, which glows. Most mercury lamps give a bluish-green light. Under this light, red looks nearly black. People look unnatural.

Engineers tried fluorescent-lamp phosphors in mercury bulbs. They found that these phosphors made the blue-green mercury light turn whiter. These color-improved mercury lamps are very acceptable for street and highway and parking-lot use.

Inside lighted mercury and fluorescent lamps, there are ultraviolet light rays. But these do not reach us because the glass does not let them through. Ultraviolet rays are the

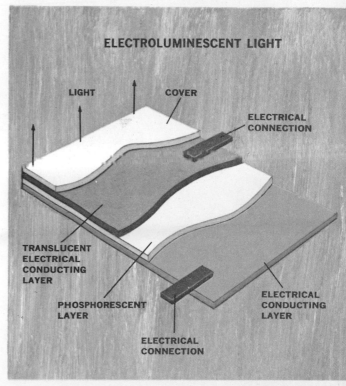

ELECTROLUMINESCENT LIGHT

LIGHT

COVER

ELECTRICAL
CONNECTION

TRANSLUCENT
ELECTRICAL
CONDUCTING
LAYER

PHOSPHORESCENT
LAYER

ELECTRICAL
CONNECTION

ELECTRICAL
CONDUCTING
LAYER

light rays that cause skin to tan. The sunlamp, a special kind of mercury lamp, has a bulb made of quartz. This allows the ultraviolet rays to pass through. Because of this, sun lamps are used for tanning. However, users should keep their eyes shielded from the ultraviolet light, as it is too strong for the eye tissues.

▶ NATURAL SOURCES OF LIGHT

The greatest natural source of light is the sun. Others in the heavens are the stars, the planets, lightning, and on rare nights the northern lights. Fireflies and phosphorescent wood are natural light sources, too. That is, they are bioluminescent. They are not very bright. However, they are very interesting to scientists, who study them for their secrets of "cold" light.

We think of fireflies as something to look at in the dark, not particularly as light to see by. But when a number of fireflies are brought together, the light is surprisingly bright. It was once an African custom to carry live fireflies in tiny, woven sacks tied to a man's ankles. This must have been a weird-looking way to light a path in the jungle at night! Perhaps it frightened wild animals the way a flashlight beam does. Fireflies were also used as lighting in Japanese and American Indian festivals.

▶ RULES OF GOOD LIGHTING PRACTICE

Rules of good lighting are best understood when we can measure lighting and have some idea of how much light we need. We think of a moonlit night as being very bright compared with a pitch-black night. But if you measured moonlight with a sensitive light meter, it would be only about $\frac{1}{25}$ footcandle. Moonlight is the same as the light 5 feet away from a lighted candle. After about 10 minutes in moonlight, your eyes get used to the low level. Some people can read a newspaper by moonlight. Try it some night when the moon is full. Your eyes may soon tire, and you will learn one principle of good lighting in a short time: that it is necessary to have plenty of light to read easily.

In contrast, bright summer sunshine outdoors in most parts of the United States is between 8,000 and 10,000 footcandles. In the Swiss mountains, where the air is clearer, sunshine measures 12,000 footcandles. Indoors, near a window on a bright day, it may be 400 or 500 footcandles. On dull days the light in a schoolroom may be only a few footcandles. Turning the lights on should bring it up to 70 or more.

Glare should be avoided. It is uncomfortable for eyes and makes them red and tired. Glare is present when you look at a bright bulb, for example. Avoid glare reflected from your work, too. Do not place a table lamp in front of you so that the rays are reflected toward your eyes, reflecting off the page. If you work near a window, place your chair so that you do not directly face the window or shadow your work. Remember this: "Use plenty of light. Light is cheap. Eyesight is priceless."

Always leave a light on when watching television. Otherwise, the contrast between the dark room and the brightly lit television set is hard on the eyes. A reading lamp should be placed so that it does not cast a shadow on the page.

HIGH-INTENSITY LIGHT

SPOTLIGHT

FLASHLIGHT

RECHARGEABLE NICKEL-CADMIUM BATTERY FLASHLIGHT

SPOTLIGHT AND FLOODLIGHT COMBINATION

TABLE LAMP

STANDING LAMPS

DRAFTSMAN'S LAMP

DESK LAMP

DRESSER LAMPS

HANGING LAMP

DIFFERENT TYPES OF MODERN LIGHTS

▶ **ILLUMINATING ENGINEERING**

Electric lighting has developed in so many ways that it plays a part in nearly every activity of man. The study and practice of electric lighting has become a profession in itself. It is called illuminating engineering and is a branch of electrical engineering. The Illuminating Engineering Society of America states that its object is "to advance the science and art of illumination." Most of its members are scientists and engineers and architects. They design buildings so that the people working in them have abundant light without glare. In modern buildings, lighting is a part of the architecture. The lighting can make a building more useful and beautiful by day and by night.

Doctors and physicists connected with the Illuminating Engineering Society investigate eye health and the benefits of improved seeing. Lamp and lighting-equipment manufacturers are also members of the society. Together with paint manufacturers they study how light is reflected from walls and ceilings and furniture. The colors and materials in a room can affect the seeing comfort of the people in it.

▶ **THE FUTURE OF LIGHTING**

In the future there will probably be ever better types of lights. New forms of lamps and lighting equipment will probably be invented. Lighting systems of tomorrow will commonly include lighting, heating, and air-

Homes in the future will be lit by wall and ceiling paneling that eliminates glare.

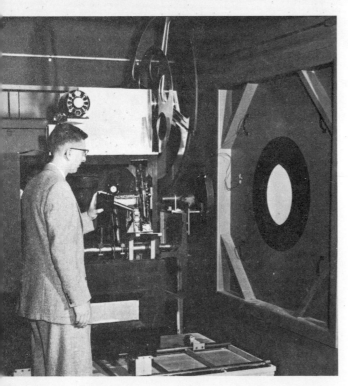

Left: A scientist tests the amount of light needed for proper visibility.

conditioning services all together. The goal will be natural outdoor lighting conditions indoors. In the future, our streets, highways, parks, and recreation and shopping centers will all be brighter. And because they are brighter, they will be safer and more colorful places in which to shop, work, play, and travel.

In the home of the future there will be indoor lighting with outdoor quality, quantity, and seeing comfort. Luminous stairways, self-illuminated walls, and whole ceilings of light in rooms where reading, studying, and sewing are done will be possible in homes. People will have seeing pleasure and eye comfort.

KARL A. STALEY
Fellow, Illuminating Engineering Society

See also CANDLES; LIGHT.

LIGHTNING. See THUNDER AND LIGHTNING.

LIME. See LEMON AND LIME.

LIMERICKS. See NONSENSE STORIES AND RHYMES.

ABRAHAM LINCOLN (1809–1865)

16TH PRESIDENT OF THE UNITED STATES

LINCOLN, ABRAHAM. The election of a Republican president in 1860 provoked the Southern states to secede from the Union and led to 4 tragic years of civil war. In this time of grave crisis it at first seemed unfortunate that the American people had not chosen a more experienced leader. Yet the tall, awkward man from Illinois who took the presidential oath proved equal to his enormous responsibilities. Gradually, as the war progressed, Abraham Lincoln placed the mark of his greatness upon American history. He guided the nation through the perils of war to peace and reunion. He struck the fatal blow at Negro slavery. He re-affirmed the dignity of free men in language of simple beauty. Death came to him with dramatic violence before his work was done. But death only hastened his elevation to a place beside George Washington in the memory and gratitude of his countrymen.

▶ BOYHOOD

Abraham Lincoln was born on February 12, 1809, in a rude log cabin near present-day Hodgenville, Kentucky. His parents, who already had a little daughter named Sarah, were hardworking, uneducated pioneers. They probably saw nothing unusual about their son, except that he grew unusually fast. Thomas Lincoln, Abraham's father, was a man of ordinary abilities whose ambition apparently did not extend beyond owning a good farm. Like many Western settlers, he tended to believe that there were better opportunities somewhere over the horizon. Of Abraham's mother, Nancy Hanks Lincoln, little is known. She and her two small children experienced the usual hardships and few pleasures of pioneer life. She must have left a mother's mark upon Abraham's character, but the exact nature of her influence is lost to history.

In December, 1816, the Lincolns packed their belongings and migrated about 100 miles to southwestern Indiana. They spent the first winter in a hastily built shelter with an open side. The forest, full of wild game, surrounded their lonely new home. Abraham later remembered shooting a turkey, watching for bears, and listening at night to the "panther's scream." In the spring Abraham, now 8 years old, began to help his father in the hard daily labor of pioneering. They had to clear the land of trees, plant crops, build a permanent cabin, and split rails for fences.

WHEN ABRAHAM LINCOLN WAS PRESIDENT
The Homestead Act of 1862 helped open up the West by providing free land to settlers. The Civil War raged during almost all of Lincoln's time in office. Lincoln's Emancipation Proclamation was the first great step toward the abolition of slavery.
Lincoln's birthplace was near present-day Hodgenville, Kentucky.

Abraham became skillful in the use of the ax but apparently never cared much for hunting and fishing. He acquired no love for the life of a farmer. It seemed to be all heavy toil with small reward.

The saddest days of Lincoln's childhood came in 1818, when his mother died and was buried in the nearby forest. A year later Thomas Lincoln married Sarah Bush Johnston, a widow with three children of her own. Between the boy and his stepmother there grew a bond of deep affection, and she lived to see him become president.

Much of Lincoln's learning was the practical kind that boys picked up from their work and play in a backwoods community. Lincoln attended school, in his own words, "by littles"—that is, only occasionally and for just a few weeks at a time. But he soon knew more than either of his parents about reading, writing, and arithmetic. In each case, school was probably a "blab school." Pupils studied their lessons aloud, and the noise could be heard some distance away. Lincoln later said that his total schooling did not amount to more than 1 year. Yet he read whatever he could lay his hands on. At home there was the Bible, and he walked miles to borrow books like *Robinson Crusoe, Aesop's Fables,* and Weems's *Life of Washington.* In the end Lincoln not only educated himself but became a master of the English language.

▶ YOUNG MAN IN ILLINOIS

In 1830 the Lincolns moved again, this time to Illinois. They traveled in ox-drawn wagons, with Abraham as one of the drivers, and built a cabin on the prairie near Decatur. Dissatisfied there, Thomas Lincoln moved a year later to Coles County. But this time his son did not go along. Now 22 years old, 6 feet 4 inches tall, very thin and yet physically strong, Abraham Lincoln still had no definite ambition. He was ready, however, to start life on his own.

When he was 19, Lincoln had made a trip to New Orleans as a hired hand on a Mississippi River flatboat. Now, in the spring of 1831, he undertook a similar journey down the Mississippi. On his return he took a job as a storekeeper in the village of New Salem, Illinois, 20 miles northwest of Springfield. His friendliness, honesty, and talent for story-telling soon made him a popular local figure. So he decided to enter politics and in March, 1832, announced his candidacy for the state legislature.

At this point the Black Hawk War, an Indian war, began in northern Illinois. Lincoln volunteered and served for 3 months, first as the elected captain of his own company, then as a private under other commanders. He engaged in no actual fighting with the Indians. Back home by July, he had only a few weeks for his political campaign. Election day brought defeat, but Lincoln was encouraged by the fact that he had run eighth in a field of 13 candidates. Next, he and a partner opened a store in New Salem. Lincoln also became the village postmaster. The store was a failure, however, and he took up surveying to earn a living and pay his debts. In 1834 the 24-year-old Lincoln ran again for the legislature. This time he won, and the voters later re-elected him for three more terms.

▶ SPRINGFIELD LAWYER

It was in 1834 that Lincoln began to study law. Here again he educated himself, reading borrowed lawbooks in his spare time. He passed the bar examination 2 years later. Early in 1837, with Lincoln playing an important part, the legislature voted to make Springfield the state capital. There he moved on April 15 and entered a law partnership with John T. Stuart, an established attorney and fellow legislator.

For the next 24 years, with one brief interruption, Lincoln practiced law in Springfield. He did not grow wealthy but always earned a comfortable living. Fair and conscientious, he gave clients a feeling of confidence. Never very learned in the law, he nevertheless knew the fundamentals. His greatest asset in court was the ability to go directly to the heart of a matter. Long before the presidential election of 1860 he had become one of the most distinguished lawyers in Illinois.

In 1844 Lincoln began his lasting partnership with William H. Herndon (1818–91). A rather strange and excitable man 10 years younger than Lincoln, Herndon nevertheless proved to be an excellent choice. The two of them worked well together in both law and politics. Herndon's biography of his famous partner, written many years later, is one of the classics of Lincoln literature.

Lincoln's law practice took him regularly to other towns where courts were held. This travel on the legal circuit was arduous, but it enlarged his circle of friends and helped make him better known in politics.

▶ HUSBAND AND FATHER

Lincoln's famous romance with Ann Rutledge is apparently just a legend. He knew Ann in New Salem and was undoubtedly saddened by her death in 1835. But there is no reliable evidence that they were ever in love with each other. He did court a young woman named Mary Owens. There was a lack of enthusiasm on both sides, however, and she refused to marry him. At Springfield, Lincoln met Mary Todd, daughter of a prominent Kentucky family. She was a popular girl in local society—attractive, gay, and intelligent, but somewhat temperamental. Her short and rather plump figure contrasted sharply with Lincoln's lank frame when he acted as her escort. They became engaged in 1840, then broke apart when Lincoln went through a long period of doubt and melancholy. Reconciled after a time, they were married at last on November 4, 1842.

Mary Lincoln, although not always easy to live with, was a good and loyal wife who probably spurred her husband's ambition. Their marriage had its troubled moments, but on the whole they were happy together. In 1844 Lincoln bought a house, which still stands at Eighth and Jackson streets in Springfield. There the Lincolns lived until their departure for Washington in 1861. Four children, all boys, were born to them. Robert became a corporation executive and secretary of war under two presidents. Edward died in his 4th year. William died in the White House when he was 11. Thomas, nicknamed "Tad," survived his father but died in 1871 at the age of 18. Lincoln was a loving and indulgent parent, but his frequent absences from home on his law practice placed the upbringing of the boys largely in Mary's hands.

▶ POLITICAL CAREER

In the legislature Lincoln became a loyal member of the Whig Party, whose most prominent national leaders were Henry Clay and Daniel Webster. Lincoln's major interest at this time was the promotion of better transportation facilities. He soon advanced to the front rank of Illinois Whigs and by 1842 had emerged as a candidate for Congress. Two other men claimed the party's nomination, however, and Lincoln had to wait his turn. Finally, in 1846 he was elected.

Lincoln's congressional term began in

Mary Todd Lincoln.

President Lincoln in 1864, with his son "Tad."

EXCERPTS FROM LINCOLN'S SPEECHES, LETTERS, AND OTHER WRITINGS

. . . [as] soon as I discover my opinions to be erroneous, I shall be ready to renounce them.

Lincoln's first political address, as candidate for the Illinois legislature, March 9, 1832

The legitimate object of government, is to do for a community of people, whatever they need to have done, but can not do, *at all,* or can not, so *well do,* for themselves . . . .

In all that the people can individually do as well for themselves, government ought not to interfere.

Fragment, probably 1850's

As a nation we began by declaring that *"all men are created equal."* We now practically read it "all men are created equal, *except negroes."* When the Know-Nothings get control, it will read "all men are created equal, except negroes, *and foreigners, and catholics."* When it comes to this I should prefer emigrating to some country where they make no pretence of loving liberty . . . .

Letter to Joshua Speed, August 24, 1855

I will say here . . . that I have no purpose directly or indirectly to interfere with the institution of slavery in the States where it exists. I believe I have no lawful right to do so . . . .

Lincoln-Douglas Debates, Ottawa, Illinois, August 21, 1858

. . . he who would *be* no slave, must consent to *have* no slave. Those who deny freedom to others, deserve it not for themselves, ...

Letter to Henry L. Pierce and others, April 6, 1859

In *your* hands, my dissatisfied fellow countrymen, and not in *mine,* is the momentous issue of civil war. . . . We are not enemies, but friends. We must not be enemies.

First Inaugural Address, March 4, 1861

With malice toward none; with charity for all; with firmness in the right, let us strive on to finish the work we are in; to bind up the nation's wounds; to care for him who shall have borne the battle, and for his widow, and his orphan—to do all which may achieve and cherish a just, and a lasting peace, among ourselves, and with all nations.

Second Inaugural Address, March 4, 1865

December, 1847, when the Mexican War was nearing its conclusion. Soon after taking his seat, he joined the Whig attack upon the war policy of President James K. Polk. Lincoln also introduced a moderate bill for the gradual emancipation, or freeing, of slaves in the District of Columbia, but it got nowhere. On the whole, his 2 years as a congressman were undistinguished.

His criticism of the Mexican War was unpopular in Illinois, and Lincoln was not renominated for Congress. He then campaigned for Zachary Taylor, helping him win the presidential election of 1848. Offered the governorship of the Oregon Territory as a reward, Lincoln declined the appointment and resumed the practice of law. His political career had apparently reached a dead end.

▶ THE REPUBLICAN PARTY

Five years went by, and then in 1854 came a decisive turn of events. Senator Stephen A. Douglas of Illinois, a Democratic leader in Congress, secured passage of the Kansas-Nebraska Act. The measure created the two new federal territories of Kansas and Nebraska and permitted the people there to have slavery if they wanted it. This policy, which set aside the Missouri Compromise, was called "popular sovereignty." Throughout the North there were angry protests against the Kansas-Nebraska Act from many Democrats and from most Whigs, including Lincoln. He had long considered slavery morally wrong, yet he respected the constitutional rights of slaveholders. If slavery could just be prevented from expanding, Lincoln reasoned, it might eventually die away in the Southern states. To such hopes the Kansas-Nebraska Act was a serious blow.

Soon the opponents of slavery expansion began to form a political alliance. Lincoln became a leader of this "anti-Nebraska" movement in Illinois, and his supporters almost elected him to the United States Senate in 1855. A year later, with the Whig Party breaking up, he helped organize the various anti-Nebraska groups into the Republican Party of Illinois. At the Republican national convention in June, 1856, Lincoln received strong support for the vice-presidency, though he did not win the nomination. He campaigned vigorously for the new party's presidential candidate, John C. Frémont, but Frémont was defeated by James Buchanan, the Democratic candidate.

In 1858 Illinois Republicans nominated Lincoln for the Senate seat held by Douglas.

Lincoln responded with his famous "House Divided" speech, in which he said: "I believe this government cannot endure permanently half *slave* and half *free*." The high points of the exciting contest that followed were seven debates between the two candidates. Douglas clung to his doctrine of popular sovereignty. Lincoln insisted that slavery must be prohibited in Western territories. The election itself was very close, but Douglas emerged the winner.

▶ ELECTED PRESIDENT

Defeat did not hurt Lincoln's growing prestige. The debates with Douglas had brought him national attention, and before long he was being mentioned as a presidential prospect. During the next year he gained further recognition by making speeches in many states. The climax of his efforts was an address delivered on February 27, 1860, at Cooper Institute in New York City. When the Republican national convention met at Chicago in May, Lincoln had more support than any other candidate except the favorite, William H. Seward (1801–72) of New York. Seward took the lead in the first round of balloting, but then Lincoln pulled almost even, and on the third ballot he was nominated for the presidency.

Meanwhile, the Democrats were split over the slavery issue. The Northern Democrats nominated Douglas. The Southerners chose John C. Breckinridge (1821–75). Still another candidate, John Bell (1797–1869), was put forward by a remnant of the Whigs called the Constitutional Union Party. Thus Lincoln had three opponents in the race. Following the custom of the time, he did no active campaigning himself but directed strategy quietly from Springfield. Out of the South came ominous warnings that his election would mean the end of the Union. At the polls on November 6 only about 40 percent of the ballots were cast for Lincoln. But since most of them were concentrated in the heavily populated free states, he won a clear majority of the electoral votes. The Republican Party had elected its first president.

▶ SECESSION AND CIVIL WAR

South Carolina promptly seceded from the Union, in December, 1860. When efforts at compromise failed, six other Southern states followed its example. Together they formed the Confederate States of America. All this happened before Lincoln became president on March 4, 1861. In his inaugural address he pleaded for harmony and insisted that the Union could not be dissolved. He hoped for a peaceful solution but was prepared to risk war rather than see the nation permanently divided.

The critical spot was Fort Sumter in Charleston Harbor in South Carolina. This was one of the few places within the Confederacy still held by Federal troops. Lincoln, proceeding cautiously, planned to send supplies but not re-inforcements to the garrison there. Early in the morning of April 12, however, Southerners opened fire on the fort and soon forced its surrender. Lincoln immediately proclaimed a blockade of the Confederacy and issued a call for volunteers to suppress the rebellion. This provoked the secession of four more Southern states. As spring gave way to summer both sides were preparing hastily for war.

▶ THE WAR PRESIDENT

From the beginning, Lincoln understood the essential nature of the Civil War better than most of his generals. The Confederacy could gain independence merely by defending itself successfully. The Union forces, how-

---

IMPORTANT DATES IN THE LIFE OF ABRAHAM LINCOLN

1809	Born near present-day Hodgenville, Kentucky, February 12.
1816	Moved to Indiana.
1831	Settled in New Salem, Illinois.
1834–1842	Served in Illinois legislature.
1837	Moved to Springfield; began law practice.
1842	Married Mary Todd.
1847–1849	Member of United States House of Representatives.
1855	Defeated for United States Senate.
1858	Debates with Stephen A. Douglas.
1860	Nominated for president, May 18; elected, November 6.
1861	Inaugurated 16th president, March 4; call for volunteers marked beginning of Civil War, April 15.
1862	Issued preliminary Emancipation Proclamation, September 22.
1863	Issued final Emancipation Proclamation, January 1; Gettysburg Address, November 19.
1864	Appointed General Ulysses S. Grant commander of Union armies, March 12; re-elected president, November 8.
1865	Second inauguration, March 4; Lee surrendered to Grant, April 9; Lincoln shot by John Wilkes Booth, April 14; died in Washington, D.C., April 15.

ever, had to conquer the enemy in order to win. Most of the material advantages were with the North. It had greater manpower, wealth, and industrial strength. Lincoln's task was to mobilize Northern superiority and make it effective on the battlefield. He favored pressing forward on several fronts to prevent the Confederates from concentrating their defenses. He also believed that the primary aim of Union strategy should be the destruction of Southern armies rather than the capture of Southern cities like Richmond, Virginia. In the early part of the war, however, Lincoln was unable to find a general capable of maintaining an offensive against the great Confederate commander Robert E. Lee.

The battle of Bull Run in July, 1861, was only the first of many Union defeats and disappointments on the Virginia front. More successful in the west, Union forces captured New Orleans and were gaining control of the lower Mississippi. At the end of 1862, however, the war was obviously still far from over.

Although military affairs occupied much of his attention, Lincoln had many other presidential duties to perform. On the whole he was content to allow his cabinet members a free hand in the administration of their departments. He rarely sought to influence Congress and seldom used his veto power. Among the important pieces of legislation that he signed were the Homestead Act, which provided free land in the West to settlers; the Pacific Railway Act; and the National Banking Act.

▶ EMANCIPATION

Despite his own strong antislavery feelings, Lincoln insisted at first that the purpose of the war was to save the Union, not to destroy slavery. But pressure from abolitionists, who demanded an immediate end to slavery, steadily increased, and the President decided that emancipation could be justified as a military measure to weaken the enemy. It would also make the Northern cause more noble in the eyes of the world. After announcing his intention in August, 1862, Lincoln issued the famous Emancipation Proclamation on January 1, 1863.

Since it applied only to the areas still under Confederate control, the proclamation did not actually free many Negroes from bondage. Yet it was a symbol and a commitment that changed the nature of the war. After that date everyone knew that a Northern victory would mean the end of slavery. Emancipation became complete and final with the Thirteenth Amendment to the Constitution. Approved by Congress at Lincoln's urging, it was not ratified by a sufficient number of states until after his death.

▶ TOWARD VICTORY

The responsibilities of his office and the mounting toll of battle casualties weighed heavily on Lincoln's spirit. For relaxation he swapped jokes, read books of humor, and visited the theater. In his more serious moments, however, he turned to Shakespeare and the Bible. Pondering the causes of the war, Lincoln came to believe that it was a divine punishment of all Americans for the sin of slavery. The bloodshed would not end, he decided, until peace suited God's purpose.

The turning point of the war came during the first days of July, 1863. Lee's army, attempting a second invasion of the North, was defeated at the battle of Gettysburg in Penn-

Lincoln in 1862 with General George B. McClellan, then general in chief of the Union forces.

sylvania. At the same time, General Ulysses S. Grant captured Vicksburg, the last important Confederate stronghold on the Mississippi River. Later that same year Lincoln helped dedicate the military cemetery at Gettysburg. His memorable address of only a few hundred words summoned the nation to complete the great task in which so many men had given "the last full measure of devotion. . . ."

Early in 1864 Lincoln promoted Grant to the command of all Union armies. Grant then began the hard, bloody work of driving Lee back toward Richmond. Meanwhile, General William T. Sherman launched an invasion of Georgia. When his troops occupied Atlanta in September, 1864, the war entered its final phase.

Now the time for another presidential election had arrived. Lincoln, although opposed by some dissatisfied Republicans, won renomination without much trouble. The Democrats chose General George B. McClellan (1826–85) as their candidate, with a platform demanding immediate peace. For a time Lincoln despaired of victory, but Sherman's progress in Georgia helped his cause. Union soldiers voted overwhelmingly for Lincoln, and he was re-elected.

▶THE LAST FULL MEASURE

As the Union armies pressed forward Lincoln gave increasing attention to the problem of restoring peace when victory was achieved. It must be done, he said in his second inaugural address, "With malice toward none; with charity for all . . . ." Desiring the speedy reconstruction of a united republic, he set forth a simple plan. Ten percent of the voters in a Confederate state, if they took an oath of allegiance to the United States, could organize a government and resume their old place in the federal union. By 1865 several states were putting the plan into operation. But strong opposition had developed in Congress. Many Republicans believed that such generosity was unrealistic. They felt that there should be more punishment for Southern traitors and more protection for freed slaves. The whole question of Reconstruction remained unsettled at the time of Lincoln's death.

On April 9, 1865, Lee surrendered to

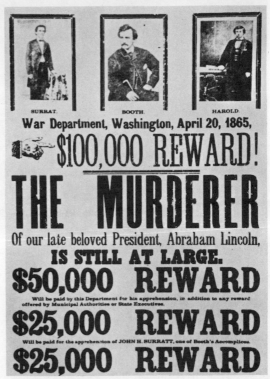

Handbill offering a reward for the capture of Booth and his accomplices.

Grant at Appomattox Court House in Virginia. Throughout the North there were joyful celebrations. Five nights later, Lincoln attended a play at Ford's Theater in Washington. There he was shot by John Wilkes Booth (1838–65), an actor devoted to the Confederate cause. The President never regained consciousness and died the next morning, April 15. Booth escaped to Virginia but was trapped and killed. While the news of the assassination sped across the country, Vice-President Andrew Johnson hastily took the oath of office as president. The war had ended, but the war leader had fallen.

A crowd of mourners gathered at each railway station as the funeral train rolled westward toward the Illinois prairies. In Springfield, his home, Abraham Lincoln was buried. It was a tragic ending but also a triumphant one; for he left behind a nation reunited and a people set free.

DON E. FEHRENBACHER
Author, *Prelude to Greatness: Lincoln in the 1850's*

See also CIVIL WAR, UNITED STATES; DOUGLAS, STEPHEN A.; EMANCIPATION PROCLAMATION; KANSAS-NEBRASKA ACT; LINCOLN-DOUGLAS DEBATES; MISSOURI COMPROMISE; RECONSTRUCTION PERIOD.

LINCOLN CENTER FOR THE PERFORMING ARTS

Lincoln Center for the Performing Arts, located in New York City, is made up of Philharmonic Hall, the New York State Theater, the Metropolitan Opera House, the Vivian Beaumont Theater, the Library and Museum of the Performing Arts, and the Juilliard School of Music and Alice Tully Hall. The center was completed in 1969, at a total cost of $185,000,000. This money was raised from many sources: city, state, and federal funds; foundations; American industry throughout the nation; foreign governments; national organizations; and individuals.

In 1962 the first president of Lincoln Center, the American composer William Schuman (1910–   ), set to work putting the creative aspects of the center into operation. The Lincoln Center Fund for Education and Artistic Advancement was set up. Its purpose is to commission new works in all the arts, to organize festivals, and to develop a widespread educational program. The student program was organized with the help of the New York City Board of Education.

The opening of Philharmonic Hall in September, 1962, began a week of special concerts by some of America's leading orchestras. The hall, which seats almost 3,000, was designed by the architect Max Abramovitz.

The New York State Theater is the home of the New York City Ballet and the New York City Opera. It was opened in the spring of 1964, at the time of the launching of the New York World's Fair. This theater, seating 2,729, was designed by Philip Johnson.

The Vivian Beaumont Theater opened in 1965. The designers were Eero Saarinen Associates, with stage designer Jo Mielziner (1901–   ) collaborating. The main theater seats over 1,000, and the Forum, a small amphitheater, seats 299. The Beaumont is the home of Lincoln Center's Repertory Theater. A film theater and archives will be added.

The Library and Museum of the Performing Arts was designed by Skidmore, Owings & Merrill. Its auditorium seats over 200, and it also contains the Hecksher Children's Oval, seating 100. It houses the New York Public Library's performing arts research materials. It offers film and record programs, concerts, dramatic readings, dance performances, lectures, exhibitions, and discussions.

The Metropolitan Opera House was designed by Wallace K. Harrison. It seats over 3,700, and its stage is a very modern one. South of the opera house are Damrosch Park and the Guggenheim Band Shell.

The designers of the Juilliard School are Pietro Belluschi and Catalano & Westermann. It contains the Juilliard Theater, Paul Recital Studio, and the Juilliard Drama Workshop. It also houses Alice Tully Hall, home of the Lincoln Center Chamber Music Society.

Throughout the nation cities are planning and building arts centers. Lincoln Center is among the largest and most ambitious.

Reviewed by WILLIAM SCHUMAN
Former president
Lincoln Center for the Performing Arts

LINCOLN-DOUGLAS DEBATES

The Lincoln-Douglas Debates took place in seven Illinois towns and cities in the summer and fall of 1858. The debaters were Abraham Lincoln, Republican candidate for the United States Senate, and Stephen A. Douglas, Democratic Senator up for re-election to the Senate.

Of the two men, Douglas was far better known. At 45 he had held important state offices. He had served two terms in the United States House of Representatives and 11 years in the Senate. Lincoln, 49 years old, had been a state legislator and a Congressman for one term. In 1850 he had given up politics. He might have remained a lawyer hardly known beyond Illinois if Douglas, in the Senate, had not offered a bill that changed the course of American history.

Called the Kansas-Nebraska Bill, it was meant to provide governments for the territories of Kansas and Nebraska. At once Douglas ran into the problem of slavery. Both territories were in parts of the country where slavery had been prohibited under the Missouri Compromise (1820). Douglas proposed to repeal the prohibition and allow the settlers to decide whether or not they wanted slavery. This policy he called "popular sovereignty."

Large numbers of Northerners greeted the Kansas-Nebraska Bill with anger. They had believed that slavery would die a natural death if its growth were stopped. But the Kansas-Nebraska Bill would give slavery a chance to enter free soil. In spite of the protests Douglas pushed the bill through Congress (1854). Opponents of the bill formed the Republican Party, and Lincoln re-entered politics.

In 1854 Lincoln made only a few speeches, but they had new depth and seriousness. Two years later he joined the Republican Party and took an active part in the presidential campaign. By 1858 he had become the leading Illinois Republican and the choice of the party to oppose Douglas in the approaching senatorial election.

Lincoln opened his campaign with his "House Divided" speech at Springfield on June 16, 1858. "A house divided," he asserted, could not stand. The nation could not "endure permanently, half slave and half free."

At Chicago on July 9, Douglas charged Lincoln with stirring up disunion. Lincoln denied the charge the next night. On July 17 both men spoke at Springfield. A week later Lincoln challenged Douglas to a series of debates in Illinois. Douglas accepted the challenge, and debates were set for Ottawa (August 21), Freeport (August 27), Jonesboro (September 15), Charleston (September 18), Galesburg (October 7), Quincy (October 13), and Alton (October 15). In each debate there was an opening statement one hour in length, a reply of an hour and a half, and an answer of 30 minutes by the first speaker. Lincoln and Douglas also spoke almost daily, from early August to November, at their own party rallies.

In the campaign Lincoln took the position that slavery was evil. He would allow it to remain in the states where it existed, but he opposed its spread. Therefore, the federal government must prohibit slavery in the territories. Douglas wanted the new settlers to decide the question. To him "popular sovereignty," or self-government, was more important than stopping the spread of slavery in the United States.

The debaters differed on Negro rights. Though unwilling to grant the Negro either social or political equality, Lincoln held that he was entitled to freedom and that he had the right "to eat the bread, without leave of anybody else, which his own hand earns." Douglas was unwilling to grant the Negro any rights.

On election day, November 2, voters cast their votes for members of the legislature, who at that time elected United States Senators. The Republicans outvoted the Democrats at the polls, but Douglas won more legislative districts, thus making his re-election to the Senate certain.

Lincoln, though failing to win the office he had sought, became a national figure. Large crowds had attended the debates and the party meetings, and newspapers all over the country had reported the campaign. To say that the debates made Lincoln president of the United States would be going too far, but without them he would not have been thought of for the office.

PAUL M. ANGLE
Director, Chicago Historical Society

LIND, JENNY (1820–1887)

Jenny Lind, "the Swedish Nightingale," was a famous concert and opera soprano. She was born in Stockholm, Sweden, on October 6, 1820, and began her vocal training when she was only 9 years old. At 17 she made her debut at the Stockholm Opera in *Der Freischütz.* Shortly afterward she was made a member of the Royal Swedish Academy of Music and was given the honorary position of court singer.

In 1841 Jenny Lind went to Paris to study voice with Manuel Garcia (1805–1906). She quickly learned all that any singing-master could teach her and the following year returned to the Stockholm Opera.

In 1844 the opera composer Giacomo Meyerbeer (1791–1864), whom she had met in Paris, arranged a debut for her in Berlin. The debut was very successful and started her on a career of opera and concert tours all over Europe. Whether she sang grand opera or simple Swedish folk songs, audiences were thrilled with her brilliant coloratura voice.

In 1850 the famous circus manager P. T. Barnum brought Jenny Lind to the United States. She was enthusiastically received by both the public and the critics. Audiences loved her not only for her voice but also for the many things she did for other people. She gave almost the entire income from her American tour to establish schools and scholarships in Sweden. Before leaving the United States she married the composer Otto Goldschmidt (1829–1907), who had conducted the orchestra on her tour.

In 1852 she returned to Europe and continued her tours there until 1856, when she and her husband settled in England. After this, her public appearances were less frequent and were only for special occasions or for charity. Her final public performance was a benefit concert in 1883. From 1883 to 1886 she taught at the Royal College of Music in England.

Jenny Lind died on November 2, 1887, at her home in Malvern Wells, England. In 1894 a medallion in her honor was unveiled in Westminster Abbey, London.

LINDBERGH, CHARLES (1902–   )

Charles Lindbergh, one of the world's greatest aviators, was born in Detroit, Michigan, on February 4, 1902. He was raised in Little Falls, Minnesota. In 1920 he went to the University of Wisconsin to study mechanical engineering. But he left the university in 1922 to go to flying school.

After flying school, Lindbergh worked as a stunt flier and then as an airmail pilot. In 1926 he decided to try for a $25,000 prize that was being offered for the first successful nonstop transatlantic flight. The following year he bought an airplane with money that he got from a group of St. Louis businessmen who were interested in gaining publicity for the city of St. Louis. Lindbergh therefore named his plane *Spirit of St. Louis.* On the morning of May 20, 1927, Lindbergh took off from Roosevelt Field on Long Island, New York, and flew the first solo nonstop transatlantic flight. He landed near Paris 33½ hours later and became a world hero. This flight was important not only because it was a new record, but also because it helped people to understand the usefulness of the airplane. As a result of Lindbergh's flight millions of people read how this new form of transportation could cover great distances in a short time.

In 1929 Lindbergh married Anne Morrow. Anne Lindbergh also enjoyed flying and was Charles's co-pilot on flights to many parts of the world. She wrote about these trips in her books *North to the Orient* and *Listen! the Wind.*

In 1932 the Lindberghs' 20-month-old son, Charles, was kidnapped and murdered. The whole world was saddened by the tragedy, and the Congress of the United States passed the "Lindbergh law." This law provided that kidnapping could be punishable by death. During World War II, Lindbergh's knowledge of aviation helped his country a great deal. In his books *We, Of Flight and Life,* and *The Spirit of St. Louis,* he wrote about his life and his flying experiences.

LINEN. See FIBERS.

LINGUISTICS

Linguistics is the scientific study of language. The scientists who study and teach linguistics are called linguists or linguistic scientists. Some people are able to speak or read several different languages, but they are not necessarily linguists. Linguists study what languages are like and how they work. They try to find out in what ways all languages are the same and in what ways they are different.

Descriptive Linguistics

There are more than 2,000 different languages spoken in the world today. Linguists hope eventually to get each and every language described as completely and accurately as possible. This important work is called descriptive linguistics.

How would a linguist describe the English language? First, what English language would he describe—the language we speak or the language we write? For these are not exactly the same. The linguist starts his work with a description of the spoken language because spoken language is learned before written language. Next, what kind of English would he describe? The British, the Americans, the Australians, and others speak slightly different kinds of English, called dialects. The same word may be pronounced in different ways; for instance, when the Englishman pronounces the word "clerk," he makes it rhyme with "dark," while the American makes it rhyme with "perk." They may use different words for the same thing, the way the Englishman says "lift" for what Americans call an elevator. The linguist has to describe each dialect separately and look for similarities between them.

In any one country like the United States, there are different dialects of English, and highly educated people tend to talk differently from people with less education. Yet they all speak the English language, and most of the time they can understand each other. The descriptive linguist studies the system of sounds and words that makes it possible for people who speak the same language to understand each other.

Sounds. To describe the system of sounds in a language, the linguist has to find out what the basic sounds are. To do this, he pays no attention to the letters with which words are spelled; instead he listens carefully to words, and he notices what happens to the lips, tongue, and other parts of the mouth as the words are pronounced. For instance, pronounce the word "thing," and you will hear three basic sounds: first the mildly hissing consonant sound represented by the letters TH, then the vowel sound of the letter I, and then a nasal sound represented by the letters NG (and this is not a combination of the sounds of N and G). Basic sounds like these are called **phonemes**, and they are the basic building blocks for the language. They enable us to tell one word from another. For example, by changing the first phoneme of "thing" we can get "sing"; by changing the second, "thong"; or by changing the third, we can get "thin." We can add the phoneme K at the end and change "thing" into "think."

Each language has a particular set of phonemes, that is, sounds that are its building blocks. Common varieties of American English have 20 consonant phonemes, 4 semivowels (W, R, H, Y), and 9 vowel phonemes. (People who say there are five vowels in English are talking about the written letters A, E, I, O, and U, not the sounds.) Each phoneme can be written with a single letter or special symbol in what is called a **phonemic transcription**. If you want to work an interesting puzzle, see whether you can read the following sentence written in a phonemic transcription, and then figure out what sound each symbol stands for. The sentence contains all the vowel, semivowel, and consonant phonemes of a common variety of American English. (If you have trouble reading it, it is printed in the ordinary way at the end of this article.)

> mɪɛɪə gcyǰ mɛžɹd awt ænd
> pækt fayv bušəlz əv striŋ biynz,
> θriy əv hwič wər ðen sowld tuw
> ə lɔhyər.

There are other kinds of phonemes that make a difference in the way we say words. For instance, read these three sentences aloud: "You don't go there." "You don't go there?" "You! Don't go *there!*" Even though the words are the same, you use phonemes of emphasis, pitch, and pause to show that you mean different things.

Other languages have their own sets of phonemes, many of them quite different from those of English. In learning a foreign language, you have to learn to hear its special sounds and to make them properly. For instance, the sound of the letter R in French is normally very different from the sound of R in English. The description of these sounds and of the way in which they are produced is treated in **phonetics,** which is another branch of linguistics. The languages of the world contain hundreds or perhaps thousands of different speech sounds.

Grammar. Linguists also work on the description of what is called the grammar of a language. Notice how in English certain words can change their form to show changes in meaning. "Song" changes to "songs" to mean "more than one song" and to "songstress" to mean "a lady who sings." An action word like "sing" (a verb) changes to *sings, sang, have sung, had sung, will sing,* and *to be singing* to mean different times and conditions of singing. The linguist tries to find changes that are the same in large numbers of words. He might notice, for example, that the change from *sing* to *sang* is similar to the change from *ring* to *rang,* but that it is different from the change from *bring* to *brought* or the change from *ask* to *asked*. He does not make the rules of the language; the language makes these for him, and few of the rules of real languages are without exceptions. The study of changes in word form is called **morphology** (from the Greek *morph-,* "form, shape"). The way words are strung together is called **syntax** (from the Greek words for "together-arrange"). In English the order of words is very important. Take the same set of words and put them in a different order: *The hare beat the tortoise* and *The tortoise beat the hare*—they mean quite different things.

Every language has a grammar of its own. In Latin, the language of the ancient Romans, the order of the words was not so important as it is in English, but there was a more elaborate way of making different word forms. In Eskimo most of the words are much longer than English words, and they wrap up many different ideas in one word. Some languages use ideas in their grammars that English pays no attention to; for instance, Hopi (an American Indian language) makes a special form of the verb when the action occurs again and again. And some languages pay no attention to things that are important in English grammar: Chinese has no regular way of showing whether there is one or more than one of anything. For instance, it ordinarily uses the same word for "book" and for "books."

As a scientist the linguist does not worry about whether one way of saying something is more "correct" than another. The fact that some people say "he doesn't" while others say "he don't" means to the linguist only that these people may have had different amounts of education or may have grown up in different parts of the country. He will tell you, however, that if you want to talk to most educated people and not have them think you uneducated, you'd better say "he doesn't."

Vocabulary. The linguist studies the words of a language and their meanings, that is, its vocabulary. Some words have many meanings: in English a tie can be an article of clothing, a part of a railroad track, or a musical sign. In another language, such as French, each of these meanings is conveyed by a completely different word.

Sounds, grammar, vocabulary—these are the chief parts of a language system. Language systems are very complicated, however, and even now linguists continue to discover new truths about English and other languages.

Writing Systems. Writing systems can also be studied by the linguist. English, like many other languages, uses the Roman alphabet with its 26 letters—not enough to represent all the different sounds in English, however good it might have been for Latin. For this and other reasons, English has a rather irregular system of spelling, and the same sound is often spelled in many different ways. For example, the sound of F is spelled F, FF, PH, and GH (as in "tough"). The linguist can make up a simple way of writing English that would be easy to read and spell, but this would not be very practical because we already have millions of books spelled in the old-fashioned way. There are many other alphabets besides the Roman alphabet. For example, Russian uses the Cyrillic alphabet of 32 letters. Chinese does not have an alphabet, but instead uses a special sign, called a character, for each syllable (and often for each meaning of the syllable).

Historical and Comparative Linguistics

Another branch of linguistics is historical and comparative linguistics. Languages change, slowly but surely, and for many reasons. Society changes, and new ways of saying things have to be found. Different people learning to speak a language introduce different pronunciations and expressions. Changes are occurring in our own language all the time.

With careful study linguists can trace the history of languages as they split off from one another and went their separate ways. They can do this by noticing how words change their sounds as the centuries go by. For instance, the word for father was *pater* in Latin and became shortened to *père* in French.

Most of the languages of Europe, including English, belong to what is known as the Indo-European family because they can all be traced back to a single language that seems to have existed some thousands of years ago. The people who spoke this language became separated, and gradually several different languages developed—Hittite (a language of Turkey around 1500 B.C.), Latin, Greek, Sanskrit, Albanian, Celtic, Germanic, and Slavic. The Latin of the pre-Christian era in turn split up into the various Romance languages—Italian, French, Spanish, Rumanian, and others. Our English language can be traced back to Anglo-Saxon, a language in the Germanic family.

Linguists have studied the history of many other families of languages, such as the Semitic family (which includes Hebrew and Arabic) and the families of American Indian languages and the languages of the Pacific Ocean islands.

Of what use is linguistics? The study of language is fascinating in itself, but it also helps us understand the peoples who use these different languages. The science of linguistics helps us to learn languages, too, for it tells us exactly what we must learn and how the foreign language differs from our own.

JOHN B. CARROLL
Harvard University

See also GRAMMAR; LANGUAGES; SPELLING; UNIVERSAL LANGUAGES.

Here is the answer to the puzzle given in the middle of the article: Mrs. Gage measured out and packed five bushels of string beans, three of which were then sold to a lawyer.

LINNAEUS, CAROLUS (1707–1778)

Carolus Linnaeus was a Swedish naturalist, known particularly for his work in botany—the study of plants. "Carolus Linnaeus" is the Latin form of his Swedish name, Carl von Linné. At the time he lived, most scientific books were written in Latin. Because he, too, wrote in that language, he used his Latin name in his scientific work. He is generally known by this name.

Linnaeus was born in southern Sweden on May 23, 1707. His father was a country clergyman. From the time Carl was a little child, he showed an unusual interest in flowers. His father, very fond of flowers himself, taught his son about them. Carl enjoyed growing unusual plants in his garden.

When Carl was 7 years old, his parents hired a teacher to educate him at home. But this did not turn out to be successful. After 2 years Carl was sent to school in the town of Växjö, about 25 miles away. His father hoped his son would become a clergyman like himself. But because Carl did poorly in school, this did not seem likely. His science teacher,

however, thought Carl was the most promising of all his students. He urged the boy's parents to let Carl attend a university to study to become a doctor.

Linnaeus went first to Lund University in southern Sweden. After a year he moved to Uppsala University, near Stockholm. Here, while a student, he began scientific research. He spent a summer in Lappland, in the far northern part of Sweden, studying the plants and animals there. In 1735, after several years of study at Uppsala University, Linnaeus went to the Netherlands. He received the degree of doctor of medicine at Hardewijk University that same year.

Also in that year, 1735, Linnaeus published a book called *Systema Naturae* ("The System of Nature"). This book explained a system he had invented for classifying plants and animals. According to this system, each plant and animal had two Latin names, one telling its group (genus) and the other its kind (species). This made it simple for scientists to recognize the name of a plant or animal, no matter what its common name was. Linnaeus'

system of classification was quickly accepted throughout Europe.

Whenever Linnaeus saw a collection of things, he had a burning desire to arrange them in an orderly way. He became famous for his systems of arranging animals, minerals, and most of all, plants. The *Systema Naturae* was only the beginning of his work in classifying living things.

Linnaeus returned to Sweden in 1738. During his 3 years abroad he had become very well-known among European scientists. He was appointed professor of medicine and of natural history at Uppsala University and physician to the King of Sweden.

People from all over the world sent Linnaeus specimens of shells, insects, minerals, and plants. His collection of dried plants was the largest in the world. It was sold after Linnaeus' death and is now in England.

Linnaeus died on January 10, 1778, having become known as the "prince of botanists."

DUANE H. D. ROLLER
The University of Oklahoma

See also TAXONOMY.

LINOLEUM. See VINYL AND OTHER FLOOR COVERINGS.

LINOLEUM-BLOCK PRINTING

Linoleum—used for covering floors—is a good material for making prints. Linoleum prints, called **linocuts**, make good-looking Christmas cards, small posters, and pictures. One carved linoleum block can print 50 to 100 copies clearly.

Linoleum blocks bought in an art-supply store should be used for your first linocuts. The linoleum is mounted on blocks of wood and may be coated with white film. After you have made a few linocuts, you no longer need to use mounted blocks. Instead, you can buy scraps of linoleum in a store that sells floor coverings. These scraps cost much less than mounted blocks and can be cut to any size.

In an art-supply store, buy one tube of black, water-base printing ink, a small cutting tool (gouge), a few sheets of inexpensive rice paper, one newsprint tablet, and a rubber roller about 4 inches wide. In addition to these materials, you will need a wooden salad spoon and a palette. A sheet of glass—its edges taped for safety—makes an excellent palette.

Cutting the Linoleum

First, draw a picture on your mounted linoleum block. Remember that your print will be made from the parts of the block that you do not cut away. Following the lines of your drawing, gently cut lines into the linoleum. Cut only the general shape of your design at first, leaving the details for later.

Everything that you cut will appear backward when you print your linocut. Therefore, if you decide to print your initials, draw them in reverse.

Linoleum is very easy to cut, but there is one safety rule to keep in mind: always cut away from your body. If you must cut in another direction, turn the linoleum, not your hand.

Printing the Linocut

After you have cut the general shape of your design, you are ready to pull a proof, or sample print. Squeeze a little ink on your palette. Spread the ink with the roller, which

LINOCUT TOOLS

ROLLER   INK   WOODEN SPOON   GOUGE

MOUNTED LINOLEUM BLOCK

GLASS PALETTE

PAPER

A design is cut into the linoleum. To cut safely, always cut toward the far edge of the block.

The roller applies ink to the uncut surface of the linoleum block.

Paper is placed on top of the inked block. Rubbing the paper with the spoon prints the design.

The paper is removed from the block. Notice that the design has been printed in reverse.

must then be rolled over the linoleum. Place a piece of newsprint over the block, smooth it with your hand, and rub the whole surface with the back of a salad spoon. Now lift off the paper and study your proof. Go back to work on your linoleum, making changes and adding details. Pull a proof whenever you want to see how the linocut looks. When you are satisfied, decide how many prints to make, and use the rice paper.

Advanced Linocuts

After you become more experienced, you can use more difficult techniques. For a reasonable price you can buy a linoleum cutting set, which includes one handle and a variety of gouges (each cuts a different kind of line). Colored, oil-base inks are messier but much better than water-base ink. The roller can be cleaned with turpentine after you use each color, but three or four rollers save time.

Linocuts of more than one color are made with several linoleum blocks. A different block is needed for each color. A great deal of experimentation is necessary, but the results are worth the effort.

See also GRAPHIC ARTS.

A family of lions resting. Only the male lion grows a bushy mane about his neck.

LIONS

Lions are very large, strong cats. The male lion may weigh 400 pounds or more. The female weighs somewhat less—usually no more than 300 pounds. A lion's coat is sandy brown in color.

Male lions are the only members of the cat family that have manes. The mane is usually the same color as the coat but can be black. Both male and female lions have a tuft of dark hair at the end of their tails. Inside this hair is the so-called claw—a tough, naked patch of skin at the tip of the tail. No one knows what function this serves, if any, but no other cat has it.

Lions are meat-eaters, and they are well suited to a life of hunting. They can run fast for short distances—up to 40 miles an hour or more when charging their prey. They have powerful muscles for leaping and springing. Their sharp, hooked claws are dangerous weapons. Like other cats, a lion can sheath its claws and walk very quietly on the soft pads of its feet.

Like the rest of the cat family, lions hunt mostly at night. But unlike most other cats, lions hunt in groups. Their favorite prey are zebras and antelopes. Males and females often work together. The females may lie hidden, waiting quietly while the males round up the prey. The males drive the antelopes or other animals toward the females. When the antelopes are nearby, the females spring out and attack. When a kill is made, the lions usually feed from it for several days. When they have used up their food, they make a new kill. Lions kill only for food or when defending themselves or their young.

Young lions, or cubs, are born about 3½ months after the parents have mated. From two to six cubs are born at one time. They are about the size of small house cats and are spotted and striped. When half grown, lions are good climbers. But as they grow older and heavier, they rarely climb.

Young lions grow quickly. At the end of a year their spots have faded or disappeared completely. By this time they have begun to join in the hunt. Now they begin to make their own kills. In 2 years they mate and start to raise families. Their manes begin to grow when they are about 3. Lions may live to be 15 to 20 years old.

Lions are usually found in fairly open country, such as plains or grasslands. They once lived in Greece, Asia Minor, and Syria. Now almost all of them are in Africa, south of the Sahara desert. A few remain in the northwest part of India.

Reviewed by ROBERT M. McCLUNG
Author, science books for children

See also CATS.

LIPREADING. See DEAF, EDUCATION OF THE.

LIQUID OXYGEN AND OTHER LIQUID GASES

Almost any gas can be turned into a liquid if it is made cold enough. This is an important fact because liquid gases have many uses in science and industry.

The most common liquid gases are oxygen, nitrogen, hydrogen, helium, and neon. All of them are extremely cold in their liquid forms. They are sometimes called cryogenic gases. **Cryogenics** is the science that deals with temperatures below −238 degrees Fahrenheit. The name comes from the Greek word *kryos,* which means "icy cold."

Nothing you usually see is even close to being as cold as −238 degrees. It is as cold as that on the unlit side of the moon. On earth the coldest weather ever recorded was −127 degrees, in the Antarctic in 1960. Dry ice (solid carbon dioxide) is only −110 degrees. Alcohol freezes at −170 degrees.

The temperatures at which these gases **boil** give some idea of just how cold liquid gases are. Methane boils at −258 degrees, oxygen at −297 degrees, argon at −302 degrees, fluorine at −306 degrees, nitrogen at −320 degrees, neon at −410 degrees, hydrogen at −423 degrees, and helium at −452 degrees.

One of the most important fields for the use of liquid gases is missile and rocket aviation. Liquid gases are used to test the operation of spaceships and their electronic equipment in the very low temperatures they will meet in outer space. Liquid nitrogen, hydrogen, and helium are used to chill the test chambers. Liquid hydrogen is the most powerful rocket fuel known. Liquid oxygen, called lox, is used to release the energy in the hydrogen fuel. Liquid nitrogen helps cool the tanks and compartments of a missile during countdown.

The extreme cold of liquid gases makes them ideal for use in refrigeration. Refrigerated trucks and railway cars use liquid nitrogen to cool fruits and vegetables. Medical laboratories store serum and blood plasma in containers refrigerated by liquid gases. Before some surgical operations the area to be operated on is frozen with liquid gas. The very low temperature makes all normal biological activity stop.

Cooling electrical conductors is another important job of liquid gases. At cryogenic temperatures (below −238 degrees) some electrical conductors have no resistance at all to the flow of electric current. This is called superconductivity. Superconducting electrical devices, such as electromagnets and computers cooled by liquid nitrogen and liquid hydrogen, take only a fraction of the power that is needed to run ordinary types.

Familiar substances take on strange new properties at cryogenic temperatures. Mercury freezes so solid that it can be used as a hammer. Rubber becomes stiff and brittle. Soft, flexible plastics become rigid and can be shattered to pieces by a hammer blow.

Liquid gases are used in many scientific research laboratories. They are also used by many big industrial companies in testing and developing new materials. The research laboratories of some companies have special storage tanks for liquid gases, in order to have a supply at all times. Other companies install special pipelines from the liquid-gas producing plant to their laboratories.

Making Liquid Gases

Liquid gases are made in devices called **cold boxes**. The technical name of the cold box is **liquefaction fractional distiller**. Some are as large as a house; others can fit into a small laboratory. All of them work in much the same way, however.

Air is compressed and cooled. It is then let through a valve into a tank where it can expand. As the air goes through the valve and expands, its temperature drops. The slightly cooled expanded air in the tank is used to precool new compressed air coming through the valve. This makes the temperature drop still further. The temperature of the air slowly gets lower and lower until the air begins to condense, at −312 degrees. When all of the gases in the air have condensed, they can be evaporated one at a time, to separate the nitrogen, oxygen, and other gases. The separated gases are then recondensed into liquid form.

There is a problem in keeping the gases liquefied. A certain amount of liquid gas is always boiling off at room temperature. Fortunately, it takes a great deal of heat to boil off even 1 pound of liquid gas, so the loss from evaporation is low.

Storing liquid gas in outer space will be easier. Temperatures out there are also at the cryogenic level. The main problem will be to shield the liquid gas from the radiant heat of the sun and other planets or from space capsules that are heated. To solve this problem, thin sheets of aluminum-coated plastic can be wrapped around the liquid-gas tanks. It is estimated that in this way liquid hydrogen could be kept in outer space for 5 years.

FRANKLIN D. YEAPLE
TEF Engineering Company

See also FUELS; GASES IN INDUSTRY; ROCKETS.

LIQUIDS

Liquids are one of the three states of matter. (The other two are gases and solids.) The most common and familiar liquid is water.

A liquid is made up of tiny particles, as solids and gases are. In some ways the behavior of the particles in liquids is like that of the particles in solids. In other ways it is like that of the particles in gases.

For instance, the particles in liquids remain close together, as those in solids do. This means that a particular quantity of liquid takes up a particular amount of room. Liquids have a definite **volume**, just as solids do.

But the particles in liquids are not fixed firmly in place. They can slide over and under and between their neighbors, as those in gases do. This means that a liquid does not have a definite shape. If liquid is poured into a container, it takes on the shape of the container. If a liquid is poured on a tabletop, it spreads out flat.

(1) Particles in a solid are densely packed. Heating a solid causes the particles to move apart. (2) The solid becomes a liquid. Heating a liquid makes the particles separate even further. (3) The liquid becomes a gas, which easily changes shape and volume.

PARTICLES IN A SOLID   PARTICLES IN A LIQUID   PARTICLES IN A GAS

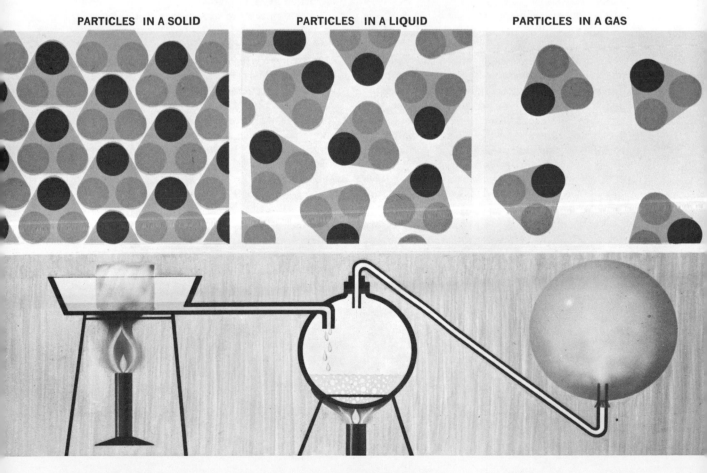

Because liquid changes shape so readily, it can flow, just as a gas can. Liquids and gases are therefore called **fluids**. ("Fluid" comes from a Latin word meaning "to flow.")

The particles in liquids tend to stick together. This sticking together is called **cohesion**. The particles in liquids are also attracted to other substances. For instance, they are attracted to the walls of a container. This attraction is **adhesion**.

Water particles are more strongly attracted by a clean glass surface than they are by one another. That is why water wets glass. The water level in a glass container curves up where it touches the glass. The narrower the glass container is, the higher the water creeps. This creeping is called **capillary action**.

Water creeps up among the fibers of a blotter through capillary action. It creeps up the stems of plants partly through capillary action.

On the other hand, water particles are less strongly attracted by wax than by one another. That is why water does not wet wax. The water level in a container with waxed walls curves downward where the water touches the walls.

The particles in the interior of a liquid are attracted by other particles on all sides. These attractions balance out. As a result, the interior particles can move about freely. But a particle in the surface is pulled inward by the particles inside. There is no balancing pull outward. This inward pull on the surface is called **surface tension**.

Surface tension always acts to reduce the amount of surface present. For that reason, small bits of liquid take the shape of spheres. (Of all shapes, a sphere has the smallest surface for its volume.) However, the pull of gravity usually flattens the spheres. For example, it flattens the surface of a glass of water. However, the tiny droplets of water in a mist are too small to be affected much by gravity. They are perfect spheres.

Some solids break up and spread out finely and evenly within a liquid. That is, the solid **dissolves** in the liquid; the process is called **solution**. Water will dissolve a large variety of solid materials; that is, it is an excellent **solvent**. Chemical reactions take place most easily among substances in solution. For that reason, the life processes go on in water solution. Living creatures may seem solid, but they are usually at least three-fifths water.

When some solids dissolve in liquid, they lower the attraction among the particles of liquid. This lessens the cohesion of the liquid. And so it becomes easier for the liquid particles to be attracted to other substances.

That is what happens when soap or detergent is dissolved in water. The water will then wet oily or greasy particles, which it would not ordinarily do. And the oily and greasy particles can be washed away. That is why it is much better to wash your hands with soap and water than with water alone.

Soap also reduces surface tension. As a result, the surface can then be stretched out to form a bubble. That is why anyone wishing to blow bubbles uses soapy water.

If a liquid is heated strongly enough, its particles pull apart and lose contact. The liquid will **boil** at that point and turn into a gas. Water, for instance, turns into steam. If a liquid is cooled enough, its particles lose the ability to move about freely; they become fixed in place. The liquid will **freeze** at that point and turn into a solid. Water turns into ice when it is cooled.

The temperature at which a liquid boils is its **boiling point**. The temperature at which it freezes is its **freezing point**. The boiling point of water is 212 degrees Fahrenheit and its freezing point is 32 degrees. Every liquid has its own particular boiling point and freezing point.

Solids can be turned into liquids, if heated enough. Gases can be turned into liquids, if cooled enough. In this way you can have blazing-hot liquid iron and super-frigid liquid air.

In addition to water, common liquids include **alcohol** and **gasoline**. Alcohol is an example of a liquid that mixes freely with water. Gasoline is an example of a liquid that does not. Alcohol and gasoline will both burn. Water will not.

A very unusual liquid is **mercury**. It is a metal, but it has such a low melting point that it is liquid even at room temperatures. It is 13½ times as dense as water—so a quart of mercury would weigh about 30 pounds.

ISAAC ASIMOV
Boston University School of Medicine
See also GASES; MATTER; SOLIDS; WATER.

LISTER, JOSEPH (1827–1912)

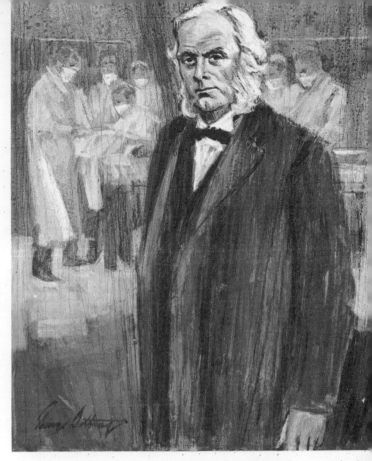

Joseph Lister, the English doctor who developed the idea of germ-free, or antiseptic, surgery, was born at Upton in the county of Essex, England, on April 5, 1827. His father was a merchant who was interested in science. He awakened an interest in science in young Joseph.

After attending private school, Joseph went to London in 1844 to study at University College, London University. While still at college he decided to become a surgeon. He graduated from University College in 1847 and prepared to enter medical school, but he was stricken with smallpox and did not start his medical studies until the fall of 1848.

In 1853 Lister graduated from medical school and went to Edinburgh, Scotland, to work as an assistant to James Syme, a famous surgeon. A few years later Lister married Syme's eldest daughter, Agnes. He stayed in Edinburgh for 7 years and then went to Glasgow University as professor of surgery, in 1860. That same year he was elected a fellow of the Royal Society of London, the leading society of British scientists. A year after his arrival in Glasgow, Lister became a surgeon at the Glasgow Infirmary, the biggest hospital in that city.

While at the Glasgow Infirmary, Lister had to treat many people who had been hurt in accidents. The wounds of these patients frequently became infected. The area around the wound would become swollen and inflamed, and pus would begin to form.

Lister became interested in preventing such infections. At first he tried to clean the wounds, but this did not seem to help. Then, in 1865, he learned that the French scientist Louis Pasteur had shown that germs caused the spoiling of milk and the rotting of meat. The tiny germs floated in the air and settled in the milk or on the meat. Lister thought that infections in wounds were also caused by these airborne germs.

Lister tried to kill the harmful germs by putting a chemical called carbolic acid on the wounds. He was very successful in reducing the number of infections and was convinced that his germ theory of infection was correct.

In 1867 Lister wrote an article for an important medical journal. In this article he wrote about his theory concerning infections and described his method for preventing them.

At first, Lister's theory was not readily accepted. But within 25 years most surgeons were using antiseptics (germ killers) in treating wounds and during surgery.

Lister moved to London in 1877 and became a professor of surgery at King's College. He devoted much of his time to developing better methods for antiseptic surgery. He was one of the founders of a medical research institute now known as the Lister Institute of Preventive Medicine. Lister's wife, who had kept his notebooks and often acted as his secretary, died in 1892.

In 1897 Lister was made a baron. He also received a privilege accorded few Englishmen of modern times. Before his death he was offered the honor of being buried in Westminster Abbey. But he refused, saying that he wanted to be buried alongside his wife. He died on February 10, 1912. Because they had no children, the title of baron died with him.

DUANE H. D. ROLLER
The University of Oklahoma

LISZT, FRANZ (1811–1886)

Franz Liszt, one of the greatest pianists of all time, was also a celebrated conductor and composer. He was born on October 22, 1811, in Raiding, Hungary. When Franz was 6 years old, his father started teaching him the piano. At 9 he gave his first public performance. A year later he went to Vienna, where his genius was recognized by the aging Beethoven. In Vienna, Franz studied piano with Carl Czerny (1791–1857) and composition with Antonio Salieri (1750–1825). At the age of 12 he set out on his first concert tour, which covered Germany, France, and England.

In 1827 Liszt settled in Paris, where he met the most important artists, writers, and musicians of the time, including Frédéric Chopin, Hector Berlioz, and Niccolò Paganini (1782–1840). The stirring, romantic works of Chopin and Berlioz influenced many of Liszt's later compositions. And Paganini's mastery of the violin inspired Liszt to a like mastery of the piano. In 1839 Liszt started on a concert tour of Europe that lasted 9 years and established his fame and fortune.

In 1848 Liszt accepted the position of court music director in Weimar, Germany. Here he wrote his greatest compositions—the popular *Hungarian Rhapsodies,* the *Faust* Symphony, and his first piano concerto. He also developed a new orchestral form, the symphonic poem. The symphonic poem is a one-movement work that either tells a story or describes a picture in music. *Les Préludes* is a famous symphonic poem by Liszt.

Liszt was always interested in helping young composers and used his position at Weimar to perform their compositions. He conducted the first performance of Richard Wagner's opera *Lohengrin* and was one of the first to recognize Wagner's greatness.

In 1859 Liszt resigned his position in Weimar, and 2 years later he settled in Rome. In 1866 he became an abbé of the Catholic Church, but continued teaching, traveling, performing, and composing. During this period he wrote many songs and choral works, as well as piano and orchestral compositions.

Liszt died on July 31, 1886, in Bayreuth, Germany, while visiting his daughter Cosima, who was Richard Wagner's widow.

LITERARY CRITICISM

Finding fault with something is the idea most commonly associated with criticism, an act we think of ordinarily as the passing of judgment, especially unfavorably. In a more limited meaning, criticism is the process of judging the merits of any kind of work of art. In this sense it may be as much an act of praising as of faultfinding. A man whose profession is giving opinions about art is called a critic, a word whose Greek and Latin roots mean "to judge" or "to decide."

Literary criticism judges the good and bad qualities of writing. To criticize a literary work is an act of appreciation, or the setting of values. When we say that we appreciate a man's character, or what someone has done for us, we mean that we set a value on these things. In the same way critics set a value on works of art. Many schools offer courses in appreciation of the fine arts. Like criticism, such courses set up standards and comparisons that help us to form judgments.

The first great literary critic was the Greek philosopher Aristotle (384–322 B.C.). His essay called *Poetics* is criticism at its highest level. In it he judged the merits of the plays of the Greek writers Aeschylus, Sophocles, Euripides, and others who had carried dramatic poetry to heights perhaps matched but never since surpassed. He also made an important extension of the critic's task: the study of literary forms and techniques. By examining how the authors achieved their effects, Aristotle set up certain general rules, or principles, of dramatic art.

These principles are not laws as to how a writer must work; they are, instead, valuable demonstrations of how some great writers did work. By studying the methods of these writers, we better understand their works. We are also better equipped to form our own opinions of other writings.

The critic performs a valuable service, though a writer who has felt his sting may regard him as a natural enemy. Some literary critics confine themselves to this work of judgment, but many—indeed most—of the greatest of them have also been poets, novelists, or playwrights themselves. Good criticism is itself a valued kind of literature.

▶ CRITICISM IS INDIVIDUAL OPINION

It is important to remember that criticism, even at its best, is individual opinion. No one critic can pronounce once for all on the merits of any work of art. Violent disagreements among qualified critics often occur. Thus no one should lean upon any critic's verdict to avoid reaching an opinion of his own.

Criticism rests upon individual judgment and taste. These qualities, in turn, partly rest upon a broad knowledge of the field and forms with which the critic deals. It is impossible to judge a single achievement without wide familiarity with other similar accomplishments by which to compare and contrast. A literary opinion from a man who had read little would be worthless. Equally useless as criticism is the statement, "I don't know anything about art, but I know what I like."

Criticism is concerned with both what a work says and how it says it, though some critics emphasize one element more than the other. A literary critic seeks to grasp the author's intention and measure the degree to which it has been achieved. The critic's concerns include the meaning of the work, its moral value, its form (poetry, prose, drama), its technical devices, and its style. (Style is the fruit of the writer's skill combined with his individual qualities of personality.)

There is a special aspect of criticism called reviewing, which is a matter of news about books, music, art, or theater. A book review lists the title, author, publisher, and price of a book. The reviewer tells us what kind of book it is and something of its subject and the nature of its story, with an opinion of its merits. Reviewing is chiefly reporting, yet a good review can be a nugget of criticism, referring us from the book at hand to a larger frame of reference.

Among the finest literary critics in the English language are John Dryden, Samuel Johnson, Samuel Taylor Coleridge, George Bernard Shaw, Edgar Allan Poe, and T. S. Eliot—all of them also distinguished writers in other fields as well. The roster of critics is vast, and theirs is one of the most important rooms in the mansion of literature.

EDMUND FULLER
Author, *Man in Modern Fiction*

LITERATURE

A simple definition of literature is: writing in prose and verse. On the basis of this definition a mail-order catalog and a first-grader's poem could be called literature. More exactly, literature is good writing that has form, a point of view, and ideas of lasting interest.

Schools offer courses in literature so that students can profit by great writers' thoughts. In many instances the thoughts are so beautifully expressed that the language gives added pleasure. True literature serves for generations, sometimes for thousands of years, as in the case of Homer's *Iliad* and Vergil's *Aeneid.*

Fiction and Nonfiction. Basically, literature is divided into two classes: fiction and nonfiction. "Fiction" comes from the Latin *fingere,* which means "to form." Fiction is something that the writer makes up. Technically, of course, every writer makes up something—namely, his book, story, or report. But the novelist uses his imagination. He is not required to be as accurate in his details as, say, the scientist. Although fiction is usually in the form of prose—a novel or short story, for instance—fiction also takes other forms. It can be a play, like William Shakespeare's *Hamlet,* or a poem, like Robert Browning's *Pied Piper of Hamelin.*

The second main division of literature is nonfiction. The writer of nonfiction tries to stick to facts as he knows them. He does not invent an interesting story. Biographies, autobiographies, diaries, histories, and essays fall into the category of nonfiction.

An autobiography gives the author's own life-story. Biography is a life-story of somebody other than the author. An essay, a short piece of prose, discusses something from a personal point of view. History quite often enters the realm of literature, when its content and style are superior.

Sometimes a book on science, if the ideas and facts are beautifully expressed, becomes nonfiction literature. In the mid-19th century the Englishman Thomas Henry Huxley wrote essays on science that are outstanding both as science and as literature.

The Novel. A novel is a long story, often with many characters in an involved plot. Novels can be serious, like Dickens' *Tale of Two Cities;* romantic, like Stevenson's *Treasure Island;* or comic, like Twain's *Adventures of Tom Sawyer.* Some books have great social influence. Harriet Beecher Stowe's *Uncle Tom's Cabin,* for example, moved many readers to help put an end to slavery.

Before prose became the usual form of the novel, verse was the medium of long fiction. Outstanding narrative poems are Homer's *Odyssey* from Greek classical times and the French medieval romance *Song of Roland.* In the 18th century, prose novels began to be popular in English. They have gradually replaced long fiction in verse.

The Short Story. A short story usually has a few characters in a single setting and focuses on a single incident. A fine example of the form is "The Necklace" by Guy de Maupassant. Short stories vary in length. Edgar Allan Poe, one of the world's greatest short-story writers, felt that a short story should be read at a single sitting. Longer short stories may be up to 30,000 words in length. These stories are usually called novellas or novelettes. Short fiction has existed for thousands of years—in fables, ballads, and various other forms of folklore.

Drama. A drama is a story, in either prose or verse, meant to be acted out on the stage. The ancient Greek playwrights wrote in poetic form. So did Shakespeare in the 16th century and Dryden in the 17th century. In more recent times most playwrights have written in prose, with the exception of playwrights such as Maxwell Anderson, Christopher Fry, and T. S. Eliot.

Poetry. Poetry differs from prose in having a regular rhythm, sometimes using rhyme, and employing a more careful and beautiful selection of words. Lyric poetry is short, very personal, and songlike. The ode, a form of lyric poetry, is dignified in style and does honor to a person or thing. Narrative poetry tells a story. Epic poetry relates the deeds of a hero of history or legend, Didactic poetry teaches. Elegies express sorrow, usually for one who is dead. A sonnet is a poem of 14 lines written according to a certain rhyme scheme.

JOSEPH MERSAND
Author, *Attitudes Toward English Teaching*

See also AMERICAN LITERATURE, ENGLISH LITERATURE, etc.; DRAMA, FICTION, POETRY, etc.; articles on individual authors, such as ALCOTT, LOUISA MAY.

LITERATURE FOR CHILDREN. See CHILDREN'S LITERATURE.

LITHOGRAPHY

Lithography is a printing technique used by artists to make several copies of a drawing. The process was invented in Germany in 1796 by Aloys Senefelder (1771–1834), who wanted to print copies of musical scores. Lithography was never widely used for that purpose. But during the 19th century artists began to experiment with lithography. Honoré Daumier (1808–79) used lithography to reproduce his cartoons in French journals. Henri de Toulouse-Lautrec (1864–1901) lithographed posters that advertised the Paris café Moulin Rouge.

To make a lithograph, the artist draws on a slab of stone with a greasy crayon. Next he treats the stone with a special chemical solution, so that grease will not stick to it. Then the artist rolls ink over the stone. Because the ink is greasy, it sticks only to the drawing. When the stone is printed on the press, the paper lifts the inked drawing.

Lithography is different from older printmaking techniques, such as engraving, etching, and wood-block printing. Using the older methods, the artist must scratch or cut his drawing into a metal plate or wood block. But to make a lithograph, he draws directly on his stone. An endless number of prints can be

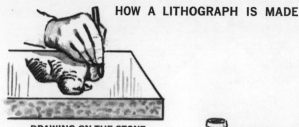

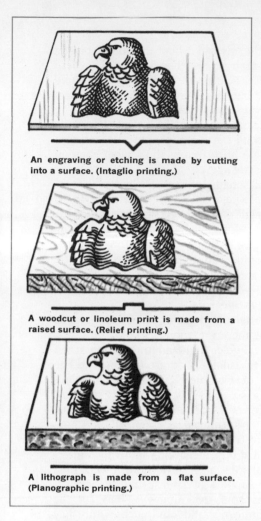

An engraving or etching is made by cutting into a surface. (Intaglio printing.)

A woodcut or linoleum print is made from a raised surface. (Relief printing.)

A lithograph is made from a flat surface. (Planographic printing.)

DRAWING ON THE STONE

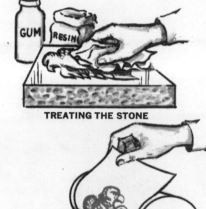

TREATING THE STONE

INKING THE STONE

PRINTING

made from each stone. The stone is then rubbed clean and used again. In modern times zinc metal has also come into use.

Lithography has become a useful tool of the commercial printer as well as the artist. Color prints can be made by using a different stone for each color. Today even photographs can be impressed on lithograph plates and printed in books and magazines.

See also GRAPHIC ARTS.

LITHUANIA. See UNION OF SOVIET SOCIALIST REPUBLICS.

LITTLE LEAGUE BASEBALL

Little League Baseball is a nonprofit organization providing organized baseball for boys between the ages of 9 and 15. It is the only agency of its kind to hold a charter. This charter was granted by act of Congress and signed into law by President Lyndon B. Johnson on July 17, 1964. There are two divisions in the Little League. One is for boys 9 to 12. The other is for boys 13 to 15 (seniors).

Beginning at Williamsport, Pennsylvania, with one league of three teams in 1939, the organization has spread across the United States and to foreign countries. There are over 6,000 leagues, with about 40,000 teams and 1,500,000 Little League players. As a rule, there are four teams in a league, but five-, six-, and eight-team leagues are now common.

Playing Field and Equipment

The bats and balls are lighter in weight than regular baseball equipment. The players wear

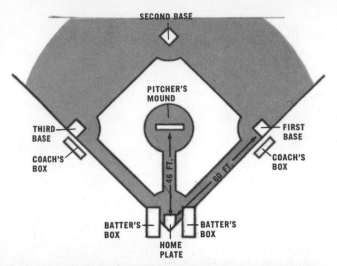

regular uniforms and rubber or molded plastic cleats on their shoes. The batters and base runners also wear protective helmets. A game consists of only six innings, and every league must play at least 36 games in a season. The winning team becomes the champion of its league. An all-star team composed of the best players from all teams in the league goes on through various levels of play to compete for the regional championship. Eight teams from among these regional champions play in the Little League's yearly World Series, which is held in Williamsport, Pennsylvania. The United States is represented by four regional championship teams. Japan, Europe, Latin America, and Canada each send one team.

Little League Sponsors

There are no owners of Little League teams, but there are sponsors. The sponsors, who have no voice in the administration of the leagues, are usually civic groups, such as the Chamber of Commerce, the Young Men's Christian Association, B'nai B'rith, veterans' organizations, or police and fire departments, as well as various business organizations in the community. Usually a local league is started by a small group of parents and other interested adults in a neighborhood, who then enlist the support of sponsoring agencies.

The sponsors give money to pay for the players' uniforms and equipment. But they neither own nor run the team they sponsor. They cannot appoint managers or coaches, or otherwise dictate rules or policy. The man-

A Japanese team waits to go to bat in Little League World Series.

Little League baseball games draw large and enthusiastic crowds.

agers and coaches for each team in the league are chosen by a committee of volunteer adults.

A league has four or more sponsors, one for each team in the league. It costs several hundred dollars to outfit a four-team league. The sponsors of the four teams split the expenses among themselves. At the end of each season all the playing gear is turned in to the League officials, except for the players' caps. These the boys are allowed to keep.

Whenever a new league is organized, it must apply for a certificate of charter (right to play) from Little League Baseball. The national headquarters of Little League at Williamsport, Pennsylvania, will send all necessary information to any group wishing to form a new league.

Candidates for Little League

Tryouts are held every spring for all four teams of a league. Every eligible boy in the neighborhood between the ages of 9 and 12 receives notice of a call for candidates.

During spring training each boy is allowed to bat and field in the position of his choice. He competes with boys of his own age, and the managers of all the teams in his league watch and judge the boy's ability. Later a player auction is held, and the managers bid for the purchase of the players. Instead of money, credits are used by the managers in bidding for the boys. Each team has the same number of credits to spend. Every boy must have his parents' written permission and a physician's approval to be a candidate.

A team may have anywhere from 12 to 15 players. The teams must be balanced so that all the best players are not on the same team. No team may have more than seven 12-year-old players, nor less than two players whose age is under 11.

If a boy does not make the first team, he is eligible to become a member of a minor, or farm team, league. In this way every boy who wants to play baseball is given the chance.

Reviewed by ROBERT H. STIRRAT
Little League Baseball

LIVINGSTONE, DAVID. See STANLEY, HENRY MORTON, AND DAVID LIVINGSTONE.

LIVING THINGS. See KINGDOMS OF LIVING THINGS.

LIVY (59 B.C.—A.D. 17)

Titus Livius, or Livy, as he is called in English, was born in Padua, Italy, in 59 B.C. and died there in A.D. 17. He spent most of his life in Rome. He was a friend of the emperor Augustus and encouraged Claudius, who later became emperor, to study history.

Livy wrote several books on philosophy and literary criticism, but his masterpiece was his history of Rome. He worked on it for 40 years. In 142 volumes he covered more than 1,000 years, from the legendary period of Aeneas down to his own time. He undertook this enormous work because he believed that the Romans had become rulers of much of the Western world through their strength of character, and he thought the men of his own time had lost the patriotism, unselfishness, honesty, and simplicity of their ancestors. By telling how the early Roman heroes had built up their fatherland into a great empire, he hoped to inspire his contemporaries to imitate the heroes' virtues.

Livy was saddened also by the collapse of the Roman republic. Although he thought

Augustus was a skillful statesman, he felt that something noble had been lost forever when the republic was changed into a monarchy. In writing Rome's history, he consoled himself by looking back at its past greatness.

His history was called *From the Foundation of the City*. It came out in installments and brought him great fame. Only Books 1 through 10 and 21 through 45 still exist, but extracts from the other books and summaries of their contents have been preserved. These give us an idea of the missing sections.

Livy gathered his material from many earlier Greek and Roman writers and molded it into a single story. He was sometimes careless about checking facts, but he wrote with wonderful energy and color. He invented bold, dramatic speeches for his chief characters, and he loved describing exciting crowd scenes, debates, and battles. His history can be put next to Vergil's *Aeneid* as an epic in prose.

GILBERT HIGHET
Columbia University

Left: A Komodo monitor, the largest lizard. Right: Gecko, smallest of lizards.

LIZARDS AND CHAMELEONS

Lizards are reptiles, a class of animals that also includes crocodiles, turtles, and snakes. There are about 3,000 kinds of lizards. About 80 of these kinds are chameleons. Some lizards look like dragons; others look like worms.

A typical lizard is four-legged, short-bodied, and long-tailed. All lizards shed their scaly skins. They may do this several times a year. Their skin may come off in patches, but some lizards shed it in one piece, as a snake does.

Lizards are found in all parts of the world except the polar regions. They thrive in tropical regions but are also found in the temperate parts of the world. Lizards of the temperate regions must hibernate in the winter. When the weather gets really cold, lizards need a warm, protected place to keep them alive.

Most lizards are small—usually less than 2 feet in length. Some chameleons and geckos are only a couple of inches long when full-grown. The largest lizards are the Komodo monitors of Indonesia, which may grow to 10 feet in length and weigh 300 pounds.

As a rule, lizards have short life spans. Chameleons live only 2 or 3 years, for instance. The record age for lizards in captivity is about 25 years.

▶ CHAMELEONS

Some lizards are kept as pets. Of these, the most familiar is the anole, usually sold as a chameleon by pet stores. However, it is not a true chameleon.

Anoles and many other lizards can change color, as can the true chameleons, a large family of African and Asian lizards. In Africa and Asia most of these slow-moving lizards live in trees. They grip the branches with their plierlike toes and tail. They adopt the color of the leaves and branches around them, which may protect them from other animals.

When hunting insects, chameleons move very slowly. Their eyes search around in all

Chameleon uses long tongue to catch insect.

The anole, sometimes sold as a chameleon in pet stores.

The horned lizard is sometimes called the horned toad.

directions, moving independently of each other. When an insect comes near, both eyes focus on it, gauging its distance. Then the chameleon's long tongue—often longer than its body—shoots out like a released spring. The insect is caught and held on the tongue's sticky tip.

The chameleon is a lizard that is well adapted to living in trees. Some Asiatic lizards are tree dwellers that can actually glide through the air from branch to branch. Thin folds of skin along the sides of their bodies are supported by long, folding ribs and act as "wings." Other types of lizards have adapted to life on the ground and underground. Some live in the desert. Some even spend part of their time in the ocean. Lizards as a group have been very successful in adapting to the most varied surroundings.

FOOD GETTING

Most lizards eat insects that they catch with their tongues or snap out of the air. They usually eat food that can be swallowed whole. Lizards have teeth that help hold their food. They rarely use their teeth to bite off mouthfuls.

Lizards often sample food with their tongues before swallowing it. A lizard's tongue not only tastes food but also smells it. Tiny particles of food may be carried by the tongue to two little pits in the roof of the mouth. These pits, called Jacobson's organs, aid the smelling sense.

Some lizards have quite specialized diets. The horned lizard (often called the horned toad) of the American southwest usually eats only ants. Other lizards eat plants or perhaps only fruit. The large monitor lizard is one of the few meat-eating lizards. It eats dead animals and occasionally catches small wild pigs, which it swallows whole.

The marine iguana is a lizard that gets its food from the sea. It inhabits the rocky Galápagos Islands off the west coast of South America. The marine iguana's powerful flattened tail equips it for swimming offshore at low tide. Here it finds the seaweed that is the sole item of its diet. The marine iguana is further adapted to its way of life by strong, clawlike feet. These enable it to clamber out of the sea onto the coastal rocks when it is not feeding.

HOW LIZARDS ARE BORN

Most kinds of lizards are born from eggs, although many are born alive. The eggs are buried in the soil or hidden in decaying logs. Often the female guards the eggs against animals that might feed on them. The young have a special "egg tooth" that grows up from the tip of the upper jaw. The tooth is used to cut through the eggshell at the time of hatching. It is lost shortly thereafter.

The common lizard of Europe may either lay its eggs or keep them inside its body and hatch them there. Which it does seems to depend on climate. This lizard is found in the colder northern parts of Europe as well as in the warmer south. In southern Europe it generally lays its eggs. Farther north its eggs need protection from the cold. The common lizard protects them by keeping them warm inside its body until hatching time. In this way the northern lizard has adapted to the harder climate.

DESERT-DWELLING LIZARDS

Lizards have adapted in many other ways to difficult surroundings. Many lizards live in deserts. They can withstand the heat and dryness that make it impossible for most other animals to stay alive there.

The body temperature of all lizards changes with outside temperature. To regulate body temperature, desert lizards move frequently in and out of the shade. Thirty minutes in the desert sun would be fatal to any of these desert dwellers. Some, like the chuckwalla of Arizona, California, and Mexico, take shelter in rock crevices. The horned lizard and others wriggle into loose soil or sand to escape the sun's rays. Some of them travel from place to place in this way. This adaptation to desert life is known as sand swimming. Sometimes lizards crawl into the burrows of other animals to get out of the sun, or they dig their own burrows.

Gila monster, only poisonous lizard in the United States.

Desert lizards are well adapted to the dryness of their surroundings. They are usually able to get the water they need from their food. Not all nondesert lizards can do this; some must have water to drink.

The feet of some kinds of lizards are specially adapted for running in the desert. The fringe-toed lizard of the American southwest has rows of spiny scales on its toes. These act as snowshoes, to enable it to move quickly over the sand dunes that it always chooses for a home. The scales also aid in sand swimming.

The fringe-toe has sharp eyesight for a lizard. From the top of its dune it may sight an intruder 100 feet away. It reacts by scrambling down the far side of the dune to hide by "swimming" into the sand beneath a dune bush or by entering the burrow of a kangaroo rat.

▶ **UNDERGROUND LIZARDS**

Some lizards are adapted to living permanently underground. These curious lizards break the general rule for their kind. They have no legs. They are wormlike in appearance and are often taken for worms. One exception is the ajolote of Lower California. It has two front legs but no rear ones.

Burrowing lizards rarely use their eyes. The eyes are greatly reduced in size in the worm lizards of Florida, for instance. Worm lizards are whitish or pale in color. Underground they do not need dark-colored skin to protect them from the sun.

▶ **PROTECTIVE BEHAVIOR**

Lizards are the prey of many animals— hawks, badgers, wild dogs, and snakes, to name a few. When an enemy is near, lizards usually "freeze" to avoid being seen. The trick is often successful. Because lizards have body colors and shapes well matched to their surroundings, they are very hard to see when they are still.

If freezing doesn't fool the enemy, most lizards will dart away as quickly as possible. They are as expert at quick and agile running as they are at concealment. Even if caught, many lizards can still bite and claw. The Gila monster of the southwestern United States and its Mexican cousin, the beaded lizard, are the only lizards whose bite is poisonous, however.

The horned lizard (and some others) is covered with spiny scales. These usually keep snakes from attacking it. The horned lizard defends itself in another way that is unique. It is able to squirt blood from broken vessels in its lower eyelid. If the blood is squirted in the face of a hungry coyote, he may seek another meal. The blood may be repulsive to wild dogs.

Many lizards, such as the American glass

The frilled lizard spreads its frill when alarmed.

The banded gecko, if caught by the tail, can drop it off.

snakes, are able to drop their tails when they are grabbed. When left behind, the tail continues to twitch on the ground. If the enemy stops to eat it, the lizard can often escape. It soon grows another tail.

Bluffing behavior is highly developed in many lizards. These lizards, though harmless, will make a great show of fierceness when approached. Some rear up and throw open their mouths as if to bite. Others bob about and hiss or display colored areas of their bodies. Often an enemy can be put off or turned away by a lizard's bluff.

Jeweled lacerta gets its name from blue spots on skin.

▶ RELATIONS TO MAN

Lizards have a definite economic value to man in some parts of the world. Many are eaten. The chuckwalla was hunted by certain American Indians. Land iguanas are eaten in Mexico and in Central and South America. Monitor meat is prized in southern India and Ceylon. Lizard eggs may also be eaten.

In India there is a thriving trade in lizard skin. A tanned skin makes high-grade leather that is often used for expensive shoes.

Crops are protected by lizards that dine on harmful insects. The sugar-beet crop in Utah is safeguarded by lizards that eat the beet leaf-hopper. In Ceylon, monitors eat crabs that destroy the banks of rice fields. Monitors also do away with rats.

Reviewed by RICHARD G. ZWEIFEL
The American Museum of Natural History
See also REPTILES; SNAKES.

LOBSTERS. See SHRIMPS, LOBSTERS, AND OTHER CRUSTACEANS.

LOCKE, JOHN (1632–1704)

John Locke, one of the greatest of English philosophers, was born on August 29, 1632. He spent his childhood near Pensford in southwestern England, where his father was a country lawyer.

After attending the Westminster School and Oxford (where he became a lecturer), Locke had a brief taste of the diplomatic service in Europe. He returned to England in 1666 to study medicine. Shortly afterward he became family adviser and physician to the Earl of Shaftesbury. Shaftesbury was an important public figure but an enemy of the Stuart kings. When Shaftesbury fell into disfavor with the government, Locke was forced to flee to Holland. In Holland he studied, wrote, and discussed philosophy with friends. King James II offered to pardon him, but Locke refused the offer because he had committed no crime. He did not return to England until the revolution of 1688, when William and Mary came to the throne.

Locke published his famous *Essay Concerning Human Understanding* in 1690. In it he expressed the belief that man's mind at birth is a blank tablet and that almost all his knowledge is gained from experience. This theory is called empiricism.

Lock's most important political work is his *Two Treatises Concerning Government* (1690). In these treatises Locke challenged the idea of the divine right of kings and said that a government should exist only with the consent of the governed. Locke believed that a ruler who loses the confidence of the people has lost the right to govern them.

Locke's political ideas had a strong influence on the American colonies. His belief that a government must protect its citizens' "natural rights" to life, liberty, and property is the basis of American government. Thomas Jefferson used many of Locke's ideas in the Declaration of Independence.

For many years Locke's health was weak, but he kept up a busy schedule of writing and philosophical discussion until his death on October 28, 1704. Among his other works are *Letter for Toleration* (1689), *Some Thoughts Concerning Education* (1693), and *The Reasonableness of Christianity* (1695).

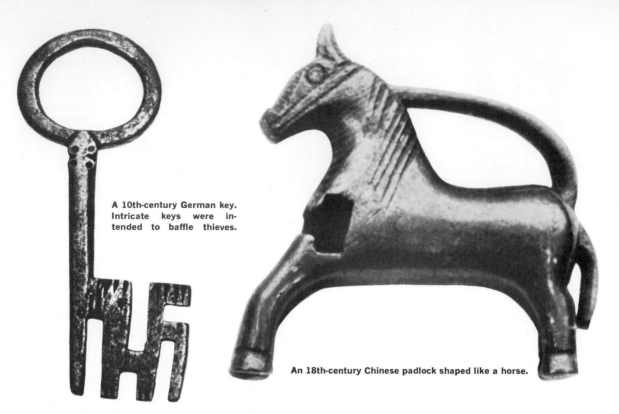

A 10th-century German key. Intricate keys were intended to baffle thieves.

An 18th-century Chinese padlock shaped like a horse.

LOCKS AND KEYS

As soon as early man had a few possessions, he began to worry about keeping them safe. He rolled a large stone in front of the opening of his cave to protect his food supply and animal skins while he was away hunting. Thousands of years passed before even a very small improvement was made in this system of protection.

Historians do not know exactly when the first lock was used to bar a door. The Assyrians and other early peoples locked their doors with personal seals. They tied a rope to a peg in the doorpost and covered the knot with clay. The clay was stamped with the owner's seal, which was covered with pictures of the Assyrian gods. The thief who broke the seal was supposedly in danger from the anger of the gods. Also, when the owner found his seal broken he could report it at once to the proper authorities.

The Egyptians used a lock that depended on more than respect for property or fear of magic. The Egyptian lock was made up of a wooden bolt that fitted into a slot. Movable wooden pins known as **tumblers** were fastened in the top of the slot. When the bolt slid into place, the wooden tumblers dropped into

holes cut in the bolt. The bolt was held fast until the tumblers were lifted up with a key. The first known key did not look at all like a key as we know it today. It looked more like a giant-sized toothbrush with pegs instead of bristles on one end. When the key was put in the slot, the pegs went under the tumblers. By raising the key, the tumblers were forced out of the bolt, which was then easily drawn back.

The Egyptian key could only be used on that side of the door where the bolt was placed. The Greeks discovered a way to slide back the bolt from the other side of the door. They slid their key through a hole in the door above the bolt until its tip touched a notch in the bolt on the inside. The Greek key was a curved bar, in shape and size much like a farmer's sickle. Some of these keys were over 3 feet long and were carried over the shoulder. By jerking or twisting the long handle, the bolt could be slid back.

With their wonderful talent for combining the inventions of many civilizations, the Romans became the most skillful lockmakers of the ancient world. They made locks that included features of both the Egyptian pin-tumbler lock and the Greek keyhole lock. They added another important improvement. The pegs on the end of the Roman keys were cut in many different shapes. Now the thief had to make a key with pins not only in the right position and of the right length but also of the right shape.

The Romans worked out a small lock that could be carried from place to place. We call such locks **padlocks** today. The small padlock keys were often made in the shape of rings, so they could be worn on a finger. The beautiful designs and shapes in which they were cut made them very handsome rings indeed. The Romans were very practical people, however, and it was not just for appearance that they made keys into rings. They had no pockets in their robes where they could carry keys.

The Romans also may have invented **wards** in locks. A ward is a guard put on the inside of the lock. Only a key with notches or slots cut in it to match the wards can move around them and slide the bolt. Unfortunately, ward locks are easy to open because a straight piece of wire can move around the guard. However, ward locks are still in use today for closets, cupboards, drawers, and doors to rooms.

After the fall of the Roman Empire there was no truly important advance in the art of lockmaking for nearly 1,000 years. Instead, locksmiths of medieval Europe made the wards of their locks more and more elaborate. The keys were cut in intricate and often symbolic designs. Even the **bits** (the notches in the key) were made into odd shapes. The keys were works of art, but they did not make

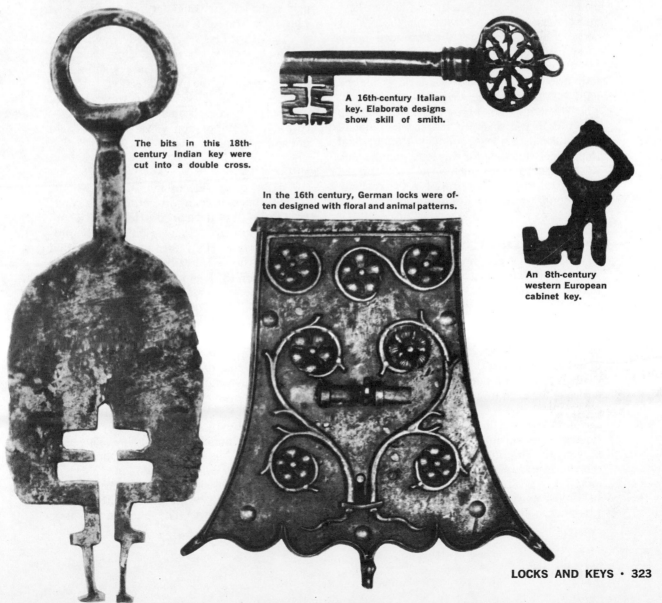

The bits in this 18th-century Indian key were cut into a double cross.

A 16th-century Italian key. Elaborate designs show skill of smith.

In the 16th century, German locks were often designed with floral and animal patterns.

An 8th-century western European cabinet key.

the locks any harder to pick. Opening a lock without the proper key is called **picking the lock**.

Since not much progress was being made in improving lock design, craftsmen invented some amazing ways to protect belongings. One famous example was a chest that held quite a surprise for the skillful thief who broke open the lock. Inside the chest was an empty tray with several holes for lifting the tray. When the burglar put his fingers into these holes, a spring snapped shut on his fingers and the thief was fastened tightly to the chest. There he remained until he was found. Another imaginative locksmith made a chest that shot a pistol directly at anyone touching the lock. The rightful owner knew how to unhook the pistol by turning a secret knob before using his key. Secret knobs and hidden keyholes were popular devices in those days because locks could not be depended upon.

Towards the end of the Renaissance, lockmakers made one improvement. They fitted a thin strip of metal inside the lock. When the bolt was in place, the strip fell into a notch. The bolt could not be moved until the strip was raised and dropped into another notch. This was called a **lever tumbler**. The keys had to be specially made for this lock, and the lock was harder to pick. But thieves soon learned that by putting a pointed tool in the keyhole, they could raise the tumbler and move the bolt.

▶ **THREE IMPORTANT LOCKMAKERS**

In 1778 a very important advance was made, using the idea of the lever tumbler. Robert Barron, an Englishman, made a lock with a lever tumbler, which had a double action. If the tumbler was pushed too high, it hit a bar on the bolt which kept the bolt from moving. Now a thief could not just flip up the tumbler and slide the bolt. The bars were really wards. But putting a bar on a different level for each tumbler made it harder for a thief to pick the lock with a **skeleton key**. A skeleton key is a long straight key with one slender tooth on the end. There is nothing to prevent the smooth key from passing around the wards and raising the tumbler of a simple lock.

Almost as soon as Barron had introduced his lock, Joseph Bramah (1748–1814)

worked out a very different kind of lock. Bramah did away with wards completely. Instead, his lock had two barrels. The inside barrel was made up of several sliding plates. These were notched in different places, and only the right key could raise them so they formed a flat surface. The inside barrel could then turn smoothly around and pull the bolt back.

In 1818 a third Englishman, Jeremiah Chubb, using the lever-tumbler principle, invented an almost pick-proof lock. Inside the lock casing, six tumblers had to be raised to exactly the right height, just as in Barron's lock. However, Chubb put in a detector tumbler that was sprung if any tumbler was raised too high. The detector tumbler jammed the lock. No matter how skillfully the thief jiggled the lock he could not free the tumblers. The lock stayed fastened until the owner released it with his key. The only way to open a Chubb lock when the detector lever was working was to put in the right key and turn it in the opposite of the usual direction.

These English locks worked very well, but they were so complicated to make that they cost a great deal of money. Most people could not afford them.

▶ **MODERN LOCKS**

On the other side of the Atlantic, in the United States, a young inventor, Linus Yale, Jr. (1821–68), developed a lock that could effectively protect belongings and also be produced cheaply. His father was also a gifted inventor, who had already set up a lockmaking business. In 1861 and 1865 young Linus received patents for the **pin tumbler cylinder lock**, which with modern improvements is still the most secure key-operated lock. Its small, flat key and basically simple parts made mass production possible. A high-security lock was at last available to everyone.

Amazingly enough, the Yale lock was based on the ancient Egyptian tumbler lock that had been developed nearly 4,000 years before. The Egyptian lock worked by raising a series of pin tumblers with a key. The tumblers in the Yale lock are set in holes in a rotating plug or cylinder. The plug is enclosed in a **shell**, or case. The pins lie partly in the plug and partly in the shell, with springs pressing them down. The plug cannot turn past the pins. But a slice called a **joint** has been cut across each pin at a different point. The joint divides the pin into two parts, the lower pin and the upper **driver**. When the correct key is put in the keyhole, its point passes under the pins and raises them until they rest in the notches, or bits, of the key. Each pin is pushed up just enough to make the joint between driver and pin match with the boundary between the plug and the shell. The key can then turn the plug. When the plug turns, a **cam**, or small arm, on the inner end of the plug also turns and pulls back the bolt of the lock.

The most common cylinder lock has five pin chambers. It is very difficult to operate this lock without the proper key. If a key with incorrect bits is put in the lock, it will not raise the pins to the right height to make the joints match. The plug remains blocked, and the bolt stays in place. These locks can be made with additional pin chambers for an even higher degree of security.

The pin tumbler cylinder lock has another important advantage in this day of tall office buildings, sprawling factories, and large hotels. A whole system of locks can be designed that one special key called a **master key** can open. A second joint is added to one or more pins. When the master key raises that pin, the plug moves around the second joint. By adding a third joint, the locks can be opened by a third key called the **grand master**. Thus the owner of a building can open every door

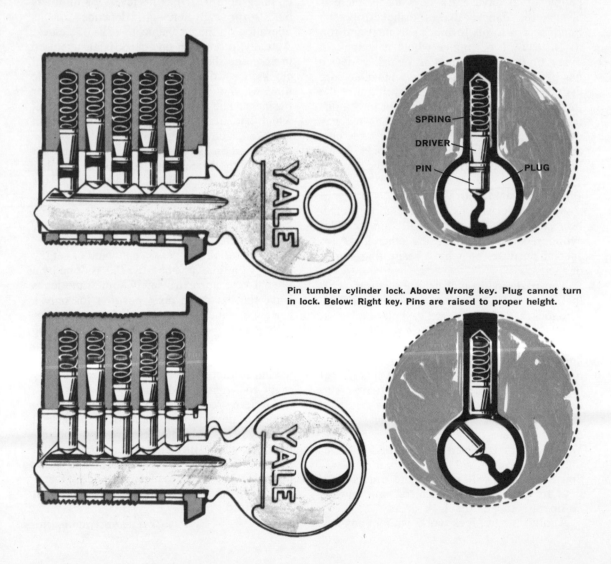

Pin tumbler cylinder lock. Above: Wrong key. Plug cannot turn in lock. Below: Right key. Pins are raised to proper height.

SPRING
DRIVER
PIN
PLUG

IMPORTANT DEFINITIONS

Bits—Notches cut in a key to allow it to pass around the wards, operate levers, or raise pins in a lock.

Master key—Key specially designed to open all the locks in one system.

Skeleton key—Key with most of the bits cut away so that it is not blocked by the wards.

Tumbler—Peg that must be moved before a lock can be opened.

Ward—Metal fence, or guard, put on the inside of the lock.

with the grand master. The maintenance personnel can open the locks only on the floors to which they are assigned. The keys of individuals open only their own rooms.

Many huge buildings have so many locks that have to be changed as people move in and out that they hire their own locksmiths. Since people often have extra keys made, there is always the danger that a dishonest person might return to his former apartment and rob it. Instead of putting a whole new lock in every time an apartment is rented, a device has been developed called the **removable core cylinder**. The cylinder can be taken out of the lock with a special key and be put into a different lock. The former tenant has no way of knowing which apartment lock his key now fits. The owner can change the locks in his building without having to reset the pins.

Other Types of Modern Locks

Most modern locks that give good protection are based on the Yale pin tumbler cylinder. However, there are other locks for special purposes that have interesting stories of their own.

The **partnership** lock is one of these. This lock is used for safe-deposit boxes in banks. The lock has two separate keyholes and must be worked with two separate keys. One is kept by the person who rents the safe-deposit box and the other by the bank itself. The guard on duty in the safe-deposit vault first puts in and turns his key. This raises the lever tumblers to a certain height. The tumblers are not high enough to throw the bolt, but they are high enough to clear the way for the renter's key. When this key is turned in the second keyhole, the levers are raised and the bolt thrown. Since the lock will not operate unless both keys are used, the two "partners" must always co-operate to get the lock open.

Another sort of lock works without any key

at all. This is the familiar **combination** lock, which can be opened only by turning a dial to the right numbers or letters. There is no key to be lost or stolen or copied. There is no keyhole through which picking tools can be inserted. The mathematical odds against guessing the right order of numbers or letters are very great.

A combination lock works this way. When the dial is moved the correct distance in the right direction, a series of levers, or disc tumblers, move one by one into an open position. When all the tumblers are lined up, another turn of the dial will move an arm that turns the locking device.

The only truly pick-proof lock is the **time lock**, which is used on the great vaults of banking houses. It has no levers or tumblers but, surprisingly enough, depends for its operation on the mechanical works of a clock. Actually, more than one clock is always used in case one should break down. These special clocks are wound until their dials show the time when the vault or safe is to open for business. The clocks are set in a large case, which has a hole in one side. When the vault is locked, a cover slides automatically over the hole. As soon as the clocks reach the time set for opening, the cover slides back. A steel bar connected to the lock mechanism enters the hole and fastens onto the handle on the outside of the vault door. The handle can then be turned to move back the bolt, and the door can be opened.

No unauthorized person can wind or set the clocks of a time lock because this is done by a special key. For extra safety some time locks leave the bar in an open position for only a certain number of minutes before automatically locking it in place again. The timing device can be set for different periods between openings. For instance, the clocks can be wound so that they will not open from Friday night to Monday morning.

Modern research and engineering have helped to develop many new locks for special security needs. Among these are keys controlling the firing mechanism of rockets and missiles. The uses of locks are almost innumerable, but today's locks provide greater protection in a greater variety of ways than ever before.

YALE AND TOWNE, INC.

LOCOMOTIVES

Few machines have fascinated people more than the locomotive, and few have had a more exciting history. In the 19th century the locomotive in effect made the world smaller by making travel faster. Overland travel times were cut from days to hours. Locomotives also made it possible to ship heavy loads of freight overland. Despite the competition of airplanes, trucks, and ships, the locomotive is still one of the most important means of transportation.

▶ **TYPES OF LOCOMOTIVES**

A locomotive is a self-propelled vehicle that draws cars over railroad tracks. It is basically an engine connected to wheels. For this reason, locomotives are often called engines. There are three chief types of locomotives: steam, electric, and diesel. All types except electric locomotives manufacture their own power. Electric locomotives get their power from third rails or overhead wires.

Steam Locomotives. Steam locomotives were the first type invented, and for three fourths of a century they were the only locomotives. Steam locomotives use the heat energy of burning fuel to turn water into steam. The expanding steam pushes a piston back and forth in a cylinder. The piston turns the driving wheels through a system of rods and cranks. Fuel and water are carried in a special car called a tender, which is coupled right behind the locomotive.

The driving wheels are the ones that move the locomotive. They may be anywhere from 3 to 7 feet in diameter. Steam locomotives usually also have smaller wheels in front of and behind their big drivers. These small wheels help carry the locomotive's weight and guide it around curves. They do not help to drive the locomotive, since they have no power. The small wheels are set in frames called **trucks**, which are pivoted underneath the engine frame so that they can swing right or left.

Steam locomotives are classified according to the number and arrangement of their wheels. For instance, a locomotive with four small leading, or pilot, wheels, six driving wheels, and two trailing wheels is a 4-6-2. Switching locomotives usually have only driving wheels. These locomotives are used to move freight and passenger cars in the railroad yards.

CLASSIFICATION OF STEAM LOCOMOTIVES
(by wheel arrangement)

2-6-0	Mogul	4-4-2	Atlantic
2-6-2	Prairie	4-6-0	Ten-wheeler
2-8-0	Consolidation	4-6-2	Pacific
2-8-2	Mikado	4-6-4	Hudson
2-8-4	Berkshire	4-8-0	Twelve-wheeler
2-10-0	Decapod	4-8-2	Mountain
2-10-2	Santa Fe	4-8-4	Northern
2-10-4	Texas	4-10-2	Southern Pacific
4-4-0	American	4-12-2	Union Pacific

Note: Locomotives with a two-wheeled leading truck were used for freight. Locomotives with four leading wheels were usually used for passenger or fast freight service. The 4-4-0 American type, however, was used for all kinds of service.

Steam locomotives are the simplest type and the easiest to build. They last a long time and are very dependable. They can work even when overloaded. They are expensive to operate, however, for normally they can put to use only about 6 to 8 percent of the energy in their fuel. Steam locomotives also need frequent servicing, since boilers and fireboxes get dirty and must be cleaned out. The up-and-down motion of the heavy main and side rods and the thrust of the pistons tend to make steam locomotives pound the track with hammerlike blows each time the wheels go round. This is bad for the track. For these reasons steam locomotives have been replaced by other types in many parts of the world.

Diesel Locomotives. An oil-burning internal-combustion engine is the heart of the diesel locomotive. The oil is not burned under a boiler to make steam. Instead, it is sprayed into the cylinders of the engine, where it burns with almost explosive force. The rapidly expanding gases from the burning oil drive the pistons. The diesel engine usually drives an electric generator, supplying power to electric motors that turn the wheels. In some locomotives the diesel engine turns the wheels directly through gears or a hydraulic transmission.

Diesels can run without servicing for much longer periods than steam locomotives. They are also much more efficient. Diesels convert from 24 to 40 percent of the energy in their fuel into useful work. Also, diesels damage the track less at high speeds. On the other hand, a diesel costs far more than a steamer of equal power, it cannot haul as heavy a load as fast, and it cannot stand being overloaded except for very short periods.

Electric Locomotives. Powerful electric motors connected to the wheels drive electric locomotives. Power comes from a central power plant through a third rail or an overhead wire. Contacts on the locomotive pick up the electricity. Big transformers and rectifiers inside the locomotive change the current from the powerhouse to the form best suited to the motors. In many electric locomotives the driving wheels are set in swiveling trucks underneath the body of the locomotive, like the pilot of a steam locomotive. The motors are generally mounted right on the trucks and drive the wheels through gears.

Electric locomotives are fast, powerful, and dependable. They make no smoke or fumes, so they are good for use in cities and built-up areas. But it is very expensive to install an electric power system. Electric railroads can pay their own way only where electricity is cheap and there is enough traffic to earn money.

Gas-Turbine Locomotives. A gas-turbine locomotive looks like a diesel and works in much the same way. But instead of a diesel engine it has a rapidly spinning turbine as the source of power. The turbine is driven by expanding gases from burning oil. Some turbines burn other fuels, such as powdered coal.

Gas-turbine locomotives can haul heavy trains at high speeds, and they cost less to keep in shape than either diesels or steam locomotives. However, they are very expensive to build, for a turbine must be made as carefully as a fine watch. And gas-turbine locomotives use about twice as much fuel as diesels of the same power.

TWO FAMOUS EARLY LOCOMOTIVES

"STOURBRIDGE LION" (1829)

The first locomotive to run on a regular railroad in the United States was the English-built "Stourbridge Lion." This engine was given a trial run on a short railroad line in Pennsylvania on August 8, 1829. However, the engine proved to be too heavy for the flimsy tracks, and it was not put into regular service.

"BEST FRIEND OF CHARLESTON" (1830)

The first locomotive to perform regular service on an American railroad was the "Best Friend of Charleston," which went into scheduled operation on December 25, 1830. The "Best Friend of Charleston" was destroyed by a boiler explosion the following year, but it was later repaired and restored to operation.

The locomotive was born in England early in the 19th century. Two earlier inventions, the railway, or "road of rails," and the steam engine, were combined to produce it.

Since the early 17th century, horse-drawn wagons had rolled on crude systems of wooden tracks in England's mining districts. At first these tracks were simply broad planks nailed along wooden cross-pieces, wide enough apart to fit the wagon wheels. In time, improvements were made. To save wood, narrow rails replaced the wide planks. Flanges, or projecting rims, were added to the wagon wheels to keep them from slipping off the rails. Iron strips were fastened to the tops of the rails to keep them from wearing out.

The steam engine, the locomotive's other ancestor, was invented about the beginning of the 18th century. The first steam engine could not possibly have been used for locomotives. It was big and clumsy and slow, with a boiler the size of a small house. It was good only for pumping water out of mines. Then James Watt (1736–1819) made a number of inventions that changed the steam engine. Thanks to Watt, steam engines became steadily smaller, lighter, faster, and more powerful. By the end of the 18th century, steam engines were being used to drive machines in factories and to do many other kinds of work. It occurred to many people that steam could be used to pull loaded wagons as well as to drive machines in a factory.

The First Locomotive

The first locomotive designed to pull loads on a track was invented by an adventurous mine engineer from Cornwall named Richard Trevithick (1771–1833). (Cornwall is the region at the southwestern tip of England.) Trevithick had already invented a new type of steam engine that worked at high pressure. He had also built a steam-powered carriage that ran on the road. In 1804, together with his cousin Andrew Vivian, Trevithick built a locomotive to run on a mine railway.

The tiny locomotive had just one cylinder, which turned the driving wheels through gears. It looked like an oversize mechanical toy. But on its first run it is said to have pulled five mine cars carrying 10 tons of iron and 70 passengers who went along for the exciting ride. In 1808 Trevithick built another locomotive, which he called "Catch-Me-Who-Can." He took this locomotive to London, where he set it up on a circular track. For a 1-shilling fee, thrill-seeking passengers could ride on open cars behind the engine.

Trevithick's locomotives had two features that were to become standard for steam locomotives. One was piping the exhaust steam from the cylinders up the smokestack. This gave the fire a better draft—that is, it sucked more air into the firebox. The fire burned hotter and made steam faster. The other feature was the use of smooth driving wheels on smooth rails.

Strangely enough, many people refused to believe that a smooth wheel could grip a smooth rail firmly enough to pull a heavy load, even though Trevithick had proved that it could. They feared that the wheels would just spin around and the locomotive stand still. But in 1813 William Hedley's locomotive "Puffing Billy" proved again, and without a doubt, that with enough weight on them, smooth wheels will take hold of smooth rails instead of slipping and spinning. However, a number of inventors designed and built locomotives that were driven by a toothed wheel, or **pinion**, that meshed with a toothed third rail, or **rack**. This principle is still used on a few railroads that climb very steep mountainsides. But for ordinary use, smooth wheels on smooth rails have plenty of pulling power. And a smooth-rail system is much cheaper to build.

A few mines around the coal center of Newcastle began to use locomotives to haul coal from the mine to the docks, where it was loaded onto ships. With all their faults, locomotives cost less to keep up than horses, and they burned cheap coal from the mines instead of eating expensive grain that had to be bought from farmers.

A sharp-eyed engine-wright (mechanic) named George Stephenson (1781–1848) followed these developments closely. Stephenson came of a family so poor that they could not afford to send him to school. Instead, he went to work when he was very young. At 14 he became assistant fireman for the big pumping engine at a coal mine. Stephenson was fascinated by steam engines and wanted to learn more about them. He went to night school,

How did the cowcatcher get its name?

Farm animals wandering onto the unfenced tracks were a constant problem for early American railroads. Colliding with a cow or pig could easily derail the light locomotives of that time—and often did. So in 1831 Isaac Dripps, master mechanic of a New Jersey railroad, fixed a V-shaped iron framework to the front of a locomotive. The iron V passed underneath the body of the stray animal, lifted it, and pushed it off the track to one side. Because it caught cows in time to keep the engine from going off the track, Dripps's invention became known as a cowcatcher.

where he learned to read and write. Then he studied everything he could about science and engineering.

Stephenson studied the locomotives being used at other mines. He became convinced that he could build a better locomotive. The owners of the coal mine where he worked put up the money. Stephenson's first locomotive, the "Blucher," began hauling coal in 1814. In 1815 he built an improved locomotive. He kept on turning out locomotives, each one a little better than the last one. In 1824 he was appointed chief engineer of the new Stockton & Darlington Railway, the world's first railroad to serve the public.

Englishmen gradually lost their fear of the new steam-powered trains. Railroads began looking for faster, more powerful locomotives. In 1829 a historic locomotive contest was held at Rainhill, near the great port of Liverpool. Men gathered from all over Europe to see the engines pull three times their own weight at a speed of not less than 10 miles an hour. Four engines were entered in the contest. One was the "Rocket," designed by Stephenson and his son Robert. Another, the "Novelty," was designed by John Ericsson, later famous as the designer of the Civil War ironclad *Monitor*.

On the appointed day, the gaily painted engines, with carefully measured quantities of fuel and water, steamed back and forth over the 2-mile course. The "Rocket" was the first to perform. It drew a load of 12¾ tons at 13.8 miles an hour. Without a load, the "Rocket" reached 29 miles an hour, a dizzying speed for those times. The "Rocket" was neither the strongest nor the fastest locomotive in the contest. But it was the most reliable mechanically, and so it was declared the winner.

The victorious "Rocket" was the first really practical locomotive, and it set the basic pattern of locomotive design for many years. It had two cylinders, directly coupled to cranks on the driving wheels. Through its horizontal boiler ran tubes that carried the hot gases from the firebox to the smokestack. This greatly increased the heating area and raised steam faster. Exhaust steam was sent up the smokestack to give better draft. A mechanical pump fed water to the boiler. Actually most of these features had been used before by other locomotive builders. But Stephenson was the first to put them all together in one locomotive.

Locomotives Come to the United States. The Rainhill Trials proved that steam locomotives were practical and reliable. But even before, men in several countries were interested in steam-powered railroads. In the United States a wealthy amateur inventor named John Stevens (1749–1838) built a tiny demonstration locomotive in 1825. The little one-cylinder locomotive, driven by a rack and pinion, ran around a circular track on Stevens' New Jersey estate. People came from near and far for free rides, but no one was interested in building a railroad. But within a few years locomotives were pulling trains on dozens of American railroads.

"Tom Thumb" Proves a Point. Some cautious businessmen, however, still preferred horses. Among them were the directors of the Baltimore & Ohio Railroad. Peter Cooper, a wealthy New Yorker who owned land along the B & O tracks, decided to show them the advantages of steam power. He put together a tiny locomotive, which he called "Tom Thumb." Since materials were hard to get, Cooper used old musket barrels for the boiler tubing. A mechanical blower supplied air to the fire. The whole locomotive was not much bigger than a modern handcar. Still, on a trial run in the summer of 1830 the little engine pushed a car with 36 passengers and performed well enough to convince the directors that their future lay with steam.

A short time later the owners of a stagecoach line challenged Cooper to race "Tom Thumb" against one of their best horses. Engine and horse each pulled an open railroad car full of passengers. At first the horse, a spirited gray, took the lead. Then the tiny steamer pulled ahead. Just as victory seemed certain, the belt that drove the engine's blower slipped off. The fire died down, steam pressure sank, and the tiny engine wheezed to a halt. While Cooper tried frantically to fix the belt, the horse pulled ahead again. By the time the damage was repaired, the horse had nearly reached the finish line. The next year, however, the B & O began buying steam locomotives.

Locomotives Grow Bigger and Better. Steam locomotives came into general use as railroads spread, and builders constantly improved them. Pilot wheels were added to guide locomotives around curves. Headlights permitted trains to run at night. Cabs protected engineers and firemen from the weather. More driving wheels were added as engines grew bigger and heavier. More steam was needed for better performance, so fireboxes were made larger. Trailing wheels were used to carry the weight of the firebox. Some locomotives were fitted with compound cylinders to save steam. After doing its work in one set of cylinders at high pressure, the steam drove another set of pistons in a pair of big low-pressure cylinders. At the end of the 19th century came the superheater, which dried out the steam as it left the boiler and greatly increased the engine's power.

Steam's First Rival. As early as 1842 a successful battery-operated electric locomotive was tried out in Scotland. But the electric locomotive could not become practical until a good source of power was developed.

Progress was rapid after the electric generator was perfected in 1873. During the 1880's electric motors were used in streetcars. In 1890 the world's first electric subway was opened in London. In 1895 the Baltimore & Ohio used an electric locomotive to pull trains through a long tunnel in the city of Baltimore —the first use of electric locomotives on a mainline railroad. Encouraged by this success, other railroads in the United States and Europe began to electrify parts of their main lines, particularly around cities, where the smoke of steam locomotives was a real problem. But the high cost of electrification limited

GEORGE STEPHENSON'S "ROCKET" (1829)

AMERICAN LOCOMOTIVE (1856)

NEW YORK CENTRAL RAILROAD'S "999"—FIRST LOCOMOTIVE TO BREAK 100 MILES PER HOUR (1893)

UNION PACIFIC RAILROAD'S "BIG BOY" (1941)

MODERN DIESEL-ELECTRIC LOCOMOTIVE

MODERN ELECTRIC LOCOMOTIVE

its use. The real rival of steam turned out to be diesel power.

The Diesel Takes Over. In 1924 a boxlike little locomotive could be seen switching freight cars in New York City. This was the first diesel locomotive in the United States. Diesel locomotives had already been used experimentally for a few years in Europe. During the 1920's a number of diesel switchers were built and used on both sides of the Atlantic.

Railroad men found that diesel locomotives were much simpler and cheaper to operate than steam locomotives. They had fewer controls. And they did not have to have their boilers and fireboxes cleaned out every few hundred miles—a hard and dirty job.

Diesels were first used for passenger service in the mid-1930's, when a few railroads used them to pull the new, high-speed streamlined trains. But they did not come into general use until after World War II. Then, within a few years, railroads began to change over to diesel power. Even some electrified stretches of railroad were changed to diesel operation.

The thing that turned the trick was the booster unit. This is like an extra locomotive, but without a cab for the engineer. The booster unit is coupled on behind the head unit and controlled from the cab. Two, three, or more booster units may be hitched up as needed if a heavy train is to be pulled. For light work, the cab unit may operate by itself. In this way railroads do not need to keep large fleets of locomotives of different sizes, as they did with steam locomotives. The small, switcher-type diesels may also be coupled together and controlled by one engineer.

Special Types of Locomotives

Mountain railroads, with their sharp curves and steep grades, needed special locomotives. These locomotives had to have great power, yet be able to swing around curves easily. To meet this need, articulated (jointed) locomotives were invented. An early articulated type was the "double-ender" built in 1865 by Robert Fairlee, an Englishman. It had two boilers, with one big firebox in the middle and a smokestack at each end. Two separate engines were underneath, pivoted so they could swing around curves.

A more successful type was invented by Anatole Mallet, a Swiss, in 1887. Mallet's locomotives had two engines under one big boiler. The Mallet, slow but very powerful, was widely used in the United States and Canada from 1904 until steam power went out of use. The Union Pacific Railroad's 4-8-8-4 Mallets were the largest steam locomotives ever built, weighing 1,208,750 pounds and measuring 133 feet long. The firebox alone was 18 feet long—as big as an ordinary room.

Logging railroads were nearly always rough, steep, and full of sharp curves. Gear-driven locomotives were built for these rough conditions. The best-known type was the Shay, which had two or three vertical cylinders on one side of the boiler. These cylinders drove a long, geared shaft that ran along the whole length of the locomotive and tender. The gears turned the driving wheels.

Industrial plants often used compressed-air switching locomotives to avoid smoke. These were like small steam locomotives, with big compressed-air tanks instead of boilers. When air pressure dropped, the engineer could refill the tank from pipelines along the tracks.

▶ EXPERIMENTAL LOCOMOTIVES

A number of experimental locomotives have been built. Few have been successful, usually because they cost too much to operate. Most experimental locomotives have been attempts to make a more efficient steam locomotive. During the last days of steam some railroads built and ran steam-turbine locomotives. Another design had V-type steam engines driving the axles through gears. This design did away with the main and side rods of an ordinary locomotive.

Scientists and engineers have long been interested in a nuclear-powered locomotive. Such a locomotive could probably run for half a year on one charge of fuel. As in submarines, a nuclear reactor would heat water to make steam, which would drive a turbine. If nuclear power becomes cheaper and oil scarcer, this may be the locomotive of the future.

FORREST CROSSEN
Former President
Rocky Mountain Railroad Club of Denver

See also DIESEL ENGINES; ELECTRIC MOTORS; RAILROADS; STEAM ENGINES; TURBINES.

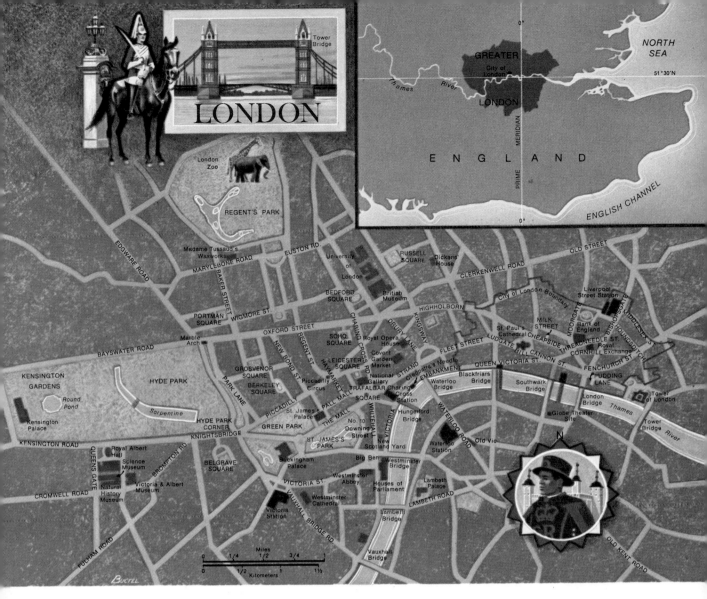

LONDON

LONDON

London is the capital of the United Kingdom and the most important city in the Commonwealth of Nations. It is a center of banking, business, and government. Parliament, the departments of state, the residence of the prime minister, and Buckingham Palace, where the Queen lives, are all in London.

London is one of the three largest cities in the world, ranking with Tokyo and New York City. In the early 1960's over 8,000,000 people lived in Greater London, which includes the city's suburbs and parts of the neighboring counties.

London means something different to each Londoner. To one Londoner it may mean the borough, or area, in which he lives. To another it may mean the West End, the shopping and theatrical center of London. To still another Londoner it may mean Westminster, the seat of government. To many visitors London is "the City," the original and most historic part of London. To sailors from all over the world, London means the Port of London with its miles of wharves and docks.

The most colorful and distinctive of Londoners are the "cockneys." True cockneys are people born within the sound of Bow bells—the bells of St. Mary-Le-Bow, an old London church. The cockneys have a special accent of their own, and their speech is difficult for visitors, and even other Englishmen, to understand. A cockney often leaves the *h* off the beginning of a word. He will say, for example, " 'Aymarket" for Haymarket. But he often puts an *h* in front of a vowel at the beginning of a word, so that Oxford Street becomes "Hoxford Street."

Not all Londoners are English-born. Many Italian and French people live in the district known as Soho. West Indians have settled in such parts of the city as Notting Hill. Some Chinese live near the docks.

Government

The government of London is divided into many units. Greater London, the largest unit, covers 616 square miles. It includes the City of London and 32 London boroughs. The boroughs occupy the county of Middlesex and large parts of Essex, Kent, Surrey, and Hertfordshire. The Greater London Council provides services required by the entire area. Local government within London is under the direction of the borough councils. The average population of a borough is 250,000. The borough council supervises education, health, and welfare agencies.

▶ HOW LONDON GREW

It is easier to understand London if we understand its history. London was not built according to a plan. It grew from many separate towns. As people built houses between them these towns spread until they ran together to make a giant city.

When the Romans came to Britain in A.D. 43, they built a town called Londinium on the banks of the Thames. They built a wall around it and put the first bridge across the Thames. Traders and craftsmen came to live in Londinium, and by the 3rd century A.D. about 15,000 people lived inside its walls.

After the Romans left Britain in the 5th century, London was deserted. But the site was too important to stay empty. In the 9th century King Alfred the Great (849–99?) rebuilt the town, repaired the old Roman wall, and put up new defenses. By the time William the Conqueror (1027?–87) invaded England in 1066, London was a stronghold inhabited by people used to running their own affairs. The Londoners accepted William as their king because he gave them a charter that promised them they could go on enjoying their independent rights and privileges.

William built a castle guarding London Bridge. This fortress, the White Tower, was the beginning of the Tower of London. Later, outer walls and other towers were built around it. No one could break in or out. The Tower was the home of the kings and later became a prison. The Tower prison is a place of grim memories. Many royal or noble prisoners accused of plotting against kings and queens were imprisoned or killed there. Visitors can still see the place where Queen Elizabeth I's mother, Anne Boleyn (1507–36), was beheaded on Tower Green.

Today the Tower is a museum where the Crown Jewels are kept. Huge black ravens perch on the walls, and colorfully dressed Yeomen Warders of the Tower, called Beefeaters, guide people around. Yeomen of the Guard, also known as Beefeaters, are the monarch's bodyguards.

The old City ran along the Thames from the Tower to just beyond St. Paul's Cathedral. The first cathedral was begun in the 11th century on the spot where an earlier church had burned down. Today's cathedral stands in the same place.

During the Middle Ages, London became the richest city in England. It was an important port and a center of shipping and crafts. Since it was no longer dangerous to live outside the walls, suburbs began springing up. Merchants and nobles built fine houses along the Strand, which is near the bank of the Thames and runs west toward Westminster. They built mansions on Fleet Street, too, where a little river ran into the Thames. Now Fleet Street is the center of newspaper publishing in England.

As trade increased, the walled City grew very crowded. Craftsmen lived over their shops and sold goods along the narrow, crooked streets. Shops where the same kinds of goods were sold were clustered together. Many street names reflect this old custom: Milk Street, Goldsmith's Row, Bread Street, Pudding Lane, and others.

A fire in a Pudding Lane shop started the Great London Fire of 1666. The fire raged through the wooden, thatch-roofed buildings for 5 days. The King sent soldiers to help put the fire out, but it burned down most of the old City between the Tower and St. Paul's Cathedral.

The fire was the second disaster in a row to strike London. Old London was a dirty, overcrowded place. About 500,000 people lived in the City and its suburbs. Poor people lived along the Thames east of the Tower, behind the docks. North and west of the wall, slums had filled the fields and grown up between the mansions. The plague broke out in one of these slums, St. Giles. During 1665 it killed almost 100,000 people—or about one out of every five Londoners.

These two tragedies changed London. The city was rebuilt according to new laws that were meant to check slums and cut down fire hazards. From then on, houses had to be built of brick or stone instead of wood. Streets were widened. But the city government was not bold enough to follow the advice of England's great architect, Sir Christopher Wren (1632–1723). Wren offered a master plan for rebuilding the whole city in a more spacious, modern way. It was rejected.

Still, Wren got his chance to change the face of London. He rebuilt about 50 City churches, as well as hospitals and other buildings. Most important, he designed the magnificent St. Paul's Cathedral that still stands today.

Among the City's other major landmarks are the Royal Exchange, which is topped by large golden grasshoppers, and the world-famous Bank of England, completed in 1734. The bank is on Threadneedle Street and is often called The Old Lady of Threadneedle Street. Every morning men wearing dignified business suits and black bowler hats and carrying rolled umbrellas come to work in the office buildings of the City. At night they go home again, and the business heart of the United Kingdom is quiet.

Much of the City that escaped bombing during World War II dates from the Great Fire of 1666. After the fire many suburbs were built around the City. London grew west along the Strand to join another town, Westminster.

▶ **WESTMINSTER**

Westminster is the most important of all the villages that became part of Greater London. In the Middle Ages, Anglo-Saxon monks built an abbey on the Thames near the present Westminster Abbey. Kings have been crowned in the Abbey since William the Conqueror's day, and many famous Englishmen are buried there. In it is the Tomb of the Unknown Soldier. Close by, King Edward the Confessor (1002?–66) built his royal palace. Westminster has remained the seat of England's government ever since. The Houses of Parliament stand where King Edward's palace once stood. Victoria Tower is at one end of the huge building, and the clock tower of Big Ben is at the other end. Big Ben strikes the hour in tones that can be heard far away.

Other palaces arose in Westminster. King Henry VIII (1491–1547) lived at Whitehall. Later this palace burned down except for the banquet hall, which is now a museum. The palace's name lives on in the name of the broad street leading to the Houses of Parliament. Most government offices are on Whitehall, and on a small street running off from it is one of England's most famous addresses—No. 10 Downing Street, the home of the prime minister.

A little farther west, Henry VIII converted an old hospital into St. James's Palace. The British court is still known as the Court of St.

London businessmen strolling in the City, London's business district.

James, although the royal family has made its London home in Buckingham Palace for more than a century. King Henry fenced off the land around St. James's to make a deer park where he could hunt. Part of his deer park became Hyde Park. Between the palace and the soldier's parade ground near Whitehall is St. James's Park. These and other parks give Londoners pleasant green places in which they can relax and their children can play. At the Marble Arch corner of Hyde Park, people gather to listen to soapbox orators make speeches on many different subjects.

King William III (1650–1702) moved to another palace because he hated city life. London was often foggy then because people heated their homes with coal-burning fires. To get away from the bad city air, William lived in a palace in the country village of Kensington. Now Kensington, like Westminster, is a busy section deep in Greater London. The King's gardens, Kensington Gardens, became a public park near Hyde Park. The adventures of Peter Pan, in the story by Sir James Barrie, begin in Kensington Gardens. Today children play around the statue of Peter Pan in the park.

Queen Elizabeth II's London home is Buckingham Palace. The palace is between Hyde Park and Westminster. It became the royal residence in the 19th century. Guards in red coats and tall black bearskin hats parade up and down in front of the palace. One of the sights of London is the changing of the guard each morning. Londoners and visitors throng to watch the colorful ceremony.

By the 16th century, Westminster and the old walled City had grown together and swallowed up the suburbs between. People who wanted country houses had to go northwest of Westminster. Today the West End is the glittering London of fancy shops, theaters, restaurants, and hotels.

▶ THE WEST END

The population began spilling over the City's ancient boundaries soon after the Great Fire of 1666. Merchants whose homes had burned built new ones west of the City. This part of London is still called the West End. It has wide, gracious streets. Many of its stately homes surround squares planted with trees, lawns, and flowers and divided by graveled paths. Some of these squares are still set off by iron railings and can be used only by the people who live in the houses around them. Others, such as Russell Square and Grosvenor Square, are open to anyone. Since most of the houses are too big and expensive for private families, they are now office buildings, apartment houses, or private hotels.

Today Knightsbridge and Marylebone are in the heart of the West End. But during the 18th century they were some distance from London. Travel was dangerous. The roads were deserted and unlighted. Highwaymen often robbed coaches. If the robbers were caught, they were hanged publicly on Tyburn gallows, near where Marble Arch now stands at the corner of Hyde Park and Oxford Street. Marble Arch is a well-known stop on the Underground (subway), where people get off in order to shop at Selfridge's, London's biggest department store.

London streets were poorly lighted until gaslights were installed in the early 19th century. This was the Regency period, the time when the Prince Regent, later King George IV (1762–1830), was the leader of London society. During this period London's fashionable West End developed. Many landmarks bear the name Regent. Regent's Park in northwestern London is one. The London Zoo is also there.

The architect who designed the park, John Nash (1752–1835), replaced a mass of twisted, narrow streets with a "Royal Mile," a graceful, curving avenue between Regent's Park and Piccadilly. He named it Regent Street for his sponsor. The place where it joins Piccadilly is Piccadilly Circus.

Piccadilly Circus is one of London's three main traffic centers. The others are the Bank, in the City near the Bank of England, and Charing Cross, near the Westminster end of the Strand. "Circus" is the Latin word for circle. Regent Street, Shaftesbury Avenue, and the Haymarket (which once really was a hay market) all lead into the Circus. Londoners say that if you stand there long enough, you are sure to meet everybody you know. All around are theaters and movie houses, including Drury Lane, London's oldest theater. Neon signs light the Circus, and advertising signs cover the buildings. People, cars, buses, and tall, black London taxis jam the circular street. They swing around a concrete traffic island where flower girls used to sell violets. On top of the fountain is a statue commonly called Eros (after the Greek god of love). It is a landmark for tourists and a mascot for Londoners.

West of Regent Street, toward Hyde Park, are the hotels, restaurants, and foreign embassies of the Mayfair district. East of Regent Street lies Soho. This is the foreign district. Though Soho is being rebuilt, parts of it are still a maze of little courts and dark, narrow streets. It is full of coffeehouses and little restaurants where visitors can get interesting foreign food.

If you walk east along Piccadilly from the Circus, you come to Leicester Square. This was once a field where gentlemen fought duels. Now it is the heart of the movie and theater district.

Still further east is Covent Garden (named for a convent garden), where the Royal Opera House stands. Near Covent Garden is one of the great London markets, which sells fruits, vegetables, and flowers. In the early morning it is a very busy place.

Going south along Haymarket from Piccadilly Circus, you come to another London landmark—Trafalgar Square. This square is named in honor of Nelson's victory over the French at the Battle of Trafalgar in 1805. In the center is a tall column topped by a statue of Admiral Horatio Nelson (1758–1805). The statue is surrounded by great fountains, stone lions, and pigeons tame enough to sit on your hand while you feed them. The National Gallery is on one side of the square.

People who disagree with the government sometimes hold rowdy demonstrations in Trafalgar Square, and the police have to be called in to keep order. On Sundays people who want to make speeches and protest sometimes go to Marble Arch, in a corner of Hyde Park.

The Strand runs into Trafalgar Square from the east, and Whitehall goes off to the south. Near Trafalgar Square is the Victoria Embankment—a park-lined drive along the Thames River. Here is another landmark, Cleopatra's Needle, an Egyptian obelisk found in the sand near the Nile. One just like it stands in New York City's Central Park. Until recently the headquarters of London's Metropolitan Police at Scotland Yard stood on the Embankment near Westminster Bridge. Although their new building is in another

Piccadilly Circus, the heart of London's entertainment area.

location, it is still called Scotland Yard. The police are called bobbies, after Sir Robert Peel, who founded the force in 1829.

▶ THE EAST END

While rich people developed the West End, working people built homes east of the City. In Queen Elizabeth's time slums began to grow up behind the shipyards below London Bridge. These shipyards were building the ships that explored the New World and fought Spain, and they needed workers. Workers' suburbs swallowed up such villages as Bethnal Green and spread east along the Thames. This part of London is called the East End. Its houses are smaller, lower, and often crowded

A view of the Thames River and the Houses of Parliament.

Left: Many parts of the City of London have been rebuilt since World War II. Right: Trafalgar Square, with the monument of Lord Nelson.

together. Many were built in the early 19th century, before people realized the need for town planning or proper sanitation. Along with cockneys, many people from other lands live and work in the East End.

THE PORT AND THE RIVER

Many of the people who work on the docks and sail the ships live in the East End. London has been a great port since Roman times. Sailing ships used to anchor in the Pool of London, downstream from London Bridge. The ships unloaded their cargoes at the city wharves. In the Middle Ages the main wharf was Billingsgate, near the Tower. At Billingsgate there is a fish market dating from the 9th century. Fish sellers sometimes quarreled so rudely that the word "Billingsgate" became a way of describing rude language.

Today's big ships can no longer use the Pool of London, though small steamers still come up with the tide and use the old wharves. The big ships now unload cargoes from every part of the world in new, modern docks farther downstream. The newest of these, the King George V Dock, can take ships up to 30,000 tons. Every year goods worth several billion dollars are imported and exported through London.

The best way to explore the river is to take a sightseeing boat. Boats start from the piers at Westminster and Charing Cross and sail past the Tower and under the impressive Tower Bridge (built in 1894). They sail through the Port of London down to the Royal Naval College at Greenwich. You can look upriver and see the many bridges that tie London north of the Thames to sections on the south bank of the Thames, such as Southwark and Lambeth.

LONDON BRIDGES AND TRANSPORTATION

Long ago most Londoners used the Thames as their main highway, for no part of London was far from the river. Many little boats carried people up and down, and houses near the Thames had private landings with stairs to the river. It was pleasanter to go by boat than through the dirty, crowded streets.

To get across the Thames, people used London Bridge, upstream from the Tower. Along the waterfront at the south end of the bridge, in Southwark, rich men built man-

sions, and slums grew up between them. Today Southwark is the site of the Old Vic theater, where people go to see performances of Shakespeare's plays.

People also got across the river by ferryboat. One went from Westminster to Lambeth, where the Archbishop of Canterbury has his palace.

Until 1750, when Westminster Bridge was finished, the only bridge was London Bridge. Old London Bridge had houses built on it. It was narrow, crowded, and jammed with carriages and people. In the mid-18th century the houses and shops were torn down to widen London Bridge and make it safer. In 1769 a third bridge, Blackfriar's Bridge, was opened. During the 19th century more bridges were built, including railway bridges to take the traffic to the new London stations. Today London has several great railroad stations, to which trains come from all over the country, as well as Heathrow International Airport, one of the largest in the world.

One of the best views of the Thames, the dome of St. Paul's, and the spires of the City churches is from the footbridge, Hungerford Bridge. It is part of the railway bridge that carries trains to Charing Cross Station, near the Westminster end of the Strand.

Coaches, Buses, and the Underground

For travel within the city, horse-drawn coaches were introduced in the early 17th century. For a small fare the passenger could jolt over the cobblestones in one of these springless carriages.

But as people began to live farther and farther from their work and from shops, museums, and theaters, they began to ride horse-drawn buses. Today the horse-drawn bus, with its driver cracking his long whip, is only a memory. Big red two-decker motor buses have taken the place of the horse-drawn buses. Buses connect all of Greater London. Londoners "queue up"—get in line—at the bus stops, waiting their turn to board. However, a city that covers about 616 square miles, with some suburbs 15 miles from the heart of town, needs faster transportation than buses can give.

London has a great network of subways. It is called the tube, or Underground, because the trains roar through tubelike tunnels under the city. The Underground is the fastest way to get from one part of London to another. Maps and directions at every station make it easy even for strangers to find their way. The fare is more for a distant station, less for one near you. Passengers pay their fare when they enter the Underground.

▶ WORLD WAR II AND AFTER

The Underground played an important part in protecting Londoners during World War II. From 1940 onward German bombers came night after night and blitz-bombed the city. In the later years of the war there were flying bombs and V-2 rockets. No one was ever safe, night or day.

Because the tubes were so far underground, many people used to take their pillows and rugs and sleep there. They never knew until they got home next morning whether their houses had been burned or bombed or were even still standing. By the end of the war, about 250,000 homes had been seriously damaged or destroyed in Greater London, and more than 30,000 people killed. Countless thousands had been wounded.

The first big raid came on September 7, 1940. In the following months bombs fell on Buckingham Palace, the Houses of Parliament, and the City, which once was a sea of flames. Much of the old City of London disappeared forever. Londoners considered it a miracle that St. Paul's Cathedral escaped. Brave volunteers guarded the dome, and some put out fire bombs with their bare hands.

London was "blacked out" at night so that bombers could not see their targets. Street lamps were not lighted. House windows had to be so heavily curtained that not even a chink of light showed. If it did, an air-raid warden knocked at the door, reminding people to turn out or dim their light. Anyone who went out had to grope his way with a tiny, dim flashlight.

Because of the bombs, fires, blackout, and shortage of food, life was hard in London. Most people sent their children away to safer places in the country or to Canada and the United States. But most of the people who worked in London stayed on. Even after the worst raids, they went to their shops or offices the next morning. All through the blitz, London's motto was "Business as usual."

▶ LONDON TODAY

London is a joy to visit—especially when the sun comes out. Until recently the fog was so thick in winter that it looked as if you could pick it up by the spoonful. Londoners called it a pea-soup fog because the fog and coal smoke mixed making the air a yellowish-green. These famous fogs no longer occur because it is now forbidden to burn fuels that produce smoke. The air is so much cleaner that London has more sunshine than before and the buildings can be cleaned of centuries of accumulated soot.

Part of the fun of visiting London is in seeing its many museums. The National Gallery and the Tate Gallery house great paintings. The British Museum has a world-famous library and outstanding Greek, Roman, Egyptian, and Assyrian collections. Near this museum is London University, which attracts students from all over the Commonwealth.

South of Kensington Gardens is a whole group of museums, where people can wander after picnicking in the park. One, the Science Museum, has a special Children's Gallery where visitors push buttons to make different exhibits work. There is a model coal mine to explore, with coal cars. Upstairs is the oldest steam engine in the world, "Puffing Billy."

Near these museums is the Royal Albert Hall, where concerts are given. London has many theaters for music and plays—the Royal Opera House at Covent Garden, the Old Vic, and Sadler's Wells for ballet. The oldest theater, the Drury Lane Theatre, is supposed to be haunted.

In the Christmas season, some London theaters give pantomimes. These are children's shows with singing, dancing, and gay costumes. They are based on fairy tales and children's books. An all-time favorite is *Peter Pan*.

A visitor or a Londoner can find almost anything he wants in London. The past, the present, and the future blend here to make this one of the most exciting cities in the world. According to the great English writer Samuel Johnson (1709–1784), "When a man is tired of London he is tired of life; for there is in London all that life can afford."

DOROTHY MARSHALL
University College of South Wales
See also ENGLAND; UNITED KINGDOM.

LONDON, JACK (1876–1916)

Jack London's life was as rugged and adventurous as the tales he told. He was born on January 12, 1876, in San Francisco. He grew up there and in Oakland. When he was 13, he left school in order to help support his family. He loved books, however, and read great numbers of them. Discouraged by working long hours in a cannery for 10 cents an hour, he borrowed money to buy a boat and became an oyster pirate. The oyster pirates were a tough gang of men who gathered oysters illegally at night and sold them in the morning. At 15 Jack was the most successful oyster pirate in San Francisco Bay and the hardest drinker of the lot.

Jack went seal hunting off the coast of Japan, worked in a jute mill, and traveled across the country by railroad as a hobo. He became interested in workers' movements and was an active socialist. When he won first prize in a story contest, he knew he could be a writer if he had more schooling. He managed to pass exams to get into college, but after one semester he left to support his family again. After prospecting for gold in Alaska, he returned to Oakland. He studied and wrote 16 to 19 hours a day, 7 days a week. He sold a few stories, but the real break came when he sold one to the *Atlantic Monthly* in 1899. A collection of stories, *The Son of the Wolf,* appeared in 1900.

In the next 16 years London produced 43 books—short stories, novels, serious studies of social conditions, essays, and autobiography. Some of the best known are *The Call of the Wild* (1903), *The People of the Abyss* (1903), *Martin Eden* (1909), and *John Barleycorn* (1913). By 1913 he was the most popular writer in the world.

London was always ready for adventure. At different times he lived in the slums of London, covered the Russo-Japanese War in Korea, sailed the Pacific in a small boat, and set up a model ranch in California. He married twice. He went into debt by giving his money away to the hundreds of people who asked him for help and by giving work and shelter to many others at his ranch. Finally, overwhelmed by his debts, he poisoned himself. He died on November 22, 1916.

LONGFELLOW, HENRY WADSWORTH (1807–1882)

The American poet Henry Wadsworth Longfellow was born in Portland, Maine, on February 27, 1807. He was the second child in a family of eight. His father was a lawyer, and his mother, who had been to school more than most girls of that time, was fond of music and poetry.

The Longfellow children all went to Portland Academy. Henry was an especially good student. He was ready for college when he was 14 and went to Bowdoin in Brunswick, Maine. His father wanted him to study law, but he was proud when poems and essays Henry wrote were published while he was still in college.

When Henry was a senior, he wrote home to say that he had chosen writing as his career. His father was disappointed, but he was pleased later when Henry wrote that he would like to be a teacher as well as a writer. He had been offered a chance to teach modern languages at Bowdoin if he would study abroad at his own expense. After graduating, Longfellow went abroad for the first time.

In Spain, Longfellow lived with a Spanish family while taking courses in Spanish. He never allowed himself to speak any English. He followed the same rule in France, Italy, and Germany. He worked very hard for long hours, and since he had a gift for words, he came home after 3 years knowing four languages.

Longfellow taught at Bowdoin from 1829 to 1834. Up to this time Latin and Greek had been the only important language studies, and there were no really good French or Spanish textbooks. So Longfellow wrote textbooks for his students—a French book of "dramatic proverbs," a Spanish book, and one in Italian.

In 1831 Longfellow married Mary Storer Potter, the daughter of a Portland judge. Three years later Longfellow was offered a position as professor of modern languages at

Harvard. He and his wife knew they would like to live in Cambridge, but first Longfellow asked for time to study abroad again. He and Mary visited London, Hamburg, Denmark, and Sweden. Longfellow studied Scandinavian poetry and translated some of it into English verse.

Up to this time Longfellow's life had been unusually successful and happy, but in 1835 Mary died in Holland. Hard work alone seemed to help Longfellow overcome his grief. He continued his journey, studying at the famous university in Heidelberg, Germany.

In December, 1836, Longfellow began teaching at Harvard. He had a way of making foreign languages interesting and exciting to his students. For the next 18 years he was one of Harvard's most famous and best-loved professors.

Longfellow rented rooms at Craigie House, a mansion built before the American Revolution. His windows overlooked the gardens and open fields that stretched down to the Charles River. He was happy but very lonely. In 1843 he married Frances Appleton of Boston. Craigie House was for sale, and Miss Appleton's father bought it for the Longfellows and furnished it with many beautiful pieces brought from Europe. Longfellow loved people, and there were many parties in the big house on Brattle Street.

Longfellow's six children were all born at Craigie House. He wrote "The Children's Hour" for them. In "The Song of Hiawatha" he wrote of Indians like those he had seen during his own boyhood in Portland, when Indians used to come to trade their furs. "Paul Revere's Ride" came from stories his Grandfather Wadsworth used to tell him. His grandfather was a general during the American Revolution and had known Paul Revere.

In 1861 Longfellow's wife died when her dress caught fire from some sealing wax she was using. Longfellow was badly burned trying to save her.

Again Longfellow turned to work for comfort. He spent years translating some of Dante's work into English poetry. He finished writing *Tales of a Wayside Inn*. He went to England again, and Queen Victoria invited him to call on her at the royal palace. Oxford and Cambridge gave him honorary degrees.

It always surprised Longfellow that his poems were so popular and that all sorts of people wanted to meet him. He welcomed everybody and helped young writers in every way he could, although, as he wrote in his diary, he sometimes wished that people would not make quite such long calls.

Longfellow was particularly pleased when schoolchildren came to see him. If he was not too busy, he asked them in and showed them around the house. In "The Village Blacksmith" he told of a blacksmith shop "under a spreading chestnut tree" in Cambridge. When the tree had to be cut down, schoolchildren gave money to have the wood made into an armchair for Longfellow. This pleased him greatly.

When Longfellow died on March 24, 1882, he was America's foremost poet. A monument to him stands in the Poets' Corner in Westminster Abbey, London. In poems like "The Belfry at Bruges" he told Americans about people in Europe, and in poems like "Evangeline" he told the Old World about life in the New.

LOUISE HALL THARP
Author, *Tory Hole, The Peabody Sisters of Salem*

Two of Longfellow's poems follow. An excerpt from "Paul Revere's Ride" can be found after the biography of Paul Revere in Volume R.

THE VILLAGE BLACKSMITH

Under a spreading chestnut-tree
The village smithy stands;
The smith, a mighty man is he,
With large and sinewy hands;
And the muscles of his brawny arms
Are strong as iron bands.

His hair is crisp, and black, and long,
His face is like the tan;
His brow is wet with honest sweat,
He earns whate'er he can,
And looks the whole world in the face,
For he owes not any man.

Week in, week out, from morn till night,
You can hear his bellows blow;
You can hear him swing his heavy sledge,
With measured beat and slow,
Like a sexton ringing the village bell,
When the evening sun is low.

And children coming home from school
Look in at the open door;

They love to see the flaming forge,
And hear the bellows roar,
And catch the burning sparks that fly
Like chaff from a threshing-floor.

He goes on Sunday to the church,
And sits among his boys;
He hears the parson pray and preach,
He hears his daughter's voice
Singing in the village choir,
And it makes his heart rejoice.

It sounds to him like her mother's voice,
Singing in Paradise!
He needs must think of her once more,
How in the grave she lies;
And with his hard, rough hand he wipes
A tear out of his eyes,

Toiling—rejoicing—sorrowing,
Onward through life he goes;
Each morning sees some task begin,
Each evening sees it close;
Something attempted, something done,
Has earned a night's repose.

Thanks, thanks to thee, my worthy friend,
For the lesson thou has taught!
Thus at the flaming forge of life
Our fortunes must be wrought;
Thus on its sounding anvil shaped
Each burning deed and thought.

THE ARROW AND THE SONG

I shot an arrow into the air,
It fell to earth, I knew not where;
For, so swiftly it flew, the sight
Could not follow it in its flight.

I breathed a song into the air,
It fell to earth, I knew not where;
For who has sight so keen and strong,
That it can follow the flight of song?

Long, long afterward, in an oak
I found the arrow, still unbroke;
And the song, from beginning to end,
I found again in the heart of a friend.

LONGITUDE. See LATITUDE AND LONGITUDE.
LORAN. See RADAR, SONAR, LORAN, AND SHORAN.

LOS ANGELES

Hollywood, famous for movies and television, is not really a city—it is part of Los Angeles. And while Hollywood films may be Los Angeles' best-known products, they are far from the only ones.

Los Angeles has been described as "nineteen suburbs in search of a city." It is actually a center surrounded by many independent cities and towns: Burbank, Santa Monica, Glendale, Long Beach, Beverly Hills, and Culver City are a few of them. Aircraft,

clothing, automobiles, chemicals, metals, electronic equipment, oil-field machinery, paper, canned seafood (supplied by a large tuna-fishing fleet), and many other things are produced. Los Angeles is also famous for 16-inch-long hot dogs, the biggest milkshakes and highest stacks of pancakes on earth, orange groves, swimming pools, and freeways. There are many jokes about the Los Angeles city limits. If you believe the signs pranksters have put up, Los Angeles' city limits include most of the United States.

The metropolitan area of Los Angeles has been expanding and the population has been growing. With about 7,000,000 people it is the second largest metropolitan area in the United States. Parts of the city of Los Angeles have been growing upward as well as outward. In the downtown area especially, much of the rebuilding has resulted in skyscrapers over 50 stories high.

Most of Los Angeles is on a plain sloping gently up from the Pacific Ocean to Hollywood and Beverly Hills. Here the plain abruptly meets the Santa Monica Mountains. Mulholland Drive runs along the crest of the mountains, and houses are built on perilously steep slopes—and occasionally slide down

Wilshire Boulevard, a major thoroughfare in Los Angeles.

them. The San Fernando Valley is north of these mountains. Most of the valley is now within the Los Angeles city limits.

To the east other mountains enclose Los Angeles in a sort of great bowl. When the wind dies and a layer of warm air settles high above the bowl, the city is covered by smog. Smog—a word coined from "smoke" and "fog"—is made up of a mixture of unburned automobile exhaust fumes, gases from chemical plants and oil refineries, and other gases. Smog makes the eyes smart and makes it hard to breathe and hard to see. However, Los Angeles is learning how to control smog, and there is much less than there once was.

The climate is pleasant. Most of the annual 15 inches of rain falls in the winter, when the temperature is very rarely below freezing. It is sometimes quite hot in summer.

There are many things to do in Los Angeles, which is really a cross-section of the United States. There is a small Mexican colony with shops and restaurants on Olvera Street. A larger Mexican colony is located in East Los Angeles. There is a Chinatown near College Street and North Broadway and a "Little Tokyo," or Japanese colony, near Main and First streets.

Los Angeles is governed by a mayor and city council, elected for 4-year terms. Each of the 15 council members represents a separate district. A controller and city attorney are also elected. Boards of commissioners, however, are appointed by the mayor. They must be approved by the city council. The more than 20 boards include city planning, police, fire, health, park, and municipal housing. Los Angeles is also the county seat of Los Angeles County.

There are many cultural activities in Los Angeles. The Music Center, the home of the Los Angeles Philharmonic Orchestra, is also a center for all the performing arts. The Hollywood Bowl is a pleasant place to enjoy an outdoor concert. Famous stars appear in theatrical productions and there are several little-theater groups in the area.

The city has two famous universities: The University of Southern California (USC) and the University of California at Los Angeles (UCLA). There are also many other, smaller colleges. There are fine museums too. The Los Angeles County Art Museum has an out-

The "stack," intersection of four freeways built to handle heavy traffic.

standing collection of paintings and sculpture. The California Museum of Science and Industry has industrial, agricultural, and recreational exhibits. The Southwest Museum has fascinating displays about the Indians of the Southwest. The Los Angeles County Museum of Natural History offers lectures, films, and historical and scientific exhibits, and owns an important collection of fossils.

The museum also administers Hancock Park, the site of the La Brea Pits.

These tar pits were once hot, bubbling cauldrons of asphalt. Saber-toothed tigers, mastodons, bison, bears, and other animals were trapped in the ooze. Their skeletons were dug up thousands of years later, and the pits are now a kind of museum with models of the extinct animals. A walk leads down into an observation pit.

The new Los Angeles County Museum of Art was opened in 1965.

Hollywood Bowl is famous for outdoor concerts.

For those who like live animals, there is the Griffith Park Zoo, with more than 1,000 varieties of animals. There is also an elephant train to ride. Marine animals can be seen at Marineland of the Pacific near Long Beach, where porpoises, which are supposed to be almost as intelligent as human beings, go through their antics. Television shows are sometimes made there.

At Disneyland, an amusement park in nearby Anaheim, Walt Disney assembled a monorail, an old train, a stern-wheeler riverboat, Conestoga wagons, Snow White and the Seven Dwarfs, horse cars, and many reconstructed old buildings. Tomorrowland has rocket ships, astrojets, a submarine voyage, and thousands of other models of things of the future. In Adventureland there is a jungle cruise with lifelike alligators, water buffalo, hippos, and other fascinating animals that perhaps do not live together in any single jungle but give a clear picture of jungle life. Frontierland has a mine, through which you can ride on ore cars, and a reconstruction of a 1790 sailing ship called a windjammer.

▶ HISTORY

Los Angeles was founded in 1781 by the Spanish Governor of California, Don Felipe

Pacific Palisades on the oceanfront near Santa Monica, a residential community of Los Angeles.

de Neve. He called the new town *El Pueblo de Nuestra Señora la Reina de Los Angeles de Porciuncula*. It means "the town of Our Lady the Queen of the Angels of Porciuncula."

The town did not amount to much until California became a part of the United States in 1848 after the Mexican War. Its population then was about 1,500. Soon farms were all around the town, and oranges, grapefruit, lemons, walnuts, avocados, and grapes were being grown. The Southern Pacific Railroad reached Los Angeles in 1876, and 9 years later the Santa Fe came in. For a time a ticket from Chicago cost only $1 (it was much more expensive to go east). This bargain was to lure new settlers to the area so that the railroads could make money shipping the town's products east.

Oil was discovered shortly after 1890. Derricks still pump it from the ground at Signal Hill, south of town, and in a number of places in the city itself.

The city began to grow after oil was discovered, but (for a time) it was very short of water. Then water was brought in from Owens Valley, over 100 miles north of the town, between the Sierra Nevada Mountains and Death Valley. Now the city also gets some of its water from the Colorado River, about 225 miles east, and a great deal of its electrical power from Hoover Dam on the same river.

Much of the Colorado River water is used for irrigation of crops in the Imperial Valley. There farmers are able to raise several crops a year because the weather is always warm. Los Angeles depends on this irrigated valley for much of its food. The Salton Sea (about 240 feet below sea level) is popular in winter as a boating and recreational area.

Early in this century moviemakers discovered that there was a lot of space in Los Angeles and that the sun shone almost every day. There was not any smog then because there were neither industries nor many automobiles. It was a perfect place for making films, and in a very few years Hollywood gained its reputation as a film center.

After World War II there was a great expansion of industry in Los Angeles. With the growth of air travel tourists and vacationers came to the area in great numbers.

Like many American cities Los Angeles has had problems and is trying to cure urban ills. In 1971 the city had to bear up under the destruction caused by the worst earthquake to hit southern California in 38 years.

ALDEN STEVENS
Field Director, *Mobil Travel Guides*

LOUISIANA

Louisiana is a land of bayous—marshy streams that thread their way through cypress groves draped in Spanish moss. Early French settlers of Louisiana formed the word "bayou" from an Indian word meaning "river" or "creek."

Many of Louisiana's bayous have French or Indian names connected with legends or events of long ago. Bayou des Oies is a French name meaning "bayou of the geese." This bayou was once a favorite resting place for wild geese. Bayou Mouchoir de l'Ourse means "bayou handkerchief of a bear." No one knows exactly where this odd name came from. Folktales say that the *loups-garous,* or werewolves—strange creatures half-wolf and half-human—hold an annual ball at Bayou Goula. People may watch the dancing, but they must beware. For safety everyone should hold a bag of salt or a few live frogs.

Bayou Teche was made by a gigantic snake—or so an Indian legend says. Brave warriors slew the snake. As it died, it wriggled down into the gumbo, cutting the bed of the bayou. The Bayou Teche area is the setting of part of Longfellow's well-known poem *Evangeline.*

STATE FLOWER: Blossom of the southern magnolia tree.

STATE BIRD: Eastern brown pelican.

STATE FLAG.

Louisiana's location alone would make it an important state. It borders on the Gulf of Mexico. It is also at the mouth of the Mississippi River. To the south of Louisiana lie the trade areas of the West Indies and of Latin America. To the north is the trade area of the vast, rich Mississippi Valley. At the docks in New Orleans, river barges from Iowa can be seen tied up near oceangoing freighters from Argentina.

It was largely to get the port city of New Orleans that President Thomas Jefferson began dealing with Napoleon I, ruler of France, in 1803. At that time France owned almost 1,000,000 square miles in the Mississippi Valley. Jefferson's agent, James Monroe, set out for Paris with instructions to pay not more than $10,000,000 for both the New Orleans area and a tract of land on the Gulf coast. When he arrived, he found that Napoleon was offering the whole Louisiana territory for about $15,000,000. He bought it at once. From this area came the state of Louisiana and all or the greater parts of 12 other states.

In many ways Louisiana can be considered one of the most international states in the Union. The French influence still exists in

Louisiana's legal system, which is based partly on the Code Napoléon—a system of laws created by Napoleon I. English common law is the basis for the laws of the other states. The celebration of Mardi Gras, which means "fat Tuesday" in French, is a custom brought to Louisiana from France in colonial times. Throughout southern Louisiana there are many Cajun settlements. The name "Cajun" comes from a local pronunciation of the word "Acadian." The Acadians were people of French origin who came to Louisiana from Nova Scotia about 200 years ago.

The flag of Spain also flew over Louisiana in colonial days. The Spanish style of building can still be seen, especially in the delicate, lacy ironwork that decorates many of the old buildings in New Orleans. In some small communities Spanish is still spoken. Local units of government in Louisiana are called parishes, rather than counties as in the other states. Originally the parishes were church units set up by a Spanish governor in 1769.

Louisiana's landscape and its industries and products are as varied as its history. In production of minerals—especially petroleum and natural gas—Louisiana ranks second in the nation, next to Texas. No other state except Hawaii produces more sugarcane. Now, as in the past, Louisiana also grows large crops of cotton and rice. But increasingly the spotlight is on industry—on factories that turn Louisiana's raw materials into a great variety of products.

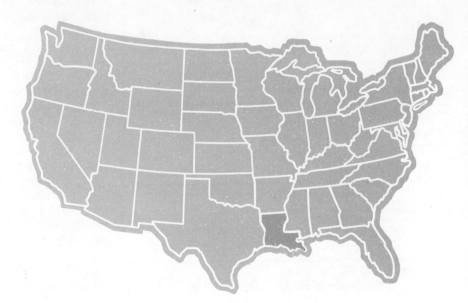

LOUISIANA

CAPITAL: Baton Rouge.

STATEHOOD: April 30, 1812; the 18th state.

SIZE: 48,523 sq. mi.; rank, 31st.

POPULATION: 3,643,180 (1970 census); rank, 20th.

ORIGIN OF NAME: Named in 1682 by Robert Cavelier, Sieur de La Salle, in honor of Louis XIV, King of France.

ABBREVIATION: La.

NICKNAME: Pelican State; Bayou State; Sugar State; Creole State.

STATE SONG: "Song of Louisiana," by Vashti R. Stopher.

STATE MOTTO: "Union, justice, confidence."

STATE SEAL: A pelican is shown in a nest feeding its young. The three words of the state motto are arranged around the pelican—the first two above and the third below. Around the border of the seal are the words "State of Louisiana."

STATE FLAG: In the center of a blue field is a pelican feeding its young, as on the state seal. The state motto appears on a white streamer beneath the pelican.

THE LAND

LOCATION: Latitude—28° 54' N to 33° 01' N.
Longitude—89° 10' W to 94° 03' W.
Arkansas to the north, Mississippi to the east, the Gulf of Mexico to the south, Texas to the west.

ELEVATION: Highest—Driskill Mountain, 535 ft.
Lowest—At New Orleans, 5 ft. below sea level.

LANDFORMS: The Coastal Plain, divided into areas of uplands and lowlands.

SURFACE WATERS: Major rivers—Mississippi, Red, Ouachita, Sabine, Pearl. **Largest natural lakes**—Pontchartrain, Borgne, Maurepas, White, Calcasieu.

CLIMATE: Temperature—January average, 56° F. at New Orleans in the southeast, 48° at Shreveport in the northwest. July average, 83° at New Orleans, 84° at Shreveport. **Precipitation**—Yearly average, 64 in. at New Orleans, 45 in. at Shreveport. **Growing season**—In the north, 220–260 days; in the south, 260–320 days.

▶ **THE LAND**

Louisiana is shaped like a short boot with a ragged toe that points toward the east. It is about one third of the way between the equator and the North Pole and about one fourth of the way around the world from the prime meridian (0° longitude). Only three other states—Hawaii, Florida, and Texas—extend farther south than Louisiana.

Landforms

All of Louisiana lies within a large natural region of the United States known as the Coastal Plain. But the land is not the same in all parts of the state. The present-day geography of Louisiana is varied and interesting. It makes a fascinating field of study for the young geographer or physical scientist.

LANDFORMS

The Uplands. There are three parts of Louisiana that geographers call uplands. One upland area lies between the Mississippi and the Pearl rivers, north of Lake Pontchartrain. Another is in northern Louisiana. The third is on the western side of the state, south and west of the Red River.

The uplands include areas of rolling hills covered with pine trees. Along the rivers and streams there are bluffs and deep ravines. Elevations in the uplands range from about 100 feet to more than 500 feet. The highest hills are in the northern uplands. One hill, named Driskill Mountain, is 535 feet above sea level. It is near Arcadia in Bienville Parish. The next highest elevation is near Athens in Claiborne Parish.

The Lowlands. The three main lowland areas are the Alluvial Floodplain, the Coastal Marshlands, and the Coastal Prairies. All the lowlands, except part of the floodplain, are in the south.

The Alluvial Floodplain follows the general course of the Mississippi, with an arm extending up the Red River. In Louisiana the Mississippi and other rivers have deposited so much sand, silt, and other material that the rivers now flow on land higher than the surrounding floodplains. The banks of the rivers make natural levees, or dikes. The higher lands sloping away from the rivers are known locally as "front lands." These lands are suitable for crops. The adjoining lands are known as backlands. Then come the swamps. The front lands and backlands drain into the swamps. The swamps also act as huge catch basins for waters that overflow the riverbanks in times of flood.

The Coastal Marshlands extend the length of Louisiana's coastline. The northern limit of this area is the 5-foot contour line—the line connecting all places 5 feet above sea level. The marshlands are flat, swampy plains covered with grass and rushes. Hundreds of lagoons and shallow lakes dot the land. There are two kinds of marshes—saltwater and freshwater. In general, the marshes closest to the coast are saltwater. Farther inland are the freshwater marshes. Alligators, muskrats, and other kinds of wildlife live in the freshwater marshes.

The marshlands are separated from the Gulf of Mexico by long, low ridges of sand and shells called barrier beaches. Throughout the marshes there are ridges, called cheniers, that once were barrier beaches. These sandy ridges support groves of oak trees. The word "chenier" comes from the French word for oak.

Hills known as land islands, or salt domes, are another feature of the marshlands. These hills rise as much as 200 feet above the surrounding marsh. They are the tops of huge domes of rock salt. Some of the hills contain sulfur and petroleum as well as salt. The best-known salt domes are five hills known as the Five Islands in St. Mary and Iberia parishes.

At the outer edge of the delta is a place called the Head of the Passes. There the Mississippi branches out like a bird's foot. The branches, or claws, of the foot are about 20 miles long. Each year they become about 300 feet longer as the river deposits more and more silt.

The Coastal Prairies occupy an area west of the Alluvial Floodplain and north of the Coastal Marshlands. This part of the state is a flat plain that slopes gently to the south. All of it is below 100 feet in elevation.

Rivers, Lakes, and Coastal Waters

Rivers have built much of present-day Louisiana. Long ago most of the area was part of the Gulf of Mexico. Gradually the land was built up as the rivers deposited their loads of sand, silt, and other materials.

The most important river is the Mississippi. It twists and turns through the state, forming part of the eastern boundary. Levees line the river. These man-made banks are built to keep the river from overflowing in times of flood. The Red River is the Mississippi's major tributary in Louisiana. It drains the northern part of the state. Other important rivers are the Ouachita and the Black in northeastern Louisiana and the Calcasieu and the Sabine in the southwest. The Sabine River forms more than half of the Louisiana-Texas boundary. In the southeast the Pearl River forms part of the Louisiana-Mississippi boundary.

Louisiana has three kinds of natural lakes—coastal lagoons, oxbow lakes, and lakes caused by flooding. Coastal lakes were formed when barrier beaches cut off large stretches of water from the Gulf of Mexico. Among the largest coastal lakes are Pontchartrain, Maurepas, and Borgne. Oxbow lakes were once part of the Mississippi River. When the river cut across its own huge bends, it formed lakes in the shape of oxbows, or half-moons. A good example of an oxbow lake is False River near Baton Rouge. Many of the lakes in northern and central Louisiana were caused by the flooding of the Red River. Among them are Caddo, Bistineau, Catahoula, and Cross lakes.

The coastline of Louisiana is very irregular. Locating the exact coastline is a difficult problem because it is constantly changing. Each year the Mississippi dumps millions of tons of silt into the Gulf. Much of this silt is then spread along the shore. Sometimes parts of the shore are built up, and sometimes they

A dredge working in the waterway known as the Mississippi River—Gulf Outlet.

Drilling for oil in the Gulf of Mexico.

are destroyed. The general coastline of the state is about 400 miles long. Counting all the inlets, bays, and islands, the total shoreline measures more than 7,500 miles.

Climate

Louisiana has a humid subtropical climate. Winters are mild and wet, and summers are long and hot. Throughout most of the state, there are only two real seasons—summer and winter. Few areas have a spring season or a fall season.

In the north the average winter temperature is about 50 degrees Fahrenheit. The average summer temperature is about 80 degrees. In the south, winters are several degrees warmer. Summers are about the same or even cooler than in the north. Frequent summer thundershowers in the south help to cool the air.

Louisiana is one of the wettest states. The average annual precipitation ranges from 45 inches in the northwest to more than 60 inches in the southeast. Snow is rare in southern Louisiana. Flakes usually melt as they touch the ground. In the north there is a measurable amount of snow or sleet almost every year.

The average growing season ranges from 220 days in the north to 320 days in the southeast. Some areas in the Mississippi Delta often have 365 days of frost-free weather.

Natural Resources

Louisiana has many natural resources. Among the most important are rich soils, an abundance of fish and wildlife, forests, and large supplies of petroleum and natural gas.

Soils. The alluvial soils along the Mississippi and other rivers and streams are among the best in the United States. Many crops, including cotton and sugarcane, are produced on these fertile soils. Parts of the uplands have sandy soils, which are good for vegetable and strawberry crops. Hill soils are usually thin and not very fertile, but pine forests and peach orchards thrive on these soils.

Forests. A large part of the total land area in Louisiana is forested. There are pine forests in the uplands and hills, hardwood forests in the river valleys, and cypress and tupelo swamps throughout the state. Most of the hardwood trees belong to the oak family. Louisiana is noted for its beautiful live oaks—so called because they keep their leaves all year long. These trees grow to a huge size.

Cypress and tupelo are hardwoods that thrive on water. These trees have large trunks. Their roots, or "knees," stand above the water to get air. Like the live oak, the cypress and the tupelo are often draped with Spanish moss, or "long moss." Spanish moss is not really a moss. It is a plant that belongs to the pineapple family. Because the plant has no roots, it uses the branches of trees as anchors. It takes its food and water from the air.

Animal Life. Louisiana has large numbers of fur-bearing animals, such as muskrat, mink, otter, and raccoon. There are many deer and a few black bears, timber wolves, and cougars.

Many North American birds and waterfowl make their winter homes in the coastal area of Louisiana. This area contains some of the largest state-owned wildlife and waterfowl refuges in the world. Native seabirds include the brown pelican, the laughing gull, and the royal tern.

The coastal waters and the many lakes and streams are filled with aquatic life. Porpoises frolic in the waters of the Gulf. Dozens of varieties of saltwater fish and shellfish live in the offshore waters and in the brackish bays and bayous. Freshwater fish are abundant throughout the state. One unusual fish is the choupique, also called bowfin or mudfish. It can breathe air and live in mud. Huge turtles and alligators are fairly common in the swamps and coastal areas.

Minerals. Louisiana's principal mineral resources are petroleum and natural gas. Most of the petroleum comes from the northwest and from the Gulf coast, but there are fields scattered throughout the entire state. The greatest natural-gas fields are in the northeast.

Salt is abundant in Louisiana. There are more than 100 known salt domes, but only a few of these are used at present to produce commercial salt. Sulfur is found in the coastal regions. The largest deposits are near the mouth of the Mississippi River in Plaquemines Parish. Louisiana also has great stores of sand, gravel, clay, shells, and stone.

▶ THE PEOPLE AND THEIR WORK

Settlement of Louisiana under the French advanced very slowly at first. In 1706 a census showed that there were only about 80 settlers living in the area. A few years later there were several hundred, including French colonists, traders from Canada who were working in the area, and soldiers. Most of the French settlers were not interested in farming. To encourage agriculture, leaders of the colony began to bring bond servants and Negro slaves from the West Indies and Africa to work in the fields. They also brought farmers from Germany, Switzerland, and other European countries. Many German farmers settled along the Mississippi above New Orleans. By 1722 the population had risen to several thousand.

Between 1764 and 1790 more than 4,000 Acadians settled in Louisiana. The Acadians were French Canadians whose ancestors had settled in Acadia, or Nova Scotia, in the early 1600's. They were expelled from Nova Scotia, beginning in 1755, because they refused to adopt British customs and to obey the laws. The Acadians settled mainly in the Bayou Teche country, west of New Orleans. Louisiana then had two different types of French settlers. The descendants of the original French settlers were called Creoles. The Acadians became known as Cajuns. Today a dialect of French, called Acadian, is spoken in many areas of southern Louisiana. It is a combination of 18th-century French and local expressions.

About 1770 a Spanish governor of Louisiana brought a group of settlers from the Canary Islands. These Spanish-speaking people made their homes in the delta country. The central and northern parts of Louisiana were settled in the late 1700's and early

Fishing boats line the shore of a bayou in southern Louisiana.

1800's by pioneers from other parts of the United States. They came mainly from the nearby states. All of these people, together with the native Indians, gave Louisiana a background of mixed customs, languages, and ancestries.

Where the People Live

In the past Louisiana was considered a rural state. Most of the people lived on farms or in very small places. Census takers now consider Louisiana an urban state. More than half the people live in the larger cities and towns. The urban population continues to grow, and the rural population declines.

Industries and Products

A favorable climate and rich soils have made Louisiana an important farming state. It is rapidly becoming an area where industry and commerce share importance with agriculture.

Agriculture. Louisiana produces a wide variety of field crops, fruits, and vegetables. Rice and cotton are important to the state's economy. Rice is grown on irrigated lands in the southwestern part of the state. Cotton is grown in the river valleys. Louisiana ranks second to Hawaii in the production of sugarcane in the United States. Sugarcane is different from most other crops in that it is not grown from seed. Cane stalks are laid in the ground and covered with soil. Buds sprout from joints along the stalks and produce a new cane crop. About three crops of cane can be produced from one planting. Corn is grown in all parts of the state except the rice area.

LOUISIANA
ARKANSAS
TEXAS
MISSISSIPPI
ALABAMA
GULF OF MEXICO
El Dorado
Springhill
Haynesville
Vivian
Caddo Lake
Benton
Mooringsport
Cross Lake
Bayou Bodcau Reservoir
Homer
Athens
Minden
Bossier City
Shreveport
Lake Bistineau
Arcadia
Grambling
Ruston
Farmerville
D'Arbonne Reservoir
West Monroe
Monroe
Driskill Mountain 535 ft.
Jonesboro
Bastrop
Lake Providence
Oak Grove
Delhi
Rayville
Tallulah
Vicksburg
Jackson
Longview
Mansfield
Coushatta
Columbia
Winnsboro
Black Lake
Saline Lake
Winnfield
St. Joseph
Natchitoches
Fort Jesup
Many
Harrisonburg
Ferriday
Vidalia
Jena
Catahoula Lake
Colfax
Pineville
Alexandria
Leesville
Marksville
Bunkie
De Ridder
Oakdale
Ville Platte
Opelousas
Oberlin
Eunice
Church Point
De Quincy
Sulphur
Goosport
Vinton
Lake Charles
Jennings
Rayne
Crowley
Lafayette
Lake Arthur
Kaplan
Abbeville
Jeanerette
New Iberia
St. Martinville
Breaux Bridge
Beaumont
Port Arthur
Sabine Lake
Cameron
Calcasieu Lake
Grand Lake
White Lake
Vermilion Bay
Pecan Island
Marsh Island
Atchafalaya Bay
Avery Island
Franklin
Berwick
Morgan City
Grand Lake
Napoleonville
Bayou Goula
Plaquemine
Port Allen
Baton Rouge
New Roads
False River
St. Francisville
Zachary
Clinton
Kentwood
Greensburg
Amite
Franklinton
Bogalusa
Hammond
Livingston
Denham Springs
Covington
Slidell
Lake Maurepas
Lake Pontchartrain
Gonzales
Convent
Donaldsonville
Reserve
Edgard
Kenner
Vacherie
Hahnville
Harahan
Westwego
New Orleans
Chalmette
Gretna
St. Bernard
Lake Borgne
Thibodaux
Lake Salvador
Houma
Daigleville
Bayou Cane
Golden Meadow
Barataria Bay
Grand Isle
Pointe a la Hache
Port Sulphur
Buras
Venice
Head of Passes
Main Pass
Southwest Pass
Mississippi River-Gulf Outlet
Breton Sound
Chandeleur
Gulfport
Biloxi
Prichard
Mobile
Mobile Bay
Laurel
Hattiesburg
Galveston Bay
Town Bluff Reservoir
McGee Bend Reservoir
Angelina River
Neches River
Trinity River
Sabine River
Red River
Little River
Ouachita River
Bayou Bartholomew
Boeuf River
Black River
Mississippi River
Calcasieu River
Bayou Teche
Intercoastal Waterway
Amite River
Pearl River
Bayou Lafourche
Leaf River
Chickasawhay River
Tombigbee River
Statute Miles
0 25 50
N
95° 94° 93° 92° 91° 90° 89° 88°
33° 32° 31° 30° 29°
A B C D E F G
1 2 3 4 5
Copyright Diversified Map Corporation, St. Louis, Mo

Louisiana ranks high among growers of sweet potatoes. Other important cash crops are spring strawberries, pecans, tung nuts, oranges, and honey. Thousands of queen bees and many packages of bees are shipped to beekeepers in other states. Two specialties of Louisiana are Easter lily bulbs and vetiver. The roots of vetiver, a grasslike plant, are used in making perfume.

Herds of cattle graze on the Coastal Prairies in the southwest and on land elsewhere that was once planted in cotton and sugarcane. Recently cash receipts from beef cattle and calves have been higher than receipts from any one of Louisiana's crops. Dairying also brings a large income, as does the raising of poultry.

Mining. In total value of mineral production, Louisiana ranks second nationally, after Texas. The chief minerals are petroleum and natural gas. Both are used as a source of fuels and as raw materials for chemicals. The salt taken from Louisiana's salt domes is very pure. It is used in chemicals and as table salt. Sulfur is mined by the Frasch process, which was developed in Louisiana. Very hot water is used to melt the underground sulfur deposits. Then the liquid sulfur is forced to the surface. Before the Frasch process was developed, much of the world's sulfur came from the island of Sicily in the Mediterranean Sea. Quantities of sand, gravel, and shells are quarried in the state. They are used mainly as materials for construction work.

Manufacturing. Petrochemicals—chemicals made from petroleum and natural gas—are the most important manufactured products. In turn, petrochemicals are used to make dozens of other products. Just a few of these are plastics, detergents, textiles, dyes, and fuels for rocket engines. Louisiana also has many plants that manufacture chemicals from sulfur, salt, and lime.

The sugar industry has been important since 1795. In that year Jean Étienne Boré, a sugar-planter, invented a process for large-scale refining of sugar. Today refineries in Louisiana produce a large part of the nation's sugar. The processing of cotton and cottonseed is another important industry. Pulp and paper mills are located throughout the state. By-products of the paper industry are chemicals, turpentine, and tar. These are recovered from the wastes of the paper mills.

Fisheries. Louisiana's most valuable fishing grounds are in the Gulf of Mexico. Shrimp and oysters caught in the Gulf and in sheltered bays are known throughout the United States. Among the commercial fish from the Gulf are speckled trout, redfish, red snapper, flounder, Spanish mackerel, menhaden, and tuna.

Freshwater fisheries have large catches of gaspergou and spoonbill catfish. "Gaspergou" is a local name for freshwater drumfish. Thousands of frogs are captured each year for a food delicacy—frogs' legs.

Transportation and Communication

The first roads in Louisiana were its rivers and bayous. Early settlers used many kinds of boats. The most common were flatboats and keelboats, propelled by oars. Travel was slow and difficult until the steamboat came into use. The *New Orleans,* the first steamboat to navigate the Mississippi River, was put into service between Natchez, Mississippi, and New Orleans in 1812. Soon the paddle-wheelers steamed up and down many of the waterways. But by the end of the 1800's most of these boats had disappeared. They had been replaced by towboats and barges.

Waterways are still important for transportation in Louisiana. Barge lines operate on the Intracoastal Waterway and on the Mississippi, Ouachita, and other rivers. The largest ports in the state are New Orleans, Baton Rouge, and Lake Charles. Oceangoing vessels dock at these ports daily. A new 76-mile waterway, the Mississippi River–Gulf Outlet, was opened in 1963. This new route between New Orleans and the Gulf of Mexico goes through St. Bernard Parish. It is about 40 miles shorter than the former route.

WHAT LOUISIANA PRODUCES

MANUFACTURED GOODS: Chemicals and related products; processed foods (especially sugar); petroleum and coal products; paper and paper products; transportation equipment; ships and boats; finished metals.

AGRICULTURAL PRODUCTS: Cattle and calves, rice, milk, soybeans, sugar, cotton, eggs.

MINERALS: Crude petroleum, natural gas, natural-gas liquids, sulfur, salt.

The tops of levees and well-worn Indian or buffalo trails were the first land roads. In some areas the pioneers built roads of heavy boards. These were known as plank roads. Today there is a network of local, state, and national highways. The new interstate and defense highway system helps to relieve heavy traffic in the more densely settled areas. Railroading started in 1831, when the Pontchartrain Railroad Company completed a line from New Orleans to a suburb on Lake Pontchartrain. On the first trip a team of horses served as an engine. At present there is a well-developed system of railroads. New Orleans, Alexandria, and Shreveport are the major rail centers. Each major urban area has a good airways network, served by a well-planned and well-developed airport.

Most of the early newspapers were French. The first was *Le Moniteur de la Louisiane* ("The Louisiana Monitor"), begun in New Orleans in 1794. The oldest and largest of present-day newspapers is the New Orleans *Times-Picayune,* founded in 1837. Each parish has at least one weekly paper. The total number of dailies is about 20.

All the cities and many of the smaller towns have at least one radio station each. All the larger cities have television stations that carry the major network programs along with news and programs of local interest.

▶ EDUCATION

The first school in the Louisiana area was opened in New Orleans in 1725. It was a school for boys established by Father Raphael, a Catholic priest. In 1727 nuns of the Ursuline order opened a school for girls, also in New Orleans. But during the 1700's there was little progress in establishing schools. Wealthy planters sent their sons to school in France. Many small private schools were opened in New Orleans and elsewhere in the colony. Usually these schools taught only elementary subjects.

Schools and Colleges

After Louisiana became a state in 1812, the state gave some money to support private and church schools. But state money was intended to help only those children whose parents could not afford to pay. Public education began in 1847, when Alexander Dimitry, state superintendent of education, organized a school system for Louisiana. The constitution of 1845 had provided for a statewide system. At present each parish has a public school system. Monroe, Bogalusa, and Lake Charles have separate city school systems. After the Civil War the laws of the state required segregation in the public schools. In 1954 a decision of the United States Supreme Court declared this requirement to be unconstitutional.

Louisiana has more than 20 colleges and universities. The largest is the state-supported Louisiana State University and Agricultural and Mechanical College in Baton Rouge. The university also has campuses in New Orleans, Alexandria, Shreveport, and Eunice. Other state-controlled colleges and universities are located in Baton Rouge, Grambling, Hammond, Lafayette, Lake Charles, Monroe, Natchitoches, Ruston, and Thibodaux.

The largest private institutions of higher education are Tulane University of Louisiana and Loyola University, both in New Orleans. Newcomb College for women is attached to Tulane.

Libraries and Museums

The Louisiana State Library in Baton Rouge provides library services throughout the state. It also lends books and films from its large collections. Most of the parishes have their own libraries, as do some of the cities. The library at Louisiana State University in Baton Rouge has a notable collection of books and documents pertaining to the history of the state. Other important historical collections are maintained by the New Orleans Public Library and by the Howard-Tilton Memorial Library of Tulane University. The library of the Middle American Research Institute at Tulane has many books on Mexico, Central America, and the West Indies. The museum connected with the library has exhibits pertaining to both ancient and modern Indians.

The Isaac Delgado Museum of Art in New Orleans includes a collection of Renaissance paintings. It also has paintings and sculpture by Louisiana artists. Louisiana State Exhibit Museum in Shreveport has displays of Louisiana's natural resources and the products produced from them. Louisiana State Mu-

LOUISIANA
PLACES OF INTEREST

seum in New Orleans consists of two historic buildings. The Cabildo, built in 1795, was once the headquarters of the Spanish governors. Among the displays in this building are Mardi Gras costumes, mementos of the pirate Jean Laffite, and an Audubon collection. Another building, the Presbytère, dates from 1793. It houses natural history exhibits.

▶ PLACES OF INTEREST

New Orleans has long been a major tourist center of the United States. Each year the city is host to people from all parts of the nation and the world. Other places that attract large numbers of out-of-state visitors are the Acadian country and the city of Baton Rouge. The people of the state and visitors alike enjoy exploring off the beaten paths, where some of the most interesting areas are found.

Forest and Park Areas

Louisiana has one national forest, the Kisatchie National Forest. It is spread out over central and northern Louisiana in six divisions. All the divisions have recreation facilities. National and state park areas preserve historic places or places of unusual beauty. Some of them also include recreation areas. The following are especially well known:

Chalmette National Historical Park was the site of the battle of New Orleans, the last major battle of the War of 1812. There the Americans, commanded by General Andrew Jackson, defeated a superior British force. The battle was fought in January, 1815.

Audubon Memorial State Park near St. Francisville preserves 100 acres of the Oakley Plantation. John James Audubon came there in the summer of 1821 to teach drawing to the daughter of the owner. During his stay he painted some of the birds for his noted work, the *Birds of America*. The plantation house and gardens have been restored as they were when Audubon first arrived.

Chicot State Park near Ville Platte contains nearly 6,500 acres of wooded hills, lakes, and cypress-filled bays. It is one of the largest state parks in the South.

Fontainebleau State Park on the north shore of Lake Pontchartrain was once a great plantation. The park is forested with live oak, magnolia, cedar, cypress, and pine. A white sand beach extends along the lake shore.

Fort Jesup State Historical Monument in the village of Fort Jesup preserves the fort that served as a base of operations for General Zachary Taylor before and during the Mexican War (1846–48). The park contains a restored building of the fort and a museum.

Fort Pike and **Fort Macomb** are state historical monuments located within 10 miles of each other in Orleans Parish. Both forts were built about 1820 to protect the water passes from Lake Pontchartrain to New Orleans.

Longfellow-Evangeline State Park near St. Martinville borders on Bayou Teche. The poet Henry Wadsworth Longfellow used the country around Bayou Teche as part of the setting of his famous poem *Evangeline*. An early Acadian house in the park has been restored as a museum.

Marksville Prehistoric Indian Museum and Park in Marksville contains several ancient burial grounds and a museum of Indian relics.

Other Places

Gardens and the many houses built before the Civil War add much to the beauty of Louisiana.

Avery Island near New Iberia is one of the state's major "land islands," or salt domes. In the area are the Jungle Gardens, a large salt mine, and a small factory that makes a famous pepper sauce—Tabasco sauce. The Jungle Gardens consist of more than 200 acres of wooded areas, tropical gardens, and a special sanctuary for egrets.

Hodges Gardens, south of Many, have almost 5,000 acres of beautiful gardens, an arboretum, and a refuge for deer, elk, and other animals. There is also a lake that shelters migratory waterfowl.

Oak Alley, a mansion near Vacherie, was built in the 1830's. It is a good example of Greek Revival architecture. An avenue bordered by live oaks extends from the mansion to the Mississippi River.

The Shadows, a plantation house in New Iberia.

The Shadows in New Iberia was built about 1830. It is considered one of the best examples of plantation house architecture in the United States.

Annual Events

Louisiana's famous festival is the Mardi Gras celebration in New Orleans. The biggest events take place during the 2 weeks before Mardi Gras, or Shrove Tuesday. Other festivals, fairs, and sports events are held throughout the year.

January—Sugar Bowl football game, New Orleans; Camellia Show, Lafayette.
February–March—Mardi Gras, New Orleans.
May—Strawberry Festival, Hammond.
June—Peach Festival, Ruston
August—Rodeo Week, Alexandria; Shrimp Festival and the Blessing of the Fleet, Morgan City.
September—Cotton Festival, Ville Platte; Sugarcane Festival, New Iberia.
October—Louisiana State Fair, Shreveport; Forestry Festival, Winnfield; International Rice Festival, Crowley; Yambilee (sweet potato festival), Opelousas.
December—Orange Festival, Buras.

▶ CITIES

All sections of Louisiana have large cities. These include New Orleans and Lake Charles in the south, Shreveport and Monroe in the north, and Alexandria in the center of the state.

Baton Rouge

Baton Rouge, the state capital, was established about 1720, when the French built a fort on the east bank of the Mississippi River. Since that time many flags have flown over the city, including those of France, Spain, Great Britain, and the United States. The name "Baton Rouge" is the French form of an Indian expression meaning "red post." It is said that the Indians had placed a reddened post at the site to mark the division of two Indian nations.

Baton Rouge is a deepwater port and a busy industrial city. One of the largest oil refineries in the world is located there. Baton Rouge is also the home of Louisiana State University. Points of special interest include the Old State Capitol, which resembles a medieval castle, and the present capitol.

New Orleans

New Orleans, the largest city in Louisiana, is an important seaport of the Gulf of Mexico. It is located about 110 miles upstream from the mouth of the Mississippi. The city was founded in 1718. It was named in honor of the Regent of France, Philippe, Duc d'Orléans. An article on New Orleans is included in Volume N.

Shreveport

Shreveport, the second largest city, is situated on the banks of the Red River in the northwestern part of the state. It was named

PARISHES

The famous French Quarter in New Orleans.

for Henry Miller Shreve, a steamboat captain and builder of steamboats. Shreve designed the first snag boats. These boats were used to remove snags—sunken trees, stumps, and logs—from riverbeds. The boats were nicknamed Uncle Sam's tooth-pullers. In the 1830's Shreve directed a project to clear the Great Raft—a huge mass of snags—from the Red River. The opening of the river was a major factor in the development of Shreveport and northern Louisiana.

Today Shreveport is a leading cotton market and the center of one of the most important oil and gas areas in the United States. Bossier City, twin city to Shreveport, has grown rapidly in recent years. Barksdale Air Force Base is nearby.

Lake Charles

Lake Charles is located on a wide part of the Calcasieu River not far from the Texas border. It has been called a Louisiana town with a Texas flair. Early settlers had a more informal name for the town—Charlie's Lake. It is one of Louisiana's three deepwater ports. Oil refining is a major industry.

Other Cities

Monroe and West Monroe, separated by the Ouachita River, are important manufacturing and trade centers of northern Louisiana. The Monroe gas field is located nearby. Alexandria, the largest city in central Louisiana, is in an important lumbering and agricultural area. Lafayette is the largest town in the Acadian country. It is located in a highly productive agricultural area. In the city are large petrochemical industries. Bogalusa is located near the Pearl River. It is known for paper and wood products and for a forestry center maintained there by Louisiana State University.

GOVERNMENT

The present state constitution was adopted in 1921. It is Louisiana's 10th constitution.

The executive branch of the government is headed by a governor. His term is 4 years, and he may succeed himself. The legislative branch has two houses. The Senate is composed of 39 members, and the House of Representatives has 105 members. In both houses, members are elected for 4-year terms. The judicial branch is headed by a supreme court. Lower courts are courts of appeal, district courts, municipal courts, and juvenile and family courts.

Units of local government in Louisiana are called parishes instead of counties. The state is divided into 64 parishes.

FAMOUS PEOPLE

Louisiana has been the home of many persons whose names are well-known. Most of them made important contributions to the state or the nation. A few are remembered chiefly because of their colorful lives.

Jean Baptiste Lemoyne, Sieur de Bienville (1680–1768), has been called the Father of Louisiana. Under the leadership of his older brother, he helped to explore the lower Mississippi and to establish the first settlement in the Louisiana area. He founded the city of New Orleans and served three times as the governor of the Louisiana colony. Bienville was born in France.

William Charles Coles Claiborne (1775–1817) was one of the two agents who received possession of Louisiana for the United States after the Louisiana Purchase. In 1804 Claiborne was appointed governor of the Territory of Orleans. In 1812 he was elected the first governor of the new state of Louisiana. Claiborne was born in Sussex County, Virginia.

Jean Laffite (1780?–1826?) became famous as the Pirate of the Gulf. His birthplace is unknown, but it was probably Bayonne, France. Around 1810 he established himself as the head of a band of adventurers at Grand Isle on Barataria Bay. During the War of 1812 he

GOVERNMENT

Capital—Baton Rouge. **Number of parishes**—64. **Representation in Congress**—U.S. senators, 2; U.S. representatives, 8. **State Legislature**—Senate, 39 members; House of Representatives, 105 members, both 4-year terms. **Governor**—4-year term; may succeed himself. **Elections**—General and state, Tuesday after first Monday in November.

offered his services to the Americans. A biography of Laffite appears in Volume L.

Judah Philip Benjamin (1811–84), lawyer and Confederate statesman, was born in St. Thomas, British West Indies. He came to Louisiana as a young man. From 1853 to 1861 he served as United States senator. During the Civil War he served the Confederacy as attorney general and secretary of state. After the war Benjamin moved to England, where he built a new career as a lawyer.

Edward Douglass White (1845–1921) was a justice of the United States Supreme Court for 27 years, 1894–1921. After serving as an associate justice, he was appointed chief justice in 1910. Earlier he had been a United States senator, 1891–94. He was born in Lafourche Parish. His father, also named Edward Douglass White (1795–1847), was governor of Louisiana, 1835–39.

Huey Pierce Long (1893–1935) was born near Winnfield. He was governor of Louisiana (1928–31) and United States senator (1931–35). While a senator, he organized a "share the wealth" plan. His slogan was "Every Man a King." Long ruled like a dictator, but his terms in office produced some benefits for the state. He was assassinated in 1935.

Authors who wrote about life in Louisiana include Lyle Saxon, who was born in Baton Rouge, and George Washington Cable, Harnett Kane, and Robert Tallant, all born in New Orleans. The historian Charles Étienne Arthur Gayarré was also born in New Orleans. One of the great American architects of the 1800's was Henry Hobson Richardson, born in St. James Parish.

Two famous actresses of the 19th century were Adah Bertha Menken, known as Adah Isaacs Menken, and Minnie Maddern Fiske. Both were born in New Orleans. This city was also the birthplace of playwright Lillian Hellman, pianist and composer Louis Moreau Gottschalk, and jazz musician and singer Daniel Louis Armstrong, known as Satchmo.

Folk singer Huddie Ledbetter was born in Mooringsport.

▶HISTORY

When the first Europeans arrived in Louisiana, they found a small population of Indians scattered throughout the area. One of the strongest and most important groups was the Caddo confederacy. The Caddoans oc-

---

IMPORTANT DATES

1541	Hernando de Soto discovered the Mississippi River.
1682	La Salle reached the mouth of the Mississippi and claimed the entire Mississippi Valley for France.
1699	Pierre Lemoyne, Sieur d'Iberville, explored the lower Mississippi as far as the Red River.
1714	Fort St. Jean Baptiste (Natchitoches) established, first permanent settlement in present-day Louisiana.
1718	Jean Baptiste Lemoyne, Sieur de Bienville, founded New Orleans.
1722	New Orleans became capital of the Louisiana colony.
1727	Ursuline nuns established a school at New Orleans.
1762	France transferred Louisiana to Spain by the secret Treaty of Fontainebleau.
1769	Spanish authority restored after a revolt by the French colonists in 1768.
1776	Governor Bernardo de Gálvez assisted American patriots during the Revolutionary War.
1795	Jean Étienne Boré invented a process for large-scale refining of sugar.
1800	Spain ceded Louisiana back to France.
1803	United States purchased the Louisiana territory from France.
1812	April 30, Louisiana admitted to the Union as the 18th state.
1815	General Andrew Jackson defeated the British in the battle of New Orleans.
1831	First railroad built in Louisiana.
1838	First Mardi Gras parade held in New Orleans.
1845	New state constitution provided for a statewide system of public education.
1849	Baton Rouge became the capital of Louisiana.
1861	Louisiana seceded from the Union and joined the Confederacy.
1862	Admiral David G. Farragut won New Orleans for the Union.
1868	Louisiana readmitted to the Union.
1901	Oil discovered near Jennings.
1905	Commercial mining of sulfur by the Frasch process begun near Sulphur.
1916	Monroe gas field discovered.
1953	Re-enactment in New Orleans of the Louisiana Purchase on the 150th anniversary of the event.
1956	New Orleans Bridge and Causeway over Lake Pontchartrain completed.
1963	Mississippi River–Gulf Outlet opened to ocean-going vessels.
1966	Amendment to the Louisiana Constitution permits the governor to run for office to succeed himself.
1970	State legislature passed tax package; first new tax legislation since 1948.

---

cupied the northern part of the state. Other smaller groups lived in the east and the south. Words from Indian languages are still used today as the names of some of the bayous, rivers, lakes, and towns.

Exploration and Settlement

The mouth of the Mississippi River probably was sighted by Spanish explorers in the early 1500's. But Hernando de Soto is thought of as the real discoverer of the Mississippi. In 1541, while searching for riches, he and his party crossed the river, probably at a point near Memphis, Tennessee.

More than 100 years passed before further exploration of the river took place. In April, 1682, the French explorer Robert Cavelier, Sieur de La Salle, reached the mouth of the Mississippi. There he laid claim to the entire Mississippi Valley. He named the area Louisiana in honor of his king, Louis XIV. Two years later La Salle was sent to establish a colony on the delta. But he made an error in calculating its latitude. As a result he sailed too far westward and landed at Matagorda Bay, Texas.

The next attempt at settlement in the Louisiana area was made by a French Canadian, Pierre Lemoyne, Sieur d'Iberville. His younger brother, Jean Baptiste Lemoyne, Sieur de Bienville, joined him on the expedition. In the spring of 1699 they rediscovered the mouth of the Mississippi and sailed up the river, probably as far as the mouth of the Red River. But they chose a place near present-day Biloxi, Mississippi, for the first settlement. Early in 1702 the colonists were moved to a better location—a site near present-day Mobile, Alabama, which was named Fort Louis de la Mobile. Bienville was named governor of Louisiana, and Fort Louis became the headquarters for the colony.

Colonial Days

In 1712 France gave control of Louisiana to Antoine Crozat, a wealthy merchant. About 2 years later Fort St. Jean Baptiste was established at present-day Natchitoches. This was the first permanent settlement in the area now known as Louisiana. But Crozat failed to develop the colony. In 1717 it was turned over to a private group—John Law's Company of the West. Many settlers came to Louisiana, attracted by stories of quick riches. New Orleans, established by Bienville in 1718, became the new capital in 1722. But bad management prevented any real development of the colony, and it was returned to the French king in 1732.

By the Treaty of Fontainebleau in 1762, France ceded Louisiana west of the Mississippi River to Spain. Louisiana east of the river was ceded to Britain. The French were glad to get rid of Louisiana. It had been a heavy drain on the French treasury.

The people of Louisiana were unhappy about the change, and the Spanish were slow to take command. Late in 1768 the Frenchmen of New Orleans ordered the Spanish governor to leave the colony and declared their allegiance to France. But this revolution did not last long. Alexander O'Reilly, the new Spanish governor, arrived in August of 1769 to restore Spanish authority. O'Reilly was an Irishman who had settled in Spain. His rule was harsh, but Louisiana progressed under it.

During the Revolutionary War, Louisiana aided the American colonies. The Spanish governor, Bernardo de Gálvez, allowed the Americans to go up and down the Mississippi and to use New Orleans as a base for sending supplies. After the war American settlers thronged to the upper Mississippi Valley. The Mississippi River became their main artery of commerce, with New Orleans as the most important seaport.

To solve shipping problems at New Orleans, the United States began negotiations to buy the "Isle of Orleans"—an area including New Orleans and the mouth of the Mississippi. By this time Louisiana was back in French hands. Spain had returned it to France in 1800. Napoleon I, ruler of France, decided to offer the entire Louisiana area for sale, and the United States purchased it in 1803.

Statehood

In 1804 the part of the Louisiana Purchase north of 33 degrees latitude became the District of Louisiana. The part to the south— the present state of Louisiana—was organized as the Territory of Orleans. In 1811 Congress passed an act allowing the Territory of Orleans to draw up a constitution. On April 30, 1812, Louisiana was admitted to the Union as the 18th state.

Almost immediately after becoming a state, Louisiana became involved in the War of 1812. In 1815 General Andrew Jackson defeated the British in the battle of New Orleans. After the war Louisiana grew rapidly. Cotton and sugar plantations flourished. Railroads were built, and steamboats came to the Mississippi. By 1840 New Orleans was second only to New York as a port.

From 1861 to 1865 Louisiana was involved in the Civil War. It withdrew from the Union in January, 1861. After a brief period as a republic, Louisiana joined the Confederacy. In 1862 Admiral David G. Farragut captured New Orleans and Baton Rouge for the federal government. During the rest of the Civil War these cities and other important areas were administered by a federal governor. The Confederate state capital was moved to Opelousas and then to Shreveport. Recovery after the war was slow. There was a long period of strife, plundering, and heavy taxation.

An event that helped the economy of the state in the 1870's was the building of a system of jetties, or piers, that deepened the mouth of the Mississippi River. Before that time the larger oceangoing ships sometimes were unable to get over the bars of silt and sand. After 1900 Louisiana began large-scale production of petroleum, natural gas, sulfur, and other minerals. The traditional crops— cotton, sugarcane, and rice—continued to be important. But many farmers turned unproductive land into pasture for beef cattle. Dairying, poultry raising, and truck farming added to the variety of agriculture in the state. Since World War II the industrial areas around the larger cities have expanded rapidly.

The Future

At present Louisiana is in a prosperous era. It is fortunate in having an abundance of fresh water, many raw materials that are needed in the space age, and good transportation. All these should help to bring many more industries to the state. With continued prosperity the state should be able to obtain the money badly needed to provide vocational training and other services for all its people.

W. C. BUCHANAN
Northeast Louisiana State College

LOUISIANA PURCHASE

By the Louisiana Purchase of 1803 the United States bought from France a vast area of some 828,000 square miles. This was one of the biggest land purchases in history. The area involved stretches from the Mississippi River in the east to the Rocky Mountains in the west and from the Gulf of Mexico in the south to the United States–Canadian border in the north. This territory makes up the central third of the United States. It included, before territorial boundary adjustments, all or parts of what were to become 15 states. These are, with the dates of their admission to the Union: Louisiana (1812), Missouri (1821), Arkansas (1836), Texas (1845), Iowa (1846), Minnesota (1858), Kansas (1861), Nebraska (1867), Colorado (1876), North Dakota (1889), South Dakota (1889), Montana (1889), Wyoming (1890), Oklahoma (1907), and New Mexico (1912).

▶ HISTORICAL BACKGROUND

This huge region was explored in the 16th century by the Spanish conquistadores Francisco Vásquez de Coronado (1510–54) and Hernando de Soto (1500?–42). A Frenchman, Robert Cavelier, Sieur de La Salle (1643–87), in 1682 named it Louisiana in honor of his king, Louis XIV (1638–1715). Early in the 18th century the French founded settlements along the Mississippi River. The most important one, New Orleans, was founded in 1718 on the east bank of the river, 90 miles from its mouth. In 1732 the French Government took possession of Louisiana.

At the end of the French and Indian War (1754–63) in North America, France lost its lands east of the Mississippi to Britain. In a

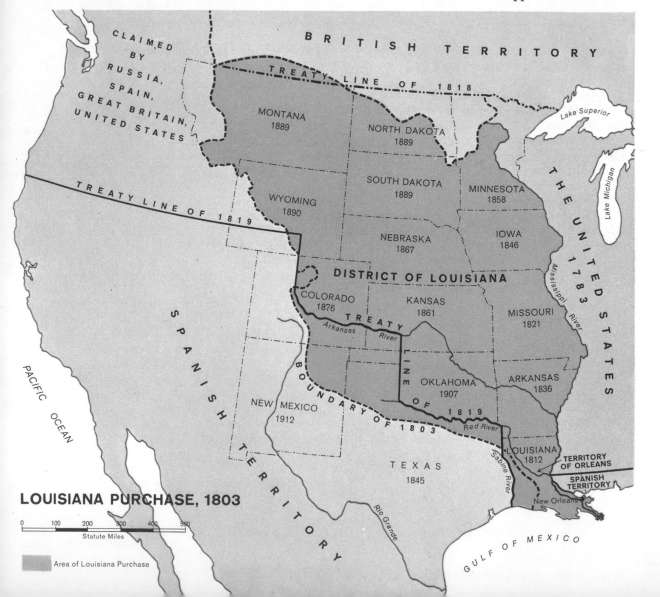

LOUISIANA PURCHASE, 1803

0 100 200 300 400 500
Statute Miles

Area of Louisiana Purchase

separate treaty France gave up Louisiana—the French lands west of the Mississippi, and New Orleans—to Spain.

In the late 18th century Napoleon Bonaparte (1769–1821) rose to become the first emperor of France. He dreamed of creating a new French colonial empire in North America. In 1800 he persuaded the Spanish rulers to sign the secret Treaty of San Ildefonso. This treaty transferred Louisiana back to France.

▶CRISIS OVER LOUISIANA

When President Thomas Jefferson (1743–1826) learned of the secret agreement, he was very worried. He did not welcome the idea of gaining a strong France as a neighbor in the west in place of a weak Spain. Jefferson was also afraid that when the French controlled New Orleans they would close the Mississippi to American trade. This happened even sooner than he expected.

On October 15, 1802, the King of Spain finally gave the order transferring Louisiana to France. But the Spanish governor in New Orleans did not know of this order. The following day he suddenly withdrew the **right of deposit**. This was the right given to American shippers that allowed them to leave their goods at New Orleans while awaiting transfer onto oceangoing vessels.

Seeing their means of making a living threatened, western fur trappers and traders demanded that the United States seize Louisiana by force. As it turned out, this was not necessary.

Jefferson ordered Robert R. Livingston (1746–1813), the American minister to France, to explore the possibility of purchasing New Orleans and a section of West Florida near the mouth of the Mississippi. Jefferson used psychology to force Napoleon's hand. He permitted to fall into the hands of French agents certain letters hinting at a joint United States-British attack on Louisiana. One to Livingston said: "The day that France takes possession of New Orleans . . . we must marry ourselves to the British fleet and nation." In March, 1803, James Monroe (1758–1831) went to Paris as a special envoy. Congress had given him the power to offer Napoleon up to $10,000,000 for New Orleans and a tract of land on the Gulf of Mexico.

Monroe did not arrive in Paris until April 12. By then Napoleon had decided to give up his plans for a New World empire. He needed all of his ships for his planned invasion of England. His treasury was nearly empty—and he wanted to prevent the United States from joining Britain against him. He decided to sell all of Louisiana.

▶THE SALE AND TRANSFER

Livingston and Monroe were startled at being offered so much more than they had come to buy. They also knew that they did not have the right to go beyond their instructions. But it would have taken many weeks to refer the matter to Washington. Moreover, Napoleon was in a hurry to finish the business.

A treaty dated April 30, 1803, and signed May 2, gave Louisiana to the United States for about 80,000,000 francs, or $15,000,000. Of this amount, 60,000,000 ($11,250,000) was for the territory itself. The rest covered debts owed by France to American citizens, which the United States agreed to pay.

At first Jefferson did not know exactly how to take the surprising news. The Constitution said nothing about acquiring foreign territory. But popular enthusiasm for the purchase swept his doubts aside. Not until October was the treaty ratified by the Senate. On December 20 a colorful ceremony was held at New Orleans. Frenchmen, Spaniards, and Americans watched as the French flag came down and the Stars and Stripes fluttered to the top of the flagpole.

For about 3 cents an acre the United States had almost doubled its area. In 1804 Louisiana was divided into the Territory of Orleans (which became the state of Louisiana) and the District of Louisiana (later divided among 14 states).

Because the boundaries had not been exactly defined in the treaty, disputes arose. In 1818 the United States and Britain established the northern boundary at the 49th parallel. In 1819 the United States purchased Florida from Spain for $5,000,000 and gave up its claim to Texas. With the Louisiana Purchase the United States took a giant step in expanding its national territory "from sea to shining sea."

MARY LEE SETTLE
Author, *O Beulah Land*

LOUVRE

The Louvre, in Paris, is the largest museum in the world. It is also one of the oldest museums, having been opened to the public in 1793. The buildings of the Louvre form a tremendous rectangle around courtyards and gardens.

The famous collections of the Louvre grew from the works of art bought by the kings of France for their own enjoyment. Ruler after ruler added more treasures. Occasionally a king sold something to pay for the expenses of war, but most of the original works remain. The Louvre is now a national, or state-owned, museum, and its collections are enlarged by gifts and purchases.

People come from all over the world to see the great works of art gathered in the huge museum, and there are more than 1,500,000 visitors every year. The Louvre owns over 250,000 works of art, including more than 5,000 paintings and 75,000 drawings.

The museum has a fine collection of the art of the ancient world. The Egyptian collection includes works sent back to France by Napoleon during his campaign in Egypt. One of the ancient Near Eastern works is a relief (sculpture carved from a background) dated about 2100 B.C. It was inscribed with the code of Hammurabi, the oldest known code of laws. Among the important pieces of sculpture from ancient Greece are the famous marble statues the *Winged Victory* and the *Venus de Milo*.

The museum contains the most extensive collections of French paintings and sculpture in the world. The work of every period from medieval to modern times is represented. Next to the collection of French paintings, the Italian collection is the largest. There are also fine collections of Flemish, Dutch, and Spanish paintings. One room contains 23 paintings by the 17th-century Flemish painter Peter Paul Rubens and his pupils. All these paintings show scenes from the life of Marie de Médicis, Queen of France (1573–1642). The collection of decorative arts includes enamels, furniture, ivories, and the Crown jewels.

The buildings that house these works of art are important in the history of French architecture and culture. Many of the most talented and famous French painters, sculptors, and architects helped to decorate these buildings. The first building, a royal fortress built about

Above: A gallery in the Louvre. The easel and canvas belong to a student copying a painting by Rubens. Right: *Mona Lisa* (1503?) by Leonardo da Vinci.

1190, was made into a royal palace in the 14th century. Francis I (1494–1547) was the first great art patron in France. When he came to the throne, the palace was in a state of decay. In 1546 he hired the architect Pierre Lescot to design a new palace. Francis I bought the most important paintings by Raphael and Leonardo da Vinci, including the *Mona Lisa,* which the Louvre owns today. By the time Francis I died, the royal collections had been enriched by many valuable works of art.

During the reign of Henry IV (1553–1610), a long wing called the Grand Gallery was added to the palace. The King allowed hundreds of artists and craftsmen to live on the lower floors of the gallery. Today some of the most famous Renaissance paintings hang there.

Louis XIII (1601–43) and his architect Jacques Lemercier tore down the last remains of the medieval fortress and added to the buildings. The next ruler, Louis XIV (1638–1715), also made additions. The most important was the famous Louvre colonnade (a series of columns supporting a roof), designed

Two famous Greek statues in the Louvre: *Venus de Milo* (*left*) and *Winged Victory* of Samothrace (*right*). Both probably were carved in the 3rd century B.C.

by Claude Perrault and completed in 1670. This colonnade is considered one of the finest examples of French classical architecture. After Francis I, Louis XIV was the most outstanding royal collector. He was, however, more interested in his great palace at Versailles, which he decorated with many of the treasures from the Louvre. When the King deserted the Louvre to live in Versailles, the people of Paris moved in, setting up ramshackle houses and shops in the big courtyards. The buildings themselves became hideouts for criminals.

By 1710 nearly 2,400 paintings were in the royal collection. People interested in the arts were upset to see the royal palace treated so badly, and plans were made to restore it. In 1793 the Grand Gallery was officially opened as a museum to exhibit the royal collection.

After Napoleon (1769–1821) became emperor, he had the huts and booths cleared away from the courtyards. He sent away the artists who had been living in the Louvre. Napoleon had his architects, Charles Percier and Pierre Fontaine, build a large triumphal arch in the courtyard. Occasionally Napoleon stayed in the palace, and for his convenience one of the halls was made into a riding ring.

The buildings of the Louvre were completed by Emperor Napoleon III (1808–73) between 1852 and 1857. Since then the Louvre has remained much the same.

LOWELL, JAMES RUSSELL (1819–1891)

James Russell Lowell, author, teacher, and diplomat, was born on February 22, 1819, in Cambridge, Massachusetts. His father was a Unitarian minister, and James was the youngest of five children. After attending a neighborhood school run by an Englishman, James entered Harvard at the age of 15. He lived at home and spent much of his time reading English poetry. He wrote poems and essays for college magazines and literary societies and was chosen class poet.

Lowell went to law school after college and graduated in 1840. The same year he became engaged to Maria White, a poet, who was a great influence on him. They were married in 1844. *A Year's Life* (1841), a collection of Lowell's poems, was followed by *Poems* (1844). In 1846 the first of Lowell's *Biglow Papers,* a series of antislavery satires, was printed in the Boston *Courier*. It was in the form of a letter from "Ezekiel Biglow," presenting a poem by his son, Hosea. Lowell collected this series into book form in 1848. A second series, published in 1866, ran in the *Atlantic Monthly* during the Civil War.

A Fable for Critics, a second series of *Poems,* and *The Vision of Sir Launfal* also appeared in 1848. Lowell and his wife spent over a year in Europe before she died in 1853, leaving Lowell with one small daughter. In 1855 he was chosen to fill Longfellow's position as professor of French and Spanish languages and literatures and professor of belles lettres at Harvard. He went to Europe to prepare for this position and began teaching in 1856. In 1857 he married his daughter's governess. That same year he became the first editor of the *Atlantic Monthly*. He next edited the *North American Review* with Charles Eliot Norton.

Lowell was sent to Madrid as American ambassador in 1877 and was transferred to London in 1880. After his second wife died in 1885, he returned to private life. He died on August 12, 1891, in Cambridge in the house where he was born.

LOYOLA, SAINT IGNATIUS (1491–1556)

Saint Ignatius Loyola founded a religious order of Catholic priests and brothers known as the Society of Jesus. Its members are known as Jesuits. Ignatius was born in 1491 in Loyola in northeastern Spain, the youngest son of a wealthy nobleman. When he was about 20 years old, he fought against the French in the Spanish city of Pamplona.

During the battle Ignatius was severely wounded in the legs. While he was recovering, he began to read the life of Christ and the lives of saints. Deeply moved by these stories, Ignatius resolved to change his former way of life and dedicate himself to God.

When his wounds had healed, he went to Montserrat, a famous monastery in northeastern Spain. After 3 days of prayer he made a vow to become a soldier of God and placed his weapons on the altar of the monastery church.

Ignatius then began a life of prayer and penance. He supported himself by begging. In 1523 he made a trip to Jerusalem. He returned to Spain the following year and began to study for the priesthood. In 1528 he went to Paris to continue his studies. There he and six other young men, all eager to serve God, took vows to lead a religious life, to teach Christianity to unbelievers, and to make a pilgrimage to Jerusalem.

In 1537 Ignatius and his companions tried to make this pilgrimage. However, war had broken out in Jerusalem. They got no farther than Italy. In Venice, Ignatius and some of his companions were ordained priests in June of 1537. Two years later they formally organized the Society of Jesus, a teaching order. Pope Paul III approved the society in 1540.

Ignatius was elected the first general of the society and spent the remaining years of his life directing its activities. By the time of his death there were Jesuits working in Portugal, Spain, Italy, France, and Germany, as well as in South America and Asia. Ignatius died in Rome on July 31, 1556. He was canonized in 1622, and his feast day is July 31.

KATHLEEN McGOWAN
Catholic Youth Encyclopedia

LUBRICATION AND LUBRICANTS

Today machines of every kind, large and small, simple and complex, work for mankind. Without proper lubrication none of these machines could operate. The main purpose of a lubricant is to reduce the friction and wear between two surfaces.

▶ FRICTION

It is harder to slide something over a rough wooden floor than it is to slide the same object over a smooth linoleum floor. That is because friction is greater on the rough floor than on the smooth floor. Whenever two surfaces move against each other, there is a force that works against that movement. That force is friction.

Any surface, no matter how smooth it may seem to the naked eye, looks very uneven and bumpy under a microscope. At one time it was thought that friction between surfaces was a result of the fact that the bumps on one surface had to be slid up and down the bumps on the other surface. Modern scientists have found that this is only part of the cause of friction. They have found that these bumps actually stick to each other under pressure. When pressure between the surfaces is increased, more of these bumps come into contact with each other and stick, and friction is greater.

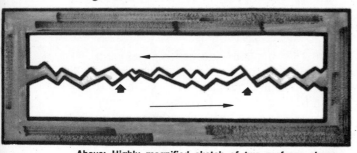

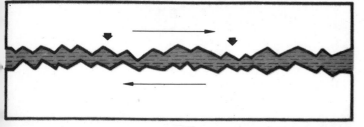

Above: Highly magnified sketch of two surfaces shows how very tiny irregularities cause friction. Below: A thin film of lubricant separates and cushions the two surfaces and lets them slide smoothly past each other.

When an oil is used as a lubricant, friction is reduced by separating the two surfaces with a thin oil film so that they do not touch. The oil film replaces solid friction—the friction between surfaces of solids—with **fluid friction**, which is much weaker than solid friction. When a fluid—a liquid or gas—separates the surfaces of two solids, and one or both of these solids is moved, the fluid between them acts like a deck of cards, moving in layers. The resistance of the fluid layers to movement over each other is called fluid friction, or **viscosity**. Liquids of high viscosity are thick and do not flow as easily as low-viscosity liquids. Molasses, for example, has a higher viscosity than water.

Sometimes friction is very useful. There must be friction between an automobile's tires and the road. Otherwise, the tires would just turn and the automobile would not move. This often happens when an automobile tries to start on an icy or other slippery surface. Walking on a slippery surface is also difficult because of the lack of friction. Many machines make use of friction. Rollers are often used to move a product through a machine; friction makes this possible. Automobile brakes also work by friction.

There are many places, however, where friction is a nuisance. Friction makes it harder to move the parts of a machine. If there is too much friction in a machine, extra power is needed to make it run. This makes running the machine very expensive. If you rub your arm with the palm of your hand, you can feel heat produced by friction. This heat can be troublesome. In some machines friction can produce enough heat to cause the parts to be welded together.

Early man knew some things about friction. He knew, for example, that it was easier to roll a log than to slide it. Very soon he learned that certain materials could be used to make sliding easier. When building the pyramids, the ancient Egyptians used mortar (a thick, slippery paste) to help slide huge stones into place. Once wheeled vehicles came into use, lubrication became more important. The Egyptians used mutton tallow (sheep fat) to make the wheels turn more easily. Many different fish oils, vegetable oils, and animal fats have been used for lubrication since ancient times in many parts of the world. In the 19th century, however, petroleum products quickly replaced other lubricants for most uses.

TYPES OF LUBRICANTS

Lubricants may be grouped into three different types: oils, greases, and solid lubricants.

Oils

Lubricating oils are made in many different viscosities. In order to cut down friction as much as possible, it is necessary to use the lowest-viscosity oil possible. However, where pressure between machine parts is great, a thin (low-viscosity) oil would be squeezed out, leaving the part without lubrication. For many purposes, therefore, it is necessary to use thicker (higher-viscosity) oil.

Greases

Lubricating greases are oils that have been thickened by the addition of special materials. Usually metallic soaps are used for this. Metallic soaps are chemicals that are in the same chemical family as the soap you wash your face with. Greases are so thick that they cannot be poured from a container. They have the advantage that they will stick to parts on which they are used. They do not run off easily, leaving the part unprotected, as an oil may. In use, the oil in the grease oozes out slowly, gradually feeding oil to the machine part. The grease acts like a storage container for the oil. Greases also help prevent wear by keeping water and dirt away from machine parts.

Most lubricating oils and greases are petroleum products. However, other materials are used for special purposes. The most important of these is a group of chemicals called **esters**. Fats, such as mutton tallow, are one kind of ester. However, other types of esters, which are man-made, are much better lubricants than fats.

Another useful group of materials are the chemicals called **silicones**. Silicones contain the element silicon. Silicone oils and greases are valuable because they work well at very high and very low temperatures, while petroleum products do not. Silicones are too expensive, however, to use where petroleum products would work as well.

Solid Lubricants

Most solid lubricants reduce friction because their molecules form very, very thin plates or sheets that slide over one another very easily.

The main advantage of solid lubricants is that they remain in place longer than oils or greases. Parts that are not easily reached are often lubricated with solid lubricants so that they will not have to be lubricated as often. The most important solid lubricant is **graphite**, a form of the element carbon. Graphite is the black material used to make the "lead" in lead pencils.

ADDITIVES

Additives are materials that are added to a product in order to improve it in some way. Lubricating oils, for example, tend to get thinner when they are heated. When cold, they tend to thicken. Additives help keep oils at the same viscosity at different temperatures. Another problem is solved by adding additives called antioxidants. Antioxidants prevent oils and greases from combining with the oxygen in the air to form acids and other chemicals that can harm machinery. Oils used in engines, such as automobile engines, contain additives called detergents. These detergents work the same way as laundry detergents. They keep the inside of the engine clean and free of dirt that can harm or clog the engine.

IMPORTANCE OF LUBRICANTS

Lubricants have thousands of uses both in the home and in industry. Low-viscosity oils are used in the home to keep sewing machines, electric fans, washing machines, and refrigerators running smoothly and quietly. Bicycles, roller skates, and coaster wagons run faster when their wheels are well lubricated. A single automobile uses several types of lubricant. All the many thousands of machines and vehicles that make life easier for us must be kept well lubricated in order to run well and not wear out. The United States alone uses over 1,500,000,000 gallons of oils and greases a year to keep its machines running.

Reviewed by T. W. HAVELY
Shell Oil Company

See also PETROLEUM AND PETROLEUM REFINING; WORK, POWER, AND MACHINES.

LUKE, SAINT. See EVANGELISTS, THE.

LUMBER AND LUMBERING

Imagine that you are walking through the woods on a clear, cold, winter's day. The air is clean and fresh, and the snow crunches under your feet. In the distance you can hear the steady chop of an ax or the whine of a power saw. You may hear the faint cry, "Timber!" Then, with a creak and a swish and a spray of snow, a tree falls through the air and settles on the ground. You know loggers are working in the woods.

The forest has served the needs of men for centuries. Wood is used to make homes and other buildings. It is used to make furniture. Wood is used to make pulp and paper. It is still used by many people as fuel. But no matter how we use wood, men must first go into the forest and log the trees.

There are forests all around the globe. The Scandinavian countries have depended on their forests for centuries. Finland's forests, for example, cover 72 percent of that country. At one time there may be 200,000 men at work in its forests. Japan and Germany also produce large quantities of lumber. But nowhere in the world have forests been more important in meeting the needs of people than in North America. The story of logging and lumbering is largely the story of logging and lumbering in North America.

Productive forests—those that can yield a continuous crop of timber—cover nearly 500,000,000 acres in the United States. In Canada productive forests cover slightly more than 600,000,000 acres. This is an area approximately equal in size to the provinces of Ontario, Manitoba, and Saskatchewan combined. The United States is the world's largest user of lumber. It is also one of the largest producers of lumber. It produces more than one third of the world's total. It produces much of the wood pulp in the world. Canada produces well over half the world's supply of newsprint.

North American forests are rich in trees that are strong, beautiful, and useful. In the northeastern states there are white pine, hard maple, oak, basswood, and beech. In eastern Canada there are spruce and balsam fir, and white, red, and jack pine. On the Pacific slope there are Douglas fir, hemlock, western red cedar, and spruce. California is known for its redwood and the South for its pine **stands** (a stand is an area on which only one type of tree grows). There are almost 1,000 different kinds of trees growing in the United States. About 100 of these kinds of trees are used for lumber.

► EARLY LOGGING AND LUMBERING

Logging and lumbering played a major role in the development of North America. The forests provided shelter, fuel, game, and furs, but they also occupied great areas of fertile land needed for crops. The work of clearing the land was difficult and wearying.

But from the earliest days there were many settlers for whom logging and lumbering provided a livelihood. Sawmills were built to cut lumber for building construction. Railroads and canals were built so that new stands of timber could be tapped. Lumber was produced for export to England.

The value of this lumber from the colonies was well appreciated in England. The great white pines made excellent masts for ships. Trees that were as tall and straight as these pines could not be found in Europe. Therefore men were sent out by the British Navy to mark the tallest trees of the colonial forests with the sign of a broad arrow. This meant that they were for the king. If a settler cut down or damaged a marked tree, he received the death sentence.

For nearly 300 years after Jamestown was settled in 1607, the white pine remained the most useful tree in the United States. The white pine stands of Maine were easily reached. So it was in this area, in York, Maine, in 1623, that the first sawmill in the United States is believed to have been built.

The forests of Canada were developed for war purposes after 1534, when Jacques Cartier claimed the land for France. The lumber was used by France to build ships of war. After the British conquered Canada in 1763, timbers from its forests were used to build the ships of the Royal Navy. Today the forest-products industry is the largest industry in Canada.

► METHODS OF LOGGING

Methods of logging vary according to the type of tree, its location, and the way in which the wood is to be used. There are four basic steps, however, that are common throughout the world. First, the tree must be cut down, or **felled**. Second, the tree must be cut, or **bucked**, into suitable lengths. It may be bucked into 16-foot lengths if the logs are going to the sawmill to be made into lumber. It may be cut into 4-foot lengths if the logs are going to a newsprint or pulp mill. Third, the bucked logs must be dragged, or **skidded**, out of the woods to a central assembly point, called a landing. A landing may be on a road, a railway, or a riverbank. The fourth major step is the **hauling**, or transportation, of the logs to the mill. Transportation may be by railcar, truck, or sled. The logs may be floated down a river. Sometimes the logs may be rafted and towed to the mill.

In many parts of the world men have completely changed logging by using machines instead of muscles. Although the ring of the ax is still heard in the woods, power saws are used increasingly in felling and bucking. In skidding and hauling, however, the change from the use of man power to machine power has been so great that some loggers say the story of modern logging is the story of transportation.

From the time of the first settlers until the end of the 19th century, men, animals, and the natural force of streams and rivers were of great importance in North American logging. Men felled the trees with powerful strokes of the ax. Horses or oxen skidded the logs out of the woods to the central assembly point, or landing. The spring river drive swept the logs to the mill in a rush of water and melting ice. Where there were no waterways, wagons or sleds drawn by mules or horses hauled the logs to the mill.

Horse skidding and stream driving are still used in many areas of eastern Canada and the United States, much as they were 100 or 200 years ago. But as good roads and new machines develop, tractors and trucks are replacing animals in skidding and hauling logs. Machines have tongs or grapples that load the logs onto the trucks at the landing.

Before logging begins, the logging manager must consider the needs of the mills in choosing the timber to be cut. Reforestation programs must be planned. Roads must be engineered. Forest fire hazards must be avoided, and fire drills organized. Campers

Logs stacked in long rows dry in a Swiss lumberyard.

and sportsmen must be encouraged to help prevent forest fires. The manager of a large operation often plans his logging program years in advance.

Sometimes **selective cutting**, or prelogging, is carried out to remove timber ready for harvesting without damaging the young, growing crop. Sometimes **salvage logging** is planned to follow the major logging operations, so that all remaining usable wood is removed from the site. The logging plan may call for all timber in an area to be logged. This is called **clear-cutting**. Other timber may be **patch logged**. In this method, cleared areas, or patches, are separated by stands of trees that serve as firebreaks or seed trees.

Some logging is done the year round. But in eastern Canada and the United States most logging takes place in the winter. Since a large part of the forest is swampy, men cannot move, or transport, wood in hot weather. In winter, snow forms white highways through the forest, and the frozen lakes can withstand the weight of a load of logs.

The loggers go into the eastern forests in the later summer or early autumn. First they must open up trails and build roads. Trees are felled to open up trails. Stumps are pulled out or blasted. Hollows are filled and streams bridged. In winter the snow is rolled until it is packed hard. Then it is sprinkled with water to give it an icy surface so that horses or machines can pull larger loads.

The fellers and buckers go into the woods alone or in pairs. Fellers must have great skill. A skilled feller can drop a tree exactly where he planned it to fall. After being felled, the trees are bucked and skidded to the landing point.

Time is important in winter operations, for the wood must be ready to move with the spring freshets, which come after the snows melt. Sometimes the logs are piled at the riverbank. Sometimes they are dumped onto the frozen surface of a lake. Then, when the ice melts in the spring, the logs are left in the water and can be rafted and towed to the river outlet. When the freshet comes, nimble lumberjacks drive the logs down the river, jumping from one to another of the big, slippery logs as they swirl through the waters.

On the Pacific slope logging is done in the summer or in all but the snowiest months of the year. Railroad logging was developed in the period from 1890 to 1930 to tap the remote stands of timber in the West. Here the trees were too big and the mountain streams too fast and furious to permit stream driving. The railroads usually ran along the mountain valleys or along the lower mountain slopes. Trees were logged as far up a mountain as the cables could reach from the railcars. From some of these valleys you can today still see on the mountainsides the ribbonlike lines that mark the limits of rail logging. Sparks from the engines started vast and terrible forest fires, and the scars still show on the mountain flanks.

The rugged landscape and the giant trees of the western timber stands made it very difficult to skid and haul logs. Because of this, machines to do these jobs were developed.

Steel cables now swing the logs over narrow canyons or up steep mountain slopes. Cable logging is called **high lead** or **skyline** skidding. One end of a cable is attached to the log to be skidded. The other end is fastened to a tall spar tree. By means of a diesel-powered donkey engine the log is dragged over the ground or swung through the sky to the landing. There it is lowered to a waiting truck. Normally the truck hauls the logs to the riverbank or seashore, and the logs are dumped into the water. Here they are sorted and **boomed** (guided or carried into position) and towed to the mill. While railways are still used to haul logs in a few operations, the era of rail logging belongs to the past.

In cable logging the **rigging cable** is attached to a spar tree chosen for its height and its central location. The job of cutting off the top of the spar tree so that the rigging may be attached belongs to the **high rigger**. With his safety belt slung around himself and the tree, the high rigger scrambles up the tree, cutting off branches as he goes. He reaches a height of 175 to 200 feet. Then he digs his spiked boots into the bark for a foothold and saws off the top of the tree. The moment the top is chopped loose, the high rigger drives his ax into the top of the trunk that is left. There he "rides" it as it whips back and forth. When the tree is still again, he attaches the rigging. The high rigger's job is dangerous and exciting.

Gradually the machine-made steel spar tree is replacing the wooden tree and the high rigger. The steel spar can be moved from place to place because it is mounted on wheels or tracks. It can be rigged more quickly than the wooden spar. Specially equipped tractors are replacing cables for logging where the ground is not too steep. Machines with long steel arms reach into the woods and scoop up the bucked logs. Huge log barges transport the logs from the tidewater to the mills.

The elements of logging and lumbering are essentially the same over the world. However, many countries use special features to meet their own requirements. Heavily populated countries, such as Pakistan, use people instead of machines to a much greater extent than countries of North America. In some Asian countries elephants are used to skid (drag) the logs out of the forests. In other parts of the world, such as Finland, horses are still used.

However, the trend toward using trucks and other machines is increasing everywhere.

▶ CAMP LIFE OF LOGGERS

Camp life has also changed. Thirty or forty years ago a lumberjack who went into the woods to earn a little money might walk from 25 to 50 miles along bad roads, carrying the 30 pounds or so of luggage that he needed to winter in the bush. Now he takes a plane, a bus, or a snowmobile. Many lumberjacks in eastern operations are farmers who turn to logging to earn some money in the winter. Others are professional loggers, for the introduction of machines calls for men with a high degree of skill.

Some loggers live in comfortable, well-equipped camps, although the construction of roads into the bush has turned some loggers into commuters who live in town and go to the woods each day. Some large camps have television and other recreation facilities for the men. In small bush operations the men may be housed in cabins built of fresh-sawn lumber. In each cabin are iron cots, a stove, a shelf or a table, and some nails in the walls on which to hang clothing.

A power saw is used to cut through a huge ponderosa pine in California.

Lumbering is an important industry in the state of Washington.

In Burma and Thailand elephants are an essential part of the lumbering industry.

The typical cookhouse has a shiny, big stove, presided over by a cook in a fresh white cap. The spotless dining room smells of strong coffee and fresh-baked bread. The men sit at long tables in the dining room, plates and cups neatly stacked upside down on the tabletops in front of them. The food is good and plentiful, for loggers have big appetites. Tales of loggers who eat seven steaks for lunch are not uncommon and are possibly true!

▶ **SAWMILLING**

The sawmiller takes over from the logger when the logs reach the millpond or yard. Summer is normally the busiest season for sawmills. However, the industry is gradually becoming a year-round operation in regions where the sawmills are part of large, integrated forest-products companies.

The logs are lifted from the water to the mill by means of a moving **jack ladder** (an endless chain with hooks along it) and put through the head saw. The **band saw** and the **circular saw** are two common types of saws. These either cut the logs into planks roughly 3 inches thick or **slab** the logs on two sides (remove the thick outside slices). The slabbed

log moves along a series of rollers and chains. It goes through the **gang saws**, which cut it into several boards. **Resaws** are used in some mills to slice the thick planks or boards into thinner sizes. Because the blades of the resaws are thin, they reduce the amount of the log turned into sawdust in the sawmilling process.

Then the boards go through the **edgers** and **trimmers**, which trim off the bark and reduce the boards to standard widths. To be planed, they go to the planer mill, which may be either next to the sawmill or some distance away. When the boards leave the planer mill they are smooth and lustrous. In the mill yard the lumber is stacked in neat rows.

Lumber must be sorted and graded, for boards sawn from average logs vary widely in quality. A perfect board is free of knots and has a nice, straight grain. A poor board may be scarred, stained, or knotty.

In the raw state of the wood the water content of a board may equal the weight of the wood itself. This moisture must be removed or reduced before lumber is used. Also, moisture encourages rot and stain and increases the cost of shipping lumber.

Sometimes lumber may be dried well enough in the open air. But if the lumber is to be used in flooring or furniture or for general interior use, air drying alone is not enough. Lumber for these uses is stacked in an airtight structure called a **dry kiln**. Here it is artifically dried to the correct moisture content. Drying by kiln can accomplish in hours or days what air drying would accomplish in weeks or months. After the drying process the lumber is ready to be shipped to market.

Sawmills may range in size from huge lumber factories to small, open-air, portable mills. The small mills are often used in the southern pine region of the United States and the interior of British Columbia. The basic steps in sawmilling are essentially the same throughout the world. The process has not changed much since the industry began.

Still, mechanization has had important effects on sawmills. As ways of using new kinds of woods are found, new ways of treating logs in the sawmill must be developed. The modern sawmill may have special machines called **chippers** and **barkers**. These salvage the chips, bark, and other parts of the

A boom of logs outside a sawmill in British Columbia. The logs are enclosed by connected floating timbers.

log wasted in the sawing process and prepare them for use in pulp mills. There is closed-circuit television in some mills. This permits the men to watch the progress of the boards along the rollers and chains. Machines that substitute for man power are constantly becoming a part of the lumber industry.

▶ **TRENDS**

The rapid changes in sawmilling and logging reflect our growing knowledge about wood and its uses. New pulpmaking and papermaking processes have led to the use of some varieties of trees previously left in the woods. Some countries are planting new varieties of trees to suit special needs. For instance, Australia and other countries in the Southern Hemisphere have started tree-plantation programs to grow softwood species. There are many needs for which the native hardwoods, such as eucalyptus, are not suited.

New roads, railroads, and man-made reservoirs behind hydroelectric dams have opened up stands of timber that men could not get to before. New, more efficient machines have made it possible to log timber that once was too difficult and costly to log. Modern loggers work the mountainsides in places where their grandfathers logged only the valleys. Methods of logging by helicopters and by balloons have been studied extensively. When better methods are developed for them, helicopters will be used. Balloons have already been used on an experimental basis.

Specially equipped airplanes are being increasingly used to locate and fight forest fires. When the size and number of forest fires are further reduced, there will be more timber available for cutting. Some foresters look ahead to the day when satellites will report forest fires and missile-mounted fire extinguishers will put them out. In the future, lumbermen may possibly use a machine with high-intensity rays of light—a laser beam—to saw off trees at their bases.

The more we learn about wood, the more we discover ways to use it. The challenge to develop new machines and new ways to harvest and manufacture lumber is becoming greater.

PAT CARNEY
Business columnist, Vancouver *Sun*

See also BUILDING CONSTRUCTION; FORESTS AND FORESTRY; WOOD AND WOOD PRODUCTS.

LUTHER, MARTIN (1483–1546)

Martin Luther was the first and most important leader of the reform movement in European Christianity known as the Protestant Reformation. Except for a brief trip to Rome, Luther spent his busy life—studying, teaching, preaching, and writing—within a small circle of towns in central Germany. From there his name and influence spread throughout Europe. By the time of his death he was the best-known and most talked-about figure of his time.

Luther was born in Eisleben, Germany, on November 10, 1483. He was given a better than average education by his father, who wanted his son to study for the law. At the age of 18 Luther entered the University of Erfurt. He received his master of arts degree in 1505 but gave up his law studies and entered a monastery in Erfurt. In 1507 he was ordained a priest in the Roman Catholic Church. He became a doctor (professor) of theology in 1512 at the University of Wittenberg.

Deeply disturbed by his struggle to find the meaning of faith and salvation, Luther became restless with the traditional ways of thinking. Gradually he turned to the teachings of the Bible, especially the epistles of the Apostle Paul, and to the writings of the early church father Augustine. Luther was not, at first, in rebellion against the Church. But he was dissatisfied with the religious ignorance and immorality of the time. A pilgrimage to Rome about 1510 left him disappointed with the Church's lack of spiritual truth in contrast to its material wealth and power.

A basic issue that aroused him to action was the Church's sale of indulgences. These were documents sold for cash by representatives of the Pope, promising forgiveness for sins. Luther argued that forgiveness is not something one can buy or deserve but is the free gift of God. He prepared a list of 95 theses, or statements, on the subject of indulgences and nailed them as a public notice on the church door in Wittenberg. The date—October 31, 1517—is often considered as marking the birth of the Reformation.

Luther, against his original intentions, was now thrust into a debate with the Church on fundamental issues of Church authority and religious truth. He came to be regarded as a dangerous heretic, unbeliever, and revolutionary. In a series of public hearings Pope Leo X tried to persuade Luther to change his mind and withdraw his objections against the Church. The most famous of these hearings was held in the city of Worms, Germany, in 1521. There Luther defended his position, claiming the authority of the Bible as higher than the authority of the Pope. He refused to alter his views, saying: "My conscience is bound by the Word of God; I cannot and will not recant anything. . . . Here I stand; I cannot do otherwise." Excommunicated from the Roman Catholic Church by the Pope's decree, Luther became the leader of the growing protest, or Protestant, movement throughout Germany.

Luther's translation of the Bible into German was of great importance in the early days of the Reformation. For the first time people could read the Bible for themselves in their own language, rather than hearing it read in church in Latin. He also wrote many books and essays and the hymn "A Mighty Fortress is Our God," which is sometimes called the battle hymn of the Reformation.

Luther's religious views developed out of his own troubled conscience about the meaning of salvation. He came to understand that God freely offers forgiveness, faith, and new life to anyone who puts his trust in Jesus Christ as the Son of God and as the Mediator between man as sinner and God as Savior. This view became known as the doctrine of justification by faith.

The last years of Luther's life were marked with difficulties. These arose not only with Rome but within Protestantism and even within the emerging Lutheran Church itself. Though he won the political protection of the German rulers, Luther suffered loss of prestige with many of the common people. Stubborn and unyielding, he frequently came into conflict with other reform leaders.

Luther was married in 1525 to Katherine von Bora, who bore him six children. His family life was happy, intimate, and warm, and he always enjoyed a large circle of friends and associates. He died at Eisleben on February 18, 1546.

HUGH T. KERR
Princeton Theological Seminary

See also REFORMATION.

LUXEMBOURG

The Grand Duchy of Luxembourg has been called The Land of Haunted Castles. This tiny country covers only 999 square miles, but it has over 100 castles. Most of the castles have partly tumbled down and rise on hilltops like huge gray ghosts. Luxembourg was once a land of warlike feudal knights who were quick to attack their neighbors' lands or to defend their own. Today Luxembourg is a bustling industrial nation and a center of the movement for European unity.

▶ THE PEOPLE

Most Luxembourgers come from peasant stock. It has been said that the great-grandfathers of almost all living Luxembourgers ploughed the fields, chopped down trees, or pressed grapes. This is changing as more and more people move into the growing cities. The most important of these is the capital, Luxembourg City.

Nearly all Luxembourgers speak several languages. They all speak Letzeburgesch, a Germanic language with some French added. Children start learning German in the first grade. French, Luxembourg's official language, is begun in the third grade. High-school students also learn English.

Children start school when they are 6 years old and must attend for at least 8 years. As there are no universities in the country, boys and girls go abroad to study.

Luxembourgers are travelers. Many of its people have moved to other nations. In fact, there are more people of Luxembourgian origin living in the United States than in the Grand Duchy. The Luxembourgers who have remained at home take pride in their beautifully kept homes and attractive countryside. Throughout Luxembourg there are roadside shrines decorated with flowers. Most Luxembourgers are Roman Catholics, but there is complete freedom of religion.

▶ THE LAND

The northern part of Luxembourg is known as the Oesling or the E'sleck. Here the forested Ardennes plateau reaches 1,700 feet above sea level. Today only about one third of Luxembourg is forested. But 150 years ago,

when Luxembourg belonged to France, it was called the Department of Forests because three quarters of the land was wooded.

The southern part of Luxembourg is called Le Bon Pays, which means "the Good Earth." About 20 percent of the population live on farms in these fertile lowlands and river valleys. Most farms are small, usually about 30 acres in size. Farmers grow wheat, rye, oats, beets, potatoes, vegetables, and fruits. Wine grapes are grown along the Moselle

Clervaux, the leading town in northern Luxembourg.

River, which divides Luxembourg from Germany. Farmers also raise livestock, and there is a flourishing dairy industry.

The southern part of Luxembourg, along the French border, is known as the Red Earth because of the rich veins of iron ore that were discovered there in the 1870's. Iron ore is Luxembourg's most important natural resource. Esch-sur-Alzette, the center of the steel industry, is the nation's second largest city.

▶ INDUSTRY AND PRODUCTS

The iron and steel industry is the basis of the economic life of Luxembourg. Despite its small size, Luxembourg is an important steel-producing country. Steel, agricultural products, wine, and tourism are Luxembourg's chief industries.

Luxembourg has a modern transportation and communications system. Highways are excellent, and railways and planes connect the country with all of Europe. Radio-Tele Luxembourg is the largest private commercial radio and television station in Europe.

▶ HISTORY

Luxembourg is an old country, which had its beginnings about 1,000 years ago. In A.D. 963 a young count named Sigefroi became the owner of some land and an old fortress called Lucilinburhuc, or "little fort." Sigefroi rebuilt the fort, which was at the place where Luxembourg City stands today.

Under Sigefroi and the nobles who followed him, Luxembourg grew and became an important power in the Middle Ages. Some of its rulers became kings of other countries too, and some led or took part in the Crusades.

Luxembourg's favorite hero, Jean l'Aveugle—John the Blind (1296–1346)—became Count of Luxembourg in 1309. He and his army waged war throughout Europe. In about 1340 he was blinded. According to legend, he pretended that he could see and kept fighting until he died in battle in 1346.

The wars continued, and Luxembourg grew bigger. It also grew poorer and less able to defend its large territory. Philip the Good, Duke of Burgundy (1396–1467), conquered Luxembourg in 1443. For the next 400 years many nations fought to control this fortress stronghold. Luxembourg became an independent constitutional monarchy in 1839.

When World War I began in 1914, Germany broke its promise to respect Luxembourg's neutrality and independence. German armies invaded Luxembourg and then proceeded to attack France. In World War II, Germany's armies again invaded Luxembourg. In 1944 the United States Army freed Luxembourg from the Germans after long, hard fighting, which destroyed much of the northern half of the country.

Since World War II independent Luxembourg has been a leader of the important new movement toward peaceful unity in Western Europe. Luxembourg is an active member of the North Atlantic Treaty Organization (NATO), the European Coal and Steel Community (whose headquarters were in Luxembourg until 1966, when they moved to Brussels, Belgium), the European Economic Community (Common Market), and the European Atomic Energy Community (EURATOM). Through such organizations Luxembourg is working to remove the barriers that kept nations apart and at war for so many centuries.

Susan C. Stone
Former consultant, U.S. Government
Reviewed by André Claude
Press Attaché, Grand Duchy of Luxembourg

FACTS AND FIGURES

GRAND DUCHY OF LUXEMBOURG is the official name of the country. It comes from *Lucilinburhuc*, meaning "little fort."

CAPITAL: Luxembourg City.

LOCATION: Western Europe. **Latitude**—49° 27′ N to 50° 11′ N. **Longitude**—5° 45′ E to 6° 30′ E.

AREA: 999 sq. mi.

POPULATION: 340,000 (estimate).

LANGUAGE: French (official), Letzeburgesch, German.

GOVERNMENT: Constitutional monarchy. **Head of government**—prime minister, president of the government. **Titular head of state**—grand duke or grand duchess. **International co-operation**—United Nations, North Atlantic Treaty Organization (NATO), European Coal and Steel Community (ECSC), European Economic Community (Common Market), European Atomic Energy Community (EURATOM), Organization for European Economic Co-operation (OEEC), Council of Europe, Benelux.

NATIONAL ANTHEM: *Ons Hemecht* ("Our Homeland"), sung in Letzeburgesch.

ECONOMY: Agricultural products—potatoes, hay, fodder, beets, wheat, oats. **Industries and products**—iron, steel, agricultural products, wine, tourism. **Chief minerals**—iron ore, slate, gypsum, lime. **Chief exports**—steel, pig iron, chemicals, rubber, cement. **Chief imports**—coal, petroleum, automobiles, cotton, food products. **Monetary unit**—Luxembourg franc.

L, twelfth letter of the English alphabet **L** 1
  See also Alphabet

Laban (LAY-ban), father of Leah and Rachel. According to the Old Testament story, he was a crafty man who cheated Jacob into working for him for 14 years. As a reward for 7 years' labor, Jacob was to receive Rachel as his wife. Laban gave him Leah instead, and Jacob had to work another 7 years for Rachel. When Laban tried to detain Jacob further, the two quarreled. Finally agreeing to make peace, they set up a mound of stones to separate their two regions. The story is considered by some to be an allegory of Syrian-Israeli relationship.

Labels, on food containers
  government-required information **F** 350
Labor **L** 2–10
  agriculture **A** 89, 92, 96
  automation **A** 528–34
  child labor **C** 235
  contract and wage agreements **L** 12
  discrimination in employment prohibited **N** 104
  economic factor of production **E** 48
  government regulation **L** 14
  guilds **G** 401–03
  Industrial Revolution **I** 238–41
  International Labour Organisation (ILO) **U** 85
  iron and steel employment statistics **I** 408
  labor and management **L** 11–18
  Labor Day **H** 154
  labor reserve schools of Soviet Union **U** 30
  May Day, or International Labor Day **H** 153
  occupational health and safety **O** 15–16
  rotos, Chilean workers **C** 250
  serfs under feudalism **F** 102
  service industries and occupations **S** 124–25
  slave labor **S** 195–200
  sweat shops in early clothing industry **C** 353–54
  trade, productive factor in **T** 242
  unemployment and unemployment insurance **U** 25–26
  work, the world of **W** 251–53
  working conditions in Industrial Revolution **I** 238–41
  workmen's compensation **W** 253
  work songs of occupations, in folklore **F** 304, 319
Labor, U.S. Department of, established 1913 **L** 5
  handicapped persons helped by **H** 29
Laboratories (LAB-or-a-tories)
  floating laboratory for oceanographic research **O** 26
  high school chemistry laboratory, picture **E** 72
  IBM laboratories, picture **N** 216
  language laboratories **E** 78; picture **E** 79
  medical laboratory tests **M** 201–02, 209
  Skylab, in space **S** 343
  underwater laboratory, Sealab I **U** 19–20
Labor camps, for criminals **P** 468
Labor contracts **L** 15; picture **L** 16
Labor Day **H** 154
  See also May Day, International Labor Day
Labor-Management Relations Act (Taft-Hartley Act), 1947
    L 6, 15
  Truman, Harry S **T** 301
Labor-Management Reporting and Disclosure Act
    (Landrum-Griffin Act), 1959 **L** 15
Labor mediators **L** 18
Labors of Heracles (HER-a-clese), in Greek mythology
    G 363
Labor unions **L** 2–10
  capitalism modified by **C** 104
  changes in the world of work **W** 252–53
  clothing industry **C** 354
  folk song, words and music, "Solidarity" **F** 320
  Gompers, Samuel **G** 263

guilds **G** 401–03
Industrial Revolution **I** 241
Lewis, John L. **L** 161
newspapers **N** 205
work, changes in the world of **W** 252–53
See also National Labor Relations Act (Wagner Act),
  1935; Railway brotherhoods; Railway Labor Act
Labour Party, Great Britain **P** 379
  socialism and labor **S** 220
Labrador, Newfoundland, Canada **N** 140–45
Labrador Current, of Atlantic Ocean **A** 478
  foggy conditions **C** 55
  Gulf Stream, meeting with **G** 411
  icebergs **I** 26
Labradorite (LAB-ra-dor-ite), gemstone **G** 76
Labrador retriever, sporting dog, picture **D** 253
La Brea (la-BRAY-a) **Pits,** Los Angeles, California **L** 345
La Bruyère (la bru-YARE), **Jean de,** French social critic
    F 438

Laburnums, shrubs or small trees related to the bean, cultivated as ornamental plants in many parts of the world. Laburnums have glossy leaves and an abundance of yellow flowers, growing in clusters. The plants, especially the seeds, are poisonous if eaten by people but harmless to most animals. Laburnum wood is tough. It is used in cabinetwork and for musical instruments.

Labyrinth (LAB-ir-inth), in Greek mythology **G** 365
Labyrinth, inner ear
  of fishes **F** 191; picture **F** 193
Lac, a resin **R** 184
Lace **L** 19
  Belgian lacemaking, picture **B** 127
La Ceiba, Honduras **H** 197
Lacertas (la-CER-tas), lizards, picture **L** 321
Lacewood, tree
  uses of the wood and its grain, picture **W** 223
Lachaise (la-SHEZ), **Gaston,** French-born American
    sculptor **U** 116
  20th century sculpture **S** 103–04
Laclède (la-CLED), **Pierre,** French fur trader **F** 522–23
  early settlement of St. Louis **S** 17

Lacombe (la-COM), **Albert** (1827–1916), Canadian missionary, b. St. Sulpice. He was ordained a priest (1849) and ministered to Indians in Northwest territory. He helped draw up treaty with Indians (1898), and he wrote a dictionary and grammar of Cree language.

La Condamine (la con-da-MENE), **Charles de,** French
    scientist **R** 340
Lacquers (LAC-ers) **V** 280
  Japanese box, picture **D** 74
  lacquered wood statue, picture **O** 218
Lac resin **V** 279
Lacrosse **L** 20–21
  Canada **C** 67
  Indians playing lacrosse, picture **I** 188
La Crosse, Wisconsin **W** 205
Lactose, or milk sugar **M** 311; **S** 453
Lactic acid, in sour milk **M** 311
Ladd, Edwin Fremont, American chemist **N** 335
Ladd, William, American worker for peace **P** 104
Ladder-back chair, picture **C** 389
Ladder ditchers, machines **B** 448
Ladder division, in arithmetic **A** 401
Ladders
  on fire engines, pictures **F** 146, 147
  superstitions about **S** 474
Ladies' Home Journal, The, magazine **M** 14
Ladies Professional Golfers' Association **G** 262

Ladino (la-DI-no), popular name for Judeo-Spanish language spoken by descendants of Jews who were expelled from Spain in 15th century and who settled along the Mediterranean. Ladino is basically 15th-century Spanish, with many words borrowed from Turkish, Greek, and Hebrew. It is written with modified Hebrew alphabet. The term also refers to a Spanish-speaking Latin American of mixed Spanish, Indian, or Negro blood.

Ladoga (LA-do-ga), **Lake,** northwestern European U.S.S.R. **L** 32
Lady, British title **K** 277
Lady and Tramp, cartoon characters, picture **A** 297
Ladybird beetles, or lady bugs, pictures **I** 269, 276
Lady Day, or Annunciation Day, religious holiday **R** 154
Lady of Shalott, poem by Alfred, Lord Tennyson **T** 101
Lady's slipper, flower, picture **W** 170
   state flower of Minnesota **M** 323
Laënnec (laen-NEC), **René,** French doctor **M** 206–07
La Farge, John, American painter and glassmaker **S** 395

La Farge, Oliver Hazard Perry ("Oliver II") (1901–1963), American novelist and anthropologist, b. New York, N.Y. He is noted for his special interest in American Indians and for his efforts to improve their living conditions. He served on archeological expeditions to Arizona, Mexico, and Guatemala. He was president of Association on American Indian Affairs (1937–42, 1948–63) and was awarded the Pulitzer prize (1929) for novel about Indians, *Laughing Boy.*

Lafayette, Louisiana **L** 360–61
La Fayette (la-fay-ETT), **Marie, Comtesse de,** French novelist **F** 438; **N** 348
Lafayette, Marquis de, French soldier **L** 22–23
   feted in Independence Hall **I** 113
   in American Hall of Fame **H** 14
   National Guard so named to honor Lafayette **N** 42
   Revolutionary War **R** 202
Lafayette, U.S. nuclear submarine, picture **S** 442
Laffite (la-FEET), **Jean,** French-born American pirate and
   adventurer **L** 23
   Louisiana, early history of **L** 361
La Follette (la FOLL-ett), **Philip F.,** American statesman **W** 205, 208
La Follette, Robert, American statesman and political reformer **L** 24
   Wisconsin Idea, progressive government **W** 208
La Follette, Robert, Jr., American legislator **L** 24
La Fontaine (la fon-TAIN), **Jean de,** French writer of fables **F** 3, 438
Laforet (la-for-EH), **Carmen,** Spanish writer **S** 372
LAFTA see Latin American Free Trade Association
Lagan see Flotsam, jetsam, and lagan, or ligan
Lagash (LAY-gash), city of Babylonia **A** 217
Lager (LOG-er) **beer** **B** 116–17
Lagerkvist (LOG-er-kvist), **Pär,** Swedish author **S** 51–52 53
Lagerlöf (LOG-er-lerv), **Selma,** Swedish author **S** 53
Lagomorpha (lag-o-MORPH-a), order of mammals **M** 62, 69; **R** 22

Lagoon, area of water protected from the open sea by a sandbar or coral reef. Biscayne Bay between Miami Beach and Miami, Fla., and Great South Bay between Fire Island and Long Island, N.Y., are lagoons. Venice, Italy, is built in a shallow lagoon. The circular body of water enclosed by an atoll is also a lagoon.

Lagos (LAY-gos), capital of Nigeria **N** 255; pictures **A** 60, 68
Lag screws **N** 3; picture **N** 2

La Guardia (la gu-AR-dia), **Fiorello,** American lawyer and political leader **L** 24
La Guma, Alex, South African novelist **A** 76b
Lahaf (LA-haf), robe of Libyan women, picture **L** 201
Lahaina (la-HA-i-na), **Maui,** Hawaiian Islands **H** 66
Lahontan (la-HON-tan), **Lake,** Nevada **N** 124–25
Lahore (la-HORE), Pakistan **P** 40
   Badshahi mosque, picture **P** 37
   dyed fabric, picture **A** 463

Laird, Melvin Robert (1922–   ), American politician, b. Marshfield, Wis. He served in the Wisconsin state senate (1946–52), the U.S. House of Representatives (1953–69), and as secretary of defense (1969–73). In 1973 he became chief domestic adviser to President Nixon.

Laissez-faire (les-say-FAIR) (French, meaning "let do" or "let things alone"), principle of allowing problems to work themselves out without interference or regulation. As an economic doctrine opposes state interference in economic affairs. It originated among 18th-century French economists and was later expanded by English economist Adam Smith. The concept is based on belief in a natural order, in which individual interests are in harmony with economic progress.

Lake, chemical compound used in dyeing **D** 371
Lake Charles, Louisiana **L** 360
Lake District, in northwestern England **E** 212

Lake dwellers, people who live in houses built on piles in water. In ancient times, farmers in alpine areas of Europe built dwellings along the margins of lakes in order to save land for agriculture and pasturage. Irish, Scottish, and English people of olden times built dwellings on man-made islands called crannogs.
   homes of the past **H** 177

Lake Isle of Innisfree, The, poem by Yeats **Y** 344
Lake of the Woods, Minnesota-Ontario **M** 325; **O** 120a
   territorial boundaries, Northwest Angle **T** 108, 109
Lake Placid, New York, Van Hoevenberg bobrun **B** 265

Lake poets (Lake school), term applied to the romantic poets Wordsworth, Coleridge, and Southey, who lived in the Lake District of Cumberland and Westmorland in England. They gained inspiration from nature and viewed poetry as a means of emotional expression. The title originated as a term of contempt in the *Edinburgh Review* but later lost its scornful connotation.

Lakes **L** 25–34
   dams create man-made lakes **D** 19
   Glacier National Park, Montana, pictures **G** 221, 222
   Indiana Dunes National Lakeshore **I** 146; picture **I** 147
   Kashmir, picture **K** 199
   national lakeshores, list **N** 52
   North America has largest number **N** 288–89
   See also land section of country, province, and state articles; lakes by name, as Erie, Lake
Lakeshores, National, list **N** 52
   Wisconsin's Apostle Islands National Lakeshore **W** 203
Laki (LA-ki), volcano, in Iceland **I** 45
La Libertad (la li-ber-TOD), El Salvador, picture **E** 182
Lalique (la-LEEK), **René,** French jeweler **J** 97
L'Allegro, poem by John Milton **M** 311
Lalo (la-LO), **Edouard,** French composer **F** 446
Lamaism (LA-ma-ism), religion
   Bhutan **B** 150
   Mongolia **M** 413

Sikkim, state religion of **S** 176
Tibet **T** 175, 178
Lamar, Lucius Q.C., American statesman **M** 361
Lamar, Mirabeau B., American statesman and soldier **T** 135
Lamarck, Jean Baptiste, Chevalier de, French zoologist **B** 192
Darwin influenced by **E** 344
Lamarckian theory of evolution questioned **S** 73
Lamartine, Alphonse de, French poet **F** 440
Lamb, Charles, English critic and essayist **L** 34
children's literature **C** 237
English literature, romantic period **E** 261–62
Essays of Elia **E** 292, 293
Lamb, Mary, English writer **L** 34
children's literature **C** 237
Lamb, meat of young sheep **C** 151; **M** 192; cuts of, picture **M** 194
outdoor cooking **O** 248
Lambaréné (lon-ba-ren-AY), Gabon, central Africa **G** 3
Schweitzer, Albert **S** 59

Lambeau, Earl ("Curly") (1898–1965), American football coach, b. Green Bay, Wis. A Notre Dame halfback (1917–18), he formed the Green Bay Packers when working for the Indian Packing Company. He played for the Packers (1919–28) and was their coach and, later, owner (to 1950). He then coached the Chicago Cardinals (1950–51) and Washington Redskins (1952–54) and was elected to the Professional Football Hall of Fame (1963).

Lambert, Albert Bond, American army officer **M** 374

Lambert, Johann Heinrich (1728–1777), German mathematician and physicist, b. Mülhausen. Lambert became a favorite of Frederick the Great, King of Prussia. He performed basic research in mathematics, astronomy, heat, light, and color. The basic unit of brightness, the lambert, was named in his honor. Among his achievements was his proof of the irrationality of the number pi (the ratio of a circle's circumference to its diameter).

Lambert, Louis, pen name of Patrick S. Gilmore **B** 40

Lambert, Richard Stanton (1894–   ), Canadian writer, b. Kingston-on-Thames, England. After serving as head of the adult-education section of the BBC (1927–28) and editor of its publication *The Listener* (1928–39), he went to Canada (1939) and became educational adviser to the CBC (1940) and supervisor of its educational broadcasts (1943–60). His books for young people include *Franklin of the Arctic* and *Mutiny in the Bay.*

Lambeth, section of London **L** 339
Lambs, young sheep **S** 145
fur **F** 518
symbol of Christian Easter **E** 41
Lambton, John George, English statesman **O** 125, 127
Canada, history of **C** 73
Lame duck amendment, to the U.S. Constitution *see* Twentieth Amendment
Lamentations, book of Bible, Old Testament **B** 156
Laminae (LAM-in-e), thin plates or scales
turtles **T** 331
Laminar airflow A 39
Laminates, layers bound together
laminated wood **W** 227
plastics **P** 330
Lamington, Mount, New Guinea **V** 382
Lamont, J., Scottish astronomer **A** 476
Lampblack
India ink made of **I** 256

Lampedusa (lom-pay-DU-za), **Giuseppe Tomasi di,** Italian novelist **I** 481
Lamplighters, for lighthouses **L** 278
Lampreys, eel-like fishes **F** 182; picture **F** 181
control measures in Wisconsin **W** 196
invasion of the Great Lakes **M** 265–66
little in common with true eels **E** 86–87
Lamps L 279–90
miner's safety lamps **C** 364
Lamy (la-ME), **John Baptist,** French missionary **N** 193
Lanai (la-NA-i), one of the Hawaiian Islands **H** 59
Lancaster, House of, English royal family **U** 77
War of the Roses **E** 220
Lancaster, Pennsylvania **P** 128; picture **P** 135
Lancelot, knight of King Arthur's court **A** 442
Lances, weapons **K** 272
Lan Chang (Lan Xang), former kingdom of Laos **L** 41, 43
Land
agricultural management **A** 92–93
clearing of land by pioneers **P** 252
climate and land areas **C** 346
conservation **C** 482–89
economics **E** 48
environment and overcrowding **E** 272b
feudal system of serfs working the land **F** 102
food chains **L** 241
irrigation **I** 408–10
land laws for pioneers **P** 260
land use studied in agricultural geography **G** 107
life, distribution of plant and animal **L** 233
proportion for agriculture **A** 93
public lands **P** 506–07
real estate **R** 112–13
surveying **S** 479–80
See also Agriculture; Soils; and agriculture section of country and state articles

Land, Edwin Herbert (1909–   ), American scientist and inventor, b. Bridgeport, Conn. A founder of Polaroid Corporation (1937) in Cambridge, Mass., he developed a method of polarizing light for cameras, a way to produce three-dimensional effect, and a new method of color photography. He is best-known for development (1947) of Polaroid Land Camera, which takes, develops, and prints photographs in seconds. He also developed a way to observe living cells in their natural color, thus advancing cancer research. **P** 203

Landau (lon-DOW), **Lev Davidovich** (1908–68), Soviet physicist, b. Baku, Azerbaijan. During the 1930's he specialized in the investigation of magnetism and of magnetic domains. These are tiny "islands" of magnetic force found in magnetic materials such as iron and cobalt. Later Landau became interested in the behavior of materials at very low temperatures. For this work he was awarded the 1962 Nobel prize in physics.

Land bank associations, federal B 50
Land Between the Lakes, TVA recreation area, Kentucky-Tennessee **K** 221; **T** 84
Land bridges, linking continents **L** 236–37
Middle East **M** 300
Lander *see* Lunar module, of Apollo spacecraft
Lander, Richard, English explorer **N** 258
Landfills, burying of refuse **S** 34
Land flowing with milk and honey, name for Canaan **M** 468
Landforms, of earth's surface **G** 96
elevations on maps **M** 90; picture **M** 91
world patterns **W** 254
See also land and landform sections of continent, country, province, and state articles

Land-grant colleges A 95; U 205
  in the history of education E 73
  Morrill, J. S., sponsor of land-grant act   V 316

Land grants, government land allotted for construction of roads, railroads, and public works or for establishment of agricultural or technical colleges. Term also refers to public lands distributed to private citizens for settlement. In United States, land-grant legislation includes the Pacific Railway Acts (1862–64), the Morrill Act (1862) for state agricultural colleges, and the Homestead Act (1862) for private settlement.
  railroads, history of R 90

Landing, moon E 368; S 339–340a, 340g–340i
Landing gear, of airplane A 556–57
Landini (lon-DI-ni), **Francesco**, Italian composer I 483
  Middle Ages, music of the   M 299
Landis, Kenesaw Mountain, American baseball commissioner B 81
Land of Enchantment, nickname for New Mexico N 180
Land of Haunted Castles (Luxembourg) L 379
Land of Lincoln, official nickname for Illinois I 70

Land of Nod, in Old Testament, the land, east of Eden, where Cain took refuge after killing his brother Abel (Genesis 4:16). The term is thought to be derived from the Hebrew word meaning "wanderer," and it signifies a condition of sleep.

Land of Sky-blue Waters, a nickname for Minnesota M 323
Land of Steady Habits, nickname for Connecticut C 467, 481
Land of 10,000 Lakes, a nickname for Minnesota M 322
Land of the Dakotas, nickname for North Dakota N 323
Land of the Midnight Sun, Arctic region P 364
  Eskimo life E 284
  nickname for Alaska A 129
Land of the Pagodas (Burma) B 454
Land of the Shining Mountains, Indian name for Montana M 428
Landon, Alfred Mossman, American statesman K 190
  anagrams on his name W 236

Landowska (lon-DOF-ska), **Wanda** (1879–1959), Polish harpsichordist and pianist, b. Warsaw. She taught harpsichord, upon invitation, in Berlin (1912–19) and founded and taught at Saint-Leu-la-Forêt, near Paris, a school for the study of baroque and classical music (1925–40). She made numerous concert tours in Europe, North and South America, and Africa, and she composed songs, music for string orchestra, and pieces for piano. She wrote (with her husband) *La musique ancienne* on the music of the 17th and 18th centuries.

Landrum-Griffin Act see Labor-Management Reporting and Disclosure Act
Landscape gardening G 26, 29
Landscape painting
  American wilderness painters U 121
  Dutch and Flemish art D 357
  English E 238, 240
  Sung dynasty of China O 216
  Turner, Joseph Mallord William T 329
Landscape with the Flight into Egypt, painting by Claude Lorrain B 58, 60

Landseer, Sir Edwin Henry (1802–1873), English painter, b. London. Noted for his paintings of animals, he modeled the lions at base of Nelson Monument in Trafalgar Square, London. His paintings include *Stag at Bay*,
Dignity and Impudence, and *Cat's Paw*. Some paintings were engraved by his elder brother Thomas.

Land's End, England E 213
Land snails, mollusks O 276
Landsteiner (LAND-sty-ner), **Karl**, Austrian physician, classified blood types B 257
  blood transfusions T 251
Land use
  studied in agricultural geography G 107

Landy, John (1930–   ), Australian track star, b. Melbourne. He ran the mile in a record 3 min. 58 sec. in Turku, Finland (1954), surpassing Roger Bannister's record of 3 min. 59.4 sec. He lost to Roger Bannister in British Empire Games in British Columbia (1954) and retired in 1957.

Lane, Harriet, acting first lady in Buchanan's administration see Johnson, Harriet Lane
Lane, Ralph, English seaman A 181
Lang, Andrew, Scottish writer S 435
Langer, William, American political leader N 335
Langland, William, English poet E 248
Langley, Samuel, American astronomer and aeronautical pioneer A 568
Langmuir, Irving, American scientist and engineer L 35
  cloud-seeding experiment for weather control W 92
  filament lamps L 284
Langrenus, Belgian astronomer M 449

Langston, John Mercer (1829–97), American educator and diplomat, Negro, b. Louisa County, Va. Orphan son of a plantation owner and a freed slave, he was raised by a family friend. After graduating from the theology department of Oberlin College, he read law and was admitted to the bar. Chosen clerk of Brownhelm township, Ohio (1855), he was probably the first Negro to win an elective office. He later served as dean of Howard Law School, minister to Haiti, and chargé d'affaires in Santo Domingo. He won a Republican Congressional election (1888), but the election was contested and he was not seated for 2 years. His autobiography is entitled *From the Virginia Plantation to the National Capital*.

Langton, Stephen, English theologian E 218
  Magna Carta, an author of M 22
Language and languages L 37–40
  Africa A 55–56
  African tone languages A 79
  alphabet A 170–73
  Anglo-Saxon (Old English) in *Beowulf* B 141
  animal signals A 275–76
  anthropological studies A 300, 308
  Asia A 459–60
  Bible translations B 152–54
  child development C 232–33
  Chinese C 258–59
  communication by speech C 429–30
  computer programing languages C 457
  days of the week in five languages D 47
  dialects D 152
  dictionaries D 164–65
  Europe E 317
  French official language of many countries F 433–35
  grammar, the way a language works G 288–90
  Grimm brothers, first scientific study of German grammar G 376
  Hawaiian H 63
  India's regional languages I 119
  international trade problems I 328
  Japanese J 27–28

laboratories in schools   E 78; picture E 79
Latin once a world language   L 76
linguistics   L 301–03;   R 182
North America   N 297
phonics   P 193–96
population geography studies distribution of languages
   G 108
pronunciation   P 478
Romany, or gypsy   G 434
semantics   S 117–18
slang   S 194
South America   S 282, 288
speech   S 376–78
spelling   S 378–79
taxonomy, a kind of universal language   T 29
television production   T 70a
treaties   T 272
universal languages   U 194–95
word origins   W 238–41
writing   W 317–21
See also Alphabet; Dialects; Grammar; Linguistics;
   Semantics; Speech; Universal languages; Writing;
   articles on individual countries; names of principal
   languages and language groups
Language arts   L 36
   handwriting   H 31–33
   punctuation   P 530–33
   reading   R 107–11
   speech   S 376–78
   spelling   S 378–79
   vocabulary   V 371–72
   See also Compositions; Grammar; Handwriting; Letter
     writing; Reading; Reports; Spelling
Languages, universal *see* Universal languages
Languedoc Canal *see* Canal du Midi
Langwelser Viaduct, Switzerland, picture   E 328
Lanier (la-NIER), **Sidney,** American poet   A 204;
   G 146
   was prisoner in Maryland in Civil War   M 128
Lanolin, fat from wool   W 235
   use in cosmetics   C 510
   wool wax   W 69
L'Anse aux Meadows, Newfoundland   N 143
Lansing, capital of Michigan   M 269–70
Lanston, Tolbert, American lawyer   P 465
Lantern Festival, China   H 154

Lanternfish, any member of a family of small, club-
shaped fish found in the deep waters of the Atlantic
Ocean and the Mediterranean Sea. Lanternfish live at
depths of about 2,500 feet, often surfacing at night. All
have large eyes and wide mouths, and most are from 3
to 6 inches long. Luminous dots are found along the side
of the body, and in one species the front of the head
also gives off light.

Lanterns, Feast of, Japan   J 31
Lanterns, outer casings for lights   L 281–83
Lanthanide (LANTH-an-ide) **series,** of rare earth elements
   E 159
Lanthanum, element   E 154, 162

Laocoön (la-OC-o-on), in Greek mythology, Trojan priest
who warned citizens of Troy to be on guard against
wooden horse presented by Greeks as gift to Athena.
According to one story, for his distrust of the gift horse
Athena sent two serpents to crush him and his two sons.
His death was taken by the citizens of Troy to mean that
his warnings were false and that the horse was indeed
sacred. Ancient sculpture depicting his death (discovered
1506) is now displayed in the Vatican.
   Trojan War   T 293

Laos (LAY-os) or (LOUS)   L 41–43
   flag   F 238

Lao-tzu (LA-o-DZU), or **Lao-tse,** or **Lao-tsze,** Chinese
philosopher and reputed founder of Taoism. Traditionally
believed to have been born in Nonan province during 7th
century B.C., he served as librarian in Chou court. As
reputed author of *Tao Tê Ching (The Way and Its Virtue),*
he advocated doctrine of naturalness and spontaneity,
by which man achieves ideal or oneness with universe
by renouncing artificiality—forms and ceremonies.
   Chinese literature   O 220a
   religions of China   C 260–61
   Taoism, a great mystic faith   R 148

La Paz (la POS), capital of Bolivia   B 302, 306; pictures
   B 305;   L 47;   S 274

Lapchick, Joseph (1900–1970), American basketball player
and coach, b. Yonkers, N.Y. He played with N.Y. Celtics
(1922–27) and later helped organize and played with
the Original Celtics (until 1936). He coached the St.
John's University's Redmen (1936–47, 1955–65) and
participated in National Invitation Tournament, winning
the 1943, 1944, 1959, and 1965 championships. He
coached the New York Knickerbockers (1947–55). He was
elected to Basketball Hall of Fame (1961).

La Peltrie, Marie Madeleine de (1603–1671), French nun,
b. Alençon. She founded Ursuline convent for French and
Indian girls at Quebec (1639) and accompanied a group
of colonists who founded Montreal (1642). She returned
to Quebec (1643), becoming an Ursuline novice.

Lapis lazuli (LAP-is LAZ-u-li), or lazurite, gemstone   G 76
Laplace (le-PLOS), **Pierre, Marquis de,** French mathemati-
   cian and astronomer   S 247
Laplace theory, of origin of solar system   S 247
La Plata, Rio de *see* Plata, Rio de la
Lapland   L 44–45
   children playing with lassos, picture   A 304
   Lapland family, picture   F 39
   taiga   T 11
Laps, rolls of raw cotton   C 525
Lapstone, shoemakers' stone used in leatherworking
   S 162
Laptev (LOPT-yef) **Sea**   O 48
Laramie, Wyoming   W 335
Larboard, port or left side of a ship   S 155

Larcom, Lucy (1824–1893), American poet and story
writer, b. Beverly Farms, Mass. She compiled and edited
Roadside Poems and *Hillside and Seaside in Poetry* and
collaborated with Whittier on editing anthologies. Her
works include *Similitudes from Ocean and Prairies,*
Ships in the Mist, Poems, and an autobiography, *A New
England Girlhood.* She was a teacher at Wheaton College,
Mass. (1854–62), and an editor of magazine *Our Young
Folks.*

Lard, fat obtained from hogs   O 79
Larderello (lar-der-EL-lo), Italy
   natural steam runs generators, picture   E 203
Lardner, Ringgold Wilmer ("Ring"), American writer
   M 272
   short stories   S 167

Lares (LAY-rese) **and penates** (pe-NAY-tese), in ancient
Rome, protective household gods (each family had a *lar*
and several *penates*). *Lares* were usually deified spirits
of ancestors, and *penates* were gods and guardians of
hearth and storehouses. They were also deities of the

Lares and penates (continued)
state and were therefore worshiped publicly as well as privately. The term has come to mean one's most valuable personal and household possessions.

Lariats R 333
honda knots used for K 290
roping R 334

Lark, any of several small brown- or gray-streaked birds noted for their songs, which are especially beautiful when the birds are in flight. Larks live in fairly open country and usually nest on the ground. They walk or run, but they never hop. Larks are found chiefly in the Old World, from tundra areas south.

Lark buntings, birds, picture B 236
state bird of Colorado C 401
Larkin Building, Buffalo, New York W 315
Lark in the Morning, folk song F 320

Larkspur, or delphinium, flowering plant of the Northern Hemisphere that has long been a favorite with gardeners. It grows to a height of 3 to 4 feet and has a spirelike cluster of flowers. The flowers are usually blue, but some varieties bear white, pink, lavender, or purple blossoms. Plant's sap is poisonous. Pictures G 27, 49.

La Rochefoucauld (la rosh-foo-CO), **François, duc de,** French writer F 438
Larra, Mariano José de, Spanish writer S 370
Larsen, Don, American baseball pitcher B 80
Larsen, Henry A., Royal Canadian Mounted Police officer commands trip through Northwest Passage N 338
Larvae (LAR-ve), early forms of animals that must undergo metamorphosis M 234
ants A 323, 331
bees B 122–23
butterflies and moths B 469
clothes moths H 261
eels E 86
eggs and embryos E 89
frogs, toads, and other amphibians F 470–78
insects I 264–65; pictures I 276, 277
plant enemies P 284–87
plankton, animal P 281
Laryngitis (la-rin-JITE-is), inflammation of the larynx D 195
Larynx (LARR-inx), voice box V 375
speech S 377
La Salle, Robert Cavelier, Sieur de, French explorer L 46
Canada C 69
exploration of the New World E 384
Saint Lawrence River S 16
La Scala (la SCA-la), opera house, Milan I 486
Lascaux (la-SCO) **Caves,** France, pictures P 440, W 217
laser mirror on moon S 340a, 340i; diagram S 340i
Lasers (LAZE-ers), devices for amplifying light waves M 131–33
electronic communication E 142f
gas lasers, for projecting light beams G 62
holograms, pictures P 208
laser mirror on moon S 340a, 340i; diagram S 340i
new discoveries in physics P 239
telephone, uses in T 60
welding W 119

Lasker Foundation, Inc., Albert and Mary, organization that donates funds for medical research. It encourages research in the areas of cancer, heart disease, and mental illness. The organization presents Lasker awards yearly for important contributions in medical research

and writing, as well as in public health administration. Founded in 1942, its headquarters are in New York, N.Y.

Lassen Peak, California V 380
only active volcano in the first 48 mainland states C 16
Lassen Volcanic National Park, California C 24
Lassoing, roping R 333–35
children playing with lassos, picture A 304
honda knots used for K 290
Lassus, Roland de, Belgian composer D 365; F 444
Renaissance music R 173–74
Last, block used in shoemaking S 162–63
Last Frontier, nickname for Alaska A 129
Last Judgment, fresco by Michelangelo M 257; picture M 256
Last of the Mohicans, The, novel by Cooper C 498
Last Supper, of Jesus Christ J 84
Holy Thursday commemorates events leading to Easter E 41
See also Holy Communion
Last Supper, painting by Tintoretto I 470, 471
Last Supper, The, painting by Dierik Bouts D 354
Last Supper, The, painting by Leonardo da Vinci A 332
Last Word of a Bluebird, The, poem by Robert Frost F 480
Las Vegas (los VAY-gas), Nevada N 133–34
Latakia (lat-a-KI-a), Syria S 508
Lateen (la-TEEN) **sails** T 261
Latent (LATE-ent) **heat** I 4
Lateral moraines I 19; picture I 18
Lateral pass, in football F 360
Lateran Councils, of the Roman Catholic Church R 292, 294
Lateran Treaty, 1929 V 280
Latexes (LAY-tex-es)
rubber R 340, 343–45
synthetic latexes, paints P 32

Latham (LAY-tham), **Jean Lee** (1902–), American author and playwright, b. Buckhannon, W.Va. She was editor in chief of Dramatic Publishing Company (1930–36) and worked as a free-lance writer (1936–41 and since 1945). Her career was interrupted during World War II, when she trained women inspectors for the Signal Corps, U.S. War Department (1943–45). She is best-known for fictionalized biographies of prominent Americans, including *Carry on, Mr. Bowditch,* which won the Newbery award (1956), *The Story of Eli Whitney, Medals for Morse,* and *Trail Blazer of the Seas.*

Lathes, machine tools T 217; picture T 218

Lathrop (LAY-throp), **Dorothy Pulis** (1891–), American illustrator and author of children's books, b. Albany, N.Y. She wrote and illustrated *The Fairy Circus* and the first book to win a Caldecott medal (1938), *Animals of the Bible.*

Latimer, Hugh (1485?–1555), English prelate and reformer, b. Thurcaston, Leicestershire. An ardent defender of reformed Anglican doctrine, he was periodically out of favor at court during reigns of Henry VIII and Edward VI. He was consecrated bishop of Worcester (1535) but resigned (1539) when he could not sanction the Act of the Six Articles. He was accused of heresy under Mary Tudor, an ardent Catholic. Convicted, he was burned to death at Oxford.

Latimer, Lewis Howard (1848–1928), American inventor, Negro, b. Chelsea, Mass. He was employed by Alexander Graham Bell to make patent drawings for the first telephone. He invented (1881) the first incandescent electric bulb with a carbon filament. As an engineer for the Edison Company, he supervised the installation of light systems in New York, Philadelphia, Montreal, and London.

Latin American Free Trade Association (LAFTA), organization formed by nine Latin-American countries to further economic development by reducing trade barriers. It was founded in 1960 when Argentina, Brazil, Chile, Mexico, Paraguay, Peru, and Uruguay signed the Treaty of Montevideo, later adhered to (1961) by Colombia, Ecuador, Venezuela, and Bolivia.
  trade in South America **S** 293

Lattimore, Eleanor Frances (1904–), American author of children's books, b. Shanghai, China. She is known for books about Chinese children, including *Little Pear* and *The Chinese Daughter.*

Laubach, Frank Charles (1884–1970), American missionary and educator, b. Benton, Pa. He was a missionary in the Philippines (1915–40), where he developed a system for teaching illiterates to read using phonetic symbols and pictures. Students became teachers according to his motto, "Each one teach one." Laubach directed the Maranaw Folk Schools in the Philippines (1929–40) and wrote *Toward a Literate World* among other books.

Laud, William, English prelate **E** 223

Laugh-In, a television comedy show. Introduced in 1968, this program offered a totally different format from the usual TV fare. The comedy team of **Dan Rowan** (1922–) and **Dick Martin** (1922–) head a cast that specializes in poking fun at the American way of life by means of rapid-fire jokes and comedy sketches.

Laurel and Hardy, American film comedy team. Stan Laurel (Arthur Stanley Jefferson) (1890–1965), b. Ulverson, England, and Oliver Norvell Hardy (1892–1957), b. Atlanta, Ga., were both vaudeville performers before their paths crossed in 1926. In over 100 feature films, among them *Pardon Us, Pack Up Your Troubles, Blockheads,* and *Babes in Toyland,* timid Laurel suffered the insults of Hardy, the blustering bully. A short, *The Music Box,* won an Academy Award.

Lausanne, University of S 496
Lauth, Bernard, Alsatian-born American inventor of a
    method of cold-rolling steel I 406
Lava, volcanic molten rock R 264; V 378; picture
    R 265; V 379
  caves C 156
  diamonds formed in D 153
  earth formations of E 13–14
  intrusion and extrusion of, diagram G 111
Lava Beds National Monument, California C 25
Lava Hot Springs, Idaho I 65
Laval (la-VOL), Carl Gustav de, Swedish engineer T 320
  cream separator inventor M 310
Laval, François, French bishop Q 17

Laval (la-VOL), Pierre (1883–1945), French politician and
lawyer, b. Chateldon. He shifted his political sentiments
from socialist to republican and finally to fascist. He
served as France's prime minister and minister of
foreign affairs (1931–32, 1935–36), minister of labor
(1932), and minister of foreign affairs (1934–35). He became premier (1942–45) of the Vichy government and
after the war was executed as a Nazi collaborator.
  Vichy government W 289

La Valette, Jean de, French knight of Malta M 60
Lavalleja, Juan, Uruguayan patriot U 239

Laval-Montmorency (la-VOL MON-mo-RON-cy), François
Xavier de (1623–1708), first Bishop of Quebec, b. Mon-
tigny-sur-Avre, France. He came to Canada as vicar apos-
tolic (1659) and later was appointed Bishop of Quebec
(1674–88). The seminary he founded (1663) was the core
of Laval University, founded later.

Laval University, Quebec City, Canada C 62; Q 10b, 17
Lava River Caves, Oregon, picture C 156

Laver, Rod (Rodney George Laver) (1938–), Australian
left-handed tennis player, b. Rockhampton. He won the
Australian, French, British (Wimbledon), and United
States championships in 1 year (1962), to make the
second "grand slam" in history (first made by Don
Budge, 1938). He was a member of the Australian Davis
Cup team (1959–62), and then turned professional. In 1969
he became first man to capture a second "grand slam."

La Vérendrye (la vai-ron-DRE), Pierre Gaultier de
Varennes, Sieur de (1685–1749), French explorer, b.
Three Rivers, Canada. In search of the Western Sea, he
explored the area west of Lake Superior. Besides
establishing five forts, he explored Manitoba and the
northwest territories of Canada.

Lavinia, painting see Girl with a Bowl of Fruit
Lavoisier (la-vwa-si-AY), Antoine Laurent, French chemist
    L 86; picture C 211
  chemistry of breathing M 206
  law of conservation of matter C 212
  phlogiston theory disproved C 210–12
  the new chemistry in the history of science S 72
Law, Andrew Bonar, Canadian-born British statesman
    N 138c
Law and law enforcement L 87–89
  adoption laws A 26
  Anglo-Saxon basis of English law E 216, 217–18
  Bill of Rights B 177–80
  Canadian courts C 77–78
  child labor laws C 235
  civil rights and civil liberties protected C 316
  codes see Codes, of law
  corporation law and trusts and monopolies T 304

courts C 526–30
divorce D 234–35
FBI training of officers F 77
fishing laws F 223–24
food regulations and laws F 350–52
French civil law in Quebec, Canada C 71
Holmes, Oliver Wendell, Jr., the "Great Dissenter"
    H 160–61
immigration, legislation on I 99–102
income tax I 111
insurance I 296
international law I 320–21
interstate commerce I 331–32
jury J 159–60
lawyers L 92–93
legislation U 140–41
legislatures L 135–36
Magna Carta E 218; M 22
marriage laws W 101
Marshall, John M 112
mentally ill, problem of the M 224–25
municipal government M 503
narcotics, legal measures to control use of N 14
"no conflict" principle, layers of law S 412, 414
oldest written laws A 220; picture A 219
pioneer life P 260
police P 372–77
president's executive ordinances P 453
prisons P 468–70
Roman law A 232
Supreme Court S 476–77
trademarks and copyright T 244–45
United States Constitution U 145–58
What is meant by "Possession is nine points of the
    law"? L 93
wills W 174–75
women, role of W 211, 212a–213
See also Civil liberties and civil rights; Lawyers
Law Courts, London, picture E 241

Law Day, U.S.A., national observance to foster respect
for and understanding of U.S. democratic rule of law—in
contrast to law under a Communist system. It is
sponsored by the American Bar Association and is
proclaimed annually by the president of the United
States. It began in 1958 and occurs on May 1.

Lawless, Theodore Kenneth (1892–), American dermatologist, Negro, b. Thibodeaux, La. A distinguished
dermatologist and syphilologist in Chicago, he is a
member of the Chicago Board of Health and of the
Chicago Civil Liberties Committee. He has received a
number of awards for outstanding work in medicine.

Lawman see Layamon, English priest
Lawn bowling, or bowls B 349
Lawn games
  badminton B 13–15
  bowls or lawn bowling B 349
  croquet C 536–37
  lawn tennis T 90–99
Lawns L 90–91
  lawn and garden tractors F 57
Lawn sprinklers
  show reaction principle of jet propulsion
    J 85
Lawn tennis see Tennis
Law of see inverted form as Moses, Law of
Lawrence, Andrea Mead, American athlete O 113; pic-
    ture O 112
Lawrence, D. H., English novelist E 267
  themes of his novels N 347

Lawrence, Ernest Orlando (1901–58), American physicist, b. Canton, S. Dak. A pioneer in nuclear research, he invented the cyclotron in 1930 and in 1932 turned lithium into hydrogen by bombardment with a high-energy proton beam. In World War II he adapted the cyclotron for use in extracting uranium-235 for the first atomic bomb. For his invention and development of the cyclotron he received the Nobel prize in physics in 1939. The man-made element lawrencium is named for him.

particle accelerators **N** 366

Lawrence, Jacob (1917–), American painter, Negro, b. Atlantic City, N.J. His works have appeared in many exhibitions and are included in the collections of major museums. From 1958 to 1965 he taught at the Pratt Institute art school. He was represented in an exchange exhibit with the Soviet Union in 1959. In 1965 he was artist in residence at Brandeis University.

Negro Renaissance **N** 98

Lawrence, James, American naval officer **N** 178, 179

Lawrence, Robert (1936–67), American astronaut, Negro, b. Chicago, Ill. A major in the Air Force, he was a flight instructor and a service research scientist at the Air Force Weapons Laboratory. He was one of the final four chosen from sixteen prospective astronauts for the Defense Department's Manned Orbiting Laboratory program. Lawrence was killed in a crash of an F-104 Starfighter jet as it landed after a routine training flight. He held a doctorate in physical chemistry from Ohio State University.

Lawrence, Thomas Edward ("Lawrence of Arabia") (also wrote under pseudonym T. E. Shaw) (1888–1935), British archeologist, soldier, writer, and diplomat, b. Tremadoc, North Wales. He was associated with the British Museum in excavation expeditions (1910–14), was a member of the intelligence service in Egypt during World War I (1914–16), and made intensive studies of feasibility of Arab revolt against the Turks. He organized and led Arabs to victory over Turks at Damascus in 1918. Lawrence was a member of the Arab delegation at the Paris Peace Conference (1919) and adviser on Arab affairs, Middle East division of the British Colonial Office (1921–22). An enigmatic personality, he joined Royal Air Force and Royal Tank Corps under assumed names. His best-known book is *Seven Pillars of Wisdom.*

World War I in Syria **S** 508

Lawrence-Haverhill Metropolitan Area, Massachusetts
M 147
Lawrencium (law-REN-ci-um), element
E 154, 162
atomic number **A** 487
Laws see Law and law enforcement
Lawson, Harry J., English builder of first safety bicycle
B 173

Lawson, Robert (1892–1957), American author and illustrator, b. New York, N.Y. He worked as stage designer for the Washington Square Players and as a magazine illustrator (1914–17) before devoting his time to children's books. He illustrated the classic *The Story of Ferdinand,* by Munro Leaf, in addition to his own works for children, including *Ben and Me, They Were Strong and Good* (Caldecott medal, 1941), and *Rabbit Hill* (Newbery medal, 1945).

Lawton, Oklahoma **O** 92
Lawyers **L** 92–93
complaints and pleadings for court cases **C** 527

divorce **D** 234
insurance **I** 297
jury trials **J** 160
patent lawyers **I** 347
patron saint of Catholic lawyers, Sir Thomas More
M 456
See *also* American Bar Association; Law and law enforcement
Laxatives, from medicinal plants **P** 314
Lay, short epic poem
related to ballads **B** 23
Layamon (LAY-a-mon), English priest **A** 445
Middle English literature **E** 247
Layard, Sir Austen Henry, British archeologist and diplomat **L** 192
Laye, Camara, Guinean novelist **A** 76c
Lay investiture, in Roman Catholic Church **R** 291
Layouts, in bookmaking **B** 322, 324; picture **B** 325
commercial art **C** 425
magazines **M** 15–16
planning a layout, picture **P** 464

Lazarus (from Hebrew name Eleazar, meaning "God has helped"), brother of Mary and Martha at whose house in Bethany Jesus was a guest. Lazarus fell sick and died while Jesus was elsewhere, but 4 days after his death Jesus resurrected him (John 11:1–44). The miracle resulted in heightening Jesus' fame among the populace while provoking anger of the Sadducees and Pharisees. Only other mention of Lazarus in the Bible states that he attended a supper with Jesus (John 12:1–2).

Lazarus, Emma (1849–87), American poet and essayist, b. New York, N.Y. Her concern over the unjust treatment of the Jewish people is reflected in her later writing. Author of the sonnet inscribed on the base of the Statue of Liberty, she wrote *Admetus and Other Poems* for her close friend Emerson and *Songs of a Semite,* containing the celebrated poem "The Dance to Death." Other works include *By the Waters of Babylon* and a translation, *Poems and Ballads of Heinrich Heine.*
poem for plaque on the Statue of Liberty, excerpt
L 168

Lazurite, or lapis lazuli, gemstone **G** 76
Lazy daisy stitch, in embroidery **E** 188
Lazy stitch, in beadwork **I** 158
LCD see Lowest common denominator
Leaching, of ores **M** 228
Leacock, Stephen, Canadian economist and humorist
O 127
Canadian literature **C** 64
Lead **L** 94–95
atom **A** 488
elements, some facts about **E** 154, 162
galena, ore, cleavage of **R** 270; picture **R** 271
glass, used in making **G** 226
Missouri deposits **M** 370
lead-free gasolines **G** 63
lead-producing regions of North America **N** 293
metals, chart of ores, location, properties, uses **M** 227
pencils **P** 147–48
poisoning **P** 356
radioactive elements break down to form lead **R** 64
Roman plumbing systems of lead pipes **P** 343
tetraethyl lead added to gasoline **G** 63
white lead a pigment in paints **P** 32
Lead (LEED), South Dakota **S** 320–21
Lead (LED) **crystal,** glass **G** 230
Lead pencils **P** 147–48
development of writing tools **C** 433
What is the "lead" in a lead pencil? **L** 95

Leaf, Munro (1905–), American author and illustrator, b. Hamilton, Md. His best-known children's books are *Grammar Can Be Fun, Manners Can Be Fun,* and *The Story of Ferdinand.* He is also noted for the book *You and Psychiatry* (written in collaboration with William C. Menninger) and for an army manual on malaria.

League of Women Voters of the United States (LWVUS), nonpartisan women's organization formed as successor to National American Woman's Suffrage Association. Its purpose is to guide women in using voting privilege. It also attempts to cultivate citizen interest in voting. The organization was founded in 1920, has its headquarters in Washington, D.C., and publishes the *National Voter.*

Leah (LE-ah) (Hebrew, meaning "mistress"), elder daughter of Laban, older sister of Rachel, and Jacob's first wife through trickery of Laban (Genesis 29). She was the mother of his sons Rueben, Simeon, Levi, Judah, Issachar, and Zebulun and his daughter Dinah. She died prior to Jacob's departure for Egypt.

Leahy (LAY-he), **Frank** (1908–), American football coach, b. O'Neill, Nebr. A graduate (1931) of Notre Dame University, where he played under Knute Rockne, he became Notre Dame's head coach (1941–54) and built up a record that was second only to Rockne's. His team won 87 games, lost 11, and tied 9.

Leap year, 366-day year that, according to legend, was so named because during each such year February has one extra day, the 29th, causing each date following to skip, or "leap over," the day upon which it would otherwise have fallen. In Scotland a law is said to have been passed in 1288 granting women the right during leap year to propose marriage to the man of their choice. The man could not refuse unless he was willing to pay a sum of money or could prove himself bound to someone else. The custom has since been adopted in many countries.

Lebanon (LEB-an-on) **L** 121–24
  coastline, picture **E** 12
  flag **F** 238
  Middle East region **M** 300–01
Le Bris (l' BRI), **Jean-Marie,** French inventor **G** 239
Le Brun (L'BRURN), **Charles,** French baroque artist
    B 62; **F** 425
  tapestry **T** 24

Le Corbusier (L'cor-boor-si-AY) (pseudonym of Charles
Edouard Jeanneret) (1887–1965), French architect and
city planner, b. La Chaux de Fonds, Switzerland. He
headed the international committee that designed United
Nations Headquarters, N.Y. (1947–50), and designed
urban projects in Antwerp and Stockholm, the city of
Chandigarh in India, and the Ronchamp chapel, Haute
Saone. He is author of *The City of Tomorrow.*
  apartment with nursery school, picture **S** 56
  modern architecture **A** 386–87; **F** 432
  Monastery of La Tourette, picture **F** 432

Leda (LE-da), in Greek mythology, mother of Helen of
Troy, Clytemnestra, and Castor and Pollux. Helen was
the daughter of Leda and Zeus, and Clytemnestra the
daughter of Leda and Tyndareus, King of Sparta. According to one account Castor and Pollux sprang from
an egg as offspring of Leda and the swan, the form in
which Zeus appeared to her. A conflicting story states
that Pollux is the son of Zeus and Castor the offspring
of Tyndareus and Leda.

Lederberg, Joshua (1925–), American geneticist, b.
Montclair, N.J. Together with E. L. Tatum he found that
bacteria can reproduce sexually and thus recombine
their genetic material in ways biologists had not believed
possible. Later he found that certain viruses could transfer
genetic material from one bacterium to another. Lederberg
shared the 1958 Nobel prize in physiology and medicine
with Tatum and G. W. Beadle.

Ledger lines, in musical notation **M** 526
Ledgers, in bookkeeping **B** 312

Ledyard (LED-yard), **John** (1751–89), American explorer,
b. Groton, Conn. He sailed with Captain Cook's third
voyage to Pacific (1776–80). After the American Revolution, he failed to gain American aid to open fur trade
with China. He next attempted to cross Russia and
Siberia on foot. He reached Irkutsk, where he was
arrested and ordered from the country (1788). Ledyard
died on an expedition to explore the source of the Niger
River in Africa. He wrote *A Journal of Captain Cook's
Last Voyage to the Pacific Ocean.*

Lee, Canada (Leonard Lionel Cornelius Canegata) (1907–
1952), American actor, Negro, b. New York, N.Y. He was
a jockey and a boxer before he organized a dance band
that played in theaters, where he became interested in
acting. His most notable roles were as Bigger Thomas in
Native Son (1941), Caliban in Margaret Webster's
production of *The Tempest* (1945), and in whiteface,
opposite Elizabeth Bergner in *The Duchess of Malfi.*
  Negro Renaissance **N** 98

Lee, Charles, American soldier **R** 204

Lee, Doris (1905–), American painter, b. Aledo, Ill. She
is best known for paintings of rural scenes. Her works
include the mural *Rural Postal Delivery* in Washington,
D.C., post office, paintings *Thanksgiving Dinner* and
Country Wedding. She illustrated James Thurber's *The
Great Quillow.*

Lee, Francis Lightfoot (1734–1797), American statesman,
b. Westmoreland County, Va. He served in Virginia's
House of Burgesses (1758–76) and was a member of
the Virginia convention (1775), in which the Virginia
revolution is said to have begun. He was an influential
member of the Continental Congress (1775–79) and a
signer of the Declaration of Independence.

Lee, (Nelle) **Harper** (1926–), American novelist, b. Mon-
roeville, Ala. She won fame with her first novel, *To Kill a
Mockingbird,* about a contemporary southern town. She
was awarded a Pulitzer prize for fiction (1961). The book
was made into a motion picture (1963).

Lee, Henry ("Light Horse" Harry Lee), American officer
  originated the "First in war, first in peace" description
  of George Washington **W** 36
Lee, Jason, Canadian-born American pioneer **O** 205
  missionaries followed the overland trails **O** 260
Lee, Manfred, see Queen, Ellery
Lee, Richard Henry, American Revolutionary War leader
  and statesman **A** 9
  Declaration of Independence **D** 61
Lee, Robert E., American military leader **L** 125–26
  Civil War **C** 321, 324–27, 460
  Grant and Lee **G** 295
  holiday on his birthday **H** 147
  North Carolina nickname (Tarheels) first used by
    N 306

Lee, Tsung-Dao (1926–), Chinese-American physicist,
b. Shanghai, China. In 1957 Lee and a colleague, C. N.
Yang, challenged the principle of the conservation of
parity, a complex theory dealing with the behavior of
subatomic particles. For their work Lee and Yang shared
the 1957 Nobel prize in physics.

Leeches, worms **W** 310, 312

Leek, plant closely related to the onion but with a milder
flavor. It has broad, thick leaves and a long, narrow
bulb. The upper parts of the leaves are used to spice
soups and stews. The bulb is eaten, cooked or raw, as a
vegetable. The leek is native to the eastern Mediterranean region and has been used as food and medicine
since prehistoric times. It is the national emblem of
Wales. Picture **O** 118.

Lee Kuan Yew (Lee Kwan Yew) (1923–), Singapore
statesman, b. Singapore. He helped found the People's
Action Party (1954), which demanded self-government
from Britain, and helped negotiate self-rule agreements
with Great Britain (1957, 1958). Elected first prime
minister of Singapore (1959), he helped bring about the
merger of Malaya, Sarawak, North Borneo, and Singapore into Great Malayasia Union (1963), from which
Singapore has since withdrawn (1965). **S** 184a

Lee Mansion, in Virginia **N** 28–29
Leeuwenhoek (LAY-ven-hook), **Anton van,** Dutch naturalist
    L 127; **M** 206
  advances in biology **B** 190
  lenses, histoy of **L** 141
  microbiology, a new world **M** 274
Leeward, away from the wind **S** 13
Leeward Islands, Caribbean island group **C** 118
Leeward Islands, of the Society Islands group, Pacific
    Ocean **P** 8
Left, political term, origin of **P** 379
Left Bank, of the Seine, Paris **P** 73–74
Left-handedness
  how to write easily **H** 33

Left wing, political groups or branch of a political group whose views are more radical than, or in advance of, the general level of political action and thought. The term originated in France after the Revolution, when conservative members of the legislature were seated to the right of the speaker, and more radical ones to the left. Today the left wing is often identified with socialism or communism.

Legal holidays, United States **H** 147

Le Gallienne (l'GAL-yenn), **Eva** (1899–   ), American actress, b. London, England. She is noted for interpretations of Henrik Ibsen's plays. Founder and director of the Civic Repertory Theater in New York (1926–32), she helped found the American Repertory Theater (1946). She has appeared in *Hedda Gabler, The Cherry Orchard, Liliom,* and *Peter Pan.* She has written two autobiographies, *At 33* and *With a Quiet Heart.*
  theater in the United States **T** 161

Legal profession see Lawyers
Legal tender see Paper money
Legato, or slurred notes, in musical notation **M** 531
Legazpe, Miguel López de see López de Legazpe, Miguel
Legend of the Blue Plate, The **L** 133
Legend of the White Deer **L** 134
Legends **L** 128–35
  Alfred and the cakes **A** 154
  Arthur, King **A** 442–45
  Boy Prisoners in the Tower **E** 220; **P** 470
  early form of fiction **F** 109–10
  Faust **F** 72–73
  folklore of place and personal names **F** 310
  glassmaking, origin of **F** 144; **G** 226
  Groundhog Day in February **F** 74
  Holy Grail in early French literature **F** 436
  Japanese legend of the Sun Goddess **J** 42
  "Pied Piper of Hamelin, The," poem by Browning, excerpt **B** 413–14
  Prometheus stole fire **F** 144
  Robin Hood **R** 253
  Song of Roland **C** 189
  writing, how it began **W** 317
  See also Folklore; Mythology
Legends, on maps **M** 88
Legge (LEG), **Robert T.,** American doctor **O** 16

Legion, body of soldiers making up chief unit of the Roman army. A legion originally consisted of cavalry and 3,000 footsoldiers. Under Roman consul Gaius Marius (155–86 B.C.) the number of footsoldiers was increased to 6,000.

Legionary ants **A** 331
Legion of Honor, French award, picture **M** 200
Legion of Merit, American award, picture **M** 199
Legislation, lawmaking **L** 87–88
  direct see Initiative, referendum, and recall
  how legislatures function **L** 135–36
  presidential leadership **P** 453–54
  United States **U** 140–41
Legislatures **L** 135–36
  Ethiopia's, picture **A** 68
  Kansas' Legislative Council **K** 188–89
  Nebraska's unicameral state legislature **N** 85
  single national legislative bodies **K** 233; **U** 6
  state legislatures **S** 415
  See also country and state articles for detailed information on national and state legislatures
Legs, of animals
  bones of the human leg, diagram **F** 79

insects **C** 167; **I** 262–63, 273
  locomotion **A** 291–92, 293
Leguía (leg GHE-a), **Augusto,** president of Peru **P** 166
Legumes, plants of the pea and bean family
  fertilizers **F** 96
Lehár (LAY-har), **Franz,** Hungarian composer
  O 156
  Merry Widow, The, operetta **O** 158
Lehman (LEE-man), **Herbert H.,** American statesman
  L 136
Lehman Caves, Nevada, picture **C** 155

Lehmann (LAY-monn), **Lotte** (1888–   ), German-American soprano, b. Perleberg, Germany. She was one of the finest Wagnerian singers of her day. When she was with the Vienna Opera (1914–38), Richard Strauss selected her to sing the Young Composer for the premier of *Ariadne auf Naxos* and Barak's wife for the premier of *Die Frau ohne Schatten.* He wrote *Arabella* for her and invited her to create the role of Christine in *Intermezzo.* She sang Octavian and then the Marschallin in *Der Rosenkavalier.* Her first appearance (1934) with the Metropolitan Opera Company was as Sieglinde in Wagner's *Die Walküre,* and as a member of the company (1934–45) she sang chiefly Wagnerian roles.

Lehmbruck (LAIM-broock), **Wilhelm,** German sculptor
  S 103
Lehr (LEER), cooling oven for glass **G** 232
Leib (LAIB), **Mani,** Yiddish author **Y** 351

Leibniz (LIPE-nits), **Gottfried Wilhelm** (1646–1716), German philosopher and mathematician, b. Leipzig. He developed a system of infinitesimal calculus independently of Newton and at about the same time. (Followers of the two men later stirred up a bitter rivalry between them over who had been first.) Leibniz also invented an ingenious calculating machine. In philosophy his theory of monads (tiny particles that make up all matter) was a forerunner of modern atomic theory. He has been ranked with Newton as one of the two greatest thinkers of the 17th century.
  calculus created **M** 157

Leicester, earl of see Dudley, Robert
Leiden (Ly-den), Dutch colony on Staten Island, flag of
  F 228
Leiden, the Netherlands **N** 118
  Separatists settlements form the Plymouth colony
  P 344
Leif Ericson, or Leif the Lucky see Ericson, Leif
Leigh (LE), **Vivien,** English actress, picture **M** 475

Leinsdorf (LINES-dorf), **Erich** (1912–), American conductor, b. Vienna, Austria. He went to United States (1938), where he was chief conductor of Rochester Philharmonic Orchestra (1947–56) and Metropolitan Opera (1957–62). He was conductor and musical director of Boston Symphony Orchestra (1962–69).

Leipzig (LIPE-tzig), Germany **G** 157
  book and fur fairs **F** 11
Leisure activities see Hobbies; How to; Sports
Leitmotivs (LITE-mo-teefs), melodic themes in music drama **G** 187–88
  in opera and musical drama **O** 136
Lei-tsu see Hsi-Ling-Shih
Leixões, Portugal **P** 401
Lely (LE-ly), **Sir Peter,** English painter **E** 237
Le Mans (l'MON), France, sports-car race **A** 539; picture **F** 404
Lemmings, rodents **R** 278–79

Lemnitzer, Lyman Louis (1899–   ), American army officer, b. Honesdale, Pa. He served as assistant chief of staff to General Eisenhower (1942), directed foreign military assistance in Department of Defense (1948–50), and commanded forces in Korean War (1951–52). After serving as Army chief of staff (1959–60) and chairman of Joint Chiefs of Staff (1960–62), he was appointed commander in chief of European command (1962) and supreme allied commander in Europe (1963). He held both posts until 1969.

Lemnos, Greek island in the Aegean **G** 333
Lemon, citrus fruit **L** 136–38
Lemon sharks **S** 143
Lemoyne, Jean Baptiste see Bienville, Jean Baptiste Lemoyne, Sieur de
Lempa, major river in El Salvador **E** 181
Lemus, José María, former president of El Salvador **E** 184
Lemurs (LE-murs), animals related to monkeys
  flying lemurs, gliding animals **B** 96
  have four hands **F.** 83
  primates, true lemurs **M** 418, 422

Le Nain (l'NAN) **brothers,** family of French painters, b. Laon. All were elected to Royal Academy of Painting and Sculpture (1648). **Antoine** (1588?–1648) primarily painted miniatures on copper and wood, including *The Annunciation.* **Louis** (1593?–1648) is remembered for paintings of peasant families, such as *The Peasant Supper* and *The Dairyman's Family.* **Mathius** (1607?–77) is associated with paintings of historical and religious subjects, such as *The Guard.*

Lena River, Union of Soviet Socialist Republics **R** 244

Lend-Lease Act, act prepared by President Roosevelt and passed by Congress (1941) to render any aid, except troops, to Allied forces. The act resulted from heightened German aggression and Britain's inability to pay for American defense materials. It provoked heated opposition of isolationist faction in Congress. Lend-Lease allowed the President to order manufacture of arms and defense materials to be sold or loaned to nations in combat with Axis powers. Its chief beneficiaries were Britain and Soviet Union. Aid was terminated (1945) by President Truman.
  Roosevelt's provision for aid to the Allies **R** 324

L'Enfant (L'on-FON), **Pierre Charles** (1754–1825), French army officer, engineer, and architect, b. Paris. He joined the American forces (1777) and rose to rank of major (1783). After redesigning a New York City site for federal government headquarters (1789), he was commissioned by Washington to lay out plans for the new capital city (1791). The city of Washington developed in the 19th century partly in accord with his concepts. His plan was later fully acknowledged by the Washington Park Commission (1901) as a guide for urban renewal.
  Washington, D.C., history of **W** 35
  White House (President's House) included in the plan **W** 162

L'Engle, Madeleine (1918–   ), American author, b. New York, N.Y. She acted in New York theater (1940's). Her books include *Ilsa, A Winter's Love, Meet the Austins, The Moon by Night,* and *A Wrinkle in Time,* which was awarded the Newbery medal (1963).

Lenglen (lon-GLEN), **Suzanne** (1899–1938), French lawn-tennis player, b. Compiègne. French champion (1920–23, 1925–26), she was women's world champion in singles (1919–23), doubles (1925), and mixed doubles (1920, 1922, 1925).

Length, measurement **W** 108, 115
  wave length of light, a modern standard, picture **W** 110
Lenin, Vladimir I., Russian leader **L** 138
  birthday U.S.S.R. holiday **H** 148
  communism **C** 442–43
  Leningrad, U.S.S.R., named for **L** 139
  Russian Revolution and Civil War, 1917–21 **U** 50
  Stalin, warnings about **S** 395
  stamp with his portrait **S** 399
Leningrad, Union of Soviet Socialist Republics **L** 139–40
  formerly St. Petersburg, capital of Russia **U** 35–36
  Hermitage Museum **H** 119–20
  siege in World War II, 1941–44 **W** 291, 299
Lenin State Library, Moscow, picture **L** 199
Lenin (formerly Skoda) **Works,** in Czechoslovakia, picture **C** 561
Lenni-Lenape (len-ni-le-NA-pe), Indians of North America **I** 185–86
  called Delaware Indians **D** 92
  New Jersey **N** 178
Lennon, John, English rock music composer and performer **R** 262d
Leno weave, of fabrics **T** 144
Lenoir (l'NWAR), **Jean Joseph Étienne,** French inventor **A** 542
  gas engines, invention of **I** 308
Lenoir, William B., American astronaut **S** 347
Lenormand (len-or-MON), **Louis Sébastian,** French chemist **P** 59

Lenox, Walter Scott (1859–1920), American potter, b. Trenton, N.J. He served as a potter's apprentice before forming a partnership with Jonathan Cox in the Ceramic Art Co. (1889). Afflicted with blindness (1895), he nevertheless continued in his efforts to manufacture a ware similar to Irish Belleek. He organized the Lenox Co. (1906) and employed two potters who had worked at Castle Caldwell in Ireland. He succeeded in producing the creamy, richly glazed china that bears his name.

Lenses **L** 141–51
  cameras **P** 201, 203
  contact lenses **L** 151
  eye **B** 284
  lens openings and shutter speeds in cameras **P** 201–03, 215
  light **L** 263–64
  lighthouses **L** 276
  manufacture **O** 175
  microscopes **M** 283
  optical instruments **O** 166–75
  quartz crystals **Q** 6
  telescopes **T** 60–61

Lenski, Lois (1893–   ), American artist and author, b. Springfield, Ohio. She studied painting at Art Students League, New York. Author of children's books—including historical studies such as *Indian Captive* and regional books *Bayou Suzette* and *Strawberry Girl,* which won Newbery medal (1946)—she also wrote "Mr. Small" series, including *The Little Train* and *The Little Airplane.*
  picture books for children **C** 242–43

Lens puzzle **L** 148
Lent
  Mardi Gras, carnival **C** 120
  pre-Easter period **E** 41
  religious holidays connected with Lent **R** 153–54

Lentil, plant of the pea family with small, round, flattened seeds, which are used as food. Lentils were first cultivated in ancient Asian countries and in the Mediterranean regions. They are used more often in Europe and the Middle East than in North America. They are eaten as a vegetable, used in soups and stews, and ground into flour for bread.

Leo, constellation C 492; sign of, picture S 245
Leo III, pope
   Charlemagne C 284
Leo IX, pope
   church reforms R 291

Leo X (Giovanni de' Medici) (1475–1521), pope, b. Florence. The second son of Lorenzo the Magnificent, he was educated by the finest scholars and elected pope in 1513. He did much to promote literature, science, and art, but he created a huge financial debt and neglected the needs of his people. The Reformation began (1517) during his reign, and he excommunicated (1521) Luther.
   Luther's presentation of the 95 theses R 134

Leo XIII, pope L 152
   encyclicals R 297–98

Leo I, Saint (the Great) (390?–461), pope (440–61), b. probably Rome. One of only three popes called Great, he sustained the unity of the Catholic Church at a time of great disorder in the world, combating heresies and maintaining strict church discipline.

León (lay-OHN), **Fray Luis de,** Spanish writer S 368
León, Nicaragua N 247
León, Ponce de see Ponce de León

Leonard, Benny (Benjamin Leiner) (1896–1947), American boxer, b. New York, N.Y. He turned professional at 16, won the lightweight title in 1917, and held it for 7 years. A great scientific boxer, he was elected to the Boxing Hall of Fame in 1955.

Leonardo da Vinci (lay-o-NARD-o da VEEN-chi), Italian
   painter, architect and inventor L 152–55
   air conditioning principle A 102
   auto-type vehicle, plan for A 541
   aviation, history of A 567
   biology during Renaissance B 188
   canals, miter gate of, invented by C 84
   diving equipment, idea for D 79
   drawings of human skeleton B 188
   first to understand what fossils are G 112
   Ginevra de Benci, painting R 168
   helicopter, idea for a H 105
   Last Supper, The, painting A 332
   Madonna of the Rocks, painting P 21
   medicine and anatomy, interest in M 204
   Mona Lisa, painting L 367
   painting, history of P 21
   parachute, idea for P 59
   Renaissance man R 162, 167
   scenery for court masques D 25
   Self Portrait L 153
   Virgin and Child with St. Anne and the Infant St.
     John L 153
   Virgin, Jesus and St. Anne, The, painting I 466, 469
Leoncavallo (lay-ohn-ca-VA-lo), **Ruggiero,** Italian operatic
   composer I 486
   Pagliacci, I, opera O 150
Leoni (lay-O-ni), **Raúl,** president of Venezuela V 300
Leonid (LE-o-nid) **storm,** meteor shower, 1833 C 420;
   picture S 246

Leonov, Aleksei Arkhipovich (1934–), Soviet astronaut, b. Listvyanka, Siberia. On March 18–19, 1965, he took part in the flight of the spacecraft Voskhod 2, with Pavel Belyayev commanding. The craft remained aloft 26 hours, completing 17 orbits. While in orbit, Leonov left the capsule and floated in space at the end of a 16-foot lifeline, the first man to leave a spacecraft in space. This feat was seen on television in Communist countries.
   space flight data S 344, 345

Leopard, The, book by Lampedusa I 481
Leopardi (lay-o-PAR-di), **Giacomo,** Italian poet I 480
Leopards L 155
   cat family C 137–38
   furs F 519
Leopard seals, or sea leopards, animals W 8
Leopold I, king of the Belgians B 131
Leopold II, king of the Belgians B 131
   royal claim to Congo Z 366d
Leopoldville, capital of Zaïre see Kinshasa
Lepanto (le-PON-to), **battle of,** 1571 S 159
Lepchas, people of Sikkim S 176
Leper see Leprosy
Lepidoptera (lep-i-DOP-ter-a), scaly-winged insects B 468
Lepidus, Marcus Aemilius, Roman general M 100
Le Play (l'PLEH), **Frédéric,** French economist S 227

Leprechauns (LEP-re-cauns) (from the Gaelic *liepreachan,* meaning "little body"), mythical Irish dwarfs generally thought of as shoemakers. According to legend, leprechauns possess secret treasure. If they are caught, they can be forced to reveal where the treasure is buried. However, if leprechauns can escape by tricking their human captors into looking away, the hiding place of the treasure remains a secret.

Leprosy (LEP-ro-se) (also called Hansen's disease, after discoverer of causal bacterium), disease, recognized in ancient times, that attacks the skin, mucous membranes, and nerves. In general, its characteristics include skin ulceration, loss of feeling, and, in some cases, deformity of fingers and toes and paralysis. It progresses slowly and is not highly contagious. Treatment includes prolonged use of sulfone drugs. The disease may be cured, in most cases, if treated in early stages. Leprosy's highest prevalence is in tropical areas.
   chaulmoogra treatment P 313
   Hawaii's Kalawao County H 59

Leptis Magna, Libya, Roman theater, picture L 204
Leptons, a group of subatomic particles N 370
Lermontov, Mikhail, Russian poet U 60
Leroux (ler-OO), **Gaston,** French writer M 555
Lesage, Alain René, French novelist F 439
Lesbos, Greek island in Aegean Sea G 333
Lesotho L 156–156a
   flag F 235
Lesseps (LESS-eps), **Ferdinand, Vicomte de,** French
   diplomat and engineer L 156a
   Panama Canal attempt P 48
   Suez Canal S 450–51
Lesser Antilles (an-TILL-ese), Caribbean island group
   C 118
   Barbados B 53
Lesser Sunda Islands, Indonesia I 219–20
Lessing, Doris, Rhodesian-born English novelist
   A 76b
Lessing, Gotthold, German critic and fabulist F 4
   German drama D 297; G 175
Lesson books, for children C 236
Lester, Harry, American ventriloquist V 301
Let, in tennis T 97

Lethbridge, Alberta, Canada **A** 146f–146g

Lethe (LE-the), in Greek mythology, mythical river of forgetfulness that flows in Hades. Souls entering Hades, and those preparing for return to mortal world, drink from river to forget former life.

Leto (LE-to), Greek goddess **G** 360
Lettering, in commercial art **C** 426

Letter of credit, order from a bank addressed to one or more foreign banks instructing them to make payment up to a certain amount to the holder of the letter upon proper identification. The traveler deposits a sum of money with the bank or arranges a loan before receiving credit. Each payment is noted on the letter to show how much of the total credit remains.

Letterpress printing **P** 459–60

Letters of marque (MARK) (letters of marque and reprisal), in international law, written permission given by a government to a private person or group to appropriate the property of a foreign government or of citizens of a foreign government. Such seizure is a retaliatory action for injuries inflicted by the foreign state or its citizens. The term generally applies to private armed ships delegated by the government to retaliate against foreign ships. Congress has constitutional authority to grant letters of marque.

Letters of the alphabet see Alphabet; individual letters
Letters patent, rights granted by a government **P** 97
Letter writing **L** 156b–160
  address, forms of **A** 19–21
  autographs **A** 527
  Committees of Correspondence in American colonies
    C 436
  epistolary novels (novels in form of letters) **E** 260;
    N 346
Lettish, language of Latvia **U** 43
Lettuce **V** 291
Let us cross over the river, and rest in the shade of the
    trees, last words of Stonewall Jackson **J** 8
Leucippus (leu-CIP-pus), Greek philosopher **S** 62
Leukemias (leu-KE-mias), cancers **C** 90; **D** 200
Levant (lev-ANT), region bordering the eastern Mediter-
    ranean **M** 300
Levassor (ler-va-SUR), **Émile,** French engineer and auto-
    mobile racer **A** 538
  automobiles, history of **A** 543
Levees (LEV-ees), to control floods **F** 256; picture **F** 257
  embankment dams **D** 16
  Louisiana **L** 351
  Mississippi **M** 353
  natural levees of rivers **R** 239
Level, measuring tool, picture **T** 216
  surveyor's level **S** 479
Leverrier (lev-er-i-AY), **Urbain,** French astronomer
    A 475
  made calculations leading to discovery of Neptune
    P 277–78
Levers, simple machines **W** 247–48
  inventions of mechanical devices **I** 335
Lever tumblers, in locks **L** 324

Levi (LE-vi) (Hebrew for "joined"), third son of Jacob and Leah. He and Simeon led attack on the Shechemites to avenge the rape of their sister Dinah. Levi's sons were Gershon, Kohath, and Merari, patriarchs of three houses. The tribe of Levi's descendants, known as Levites, produced the priests of the nation of Israel.

Leviathan (lev-Y-ath-an), in Old Testament, a crocodile (Job 41) or a sea monster resembling a dragon or serpent (Psalms 74:14–17). It was a symbol of wickedness, to be destroyed by God. In creation myths of the Phoenicians, it was a sea monster with seven heads that was slain by Baal.

Leviathan, ocean liner **O** 24
  first commercial ship-to-shore radiotelephone service
    E 142a
Leviticus (lev-IT-ic-us), book of Bible **B** 154
Levitski (lev-IT-ski), **Dimitri,** Russian painter **U** 55
  portrait of Princess Dashkova **U** 55
Levita (le-VY-ta), **Elias,** Yiddish author **Y** 350
Levulose (LEV-u-loce), or fructose, fruit sugar **S** 453

Levy, Asser (Asser Levy van Swellem) (?–1681), colonial American merchant. One of the first Jews to settle in America, Levy arrived in New York with 23 immigrants from Brazil, who comprised the first Jewish community in the North American colonies (1654). He circulated a petition (1655), asking equal opportunity for Jews to have guard duty and exemption from tax imposed on them in place of guard duty. He was known as an ardent defender of Jewish rights in the colonies.

Lewes (LEW-es), Delaware **D** 97
Lewes, George Henry, English editor and writer **E** 177

Lewis, Cecil Day (1904–), British poet, b. Ballintogher, Ireland. Associated with British poets W. H. Auden and Stephen Spender of the "poetic political" school of 1930's in England, his verse includes *Overtures to Death and Other Poems.* He also writes detective stories under pseudonym of Nicholas Blake. He was named poet laureate in 1968.

Lewis, Francis (1713–1802), colonial American merchant in New York and signer of the Declaration of Independence, b. Llandaff, Wales. A delegate to Stamp Act Congress (1765) and a member of the Sons of Liberty, he was also a representative to the Continental Congress (1774–79) and a commissioner on the Board of Admiralty (1779–81).

Lewis, Gilbert N., American scientist **C** 216
Lewis, Jerry, American movie comedian, picture **M** 483
Lewis, John L., American labor leader **L** 161
  labor movement, history of **L** 6
Lewis, Meriwether, American explorer **L** 162
  monument near Hohenwald, Tennessee **T** 83
Lewis, Sinclair, American novelist **L** 161
  American literature **A** 208
  novels of the 1920's **N** 349
Lewis and Clark Centennial Exposition, 1905, Portland,
    Oregon **F** 12
Lewis and Clark expedition **L** 162–63
  assists U.S. competition for fur trade **F** 522–23
  Fort Clatsop National Memorial, site of winter en-
    campment **O** 203
  Idaho **I** 54, 66, 67
  overland trails and waterways **O** 256

Lewisohn (LEW-is-ohn), **Adolph** (1849–1938), American industrialist and philanthropist, b. Hamburg, Germany. He established a mining industry and sales agency for copper and other metals, but he withdrew from business concerns and turned his attention to philanthropy, the arts, and improvement of prison conditions. His donations included funds for establishment of Lewisohn Stadium in New York City and for a building for Columbia University's School of Mines.

Lewiston, Idaho I 66
Lewiston, Maine M 44
Lexington, Kentucky K 224
Lexington, Massachusetts
  Revolutionary War begins R 198

Ley (LAY), Willy (1906–69), American rocket expert and author, b. Berlin, Germany. He was a founding member in 1927 of the pioneering Society for Space Travel in Germany and was its vice-president (1928–34). He is best known for his books for the non-scientist. These books include *Conquest of Space*.

Leyden (LY-den) jar, simple device for storing electricity. Developed in the mid-18th century, it consists of a glass jar partly coated, inside and out, with metal foil. Separated by nonconducting glass, the two coatings form the electrodes of the device. A charge is introduced to the inner electrode through a metal rod, which passes through the stopper of the jar. An opposite charge is thus induced in the outer electrode, which is grounded. If a wire attached to the outer foil is brought close to the metal rod in contact with the inner foil, a spark is produced.
  possibility of use for communication T 51

Leyte (LAY-te) Gulf, battle of, 1944 W 302; picture W 301
Lhasa (LA-sa), capital of Tibet T 177; picture T 175
Liabilities (ly-a-BIL-it-ies), shown in bookkeeping statements B 312
Liability insurance *see* Insurance, liability

Libby, Willard Frank (1908–), American chemist, b. Grand Valley, Colo. He is best-known for his discovery of radioactive dating, using carbon-14, a radioactive form of carbon. He began this work in 1945 and perfected the technique by 1947. In 1960 he received the Nobel prize in chemistry for his work.

Libel (LY-bel), statement harmful to a person's reputation
  case of John Peter Zenger Z 369
  case of Oscar Wilde W 167
Liberación Nacional (li-bair-ah-si-OWN nah-si-o-NAL), social-democratic party, Costa Rica C 518

Liberalism (LIB-er-al-ism), social and political philosophy formulated in 18th and 19th centuries in Europe. During the Industrial Revolution, liberalism favored an end to privileges held by the aristocracy and state churches; a limit on central government; an extension of political and civil liberties for each individual; and an economic policy of laissez-faire. Today it favors a firm central government to check power of business and other private groups in order to insure individual civil liberties, and it encourages more government spending for wider health, education, and welfare facilities.

Liberal Party, British P 379
  Gladstone's career G 225
Liberal Party, Canadian C 77
  King, William Lyon Mackenzie K 248
  Laurier, Sir Wilfrid L 85
  Pearson, Lester P 115
  St. Laurent, Louis Q 13
Liberation Day, Italy H 150
Liberia (ly-BEER-ia) L 164–67
  colony for ex-slaves and free-born American Negroes N 94
  flag F 235
  Perry, Matthew C. P 156
  U.S. merchant marine flying "flags of convenience" U 184

Liberty, Equality, Fraternity, watchwords of French Revolution F 466
Liberty, Statue of L 168
  view from a helicopter H 105
Liberty Bell L 169
  how bells are made B 135
  Independence Hall I 113
Liberty Bell, Mexican M 251

Liberty cap (Phrygian cap), soft conical hat used as a symbol of freedom. In ancient Rome the cap was presented to slaves at their emancipation. The term also refers to red caps worn as emblems of liberty by French Revolutionists.
  Phrygian bonnet, picture H 55

Liberty Island, New York Harbor, site of Statue of Liberty L 168
Liberty of the press *see* Freedom of the press
Liberty Party, United States P 385
Liberty ships
  named for famous Negroes N 101
Liberty Song, by John Dickinson N 22
Liberty Tree flag, 1775 F 229
Libra (LY-bra), constellation C 491; sign of, picture S 245
Librarians and librarianship L 188–92
Libraries L 170–200
  ancient Assyrian civilization A 225
  book exhibits for National Library Week B 316
  books: from author to library B 329–34
  Carnegie, Andrew C 119
  Coonskin Library, Ohio O 68
  Crane Memorial, Quincy, Massachusetts U 124
  elementary school buildings E 79
  first circulating library in United States P 137
  first free tax-supported public library in United States N 157
  history of L 192–200
  how to use your library L 180–88
  importance to the school's reading program R 111
  influence on children's literature C 242
  librarians and what they do L 188–92
  Mexico, University of, Mexico City M 253
  modern library services L 170–79
  Nairobi, Kenya, University College in, picture K 231
  Oklahoma, University of, picture O 87
  oldest public library in Europe U 71
  paperback books P 58a
  presidential *see* Presidential libraries
  record library, basic R 125
  reference books R 129–31
  research methods R 182–83
  storytelling S 435; picture S 434
  talking books for the blind B 253
  Working Men's Institute Library, New Harmony, Ind. I 143
  See also Indexes and indexing; education section of country, province, and state articles

Library Association, The, founded (1877) as Library Association of the United Kingdom (renamed, 1896). Granted a royal charter (1898) to unite all persons engaged or interested in library work and promote the better administration of libraries, it was reorganized in 1962 and became fully professional. It publishes books and pamphlets, and the official *Library Association Record*. Headquarters are in London.
  admission by examination L 191
  book award, Carnegie Medal B 310

Library associations L 191–92

Library of Congress, Washington, D.C.   **L** 177, 200;
  picture **L** 179
  books for the blind   **B** 253
  Copyright Office of   **T** 244–45
  points of interest in Washington, D.C.   **W** 31–32
Library Services Act, 1956   **L** 173
Library Services and Construction Act, 1964, 1966   **L** 173
Libraries, motions of the moon   **M** 447
Librations, motions of the moon   **M** 447
Librettos, words of an opera or other long musical composition   **O** 131
Libreville (LE-brev-ill), capital of Gabon   **G** 3
Libya (LIB-ia)   **L** 201–05
  agriculture, picture   **A** 99
  camel caravan, picture   **S** 8
  flag   **F** 235
  nomadic herdsmen, picture   **D** 129
Libya, University of   **L** 201
Libyan Desert, Africa   **E** 90d
  prospecting for oil, picture   **G** 106
Lice, insects   **H** 262; pictures **H** 263,   **I** 283
  carriers of typhus   **I** 283
Licenses
  amateur radio operators (hams)   **R** 63
  hunting   **H** 291; picture **H** 290
  marriage licenses   **W** 101
  television stations   **T** 70a
  to private utility companies   **P** 510
Lichens (LY-kens),   **F** 94–95
  partnership of algae and fungi   **A** 156
Lichtenstein, Roy, American artist   **P** 31
Licinius (li-CIN-ius), Roman emperor   **C** 489

Licorice, herblike plants of the pea (legume) family.
Licorice is also a product of the roots, used in candy,
flavoring, and medicines. Native to Asia and southern
Europe, the plant is up to 3 ft. tall and has blue flowers.

Liddell, Alice, for whom Lewis Carroll wrote "Alice in
  Wonderland"   **A** 164; **C** 123
Lie (LEE), **Trygve,** Norwegian statesman   **L** 205

Liebig (LE-bik), **Baron Justus von** (1803–1873), German
chemist, b. Darmstadt. He pioneered in organic chemistry, discovering and perfecting methods of analyzing
organic substances. He did basic work on the behavior of
radicals (groups of atoms that behave as one unit in
chemical reactions). In 1831 he discovered the anesthetic
chloroform. He also devised improved methods for manufacturing chemicals. After 1840 he specialized in plant
and animal physiology. He was the first to experiment
with chemical fertilizers, and he set up an experimental
farm to demonstrate his theories. At the University of
Giessen he set up the first laboratory designed for the
use of students.
  discovery of chemical fertilizers   **A** 100; **F** 98; **S** 74
  his work a major development in biology   **B** 193–94

Liechtenstein (LEECK-ten-shtine)   **L** 206–07
  flag   **F** 239
Lied (LEED) (plural lieder), German art song   **C** 333;
  M 538
  styles of singing   **V** 376

Lie detector, apparatus that records changes in respiration, blood pressure, and pulse beat, as index of
emotional tension, in attempt to determine guilt or
innocence of person under questioning, based on
supposition that a guilty person shows greater emotional
response. The instrument has proved effective but not
always accurate. Therefore lie-detector tests are almost
never allowed in court as evidence for guilt.
  police use certain new technical inventions   **P** 376

Liège (li-EZH), Belgium   **B** 129
Lieutenant governor, in Canadian government   **C** 77
Life   **L** 208–14
  adaptations in the world of   **L** 214–27
  adaptive radiation in birdlife   **B** 209–10
  aging   **A** 81–87
  altitude, vertical life zones of   **Y** 352–53;   **Z** 372–73
  bacteria in the cycle of   **B** 12
  biology, study of living things   **B** 187–96
  blood, stream of life   **B** 255
  butterflies and moths, life cycle   **B** 468–69
  cell, unit of life   **C** 159, 161
  cosmic rays, effect on   **C** 513
  cycles see **Life cycles**
  distribution of plant and animal   **L** 227–39
  eggs and embryos   **E** 88–90a
  energy and life   **E** 201
  evolution   **E** 338–47
  food chains in   **L** 239–43
  forest life   **F** 371–72
  genetics   **G** 77–88
  hibernation   **H** 121–24
  kingdoms of living things   **K** 249–59
  life belt of the sun   **E** 22; diagram   **E** 23
  living on moon or in space **M** 455–56; **S** 340a, 340d–341
  Mars   **M** 104, 107, 111
  meteorites show signs of   **C** 421
  moon, life on   **C** 421
  prehistoric animals, early life forms   **P** 436
  reproduction   **R** 176–80
  rhythms and clocks in plant and animal   **L** 243–50
  temperatures, life range in, diagram   **H** 86d
  underwater exploration of life in the sea   **U** 21–22
  vertical life zones   **Z** 372–73
  water essential to all forms   **W** 51
  webs of   **L** 250–59
Life, adaptations in the world of   **L** 214–27
  animals living in caves   **C** 157
  dinosaurs, the end of the   **D** 181
  plant defenses   **P** 282–83
  rhythms and survival   **L** 243
Life, distribution of plant and animal   **L** 227–39
  plankton   **P** 279–81
Life, early humor magazine   **C** 127
Life, food chains in   **L** 239–43
  giants of nature   **G** 204
  photosynthesis   **P** 221
  underwater exploration of life in the sea   **U** 21–22
Life, magazine   **M** 15
Life, origin of   **L** 213–14
Life, rhythms and clocks in plant and animal   **L** 243–50
  hibernation and estivation   **H** 121–24
Life, webs of   **L** 250–59
  communities of living things   **K** 257–59
  environment, problems of   **E** 272a–272h
Lifeboats, on ocean liners   **O** 24
Life cycles
  ant, life cycle   **A** 323
  bullfrog, pictures   **F** 472
  newt, pictures   **F** 476
  wheat rust, diagram   **F** 499
Life expectancy see **Life spans**
Life insurance see **Insurance, life**
Life on other planets   **P** 271
Life plant, or bryophylium, picture   **P** 300
Lifesaving see **First aid; Safety**
Life sciences
  experiments and projects (involving animals and
    plants)   **E** 356–59
Life spans, average length, for man and animals   **A** 81–84
  birds   **B** 229
  elephants   **E** 170

Life spans (continued)
   insects **I** 265–66
   life expectancies (highest and lowest countries), **list**
      P 395
   turtles **T** 335
Life-support systems, for space exploration **S** 340a,
   340L–341; diagram **S** 340L
Life zones, belts of plant and animal communities, by
   altitude **Z** 372–73
   Yosemite National Park **Y** 352–53
Liffey River, Ireland **R** 244
   Dublin's river **I** 388
Lift, upward force opposing gravity
   aerodynamics theory and demonstration **A** 38
   animals: locomotion **A** 294–95
   aviation **A** 553
   hydrofoil boats **H** 304–05
Lifts see Elevators; Escalators; Hoisting and loading
   machinery
Ligaments, cords of tissue connecting bones **B** 270
Ligan see Flotsam, jetsam, and lagan, or ligan
Light **L** 260–74
   atmosphere **A** 482
   bioluminescence, cold light **B** 197–98
   cameras and light meters **P** 213
   chemical changes caused by **C** 199
   constant speed, how shown by an interferometer
      R 140
   deep-sea fishes, light organs of **F** 198
   dust scatters **D** 348
   effects in impressionistic painting **F** 426; **M** 408
   energy **E** 199
   experiments in effect of light on plants **E** 356–57
   interferometers, instruments **O** 172
   lasers **M** 131–33
   lenses **L** 141–51
   lighting **L** 279–90
   light waves, theories of **R** 140
   matter, light a special form of **M** 171
   Michelson-Morley experiment on the ether theory
      R 140–41
   mirage, cause of **M** 341–42
   Newton's experiments with the spectrum **N** 207
   phosphorescent paints **P** 34
   photoelectricity **P** 199–200
   photosynthesis **P** 221–23
   quasars and pulsars **Q** 7–8
   radiant energy, in physics **P** 236
   radiation **R** 43–44
   rainbow **R** 98
   signals for communication **C** 437, 438
   signals for fish **A** 280
   solar energy **S** 235
   spectrum, visible and invisible rays of **E** 24
   sun **S** 458–67
   wave theory, first studies **S** 74–75
   X rays and light rays **X** 341
   See also Bioluminescence; Color; Optical instruments
Lighter-than-air craft see Balloons and ballooning;
   Dirigibles
Light heavyweight, in boxing **B** 352
Lighthouses **L** 275–78
   Cape Hatteras, picture **N** 317
   Lake Superior, picture **M** 324
   Pemaquid Point, Maine, picture **M** 37
   Pharos, a wonder of the ancient world **W** 216; picture
      W 215
   Where is the Boston Light? **L** 278
   Where is the Eddystone Light? **L** 276
Lighting **L** 279–90
   candles **C** 96–97
   Edison's electric inventions **E** 60

   interior decorating **I** 300
   lighthouses and lightships **L** 275–78
   neon and other noble gases **N** 109–10
   petroleum **P** 176
   photography **P** 216–17, 220
   plays, stage lighting **P** 339; pictures **P** 337
   Tungsten filament in light bulbs **T** 308
Lighting designers, of plays **T** 158
Light meters
   photography, use in **P** 213
Light middleweight, in boxing **B** 352
Lightning **T** 170–73
   ball lightning mistaken for flying saucers
      F 285–86
   fire and early man, picture **F** 138
   Franklin's rod **F** 453
   nitrogen in the air "fired" by lightning **N** 262

Lightning rods, sharp-pointed metallic rods set atop a
building or other such structure and connected to moist
ground or water. They protect structures from dangerous
effects of lightning stroke by conducting electric charges
into earth or water. Their invention (1752?) is usually
attributed to Benjamin Franklin.

Lightships **L** 277–78
Light-year, unit of interstellar measurement **S** 405
   quasars and pulsars, distances from earth **Q** 7
   universe, galaxies in **U** 196–204
Lightweight, in boxing **B** 352
Light welterweight, in boxing **B** 352
Lignin (LIG-nin), a substance in wood **W** 222, 227
Lignite, a soft coal **C** 362, 363
   fuel **F** 487
   North Dakota deposits burn constantly **N** 326
Lignum vitae (VY-te), tree
   bearings in machinery **W** 227
Liguest, Pierre Laclède see Laclède, Pierre
Ligurian (li-GU-rian) **Sea** **O** 48
Li Ho, Chinese poet **O** 220a
Liholiho, Alexander see Kamehameha IV, Hawaiian king
Lihue (LEEHOO-ay), Hawaii **H** 69
Lilacs, flowers, picture **G** 36
   state flower of New Hampshire **N** 149

Lilienthal (LI-li-en-thol), **David Eli** (1899–   ), American
business executive, b. Morton, Ill. He was chairman
(1941–46) of the Tennessee Valley Authority, chairman of
the Atomic Energy Commission (1946–50), chairman and
chief executive officer of the Development and Resources
Corp. (1955–62), and director of minerals and chemicals
for the Philipp Corp. (since 1962). His books include *TVA:
Democracy on the March.*

Lilienthal (LI-li-en-tol), **Otto** (1848–1896), German aeronautical pioneer, b. Anklam, Prussian Pomerania. He
studied flights of birds as preliminary to experiments
with gliders, and he built a series of gliders, which he
flew, inspiring the Wright brothers with his experiments.
   pioneer in aviation **A** 567; picture **A** 568
   early glider pilots **G** 239

Lilies, flowers **G** 46, 51; picture **G** 37
   leaves, special kinds of, pictures **L** 120
   lily, a monocot, picture **P** 292
Lilies of the valley, flowers **G** 42; picture **G** 44

Lilith, in Talmudic tradition, Adam's first wife, expelled
from Eden and believed to have borne evil spirits. In
medieval legends Lilith was a demon who threatened
infants unprotected by amulets; in Old Testament
(Isaiah 34:14) the name is associated with the owl.

Liliuokalani (li-li-u-o-ka-LA-ni), queen of Hawaii **H** 70, 71
Lille (LEEL), France **F** 406

Lillie, Beatrice (1898–   ), British actress, b. Toronto, Canada. Noted for performances as vaudeville comedienne, she appeared in *Big Top, Seven Lively Arts*, and *High Spirits*. She also appeared in *Ziegfeld Follies of 1957*, as well as in motion pictures and on radio and TV.

Lilliput, imaginary country in *Gulliver's Travels* **G** 412–13

Lilly Endowment, Inc., foundation that makes grants available for research and training in education, religion, and community services. It assists private social agencies and the United Fund in Indianapolis, Ind., and environs, and has provided funds for technical aid and literacy projects in Southeast Asia and the Near East.

Lilongwe, Malawi **M** 51
Lima (LI-ma), capital of Peru **P** 164; picture **P** 165
   Pizarro, Francisco founded Lima **P** 266

Lima, Declaration of (1930), proposal adopted at the Lima Conference in Peru to promote hemispheric unity and security. Introduced by U.S. Secretary of State Cordell Hull to thwart German Nazi influence in the Americas, it proposed to establish meeting of the American states if any of them felt threatened by foreign power.

Lima beans, vegetables **V** 289
   germination, pictures **P** 299
Limb darkening, of the sun **S** 460–61
Limbe (LIM-bay), Malawi **M** 51
Limburg brothers, Flemish painters **D** 349
   April, manuscript **D** 349
   The Belles Heures of Jean, Duke of Berry, picture from **A** 438a
Lime, calcium compound made from limestone **R** 268
   fertilizer **F** 98
   glass **G** 226
Lime, citrus fruit **L** 136–38
Limerick, Ireland **I** 385
Limericks (LIM-er-icks) **N** 273, 276
   form of humor **H** 279
Limestone **R** 267–68
   building stone **S** 433
   Carlsbad Caverns **C** 153–55
   cement made of **C** 165
   gemstones result from impurities in **G** 70
   marble **R** 209; **S** 433
   quarry in Bermuda, picture **Q** 5
   steelmaking uses **I** 404
   test to identify **R** 267
Limeys, nickname for British sailors **L** 137
   lemons and limes supplied needed food element **F** 335
   vitamins, discovery of **V** 370a

Limitations, Statute of, law, originated (1623) under James I of England, limiting the period of time during which a person or group may bring claims to court, defend certain rights, or bring action against criminal offenders. It prevents delaying trial of a case until the evidence needed for defense has been destroyed or witnesses have died. In criminal cases, it supports the principle that the offender or suspect cannot be subject to trial forever.
   war crimes trials **W** 9

Limners, artists **F** 293–94
Limoges (li-MOGE), France
   enameling artists of **E** 192

Limón (li-MONE), Costa Rica **C** 515, 516

Limón, José Arcadio (1908–72), American dancer and choreographer, b. Culiacan, Mexico. A dancer with the Humphrey-Weidman Co. of New York (1930–40), he also choreographed several Broadway shows. As principal male dancer in the modern dance theater, he and his company toured throughout the world. He last performed in 1969, but continued as artistic director for the José Limón Dance Company until his death.

Limonite (LIME-on-lte), iron ore **I** 404
Limp blimp, underwater house **U** 19
Limpets, shell-bearing mollusks, gastropods **O** 276
Limpopo River, east central Africa **R** 229
Lincoln, Abraham, 16th President of the United States **L** 291–97
   assassination, aftermath of Civil War **C** 327
   Civil War **C** 321, 324, 327, 458, 459
   Emancipation Proclamation **E** 185–86
   Gettysburg Address **G** 191
   Grant and Lincoln **G** 295
   holiday on his birthday **H** 147
   Illinois **I** 70–72, 81
   Johnson, Andrew, vice-president under **J** 124–25
   letter to Mrs. Bixby **L** 156b
   Lincoln-Douglas debates **L** 299
   Lincoln Homestead State Park, Kentucky **K** 223
   presidential leadership **P** 450
   quoted **Q** 20
   Reconstruction Period anticipated **R** 117
   Republican party, rise of **P** 380
   Thanksgiving Day proclamation **T** 154
   tomb in Springfield, picture **I** 83
   Whitman's poem "O Captain! My Captain" **W** 165–66
Lincoln, Benjamin, American military commander **R** 208
Lincoln, capital of Nebraska **N** 83–84
Lincoln, Illinois **I** 81
Lincoln, Mary Todd, wife of Abraham Lincoln **F** 171–72; **L** 293
Lincoln Boyhood National Memorial, Indiana **I** 146
Lincoln Center for the Performing Arts, New York City **L** 298
   plaza, picture **N** 235
Lincoln-Douglas debates **L** 299
   Douglas, Stephen A. **D** 287
   Lincoln opposes Kansas-Nebraska Act **L** 294–95
Lincoln Highway, transcontinental road **W** 330
   Abraham Lincoln Memorial monument **W** 333
Lincoln Memorial, Washington, D.C. **W** 32; picture **W** 34
Lincoln National Life Foundation, Fort Wayne, Indiana **I** 145
Lincoln's Inn see Inns of Court
Lincoln's New Salem State Park, Illinois **I** 81; picture **I** 80
Lincoln Trail, in Illinois **I** 81
Lincoln Tunnel, Hudson River, picture **N** 173
   construction, picture **T** 316
Lind, Don L., American astronaut **S** 347
Lind, James, English physician **V** 370a
Lind, Jenny, Swedish singer **L** 300
Lindauer, Martin, German scientist **B** 119

Lindbergh, Anne Spencer Morrow (1906–   ), American author, b. Englewood, N.J. Wife of aviator Charles A. Lindbergh, she was the first woman to be awarded the Hubbard medal (1934), given her for accompanying her husband as co-pilot and radio operator in flights covering five continents and totaling 40,000 miles. Her books include *Gift From the Sea, North to the Orient, The Wave of the Future* (criticized by some readers as antidemocratic), and *Dearly Beloved*.

Lindbergh, Charles, American aviator **L** 300
  aided Goddard's rocket research **G** 246
  airmail pilot **P** 407
  autobiography **A** 215
  aviation history **A** 573
  Charles A. Lindbergh State Memorial Park, Minnesota
    M 333
  Missouri's place in development of air transport
    M 374–75
  only civilian Medal of Honor winner **M** 200
Linden, tree see Basswood, tree
Lindenwald, New York, home of Martin Van Buren,
    picture **V** 273

Lindgren, Astrid (1907–   ), Swedish author and editor of
children's books, b. Vimmerby. Her works include
Rasmus and the Vagabond, which won the Hans Christian
Andersen medal (1958), *Nils Karlsson Pyssling,* and
Pippi Longstocking.

Lindisfarne Gospels, illuminated page from, picture **I** 87

Lindsay, John Vliet (1921–   ), American politician, b. New
York, N.Y. After receiving a Bachelor of Arts degree from
Yale University, he entered the Navy and saw active service during World War II. He returned to Yale and earned
a law degree. He became interested in Republican politics
and was executive assistant to Attorney General Brownell
in Washington. Elected to congress from New York in 1958,
he was re-elected for the following three terms. In 1965 he
was elected mayor of New York City, and again in 1969.
In 1971 he joined the Democratic party.

Lindsay, Vachel, American poet **A** 209

Lindsey, Benjamin Barr (1869–1943), American jurist, b.
Jackson, Tenn. A judge in juvenile court, Denver, Colo.
(1900–27), and in California superior court (1934–43), he
was known for his understanding of the juvenile
delinquent and for his improvements and revisions of
the juvenile court system. His public support of companionate marriage created much dispute. Among his
published works are *Problems of the Children, The Beast
and the Jungle,* and (with Wainright Evans) *The
Companionate Marriage.*

Lindsey, Philip, American educator **E** 72
Line, element in design **D** 135
Linear (LIN-e-ar) **accelerators,** atom smashers **A** 489
Linear perspective **P** 158; diagrams **P** 159
Line engraving, in printing **P** 458–59
Line games **G** 22–24
Line graphs **G** 311–12

Line Islands, 11 small, barren atolls in the central
Pacific. Formerly important as guano sources, they were
divided between United States and Britain in 1930's and
converted into air bases. Kingman Reef, Palmyra, and
Jarvis belong to United States; Washington, Fanning,
and Christmas are part of the British colony of Gilbert
and Ellice Islands.

Linen **F** 106
Linenfold, an ornamental design or pattern **F** 505
Linen-supply laundries **L** 84
Line of Demarcation **E** 378
Line officers
  United States Navy **U** 189
Lines, for fishing **F** 206, 211
Lines, geometric **G** 124
Lines of force, electric and magnetic **E** 129–32, 134
  magnetism **M** 25

Ling, Per Henrik, Swedish gymnast **P** 225
Lingonberries **G** 301
Linguistics (lin-GUIS-tics), study of languages **L** 301–03
  anthropological studies **A** 308
Lingula (lin-GU-la), stalked lamp shells **L** 224
Link, Edwin, American inventor **U** 19

Link Foundation, charitable fund that awards grants to
nonprofit educational institutions and organizations for
educational projects—especially in aerospace and ocean-
ography. It was established (1953) by Edwin A. Link and
has headquarters in New York City.

Linking verbs **G** 289
Linnaeus (lin-NE-us), **Carolus,** Swedish botanist **L** 303–04
  biologists adopt classification scheme **B** 191
  manager of Uppsala Botanical Gardens **Z** 379
  science of taxonomy **T** 29
Linné, Carl von see Linnaeus, Carolus
Linocuts (LY-no-cuts), linoleum prints **L** 304–06
Linoleum **V** 340–41
  cork used in **C** 505
Linoleum-block printing **L** 304–06
Linotype, typesetting machine **P** 463
  lines of type, casting of **T** 344–45
  newspapers use **N** 203

Lin Piao (1908–   ), Chinese government official, b.
Ungkung, Hupeh Province, China. A member of the Nationalist Party (1922–27), he joined the Communist Party
in 1927. He won important military victories (1945–49)
in the Chinese civil war and commanded the Communist
Chinese forces during the Korean War. In 1969 he was
named Chairman Mao Tse-Tung's successor.

Linsangs, animals related to genets **G** 90
Linseed oil **O** 79
  ink **I** 256
  varnishes and lacquers **V** 279
Lindsey-woolsey, home-woven cloth **P** 256
Lint, cotton **C** 525
Lintel, term in architecture **A** 374
Linters, fibers of cottonseed **C** 525

Lin Yutang, or **Lin Yu-t'ang** (1895–   ), Chinese author,
b. Changchow. He was head, Arts and Letters Division,
UNESCO (1948). He is known for writings on Chinese
culture and invented Chinese indexing method and
typewriter with Chinese characters. He collaborated on
official project for romanizing Chinese alphabet. His
works include *My Country and My People.*

Lion, constellation see Leo
Lion and the Mouse, The, fable by Aesop **F** 4
Lioness, picture **A** 292
Lion Gate, Mycenae, Greece, pictures **A** 374, **S** 94

Lionni, Leo (1910–   ), American painter and children's
author, b. Amsterdam, the Netherlands. He was named
art director of the year by the National Society of Art
Directors (1955). His books for children include *Little
Blue and Little Yellow* and *Inch by Inch.*
  Inch by Inch, page from, picture **C** 244

Lion of Judah, symbol of the Emperor of Ethiopia, pic-
    ture **E** 296
Lions **L** 307
  Africa, picture **A** 51
  cat family **C** 134–39; pictures **C** 136, 137
  Hittite art **A** 238; picture **A** 239
  in heraldry, pictures **H** 117
  mammal societies, picture **M** 70

Lions Clubs, International Association of, federation of community service clubs founded in 1917. It became an International organization in 1920 and has branches in 145 countries. It has headquarters in Chicago, Ill.

Lion's mane, jellyfish, picture **J** 70

Lipchitz, Jacques (1891–1973), American sculptor, b. Druskleniki, Lithuania. As a young man, he studied in Paris. When the Germans invaded France during World War II, he settled in the United States. One of the most celebrated exponents of cubist sculpture, he drew many of his themes from mythology and the Bible.
   modern art **M** 391
   Figure, sculpture **S** 104

Lipids, fatlike body compounds **B** 293; **V** 363
Lipizzaner horse see Lippizaner horse

Lipkind, William (1904–), American author and anthropologist, b. New York, N.Y. He spent 2 years (1938–40) in Brazil studying the Carajá and Javhé Indians. Under the names Will and Nicolas he and illustrator Nicolas Mordvinoff have produced a number of picture books, such as *Finders Keepers* (Caldecott medal, 1952), *Four-leaf Clover, The Two Reds,* and *The Little Tiny Rooster.* They also wrote and illustrated *Boy with a Harpoon, Boy of the Islands,* and *Boy and the Forest.*

Li Po, Chinese poet **O** 220a
Lippershey (LIPP-ers-hy), **Hans,** eyeglass maker **T** 60–61

Lippizaner horse, a special breed of dressage horse used in the Spanish Riding School, Vienna, Austria, and recently imported to the United States. It was named after the town of Lippiza, where the strain was first developed about 400 years ago. Black at birth, gray at maturity, and white in old age, the Lippizaner can be used as a ceremonial carriage horse.

Lippmann, Walter (1889–), American editor and author, b. New York, N.Y. He was editor of the New York *World* (1929–31) and then became a syndicated columnist for over 200 newspapers throughout the world. He won the Pulitzer prize for reporting (1958, 1962) and the Presidential Medal of Freedom (1964). His books include *Drift and Mastery, The Good Society,* and *The Communist World and Ours.*

Lipreading, of the deaf **D** 50, 52
Lipstick, cosmetic **C** 509
   beauty culture **B** 110
Lipton, Seymour, American sculptor **M** 397

Lipton, Sir Thomas Johnstone (1850–1931), Scottish businessman, b. Glasgow. As a young man, he worked in United States (about 1865–70) before returning to Glasgow to launch his business career by opening a food store (1871). He quickly expanded his interests in Britain and other countries, including United States and Germany, and developed large tea plantations in India. He was well known as a philanthropist and was knighted in recognition for his generous contributions to various charities. He was an accomplished yachtsman and a dedicated contender for the America's Cup.

Liquefaction (lik-we-FAC-tion) **fractional distiller,** for liquid gases **L** 308
Liquefied petroleum gas see LPG
Liquid air
   conversion from gas **G** 58
   industrial uses **G** 59

Liquid fuels **F** 488
   Goddard's rocket experiment with **G** 245
   missile fuels **M** 345
   petroleum **P** 169–78
Liquid gases **L** 308–09
   helium **H** 107–08
   hydrogen **H** 306
   rocket fuels **R** 257–58
   what happens near absolute zero **H** 90
Liquid measure **W** 113, 115
Liquid oxygen, or Lox **L** 308–09
   Goddard's rocket experiment with **G** 245
   oxidation **O** 269–70
   oxidizer for rocket fuels **F** 490; **R** 258
Liquids **L** 309–10
   buoyancy principle, discovery of **A** 369; **F** 252
   contrasted with crystalline solids **C** 544
   defined **C** 219
   density of fluids **F** 250–51
   detergents **D** 149
   distillation process **D** 224–26
   gases, liquefaction of **G** 58
   how heat changes matter **H** 91–94
   matter, states of **M** 170–71
   osmosis **O** 233–35
   Pascal's Law applied to hydraulic machinery **H** 301–03
   specific gravity **F** 253
   water **W** 51–55
   waves on the surfaces of water **O** 34–35

Lisa, Manuel (1772–1820), American trader and explorer, b. New Orleans, La. He traveled extensively on the Missouri River, building fur-trading posts, among them Fort Raymond (1808), the first post (later renamed Fort Manuel) on upper Missouri.
   fur traders and explorers **F** 522–23

Lisala (li-SA-la), Congo (Kinshasa), picture **C** 465
Lisboa (lees-BO-a), **Antônio Francisco,** known as Aleijadinho, Brazilian architect-sculptor **B** 376–77
   Christ at the Last Supper **L** 63
   church of São Francisco **L** 65
   Latin-American art and architecture **L** 64
Lisbon, capital of Portugal **P** 400–01
Li Shang-yin, Chinese poet **O** 220a
Listening, one of the language arts **L** 36
Listening posts, spies **S** 389
Lister, Joseph, English doctor **L** 311
   developed germ free surgery **M** 208
Liston, Sonny, American boxing champion **B** 353
Liszt, Franz, Hungarian composer and pianist **L** 312
   German music **G** 187
   romantic symphonic poems **R** 311
Litanies, prayers **O** 229
Liter (LI-ter), measure of volume **W** 116
Literacy
   Argentina, highest rate in Latin America **A** 390
   Iran's Literacy Corps **I** 372
   Japan's rate one of highest **J** 29
   Philippines has one of highest rates in Asia **P** 185
   tests required of immigrants **I** 100
   voting qualification in United States **E** 113
   women, role of **W** 211
Literary agents, for writers **W** 321
   publishing industry **P** 514–15
Literary awards and medals see Awards, literary; Book awards
Literary criticism **L** 312–13
   children's literature **C** 242
   classics in literature **C** 334
   critics in American literature **A** 211, 215

Literary Market Place, annual guide in publishing M 15
Literature L 313–14
    ballads B 22–23; P 354
    Bible, Old Testament, literary greatness of H 101
    biography, autobiography, and biographical novel
        B 185–86
    children's see Children's literature
    classics C 334
    creative writing, forms of W 319–21
    diaries D 157–58
    drama D 292–300
    duels in D 341
    essays E 292–93
    fables F 2–8
    fairy tales F 19–32
    fiction F 109–12
    folklore F 302–17
    growth of national literature during the Renaissance
        R 159–60
    humor H 277–81
    literary criticism L 312–13
    Nobel prizes N 266
    novels N 345–49
    oratory, spoken literature O 180
    poetry P 349–55
    Pulitzer prizes P 524–28
    romantic music based on novels and plays R 310
    science fiction S 85
    short stories S 165
    See also African literature; Oriental literature; lit-
        erature of countries, as German literature, and
        articles on individual authors, as Alcott, Louisa
        May
Literature for children see Children's literature
Lithium, element E 154, 162
    atom, structure of the, diagrams N 355
Lithography (lith-OG-raphy), printing technique L 314–15
    techniques and uses of the graphic arts G 302, 308
    use in the printing industry P 460–61
    posters P 404
Lithuania (lith-u-A-nia) (Lithuanian Soviet Socialist
    Republic) U 44; W 281, 288
    languages of the U.S.S.R. U 27
Litmus paper, for testing acidity or alkalinity S 234
Little America, Byrd's Antarctic base B 481; P 366,
    369
Little Bear, constellation see Ursa Minor
Little Bighorn, battle of, 1876 I 169; M 443
Little Bo-Peep, from Mother Goose, with Kate Greenaway
    illustration C 239; I 93
Little Brown Church in the Vale, Nashua, Iowa I 367
Little Dipper, star group C 491
Little Dog, constellation see Canis Minor
Little Giant, nickname of Stephen A. Douglas D 287
Little John, member of Robin Hood's band R 253
Little League Baseball L 315–17
    growing up in baseball B 78
Little Match Girl, The, story by Hans Christian Andersen
    A 248
Little Metropolitan Church, Athens, picture B 487
Little Nanny Etticoat, nursery rhyme riddle J 132
Little Pretty Pocket-Book, by Newbery, picture C 237
Little Red Riding-Hood, story, retold by Walter De La
    Mare F 29–32
Little red schoolhouse E 71
Little Rhody, nickname for Rhode Island R 212
Little Rock, capital of Arkansas A 429
Little Rose Tree, The, poem by Rachel Field F 120
Little Tear Gland that Says Tic-Tac, art by Max Ernst
    M 395
Little theaters, community theater groups T 161–62
    art theater movement in America D 300

Little Turtle (Michikinikwa) (1752–1812), American Indian, b. near present-day Fort Wayne, Ind. As chief of
the Miami Indians, he led the Indian forces that defeated
General Harmar (1790) and General St. Clair (1791). He
signed a treaty (1795) of continued peace after his
defeat by General Wayne's army (1795). Gilbert Stuart,
the famous painter, did a portrait of him (1797).

Little Women, by Louisa May Alcott, excerpt A 149–50
Liturgical drama see Religious drama
Liturgy
    hymns H 309
    Roman Catholic Church R 298; picture R 302

Litvinov (lit-VE-nof), Maxim Maximovich (Meer Moisee-
vich Vallakh) (1876–1951), Russian diplomat, b. Bialys-
tok. As a youth, Litvinov joined the Social Democratic
Party (1898), participating in the revolution of 1905. He
was appointed Soviet representative to Great Britain
(1917) but was seized in exchange for a British agent
because Britain had not recognized the new Soviet
government. He advocated disarmament at international
conferences (1927, 1928, 1929) and negotiated nonag-
gression treaties with several European nations. He
served as ambassador to United States (1941–43) and
deputy commissar for foreign affairs (1941–46).

Liu Shao-ch'i (liu SHA-o-chi) (1898?–   ), Chinese
Communist theoretician and politician, b. Hunan. He
began his career as union organizer in southeastern
China, led student movements against Japanese
(1936–42), and was vice-chairman of provisional govern-
ment (1949), vice-president of World Federation of Trade
Unions (1949), and founder of Sino-Soviet Friendship
Association (1949). He is closely associated with Mao
Tse-tung in Chinese Communist Party and has been
chairman of republic since 1959.

Livelihood, means of subsistence A 301–02
Live oak, tree
    leaves, shapes of, pictures L 116
    state tree of Georgia G 133
Liver
    cancer of C 92
    chemistry of the liver cell B 293
    digestive function in human body B 275
    fish-liver oils O 79
    hepatitis, disease, affects the liver D 198

Livermore, Mary Ashton Rice (1820–1905), American
reformer and suffragist, b. Boston, Mass. She worked
with the U.S. Sanitary Commission during the Civil War.
Later she established (1869) and edited a newspaper
advocating woman's suffrage, the Agitator, which
merged with the Woman's Journal (1870). She was
president of the Illinois and later the Massachusetts
Woman's Suffrage Association and appeared frequently
as a public speaker on temperance, women's rights, and
education. Her works include "What Shall We Do With
Our Daughters?" and My Story of the War.

Liverpool, England U 71
Liverwort, plant
    hepaticae, picture P 292
Livery, clothing in family colors H 118
Livestock C 145–52
    Asia A 451
    Canada C 58
    Chicago's International Livestock Exhibition C 230
    corn as feed C 506, 507
    dairying and dairy products D 5–13
    herding in Africa A 62, 64

pasture grasses and hay **G** 317
plant poisoning of animals **P** 323
pollution danger in rural water supplies **W** 58
specialized, extensive agriculture **A** 89, 92
veterinarians **V** 324
See *also* Meat and meat-packing; agricultural section
of continent, country, province, and state articles;
names of domestic animals
Livestock Judging Pavilion, Raleigh, North Carolina,
picture **A** 387
Live television **T** 70a
Live wires, of electricity
safety precautions **E** 135
Living fossils **E** 347
horseshoe crabs **H** 245
successful life adaptation **L** 223–24
tuatara of New Zealand **N** 240
Living obstacles, game **G** 19
Living standards see Standard of living
Livingston, Milton Stanley, American scientist **N** 366

Livingston, Philip (1716–1778), American merchant, b.
Albany, N.Y. He was partly responsible for the founding
of King's College (now Columbia University). He helped
organize the New York Society Library (1754) and was
active in New York State politics and a member of the
Continental Congress (1774–78). He was a signer of the
Declaration of Independence.

Livingston, Robert R., American patriot **N** 223–24
Louisiana Purchase **L** 365
Livingston, William, American statesman **N** 177
Livingstone, David, Scottish missionary **S** 400
African exploration **A** 68
Malawi, exploration **M** 51
Livingstone Falls, Congo River **C** 465
Livius Andronicus (LIV-ius an-DRON-ic-us), **Lucius,** Greek-
born Roman poet and playwright **L** 77
Livy, Roman historian **L** 317
place in Latin literature **L** 80
studied by Renaissance historians **H** 135
Li Yu, Chinese poet **O** 220a
Lizards **L** 318–21
compared to snakes **S** 204
dinosaurs, "large lizards" **D** 172–81
forelimb, picture **F** 80
hibernation **H** 123; picture **H** 122
life, adaptation to surroundings **L** 214
reptiles, groups of **R** 181
Ljubljana (l'YOO-bel-ya-na), Yugoslavia **Y** 357
Llamas (LA-mas), hoofed mammals **H** 210; pictures
A 252, **H** 213
grazing at Lake Milluni, picture **S** 274
pack-animals in Ecuador, picture **E** 54
Peru **P** 161
Llanos (YA-nos), grasslands of South America
Venezuela **V** 297
Lleras Camargo (YARE-as com-AR-go), **Alberto,** president
of Colombia **C** 384
Llewellyn (lew-EL-lin), Welsh prince **W** 4
Llopango, lake in El Salvador **E** 181
Lloyd, Harold, American movie comedian, picture **M** 473
Lloyd, Selwyn, British statesman, picture **E** 111

Lloyd George, David (1863–1945) British statesman, b.
Manchester. He held a seat in British House of
Commons for a record 54 years (1890–1944). He was
noted for his People's Budget (1909), his legislation for
health and unemployment insurance (1911), and his efforts to produce armaments during World War I. As prime
minister (1916–22) he set up coalition government and
was instrumental in creating the Irish Free State (1921).

He received an earldom immediately after his resignation
from Parliament (1944). Picture **W** 180.
World War I **W** 282

Lloyd's of London, insurance **I** 295–96; picture **I** 293
LM see Lunar Module, section of Apollo spacecraft
Loading machinery see Hoisting and loading machinery
Loam, soil **S** 231
Loans, bank **B** 48–49
college education **T** 44
installment buying **I** 288–89
interest: renting money **P** 149–50
Lobachevski (lob-a-CHEF-ski), **Nikolai,** Russian mathema-
tician **G** 131
non-Euclidean geometries **M** 159
Lobatse, Botswana **B** 340a

Lobbying, organized attempts by persons not connected
with government to influence opinions of legislators
through personal contact. The term arose from the fact
that persons with a vested interest in legislation
frequented the lobby of a legislative house to speak to
public officials.
lawmaking in the U.S. Congress **U** 142

Lobengula (lo-ben-GU-la), king of the Matabele people of
Rhodesia **R** 229–30
negotiations with Cecil Rhodes **R** 227
Lobes, of leaves **L** 114
Lobito (lu-VI-tu), port of Angola **A** 261
Lobola (LO-bo-la), or bride-price, amount paid for a wife
among certain African peoples **S** 268
Lobsterbacks, nickname for British soldiers **R** 196
Lobsters, crustaceans **S** 168–71
fishing fleet, Glace Bay, Nova Scotia, picture **N** 344a
lobster fishing industry **F** 221
traps, or pots **F** 217; pictures **F** 219, **M** 38,
P 456b
Lobster Trap and Fish Tail, mobile by Calder, picture
M 398
Local anesthetic (an-es-THET-ic) **A** 258
Local color, in literature
American literature **A** 204–05
short stories **S** 167
Local government see Municipal government
Locarno (lo-CAR-no) **Conference,** 1925 **W** 283
Germany signs Pact **G** 162
Location, natural settings for movies **M** 479, 480
Loch, Scottish for lake see names of lochs, as Ness, Loch

Loch (LOCK) **Ness monster,** a 40- to 50-foot sea serpent
reportedly seen in Loch Ness, Scotland, whose existence
is questionable but has not yet been disproved. The
monster was first sighted in 1933. Subsequent reports
included the noted photograph by Kenneth Wilson (1934)
showing a long neck, tapering off to a small head,
emerging from the water. It is thought by some to be a
creature similar to a massive reptile, the *Plesiosaurus*,
believed to be long extinct. Others feel reports of the
monster are based on distorted views of diving otters or
surfacing bubbles of marsh gas.

Locke, Alain Le Roy (1886–1954), American educator,
Negro, b. Philadelphia, Pa. Locke was an authority on
Negro art. He was head of the philosophy department at
Howard University (1918–54) and an exchange professor
in Haiti (1943). His works include *The New Negro, Race
Contact and Inter-Racial Relations,* and (co-editor) *When
Peoples Meet: A Study in Race and Culture Contact.*
Negro Renaissance **N** 98

Locke, David Ross, American humorist **A** 206

Locke, John, English philosopher **L** 321
  Carolina colony's government based on his plans
    S 310
  Declaration of Independence **D** 63
  experimental science, interest in **H** 87–88
  influence on law in America **L** 87–88
Lockjaw, bacterial disease **D** 200–01
Lockout, shutting down work by management in labor
    troubles **L** 18
Locks, of canals **C** 83–84
  Erie Canal at West Troy, New York, picture **E** 276
  Panama Canal **P** 47
  Sault Sainte Marie Canals, picture **M** 266
Locks and keys L 322–26
  use in animal tests **A** 285
Locksmiths, makers of locks and keys **L** 323
Lockups, places of short-term imprisonment **P** 468
Locomotion of animals see Animals: Locomotion
Locomotives L 327–32
  Diesel locomotive and train, picture **D** 168
  early history **T** 263
  first in U.S. built by Peter Cooper **C** 498
  How did the cowcatcher get its name? **L** 330
  railroads, history of **R** 79, 87–88
  railroads, model **R** 92
  Stephenson's, picture **I** 237
Locoweed, plant **P** 323

Locust, any one of several insects found in many parts of
the world. In general, a locust has long, sturdy legs and
short, thick antennae. Locusts vary in size—the largest
are tropical locusts with a wingspread of 6 in. Certain
locusts are noted for their songs. The sound is produced
by rubbing the hind leg against the forewing. Swarms
of locusts sometimes do great damage to crops.
  insect migrants **H** 189

Locust, tree
  black locust, poisonous bark **P** 322
  honey locust, prickly defenses **P** 283
Lodes, layers of rock
  gold-bearing lodes **G** 251
Lodestar see North Star
Lodestone, magnetic rock **M** 24
  early use in telling direction **D** 182

Lodge, Henry Cabot (1850–1924), American statesman
and writer, b. Boston, Mass. He was assistant editor of
the *North American Review* (1873–76) and member of
House of Representatives (1887–93) and Senate
(1893–24). One of Theodore Roosevelt's closest consult-
ants on matters of foreign policy, he led senatorial
forces in opposition to United States involvement in the
League of Nations (1919). His books include *Alexander
Hamilton, Historical and Political Essays,* and *The Senate
and the League of Nations.*
  Wilson and Lodge **W** 181

Lodge, Henry Cabot, Jr. (1902–), American statesman,
b. Nahant, Mass. Grandson of Henry Cabot Lodge, he
was reporter and editorial writer for the New York *Herald
Tribune* (1924–36), U.S. Senator from Massachusetts
(1937–44; 1947–53), and U.S. delegate to the United
Nations and the Security Council (1953–60). Lodge has
been U.S. ambassador to the Republic of Vietnam
(1963–64; 1965–67), to West Germany (1968–69) and
(1969) chief negotiator at the Paris peace talks.

Lodge, Sir Oliver Joseph, English scientist
  radio, early history of **R** 52
Lodge, organization of Gothic architects **G** 272
Lodge family, of Massachusetts **M** 147

Lodges, of beavers **B** 113–14
Lodz, Poland P 361
Loess (LESS), sandy soil deposited by wind **S** 234
  Iowa soils **I** 360
  landform region in Mississippi **M** 352
  Nebraska deposits **N** 74, 75
Loesser (LESS-er), **Frank,** American composer **N** 26
  musical comedy **M** 543

Loewy (LOE-wy), **Raymond Fernand** (1893–), American industrial designer, b. Paris, France. He started his
own design organization (1927), Raymond Loewy Associates (1945), and the firm of Raymond Loewy-William
Snaith (1961). Scope of design has ranged from building
interiors, such as that of Lever House in New York, N.Y.,
to refrigerators, trade centers, and automobiles. He wrote
an autobiography, *Never Leave Well Enough Alone.*

Lofoten (lo-FO-ten) **Islands,** northwest of Norway **I** 434

Lofting, Hugh (1886–1947), American author of children's
books, b. Maidenhead, England. He settled in United
States in 1912. He illustrated letters to his children
during World War I. He later compiled these letters into
The Story of Doctor Dolittle. Lofting wrote the Doctor
Dolittle series and won Newbery medal (1923) for *The
Voyages of Doctor Dolittle.*

Log, apparatus to measure a ship's speed **N** 65
  logs or logbooks, official daily records of data of a
    voyage **C** 417

Logan (LO-gan), **James** (John) (1725?–1780), American
Indian leader of the Mingo tribes, b. probably Shamokin,
Pa. He was named Tah-gah-jute but called Logan, probably after the American statesman James Logan. After
the Yellow Creek massacre (1774), in which members of
his family were slaughtered, he sought vengeance
against American colonists, siding with the British during
the Revolution.

Logan, Mount, Canada **C** 51; **Y** 361

Logan, Rayford W. (1897–), American educator and
author, Negro, b. Washington, D.C. Head of the history
department at Howard University (1942–64) he was United
Nations consultant for NAACP (1949) and a member of
U.S. Commission for U.N.E.S.C.O. (1947–50). He was
editor of *What the Negro Wants* and author of *The Negro
in American Life and Thought: The Nadir, 1877–1901* and
The Negro in the United States.

Loganberries, large reddish-purple acid berries of the
blackberry and raspberry group. They are named for J. H.
Logan of California, who first grew the berry from a cross
between raspberries and blackberries or dewberries. Loganberries are cultivated on the West Coast of the United
States.
  varieties of blackberries **G** 301

Logarithmic spiral, picture **G** 131
Log booms
  British Columbia, picture **L** 377
Log cabins P 252; pictures **P** 253, 258
  houses of wood **H** 171
  introduced to America by Swedes **C** 388
  origin in Delaware **D** 89
  similar wooden homes in Soviet Union **U** 29
Loge, or Loki, Norse god **N** 279
Loggerhead shrikes, birds
  bill, picture **B** 223
Loggers, lumbermen **L** 375

Loggia, a roofed open gallery within the side of a
building
Hermitage Museum, picture   **H** 120
Logging see Lumber and lumbering
Logic, science of reasoning
Aristotle's key to knowledge   **A** 397
mathematics and logic   **M** 155
symbolic logic   **M** 161
See also Probability

Logistics (lo-GIST-ics), division of military science that
involves planning, handling, and implementation facilities, both material and personnel.

Log lines, measure speed of ships   **K** 289

Logrolling, exchange of assistance or favors. Used
politically to mean congressmen's mutual support of
each other's legislation, the term also refers to lumbermen's custom of trying to remain standing on a log
rotating in water. The word is derived from an American
pioneer custom of neighbors helping to roll logs into
piles for burning when clearing land.

Logwood, tree, used for dyes   **D** 369
Lohengrin (LOH-en-grin), opera by Wagner   **O** 145
Loire (LUARE) **River,** France   **R** 244
chateaux country   **F** 407; picture **F** 414
Loki (LO-ki), or **Loge,** Norse god   **N** 279
Lo Kuan-chung, Chinese novelist   **O** 220b
Lolly Tu Dum, folk song   **F** 322
Loma Mountains, Sierra Leone   **S** 174

Lomax, Louis E. (1922–70), American writer; b. Valdosta,
Ga. After graduating from Paine University, he taught
philosophy at Georgia State College In Savannah before
becoming a feature writer for the Chicago American. He
joined a television news staff (1959) and became the
first Negro to appear on TV as a newsman. A frequent
magazine contributor, he is best known for his book
The Negro Revolt.

Lombardi, Vince (Vincent Thomas Lombardi) (1913–1970),
American football coach, b. Brooklyn, N.Y. He entered
professional football as a coach with the New York
Giants (1954). In 1959, he became head coach of the
Green Bay Packers and led them to five National Football
League titles and two Super Bowl triumphs before be-
coming general manager (1968). He returned to active
coaching with the Washington Redskins (1969).

Lombards, Germanic tribe that invaded northern Italy
under war leader Albion (A.D. 568) and set up a kingdom
with capital at Pavia. The kingdom reached its peak in
the 7th and 8th centuries, when it adopted Roman
law, Catholic religion, and Latin language. Lombards
attacked Rome (773) but were conquered by Charlemagne, who received Lombard crown of iron in Pavia
(774). Today the name refers to inhabitants of Lom-
bardy, a region in northern Italy.
Charlemagne   **C** 189

Lomé (lo-MAY), capital of Togo   **T** 203
Lôme, Enrique Dupuy de see Dupuy de Lôme, Enrique
Lomond (LO-mond), **Loch,** lake in Scotland   **L** 32; picture
L 29
Londinium (lon-DIN-ium), Roman town, now London,
England   **L** 334
London, capital of the United Kingdom   **L** 333–40; pic-
tures **C** 305, **E** 212
aerial view   **E** 232
British Museum   **M** 511, 514; picture   **M** 515

fog and smog   **F** 289
great fire of 1666   **F** 146
Hyde Park's Speakers' Corner, picture   **C** 314
Law Courts, picture   **E** 241
police   **P** 372–73
postal service   **P** 406
Shakespeare's London   **S** 131
theater   **T** 159
Tower Bridge, picture   **E** 305
Wren, Christopher   **W** 313
London, Jack, American writer   **L** 341
American literature   **A** 209
London, Ontario   **O** 125
London, Tower of   **L** 334
Christmas choristers, picture   **C** 290
London Bridge, England   **B** 395–96
London Bridge in the 17th century, picture   **E** 221
London's bridges and transportation   **L** 339; picture
L 333
London Bridge Is Falling Down, game song, origin   **B** 396
music for the harmonica   **H** 43
London Company, business company to colonize America
A 183–85
Jamestown   **J** 20
Londonderry, Northern Ireland   **U** 73
London Missionary Society   **M** 349
London Stock Exchange   **S** 430
Lone Eagle, Charles A. Lindbergh   **P** 407
Lone Star Republic   **T** 137
territorial expansion of the United States   **T** 110
Lone Star State, nickname of Texas   **T** 123
Long, Crawford W., American doctor   **A** 257
first use of anesthetics in an operation   **M** 208a
Long, Huey Pierce, American politician   **L** 361
Long-chain molecules, or polymers   **P** 324
Long Drive, of cattle over the Chisholm Trail   **O** 266–67
Longevity (lon-JEV-ity), length of life, in animals
crocodilians   **C** 535
turtles   **T** 335
See also Aging
Longfellow, Henry Wadsworth, American poet   **L** 341–42
American literature   **A** 203
Arkansas, pronunciation of the word   **A** 418
"Arrow and the Song, The"   **L** 343
Hiawatha, setting for the poem   **M** 258
"Paul Revere's Ride," excerpt   **R** 192
"Village Blacksmith, The"   **L** 342–43
Wadsworth-Longfellow House, Maine   **M** 43
Longfellow-Evangeline State Park, Louisiana   **L** 359
Longhair cats   **C** 141
Longhena, Baldassare, Italian architect
Santa Maria della Salute, church, picture   **B** 55
Longhorn cattle   **C** 146, 147
Chisholm Trail   **O** 266
Dodge City, Kansas, Queen of the Cow Towns   **K** 186
herd in national wildlife refuge, Oklahoma   **O** 90
hoofed mammals   **H** 221
Texas   **T** 122; picture   **H** 216
Longhouses, of the Iroquois Indians   **I** 184, 187, 196
anthropologists study family houses   **A** 302–03
Long hunters, hunters in distant areas   **W** 144
Long Island, New York   **N** 214–15
Long Island National Cemetery, New York   **N** 30
Long Island Sound, eastern coast of United States
Connecticut   **C** 469, 470, 477
Longitude (LON-gi-tude)   **L** 81–83
how shown on maps and globes   **M** 90
international date line   **I** 309–10
navigation, uses in   **N** 63–64
time zones   **T** 189–91
Long jump, formerly broad jump, field event   **T** 240
Long Knives, group of frontiersmen   **I** 85–86

Longleaf pine, tree **A** 113
Long Parliament, English **E** 223
Long-playing records (LP's) **P** 198
  hi-fi and stereo **H** 125–27
  record collecting **R** 124
LOng RAnge Navigation see Loran
Longshoremen, men who load and unload ships **S** 161
Long tom, for washing gold from sand **G** 251; picture **G** 252
Long ton, measure of weight **W** 114; picture **W** 113
Longway sets, dance forms **D** 28
  contra dances, forms of folk dancing **F** 299
Longworth, Alice Roosevelt, daughter of Theodore Roosevelt **F** 176
Longworth, Nicholas, American statesman
  real estate fortune **R** 112
Lon Nol, Cambodian president **C** 33
Looby-Loo, singing game **G** 11
Looking Glass, chief of Nez Percé Indians **I** 176–77
Looking-glass tree
  seeds, picture **F** 281
Lookout Mountain, Colorado **C** 410
Lookout Mountain, Tennessee **T** 85–86
Lookout Mountain, battle of, 1863, Civil War **C** 326
Lookout towers, for forest fires **F** 152; picture **F** 374
Looming, kind of mirage **M** 342
Looms, for weaving textiles **T** 140–41
  cotton industry aided by British inventions **C** 520–21
  how to make your own looms **W** 97–98
  Indian beadwork weaving **I** 158
  Industrial Revolution improvements **I** 234

Loons, water birds noted for eerie cry and their skill in diving. Loons can dive deeper and for longer periods of time than any other bird. They live in colder northern regions of the world. Heavy-bodied birds, they are whitish below and dark above, with lighter stripes or spots. The legs are set so far back on the body that the birds are almost helpless on land. They are strong fliers but must take off from water by running rapidly along the surface. Their chief food is fish, which they can pursue underwater for long distances, propelled by their feet and aided by their wings in balancing and turning. Picture **B** 236.
  state bird of Minnesota **M** 323

Loop, The, in Chicago, Illinois **C** 228
Loop knots **K** 290
  roping **R** 333–35
Loose caboose, tag game **G** 18
Loose housing, cow-keeping system **D** 9; picture **D** 6
Lope de Vega see Vega Carpio, Lope Félix de
López (LO-pez), Carlos Antonio, Paraguayan dictator **P** 66
López, Francisco Solano, Paraguayan dictator **P** 66
López Arellano, Oswaldo, president of Honduras **H** 199
López de Legazpe, or Legazpi (LO-peth day lay-GOTH-pi), Miguel, Spanish navigator **M** 75; **P** 189
López de Villalobos (vi-ya-LO-boce), Ruy, Portuguese navigator **P** 189

López Mateos (LO-pace mat-A-oce), Adolfo (1910–69), Mexican statesman, b. Atizapán de Zaragoza. Professor and director of Toluca Scientific and Literary Institute, he headed Revolutionary Institutional Party. He was a federal senator (1946–52), minister of labor and social welfare (1952–58), and president of Mexico (1958–64).
  Mexico, history of **M** 250

Loran (LOng RAnge Navigation) **R** 38–39
  aid to aviation **A** 562
  United States Navy electronics and weapons **U** 193

Lorca, Federico García see García Lorca, Federico
Lord Dunmore's War see Dunmore's War
Lord Jim, by Joseph Conrad **C** 482
Lord of the Flies, by William Golding **E** 267
Lords, House of, British Parliament **E** 219; **U** 78
  parliaments, history and function of **P** 81

Lord's Prayer (also known as Our Father, Pater Noster, or Paternoster), most familiar Christian prayer. It was taught by Jesus to his disciples, and it is used at virtually all Christian services. It is derived primarily from Biblical Sermon on the Mount.
  opening lines in Anglo-Saxon and in English **L** 38
  opening words in Esperanto **U** 194
  rosary **R** 302

Lord's Prayer, The, Bible (Revised Standard Version) **P** 435
Lord's Supper see Holy Communion
Loreal (LO-re-al) pits, of snakes **S** 208

Lorelei (LO-rel-i), precipitous cliff over Rhine River south of St. Goarshausen, Germany. In German literature Lorelei is the name of a beautiful water nymph who lived on a rock, and with her haunting melodies, lured sailors to their ruin on rocks below. Her story is told in two operas, by Mendelssohn and Lochnar, and in "Die Lorelei," by Heinrich Heine.

Lorelei's Golden Rockbottom, champion golden retriever dog **D** 262

Lorentz (LO-rentz), Hendrik Antoon (1853–1928), Dutch physicist, b. Arnhem. He made many important contributions to physics, his greatest being on the theory of light. For his study of how a magnetic field affects the wavelength of light, he shared the 1902 Nobel prize in physics with his former pupil Pieter Zeeman. He is best known for the theory known as the Lorentz-Fitzgerald contraction, which states that a moving body contracts in the direction of motion.

Lorenzini, Carlo see Collodi, Carlo
Lorenzo the Magnificent see Medici, Lorenzo de'
Lorises, animals related to monkeys **M** 422
  animal life of Ceylon **C** 180
Lorrain, Claude see Claude Lorrain
Los Alamos, New Mexico **N** 181, 188
Los Angeles (los AN-ge-lese), California **L** 344–47
  harbor, man-made **H** 37
  network of freeways, picture **C** 27
Los Angeles County Museum of Art, picture **L** 346
Los Islands, Guinea **G** 405
Los Padres National Forest, California, picture **N** 36
Lost, poem by Carl Sandburg **S** 29

Lost Battalion, group of about 600 men of the 77th Division who were separated for 5 days from the rest of American forces while fighting in Argonne Forest, France, during World War I (1918). They were encircled by German forces but refused to surrender despite lack of food, water, and munitions. The battalion, which was rescued by American forces after about 400 men had died, was led by Major Charles W. Wittlesey, who was awarded a Medal of Honor for heroic command.
  World War I, in the last German offensive **W** 281

Lost Colony, The, pageant **P** 12
Lost Colony of Virginia **A** 181
  early settlement of North Carolina **N** 320
Lost generation, phrase attributed to Gertrude Stein **H** 109

Lost Ten Tribes of Israel see Ten Tribes, Hebrew

Lot, in Old Testament, son of Haran and nephew of Abraham, b. Ur. He traveled with Abraham to Canaan and Egypt, but they parted when disputes arose over pastureland. Lot took up residence in Sodom and the plain of Jordan. He left Sodom with his wife and two daughters just before its destruction. His wife became a pillar of salt when she stopped to look back at the city. Lot's descendants were founders of the nations of Moab and Ammon.
    Abraham and Lot **A** 7

Lothrop, Harriet Mulford see Sidney, Margaret
Loti, Pierre, French novelist **F** 442
Lotions, cosmetics **C** 509
  beauty culture **B** 110
Lotteries
  draft lotteries **D** 289, 290
  New Hampshire **N** 161

Lotus (LO-tus), water plant with pink, yellow, white, or blue flowers. The sacred flower of Buddhists of India, China, and Japan, it symbolizes divine creative power, purity, fertility, and the seats of the gods, including Brahma and Buddha. In Egypt it is an emblem of fertility, the sun, and resurrection. In Homeric legend the lotus is a fruit of a North African shrub or tree. It produces drowsiness and contentment.

Lotus-Eaters, according to Homeric legend, inhabitants of the northern coast of Africa who ate the fruit of lotus trees, causing them to forget past desires and become languidly satisfied. In the *Odyssey*, when Odysseus and his men visited them, those who ate lotus fruit no longer wanted to return home and had to be forced back on ship. The story is also recounted by Tennyson in "The Lotus-Eaters."

Loudness, of sound **S** 258–59
Loudspeakers, for hi-fi and stereo **H** 126
Louis, Joe, American boxing champion **B** 353; **N** 99

Louis V ("the Sluggard") (966?–987), king of France (986–987). He was the son of Lothair and the last Carolingian king of France. When he died after a hunting accident, Hugh Capet was chosen to succeed him.

Louis VI (the Fat) (1081–1137), king of France (1108–37). The son of Philip I, he was the first of the Capetian kings to break down power of the feudal nobles. He led his armies against pillaging lords and against Emperor Henry V and Henry I of England. He protected the property of the clergy.
  kings of France in the Middle Ages **M** 291

Louis IX (Saint Louis) (1214–1270), king of France (1226–70), b. Poissy. Son of King Louis VIII, he succeeded to throne (1226), with his mother, Blanche of Castile, as regent during his youth. He tightened control in feudal and tax systems and court procedure, and he constructed Sainte-Chapelle in Paris (1245–48) to enshrine Crown of Thorns obtained from Emperor Baldwin of Constantinople. A crusader in Egypt and Syria (1248–54), on Second Crusade (1270) he succumbed to plague during epidemic in Tunis. He was canonized in 1297.
  kings of France in the Middle Ages **M** 291

Louis XIII (1601–1643), king of France (1610–43), b. Fontainebleau. The son of Henry IV, he was dominated by his prime minister, Cardinal Richelieu. Richelieu guided him into a costly foreign policy, including war against Spain, to the neglect of the welfare of his people. Richelieu also destroyed the political power of the Huguenots and centralized the government in the hands of the king.

Louis XIV, king of France **F** 416
  Bernini's statue **B** 148
  built Palace of Versailles **A** 381–82
  danced in ballets **B** 24
  Louisiana named after **L** 46
Louis XV, king of France
  diamond necklace scandal **J** 99–100
Louis XVI, king of France **F** 464
Louis XVIII, king of France **F** 417; **N** 12
Louisburg, fortress on Cape Breton Island, Canada **C** 70
Louise, Lake, western Canada **L** 32; picture **L** 30
  Banff National Park **B** 43; picture **B** 42
Louisiana (louise-i-AN-a) **L** 348–63
  Indian mound, picture **A** 356
  New Orleans **N** 196
  southern mansion, picture **H** 181
Louisiana Purchase, 1803 **L** 364–65
  Jefferson, Thomas **J** 68
  land laws and pioneer life **P** 260
  Lewis and Clark expedition **L** 162–63
  Monroe acted for Jefferson **M** 424
  territorial days of Missouri **M** 380
  territorial expansion of the United States **T** 108–09
  westward movement **W** 146
Louisiana Purchase Exposition, 1904 **S** 17
Louisiana State University and Agricultural and Mechanical College **L** 357
Louis Period styles
  furniture design **F** 508
Louis Philippe, king of France, called Citizen King **F** 417
  Paris a town of big business during his reign **P** 74
Louis the Fat see Louis VI, king of France
Louis the Pious, Holy Roman Emperor, son of Charlemagne **C** 190
  Andorra established **A** 254
Louisville (LOO-i-ville), Kentucky **K** 224
Lourenço Marques (lor-EN-so MAR-kes), capital of Mozambique, picture **M** 500
Louse see Lice
Lousma, Jack R., American astronaut **S** 347
Louvain (loo-VAN), **University of,** Belgium **B** 127
L'Ouverture, Toussaint see Toussaint L'Ouverture
Louvre (LOOV-ra), art museum in Paris, France **L** 366–68
  great museums of the world **M** 511, 514
  places of interest in Paris **P** 73
Lovebirds **P** 85–86
  feathered pets **P** 181

Lovejoy brothers, American abolitionists, b. Albion, Maine. **Elijah Parish** (1802–37), a clergyman, promoted abolitionist cause as editor of Alton *Observer* in Alton, Ill., and established Illinois chapter of American Anti-Slavery Society. He was fatally shot defending his printing press against destruction by a mob. **Owen** (1811–64), an abolitionist leader in Illinois and a representative to Congress (1857–64), formulated the bill to abolish slavery in all U.S. territories.

Lovelace, Richard (1618–1658), English poet, b. Kent. He was one of the Cavalier poets—17th-century lyric poets who supported Charles I and the Loyalists in the Civil War (1642–48). He was imprisoned twice (1642, 1648) by an anti-Loyalist Parliament. His poems were published after his death in a collection entitled *Lucasta: Posthume Poems*. His best-known poems are the celebrated

Lovelace, Richard (continued)
lyrics "To Althea from Prison" and "To Lucasta on Going to the Wars."

Lovell, James Arthur, Jr. (1928–), American astronaut, b. Cleveland, Ohio. A former Navy flier, Lovell became an astronaut in 1962. He made the Gemini 7 (1965), Gemini 12 (1966), Apollo 8 (1968), Apollo 13 (1970) flights.
space flight data **S** 344, 345, 347

Love's Labour's Lost, play by Shakespeare **S** 135

Low, Juliette Gordon (1860–1927), American founder of Girl Scouts of America, b. Savannah, Ga. She moved to England (1886) and led Girl Guides troops in Scotland and England. Returning to United States, she organized the first Girl Guide company (1912), which became known as Girl Scouts (1913). She was first president of the national organization of Girl Scouts (1915).
Girl Scouts **G** 213, 215, 219

Löw (LURV),Oskar, German doctor **A** 310
Lowboy, furniture, picture **C** 389

Low Countries, the densely populated countries situated on the northwestern European plain along the North Sea. Geographically the term applies specifically to the Netherlands and Belgium. As a political term it refers to the Benelux countries: Belgium, the Netherlands, and Luxembourg. This area is composed of very fertile and productive land, watered by three rivers that flow into the North Sea, the Rhine, the Maas, and the Schelde.

Lowell, Amy, American poet **A** 209
Lowell, James Russell, American author **L** 369
American literature **A** 203
Lowell, Percival, American astronomer
studies of Mars **M** 104
Lowell, Robert, American poet **A** 211
Lowell family, of Massachusetts **M** 147
Lowell Observatory, Arizona **A** 412–13; **T** 64
Lower California, Mexico **M** 242
Lower Canada **C** 71, 73
Quebec **Q** 14, 16
Lower-case, or small, **letters of the alphabet A** 173
Lowest common denominator (LCD) **F** 399
Low German, dialect of northern Germany **G** 172, 173
Lowry, Malcolm, English novelist **B** 405
Lows, or cyclones, in meteorology **W** 74
east-west movement of air **W** 186
Lox see Liquid oxygen
Loya Jirgeh, Great National Assembly, Afghanistan **A** 45
Loyalists, or Tories, colonial supporters of the British
R 198
political parties in colonial America **P** 379
Loyalists, United Empire see United Empire Loyalists

Loyalty Day, American national observance celebrated annually by Loyalty Day parade (May 1), sponsored by Veterans of Foreign Wars since 1947. The observance was proclaimed by Congress and approved by President Truman (1948) as a day of reaffirmation of loyalty to American tradition of freedom, to countervail Communist celebration of May Day (May 1).

Loyalty Islands, chain of three coral islands and many islets in southwest Pacific. A dependency of New Caledonia, they are administered by France. The principal exports are nickel and other metals and copra.

Loyola (loy-O-la), **Saint Ignatius,** founder of Society of Jesus, or Jesuits **L** 369

Counter-Reformation in the Roman Catholic Church
C 287; **R** 294
Roman Catholic reforms **R** 294
LPG, liquefied petroleum gas **F** 489
L.P.G.A. see Ladies Professional Golfers' Association
LP's see Long-playing records
LSD, hallucinogenic drug **D** 329, 331
Luanda, capital of Angola **A** 261
Luang Prabang (lu-ONG pra-BONG), royal capital of Laos
L 41
Luau (LU-ow), Hawaiian "cook-out," or outdoor feast
F 340; picture **H** 65
Lubrication and lubricants L 370–71
internal-combustion engines **I** 307
petroleum **P** 176
plastics **P** 327
powder metallurgy **M** 232
tallow **O** 79
Lucan (LU-can), Roman poet **L** 80
Lucas, Robert, American statesman **I** 369
Luce, Henry R., American editor and publisher **M** 15
Lucerne (lu-CERN), **Lake of,** central Switzerland **L** 32
Lucerne, Switzerland **S** 499
Lucerne Festival, Switzerland **M** 551
Lucia di Lammermoor (lu-CHI-a di la-mer-MOOR), opera by Gaetano Donizetti **O** 145–46
Lucian (LU-cian), Greek satirical writer **G** 355

Lucifer, in Old Testament (Isaiah 14:12), name applied symbolically to a king of Babylon about to fall from high rank. In New Testament (Luke 10:18), through reference to Isaiah 14:12, the name alludes to Satan, who fell as lightning from heaven. The name also refers to the planet Venus when it appears as the morning star.

Luciferases (lu-CIF-er-ases), light-producing chemicals
B 198
Luciferins (lu-CIF-er-ins), "glowing" chemicals **B** 197–98
Luck
counter-magic **S** 473
Lucknow, India **I** 122
Luck of Roaring Camp, The, short story by Bret Harte, scene from, picture **S** 167
Lucretius (lu-CRE-tius), Roman philosophical poet
L 78

Lucy, Saint (Italian, Santa Lucia) (283?–303), Italian virgin martyr, b. Syracuse, Sicily. According to tradition, she declared her belief in Christianity by distributing her wealth to the poor during Diocletian's persecutions. She was denounced by her betrothed and killed with a sword. Her feast day is December 13.
Christmas patron saints **C** 292

Ludendorff (LU-den-dorff), **Erich Friedrich Wilhelm** (1865–1937), German general and strategist, b. Kruszewina. He assisted Hindenberg in defeating Russians during World War I and was solely responsible for German victory over Rumania and Italy (1917). He fled to Sweden after German defeat but returned to Germany (1919) and took part in Kapp Putsch (1920) and Hitler's Beer Hall Putsch (1923). A member of the Reichstag (1924–28), he wrote almost fanatical anti-Semitic, anti-Catholic, and anti-Masonic material.
World War I **W** 274, 280

Ludlow casting machine
printing **P** 465
type-casting process **T** 345
Luffing, in sailing **S** 12

Luftwaffe (LOOFT-va-fa) (from German word meaning

"air weapon"), Nazi air force during World War II. It was openly established (1935) under Hitler by Hermann Goering. The name is still used for the air force of the Federal Republic of Germany (West Germany).

World War II **W** 287, 288

Lugano (lu-GA-no), **Lake of,** Italy and Switzerland **L** 32
Lugano, Switzerland **S** 499
Lugard (lu-GARD), **Lord Frederick,** British colonial administrator **N** 258
Luge (small sled) **event,** in Winter Olympics **O** 109
Lu Hsun, Chinese novelist **O** 220b

Lujack, John (1925–), American football player, b. Connellsville, Pa. He played quarterback for Notre Dame (1943, 1946–47) and won Heisman Trophy for college football's outstanding player of the year (1947). He turned professional (1948–51) and played for the Chicago Bears. He retired in 1951 and became an analyst for national football telecasts.

Luke, Frank, Jr., American aviator **A** 416
Luke, Saint **E** 335
    Christianity, history of **C** 280
    writings in Bible, New Testament **B** 160–61
Lullabies **F** 303–04
    folk music **F** 326
    "Lullaby" (Rock-a-bye, baby) nursery rhyme **N** 405
Lully (lu-LE), **Jean-Baptiste,** French composer **F** 444
    ballet music **D** 36
    baroque music **B** 63
    opera **O** 132
Lumber and lumbering **L** 372–77
    Africa **A** 64
    Alabama, picture **A** 119
    building materials **B** 430
    Burma, picture **B** 458
    log booms, picture **G** 327
    log drives, pictures **C** 59; **M** 38
    National Forests, multiple use of **N** 31, 32; picture **N** 33
    plywood and laminates **F** 503; **W** 226–27
    preparing wood for furniture-making **F** 501–02
    rain forests **R** 100
    sawmill on Vancouver Island, picture **B** 404
    shortage in Asia **A** 462
    veneers **F** 503–04; **W** 226–27
    wood products **W** 225–28
    woodworking, dimensions for **W** 234
    See also industries and products section of country, province, and state articles
Lumberjacks, lumbermen **L** 374, 375
    Paul Bunyan stories **F** 312–13
Lumbertown, U S A, near Brainerd, Minnesota **M** 333
Luminous (LU-min-ous) **paints** **P** 34

Lumumba (lu-MOOM-ba), **Patrice Emergy** (1926–1961), Congolese nationalist leader, b. Katako Kombe, Kawai Province. As leader of Mouvement National Congolais, he became prime minister of Republic of Congo when it gained independence from Belgium (June, 1960). He tried to keep Congo unified, opposing Katanga Province's independence (July, 1960). He was overthrown by Colonel Mobutu's coup (September, 1960) and put under house arrest. He escaped, was recaptured, and was flown to Elisabethville, where he again escaped but was reported to have been killed by political enemies.

Zaire, history of **Z** 366d

Luna, or **Lunik,** Soviet spacecraft, of which Luna 9 on Feb. 3, 1966 made the first soft landing on the moon. Its radio and television messages revealed the moon's surface in its vicinity is less radioactive than earth's, does not have a thick dust layer, and can support manned craft. In April, 1966, Luna 10 became the first craft to successfully orbit the moon. Moon landing sites **M** 449.

Luna 3 **S** 348
Luna 16, rock samples **S** 348
Luna 17 **S** 348
Lunik III **M** 447
Lunokhod, vehicle **S** 348

Lunalilo (lu-na-LI-lo), **William Charles** (1832–1874), Hawaiian king (1873–74), b. Honolulu. Hawaii's first elected ruler, he increased the rights of people and left his fortune to erect the Lunalilo Home for needy Hawaiians.

Lunar calendar **T** 193–94
Lunar eclipses **E** 46–47
    moon's orbit **M** 448–49
Lunar landing day, July 20, 1969 **E** 368; **S** 339–340a
Lunar module (LM), of Apollo spacecraft **S** 339–340a, 340e, 340h, 340j, 341; pictures **S** 340a, 340b, 340h
    navigation **N** 68, 69

Lunar orbiter, one of a series of U.S. spacecraft designed to orbit the moon and photograph the moon's surface. Its chief purpose was to locate possible landing sites for a manned craft. Orbiter I, launched in August, 1966, sent back more than 200 photographs and at its closest was 25 miles from the moon.

moon landing sites, choice of **M** 455; map **M** 449
    observatories **O** 14

Lunar probes, or moon probes **M** 450, 455
Lunar Rover, vehicle used on the moon, picture **S** 340g
Lunar seas, of moon's surface **M** 451, 453; map **M** 449

Lunceford, Jimmie (James Melvin Lunceford) (1902–1947), American musician, Negro, b. Fulton, Mo. He studied music under Wilberforce J. Whiteman, father of Paul Whiteman, and began his bandleading career in 1927. His group was one of the few big jazz orchestras of the 1930's to be of lasting importance. His arrangements, mostly by Sy Oliver, had influence on other bands.

Lundy, Benjamin (1789–1839), American abolitionist and editor, b. Sussex County, N.J. A leading figure in the antislavery movement during 1820's, he formed the Union Humane Society (1815), one of first antislavery organizations. He also founded The National Enquirer and Constitutional Advocate of Universal Liberty. He traveled (1825–35) to Haiti, Canada, and Texas in search of places to establish free Negro settlements.

Lunenburg, Nova Scotia, Canada **N** 344d–344e

Lungfish, any one of six species of freshwater fishes found in parts of South America and Africa and in northeastern Australia. These fishes have lungs as well as gills. Except for one species that lives chiefly in lakes, they inhabit slow-moving or stagnant waters. All but the Australian lungfish burrow into the mud when there is an absence of water in the dry season. There they cover their bodies with a mucous cocoon they secrete that keeps them moist. They breathe, with their lungs, through a hole in the top of the cocoon. Picture **F** 182.

bony fishes, kinds of **F** 183
    estivation of, picture **H** 121
    successful life adaptation **L** 224

Lungs, organs of breathing **B** 277–78
    air pollution, effect on **A** 108–09
    birds **B** 203

Lungs (continued)
cancer **C** 91–92
emphysema disease **D** 196
heart action **H** 86
pneumonia, bacteria infection **D** 203–04
smoking **S** 203
Lunik III, Russian space probe **M** 447
Lunokhod, Soviet Union's unmanned vehicle for moon exploration **S** 348

Lunt, Alfred (1893–   ), American actor, b. Milwaukee, Wis. With his wife, Lynn Fontanne, he has been a leading figure in the theater. Some of his major roles have been in *Sweet Nell of Old Drury, The Guardsman, Arms and the Man, Idiot's Delight,* and *The Visit.*

Lupercalia (lu-per-CAY-lia), Roman festival
Valentine's Day, origin **V** 266
Luque, Hernando de, Spanish priest **P** 266
Lures, for fishing **F** 206–07
Lusaka (lu-SA-ka), capital of Zambia **Z** 368
Lusiads (LU-si-ads), **The,** by Camoëns, excerpt **E** 387
Lusignan, Guy de see Guy de Lusignan
Lusignan (lu-zeen-YON) **dynasty,** of Cyprus **C** 558
Lusitania (lu-si-TAY-nia), British ocean liner **O** 24
torpedoed in World War I **W** 276
Lusitanians, early people of Portugal **P** 399
Luster, brightness
minerals identified by **R** 270
orient of pearls **P** 113
Lusterware, ceramic pottery **I** 422
Lustre, or luster, metallic glaze for pottery **P** 417
Lute, musical instrument **M** 544–45; picture **S** 438
ancient instrument **A** 245; picture **A** 244
English composers for **E** 270
in concert, picture **I** 482
Lute Player and Woman Playing the Harp, painting by Israel van Meckenem **D** 364
Lutetia Parisiorum (lu-TE-tia pa-ris-i-OR-um), ancient city, now Paris, France **P** 73
Lutetium (lu-TE-shum), element **E** 154, 162
Luther, Martin, German leader of Protestant Reformation **L** 378; picture **R** 132
Bible, translation of **B** 153
Christianity, history of **C** 285–86
demands for religious reforms divide Germany **G** 159
hymn composer **H** 311
influenced German language **G** 173
introduced chorales into church music **G** 182
Protestantism **P** 482–83
Reformation **R** 133–34
Lutheran Church
Jerusalem Lutheran Church, India, picture **P** 486
Lutheranism, religious belief **P** 483
state religion of Sweden **S** 486

Luther League of America, formerly the official youth organization of United Lutheran Church. Established in 1895, with headquarters in Philadelphia, Pa., it published *Luther Life.* It was officially acknowledged in 1918 and merged in 1962 with several other Lutheran groups

Luthuli (LOO-tu-li), **Albert John** (1898–1967), South African liberation leader, b. Groutville Reserve, Natal, Rhodesia. Chief of the Abasemakholweni (Zulu) tribe (1935–52), he was deposed by the government for his role in the "defiance [of racial segregation] campaign" (1952). He was chosen president general of African National Congress (1952) and won the Nobel peace prize (1961) for nonviolent opposition to apartheid in South Africa. He was elected rector of Glasgow University (1962). He published an autobiography, *Let My People Go.*

Luttrellstown Castle, near Dublin, picture **I** 388
Luxembourg **L** 379–80
flag **F** 239
invasion by Hitler, 1940 **W** 288
Luxembourg, Palais du, Paris **P** 74
Luxembourg City, capital of Luxembourg **L** 379
Luxembourg Gardens, Paris, France, picture **G** 32
Luxor, Egypt **E** 90f; picture **E** 90b
site of ancient Egyptian temple **E** 100, 102
Luzon (lu-ZON), Philippines **P** 186
Manila **M** 75
rice fields, picture **A** 446
Lyceum (ly-CE-um), Athens school founded by Aristotle **A** 397
Lycopodineae, division of plant kingdom **P** 292

Lycurgus (ly-CUR-gus) (lived about 9th century B.C.), Spartan lawgiver, reputed to have remodeled constitution, transforming military and civil institutions so that Sparta could remain military leader in the Peloponnesus.

Lydgate (LID-gate), **John** (1370?–1451?), English poet, b. Lydgate, Suffolk. He was court poet during reigns of Henry IV, Henry V, and Henry VI. He is often called Chaucer's disciple. His works include *Falls of Princes, Troy Book, The Story of Thebes* (meant to be an addition to Chaucer's *Canterbury Tales*), and *The Life of Our Lady.*

Lydia, ancient country of Asia Minor. Rich in minerals, particularly gold in the River Pactolus, the kingdom was a commercial center between Greece and Mesopotamia. Sardis, the capital, was a city of great affluence. Lydians are believed to have been the first people to mint coins. The wealth of Croesus, Lydia's last king, has become legendary. The kingdom was conquered by the Persians (546 B.C.).

Lydian (LID-ian) **mode,** seven-note musical scale **A** 247
Lyell, Sir Charles, English geologist **G** 113
Darwin and Lyell **D** 40
forerunner of the theory of evolution **B** 192
Lyly (LILY), **John,** English writer **E** 250
quotation **Q** 20
Lymphatic (lim-PHAT-ic) **system,** of the human body **D** 199–200
cancer of **C** 90
Lymphocytes (LIM-pho-cytes), white cells **I** 107
Lymphomas, cancers **C** 90

Lynch, Robert Clyde (1880–1931), American physician, b. Carson City, Nev. He made many important contributions to otolaryngology, the medical specialty dealing with the ears, nose, and throat. He developed the frontal sinus operation known as the Lynch operation and was the first to make successful motion pictures of the larynx and vocal cords.

Lynch, Thomas, Jr. (1749–1779), American politician, b. Prince George's Parish, S.C. When he returned to South Carolina (1772) after education abroad, he was elected to many important civil offices. He was a member of the first state General Assembly (1776) and of the Continental Congress (1776–77) and was a signer of the Declaration of Independence.
rare signatures and autographs **A** 526

Lynching, punishment by a mob, without lawful trial, of an accused person. The term appears to stem from the name of Charles Lynch (1736–96) of Virginia, who molested Loyalists during American Revolution. Historically, it has usually referred to the hanging of an

allegedly guilty person **by a mob.**
 Negro history **N 97**

Lyndon B. Johnson Library T 131, 135
Lyngenfjord (LURNG-en-fiord), Norway, **picture N 340**
Lynxes (LINX-es), wildcats **C 139; picture C 140**

Lyon, Mary (1797–1849), American educator, b. Buckland, Mass. She founded Mount Holyoke Seminary (now Mount Holyoke College) in South Hadley, Mass. (1837), the first permanent institution of higher learning for women only. She was president of Mount Holyoke (1837–49) and was elected to American Hall of Fame (1905).

Lyons (le-ON), France **F 406**
Lyra, constellation **C 492**
Lyre, ancient instrument **A 245, 246, 247; picture A 244**

Lyrebird, brownish bird of forests and scrublands of Australia. The bird is noted for its long, brightly colored tail. The lyrebird is about 37 in. long, of which some 22 in. are the tail. Males have highly ornamented tails which are colored and lacy in appearance when spread.

Lyrical voice V 375
Lyric poems, short, musical poems dealing with personal
  emotions **P 354**
  American literature **A 210**
  Greek **G 350**
  odes **O 52**
Lyrics of Lowly Life, book of poems by Paul Dunbar
  D 344

Lysander (ly-SAN-der) (?-395 B.C.), Spartan naval commander. He led his fleet to victory over the Athenians off Notium (407 B.C.), and finally caused their complete rout at Aegospotamos (405 B.C.) bringing about the end of the Peloponnesian War. He sought to gain control of all the Greek city-states. When the citizens of Boetia, a rival city-state rose against him, he was killed in battle at Haliartus.

Lysergic acid diethylamide *see* LSD

Lysippus (ly-SIP-us) (4th century B.C.), Greek sculptor. Probably the most prolific sculptor of the ancient world, he is said to have fashioned over 1,500 statues. He specialized in carvings of gods and men, and produced figures ranging in size from delicate statuettes to a 60-foot Zeus. Although none of his work survives, some statues found in Italy and Greece are said to show his influence. His work is described in the writings of Pliny and other historians.

Lysozyme, body enzyme **I 104**

Lytton, Edward George Earle Lytton Bulwer- (1803–1873), English writer and statesman, b. London. He wrote *Falkland* and other social novels, such as *Eugene Aram,* which concerns social justice. He was a member of Parliament (1831–41, 1852–66) and colonial secretary (1858–59). He turned to writing historical novels, among them *The Last Days of Pompeii* and *The Last of the Barons.* He was less well-known as a playwright, his most outstanding play being *Richelieu.*

ILLUSTRATION CREDITS

The following list credits, by page, the sources of illustrations used in Volume L of THE NEW BOOK OF KNOWLEDGE. Credits are listed illustration by illustration —left to right, top to bottom. Wherever appropriate, the name of the photographer or artist has been listed with the source, the two being separated by a dash. When two or more illustrations appear on one page, their credits are separated by semicolons.

2   Harry Harris—Wide World
4   Brown Brothers; The Granger Collection.
6   Wide World
7   Courtesy of AFL-CIO News
8   Brown Brothers
10 Inger Abrahamsen—Rapho Guillumette
13 Solidarity Photo, UAW; Solidarity Photo, UAW.
16 Gerald McConnell
17 Gerald McConnell
19 Metropolitan Museum of Art, Gift of Mrs. Frank Canfield Hollister, 1926; Metropolitan Museum of Art, Gift of Mrs. Edward S. Harkness, 1930; Metropolitan Museum of Art, Bequest of Catherine D. Wentworth, 1948.
20 Edward Vebell
26 M. Mineev, Tass—Sovfoto
27 Yu. Rahil, Tass—Sovfoto
28 Giegel—Swiss National Tourist Office
29 George Austin—Shostal; Hart Fisher—Shostal; Ray Manley—Shostal.
30 Ed Drews—Photo Researchers; Ray Manley—Shostal; Otto Done—Shostal.
31 Fritz Henle—Photo Researchers
35 General Electric Research Laboratory
41 George Buctel
44 George Buctel
45 Davis Pratt—Rapho Guillumette; Subine Weiss—Rapho Guillumette.
46 Harry Scott

47 Dana Brown—FPG; Jerry Frank.
48 Shostal; Charles May.
50 George Holton
51 George Buctel
53 Jane Latta; Esther Bubley; John Arango —Rapho Guillumette; Jerry Frank.
54 Charles May; Jane Latta; Charles Wiley.
57 Lisl Steiner
59 Charles May; Jerry Frank; George Holton—Photo Researchers.
60 Jerry Frank; Fritz Henle—Photo Researchers; Totino.
62 C. Arthaud
63 C. Arthaud
65 C. Arthaud; Mexican National Tourist Council; courtesy picture; Herbert Lanks—Rapho Guillumette.
66 The Museum of Modern Art, New York; Charles May.
68 Herman B. Vestal
73 Herman B. Vestal
78 Robin Jacques
79 Robin Jacques
81 Harry Scott
82 Harry Scott
86 W. T. Mars
88 Gerald McConnell
89 Gerald McConnell
90 Tom Eaglin
91 Tom Eaglin
94 Gerald McConnell
97 United Nations

99   Gerald McConnell
100 Henry Groskinsky, Life Magazine, © Time Inc., all rights reserved
101 Yerkes Primate Research Center of Emory University
102 David Linton
103 Animal Behavior Enterprises; Yale Joel, Life Magazine, © Time Inc., all rights reserved.
104 Arabelle Wheatley
108 Miller Pope
109 Miller Pope
111 Ron Perkins—Courtesy of Mark Cross; Courtesy of Coward Shoe Co.; Courtesy of Mark Cross; Courtesy of I. Miller; Courtesy of Miller Harness Co.
112 Herman B. Vestal
113 Herman B. Vestal
114– Arabelle Wheatley
120
121 George Buctel
123 M. Stafford—Shostal; D. Williams—Shostal; Edward J. McCabe, Jr.
124 Mary Ann Joulwan; Edward J. McCabe, Jr.
125 Granger Collection
127 Kenneth Longtemps
129 Steve Gross
131 Steve Gross
133– Steve Gross
135
139 George Buctel; Sovfoto.

140 Jerry Cooke
141– Wesley B. McKeown
147
148 Wesley B. McKeown—Fundamental Photos
149 Wesley B. McKeown
150 Wesley B. McKeown
153 Biblioteca Reale, Turin—IBM; Royal Academy of Arts, London—Art Reference Bureau.
154 IBM
156 George Buctel; British Information Services.
156b Culver Pictures; Bettmann Archive; Culver Pictures.
163 Harry Scott
164 Monkmeyer
165 George Buctel
166 United Nations
167 Monkmeyer
168 A. Devaney
169 Tom Hollyman—Photo Researchers
170 Casis School, Austin, Texas
171 Ann Zane Shanks
172 Ann Zane Shanks; Al Monner—Library Association of Portland.
173 Lawrence S. Williams—Free Library of Philadelphia; Stan Rice—Monkmeyer.
174 Micro Photo Division, Bell and Howell Co.; Kenneth Johnson—New York Public Library.
175 Federal Division, Victoreen Instrument Co.; Lisl Steiner—Franklin Junior and Senior High School, Somerset, N.J.
176 District of Columbia Public Library
177 Leonard Von Matt—Rapho Guillumette
178 United Nations; United States Information Agency; Bell Telephone Laboratories.
179 British Travel Association; Library of Congress.
180 Bruce Roberts—Rapho Guillumette; Gerald McConnell.
181 Gerald McConnell
182 Gerald McConnell
183 Gerald McConnell and Los Angeles County Public Library
185– Lisl Steiner—Franklin Junior and Senior
186 High School, Somerset, New Jersey
189 Herman B. Vestal
193 Herman B. Vestal
195 Herman B. Vestal
196 Herman B. Vestal
197 Bibliothèque Nationale; Ezra Stoller Associates.
199 Barbara M. Whitney—Peterborough Town Library; Sovfoto; A. Tessore—UNESCO; United Nations; United Nations.
200 Torkel Korling—Skidmore, Owings & Merrill
201 Courtesy of Standard Oil of New Jersey
202 George Buctel; Courtesy of Standard Oil of New Jersey.
204 Courtesy of Max Waldman—Caltex; George Holton—Photo Researchers
206 Fritz Henle—Photo Researchers
207 George Buctel
208 Lee Ames
209 Lee Ames
210 Grant Heilman
211 Walter Dawn; Harold Green—Annan.
212 Walter Dawn
213 Lee Ames
214 UPI
215 Russ Kinne—Photo Researchers; Russ

Kinne—Photo Researchers; Marineland of Florida; Russ Kinne—Photo Researchers.
216 Lee Ames
217 Dick Wolff—Photo Researchers
218 John Moss—Photo Researchers; R. Lunt —Annan; Russ Kinne—Photo Researchers; Stephen Collins—Photo Researchers; John Markham; C. G. Hampson—Annan.
220 Lee Ames
221 Lee Ames
222 Cresskill—Photo Researchers; C. G. Hampson—Annan.
223 Russ Kinne—Photo Researchers
224 Cy La Tour—Marineland of the Pacific; Russ Kinne—Photo Researchers; John Moss—Photo Researchers.
227 Tom Hollyman—Photo Researchers; Cy La Tour.
228 Lee Ames
229 Roman Vishniac; Walter H. Hodge; Russ Kinne—Photo Researchers.
230 Douglas P. Wilson; Walter Dawn; Douglas P. Wilson; Annan; Russ Kinne —Photo Researchers; Jan Hahn—Oceanall.
232 Harry Scott
233 Russ Kinne—Photo Researchers; Walter Dawn; Henry M. Mayer—National Audubon Society.
234 Herbert Lanks—Rapho Guillumette
235 Harry Scott; Russ Kinne—Photo Researchers.
236 Lee Ames
237 Harry Scott
238 Commonwealth Scientific & Industrial Research Organization, Australia
239 Terry Shaw—Annan; Runk Schoenberger —Grant Heilman; D. Mohrhardt—National Audubon Society.
240 Lee Ames
241 Lee Ames
242 Grant Heilman; Grant Heilman; Lee Ames.
244 Fish and Wildlife Service, U.S. Department of Interior
245 Jane Latta; Jane Latta; Shelly Grossman; Shelly Grossman; Lee Ames.
246 Cy La Tour; Cy La Tour; Lee Ames.
247 Lee Ames
248 Hampson—Annan
251 Lee Ames
252 Lee Ames, from Buchsbaum's *Basic Ecology,* Based on Cook and Hamilton; Lee Ames; Lee Ames.
253– Lee Ames
255
257 Shaw—Annan; Jack Dermid; Jack Dermid; Photo Researchers; Lynwood M. Chace; George Porter—National Audubon Society; Lynwood M. Chace; Hugh Spencer; Laurence Perkins—Annan; Lynwood M. Chace; Lynwood M. Chace; Lynwood M. Chace.
258 Lee Ames
259 U.S. Department of Agriculture
260 Miller Pope
261 Miller Pope
262 Miller Pope; Miller Pope—Fundamental Photos.
263– Miller Pope
270
271 University Physics by Sears and Zemansky, published by Addison-Wesley
272 Miller Pope

273 Miller Pope
274 Miller Pope
275 Annan
276 U.S. Coast Guard
277 Bruce Roberts—Rapho Guillumette; U.S. Coast Guard.
278 Robert Mottar—Rapho Guillumette
280– Miller Pope
289
290 Miller Pope; Courtesy of Illuminating Engineering Research Institute.
291 James Cooper
293 The Granger Collection
296 The Granger Collection
297 The Granger Collection
298 Morris Warman—Courtesy of Lincoln Center for the Performing Arts
302 Bettmann Archive
305 Gerald McConnell
306 Gerald McConnell
307 Leonard Lee Rue III—National Audubon Society
309 George Bakacs
311 George Sottung
315 Nes Levotch
316 Gerald McConnell; Little League Baseball Headquarters; Little League Baseball Headquarters.
318 Janet L. Stone—National Audubon Society; Cy La Tour; Jane Burton—Photo Researchers (London); Billy Jones—National Audubon Society.
319 Cy La Tour
320 Verna R. Johnston—Photo Researchers; New York Zoological Society; Robert Bustard—Photo Researchers.
321 Cy La Tour—Brookfield Zoo
322 Yale & Towne Manufacturing Co.
323 Yale & Towne Manufacturing Co.
325 Gerald McConnell
327 Union Pacific Railroad
328 Charles McVicker
331 Charles McVicker
333 George Buctel
335 Mario Carbone—Pix
337 J. Allan Cash—Rapho Guillumette
338 Shostal; Fox—Rapho Guillumette; Hans Huber—Alpha.
343 Ken Longtemps
344 George Buctel; Shostal
345 Marc Riboud—Magnum
346 P. Biro—Photo Researchers; A. Devaney.
347 Josef Muench
348 Stephanie Dinkins; Robert Meyerriecks; Color Illustration Inc.
350 Diversified Map Corp.
351 Charles Rotkin—PFI
352 B. Smith—Photo Researchers
353 Kabel Art Photo—Publix Pictorial Service
355 Diversified Map Corp.
358 Graphic Arts International
359 Jack Zehort—Shostal
360 Diversified Map Corp.; Jerry Cooke— Photo Researchers.
364 Harry Scott
366 French Government Tourist Office
367 Ricard—ZFA; Art Reference Bureau.
368 French Government Tourist Office; French Government Tourist Office.
370 Gerald McConnell
373 Comet
375 Annan; Photo Researchers.
376 Annan
377 Annan
379 George Buctel; Ken Lambert—Alpha.